Jona
An
by
Jonathan Harnisch

2

Published by

Jonathan Harnisch in association with

Etica Press Ltd
147 Worcester Road
Malvern
WR14 1ET

British Library Cataloguing-in-Publication Data

A catalogue record for this book is available from the British Library.

ISBN-10: 1499350724

ISBN-13: 978-1499350722

Printed in Great Britain

Table of Contents

Prefatory Note

Dr C's Introduction

Introductory Clause: Subject (Paresthesia and Parenthetical Pet Peeves)

To the Reader, Looking Back

BOOK ONE

Prologuery: Georgie's Big Break

Georgie Gust Takes a Stand

Proof You Can Go Home Again

Claudia Moves In (Part I)

Emptying His Pockets

Making it Count With Dr C

Claudia Goes Deep

Ah, What a Comfy Web They Weave . . .

Practice Makes Perfect

Claudia Moves In (Part II)

Dinner with the Gusts

The Fruits of His Labor

It's All in a Day's Work

Calling for Reinforcements

4

Dr C Goes Deep

Love Can Keep Them Together

Nothing But a Brilliant, Bright Prick of Light

Damned if You Do

Hunting They Will Go

Wake Up and Smell the Dopamine

Then, Unto Them

Claudia Moves Out

Waking Up With Mr Clean

BOOK TWO

The Road to Wakefield

Settling in

The birth of adult love

Heidi

School blues

The classroom

Hung over

Talking through windows

Mr Twitchy

Pushy boy

Bar cops

Fuck the bar cops

To the rescue

Passed out

On the edge of something?

The new day

At The Pen that night

Back in business

Grave company

There's no place like . . .

Misery loves company

A good thing

Once, twice . . .

Truth, lies, and lunch

Detention

Rocks for jocks

Something positive

The big game

A slight change of plans

Jump

Peacemaking

A twisted tree

How the shite hits the fan

The Other Ending

BOOK THREE

Part I: Dr C, Meet Benjamin J Schreiber
Unfinished Intro—Buffered Off a Thought
Sling-backs—Out of My Deepest of Pockets
Retirement?
Georgie Writes Back
Dr C Meets Ben (A Written Account from Dr C)
Cutting Class
Flashing Forward to Yesterday
Long Beach: The Hub of the Warp
Housekeepers Are a Blessing
Restaurant Love

Part II: From Wakefield to Rehab
Dr C Made Me Do It
What Really Happened
Mental Ward Snuff
Wax Melts

Part III: Getting Clean with Dr C
Pregnant With the Idea of Georgie Gust
What Got Me Here
Taking It to the Cleaners
A Chance Encounter: Reality?
The Emperor Concerto, Second Movement
In the Parallel Midst
Georgie's Home Is My Home
Cumming Too
Don't Be Afraid To Let Them Show
Office Bathroom
In The Shower—Water Off
History of Sex
Umbrella Makes Me Spread My Wings

Part IV: Dr C Meets Mr Clean

Mr Clean
Dr C Meets Mr Clean
Second Skins
A Man Ahead of His Time
Boy Scout Brothel
Love Beyond Dignity
Therapy
Mother's Naked Friend
Mother's Lava Soap
Waste: Notes on Ben's Novel
Family Reunion
First Date with Perplexity
From The Inside
The Slow Fade-Out
End of November
Claudia, Heidi . . . My Perplexity
More from Waste: A Novel by Benjamin J Schreiber.
Ben and Pops
Alter-Ego Claudia: Georgie's Nightmare at Noon
Easy Steps to a Perfect Pedicure (Déjà Vu)
Rehab and Mother
End the Violence
Second Skins with Footnotes
Benevolent Georgie

Part V: St Valentine's Day Massacre
Journal. . .
A Valentine Reminder
Funeral
The Narcissist
The Orange Button
Broken-hearted Jubilee
Dialogue with Self (After the Funeral)
Halloween
The New Way to Feed Solitude
Is This A New Beginning?

Part VI: Rest in Peace
Support This Troupe
Demons

8

Georgie and Dr C
Mother Ghost
To The Shore

Part VII: Postscriptum
Meanwhile, Back At Ben's New Mexico Ranch . . . .
Ben J Schreiber
Checking the Mail
On Kelly
Another Living Colorful Beauty?
Back To the Heat
Fortune
Inside

BOOK FOUR
Soliloquy (for Dr C)

Part I: A Day in the Life of Georgie Gust

Part II: Another Day in the Secret Life of Georgie Gust

Part III: Living the American Dream

Part IV: The End of a Dream?

Part V: The Crack-Up

Part VI: The Flashback

Part VII: The Fantasy, I

Part VIII: The Fantasy, II

Part IX: The Secret Love and Death of Claudia Nesbitt and Georgie Gust

Part X: Down and Out with Georgie Gust

Part XI: Epilog: The Waxworks

Part XII: Coda: Benjamin J Schreiber Writes to Dr C

Codex: Doctor C Writes Back to Benjamin J Schreiber

Appendix: Final Q & A Session between Benjamin J Schreiber and Dr C

BOOK FIVE

Glad You're Not Me
    Contract
    Mentally Ill Artist
    Sleep Dep
    Poetrusic Praise
    Never Follow An Outline
    Ode to Granny the Trannny: Nurse Natalie
    Why I Fucking Write
    To dance with "Crazy."
    Inner Child
    Who the Hell Am I Now?
    Time
    August 6, 2006
    My Santa. . . August 10, 2006
    August 18, 2006
    SMS
    Reply
    Doctor Whom?
    Band Intermission
    Queer Theory/Why I Write:
    Zen
    I am a Responsive Santa on Steroids
    Assess Up on the Cover
    Bad Days
    Mood: Total Random (House)
    Back to Reality

Prologue

Chapter 1

Chapter 2

Chapter 3

Chapter 4

Chapter 5

Chapter 6

Chapter 7

Chapter 8

Chapter 9

Chapter 10

Chapter 11

Chapter 12

Chapter 13

Chapter 14

Chapter 15

Chapter 16

Chapter 17

Chapter 18

Chapter 19

Chapter 20

Chapter 21

Chapter 22

Chapter 23

No End

BONUS NOTES: DELETED SCENES & THE UNSAID

An Afterword: The Day I Decided to Take Charge of My Life
First Draft?

Prefatory Note

I open my eyes and the room is on fire. Completely unconcerned, I, Ben, watch the fire grow larger and larger, then shrink and die out, revealing Georgie Gust, my alter ego, sitting on a matching mound of dirty clothes.

I light a cigarette.

"I thought you quit," says Georgie.

My nurse and doctor watch me, shaking their heads in disapproval.

Kelly doesn't know about my obsession with Claudia Nesbitt—or, rather, Georgie's obsession with her. I haven't told her much about the spells that haunt me either. I haven't mentioned a lot of things to her. I haven't mentioned how much I struggle to write anything original that comes from the heart. Or that all I hear is the chaos of the Devil and the angels, and the voice of Georgie dictating my every word and action. That I'm nothing but a trust fund baby with an addiction problem and a constellation of lurid sexual fetishes that shrink into petrified silence in the presence of any actual women and a half dozen psychiatric diagnoses ranging from Tourette's syndrome to schizoaffective disorder.

That I was taken into police custody for trying to rob a bank with nothing but a threateningly brandished cell phone and a reference to 9/11. That my father pulled some strings that landed me in rehab rather than prison. However, as part of one of the conditions of my release—that I must begin therapy with a court-appointed psychologist, Dr C—I haven't really talked much about it. As I began to work in therapy, the issue that came into focus was that of Georgie, my alter ego, whom I'd conceived as living a parallel life to mine that mirrors and channels my own self-aware, yet foreign, emotional highs and lows.

That with Dr C's help and encouragement, and my own intelligence and determination—well, some determination and some pure laziness—I might peel away the layers of Georgie's existence, so that I might find the *determination* to hand over to Kelly all that I've kept inside, so she won't leave me, so that I can self-actualize and get over the bitch, Claudia, and be honest with her, with Kelly, and with myself to meander out of some of the confusion. After all, sobriety has not cleared up all the fogginess; it seems to have added to it, seems to have created fucking stockpiles of it. And as the pieces of my existence have begun to emerge, they've done so with an extremely uncomfortable, agitating, transgressive, and self-loathing *clarity*. The clarity is what's frightening me more than anything. In fact, I'm scared to fucking death of all this clarity.

"I want out of the labels. I don't want my whole life crammed into a single word. A story. I want to find something else, unknowable, some place to be that's not on the map. A real adventure. A sphinx. A mystery. A blank. Unknown. Undefined." — Chuck Palahniuk

Dr C's Introduction

"Dear Ben,

What if you had such severe schizophrenia that your life was just one hallucination after another? And what if people kept trying to drag you back out of those hallucinations, to prove that you weren't living in reality, and that reality was nothing more than a psych hospital? Would you go? Would you make that leap back into reality, leave such a vivid life, for ceramic walls and metal gurneys?"

—Dr C

Dear Diary:

Not everything has to be interpreted literally; often a metaphorical interpretation is far more relevant and insightful, even if it's just some fictional nonsense.

Introductory Clause: Subject (Paresthesia and Parenthetical Pet Peeves)

I sense a tingling, fucking burning, prickling of Claudia's character defects. Prickling my skin, by reason of her particular parenthetical pet peeves. This continuous tingling and numbness in my face and back of my head I feel, therefore it must not be unreal, nor is there any other reason so remarkable as to elicit disbelief. Claudia's parenthetical pet peeves are real and therefore worthy of a name: Claudia Nesbitt, no less than what is stated, as insubstantial as her being, but my dream and inside my dream.

Example: Claudia especially hates when people add an "e" to a name ending in "y." Also, contrived spellings of common names.

Dear Diary:

History repeats itself. So does the present.

Obsession is a state of mind, so make it good.

The night is quiet and still now, and at the end . . . .

Once I encountered all these people, Claudia, Heidi, Kelly, Georgie, and myself, and my self, the fantasies of everybody and every place, and everything, they continued on. They became tragic obsessions.

Let's get the facts straight up front, to avoid any confusion later. Georgie is an alter ego. I have several of them. It's a means of leaving some room in my experience to avoid growing entirely sick of myself. I sit in this room, in this house, because I've lost myself.

I used to be all right. Back when I had a concrete hold on my place in this world, at least the people who used to make up my life. I've gone downhill, rolling down with the light feathery tumbleweed in our backyard. It's disgusting in here, as mist and smoke linger throughout this claustrophobic bachelor pad. They say Ben's 30 now, and that he's a split personality; better put: a double personality, lacking true identity, lacking any sense of self. I don't agree. I am Ben. They say a lot—the voices and hallucinations. They say Ben's skinny because he smokes crack. He's alone. He's me. He's in this living room. The landline rings all the time, often, quite a few times and they tell me to pick up, so I do.

Dear Diary:

Undoubtedly we are all capable of doing anything for 24 hours that would otherwise overwhelm us if we had to keep it up for a lifetime. We know this because we can breathe, can we not?

To the Reader, Looking Back

Looking back on it now, now that the words that come later can drain away most of the sentiment, there's a nostalgia that still lingers at the top of the Eiffel Tower, when *those kids*—three girls and two boys—defined who I was, without the slightest hint of bias or negativity.

It was the first time in my life, the first "time of my life." I was on a school trip in Paris, with the same kids who would taunt me and bully me back in New York. And although I had forgiven them, even loved them to an extent, there was so much going on at home, and in my head, and in my body, that I couldn't tell the difference between what was good and what was bad, what was appropriate and what was not. Kids can be brutal.

They say that those in the "Losers' Clubs" in school will usually show up at the reunions, years later, as glittering icons, while the popular kids turn to waste. I never went to any of the reunions.

I took a left turn by not going with my class. I got permission from the French teacher who was in charge of us to hang out with another group of kids from another junior high school; they were also in Paris from Nassau County, and, although I was away from my own crowd of popular kids (that particular crowd of waste), my new group of friends and I took off by Métro that night after dinner. We climbed most of the Eiffel Tower, as it was still open to tourists, even at the late hour.

As we gazed over the city lights, the brisk wind blowing hard, one of the kids, Wesley, who couldn't have been over 12—all wrapped up in his ski jacket, his short curly hair frozen, unaffected by the winds—smiled innocently at me, and as if it was his second nature, he said, coolly, "You seem pretty normal to me, Ben. Hey, you're one of us." And all the others bantered among themselves in agreement. I took a group photo of my new best friends, all of us arm-in-arm, holding on in the chill air, and holding on to the memory of being so free, without supervision. Looking back on everything now, the world, the universe, never looked as beautiful to me as it did during that cool breezy night on top of the world, where I was with my friends and nobody knew just how invincible we really were.

(Parenthetical Pet Peeve) The fancier the hairdo, the harder the wind will be blowing.

I haven't a clue what happened on the walk back to the hotel and, by the next day, when Wesley's and his buddies' vacation meant they'd be back in the States by sundown, I had forgotten about it. I mean, I'd forgotten about everything—my introduction—and I went back to the in-crowd as they did what they did for the rest of the trip, mostly drinking French beer from the mini-bar in the Hôtel Chateau Martine.

I find that the more I keep to myself all that I do remember from that particular night out with the group from Paris, I wonder constantly if, by now, they'd ever grown up or if they just stay the same, like in the picture I still have of them. It's under my bed, in an old shoebox—so that *I* can stay the same, somewhere, somehow way deep down inside.

Dear Diary:

There are times I'll struggle and tussle with my inner demons. Other times we'll simply cuddle and snuggle together. It's a relationship that has both feelings of love and hate. There is a bond between us that remains ever strong, perhaps based on the myth or truth of general inherent goodness or purely due to all the variants of myself and any beast or such demons, real or unreal. My inner demons are within me, and oftentimes, they end up being the ones who save me; I don't have such a need to be saved from my inner demons per se.

[Smoke Break]

—To suddenly discontinue, dissolving and dissociating breaking for a fairly ubiquitous cigarette, but to exist nowhere and do nothing—only like the fog and itty bitty bugs, to exterminate all ambiguous thoughts for a moment.

BOOK ONE

Prologuery: Georgie's Big Break

"Mr Gust?"

The secretary is standing over him. She waves her pencil in his face. "Mr Gust?"

Georgie looks up. He smiles at her. That's what people do, right? They smile?

She jerks the pencil toward the heavy wood door.

"The doctor's ready for you now," she says. She walks back to her desk, her tight little ass traveling smoothly in a clinging grey skirt. She props her yellow pumps up on the desk as she watches him. She grimaces and pulls out a nail file.

Georgie shuffles slowly over to the door, trying to keep his feet from lifting off the floor.

He leans over to open the door with his elbows, wanting to avoid the static shock he can feel rising in the roots of his hair; the electric charge traveling up his leg hair and his white, commercial-grade, psych-ward pants.

Then he realizes that sane people don't open doors with their elbows. Sane people just get shocked.

Georgie takes the shock with a snort and pushes the dark door open. Before him is Dr Abrams, a middle-aged man with salt-and-pepper hair.

"Good afternoon, Georgie," Dr Abrams says.

"Good afternoon, doc . . . Dr Abrams," Georgie replies.

Georgie raises his left foot and his right knee quivers. It's trying to hop, or something. He looks at the man seated behind the polished mahogany desk. With a silent growl, Georgie places his left foot on the floor. In front of the right. He sinks into the small leather chair and smiles tentatively.

"Well?" he says, daring the doc to say he is not cured. (Cured? Hah.)

"Well, Georgie. How are you feeling today?" Dr Abrams smiles right back, in that pseudo-friendly way he has.

"Great. Fantastic. I think I could walk right out of here today."

He stresses the word "walk."

The doc grins. "Well, there are good days and there are bad

days, Georgie."

Georgie can see this is Dr Abrams' game, and he is not going to play it.

"I got a lot of good days ahead of me, doc. And I don't want to spend them in a nuthouse."

Dr Abrams sighs. "Georgie, you committed yourself. Six months ago, you knew that you had a problem. Now you've regressed. You're in denial, Georgie. Trust me, and the other physicians. You have a long way to go yet, Georgie. A long way "

"A g-great point, Dr Abrams," Georgie says. He curses himself for letting the stutter slip. On today of all days! But Georgie perseveres. "A great point—that I committed myself. If I committed myself, I can uncommit myself."

Dr Abrams shakes his head sadly.

"This is me, uncommitting myself," Georgie insists. "Look, I'm better. I walked in here without a hop. I haven't said a word about the voices. But do you know what? They're gone. Totally gone. And the Tourette's? Well, I'm stuck with that forever, but that's hardly a committable offense—"

Dr Abrams cuts him off.

"Georgie, to tell you the truth, your therapist gave me a call this morning."

(Dr C? Is it you?)

"I looked you up. Your family. And you are a high-ticket in here."

"What do you mean?" Georgie's first hint of fear is a tic in his right cheek. Not today! Georgie commands himself.

"I'd like to keep you in here," Dr Abrams concludes.

Georgie shrugs, playing it cool. "I'm outta here. I will walk right out of here."

"Against medical advice?" Dr Abrams rolls his eyes to the ceiling. He presses his fingertips together.

It's all an act, Georgie knows. All Dr Abrams needs is to know that Georgie is not bouncing off the walls, shredding his precious books, or ripping the leather from the chairs. . . . As long as Georgie doesn't do that, he can do whatever he wants. Except leave.

If they only knew what trouble their money was going to bring, Georgie thinks, my wretched parents would have thought twice.

He laughs.

No they wouldn't have.

"Georgie," Mr Abrams continues. "Georgie, you tried to kill

yourself. For your personal safety, we have to keep you here until we are sure that you won't try to do it again."

This time that "friendly" smile is gone. Replaced with a smirk.

Georgie stares silently, not saying a word. He wants to stand, to shake Dr Abrams until his tonsils fall out on the floor, to throw him out the window, them jump out himself, and use the body as a cushion. Then steal Abram's car . . . . Georgie wonders if Abrams keeps his keys in his jacket pocket or somewhere in his desk.

No, stop it, Georgie thinks. Sane people don't think about that.

(Isn't that right, Dr C? I've always wondered.)

Dr Abrams sighs again.

"Okay, that's fine. You'll still have to wait for us to get your paperwork together."

Georgie's eyes light up. Then he sees something in the doc's face.

"How long will that take?" he asks.

"As long . . ." Dr Abrams' voice trails off, a funny glint coming into his eyes. "As long as it takes," he concludes.

Georgie screams, but there is no sound.

Dear Diary:

To worry is to waste time. Worrying doesn't change anything. It only robs one of his or her joy and peace of mind, simply keeping one busy doing absolutely nothing, when it comes down to it.

Georgie Gust Takes a Stand

Claudia, that bitch, whore, that woman I love and hate. (Who's Claudia?) She created a paradise and set it aflame. She is my world and its end, my kinky sex goddess, my creepy-crawly nemesis.

Remember her, in all her glory. Sleeping soundly under a teal-colored dream catcher in her red and white four-poster. She never stood a chance. I never stood a chance. We love and hate no matter whose face she's wearing, whose heart she's tearing.

I want to see her in those slingbacks, her perverted, cotton candy-blue toes peeking out to play.

But I won't. Not this time.

Georgie Gust loops and ties a thick piece of rope into a noose.

Not this time, not this time, not this time.

For Georgie, everything comes in threes. His stutters, his mutters, his women, his crazy step, step, hop. Everything.

(This time is different. This time, Ben controls my destiny. But this time, I end it all before any other bastard has a chance to end it for me, even Ben.)

He tosses the rope's looped end over the supporting beam in his old-world style, country living room. Then steps onto a chair and ties it tight. He cringes slightly, and lowers the loop over his head and tightens it around his neck.

He steps off the chair and kicks it away.

Georgie swings.

The rope burns his throat; he gurgles, trying to cough. His hands scrabble at his neck. His feet kick wildly, wanting to stand. Not this time.

Georgie Gust gasps, and a small trickle of air cools his throat. It's not enough. Not this time. Lightning bugs, fireworks burst behind his eyeballs. His whole body trembles and tingles and yells at him. He tries to scream again, this time emitting sound, but he cannot.

His heartbeat drums in his ears, pounding and pulsing with the blood in his eyeballs.

Thud . . . thud . . . thud.

Georgie moans, as the world turns black in his eyes.

Thud . thud . . . thud . . .

Dear Diary:

We're often asked, "How are you?" When I ask myself, and really think about it—good or bad—or in-between, it always seems to come down to the "overall" picture. Overall, I am well. Overall, I do my best. Overall, I am OK. Nothing's really black or white, but rather, overall. . .

Proof You Can Go Home Again

The black sedan pulls up to the curb outside Georgie Gust's old-style country home. The driver, Ben (Ben? Ben, again? The same Ben? You, Ben?) jumps out and runs to open the back door. Georgie pulls himself up out of the back seat.

(I thought Georgie was dead, Ben.

Well he is and he's not, Dr C. You know those creepy-crawly walking corpses—those dead but not-quite-dead people?

Like zombies, Ben?

Sure, sure. Like zombies, Dr C. If that's what helps you sleep at night.

Whatever you say, Ben. It's your story, now.)

Ben is at the trunk, pulling suitcases up and onto the sidewalk. Georgie pauses for a minute, looks at him. Then shrugs and walks up to his front door. His face is calm, peaceful. Not a tic in sight.

A brand new man, he thinks, his hand on the doorknob. Everything starts over now.

Thud . . . thud . . . thud.

A week later, a knock sounds on Georgie's front door.

He opens the door. It's Margaret, Georgie's only friend, as if he's ever had any actual friends, and true friends. He finds her annoying because she seems to care, but a tad too much, for whatever reason, though she does answer phone calls for a national crisis helpline, so it must simply be a part of her nature, to help the disenfranchised, desolate people who otherwise roam the world in their quiet introverted solitude.

Though surprised, he acts normal.

"I didn't call," he says.

"I know," Margaret says. Her perfect brown curls flood over her creamy skin. "I just wanted to see how things were going."

"Of course," he says. "Uh, come in. No, would you like to sit on the porch?"

She nods.

"Drink?"

She nods. "Water."

When Georgie comes out to the porch she is sitting comfortably on his dusty, handmade wicker chair.

"How've you been?" she begins. "I know it's only been a week, but . . . "

"Oh, great," Georgie says. He nods a little too enthusiastically. "Really. I'm like a new person." He smiles, his face a comfortable mask.

"I'm so glad to hear that," she gushes. "I had a really, really great time on the trip, you know. I can't believe it. Already, it's like a dream. We met the Dalai Lama! And trekked over the mountains. Do you remember that guy? With the chickens?" She sighs. "It was an amazing trip."

"Yeah. Amazing," Georgie nods. "The Dalai Lama. His spirit is so beautiful. Just being around him, everything felt easier, or something."

Margaret shines. "I'm so glad, Georgie, I just, you know when I found you, that day, when you were trying to . . ." Her voice fades at his blank stare.

"Well, I'm just so glad I found you. Just think, you couldn't have met the Dalai Lama if you were, well . . ." She shakes her head rapidly.

"Yeah, I know." He smiles sardonically. "Life is just great. Super."

"Yeah. Thank you, for thinking of me when your therapist recommended the trip."

Georgie shrugs. "Sure, the doc, you know, Dr C, she thought I should ask you." He doesn't say: Because you're the only person I know who actually seems to give a crap.

Margaret looks at him from the corner of her eye. She inhales, then pauses, opens her mouth.

"Georgie," she asks softly, "why did you do it?"

(You need a reason in this shitehole world?)

"I don't know. I . . . ." He can't tell her about Claudia. Claudia hasn't happened yet.

He fixes on a memory.

"It was hard to grow up with Tourette's," he says quickly. "And my parents were sh-shitey, I mean, well, even now I don't ever see them. They weren't around when I was a kid, either. All I had was this nanny."

He pauses. Margaret glows at him, so proud of herself for having gotten him to open up.

(You think you can fix this?

Why not, Ben? Are you unfixable?

Whatever.)

Georgie stifles an overwhelming urge to laugh. He coughs instead.

"Go on," Margaret whispers.

"So, this nanny, she was horrible. Bad in every way. Like, she used to pinch me and uh, grab at me and stuff. You know, inappropriately?"

Margaret leans back and inhales through her teeth. "That's horrible!" she says.

"Yeah, they had to do surgeries and stuff. To uh, make me normal-looking."

Margaret looks at him inquisitively, not getting it.

"She used to hold me in the air, by my dick. Basically, nothing but . . ."

He trails off at her fierce blush.

(Is that even possible, Ben?

I get it, Dr C, it's yet another delusion, eh?)

One day, Georgie is going to learn when to speak and when to shut the hell up.

But today is not that day.

"So, I don't know. The doc says I'm all messed up about that," Georgie concludes lamely.

Margaret shifts in her seat. Georgie suddenly notices her toes, which she painted jungle-red for the trip to Tibet. The edges are chipped now—worn out from weeks of sandals and dirt roads, from chlorinated water and unadulterated sunlight.

"Well, I think you're so, so much better now."

She smiles warmly. Then she leans over and hugs him, awkwardly, since they are sitting in separate chairs. His brain whirrs at her smell.

Then she stands.

"Thank you so much for having me over, Georgie. And thanks for the trip. It was amazing."

She smiles down on him. The bright afternoon sunshine glows at the tips of her hair, making her face a blank mask. "I'm so glad that you're doing well." With that, she leaves.

Shortly thereafter, Georgie leaves, too.

Georgie might or might not be all better. He thinks to himself: *Maybe I am, and maybe I'm not. And either way, I certainly don't seem to care much.*

(See what I mean, Doc? It's the best indication of Georgie's sanity. Sane people do not go around wondering whether or not they are crazy. They just know they have nothing to worry about.

Lucky bastards.)

Georgie wanders through the kitchen, making himself a bowl of cereal.

But crazy people, Georgie thinks, crazy people are exactly the same way.

There's only that brief transition period, somewhere between sane and insane, where a person is truly able to fear that their mind has gone.

Georgie sits down in his dark living room for a moment, then glances at the window blinds. Fortunately brief, Georgie resists the urge to descend into a catatonic stare. But he doesn't ask himself why. Instead, he stands and decides to eat his cereal on the porch. Healthy people spend lots of time outside. In the light.

In the morning, Georgie shuffles slowly into the kitchen. The coffee machine is just burbling out the last ounce of coffee; its clock reads 10:00 am. Georgie glances at the refrigerator, and his magnetized eraser board that reads: "To Do List." Beneath the line, the board is blank.

Georgie pulls a clean mug from the cupboard and pours himself a cup of coffee. He moves over to the back door, admiring his beautifully landscaped backyard with the Italian cypress, the trimmed hedges. Such a contrast to the old-world, country-feel inside. He breathes in the aroma of the coffee then walks back through the kitchen, towards the front door.

From the corner of his eye, Georgie sees that the light on his answering machine blinks red. He stops, takes a slow sip of coffee, and presses the play button.

"Hi Georgie," Margaret's voice echoes from the machine. "It's Margaret. I was just thinking about what we talked about yesterday, remember? Anyway, this morning when I woke up, it occurred to me . . . Well, I thought it would be a good idea for you to maybe, maybe find your old nanny, you know?"

Georgie frowns as he stares at the machine.

"And you could confront her about everything she did to you and maybe get some closure or something? I don't know. Talk it over with your therapist maybe, but it came into my head like lightning."

Georgie's finger plunges toward the answering machine.

"Message deleted," the machine chimes. "You have no new messages."

Dear Diary:

It's not a sprint. It's a marathon.

Claudia Moves In (Part I)

Georgie moves out the front door, his coffee in hand. He pulls the mail from the mailbox and sits on the porch. He takes a sip and then sets the coffee mug down.

A woman's voice tickles his ear.

"Come here, little boy. Come here."

Georgie turns. The woman who stares at him is in her 40s, with wild-frizzy red hair.

"Hi," Georgie says.

"Hi, neighbor. I'm Claudia. I know we haven't met yet . . . but, well, I just moved in."

"Yeah? I hadn't realized." Her gaze entrances Georgie. Then he looks down.

Her bare feet. Her big pale feet. Her perfect, long, skinny toes. Her adolescent pink nail polish partially chipped off. She intoxicates him.

"Well, it's nice to meet you," Claudia says. He looks up at her, dizzy.

"Yeah . . . I'm Georgie."

"I'll see you later, Georgie," she says.

Later that week, Georgie goes to the grocery store. Now that he has met the Dalai Lama, now that he is a new man, he goes to the store once a week. Or so he says.

When he turns the corner, there she is. Margaret.

"Georgie!" she calls. There is no escaping. He stays put, lets her approach him.

"Georgie," she says again. "How have you been?"

"Great," he says, "Just great."

"Did you get my message?" Margaret asks. "The one . . . about your nanny?"

Georgie shifts uneasily. "Yeah, yeah," he says.

"What do you think? Did you try to find her?"

"Uh, no. Well, I'm going to, you know. But it's not easy. I was going to do it to-tomorrow."

Margaret beams.

"Oh, that's so wonderful Georgie! I'm so glad."

He nods, looking around him carefully. He fixates on a can of creamed corn.

"I just know it will help Georgie, I just know it," Margaret gushes.

"Y-yeah. Me, too," Georgie says unconvincingly. "Well, uh. Gotta go " . . . ."

He gestures to the end of the aisle, then shuffles toward it, engrossed in escape. Escape from Margaret and all she wants to say. He is so engrossed, he almost forgets to check out, and is reminded by the alarm that sounds when he strides toward the door.

"Damn it," Georgie mutters. He turns around and holds his basket high in the air. "Sorry. Sorry!" he announces, showing everyone that he is not a thief.

Somewhere, Margaret is watching him. Somewhere, Margaret has seen this almost occurrence of shoplifting. Somewhere, Margaret knows exactly how not fine Georgie really is.

Georgie sighs and stands in line with the rest of his fellow shoppers.

Later that day, Georgie walks up the front walk to his home, bags of groceries slung from his fists. On his front porch is an unexpected note:

Georgie Porgie,

Having not seen you in some time, my affection toward you has cooled to mere fondness. I'm becoming indifferent. I don't want that. We've been separated from each other far too often, though you live right next door. I want to see you again, Georgie. Tonight . . . .,

XXX

Claudia

Affection? What is this woman talking about?

Georgie wonders if they have met before, maybe in another lifetime he can't remember, maybe last week at a bar. But he can't think, can't think . . . .

Georgie's mind is stuck on repeat. His balls scream for release.

Claudia is a bombshell.

That night, Georgie abandons his bright new self and rushes over to Claudia's. It's there that the two are surrounded by vanilla-scented candlelight.

(Lust always wins over self-enlightenment. That's why we are at once so prolific and so infinitely ridiculous.)

Georgie wears a light blue dress shirt with a loose tie and ripped denims.

Claudia is completely naked.

"I can't believe you've never given a girl a pedicure," she purrs.

"Believe it. I'm a virgin, Claudia." Georgie is solemn.

She sits in the candle-lit bathroom, her plump cushion perched on her toilet bowl.

Georgie holds her foot in his lap. He is in agony, and enjoying every minute of it.

(Are we being sensual? Good God damn! You bet we are!)

Claudia hands over a bright red container of Tiger Balm. Georgie massages her feet with his eyes closed.

"Mmm. That's so relaxing. It tingles. It's warm," she moans.

He removes her old pink nail polish with store-brand nail polish remover.

"Well, aren't you the quick learner?" Claudia smiles.

Georgie fills a small footbath with a vanilla-scented soak. In five minutes, Claudia is asleep. He carefully removes her beautiful, clean, pasty-white feet from the warm water and pats them dry. He greases the palms of his hands with a hefty dose of rose-scented heel balm. Then he massages her feet from the toes down to her heels. Her feet twitch a little. She shivers.

By the time Georgie finishes, Claudia's feet are cotton-soft. He kisses them, hoping she will not wake up. A sad smile passes across her face. Is she dreaming? She is heavenly and peaceful. He can't stop staring.

Her eyes flash open.

"Well done. Well done, mister." She smiles. "How do you know so much about pedicures, if you've never done one before?"

Georgie blushes. "Well, I've seen . . . I've watched how they're done. At the sa-salon."

"Good boy," Claudia says.

Georgie buffs her toenails furiously, starting to have a little fun.

"What color would you like?" he asks.

"What do you think? What would look good on me?" Claudia looks him up and down meaningfully. "What would you choose, say, if you could have my toes?"

Georgie's groin stick straightens up as though by command. Pre-cum leaks into his denim crotch. He touches it for a second, a nano-second.

"What are you doing?" She busts him. She laughs.

"Nothing." Georgie pouts.

She pouts right back at him, raising her eyebrows.

He flinches away from her all-too-knowing gaze.

He carefully paints her nails, separating her toes with cotton balls. He colors them with two coats of "Hooker Blue." He paints them rapidly, sweating and breathing heavily. When he is finished, he stands and swivels, making his way to the doorway. He has to get out of there, back across the yard to his own peaceful sanctuary . . . that sterile environment where his cum is safe to splurge. He will splash it into the bathtub and wash it down with a shower, safe. Safe to fertilize the fishes and alligators and rats of the sewer.

"Neighbor, wait!" Claudia calls.

"Gotta go. Sorry."

"But now I'm too late for the party," she exclaims.

Georgie stops in his tracks.

"I want to congratulate you on what a great job you did on my pedicure! And on such short notice, too."

He smiles, horny as all hell.

"Now it's your turn."

Georgie's face gets that dreamy look.

"Sit down," she commands. Georgie seats himself on the toilet; she sits herself on the floor. Perfectly naked. Her shaved pussy smiles up at him coyly from the cold, white, sterile linoleum.

He wants to smell it.

"Take off your clothes," she commands.

Georgie attempts to undress slowly, but misses the mark completely. When he sits again, his boner stands at attention. Claudia tsks playfully.

"This has become your night, after all," she teases. "I need to thank you for the great job you've done, neighbor."

She stresses the word "job."

"Uh, well, thank you," Georgie says awkwardly.

"You like feet?" she asks respectfully.

Before Georgie can respond, her freshly pedicured feet creep up his thigh and begin to gently rub his balls and shaft. Georgie is queasy, sick, dizzy, in heaven, in agony. He can see right into her crotch. Her shaved pussy drips wet on the tile. Her vagina looks so lonely.

Within a minute, he can't take it any longer. He cries out in a strange squeal that makes her flinch slightly.

"Claudia, you've got to make me cum!" Georgie demands. "Fast. Please? Please?"

Her feet begin to stroke his erect cock up and down. It is tall, proud, rising toward his face. All his boiling love-sap about to explode.

"Do you want to cum in my mouth?" Claudia asks.

"On your feet. Just like that. Don't stop. Don't stop," he begs.

"Are you close?"

And, before he can answer, his white nut cascades over her toes.

Georgie wakes up on the cold tile of her bathroom floor early that morning. Claudia is sleeping, leaned up against the bathtub, her jaw slack. The light slanting in through the doorway shows every line of her face. She is old, but fertile. Her hair glows like flame.

Claudia represents flashes of a future, a world on fire. Georgie, seeking his lifelong orgasm, knows that she is trouble. But that's just what he needs—a world on fire.

Forget the Dalai Lama, that happy, self-sufficient self that Georgie has always known he could be. Fuck that shite.

He just wants Claudia, and all the joy/hate/love/torture/sex she promises.

Georgie leaves her place early, while she is still sleeping.

In his kitchen, he glances at the refrigerator door. The magnetized board still reads "To Do List," and nothing else.

He doesn't hear from her at all that day.

Or the following week.

He doesn't hear from her, but he sees her. Watches her, more like it. The side of the house that faces hers?—he lives on that side of the house now. Every movement from her yard sends him running for a window. He can't help himself. That wild hair, those purple-circled eyes, that feral laugh, those toes. Those toes.

He can't see her toes without using binoculars, so he keeps the binoculars right on the windowsill.

He is sick. He has a problem.

(You're telling me? Shite.)

Georgie hardly ever leaves his cage of paradise to enter the real world. Even though he feels pretty damn good lately, even though he is a new man.

(Yeah. Right. Exactly who does he think he's kidding?)

But sooner or later, he has to eat.

Georgie shuffles through the kitchen; his countertops and sink, cluttered with dirty dishes, soggy pizza boxes. He lifts his favorite mug. Sniffs it. Not too bad, he thinks. A little grungy around the edges. The coffee machine clock reads 2:02 pm. *Fuck the swill, man,* he commands himself, *just drink the shite.*

Georgie pours the coffee into his mug and wrinkles his nose. He stands and stares at the refrigerator door. The eraser board. His hand twitches.

Georgie pushes his cart through the grocery store. Every third step, he takes a small hop. Just a small one.

He turns the corner, and there she is again.

Margaret.

He would turn and escape, but he can't. Instead, his cart slams right into hers. They are tangled now, a mess of intertwining wires.

"Georgie!" she says.

He nods. Once, twice, three times.

"Georgie," she says again, "how are you?"

"G-great. J-just great."

She looks at him from the corner of her eye and backs away a little. "You sure, Georgie?" she whispers.

He coughs. Straightens up. "Yes," he says. "Of course."

"Did you get in touch with your nanny yet?"

"Uh, yeah. Well. I'm still tracking her down. I'll let you know."

Georgie looks down at his feet, at the shelves, at anything.

Margaret wrinkles her brow. "Yeah, I guess that would be hard."

"Yeah."

She waits, but he will not speak.

"Well, uh . . . I guess I'll catch you later, right?" she says finally.

"Yeah, yeah."

"Good to see you."

"Yeah."

Georgie shuffles into his kitchen and drops a single, lightweight grocery bag on the counter. He stares at the refrigerator, at the eraser board, at the to do list, which has "GET CIGARETTES" scrawled on it in thick pen. He lifts the pen and checks cigarettes off the list.

Georgie sits on the front porch, a lit cigarette dangling from his lips. Healthy people spend time outside, he thinks to himself. He inhales smoke deep, deep into his lungs. He feels the reassurance of the thick black stuff spread from his lungs outward.

He smiles, calmed.

Georgie is a bundle of purpose, a self-made man. Self-assuredly, he steps from task to task throughout the day. By the end of each day, he is exhausted, and pleased with his progress.

Oh, yes. Georgie is a man of energy, a man whose drive to succeed, to excel, is surpassed by very few.

Really.

It's a sunny day outside, but every blind is turned down inside Georgie's home, making it feel like one gigantic, single, dark shadow. As he wanders through each gloomy room, he eventually stops in the study, and glances down at his answering machine.

The light is flashing.

When did the phone ring? Georgie wonders. Why didn't I hear it?

He presses the play button.

"Hey, Georgie," a familiar voice echoes. "It's your mo—"

Georgie's finger jams down hard on the delete button.

"Message deleted," the machine informs him coldly.

Still, Georgie can hear his mother's voice echoing in his head: "You ungrateful bastard. You never appreciated a thing I ever did."

"You have no new messages," the machine chimes.

Georgie takes a cigarette out of his pack and puts it in his mouth. He doesn't light it. The cigarette dangles loosely from his lips as he walks over to the coffee pot—always on, never off; it is still half-full of old coffee. He fills a dirty coffee mug and takes a sip. The coffee's so hot it burns his tongue. Georgie drops the mug on the kitchen floor. Coffee spills everywhere as the mug shatters into countless pieces.

Georgie stares at the spilled coffee, the remains of the broken mug, and walks to the bathroom.

On the can, Georgie looks at the silver toilet paper dispenser. The roll is empty. His bleary, worn-out face is also blank, empty.

He steps into the shower, talking to himself.

The soap drops, thudding as it strikes the porcelain tub.

Georgie bends; he slips and falls.

"God damn," he moans.

What a way to start the day, eh?

Georgie tries to start anew in the kitchen. He lines up 10 espresso cups on the counter, each filled with black liquid tar. He pours sugar into each cup, running back and forth across the lineup, an unlit cigarette dangling from his lips.

Georgie pours each cup into a large thermos. He walks out of the kitchen, stepping right into the spilled coffee and porcelain shards. Coffee splashes up over his feet, but Georgie doesn't notice.

He walks into the living room, carrying the thermos. It doesn't look quite comfortable enough, so he opts for the porch; but something doesn't feel right there either. Sipping from his thermos, burning his tongue with espresso, Georgie stumbles through the house to his bedroom.

He collapses onto the blankets, groaning as his legs and back relax into the mattress. He props a pillow under his head and sips, sips, sips away at his black liquid tar.

After downing half the thermos, Georgie steps into the bathroom. He turns on the hot water in the shower and just lets it run. Steam fills the air and moistens his lungs.

Georgie needs something to satisfy him, to give him that everlasting orgasm he craves. Claudia is caput, now nothing but a ghost. She is out of the picture.

He walks into the house, a lightweight shopping bag spinning from his fingers. He erases the check mark next to "CIGARETTES" on his to do list and then rechecks it.

Dear Diary:

I need to finally forget about being impressive and commit to being real. Because being real is impressive!

Emptying His Pockets

On a desert highway, the midday sun reflects off the tinted windows of a moving stretch limousine; its pearl-white paint muddies with the billowing clouds in the sky.

Inside the limo, up front, a street map is open.

Our driver, Ben, focuses on the long, straight road ahead. He sniffs.

Georgie has a face full of self-help literature. A pair of trendy new shoes lies on the floor beside his socked feet. Georgie takes a long breath through his nose, closing the book that he has just finished. Its cover reads *Twelve Steps for Stupid People*.

"Why are you always reading those?" Ben asks.

Georgie's right eyelid flutters exactly nine times. Georgie knows. He counts. He likes to count.

"I like to see what will happen if I do the exact opposite," he says.

Ben nods. "That sounds reasonable."

They both pause, contemplating the anti-wisdom of self-help books. The desert rolls by, silently mocking.

(Mocking Ben? Really? It's just an ecosystem.

'Course, mocking. There's no bigger "fuck you" to a man like Georgie, a man living a sterile existence, than life as an ecosystem.

A man like Georgie, Ben? Or a man like you?

Let it go, Dr C.)

"Here we are," Ben finally says.

The limousine pulls up to the iron gates of a palatial mansion. A trio of security guards in uniform open the door for Georgie. Ben is directed to a smaller outbuilding around back.

On the hot, black asphalt just within the gates, Georgie strips to nothing. The desert swelters behind him, sending up wavering gusts of invisible heat. Georgie shuffles along carefully on the burning asphalt, keeping his head down.

He is quickly joined by staff members wearing psych attire— white shirts, black belts, white pants, and shoes. They are clean, sterile people—perfect for Georgie.

"This way," one says, his lips pale against the blanched cream of his skin. Georgie steps through the open door of the mansion and turns to the right.

The patio and interior are slate and marble, clean and cool. The floor is coated with naked people, all lying on their backs. Georgie meanders through them like a zombie, unsure of his place in the carpet of bodies. The house seems dead, but is somehow breathing. The rank scent of vinegar assails his nose.

Georgie finds a small space. He lies on the floor on his back, waiting. He shivers, slightly.

A loud siren screams and screeches and a horde of young, naked women flood the room and scatter. Rushing among the naked bodies, one by one they match themselves to pairs of feet. Georgie's woman is creamy-skinned, with wild, red, frizzy hair and a scarred lip. She grins, and her scar turns the smile to a grimace.

Georgie holds back a momentary panic.

As one, the women drop to the floor. Georgie's redhead rubs his toes a few times then sniffs his feet. She grins again—that same lopsided smile. This time, Georgie is able to relax. He is in a safe arena—he and she are nothing but strangers. Their nakedness means nothing. They are surrounded by wriggling, mewling grubs.

She strokes his ankles lightly, and his dick springs to attention. She grins her approval. Then swiftly she lowers herself over his toes. His eyes zoom in on her pink crotch. It quivers, glistening wet.

She pulls his toes inside of her. Georgie gasps, jerking slightly at the feel of her. Her wet flesh sucks at him as she imbeds his foot inside her slick pussy.

"Oh, God," Georgie moans. His eyes close in ecstasy.

Around him, similar noises rise as his fellow fetishists have their dreams fulfilled. Some are having their feet bitten; others are having razors drawn lightly through their skin. Many simply enjoy a foot massage or pedicure. Most, however, most . . .

There are cries and moans and yelps around him, but Georgie seems to be at peace, as he lies on the marble floor naked, stripped of inhibitions. Everyone is so wrapped up in themselves it is like he is not even there. He is a nonentity . . . . A nothing.

Georgie's face spasms, his eyes tighten. All his peace condenses into a single, surging spark. With one last, piteous moan, Georgie cums; his dick jerks. It is like a fountain, a continuous spurt. An everlasting orgasm. Perfection. It looks to him like he has splashed the red-haired, foot-smotherer—a small spot glistens brightly on her pinky toe.

And then it is over. She stands with one last suck, a parting flex of muscle, and then she is gone. Her white, broad bottom trotting swiftly away.

Georgie sighs and smiles.

Afterward, Georgie partakes in a foot trampling, an egg stomping, a salt crystal crawl. He wanders from room to room in the mansion, feeling the cool, sweet air conditioning on his naked skin. He is not worried about his penis, which shrivels to an embarrassing size in the chilled air. In this place, Georgie feels as invisible as anyone. Everyone is invisible, in this place.

(Parenthetical Pet Peeve) Glasses that fog up when you go outside from air-conditioned room, car, or building.

The foot trampling is fun as always, but still, Georgie would prefer to lie on the ground and have someone stomp him with her feet. Crush him under her strappy sandals. Georgie seems overwhelmed with pleasure, but doesn't feel quite satisfied. He longs for something else.

Rather than stomping on eggs, feeling the messy yolk and white exploding beneath his arch, he would rather be cracking the egg over someone else's foot, rubbing it in.

Georgie's own feet hold only momentary interest for him.

By late afternoon, Georgie needs more than what the mansion can offer. After much searching, he finally finds an ample-sized woman behind a small, out-of-the-way booth in the far corner of the first floor.

"I need something else," Georgie says. "This is all very nice, but . . . Well, it's just too nice," he explains.

He gives a smile to the woman behind the booth. He reminds himself that, even though she can clearly see him, he is still invisible.

The woman smiles back at him politely. She knows more about what happens in this place than anyone, yet she seems to see nothing at all of what is in front of her.

That is the secret to being a good front-desk clerk.

"Did you try the foot smothering?" she says. "Many of our clients find the foot smothering to be entirely satisfactory."

"Well, I tried it," Georgie admits, "but it's over now. I need more, now."

She nods in agreement. "Of course. Quite understandable." She glances over the multi-tiered schedule in front of her. "You are Georgie Gust?"

He nods.

The woman scrutinizes his day's schedule.

"I would much rather be walked on by other people's feet," Georgie says helpfully.

"Oh, I'm afraid we don't have much of that here," the woman sighs. She looks at Georgie appraisingly. "But I think I've found something that will work well for you. Yes. It's just the thing, really."

She points at a small square on the schedule, and Georgie leans over to take a look. His eyebrows rise.

"Starts in 15 minutes—either on the tennis courts or in the shed. Depending on whether you'd rather do it in the dark . . ." she drifts off.

Georgie nods enthusiastically.

"Thank you," he says.

"I'm here to serve." The woman smiles vacantly, her eyes seem to look miles and miles past him, as though Georgie is not really there at all.

Twelve minutes later, Georgie is standing in the doorway of the shed. It's dark inside, but he can hear the sounds of other masochists as they shift around within waiting for something to start.

Minutes pass. Georgie takes his place against the shed wall, watching the lighted doorway as a few other stragglers come in.

Then, there is a long shushing noise as a hard and granular substance pours out of a large container and onto the floor. Salt rock crystals, Georgie remembers. The bits of mineral ping slightly as they strike the hard cement floor.

The door slides closed and Georgie is plunged into utter darkness. The other masochists, who have been whispering and muttering amongst themselves the whole time, suddenly hold their collective breath. For a moment, there is silence.

A voice booms from the darkness: "Get down on your knees, filth!"

Georgie complies with joy. The salt rocks thrust up at him mightily from the floor.

"Now, crawl, like the vermin you are!" the voice booms.

Georgie and the others begin to move around. With every motion, the crystals bite into his skin and the salt begins to burn just beneath the surface. He moans at the pain, the degradation of it all. He hears his fellow crawlers moaning likewise, their voices released by his.

Before he knows it, the room is filled with groans and moans, the pitiable cries of help from the damned; the self-hating salt-crawlers. A part of Georgie longs to get sucked into the orgiastic swirl of pain, the communal hell that they have created. But another part of Georgie (Who? Me, Ben?) floats above him, and watches the scene despite the total darkness. Georgie foreshadows how pathetic he would become if he gave into the moment, if he got carried away with the passion of the crowd. And, seeing himself so clearly, he could not possibly allow himself to become anything else . . . especially a pathetic salt-crawler.

He is both interested and uninterested, enthralled and bored. The self-doubt, the worrying, begins to make him tire of the whole experience. It all falls short of the constant, never-ending orgasm he longs for. His appetite will accept nothing less.

Afterwards, back in his limo, Georgie is dressed anew, in white shirts and shorts, a black belt. He is filthy, yet clean. He sighs, unfulfilled.

His driver Ben glances at Georgie's knees, which are badly bruised.

"What happened to your legs?" Ben asks.

"Oh, that. I crawled on a floor covered with hard salt crystals."

Ben pauses a minute, seeming to assess Georgie's mood. He's been Georgie's chauffeur for five years; he knows his boss pretty well by now. He speaks again. Quietly. "And why did you do that?"

Georgie stares at his driver, whose face is reflected in the rearview mirror. He doesn't seem to judge.

"I don't know. It feels kind of good to crawl around on the ground. To feel pain."

Georgie is lying. It feels fucking great.

"Hmmm," Ben nods.

"It does!" Georgie insists. He realizes he might sound a little crazy.

"My nanny used to do all kinds of sick and twisted things to me," Georgie says quickly and defensively. "You know, like if I didn't do my homework or forgot to flush or something. Stupid shite like that."

"Oh, man, I'm sorry," Ben says. A canned response.

"Anyway, I'm all messed up about it," Georgie finishes lamely. "You know?"

"Yeah, that makes sense. Anyone would be," Ben says, nodding again.

There is a long, uncomfortable pause.

"I bet she was just jealous of you, all your money" Ben says finally. "It wasn't your fault, man."

"Yeah. Yeah! No shite."

Ben pulls the limousine slowly over to the side of the road. Georgie sags back in his seat, and then reaches to the floor between his legs and pulls out a self-help book, which he tosses to the other side of the car.

(Parenthetical Pet Peeve) Car alarms.

The limo stops; Georgie and Ben get out and lean against the back bumper, staring out at the desert. A tumbleweed blows by as Georgie takes a drag on his cigarette.

Ben exhales. "You know, somebody actually takes the time to think up all these fucked up ways of torturing other—keeping them in brightly lit rooms for days, like in Iraq, so that they lose their sense of time. Somebody actually sits down and imagines these twisted ways to warp people."

"Nanny used to get off to the torture stuff, she must have!" Georgie blurts.

That's sick. That's perfect, Georgie decides. But how could I get into that kind of shite? I should hate it more than anyone.

I'll fake it until I make it, until it works.

(It works if you work it.)

Ben sniffs. "Yeah, probably," he says. "You can't turn around these days without bumping into one sicko or another."

He blinks as his words register in his own mind, and glances swiftly at Georgie.

"She must have," Georgie mumbles.

It is clear Ben hasn't heard a word.

He tries to redeem himself. "But that's in the past," he says, playing counselor. "Maybe it's time to move on. To make something of your life, instead of letting your past own you."

Georgie scoffs. "Yeah, I'll make a mess is what I'll do."

"What is it that you want, Georgie, for real?" Ben insists. "You have everything a person needs and more."

And Georgie responds. "The never-ending orgasm. A peak experience that will last my lifetime. That's what I really want."

Georgie's face appears dreamy. He is in some other world, a roller coaster fantasy he can't escape.

Ben snorts and takes another drag. "Speaking of which, that woman you fancy—Margaret? Is she still employed as a helpline operator?"

Georgie waves his hand in front of his face, brushing Margaret off.

"Nah, she's old news," he says.

"Huh," says Ben. "She's the one you went to Tibet with, right?"

Georgie nods.

Ben raises an eyebrow. "Did you guys, uh . . ." He sneaks a quick look at Georgie. "Yeah?"

Georgie snorts. "'Course."

He is lying. They didn't.

"But that bitch, she's just so full of herself," he continues. "Walking around with that fucking holier-than-thou attitude . . . I swear, she's stalking me."

"It was pretty cool of her to go with you on the trip," Ben says.

Georgie gets what Ben means. "Yeah, I mean, she's great and all. Whatever. It's just she likes her job too much. She's one of *those* people."

"At least she has a job," Ben mutters.

(Parenthetical Pet Peeve) The fact that people have to play such dishonest games to get a job.

Georgie continues as if he hasn't heard. "I mean, who likes their job? She's so fucking happy all the time. Happy and fulfilled. That's Margaret. It makes me sick."

(Does it make you sick, Ben? Is that what makes you sick?
Shut up, Dr C. This is my story, see?)

"Yeah, I see what you mean," Ben says.

For a long time, they stay—leaning against the limo and staring out at the desert.

"So you're seeing someone else now?" Ben sniffs and spits softly from the side of his lips.

"Y-yeah. Kind of," Georgie says. He kicks at a tumbleweed that has embedded itself in the back tire of the limo. "My neighbor. Claudia."

Ben whistles and nods. "Nice," he says.

"Yeah?" Georgie sneaks a look at him. "Yeah, she's all right. She's so clingy, though, you know? I'm thinking about calling it quits."

"Hmm," Ben mutters, holding back a cough. "Sounds like you've got it all figured out," he says.

A few hours later, the limo pulls up in front of Georgie's bungalow.

Ben opens Georgie's door.

"See you later," he says.

Georgie gives a half-hearted wave as he unlocks the front door and walks in. The door closes behind him, and he is alone again.

Georgie glances at his answering machine; it sits silent and dark. He presses the play button anyway.

"You have no new messages," the machine chimes.

Georgie turns the shower on and proceeds to shuffle around his filthy living room in the near twilight.

The room is an overkill of every fancy modernization, every electronic doodad, and every entertainment gadget he could possibly squeeze in. There are photos and drawings framed across the walls of every past girlfriend. The bookshelves boast awards, trophies, and posters from his travels. There are seriously intellectual books—endless piles of them—most of them in three copies. His video and music collections feature an equivalent overabundance.

He owns an absurd assortment of things. Sketches and notes are left lying around, some only half-complete. His drawings and paintings are scattered, unfinished, but still indicative of brilliance.

Then, there are the graph paper illustrations; intricate designs clearly drawn with some vague purpose. It's obvious that Georgie has a strong mind, maybe too strong for his own good. He also has an exorbitant number of projects in process—arbitrary projects, redundant and grandiose.

The elements of his house, although artistic, are placed according to obscure mathematical relationships. Everything somehow corresponds. Quantum physics material is neatly clustered, labeled, and placed with the complementary videos and books; an MC Escher print hangs in close proximity.

(Parenthetical Pet Peeve) The valuing of form over function, image over substance in modern society, the fact that Albert Einstein would likely have a hard time getting a job himself if he were alive today due to his messy hair and wore ratty clothing.

Similarly, his stationary bike is surrounded by trophies, workout tapes, sports magazines, and signed baseballs.

The metal ceiling fan reflects light while it spins slowly above the bike. Georgie peeks out the window, hoping to catch a glimpse of Claudia. He rushes over and crouches by the curtains when he hears the door to her house open and close. He wonders if she notices him watching, and wonders whether she counts on the fact that he stares, still waiting. Waiting for her. Waiting for something.

Maybe she is showering. Maybe she has forgotten her towel and will have to walk through the living room naked.

He thinks of sucking on her hooker-blue toenails. They taste like candy.

She is not home. Her house sits empty and dark.

Georgie returns to the running shower, which is now steaming.

He daydreams in the shower, even when the soap falls. He doesn't wash his hair today, remembering someone somewhere once told him: *You never look your best when you meet the one you've been waiting for your entire life. You are never completely prepared for that.*

Georgie resolves to never be fully prepared.

"No sex. Love," Georgie mutters in the shower. "She must've thought of me as the friendly type. That's fine. I'm used to it."

He picks up the bar of soap, runs it over his hair, and rinses out the suds.

"I enjoyed myself, that's all that matters."

Georgie can see God laughing at him, taking delight in Claudia's orchestration of him, that day. That one day, that one eternal day she and he met. The day they were together.

A pensive pause. An epiphany.

"I'll call it personal growth," he tells the walls of the shower. "I'll never hear from Claudia, ever again."

He runs the bar of soap over his hair and rinses out the suds, forgetting he already has.

"My mind ran wild with quiet confusion. It soothed the senses. I could wake up tomorrow, thinking about that day, and the next day about today," he mutters. "While I'm in love, I stop writing, for the most part. I know it won't last forever. I'm in love: I scoff at the thought. Me? In love? In love with Claudia? Me? In love with Claudia . . . ."

Georgie's alarm clock is set for 10:00 am. It blares and blares. He dreams of fires, and sirens. He tosses and turns.

Eventually, the bright white light of the afternoon light shines through his blinds.

Georgie crawls out of bed. The clock mocks him. It's 2:00 pm.

Georgie shuffles into the kitchen. He's a wreck. He pulls a mug from the sink and inspects the inside.

Not too bad, he thinks, again. Just a little grungy around the edges. Kind of like me.

Georgie mopes around and stares blankly. He can't sleep. There's no use sleeping, he thinks, when your every need is attended to. No use in resting when you never exert yourself.

For days on end he stares at the ceiling, at the wall-fan, at Claudia's driveway and her empty windows.

It all boils down to nothing, and he leaves for the grocery store.

"Georgie!" Margaret calls, waving.

(Doesn't this bitch ever go home?)

Briefly, Georgie thinks about leaving, racing out the doors and back home. Instead, he grumbles and plucks a jar of pickles from the shelf in front of him.

"Georgie," she says again, rolling her cart up to his. "How are you doing?"

"Great. Just great," he answers. "How's everything with you?"

"Oh, the same," she says. There is an awkward pause. Georgie scans the nutrition facts on the back of the pickle jar. Meanwhile, Margaret seems to be weighing whether it would be better to buy generic or go for the brand name.

"What do you think about the riots?" she finally says, at a loss.

"Huh?"

Georgie examines an entire wall of mustard.

"The riots. On the news? I'm glad that it's not on our side of town."

"I don't really watch the news." Georgie replies.

"Oh." Margaret looks stunned but only for a second.

"Well you should really look into it," she says brightly. "The east side is getting so crowded now—unemployment, you know—and they're starting to form crowds and . . . and you know they burned down the First Methodist Church, don't you?"

Georgie shakes his head.

"You don't! Georgie, you need to get up to speed. Like I said, who knows when this might start to affect our neighborhood."

"Someone actually takes the time to think up this shite," he mumbles, choosing the store brand Dijon.

"What? Well, yeah." Margaret gives Georgie a searching glance.

He tries to appear normal.

"Anyway, it's all about unemployment and the lack of services for the poor. Crime is through the roof now, on the east side, you know. There's this whole Robin Hood mentality . . . ."

"She must've gotten off to it," Georgie mumbles. "She just had to."

Margaret searches his face. "Who?"

(Claudia . . .)

"What?" Georgie looks at her face. "What are you talking about?"

Margaret blinks. Once. Twice.

"Hey, Georgie, let's get together sometime this week," she suggests, a sympathetic, almost pitying look on her face.

"Yeah, yeah. Sure." he agrees, thinking to himself it'll never happen. He'll pull his shades down, pretend he's not home.

"I'll drop by Wednesday," insists Margaret. She pats his hand lightly. "You sure you're doing okay?"

She smiles. Always with the smiling. Does she ever stop?

"Yeah, yeah. Great," he replies, convincingly.

With that, she saunters off.

Dear Diary:

I went to the doctor's office today. My doctor asked me, "Does anyone in your family suffer from insanity? I grinned and said, "No,   we   all   enjoy   it!"

Making it Count With Dr C

"Who is Margaret, really, Ben? Who is Claudia?" Dr C asks, crossing her slender legs. Her eyes are steady on me. She thinks she sees right through me, knows all my deepest, darkest secrets.

She doesn't know the worst of them.

"Whaddaya mean, Dr C," I tease her. "Margaret's Margaret. Claudia's Claudia."

She nods and leans forward. "I know that. In Georgie's world, that's who they are. But who are they really, Ben? In your world."

Dr C is going deep now. I can tell. Not that it will get her anywhere.

"They're nothing in my world, Dr C. In my world, they don't even exist. That's the beauty of it, you see?"

Dr C sighs. She often wears that dreamy expression when attempting to connect to me on a human level. She leans further forward and her breasts are almost touching my knees.

Yeah, she has my attention now. Maybe I'm the one that gets to go deep this time, huh?

But no. Her holy nipples never make contact. Nor her feet, which I notice are decked out in those red sling-backs. She wants me, wants to seduce me. Tempting me like that. With her tits. Her feet.

"What I mean, Ben," she says, "is do they represent people in your own life? Of all people, why does Georgie meet them? What does he need from them?"

"Why does anybody meet anybody, Dr C? It's all damn fool luck, as far as I'm concerned."

"What do you get out of it, Ben?" she says. It's her attempt to redirect me, put the conversation back on track, back where she wants it.

"What?" I say.

"Out of knowing Georgie. Out of being Georgie. What do you get out of it?"

I stare at her for a moment, blinking nine times. Now she is acting like the crazy one. I may like to take a hop every now and then, may have a bit of a stutter, but even I do not believe that I chose Georgie any more than I believe he chose me.

"I appreciate the company?" I suggest.

Dr C shakes her head slow and heavy. She sighs. "You are not being very helpful, Ben," she says.

There is a moment of silence between us.

"It's not like I chose him, you know," I say finally. There, Dr C. Have a gem.

"Huh?" she mutters, lifting her head slightly.

"Georgie. I didn't wake up one day and decide: 'Hey, you know what would be cool? Having an alter ego. I'll make one up. Call him Georgie.' It didn't happen that way, Dr C."

"Well, of course not, Ben. I would not dare suggest that you did this consciously."

"What happened is: One day I woke up, and there he was. Right next to me. In bed. His head on the same goddamn pillow. I was him. He was me. And that was the end of that. Bam! Now we're stuck with each other."

"You're right, Ben. I'm sorry."

At this, I reel back. The chair I'm in doesn't have wheels. It tips back and falls over, with me along for the ride.

The pain doesn't bother me so much. Not so much as hearing those words from her mouth.

"Uh, what?" I say from the floor, rubbing my head. One, two, three times.

Maybe I misheard. Maybe it's some sort of audio hallucination. Maybe it's just the concussion, talking.

"I am sorry, Ben," she repeats. "You're right. It's lousy of me to expect you'll give me all the answers. I'm just tired, I suppose."

"It's o-okay," I stutter. I lift myself back into the chair, keeping a constant eye on her.

"Why don't you just pick up where you left off?" she prompts me, smiling, "We'll figure it out sooner or later. Don't you worry."

I shrug. "Sure."

Dear Diary:

I think my latest bouts with chronic insomnia are more a mental disorder than a medical disease of the body to be solved with meds. Likely caused by my other conditions, yet appearing to be a control issue—with control being determined by the mind.

Claudia Goes Deep

Later that night, it begins to rain. Georgie rushes to the window as he hears a car door slam outside Claudia's house. He watches as she stomps to her front door with no regard for the wetness. She tears the door open and slams it shut behind her, then turns on every light in the house. He aches for a glimpse of her shadow to fall on the curtains.

(Parenthetical Pet Peeve) While getting packages out of the car, the car door swings back and swats you on the rump.

Her figure pauses, standing still for a moment. Then she's back out the door.

Georgie stares as she stomps back to her car. His groin tightens as she turns up the sidewalk and then . . . up his driveway. *His* driveway.

He looks around frantically, grabs a handful of wrappers from the coffee table, and shoves them in his pocket. He paces once, twice. The wreck of his life is too bright, too visible, to anyone who comes through the front door. He turns off the overhead light.

Claudia's fist pounds on the front door.

He opens the door wide.

"You wouldn't believe the piece of shite day I've had." She barges through the open door, shucking off her wet jacket and handing it to him.

"Yeah?" Georgie asks. He drops her jacket onto a chair by the door.

Claudia sways and barely catches herself with a hand on his sofa.

"Can I sit?" She doesn't seem to notice the squalor.

"Yeah, yeah." Georgie moves a pile of papers and books from one end of the sofa to the other. Claudia collapses into the cushions. Her eyes briefly close.

"Um, are you thirsty?" Georgie asks.

"You got any vodka?" Her voice already slurred.

"Kahlua," he answers.

"Perfect."

Quickly, Georgie pulls a dirty glass from the sink, wipes it with a wet paper towel, and fills it with ice cubes and Kahlua.

"Here" He hands it to her. She smiles and takes a long, slow sip.

"A little dark in here, isn't it?" she says slowly.

Georgie looks around. If he turns on the main light, she'll see the true depth of his slovenliness. Instead, he lights a few candle stubs on the coffee table.

"I lost my job today," she ultimately confesses. "Those fucking bastards fired me."

(Parenthetical Pet Peeve) Resume bullshite. I write, "I coordinated all company communications," when all I did was answer the phones.

Georgie racks his brains, trying to remember how normal people respond to a crisis. *(Normal? Who's normal?)*

"I'm sorry," he says, after a long pause, trying to sympathize.

(That's what normal people do, right? They sympathize.)

"What happened?" he asks.

"Those motherfuckers." She gulps the Kahlua and looks around the room. She's distracted, Georgie decides. That's all. Just distracted.

"I shouldn't have fucked him," she says. "Greg. In case you're wondering. That's who I shouldn't have fucked. It's just like my dad always said, 'Don't shite where you eat.' But who listens to their father? Jesus."

"Oh," Georgie says, as bile rises in his throat at the thought of her with another man. His penis jerks a little, a cock tic. "Who's Greg?"

"Greg was my co-worker; my boss, actually. At the clinic. Fucking pig. He was married, you know, but I didn't care. I mean it was sex. Just sex. Fucking. I couldn't have cared less 'about him or his bitch of a wife—""

Georgie interrupts. "Which clinic?"

Claudia looks at him quizzically. "Mt Shasta," she says. "I'm a paramedic."

"Oh, good," Georgie says, and then snaps his mouth shut.

(At least it's not . . .

Not what, Ben?

You'll see, you'll see . . .)

She shrugs. "Yeah, it wasn't too bad. But when I broke it off with him and Sara—"

Again Georgie interrupts. "Who's Sara?"

"His wife," Claudia says. "I was doing them both, actually. It was fun."

Georgie's mind reels. A married man and his wife? This woman is a mess. She sits there on his couch in all her mascara-streaked glory, her wild hair curling in a scarlet halo—sits there, in her perverted glory, her sexual freedom, her misery. Her overripe breasts sag just like the couch.

She's perfect, Georgie thinks.

(Parenthetical Pet Peeve) Jobs that are a professional appearance, but don't pay a professional salary to go with it—especially for young girls.

"Anyway, when it all blew up, when it all got . . . personal . . . they fired me. He fucking fired me!" She picks up a drawing from the pile of papers next to her and blows her nose into it. She crinkles up the precious thing—the fragile child of Georgie's genius, now covered in her snot—and throws it across the room.

(Perfect . . .)

"Sounds like a creep," Georgie says, in what he hopes is a sage tone. "It's probably a good thing you don't work for him anymore."

Claudia laughs, a tad hysterically. "Sure. That makes sense."

She lifts the Kahlua to her mouth and drinks deep. She sighs and relaxes into the sofa.

"I just want to hurt him," she says softly. "Punch him in the face, slice up his arm, his junk. Make him crawl naked on glass, cut him. Make him bleed. Then he'd know how I feel!" She kicks the coffee table, hard. The corner of it lifts high and the candles and a stack of papers go flying. One of the candles lands on a stack of paper and hisses out. The other lands on Georgie's lap.

"Ow!" he howls, standing and shaking the hot wax from his groin in the suddenly dark room. His heart pounds with the jolt of fear and adrenaline rushes through his veins. His cock jerks slightly.

"Oh shite, oh shite, I'm so sorry," Claudia says. She slides to her knees in front of him, wiping at the crotch of his pants with her hands, clumsily fumbling.

They're lit only by the scanty moonlight that shines through the clouds. Georgie thinks he can see her blush.

"Shite. Are you okay?"

Georgie nods, then smiles. *(Bliss.)* That rush was just what he needed, somehow.

Claudia can't know that, of course. And in the darkness she can't see him smiling.

"That hurt!" he says, crossing his arms in front of his chest and frowning down at her, wanting to see her squirm.

She looks abashed, sorrowful. "I'm sorry!"

Georgie's dick stands at attention to hear her sorrow.

She is perfect in her misery.

Why do I like her best this way? he wonders. What kind of sicko prefers to see a woman cry?

(That's a good question, Ben.

It's not me, Dr C. It's Georgie, see?)

Georgie is struck suddenly by (what he thinks is) the greatest idea of his life. He sits down next to Claudia, his thigh hot up against hers. Then he leans over and kisses her softly on the mouth.

She returns the kiss with feeling.

Georgie breaks it off. They stare at each other a minute.

"That felt kind of good," Claudia admits quietly. "When I burned you. You're not Greg, but . . . it felt kind of good, anyway. Is that sick or what?"

Georgie laughs to himself.

"I've got an idea," he says. "It might sound crazy at first but just hear me out. You're out of a job, now. You've got bills to pay. And me? Well, I need someone . . . someone like you."

He smiles again, his face almost invisible in the darkness.

When Claudia wakes up the next morning, the sun shines brightly through Georgie's slatted blinds. She reaches out her hand to the empty space beside her then sits up. Georgie is gone.

She blinks her eyes once, twice. Then she looks at the nightstand as her eyes widen slightly.

The clock reads: 9:00 am.

There is a high stack of hundred dollar bills beside it.

(Where's Georgie, Ben?

I don't know, Dr C. Can't a guy have a little privacy?)

And next to the money, a note on lined paper. Folded. Once. Twice. Three times. Claudia pulls at it, pulls at the note.

It is so bright in the light of day that she can hardly read it. She leans back into the pillow and holds the note above her head, making a shadow on the page.

Dear Claudia, (the note reads)
As per our agreement last night, here is your weekly allowance.
Claudia thumbs through the stack of hundreds, counting out a full 10. She smiles. Then she returns her attention to the note.
There are, of course, a few vital stipulations:
1. Thou shall not have sexual relationships with anyone but me.
2. Real money must be exchanged for any and all favors.
3. Failure to comply with the above shall result in double pay or loss of job.

(Parenthetical Pet Peeve) Pay cuts.

This discreet contract will never expire, until death.
Yours,
Georgie Gust
Claudia frowns as she looks at the note, then glances over at the wad of cash that has slumped slightly against her leg. She grabs the cash, thumbing through it once again. Then she crumples up the note and throws it in the trash.

Dear Diary:

Marking third day of insomnia, this condition has a mind of its own as a third party, influencing my own authenticity and reality & perhaps of our own individual colorful natures, as I see in my friends. In "confession" of mania, flitting feelings of spontaneous confessional prose spewing like Jack Kerouac writing *On the Road*, or as Carrie Fisher described her feeling as if a "light bulb in a world of moths," regardless of today's work and stresses, I continue my commitment to doing what I feel, and keeping it real, and in the now. My commitment to self: to stay in the heart of my heart, where all the healing and wholeness resides, and to remain just as I am; myself. This rare mental health condition I'm presented with often fascinates me incredibly; the mental challenges often faced & overcome. To seize the day again, in lieu of feeling guilt, apology or uncertainty for yesterday—the past, nor to anticipate tomorrow, in confession of such inspiration having derived from a product of stress & over-work . . . I move forward. I move ahead.

Ah, What a Comfy Web They Weave . . .

Georgie and Claudia get right to business. Claudia comes over later that week, with a pair of handcuffs, a feather duster, a roll of duct tape, and a waxing kit. She clinks the handcuffs together mischievously.

"Hey there, Georgie Gust," she pouts and tips forward slightly, emphasizing her breasts. "Want to come play?"

Georgie nods his head mutely. It all looks pretty kitsch to him, but then Claudia is new at the whole torture thing. In a way, she is now a virgin.

Georgie smiles up at her as she straddles him on the bed.

"What are you thinking, Mr Gust?" she says in mock shock. She closes the handcuff around one of his hands and loops the empty cuff through the holes in his headboard.

"That you're a virgin," Georgie says, wanting to share with her, to make an open forum. Like when he gave her his first pedicure. He wants it to be like that.

"Oh, hardly," Claudia grins and locks the other handcuff into place. She slides off the bed and shimmies out of her too-tight jeans.

"Not s-sexually, I mean," Georgie stutters. "Uh, an S&M virgin. A virgin torturer."

"Oh, Georgie." Claudia sinks to the side of the bed, checking the temperature of the hot wax with her hand. She smiles to find that it is right.

"This may be my first time with a pair of handcuffs . . . ." She places a hand over Georgie's mouth as he smiles.

"But that doesn't mean it's my first time torturing someone."

She slowly stuffs the feather duster into his mouth. The feathers soak up the moisture of his tongue and stick to the roof of his mouth. They flutter against the back of his throat, making him cough.

Georgie tries to protest the feathers, but all that comes out is an indistinct mumble and a frustrated moan. Clamping the feather duster down with her forearm, Claudia uses the duct tape to fix it onto his face.

"There, that should keep your gag reflex from getting in the way," she purrs. "Isn't that nice?"

Georgie rapidly shakes his head. His panic sets off another coughing fit; he chokes, coughs, and sneezes until he can't open his eyes anymore because of the tears streaming from them, until his face is red with frustration.

"If you don't calm down, you won't enjoy the rest of this," Claudia points out, pouting. She has a dipstick covered in the hot wax, letting it drip down onto Georgie's stomach.

"Just hold your breath for a while," she suggests.

He does as she asks, and eventually the feathers that tormented his tonsils are still. Georgie is now able to enjoy the feel of the warm wax as it drips onto him.

It's not too hot at all, more like a warm bath. He swims in the wax, feeling it engulf him.

He thinks of it coating his whole body, spreading up from his toes and over his genitals, up to his belly button, armpits, then up over his face, running into his mouth and locking his tongue in place, and gluing his eyeballs to a fixed stare.

Then he would be dead, but forever existing.

They could prop him up in a wax museum.

He would be famous, and he would not even have to deal with the consequences. The people. Wanting him. Wanting to be with him, touch him, get his autograph.

Georgie indulges these fantasies as Claudia spreads the wax over him. She sings a little tune under her breath as she works. After a while, Georgie is able to entirely forget that the feather duster is in his mouth. He thinks about a little girl pointing to his waxen testicles and asking: "Mommy, what are those?"

"Those are peanuts, dear," the mommy replies.

Fantasies only last so long, however, and Claudia is still spreading and spreading when Georgie runs out of imaginary material.

Georgie starts to wonder if Claudia doesn't have what it takes to be his torturer. This wax stuff is not half bad. But it's not bad enough.

Maybe Samantha, down on that place at Third Street, would be better. She gives one hell of a good foot smothering.

Then, Georgie receives a slight twinge of understanding. Claudia tugs at a bit of hardened wax down by his ankle. And it hurts. A little. The anticipation of greater pain gets him breathing faster. He almost inhales the feathers, almost chokes again.

"Better stay calm, Georgie dear," Claudia reminds him.

She crouches over his body, holding herself just inches above him. Her nose is almost touching his, her breath is on his face.

"All women are torturers," she snarls. "It's in our nature."

Without looking, she catches her nail where the wax stops at his collarbone and gives a swift yank.

"Gmma!" Georgie yells through a mouthful of feathers. Then he starts to cough again.

"We know exactly what it is you are afraid of," she continues, ignoring him. "We know exactly how to hurt you."

She tears off another small piece.

There are no strips! Georgie realizes. He doesn't know much about waxing, not any more than the average male human, but he does know that strips are involved. And with no strips . . . she is going to have to pull off every inch of it by hand. Every round little inch.

Georgie stifles a groan, not wanting the feathers to act up again.

"Men may be stronger, Georgie," Claudia concludes. "But women are the true inflictors of pain."

She rips up a quarter-sized chunk of wax affixed to his nipple, and Georgie howls. The feathers dive down his throat. He chokes, coughing and yelling and cursing Claudia in the best way he can.

Oh, what a woman! Some part of his mind praises her.

Something seems to snap in Claudia. Her eyes are suddenly full of rage. "How does that feel, huh? Does it hurt?" She tears off piece after piece, faster and faster now, until it feels like Georgie's entire torso is enflamed. She stops for a moment, gets back in his face.

"This is what women do to make themselves beautiful for you!" she screams at him, her face red and terrible. She tears off another piece, a dollar-coin sized piece right near his groin. "Am I beautiful enough for you, Georgie?"

She tears and tears at him, at the wax, not paying attention, not even caring where the wax ends and Georgie begins. His pores scream in pain. His skin is covered in thousands of tiny scratches and a few sizeable gouges from her ripping. He bleeds. It is horrible; he's terrified. At the same time, a sense of peace flows over him. He feels detached from his own body, and watches safely from a distance.

He feels sorry for Claudia, who is clearly unhappy.

Feels a little ashamed for taking advantage of her unhappiness.
But only a little.
Mostly, he feels a blissful sort of numbness.
He wishes he could ejaculate, but his cock is encased in hard wax.
Finally, Claudia collapses over him, sobbing. Incoherent. Georgie steadies his breathing, wondering what comes next.
It's almost half an hour before Claudia's breathing slows, before her shuddering ceases. Then she looks up at him, with wide, illuminated irises. Her eyes are wet and glowing. She is beautiful.
"I'm tired of this," she says. With a sniff, she stands and leaves the room.
She leaves Georgie tied to the bedpost, his legs and genitals hopelessly covered in wax, the feather duster taped securely in his mouth.
Huh, Georgie thinks as he watches her go. I wasn't expecting that.
Only minutes later, Georgie realizes that his peanuts itch.
"Biiiiiiitch!!!" he screams up from somewhere in his belly. He enunciates with his esophagus, so the whole neighborhood can hear and understand. Then he chokes and coughs, snorting and hiccupping and sobbing until exhaustion overcomes him and he passes out.

(Parenthetical Pet Peeve) Hiccupping.

Claudia hears his final screams, his despair, his infinite pain.
The shitey thing about empathy, Claudia realizes, is that even when you're torturing someone, you can feel it yourself.
Otherwise you wouldn't know how good it works.
Claudia is not sure if she can handle this job. She loves the feel of Georgie's pain, loves the preparation of it, loves his screams and the sense of vindication that it brings her.
But then there is the pain, too. Claudia's not quite sure she can handle the pain.
When Georgie wakes up, he is free of the wax, feather duster, and handcuffs.
He has no idea how that could have happened. Well, he has three ideas:
Claudia might have pulled off the rest of the wax and his

subconscious mind blocked it out.

Or:

Claudia might have drugged him so he wouldn't feel pain and peeled away the wax.

Or:

Claudia might have melted the wax, somehow, and poured it into a bucket.

(Well which is it, Ben? Inquiring minds . . .

How am I supposed to know, Dr C? You think I'm psychic or something?)

After that night, Claudia disappears. For days, Georgie stalks her house, peeking through the blinds. But she is nowhere to be seen. He calls and leaves message after message—all left unreturned. A week passes.

Georgie leaves her allowance in the mailbox.

He's afraid that maybe she took the first thousand and ran. Maybe she doesn't want to play his game. This fear of rejection— the terror of another failed relationship, no matter how forced—fills him with a mixture of hatred for her, the power she has to make him ill, and a longing that feels a little bit like love.

(Have you ever been in love, Dr C?)

Fear and uncertainty give him a pain that sets him free, that fills him with delicious, slimy horror. He can't get enough of the pain her disappearance brings him. If she abandoned him forever, he might slide deeper and deeper into the cold and empty abyss, the nothingness of self that echoes. Oh, perfectly, that everlasting moment of orgasm.

Although he is spying every moment, waiting for her, he doesn't see the moment she comes, doesn't see her remove the money. And yet it is gone the next day.

Georgie smiles to himself. A feeling even better than pain flushes through his veins.

It is triumph.

Soon after the money mysteriously disappears from the mailbox, Claudia begins to show up at her house now and then. Still, she doesn't return his calls, or come to visit, or write any notes to him. But he knows that she is there, sometimes, and she knows that he knows.

This is a new kind of torture, a new delicious pain. He knows she is still playing. The question now is not "if" but "when." And as the days drag on, Georgie becomes increasingly impatient. He makes a permanent camp in the living room, keeping everything necessary for survival next to the window, within reach of his hands. He lives for glimpses of Claudia through the blinds. Sometimes, in the dark, he imagines her naked, thinks of the softness of her sagging breasts falling to either side of her chest as she sleeps.

As the days go by with no Claudia showing up, Georgie begins to run out of food. He makes runs to the kitchen to refill his water, but when the cupboards are bare he forgets the water too, and sits and sits, watching. Slowly, he begins to starve, dehydrate, melt away into the air. He feels his skin slowly tightening around him, feels the water leaving his body to feed the atmosphere. He sighs, waiting and waiting for Claudia to show up.

Eventually, Georgie becomes too weak to leave money for her in the mailbox. He slumps against the windowpane, his gaze propped up only by his nose at the sill.

The next day, there's a knock at his door.

(Parenthetical Pet Peeve) Door-to-door salespeople.

Georgie swivels his gaze to the door, knowing somehow, just knowing that it is Claudia. But there's no need to answer it, he thinks to himself. She'll come to me.

Then the door is silent, and Georgie feels a sustained moment of terror. That was my chance, that was my only chance, and I blew it.

She's gone now, gone forever.

And I can't lift a finger.

The terror is replaced with a sense of bliss, the orgasmic nothingness of despair. Georgie melts into it, happy to disappear. God takes pleasure in this. Claudia will not miss Georgie, not his orchestration or his loving, playful orders. She'll enjoy her freedom. It is best.

The knock comes again at his door, louder and more insistent. Georgie realizes that it has awakened him from sleep. He has fallen to a heap on the floor, lacking the energy to even prop his nostrils at the windowsill.

He thinks for a moment about answering the door. He decides that he likes the numbness better. His ear sags down to the floor.

The door is pounding, shaking under the power of Claudia's fist.

"Georgie, I know you're in there!" she yells. "I know you're in there!"

Georgie flashes back to Ben's mother, to her voice feather-light in the dark doorway of Ben's childhood bedroom.

"I know you're in there," Ben's mother whispers. Georgie shivers.

"I know you're in there, Benjy . . . ."

A crash of glass and Georgie screams, his voice high like a little girl's. He feels the last bit of life in him leave with that scream. It sounds like a whisper amid the tinkling of glass all around him.

"Damnit, Georgie, what did you think you were doing?" Claudia mutters. She hoists him in her arms.

He is thin, starved, emaciated, jaundiced, and sleep-deprived. Un-showered, swollen boils and pustules adorn his thighs; he has been too exhausted to pop them. His semen-crusted pubes show a history of careless masturbation.

(Parenthetical Pet Peeve) Dieting.

"Poor little Georgie!" murmurs Claudia. "My little paranoid poopsy. I can smell you rotting away!"

He is like a child in her arms, although she never had one. A child, that is . . . .

Georgie awakens in the white sterility of a hospital bedroom. He screams, closing his eyes. His shout is loud, clear, and resounding.

"Georgie!" Claudia cries. She has been sitting next to his bed.

Well, isn't that sweet? some part of his brain snarls.

"What the fuck?" Georgie sits up straight in bed and then collapses backward. A nurse pokes her head into the room.

"Get me the fuck out of here!" Georgie yells, his eyes bulging. The nurse's head withdraws, and she scurries away.

"Georgie, calm down," Claudia tries to shush him. "You're in the hospital. You almost died. You'll be all right. Maybe in a day or two."

Georgie looks at the tangle of cords, ignoring Claudia.

"Why didn't you eat, or buy any food or anything, Georgie?" she asks.

Georgie can see from her face that she knows the answer. She wants it not to be her fault.

Fuck that shite.

Without her guilt, her repentance, this whole arrangement would be nothing better than the fetish houses he used to attend.

And at least at the houses there is a bit of variety.

He finds the clamp on his finger that measures his pulse and rips it off. He smiles sweetly as the blip-blip of the heart monitor begins to sing like a siren.

Nurses, doctors, oxygen therapists rush into the room. They glare at Georgie's sweet smile.

"Get me the fuck out of here," he tells them. "I will pay to have all of this moved to my house. See her?" He gestures to Claudia with an evil glare. "She's my live-in caretaker."

Claudia's eyes bulge, but she dares not refute him.

"I'm a paramedic," she explains. "Mt Shasta—"

The nurses sniff their disapproval, but the doctor eventually approves the arrangement. Claudia can't help but notice how much thicker the doctor's front pocket seems after his interview with Georgie.

Despite all his problems, Georgie can be very persuasive.

Hours later, Georgie is nestled snugly in his home, surrounded by wires and monitors. His heart rate beeps pleasantly. Claudia is dressed in a sexy nurse's uniform, tending to his every whim. For the occasion, she has moved into the room next to his. Just until his health returns, of course.

Once the hospital realized who he was, whose son he was, it seemed they could not get rid of Georgie fast enough. It helped that Georgie pulled a wad of hundreds out of his wallet—a wallet thicker than Claudia's wrist.

"You look good in that," Georgie leers, as Claudia leans over to place a tray of food on his lap. The heart rate monitor speeds up slightly.

"Why, thank you," Claudia simpers. She doesn't really mind the situation, and she likes the way the outfit shows off her figure.

Lunch served, Claudia sits in the chair beside Georgie's bed and crosses her legs, showing her bare thighs, visible through the slits on each side of her skirt. Freckles dotting her legs smile at him through the slits, teasing/inviting him. Her skin wrinkles slightly—just enough.

"Mind if I smoke?" she asks, already pulling the pack out of her purse.

"Does it matter?" Georgie reminds her.

She assesses him carefully, shrugs, and then lights a slim cigarette. She exhales into his face.

Georgie coughs, feeling a faint rush of happiness at his discomfort.

Claudia smiles a Mona Lisa smile, even though she feels momentary doubt when she sees Georgie cough. Part of her doesn't like to see his discomfort, but a larger part wants to hurt him and all men forever and ever (amen)—to twist him and grind him into a pitiful nothingness.

His evident pleasure reassures her that what she has done is good.

It's good for me, good for both of us, she reminds herself.

"You know what I like about taking care of you here?" she asks, smiling wickedly.

"What?" Georgie asks.

Her eyebrows raise, innocent. "The fact that we're alone," she says. Then slowly she drops her hand and grinds her cigarette butt into his arm. Georgie screams. She closes her eyes to pull his pain closer to her. She gives one last twist, feeling the ember crush into empty ash.

Claudia leans back in her chair as Georgie slumps into his pillows. She takes a few deep breaths then feels for his pulse.

His heart is still strong, despite all that he has been through.

Claudia lays herself down at Georgie's side, closing her eyes. Just for a minute . . . .

It is exhausting, taking care of Georgie. She is not just his nurse, after all. She is also his torturer—his personal trainer in pain. She has to ensure she gives him that high he craves and satisfy her own perverse longings; all the while she must be certain it's not too much for him right now. His heart must remain stable, and his body can't go into shock.

The situation requires her to summon all her knowledge as a paramedic and then to go entirely against her training.

She wonders if Georgie took into consideration her medical training when he decided to choose her for his torturer. It would be handy to have a professional on hand, someone who understood the limits of the human body.

She doubts it. It is much more likely that her body, her face, her unique situation made her far more qualified in Georgie's mind than any medical experience would.

"You're one lucky son of a bitch, picking me," Claudia whispers to him gently. "Any other bimbo would have killed you already, or have just taken the money and run."

Claudia breathes deeply and evenly, comforted by the sound of Georgie's heartbeat.

In a little while she will get back to work. But not just yet . . . .

"Georgie," Claudia whispers. He opens his eyes to see her crouched above him like a predatory animal. The buttons of her uniform are open; her simple, pink nipples loom over his forehead.

"Ah, there you are," she says quietly. She reaches down between his legs and strokes the bulge in his pants. She smiles. "Right there?"

He lifts his arm weakly; the wires drag him back down.

"It's all right, it's all right," she shushes him. With a small smile, she puts her hands on his arms, pinning him down beneath her. She kisses him full on the mouth, nibbling at his lips and drawing a little blood. Georgie moans in ecstasy.

With fingers like fire ants, Claudia unzips Georgie's pants. She fumbles his stiffening man dagger away from the hot swamp of his crotch. She pinches the soft skin of his balls with her fingernails.

Georgie cries out in pain and joy. He lifts his head and then, with a sigh, leans back into the pillow.

"That's good," he says.

"I thought you'd like that," Claudia murmurs. She pinches him again, harder. Tears ball up in the corners of his eyes.

When his lids flutter open again, Claudia slowly strips out of her nurse's uniform. Her breasts sag easily against her chest, enticing him. Her skin is pink, spotted with freckles and pores, covered in long, thin, shimmery red hairs. Her carpet matches the drapes, a wild, orange-red, waving him in. His dick is full of blood, thick with it. He thinks it might burst open at any minute.

Georgie sees her red, dangling lips that glisten, wet for him. He strains for her.

"Condoms. In the drawer," he gasps.

Claudia laughs low, almost purring. "Hm?" she says, pressing herself up against him.

"No!" Georgie moans. "The condoms. Please. God, please."

Claudia slowly, inexorably, sinks his shaft inside herself.

"Please?" he whimpers.

"Oh, no," she shushes him. "You don't get it that easy."

Georgie realizes this is part of the game. She is torturing him with contact, invading his sterile existence. What if she gets pregnant? Gets pregnant? Pregnant? Something screams inside him as she pushes against him, deeper and deeper. There is no protection between them, no safe place. If a child results from her torture, she doesn't care.

The fear of this possibility, of her not caring, of the risk—real risk—rises up in him and bursts.

"Yeeeaah?" he murmurs as he comes inside her, hard. She laughs at him. And for a moment, Georgie feels it—that sweet, endless bliss he has been searching for. He laughs along with her, pulling her face down with his plugged-in arms.

Maybe this is it, Georgie thinks. Maybe this is all I've been looking for.

I could get used to this.

Dear Diary:

I'm a narcissist. Many have pointed this out and I've assumed as such years ago, I am aware of my narcissism. "Charming, loveable, inspiring," also, might I add, and I (I-I-I-!!!) often joke about it (or feel guilty about it) but knowing that part of the definition of narcissism is one with no self-esteem (because technically one can't have low or high levels of self-esteem—one either has self-esteem, or not, as I see and know self-esteem). It's not intentional. It's perhaps the "Sheldon Cooper" in me, from *The Big Bang Theory* on TV. Zooey Deschanel's sister, Emily Deschanel, in the show Bones, as well. Many say I remind them of her character, Dr Temperance 'Bones' Brennan, too. Like with my inability to pick up social cues and the like. I think everyone has a bit of narcissism in them. I'm referring to Asperger's Syndrome, rather autism—as per the changes made in the Fifth Edition of the *Diagnostic and Statistical Manual of Mental Disorders (DSM-5)*—at least as I've heard, though I remain unsure. I haven't read it. Autism is one of my diagnoses I've collected over the years, yet I don't mention much of it, generally because within the Schizophrenic and affective, or mood spectrum involving about a baker's dozen of Axis I diagnoses per the *DSM-4*—ugh, just that it all makes me quite a rare case. The doctors all love me because I am "the most interesting person" they've ever met, they say. At least my

Tourette's has become emotionally secondary these days. As a boy, that was tough, man. But alas, here I stand!

Practice Makes Perfect

After that one, pure, perfect moment, Claudia disappears again. The first day, Georgie wanders around aimlessly, wanting her back. The second day he checks the cupboards and realizes he needs to buy food.

Georgie weakly rolls his cart down the aisle at the grocery store, leaning against the bar and shuffling along. He wonders how Claudia could leave him when he is still so weak.

He could die.

If he died, how would she get her money? She is smart enough to know that.

He smiles. Sure, she's smart enough—smart enough to know that he would get back on his feet, if only to crawl back for more.

Georgie briefly considers dying, if only to prove her wrong.

Then he smiles and tosses a few cans of pineapple rings into his cart.

That would be too easy.

Georgie bumps into Margaret on his way out of the store. Their eyes both widen.

"Georgie!" Margaret says.

Georgie keeps walking, his head twisting as he passes her. "Uh, hey. I'm, uh . . ."

Margaret frowns. "Yeah, sure. See you some other time, then."

Georgie nods. "Later."

And then he's gone.

Claudia places herself softly in the shadow of a street kiosk. The clock on her cell phone reads 2:30 pm. It has been over a day since Georgie last left his house. She knows he will need some smokes soon. She stands in the corner of the kiosk, smoking a slim and watching passersby purchase magazines, cigs, and candy.

Just as she has finished smoking her first slim down to the filter, Georgie approaches the counter. With a grin, Claudia crushes the stub beneath her shiny red sling-backs.

The clerk behind the counter hands Georgie his regular smokes. Without a word, Georgie nods and leaves a fistful of cash on the counter (way more than they are worth), and then turns. Claudia

68

sidles up behind him.

"Fancy meeting you here," she whispers in his ear. She savors a momentary thrill as he stiffens. His quick gasp is music to her.

"Claudia . . ." he breathes. He turns around.

Claudia takes a step back, smiling at him, just out of arm's reach.

"I feel like we're drifting apart," she pouts. "I don't want us to become indifferent to each other."

Georgie grins, knowing her game too well already.

"I'll call you, tomorrow." Claudia smiles and winks at him. Then, with a whiff of perfume and stale cigarette smoke, she drifts back into the shadow of the kiosk, and Georgie is alone in the bright daylight of the street.

The day passes without a call from Claudia. Georgie paces, checking the windows. He sits on his front porch, smoking and watching her house. He builds his 10 shots of espresso and gulps them down until . . .

Night falls and he is a wraith, flitting from one window to the next. For a moment, it appears that a light glimmers deep within Claudia's home. But then he blinks, and it is gone.

The next day, Georgie's alarm blares at the usual time. He slams a hand down on the ever-screeching timepiece. Morning light streams through the white blinds, splashing on his dark and dirty carpet.

When Georgie finally sits up, he blinks. The clock alarm flashes 12:00 pm. Georgie moves the blinds slightly and peers out at Claudia's house. This is now part of his morning ritual—to see if she is home, to see if she came home, to see if she has left home. Not knowing where she is, that is a sweet torture indeed.

Her car is parked out front.

He looks down at his limp dick: soft and sagging between his flat, resting testes.

Then, Georgie does something entirely uncharacteristic.

He gets out of bed.

He staggers through the lonely house. As he walks past the bathroom he decides to turn the shower on as hot as possible. The still-hot coffee, freshly percolated from earlier that morning, speaks to him.

Georgie looks around the wreck of the room—its counters scattered with broken glass and spilled coffee, the floor covered in bits of food and blue mold.

He turns and walks out, past the bathroom, which billows steam from the running shower. With bare feet, he advances to the front door. Steam pours out behind him as he goes.

Georgie stalks across the grass that separates their two homes, not caring that someone might see him violating the unspoken rule about using sidewalks.

She has upset his whole existence. He may as well upset her lawn.

Georgie pounds on the front door of Claudia's house, knowing she is inside. He is tired of the hold she has on him, tired of the games. Ever since that moment with her, after he came back to from the hospital. Ever since that moment of pure ecstasy, of unadulterated orgasm—he wants just her. He wants her with him all the time. This avoidance-torture is bullshite, it's like he is paying her for what she usually does anyway, and, even worse, it no longer gets him quite as high.

"This isn't what I paid for," he snarls, as she opens the door. Her eyes widen in surprise. "I could pay anyone to avoid me. Most people do it for free."

For a moment, Claudia looks frightened. Then she laughs. "Drives you crazy, doesn't it?"

"That's not the point," Georgie mutters.

Claudia shrugs playfully. "I'm making lunch. Would you like to come in?" she says, turning and waving. She walks to the kitchen without waiting for his answer.

Georgie follows a moment later, leaving the front door swinging open behind him.

Claudia's kitchen glows with yellow light; it is clean but cluttered. The smell of fresh food entices Georgie to step further.

The coils of the gas-burning stove glow orange beneath a flat pan, on which Claudia is frying a sandwich.

"Would you like one?" she gestures politely.

Georgie shakes his head.

Claudia shrugs and nudges the sandwich with her index finger. She flips it with a quick flash of fingertips.

Georgie is amazed at her lack of fear. He winces when, a few minutes later, she pushes the sandwich onto a plate.

"Ouch!" she cries softly, as the skin of her finger grazes the hot pan. She sucks on the finger for a moment. Then she pulls it out of her mouth and, looking at it cross-eyed, blows. Her gaze flicks to Georgie for a moment. She smiles.

"Why don't you give it a try?" she says slyly. She points at the pan with her burned finger. "Just a little touch."

With a mixture of dread and elation, Georgie slowly brings his finger close to the hot pan. Searing pain blanks his mind, followed by blissful numbness. He pulls his finger off and runs it under the cold water of her sink. The burn throbs painfully, filling him.

"Owww," he moans quietly.

"Not bad, eh?" Claudia insists.

Georgie nods, sucking on his finger. He looks at Claudia appraisingly, lingering his gaze over her hips and breasts.

"I know," she says finally, grinning. "Why don't you sit on it?"

"What?"

Georgie looks at the hot pan. A final hiss of butter burns with a wisp of smoke from its black surface. He looks back at Claudia, thinking longingly.

"Do it," she says. "Don't make me make you." She glares at him.

With one more wistful glance at Claudia, Georgie eases himself onto the hot pan. It seems only hot at first; it wobbles unsteadily beneath his pudgy bottom. Then, all of a sudden, it scorches him. With a yowl, Georgie leaps from the stove. The pan clangs to the ground behind him. Georgie feels the heat of the burn throb in his backside. He closes his eyes, waiting for the numbness and nothingness of pain to soothe his tormented soul.

"Georgie!" Claudia yells, pointing at the back of his pants. He twists, and realizes that the continued heat was not from the burn, but because his pants are on fire.

"Shite!" he screams. The flames lick up his pants, and threaten to wrap around his belt.

Georgie tugs and jerks at his pants until they crumple to the floor. He leaps away from them.

Given oxygen, the fire leaps higher.

"Jesus, Georgie!" Claudia screams. "Put it out!"

Georgie tries to pick up the burning pants and put them in the sink, but midway through the air the fire scorches his hand.

"Shite!" he yells again, throwing the fireball at the sink. It strikes the wall behind, and flames begin to climb quickly up the drapes.

"Georgie!" Claudia screams. "What are you doing?"

She runs to the pantry and grabs a small fire extinguisher. She stares at the directions on the extinguisher as the fire climbs up the drapes and begins to singe the wallpaper. The nearby cabinets begin to blacken—the laminate melts down in boiling drops that hiss as they land on the stainless steel sink. Claudia struggles with the extinguisher's pin. Unsuccessful, she shoves the extinguisher into Georgie's hands and takes a step away from the burning flames. Georgie looks at the extinguisher, trying to distinguish Step 1 from Step 3. The metal grows warm in his hands as the burning plastic of the laminate cabinets drips heavily onto the counter.

"My ass hurts," he whimpers. He watches as the fire begins to eat away at the wall surrounding the windowsill.

Claudia takes another step backwards, her eyes wide and terrified.

With a squeal, she turns and runs for the front door. Georgie follows fast behind, the extinguisher still tight in his hand.

At the doorway, Claudia suddenly stops and Georgie crashes into her.

"My pictures," she moans, and makes a move to run back inside.

Georgie stops her.

"Call the fire department," he commands, finally abandoning the pain that swelters up and down his thighs and back.

Georgie realizes that he is not wearing any pants. He looks toward the street, where a small crowd of neighbors have gathered.

"What?" he yells at them, then realizes that his underwear is singed, his legs lobster-red. He turns to the street and roars in frustration.

"Call the goddamn police!" he screams, and they scatter.

"My cell phone's inside!" Claudia wails, pulling at her hair. The smoke from the fire has begun to press heavily against her front windows now. Georgie glances at her, pleased with the smudge of smoke on her turned-up nose, and with the frantic, in-drawn terror of her brilliant green eyes. At this moment, he despises her for her idiocy, for her weakness in the face of this catastrophe. At this moment, she is perfect in her inadequacy.

Georgie pulls out the pin from the fire extinguisher with a confident jerk. He throws it on the grass, and scoffs.

"Use my phone," he tells her, pointing at his house.

Without a word, she turns and races for his front door.

Georgie walks into Claudia's burning house and stands in the doorway of the kitchen, watching as the room becomes one huge blaze. He aims the fire extinguisher at the cabinets and begins to spray; watching the white foam as it singes black spots into the fire that ignores it completely.

Like pissing down a well, Georgie thinks, and closes his eyes blissfully.

As the extinguisher runs out, the fire rages on. Georgie takes a step back from the flames, which have only grown hotter. The bulge builds in his shorts. Without warning, his huge cock peeks out between the soft flaps. It thrusts itself forward toward the flames. With a cry, Georgie erupts onto the damage he has caused. The semen spurts in short little gusts, which hiss and boil as they strike the hot floor.

Georgie takes another step back, beaten down by the scorching flames. Seeing there is no hope for the house now, his cum becomes an impossible stream, a pure, lasting orgasm that splashes wetly from the tip of his penis and dissolves into steam in the heat of the fire. Step by slow step, Georgie backs away from the fire, spewing constantly until he reaches the front doorway. The light from the midday sun warms his back, and his dick suddenly sags, lifeless. Georgie staggers backward a few more steps, an idiot grin on his face. With a drooling, gurgling sigh, he collapses backwards onto the lawn.

When the blaring red fire engines finally pull up in front of Claudia's house, flames are flickering teasingly from the attic windows. Claudia is huddled over Georgie, whom she has dragged away from the front of the building after carefully tucking his limp dick back into his shorts.

"My God," he mutters under his breath, his eyelids fluttering rapidly. "My God. Was it good for you?"

Claudia can't help but think that Georgie is delusional.

"Not that great," she mutters. She watches as the firefighters' hoses do nothing against the roaring inferno that was once her home. "Shite. What am I going to do now?" she wonders out loud.

Georgie's eyes open wide. He grins a slow grin.

"You can stay with me," he says quite lucidly. Then he laughs, so quietly, and coughs the last bit of smoke from his lungs.

Dear Diary:

I've got to stop being unhappy with myself. I am perfect. I've got to stop wishing I looked like someone else. I've got to stop hating my body, my face, my personality, and my quirks. I should love them. Without these things, I wouldn't be myself. Why would I want to be someone else? I've got to have confidence in who I am. If anyone hates me for being . . . myself, that's their problem. I can't let my happiness depend on others. I have to love who I am and be happy. Happiness is simple. Simple is difficult. I guess everybody has their own flaws and imperfections. That's what makes us all special and beautiful. Therefore, to love what it is that makes me different must be the answer because I'm pretty amazing!

Claudia Moves In (Part II)

Claudia skips over to Georgie's California bungalow. Her house is a charred pile, and the insurance company is balking at payment. It's not the first time she has ever moved in with a guy, but it's a step forward in her and Georgie's relationship.

It's not really a relationship, Claudia has to remind herself constantly. It's an arrangement. A purely financial arrangement.

It is only going to last until the insurance money comes through on her house.

But that could take years, Claudia thinks, with a sly nod. Years . . . .

Georgie glances up slowly from his perch on the porch when Claudia crosses the lawn.

She is skipping—actually skipping.

She leaps up the front stairs with a single bound then spreads her arms above her head in a 'V' for victory.

Not bad, for a lady in her 40s, Georgie thinks. This bodes well on the prospects of their sex life.

"It's just until the insurance comes through," Georgie points out. "Nothing to get excited about."

Claudia hangs her head, her mood crushed.

Hey, I thought I was the one supposed to be torturing you, Mr Georgie, she thinks.

She tries out an evil grin, and the look of shock on his face cements her instinct. Lesson number one learned: Never show Georgie your true feelings.

"I'm just thinking of all the fun we're going to have," she says, pouting at him.

Georgie shudders and gives a small smile of anticipation.

Claudia laughs. It was just the reaction she was hoping for.

Asking Claudia to move in was probably the best, and worst, decision of his life. Georgie ponders this epiphany as she plucks the hair from his forearms, one by one, with a pair of tweezers. It was the best decision because now she can't torture him with her absence, which anyone—and everyone—could do. Now, Georgie feels like he is getting what he pays for. And maybe even a little extra.

However, it's the worst decision because he has to see every side of her now. Sometimes she is happy or silly, even though he can tell she tries very hard to be neither of those things when he is watching. Still, no one is perfect. Seeing Claudia in a pleasant mood, in a celebratory mood, kills for Georgie the little sadomasochistic fantasy he is trying to live out with her. It's a buzz kill, is what it is.

Georgie has the chance to examine Claudia from all angles, now. He knows about the tiny wrinkles on the underside of her butt cheeks. He knows about the shining yellow earwax that adorns the outer rim of her ear canal. He knows the yellow glow of the whites of her eyes, and the myriad arteries that grace them.

In short, he knows too much. Much too much.

On the plus side, Georgie gets to torture Claudia a little, too. After all, she is living under his roof. And it is in his nature to do so.

"Hey Claudia, you want to get me a glass of water?" he says lazily one afternoon.

"Do I look like your damn housemaid?" she fires back in reply.

"No . . . although you are on the payroll," Georgie muses. "Unless you'd rather not be?"

Claudia slams shut the book she was reading and stands up. She glares at the back of his head. Georgie is not exactly sure how he knows this, but he does. Claudia stomps into the kitchen, muttering. When she returns, she is holding a tall glass of water. She holds it high above him, presenting it to him like a bottle of wine. Georgie nods, smirking.

With an expression that echoes the contempt of his, Claudia pours the water into his lap.

It is scalding hot. Georgie howls with pain (and pleasure).

"Bitch!" he yells. "Ah . . . !" He sucks air in through his teeth.

Claudia's smile falters slightly. He can see he has an opportunity.

"My balls," Georgie groans. "Damn it . . . I think . . . Ow!" he screeches. "Damnit, Claudia, you burned my nut sack! Shite!" He bends over his crotch protectively.

"Oh God, Georgie—are you okay? I didn't think " . . . ," she sputters.

"Ah. Ah!" Georgie yells. "I might never have an erection again. What if you broke it? Fuck!"

Claudia is crying now, really scared. "Georgie, I didn't know," she sobs. "You've got to believe me. I wouldn't have done it if I knew. God, it was such a stupid, petty thing to do. Stupid. Georgie, I'm so sorry." Tears pour down her cheeks. "Please, please forgive me," she begs him.

"Eh, it's probably nothing," Georgie says simply, and sits back in his chair. He smirks in her direction once again.

Claudia rocks back on her heels, shocked, as she realizes she's been duped.

Lesson number two, she thinks. Never believe a thing that Georgie says.

For days, Claudia mopes around Georgie's house. At first, she was excited to move in with him. Now, there is no excitement left. Just drudgery. For one thing, neither she nor Georgie have a job. The closest thing Claudia has to a job is the perpetual torment of Georgie. This was easy when she could do so by absenting herself. But at this point, living with him, she has nowhere else to go. She has to actually . . . do stuff.

Claudia drifts into the kitchen, which she has managed to scrub to a pleasing, sterile shine. The appliances glint miraculously. Yet, when she opens the refrigerator, all that greets her is ketchup and steak sauce, a pizza box with one dry slice left, three beers in an ancient 12-pack, and a sadomasochistic porno mag.

She picks up the pizza slice, leaving the empty box, and grabs a beer. Thinking twice, she nips the S&M magazine off the middle shelf, thinking it wouldn't hurt to get a few new ideas. Georgie seems pretty tired of the cigarette burning and pinching bit—he may even have left the magazine in the refrigerator for her to find. Or absentmindedly set it down and forgot it. Or, for some unknown reason, decided that porn belongs in the refrigerator. With Georgie, it is impossible to know.

Georgie enters the room just as she is leaving, and they both avoid each other's gaze. For the last several days, they have been floating around like this, pretending to be invisible. It is easier, somehow, easier than reconciling her paycheck with the attachment that would otherwise grow between them.

That has been growing, whether we like it or not.

She slides past him in the doorway, looking down at the molding that lines the hall floor. Keeping her eyes on her toes, she walks up the stairs to the red bedroom that she has made her own. She flops against the red and white gauze canopy bed, enjoying the sense of disorientation and dizziness that comes over her from days and days of nothing stacked together all in a row and begins to gnaw at the pizza.

Claudia flips through the magazine as she tears at the stale pizza with her teeth, looking at the pictures with a combination of loathing and embarrassment. When it comes down to it, the pictures are just funny—she wants to laugh. But when she thinks about actually trying the whip and thumbscrews, it makes her feel a little sick.

She licks the crumbs from her fingers and softens the last bit of dry crust in her throat with a long, cool gulp of beer. She laughs, softly, and tries to blink small tears from her eyes. She chugs half the beer and turns the page.

The face on the man in the next page makes her gasp for a moment, until she realizes that it is not Greg. Not really . . .

"Oh . . . ."

She moans in disappointment. She examines what he is doing, and finally notices the woman in the picture. They are twisted into crazy, deformed shapes—his face is marked with pain, hers crazed with triumph. The blood glistens so moistly on his skin that Claudia can almost hear it drip onto the hard wood floors.

Claudia polishes off the last of the beer, touching the picture lightly with her fingertips. With a flash, she sees herself as the girl in the picture, and Greg below her whimpering in pain and desire. She sees herself standing triumphantly over him . . . with a small moan she presses herself against the pillows, touching herself carefully, a small smile spreads across her face.

When she's done, she tiptoes to the doorway, still naked.

"Georgie."

Claudia's voice is a chime that echoes in Georgie's ears as he rummages through the cupboards to figure out where she hid all the damn coffee cups. He perks up; he percolates.

He moves over to the stairs with two long steps. "Yeah?" he calls.

"Would you come up here, darling?" she says, in a deep, seductive voice.

Georgie shrugs and trudges up the stairs.

"What is it?" he says before he turns into the room. As he takes a step inside, the light goes out. He is plunged into darkness.

Claudia's voice seems to bleed out of the walls. "Just one more step in, Georgie," she coaxes him. "Wait, stop! Now one to your right."

Georgie breaks into a sweat. A low rumble sounds in the darkness before him, seeming to come from the floor.

"Watch out," Claudia purrs. "You don't want to wake it up, do you?"

Georgie feels himself shrinking, but as he is shrinking the walls close in on him—he can't see them but he can feel the air of the room grow tighter, denser. The air wraps around him, trapping him in place. He can't breathe.

"Claudia!" he screams. "Let me out!"

Claudia's laugh echoes from the walls. She is not in the room with him. There is no room.

"Claudia!" Georgie screams. He flails with his arms and strikes hard wood on every side. His wrist tingles where it has struck the wall—his elbow explodes in a series of sparked nerves. He turns back around, beating at the door behind him, which is not a door any more but a wall—not a room but a box, a dark, airless box.

This is my coffin, Georgie realizes, with a terror that chokes him and brings him to his knees. I'm dying, I'm dead; she killed me.

(Who killed you, Ben?

Not me, Dr C, not me . . . .)

Georgie collapses into dark nothingness. His slumping body knocks the side of the coffin, bringing it crashing down to the floor. Georgie lies in it helplessly, in a daze, his fingers twitching feebly against the wood.

When Georgie wakes up, he's in his bed with Claudia. The sheets around him are thrashed, twisted up like a thick rope.

The ones around Claudia are somehow unmoved, as smooth as sand dunes in moonlight.

A dream? He wonders. Or did she wait until I passed out and haul me into bed?

Claudia rolls over, and even asleep the look on her face is triumphant, gloating.

Georgie will never know if it was a dream or not.

(Well, wait, Ben—was it a dream or wasn't it?

How am I supposed to know, Dr C? When I'm Georgie, and he's me—I only know what Georgie knows, and he . . .

Does Georgie know what you know, Ben?

Sheesh, Dr C, lighten up a bit, will ya? I can't tell you, yet . . . can't tell yet.)

Georgie feels a cold hand wrap around his heart. He rolls himself over and attempts to go back to sleep.

The blue full moon lights up Georgie and Claudia on the white sand beach. They are a happy-go-lucky, fun couple: all white-toothed smiles and sleepy bedroom looks. It's as if though they are posing for cheap promotional brochures for some ritzy beachside resort or spa.

Georgie and Claudia chase each other playfully around the big white sand dune. Claudia dips her feet in the white-foamed seawater as she sits at the edge, where the water mixes with the sand. Georgie tries to lick her wet, gritty feet, but she grinds his face into the salty tidewater, using her perfectly-manicured, stylish feet to hold his head down. Georgie's hair bobs up and down with the rising and falling waves as Claudia laughs.

As the sun sets, Georgie and Claudia dance in the empty beach parking lot, near his sporty gull-winged car. The car's CD player is set on high volume, playing '80s disco music with a pulsing, throbbing beat.

In the background, a silent fire alarm wails.

During the day, Georgie is a zombie. His dreams unsettle, unnerve him. He's terrified they are real, and that he doesn't know it. He is afraid that they are false, and the daytime is what's actually real. He is afraid to sleep, afraid to wake up.

He is fearful he might be going crazy.

Georgie zombies through the kitchen, the living room, the front porch, onto the back stoop, and over again. Sometimes he zombies out on the couch, just staring at the wreck of Claudia's burned-down house.

That must be real, if he can see it, if it's there all the time. That must be real, at least.

Georgie is so out of it that when the house phone rings, he actually answers it for once.

"Geow-gie boy!" his mother's voice cries out joyously over the line. "Lord, I thought I would never hear your voice again! How you been, Geow-gie?"

Of all the times to forget to let the answering machine get it! "Hi, Ma," Georgie mutters.

Claudia, in the next room, pricks up her ears. Georgie can see mischief brewing in her brain, and he makes haste to avoid it.

"Hey, I can't talk right now, Ma," he says. "I'm pretty busy."

"What, ya think you're some kind of big shot, Mr Geow-gie?" his mother teases. "Mr Big Shot don't have time for his own muh-thah?"

Claudia's hand snakes around the side of his head and plucks the receiver from his hands.

"Mrs Gust!" Claudia says pleasantly. "I am so glad you called." Her eyes narrow wickedly.

Georgie can hear his mother asking "And who might you be?"

"I can't say I'm surprised Georgie hasn't mentioned me to you yet," Claudia schmoozes. "He's such a secretive little devil, isn't he?"

Georgie can hear his mother most rapidly assenting, and knows that the battle is lost before he can even begin fighting. His mother will love Claudia. Discussing Georgie's many faults is something she can go on about for hours.

He sits down heavily on the floor and looks up at her, begging her not to do damage she can't undo.

For God's sake, please don't invite us to dinner, he prays.

"I'm Georgie's girlfriend," Claudia reveals. "His live-in girlfriend."

The sound of his mother babbling in disbelief rises so much that Claudia has to hold the receiver away from her ear. She grins wickedly at Georgie.

"I know, Mrs Gust. Georgie's quite the catch." She winks at him. "Yes, yes. *Your* Georgie. Georgie Gust." Claudia nods. "That's the one."

Georgie can make out the sound of his mother inviting them: "Oh, we must have you over for di-nah."

"I'd be so pleased to meet you and your husband. Oh, yes. Georgie is delighted too. Next Thursday? Perfect."

Claudia laughs. "Oh, yes, I'm writing it on the calendar. Next Thursday. I promise. Bye, Mrs G."

With a triumphant smile, Claudia hands the phone back over to Georgie. "She wants to talk to you," she says.

"Geow-gie!" his mother yells at him. "Howdja get such a nice goyil-friend? I can't wait to see you two on Thursday. I love her already!"

A pause.

"She's not one of those vegetarians, is she?"

"Georgie." Claudia's voice is a raspy, raw edged thing that sets Georgie's heart beating. He runs to the stairs, knowing what's to come and wanting it anyway. "Yeah?" he calls.

"Would you come up here, darling?" she says in a deep voice that is not quite her own.

He takes the stairs two at a time.

"What is it?" he says, before he turns into the room.

He sees her.

She's lying on her side, facing the doorway. Naked. She pats the bedspread beside her.

"Just more of the same," she says, with an evil gleam in her eye.

He takes two steps and a hop that lands him on the bed. He grins.

"You just lie back," she commands.

Georgie complies.

With a few deft gestures, she frees his already hard cock from his khakis. A nip of his nipple and a quick, bruising pinch of nails at his pudgy sides, Claudia then lowers her face to his groin.

"Ah . . . all right," he stutters, watching her intently.

She goes down, pulling his shaft up, up inside her mouth. Her tongue is moist and does a little dance around him. He moans as his blood rushes to the very ends of him.

Slowly, Claudia clenches her teeth against him.

"Ah! Ow," Georgie warns her.

She laughs, the sound muffled by his big pussy-spear. She sucks him hard and he moans.

"Oh . . . !"

Then her teeth scrape him again.

"Ow!" Georgie yells.

Claudia swiftly pulls her head up. She glares at him with her glittery green eyes. Shut up," she commands.

He opens his mouth and then snaps it shut.

She sucks him down again and Georgie can feel himself starting to disappear inside of her, down the black tunnel of her throat. She is scraping, scraping him away like a cheese grater, and soon he will be nothing but a tiny little carrot . . . and then a stub . . . and then nothing.

He cries out with terror and pain, but the blood pounds faster and faster into his dick. He feels the pain as a kind of ecstasy. It moves his blood. Everything throbs. The pain and the pleasure. Together. Pounding. Pounding in his ears.

Georgie screams, "Oh God, oh fuck!" as everything rises up in him all at once.

82

Claudia jerks her head up with one final slash of her teeth. She wipes her mouth and grins.

"What . . . what? No! I'm so close!" Georgie pleads.

Again, she flashes him a wicked, evil grin. "Aww, what a shame," she says, lifting herself off the bed and swiftly pulling her clothes back on. Georgie's dick and balls are screaming at him, throbbing still. He looks down, expecting the whole thing to be in shreds.

Instead it pulses purple at him, an angry tower.

Now even my cock hates me, Georgie thinks, as Claudia gives one last flip of her hair.

At the doorway, she looks over her shoulder for one final gloat. "You didn't think it would be that easy, did you?" she taunts him.

And then she is gone.

Dear Diary:

Life seems to give me answers in three ways. It says, "Yes" and gives whatever we want. It says, "No" and gives me something better. It says, "Wait" and gives me the best. If I'm committed to my dreams, I'll win anyway—to not just dream, but to live our dreams, and to keep moving towards them.

Dinner with the Gusts

"Geow-gie!" Mrs Gust screeches when she opens the door to her son. "Geow-gie, you haven't been over in ages!"

Mama Gust is a huge woman dressed completely in purple spandex. Her hair poofs around her thick jowls like a ball of cotton. One forgotten curler hangs from a lock behind her ear, like jewelry.

When she wraps Georgie in a hug, her body engulfs him, sucking him into the fat rolls of her enormous belly. For a moment, he cannot breathe.

"And Claw-dia!" she yells. Georgie snorts at the accuracy of her misnomer. Claw-dia has claws, all right. "Claw-dia, you're so old!"

Georgie laughs out loud at the look on Claudia's face. It looks like she is about to get a little more than she bargained for.

"Well, I'm sorry, dear, but you must know that Georgie here is only 32." Then Georgie's mother seems to remember what a "lovely goyil" Claudia is. "But who am I to judge?" she concludes. "You two are happy, arentcha?"

Georgie and Claudia nod uncomfortably, without looking at each other.

"Well, that's that, then!" Georgie's mother brushes her hands together and shifts herself out of the doorway so Claudia and Georgie can enter.

The front hall is enormous. It is clear to Claudia that the Gusts have money. A curving marble staircase ascends to her right. A chandelier hangs from the vaulted ceiling, dripping money.

"Your father's at the table," Georgie's mother yells to them as she disappears down a long hall. "Dinner will be out in a minute."

"Not my father!" Georgie mutters, glancing at Claudia. "Not my father, too! You know I can't stand him, Claudia!"

She just shrugs. "I know."

Georgie leads her into the dining room, where they are greeted by another crystal chandelier, a shining dark-wood dining table large enough to seat twelve, and Georgie's father, who rises up from his third martini. The flush in his face and the gleam in his eye gives him dead away.

"Georgie-boy!" he says, a little too loudly. "Georgie-boy, you finally came! And with a girl, too." He appraises Claudia with a knowing eye. "A pretty little thing, isn't she?" he says finally.

"She's in her 40s," Georgie's mother screams from the kitchen. Claudia flinches.

"Now don't listen to her," Georgie's father says in a low voice, taking Claudia by the elbow. "She's just jealous."

He winks and guides her to her place at the table.

Georgie pops open the bottle of wine they have brought for the occasion and serves Claudia, himself, and his mother a glass. Georgie's father declines, gesturing to the martini pitcher on the sideboard.

"Gotta dance with the girl that brung ya," he jokes.

In a few minutes, Georgie's mother sails from the kitchen with a rolling cart packed with food—a glazed ham, scalloped potatoes, asparagus wrapped in prosciutto, tomato slices topped with basil and broiled mozzarella, and a huge bowl of fresh garden salad.

"Well, help yourselves," Georgie's mother cries. "You both look about half-starved."

"Thank you, Mrs Gust. This looks amazing," Claudia says politely, hiding her smile.

Georgie's mother heaps an extra spoonful of potatoes on Claudia's plate. "Oh, I do what I can," she says.

There is only the sound of chewing and the mumbling of appreciative comments for a while. Then:

"So where didja two meet, then?" Georgie's mother asks.

"Oh, we were neighbors," Claudia explains.

"Didn't have too far to move, then, didja?" Georgie's mother jokes.

Georgie and Claudia both nod.

"Hm," Georgie's father mumbles into his ham.

"So Georgie's Tourette's doesn't bother ya, then?" Georgie's mother continues. "It runs most of the goyils off. Then again, with you being so old and all."

"Ma," Georgie whines. "Claudia's not old."

"Well, the goyil knows her age," Georgie's mother says huffily. She turns back to Claudia. "Anyway, we are just so glad that you gave our Geow-gie a chance. He needs a lady around, someone to pick up after him. You take good care of our boy, dontcha Claw-dia?"

Claudia grins. "Of course, Mrs Gust. Georgie's a little rough around the edges, but he cleans up real nice." She reaches over and ruffles his hair.

Both Georgie and his mother stare at the affectionate gesture. Georgie's father snickers slightly.

"The Tourette's isn't catching, you know," Georgie's mother says, continuing on her favorite topic. "You don't need to worry about coming down with it. Though your kids might."

"Ma!" Georgie snaps. The last thing he needs is his mom putting ideas in Claudia's head.

"Ma," he continues, changing the subject, "How is everything down at the club?"

"Oh, same as ever, Geow-gie dear," she says, patting his hand with her own. "Those same bitches always sniffing 'round with their noses in the air, and your father's tennis game is as bad as ever. I don't know why we bother to keep up our membership, Huey, it's so damn expensive."

"Dear, it doesn't matter that it's expensive," Georgie's father says very carefully. "We already have more money than we know what to do with."

Claudia glances over at Georgie to confirm that this is true. His face is still as stone, but she can tell that Georgie knows his father is right. This explains so much. Like why Georgie never seems to worry about not having a job.

"So, Mr and Mrs Gust," Claudia breaks the tension, "where did you two meet?"

"Oh, it was so romantic," Georgie's mother gushes. "We met at the beach, under the moonlight. Do ya remember it, Huey?"

"No, no. We met at the restaurant. Remember?" Georgie's father shakes his head disdainfully and turns to Claudia. "Well, we knew each other in high school, of course. But we met up again at a restaurant here in town."

"Aw, I like the beach story better, Huey," Georgie's mother whines playfully.

"Well, you can't make it more real just because you like it better," Georgie's father snaps.

Claudia and Georgie begin to pay very close attention to the food on their plates.

"Gosh, Huey, don't get so upset," Georgie's mother says in a hushed voice. "We've got company."

Georgie's father mumbles, polishes off his martini, and attends to his potatoes.

"We met at the beach," Georgie's mother continues, as if nothing at all had happened. "At a party. We were so young back then! But even then, I knew that Huey would ask me to marry him . . . someday. Oh, we danced all night"—"

She stops abruptly and looks at Claudia and Georgie. "Do you two go dancing?" she asks. "You really should. Maybe Geow-gie's got two left feet, but you should still go dancing."

Georgie shrugs.

"Maybe sometime," Claudia says.

Georgie's mother nods (once, twice, three times).

Finally, she says, "Are ya ready fer some dessert? I bet yer ready fer some dessert." She stands up and waddles from the room.

Georgie's father helps himself to the martini pitcher on the sideboard, while Claudia tries to catch Georgie's eye. She had come here to humiliate Georgie in front of his family, to torture him with their disapproval and disgust. But she finds that she is too late. They already have plenty of disapproval and disgust with Georgie. They can hardly stand each other, let alone him.

Having dinner with his parents is torture enough for him.

Claudia wonders if there is a way to utilize dinner-with-the-parents torture without her actually having to be there, but she suspects that if she is not there to drag Georgie along, he probably wouldn't go.

She can't really blame him.

"Here it is," Georgie's mother sings out as she comes back through the door. She has a three-tiered cake on a beautiful silver pedestal, blazing with candles. "It's for your birthday, Geow-gie!"

She sets the cake down on the table. The top is decorated with racecars and checkered flags.

"It's not my birthday," Georgie says sullenly. Still, his eyes light up as he looks at the cake. It might just be the glow of the candles, though.

"It's for all the birthdays ya missed having with us," Georgie's mother said. Claudia wonders if the guilt trip is on purpose, but all she can detect in the woman's face is a happy glow.

Georgie's mother exudes guilt. It's not that she tries to make people feel bad, just that her very existence makes people feel bad.

"When Geow-gie was little, he always wanted to be a racecar driver," Georgie's mother explains to Claudia. "Ever since he was little, he wanted to be a driver."

"Who wouldn't?" Claudia exclaims.

When no one is looking, Claudia sneaks one of the candles off the top of the cake. She holds it at an angle under the table, so that the hot wax drips slowly on the crotch of Georgie's pants. She knows it doesn't hurt him, not much at least. It is more like a pact, of sorts. Or a gesture of friendship.

Georgie finds her free hand with one of his and squeezes it, tight. She can see a tiny tear glimmering in the corner of his eye. Then, with a long-suffering sigh, Georgie blows the candles out.

Dear Diary:

Yikes, when someone is just here—or there—for me, it can sometimes bring even just some hope when all else seems completely hopeless. I trudge on.

88

The Fruits of His Labor

(Isolate me. Destroy me. Tear out my eyeballs and do your dance in the sockets.

You know you love me. I know you hate me. Let's love and hate our way to the bank to the grave to the back of my shiny new car.

Trap me. Smother me. Strangle me into nothingness.

I want your blood and flesh to become apparent to me. I want to meet your hungry, tearing inner ego. There's only one way to go, now, and that is to disappear in your loving strangle, your twisting dark galaxy.

Isolate me. Love me. Destroy me.)

Georgie opens his eyes and realizes that everyone is staring at him. Everyone. Who are these people? Why am I here?

"Don't you remember?" Claudia's voice taunts him. "You wanted this."

Georgie blinks and looks around, not finding Claudia anywhere. Instead, he is surrounded by a wall of faces. They all stare at him, mouths agape.

A child makes a small sound and its mother pulls it close, protecting its face with her hands.

"What . . . ?" Georgie finally croaks.

A man steps out from the crowd.

"Just what do you think you're doing?" the man demands. His voice is angry, though his eyes convey something of an understanding smile.

"I . . . I don't know," Georgie says.

The man's face distorts with mockery, with hatred.

"There's obviously something wrong with him," a woman to his left whispers.

Georgie looks down at himself.

He is naked.

Georgie staggers away from the people, trying to hide himself behind his hands. His face is a ball of fire that ends in bright splashes on his back.

"Fuck," Georgie mutters. "Fuck, fuck, fuck."

He has no idea how he came to be naked in the streets, only the vague sense that it is Claudia's fault.

He doesn't even know where he is. He steps into three different stores before finding someone who will not scream and shove him back out into the street again. Finally, he steps into a dingy corner drug store, which is being watched over by a wrinkled old clerk who has probably seen everything there is to see.

"Can I use your phone?" Georgie asks, desperately, panting. The clerk eyeballs him, from the slight fat rolls of his neck to his thick ankles.

"You better cover up," the clerk says slowly. His face doesn't twitch—not even an inch.

Georgie gapes at the man. He gestures up and down the length and width of his naked body.

"I can't," he squeaks. "I just woke up like this."

The clerk shrugs. He points to the bargain bin in the corner, which overflows with t-shirts.

"Buy a t-shirt. Then you can use the phone," the old man suggests.

"Does it look like I have my wallet on me?" Georgie gestures frantically to his pocket-less, bare legs.

The old clerk raises his eyebrows then points at Georgie's right hand. Georgie lifts his hand and realizes that he has been holding his wallet the entire time.

Really, he wonders.

(What's real, really?)

Georgie pulls out a 10 and buys a t-shirt. It is so long that the cotton falls around his knees. He feels like a little kid in an old-fashioned nightie.

The old man smiles. "Phone's back here," he says, gesturing behind the counter.

Georgie comes around to the back of the counter and feels an instant sense of relief. From behind the counter, his legs are hidden. To anyone on the other side of the counter, he is just a guy wearing a really long t-shirt.

"Hello?" Ben's voice speaks into his ear through the phone.

"Ben," Georgie gasps with relief. "Ben, you gotta to come get me. I'm . . . I'm . . . Claudia . . . Shite, you just have to come get me. Now!"

There is a muffled sound on the other end of the phone. "Sure thing, Mr Gust. Where are you?"

"Uh . . .," Georgie looks around him then lifts his mouth over the top of the receiver. "Hey," he asks the clerk. "Where am I?"

The old man snorts unbelievingly. "Don't ask me," he says.

"What? You don't know where we are?" Georgie exclaims. "It's your store, isn't it?"

"Oh, I know where *I* am," the old man says, a smile tugging the corner of his wrinkled old mouth. "But as for you . . . I thoroughly believe *you* are somewhere else entirely. Yessiree . . . ."

Georgie sighs. "Just the address please," he tells the clerk. "Please."

When Georgie hangs up the phone, the clerk gestures towards the door.

"No pants, no service," he says. "Bad for business."

"But you don't sell any pants," Georgie points out.

The shopkeeper crosses his arms and sighs audibly through his nose.

"What if I stay behind the counter?" Georgie pleads. "No one can tell I'm not wearing pants when I'm back there."

The old man shakes his head. "Last thing I need is a man swinging loose behind my counter," he says gruffly.

Georgie suddenly gets the idea that this might be one of those stores that carries a shotgun somewhere behind the counter. He whisks himself out to the street and leans against the corner of the building, trying to hide in its narrow shadow.

Finally, finally, finally, Ben pulls up in the limo.

When Georgie arrives back at his house, Claudia is reading a book in the living room.

"Did you have a nice time?" she asks, without looking up.

"What d-do you think!" Georgie yells. He gestures to the long t-shirt, which drifts around him like an old-fashioned nightshirt.

Claudia looks at him finally. She snorts.

"Th-this isn't what I wanted!" Georgie wails. He sits down across from her. The shirt rides up to his waist, exposing his balls. They look shriveled and sad, peeking out from beneath the cotton drape.

He doesn't seem to notice. Or if he does, he doesn't seem to care.

"How did you do it?" he asks her.

Claudia points her chin at the bookshelf. One of the books has been pulled from its place and lies face down on the shelf, its binding facing outward.

"*Everyday Hypnotism*," Georgie reads out loud. "Christ . . . ."

With a sinking feeling, Georgie realizes Claudia could do the same thing to him again. Every day, if she wanted. He doesn't even know what the trigger is. The special phrase that'll send him into the streets naked again. There is no way to stop her, to undo what she has done. From this moment onward, Georgie's nakedness is her plaything, her bare plastic doll. She can dance his boys out on the street any time she wants.

The fear of her power over him tightens his gut. This is part of the torture.

"You can't do this kind of stuff," Georgie explains. "What will people think?"

Claudia looks at him steadily. "Since when do you care what people think?"

"C-cunt," Georgie mutters.

"You love it," she insists.

Georgie pulls out his wallet and gives her an extra grand for the month. Although he would never say it out loud, the money is proof enough. She has earned it.

"Where do you come up with this shite?"

Claudia smiles vacantly, her eyes cold and unrevealing. She says nothing.

Shuddering, Georgie turns from her and moves carefully upstairs.

Later that afternoon, Georgie hears the doorbell ring. He doesn't move. Maybe it is the police, to take him in for public exposure. If not this time, sooner or later they will come. The doorbell rings again, and he realizes that Claudia has not answered it. Grudgingly, he trudges downstairs. He can hear voices in the doorway. When he reaches the bottom of the staircase, the door clicks closed. The hall is empty.

(Parenthetical Pet Peeve) Door-to-door salespeople.

Georgie moves to the window that overlooks the front porch. Who is she talking to? Rage and injustice course through him as he considers the thought that Claudia might have struck up acquaintance with an old lover. He peeks carefully between the blinds.

She is talking to a woman, whose back is to Georgie.

"I just wanted to make sure he's okay," the woman says. The

voice is Margaret's. Georgie's heart skips a beat. "A friend of mine saw him downtown earlier today."

"He's fine," Claudia says, with a slippery smile. The afternoon sun slides across her cheek. "Really. I mean, of course he's embarrassed about it, but he's taking the whole thing awfully well."

Margaret sits down on a wicker chair, turning so Georgie can see her face. She frowns. "I just don't understand how it could have happened. It's not the sort of thing that happens by accident."

Claudia looks at Margaret with something close to pity. "Georgie has issues, Margaret," she says. "You can't just take a person to meet the Dalai Lama and assume he'll be magically healed."

"Then he's not doing 'awfully well,' is he?" Margaret says heatedly.

Claudia cuts her off with a gesture. "He's seeing someone. It's being taken care of."

"Well, I . . . I just want to make sure he's okay, that's all," Margaret stutters.

"Of course you do," Claudia sniffs. "You spend two weeks 'nursing' him back to health in an exotic location and the second you get back you abandon him. You want to make sure that he's okay, only as long as that means that you don't have to do anything."

Georgie feels a pang in his stomach as he watches Margaret's face twitch with guilt. He wants to yell: "Don't hurt my friend!" But he doesn't. He just keeps watching.

"I . . . I," Margaret stutters.

"You have no stake in his future anymore," Claudia insists. "I'm taking care of Georgie now. Full time."

Claudia stretches herself up tall, and Georgie is amazed by how imposing she is.

Margaret's face fills with a suppressed panic. "Oh?" she says creakily. Then she seems to find some strength in herself. "Well, then, I can only hope he's in good hands," she says, then flees the porch before Claudia can say another word.

At the sight of Margaret's small figure turning swiftly up the street, Georgie feels the dark knot inside of him grow bigger. Margaret . . . he thinks. But he can't quite finish the thought.

Claudia turns back toward the house, a satisfied smirk curling her lips. She notices Georgie peeking out at her from the blinds and laughs. Georgie looks up at her in horror.

"She's my friend!" Georgie yells at her through the window.

She frowns for only a second. Then she mocks him, her voice muffled by the glass.

(Parenthetical Pet Peeve) Grown women with voices like a 6-year-old. "Aw, poor Georgie. Your friends don't like you anymore, is that it?" she says in a sing-song voice.

He gapes at her.

She steps inside the front door. "It's your own damn fault," she hisses, her face coming close to his.

The sad truth is she's right. Georgie sinks into the despair that is clamoring inside him, trying to find peace in numbness. Instead, he finds only turmoil and fear. The misery is part of the torture, he reminds himself. But still he finds it difficult to believe. This is not what I wanted, something insists.

(Yes, it is.)

"You're so pathetic," Claudia continues. She can see that he is sinking, but wants to plunge him under. "You care so much about what other people think that it even makes you look desperate."

The well-trained Georgie tries to argue. "No, I'm an individual!" But the secret, drowning Georgie knows that what she is saying is true. He despises himself.

"You're so pathetic. You beg for love and attention, but don't even know how to get it," Claudia continues. "You're such an idiot, hopping around in that silly blue hat, moping after your cigarettes like a fucking zombie. If you want people to like you, why don't you just act like a normal person?"

Georgie tries to straighten up as an overwhelming rage builds in him.

"F-f-f . . . f-f-fuck you!" he shouts.

He charges out the front door, turning up the street in the direction where Margaret went. She is nowhere to be seen, but he keeps walking anyway.

Dear Diary:

Just a thought of the day—always be willing to change!

It's All in a Day's Work

Claudia dreams that she is having dinner with the Gusts. Except that instead of a ham, there is an entire roasted pig on the table, an apple shoved in its snout. And there are tall, slim candles lighting the dark wood table, dripping rivulets of wax. Wasted wax, Claudia thinks in the dream.

Georgie's mother comes to the table with a pair of thick, round goggles over her eyes and a leather helmet on her head. She sits. "Geow-gie always wanted to be a driver," she says.

"Ma!" Georgie whines. In Claudia's dream, he is only five years old, although everyone treats him like he is 30.

"Georgie and I are lovers!" Claudia blurts out. Everyone looks up at her. Now she's done it.

"Well, why wouldntcha be, dear?" Georgie's mother asks, dishing out more potatoes.

Through the dream, Claudia realizes that Georgie is not married. He is not Greg. She can't hurt Georgie in the same way that she wants to hurt Greg. And hurting Georgie will not hurt Greg—not one bit.

Claudia wakes up from the dream filled with an aching sense of loss. For some reason, she can't say why, it feels like someone she loved very dearly has just died.

"Georgie," Claudia says quietly, kindly, one evening.

He looks up at her in surprise. Her eyes are wide, her expression innocent and caring. Georgie feels a sudden certainty that everything they have been through in the last few months has just been a dream. He will wake up any minute and discover that they are actually happy together, and considerate—the American Dream couple, on the outside and in. Maybe they will go for a drive in his shiny black car and dance together on the beach. He is surprised at the sudden bliss this thought gives him, that a satisfying, loving relationship with Claudia is the dream. The nightmare is the reality. He realizes that the bliss between the moments of torture—just an accidental current of happiness—is what makes up his orgasm now. His life is just one torturous sexual act interspersed with brief spurts of joy and relief from pain.

"I was thinking," Claudia continues, looking on him with eyes filled with adoration—maybe false adoration, but Georgia will take it, "what if we went out for dinner tonight?"" You know, like, an actual date?" Her voice sinks down to a whisper. "Like real couples do."

Georgie wonders again if the whole arrangement is a lie. His mind could have created all the torment during an episode, a way to explain all the pain of their normally loving relationship.

But that is impossible.

(Is it, Ben? Is it really?)

"Y-yeah. Sure," he stutters, looking up at her with hope.

"Wonderful." Claudia seems to glow. She drops down and plants a lingering kiss on his forehead. "I have to take a shower. Shouldn't we look nice?"

Georgie can only nod in silence.

Georgie and Claudia step out of his shiny black sedan in front of the neighborhood's premier Italian restaurant. Claudia is dressed to the nines in a slinky green dress that shimmers with her eyes. Her hair falls in soft, red waves down her back. Georgie wears a dark gray suit with pale blue pinstripes. They glide together to the front door of the restaurant. A doorman in a tuxedo opens it as they arrive.

"Georgie, it's beautiful," Claudia says in a hushed tone, as they enter the dining room. It is dimly lit, but filled with mirrors, lighted candles, and glinting crystal. The two are seated in red leather chairs in a corner near the window, where the glow of nearby shops lights their faces.

"Thank you, Georgie," Claudia says, after a sip of water. Her eyes seem to shine. Almost, almost, Georgie convinces himself that their arrangement is a lie, that this momentary connection and consideration are truth. Almost.

Their conversation is light and pleasant, without any bitterness or mention of what has passed between them in the last weeks. Claudia's face seems to glow in the candlelight. Her freckles have all but disappeared. When Georgie squints, he decides that Claudia's hair looks almost like Margaret's.

Their waitress is attractive, tall, and graceful. Her eyes shine, too, as she meets Georgie's gaze. His momentary happiness overflows, and he smiles at her radiantly. He includes Claudia in his smile, feeling suddenly like the three of them wholly understand each other, that the world is at peace and that they are at one with themselves and with the universe.

When the waitress glides off, Georgie sets his hand on the table, halfway between himself and Claudia. He beckons her with his fingers.

"This was a good idea," he says.

"I can't believe you," she hisses.

"What?" Georgie frowns. For a moment, he disbelieves his ears. But her face is a horrible sight, despite the hours she spent making it up. It is twisted into some horrible snarl, an evil mask. She looks like a demon, a gargoyle. "What do you mean?"

He tries desperately to hang on to his earlier happiness.

"I saw how you were acting with the waitress," she says. "Do you think I'm blind?"

She's insane, Georgie realizes, in a moment of inspiration. Completely nuts.

"What are you talking about?" Georgie replies, his voice rising slightly.

"You know what I'm talking about. You were flirting with her," Claudia says, accusingly. An older couple at the next table looks at them disapprovingly.

"I was not," Georgie says. "I didn't say anything."

"Like you need to speak." Claudia scoffs. "You, of all people, should know that you're more attractive when you keep your mouth shut."

"W-where do you . . . how . . . Christ, Claudia! We are at one of the nicest restaurants in town and all you can do is insult me."

"Don't change the subject," she insists. "You were flirting with that girl. She's young enough to be your daughter."

Fellow patrons are becoming tense at Georgie and Claudia's display. Some of them stare at Georgie openly, hostility etched on their face.

"She's young enough to be your daughter," Claudia repeats.

One of the women at the table nearby gasps. She glares at Georgie then stares pityingly at Claudia.

"Men are scum," the woman mutters to her companion, who nods.

"I can't believe you," Claudia says a little louder. "All I want is to have a nice dinner with you . . . ."

"That's what I want, too," Georgie interrupts.

"And all you can do is ogle the waitress." Claudia barrels forward like a freight train. "You disgust me."

At that moment, the waitress brings their food, and Georgie no longer cares about Claudia's disgust. Instead, he stares unflinchingly at the woman's breasts. She seems nice, he thinks to himself. When he turns to his dinner, Claudia slaps him hard across the face.

"You're embarrassing me," she screams. "I spent hours trying to look beautiful for you and in front of all these people you just ignore me and stare at that girl like you're at Hooters or something!"

"These people wouldn't have a clue about it if you weren't yelling so loud," Georgie roars back, losing his temper.

"So you admit it. You were flirting with her," Claudia screeches, triumphant.

"So what if I was?" Georgie returns. "What's the big fucking deal?"

The woman at the nearby table looks sharply at him and he returns her glare. "What the fuck are you looking at?" he snaps.

"You're always doing this to me," Claudia yells. "You have no respect for me or for any woman."

She turns to the sympathetic woman nearby. "He walks around naked, you know," she reveals. "Downtown. It's disgusting."

The woman gasps. "That was him?" she murmurs. She whispers something to her partner. With a glare, they both stand up and leave.

"Sexist," one of the women hisses as they pass.

"Bitch," Georgie mutters. He looks down at his food, his appetite gone.

"You really are something else," Claudia starts in on him again. "What does she have that's so great, huh?"

Georgie rolls his eyes. "Nothing, Claudia. You're perfect just the way you are."

She grunts, unsure what to make of his sarcasm.

"Can we just eat?" Georgie asks, poking at his food with a fork.

"That's all you think about," Claudia says, slamming her napkin down on the table. "Your stomach . . . and your dick."

Bumping the table with her hip as she stands, Claudia glowers down at him. Then, she walks out of the restaurant, leaving Georgie alone in front of two lukewarm plates of food.

Claudia scurries down to the car, her heels clacking against the sidewalk. The secret to Claudia's fake-outs is that they're not really fake. There is a small, secret Claudia inside her, who's actually kind of pissed about the way Georgie and the waitress seemed to have a special moment back there. She doesn't think about the fact that she was included in that moment, too. If she did, it probably wouldn't help Georgie's case, anyway.

A second after she slides her feet across the smooth carpet of Georgie's shiny black car, she doesn't give a shite about the waitress or about Georgie anymore. Or so she tells herself. Instead, she laughs a quiet chuckle and leans back against the seat. She rolls down the divider that separates her from the driver.

"Hey, Ben," she says, her voice throaty and seductive. "How about a drink?"

When Georgie comes home, the lights in the house are blazing. Music plays loudly over the wireless sound system. Claudia is nowhere to be seen. Georgie briefly wonders what horrors are in store for him now. He wonders if an apology would stave off the torture. An apology would be more likely to cause pain, he decides. Claudia would use the moment of weakness to shred his heart.

He pays the bills, after all. What does he need to apologize for?

Georgie stands indecisively in his own front entryway. He could turn around and leave. He could run away, and she would never find him. The Galapagos are nice, this time of year. Any time of year. Maybe he should do it. She can have the house as long as he is free of what is in it.

(He won't.)

Even if I did run away, Georgie thinks, there would be someone else, someone else like her to torture me. There's always a Claudia, no matter what I call her. In that case, Georgie would not be in control. The torture would be part of the love–hate relationship that he is doomed to always repeat. But with Claudia, at least, Georgie is in control. After all, she is only doing what she does because he pays her to.

Georgie fingers his wallet, wondering if he could pay her to stop.

He is afraid of that question, afraid of the answer.

He goes upstairs.

On the covers of his neatly made-by-Claudia bed, Georgie finds a note.

Dearest Georgie, (the note reads)

My dismay at your behavior at dinner this evening, and my own, can know no bounds. You and I have hurt each other so many times that there is nothing left for us to do. It is obvious, as well, that your affection for me has dwindled, and there can be no reviving it. What else is there for me but despair? You are my shelter and my sustenance. I should so much rather lose my life than my heart.

Remember me fondly.

Love ever,

Claudia

Georgie's mind whirls and he considers the note. What does it mean? Has she left him for good? At once his stomach sinks into his groin and his brain rips free of his skull. His thoughts float happily for a second when he thinks about life without Claudia's torture. He feels himself becoming aroused at the thought, all his past rationalizations, for a moment, far behind him.

Then he looks at the note once more, and is filled with terror. Has she? Could she? He races to the bathroom.

She lies within the flame, on the still-cold tile in a pool of blood. The fire, it's happening again. Her arms are sticky with the plasma and platelets; her eyes are glassy and horror-filled. Georgie drops to his knees. He dreams without sleeping.

In Georgie's dream, Claudia's slumped against the counter, and as dreamscapes change, the counter blends and transforms. She's in the kitchen, flooding, too. And the entire kitchen counter's contents, from leftover coffee mugs filled with black coffee bean soot, to the salt and pepper containers, mostly salt.

Salt is the omen of discordance, everything having gone awry with quarrels and discontent. Georgie and Claudia adore salt, they're addicted to love and salt. Everything falls down and apart, slipping and falling over and over back to the bathroom and back to everywhere and nowhere, just like the completely awry love and salt of Georgie and Claudia's discordant relationship.

The kitchen sink water pours like a river, flooding the room—all of the rooms—into a saltwater ocean. Claudia remains on the floor and still in the kitchen. Her kitchen. She falls again, gets up, and falls again, over and over, just like Georgie, freely under the influence of gravity, together they blend into yet another overlapping dream. This entangled and intertwined nightmare, together. The wasted wax, the jealousy, and now the remembrance of Claudia's house fire storms into their combined dream.

Georgie's perspective nearly wakes him. He's lucid now, and can telepathically control this mutual dream, controlling something for once, and once for the benefit of himself, not Claudia. He flickers flashbacks of her house fire. She's burnt. Georgie lights up her middle brain, the place where dreams take place—the emotions, in particular. The sea of saltwater Georgie has created as God said, "Let there be water," as Georgie seems to know, though God wanted an expanse between waters, Georgie just wanted water. All the water coats Claudia's blackened, charred skin, as she remembers, as if she had been inside her own burning home. Fear, lots of fear and discontent, exacerbates the still-sparking hair dryer. It rests just beside her fingertips.

Blending back to the bathroom, Claudia's face is bloated soaked and strange, her hands limp at her sides, her toes pointed down just an inch from the lid of the toilet seat. Georgie rises from his knees. The fire and flood stops dead.

Claudia lay in the bathtub with a broken heart, her arms limp over her face, white and empty against the still water. A nearly empty prescription bottle holds a few white pills. Georgie drops to his knees again. Nobody dreams. They're both wide awake, now, with mere distorted memories as dreams do upon awakening at last.

"Claudia!"

Georgie's voice makes a gargling sound; his tongue seems trapped in his throat. His thoughts are filled with horror, his heart a bleak, terrified thing, and yet the hope, the small hope that now she has disappeared forever tugs softly at him.

"Claudia!"

He feels her slippery hand and finds a pulse. The hope disappears in a cloud of impossibility and guilt. Georgie slaps her across the face. The dreams that were have become real.

"Jesus, Georgie," she yells, sitting bolt upright. "I'm not really dying, you dolt. There was no dream. It's all real, Georgie. What's wrong with you? What in the hell is wrong with you?

She rubs her face with her hand.

"Ow. Sheesh," she says, "Look at what you've done. Look what you've created!"

Georgie gapes at her like a fish. "But . . . the pills . . . the note . . .," he babbles.

Claudia sinks back in to the tub and smiles lazily. She lifts a glass of wine from the rim and brings it to her lips.

"You really think I'd give up all this?" she says finally.

"But what about the waitress? Our date?"

The so-called reality sinks in. Georgie's in la-la land.

"What the hell do I care if you flirt with the waitress or if you don't?" Claudia says with a wave of her hand. She closes her eyes. "I don't kid myself that I have any hold on you."

"Yeah?" Georgie looks at her unflinching face. He tests the waters. "I guess you don't have a hold on me," he says thoughtfully.

He hopes it hurts her. Even if it doesn't hurt her, he is glad to say it out loud. If only to show that he doesn't give a shite, either.

As Georgie leaves her there, he thinks—for just a moment—that he hears her sob. But as he looks back into the tub, Claudia's face is pure, serene, calm. He decides that it was just his imagination, that's all, la-la land or not. It's his damned imagination. It always is. Moonshine penetrates through the window. Beddy-bye time and time to wake up.

Awakened the next morning, all he sees is darkness, darkness again, this time literally. He blinks for a moment, waiting for his eyes to adjust. But there is no light. None at all. Before him is only a vast wall of blackness. Georgie pushes his hands up before his face and sits up straight, adrenaline coursing through him. He cries out.

One hand brushes against soft cloth, the other clutches the matted substance to his side. He is sitting on carpet. He stands and hits his head on something hard, which vibrates with a soft dong when he strikes it. Where am I? Georgie thinks wildly. Is this hell? Am I dead?

"Claudia," he screams.

The light switches on. He is in the closet.

"Sheesh, Georgie," Claudia says, rubbing her eyes. She is wearing her pajamas. "What are you doing in the closet?"

Georgie shakes his head.

Claudia shrugs. "Can you hand me my robe?"

Without a word, he hands it to her. Claudia closes the door. After a moment, she turns out the light. Georgie sits on the floor in the closet, staring into the darkness. It is quiet, and still. A night with no stars, no moon to confuse it. It is a new kind of nothingness. He likes it all right. He is the dreamer who doesn't sleep and the sleeper who never dreams.

Georgie walks down to the kitchen. Claudia is huddled over the coffee-maker, making small noises. Her shoulders are shaking a little.

Georgie wonders if she is crying. Again? What does she have to be sad about, anyway? She is not the one who has to undergo daily torture. Georgie scoffs softly and Claudia straightens up.

"You put me in the closet?" he says grumpily, grabbing a coffee cup.

Claudia sends him a withering glare. Georgie wonders for a moment whether he has begun sleepwalking or if it was just another one of Claudia's hypnosis tricks. Judging from Claudia's face, he figures that he will never know. He decides to laugh.

"That was pretty stupid," he tells her. "I mean, the closet? It's not like I'm claustrophobic or anything."

Claudia shrugs. "Yeah, you sounded pretty calm and collected when you were thrashing around in there," she says sarcastically.

"Hmm," Georgie mutters. He pours himself a cup of coffee and stares at her. He remembers the nothingness of the closet. It was not orgasmic, but it was peaceful. It was all right, he thinks.

(Define "all right," Ben.

You're supposed to be the doctor, Dr C. You tell me.)

"I'm tired of the way you've been treating me," Georgie says. "Last night, this morning. I mean, can't you let up even a little?"

Claudia stares at him. "You don't pay me to let up," she says finally. "I don't even get weekends."

"So am I supposed to feel sorry for you? You're the one who's torturing me. You've done the most despicable things to me, isolated me from my friends. I can't even trust myself right now. I never even know where I'm going to wake up, anymore."

Georgie realizes he is screaming.

"What do you want me to do, Georgie?" Claudia screams back. He is shocked to find that tears are streaming down her face. Her face is shining red and mottled like a cherry. "I'm just doing my job. Now you're telling me I can't even do that right?"

Georgie squirms under her despair.

"It's just that I'm doing it all too well," Claudia accuses him. "You can't handle it, is that it? How is it my fault if you can't make up your mind?"

He can't believe the storm that he has unleashed.

"You can't ask me to do something and then bitch at me when I do it," Claudia screams. "You can't have it both ways, Georgie."

"I can have it any way I want," Georgie insists meanly, irrationally. "I'm the one who's paying you."

Claudia stares at him for half a second then bursts into fresh tears.

"You are so cruel," she sobs.

"Oh, shut up," Georgie says, tired of the guilt trip, not believing her tears are genuine. "You love it. You know you do."

Claudia buries her face in her hands. The sound of her crying fills the kitchen, the whole house.

Georgie can't handle her misery. He leaves.

"I need a smoke," he mutters to himself, slamming the door behind him.

Dear Diary:

The truth is the truth—the present is the present.

Calling for Reinforcements

Georgie wanders up and down the aisles of the grocery store, a pack of cigarettes and a small sack of limes in his hand. He watches the shelves of goods slide past him. Red, green, yellow colored labels. It's a rainbow, Georgie thinks. A rainbow. He stands for a moment, staring dumbly at a can of fried onions.

"Georgie," Margaret calls. "Georgie, over here!"

When Georgie hears her voice, something in him lifts. He turns to see her waving from the end of the aisle.

"I stopped by your house the other day, but . . ." Margaret pauses.

"I wasn't feeling well," Georgie supplies.

"I heard about, um, what happened. Downtown . . . ."

"Yes, that?" Georgie pauses, rubbing his chin meaningfully. "That was embarrassing, wasn't it? Well, I've just had some trouble sleeping, lately. Actually, I've been sleepwalking, Margaret. That's what it was."

Pleased with this fabrication, Georgie asks Margaret how she's been.

"Oh fine, fine," she says, smiling. "Work, you know. Well, I signed my first book deal. I guess you wouldn't have heard about that though, right?"

"That's great," Georgie exclaims with a big smile, wondering since when Margaret wrote.

"What is the book about?" he says finally.

Margaret looks confused for a moment. "Oh my God, I never told you about it?" Margaret beams. "I wrote it years ago, and I've have been submitting it for publication. I had all but given up, but it was finally accepted," she says. "It's about, well, it's about a girl, like me, but with Tourette's and schizophrenia, and well, things get really bad for her, one thing after another, you know. And then she meets a man who can support her, who has the time to care for her, and the money, too."

"Well, that's just great." Georgie's smile is frozen on his face. "Really. What a great story."

"Thank you Georgie." Margaret smiles. "So, uh . . . I met your girlfriend the other day, when I came to meet you?" She says it like a question, like she is not sure whether Claudia is his girlfriend or not.

"Yes, Claudia," Georgie says. "She's just great, isn't she?"

Margaret starts. "Oh yeah," she mumbles. "So, you guys are really happy, huh?"

"You bet." Georgie grins. He is playing the part of a lifetime. "She's like, my soul mate. She's so thoughtful all the time. Really takes care of me, you know?"

Every word pierces her heart. She actually flinches.

"Well, as long as you're happy," she says.

"Oh, I am," Georgie assures her.

His utter bliss gives her no room for doubt; she puts on her happy face, and the mask is complete.

"Well, all right, Georgie. Make sure you tell her that I'm glad she's taking such good care of you." Margaret pauses a moment, and a light flashes in her mind: "Did you get in touch with your nanny, yet?"

"What?" Georgie looks at her blankly.

"Your nanny. The one who used to . . . you know. I thought you were going to confront her?"

"Oh, yeah," Georgie says. "Well, no, I haven't found her yet. She's really hard to find, you know?"

She can tell that Georgie's lying, but drops it for now. She places her hand lightly on his arm. "I'm glad that we're still friends," she says, smiling up at him.

He smiles back with real pleasure. "It sucks to hold a grudge, doesn't it?" he says.

She nods. "If you need anything . . . anything at all," she says quietly, "well, you know you can count on me."

And with that, she turns and rolls her cart down the next aisle without a backward glance.

Georgie knows that Margaret doesn't buy his story about Claudia and his everlasting bliss. But he would not have it any other way. What is the point of being miserable if everyone knows about it?

The house is rocking when Georgie gets back from the store. The windows are blazing light, with only shadows of the people who crowd his living room. Music booms from the windows and walls; the frame seems to shake and creak from the sound waves.

Someone yells at him from his own porch, "Hey, buddy!"

Georgie sneers at the man.

"Sheesh, what's his problem," the man snickers. "Hey, who the hell invited you, anyway?" he yells at Georgie's back.

Georgie slams through the open front door and bumps into a teenaged-looking partygoer on her way out to the porch. She smiles up at him drunkenly, her eyes shining with bright blue makeup.

"Hey, you got a light?" she giggles. "I need a smokes." She laughs again and looks over her shoulder at no one. "Did you hear that? A smokes?"

She takes one look at Georgie's face and then slides past him, bumping arms with the man on the porch. "A smokes!" she snickers, and he laughs loudly with her, dropping an arm lightly on her shoulders.

Ordinarily, Georgie would be all over this party. He would be its wildest fiend.

"Hey, party," he would mumble drunkenly, punctuating the air with a pack of smokes. "Hey, party, you ain't seen nothing yet."

But not here, not in his own little sanctuary, the cave that he has made for himself (and Claudia). Oh no. Instead he is angry, crazy mad; he wants to go ballistic on Claudia, smack her around a little, something–anything. Strange alcoholics and druggies have invaded his untidy little world. Some are knocking over the stacks in the living room; others are raiding the almost empty refrigerator for mayonnaise scrapings and a last warty pickle. Worst of all, with all the people, he can't even find Claudia.

"Fucking bitch," he mutters.

Georgie walks into the kitchen, where there is a blender whirring in the corner. He wonders if it's his blender. Does he even have a blender?

The man at the controls takes his hand off the top for a moment to grab the belt loop of a pretty little blonde standing next to him. With a triumphant rush, the contents of the blender free themselves, sending an explosion of orange liquid and crushed ice all over the counters and floor.

Georgie gapes at the mess, the orgasmic spurt of alcohol that has tainted his otherwise sterile environment.

"Don't worry, man." The guy who took his hand off the top leans his face close to the blonde, although he is talking to Georgie. He fingers a lock of her hair, basks in her willing smile. "I'll take care of it. First thing tomorrow."

Then he addresses the girl like no one else is even there.

"Shots?" he suggests.

Georgie stomps out into the back yard, where a crowd of 20- and 30-something men and women dance together to the blaring of music from a fat set of speakers. The crowd gyrates, crooning and moaning together. The muscle heads have all taken their shirts off, and so have some of the skinnier girls. One girl, her waist a long, slender board, wanders around in nothing but a purple lace bra and matching panties—bouncing from chest to chest as she tries to dance.

It is like one big orgy in Georgie's backyard, reminding him of the fetish houses where he used to play.

Except the people at this party are almost all, without exception, remarkably attractive. Georgie sees a flash of red. Curly, wild, orangey-red.

Claudia!

He weaves his way through the bodies, bumping elbows and pushing past the naked flesh of the pulsing, sweating dancers. The stench of collective body odor shoves its way up his nostrils. He tries hard not to gag.

The dancers part a minute and he sees Claudia wedged between two well-muscled young men and doing a good job on both of them. Neither of the men can take their eyes off her, and Georgie can hardly blame them. She is wearing her most fetching black leather halter, her tightest and lowest-cut black leather pants. A shimmering red thong pokes up from her ass crack.

Claudia sees Georgie and winks at him. She flicks the whip she is holding in her right hand so that it curves gently around the cheek of the young man who rides her belly button.

"It's a party, Georgie," she cries drunkenly, flinging her head back. Her hair rises above her face, swirling like flame. "I threw you a party."

"I didn't want a fucking party, Claudia," he yells, grabbing at her elbow. Her eyes open wide, like she is surprised by his anger. He tries to pull her away from the two hunky young men and out of the pumping, thrusting crowd, but one of the men steps in front of him.

"Give the lady some respect," the man says. He crosses his arms over his ridiculously bulging pectorals.

"Yeah," the other man chimes in. He is stockier than the first and still bigger than Georgie.

"Hey, guys," Claudia laughs, trying to lighten the mood. "Let's just dance, huh?"

With one last glower, the two boys turn back to their sexy cougar and resume their half-frenzied attempts to fuck her leather-bound ass.

They will probably both do it, too, once the sun goes down.

Georgie pictures the two of them riding his Claudia, their sweaty and strong young bodies working in tandem with her, forming a cage of flesh around his Claudia . . . . Jealousy twists through his heart like a thick, rusty wire, shoving in deeper than he knew existed.

Why does she bother with me if she can get that? Georgie revels in disgust and self-hatred. Because you're paying her to, dumbass, is the obvious reply. And that brings along a whole new brand of pain.

Georgie thuds noisily up the stairs. In the bedroom, some black-haired bimbo is giving a surfer dude a back massage in Georgie's bed.

"Get the hell out," he yells, and they scram.

"Christ," he mumbles, climbing into the bed with his shoes on. In 10 minutes, he is asleep.

When Georgie sleeps, he dreams of the deep dark of the closet. The silence and peace, the strange anonymity of blackness, soothe his rattled nerves. My dear, my deepest love, your peace is music to my senses. Come and be nothing with me, sink into the bliss of blackness, of a world without us. When Georgie dreams, Claudia is his slave. He strings her up until she is hanging from the ceiling—her wrists chafing from the rope.

"Georgie, please," she screams, terrified. She is not paying him to torture her, after all. He is just doing it for fun.

"Please, Georgie. Just let me down."

"Who's Georgie?" he answers, then laughs. "There's no Georgie here."

Georgie sharpens a knife carefully as he watches her swing. Her eyes saw back and forth with every swipe of the blade.

"Georgie, I couldn't help it," she gasps. "You made me do it. You wanted me to. I just did what you wanted me to do."

Georgie takes the tip of the knife and embeds it into her calf. She screams.

"You wanted to do it," he says finally. "I may have asked you for it, but you wanted to do it."

He slowly drags the blade down to her ankle. He has to tug on it when he gets towards the bottom. Then he slices her Achilles' tendon, psycho-style.

Georgie gets nothing from Claudia now but a series of screams and weeping. "No, no, no, no," she moans, sobbing between cuts.

"How could you do it? How could you know how far to go? How can you know when to stop if you don't know what it's like, Claudia?" he argues with her. He grabs each side of the cut with his fingers and begins to tear the skin away from the muscle, tearing slowly from the back of the calf all the way to her shinbone.

Claudia's screams are a constant, never ending nightmare of pain.

"Shhhh," Georgie soothes her as he gives the skin one last tug, ripping it from her leg. Blood drains from her and pools on the floor.

"This is for your own good," Georgie soothes her.

Then he starts to work on her other leg.

When Georgie comes back to reality *(reality?)*, it is in the strange half-darkness of morning. A searing pain in his arm brings him full awake. Georgie tries to sit up, but a heavy weight holds him down.

Claudia straddles him, naked. She grins fanatically, her hair a glowing orange halo.

"Good morning, lover," she murmurs. Then she slashes at him again with a razor blade, in the chest this time.

"Ow," Georgie cries. But as the blood seeps from the cut, the exclamation turns to a low moan. The numbness and nothingness of this pure, blessed pain is all that he has missed and more.

"Again," he begs.

Georgie doesn't hear the Mexican cleaning crew when they arrive. But they can hear him. They stand uncertainly on the front porch as his voice drifts down from the upstairs window. Georgie is moaning and groaning. Sanchez looks over at Rueben, gives him a swift shrug.

"Sounds like fun, hey?" he mutters.

Rueben just grunts.

"Hey, Maria, why don't you get the coffee started?" Sanchez suggests. He tosses her the keys.

She stares up at the upstairs window with eyes large in fear.

"*Por favor,*" she whispers.

Sanchez gives her no pardon. With trembling fingers, she puts the key in the lock. She enters the house of pain, which echoes with Georgie's cries. Then the door closes behind her, and Rueben and

Sanchez each light a cigarette, occasionally glancing upward and snickering.

Margaret stands uncertainly at the threshold of Georgie's house. The door is slightly ajar. Inside, the sounds of thumping and knocking echo, along with whispered words in Spanish. More worrisome are the sounds of screaming and moaning from upstairs.

Sanchez pauses when he sees her. A mop is in one hand and a bucket filled with cleaning supplies is in the other.

"Excuse me," he says finally. She moves away from the door to let him through. "Just cleaning up?" she asks as Rueben passes by, closely followed by Maria, who keeps her head down. She is shy.

"Oh, yeah," Rueben whistles through his teeth. "What a riot in there last night, hey?" he winks at Margaret. "Not so quiet this morning, either."

Margaret returns his attitude with a cold smile, and he shrugs boyishly. Then Rueben, Sanchez, and Maria load up the van and drive off.

The screaming and moaning continue from upstairs. It is Georgie. Margaret knows it is Georgie. What is that woman doing to him? she thinks frantically. Whatever it is, it can't be good. Steeling herself, Margaret rings the doorbell. The moaning cuts off mid-gasp. Margaret hears the slamming of a door and a gentle thumping from inside the house. The front door swings open.

It's Claudia.

The woman's hair floats around her head like fiery-orange snakes. Her eyes are shadowed with purple circles, her freckles strain to jump off of her parchment-white skin.

"Uh, hi ". . . ," Margaret begins.

"What do you want?" Claudia interrupts.

Margaret stares open-mouthed at the woman. "Georgie," she finally sputters. She stands up a little straighter. "I wanted to talk to Georgie?"

"He's not home," Claudia says impatiently. Her eyes narrow, her message clear. *Scram.*

"But I heard him," Margaret insists, almost choking on the words. Claudia's eyes are like smoldering coals. Margaret cringes back from them but refuses to leave.

"Did you?" Claudia raises an eyebrow. Then she sighs. Her face softens into a small smile. "I suppose you did."

Margaret can't help but relax slightly at Claudia's sudden change of attitude, although she is still terrified of the woman.

"Why don't you sit down?" Claudia gestures gently to one of the porch chairs. Margaret collapses into it weakly; Claudia's smile increases slightly. To Margaret, the woman's canines seem pointed, wolf-like.

"Georgie has not been feeling very well lately," Claudia explains.

Margaret raises her eyebrows and opens her mouth to express her worry, but Claudia cuts her off.

"Not that. Mentally, he is fine. It's just, uh, the flu. A really bad case of the flu. That's what the noise is from. It's hurting him a lot."

Margaret gasps. "Shouldn't he be in the hospital, if it's that bad?"

Claudia shakes her head. "I took him there last night. But you know Georgie—he can't stand the hospital." She smiles. "They sent me home with instructions for caring for him, and I know who to call if he takes a turn for the worst. But they say he should pull through all right. It just has to hurt him a bit, first, before he can get better."

"Can I see him?" Margaret says.

"No," Claudia says, her breathing becomes short, and her eyes go wild for a moment. "He's really contagious." Claudia's eyes narrow evilly. "Trust me; you don't want to catch this one."

Margaret nods slowly; then her own eyes narrow with suspicion. "I just saw Georgie yesterday, at the grocery store," she says. "He seemed fine."

Claudia seems shocked for a moment. And then . . . Is that jealousy? Is she actually jealous of Margaret?

(I don't know, Ben. Is it? Does Claudia love Georgie, really?

Who can really love Georgie, doc? He isn't real. Remember? Who can love what isn't even there?

And what does love have to do with jealousy anyway?)

Margaret starts. What can Claudia have to be jealous of?

"It came on quickly," Claudia says, her smile stiffening, her sharp teeth glistening. Margaret shudders. "In the afternoon. I took him to the hospital last night; they sent him home this morning."

Margaret nods again. What else can she do? Claudia's story is airtight.

"Will you tell him I came by to see him?" Margaret says. "Tell him that I'm worried about him and I hope he gets better soon."

Claudia's grin widens triumphantly. "Oh, I will. I'm sure that he'll be back on his feet in no time." Claudia rises from her chair.

Margaret stands with her but doesn't move away. She hesitates a moment, looking up to the bedroom window, wondering.

Georgie has been absolutely silent since Claudia came to the door. Almost as if . . .

"Goodbye," Claudia says pointedly, showing her teeth.

(Parenthetical Pet Peeve) People who say "Bub Bye."

"Yes." Margaret jumps a little, and takes a few steps back. "Yes, goodbye."

. . . as if Claudia is the one who is causing his pain.

Margaret puts as much feeling as she can into her next words. "I'm sure we'll see each other again soon," she says.

Claudia's face seems to indicate that she would rather not, but Margaret doesn't see; she is already halfway down the sidewalk, running for the street.

When she hears the front door slam, Margaret sneaks back up to the side of the house. After a moment, she hears Georgie begin to moan again. He actually screams. The sound reminds her of a terrified child.

With this proof in her pocket, Margaret flees the sounds of her friend's pain.

That night, Georgie dozes on his bed. He feels his cuts oozing slowly into the bandages Claudia applied so expertly. The tingling, burning pain consumes his whole mind. He relaxes into the sensation, wrapping it around him like a blanket. A fuzzy, pinching, biting blanket.

The doorbell rings. Georgie dimly hears Claudia's voice as she answers.

A loud, booming male voice answers hers. Georgie perks up a little. He wonders if it is an old boyfriend. Claudia answers the voice, but it insists. The door opens, and two sets of loud footsteps clomp on the hardwood floors.

A soft knock on the door, and Claudia pokes her head in.

"I'm so sorry, dear, but there are some officers here to see you," she says, in the kindest, most gentle voice that Georgie has ever heard her use.

"What?" he says groggily.

"He's sick," she explains to someone behind her. "You can't just come in. You might catch it."

"We'll take our chances, Ma'am," the booming voice says.

Georgie sighs. "They can come in, Claudia," he says.

Two blue-suits tromp into the room in heavy black shoes. When they see Georgie lying on the bed, they exchange glances.

"We're sorry to bother you, sir," says the first suit. His voice is quiet, but serious. "I am Detective Marley, and this is my partner, Officer Carver."

Detective Marley is thin, with a mustache. Georgie wants to laugh at him, but remembers to play his part.

"Is everything okay? What's wrong?" he says weakly.

"There's been a report of domestic violence," Carver begins, his voice filling up the room. He is a large man, with a shock of black hair that sticks straight up towards the ceiling.

"What? Claudia?" Georgie looks over at her.

"It wasn't me, darling," she says innocently.

He wonders if this is a new sort of torture. Maybe she will send him to jail, and let the inmates and the guards do the torturing for her. He would have to pay her double for that, maybe even an extra grand as congratulations for her genius. She's riding me all the way to the bank, he thinks lazily. Then Georgie realizes that the cops are staring at him.

"I never hit her," he stammers. "Not once."

The officers glance at one another. Detective Marley turns around.

"Would you mind leaving us, Ms Nesbitt?" he says calmly.

Claudia looks at Georgie. He shrugs weakly.

"Don't be too hard on him," Claudia says. "He's in very fragile condition."

She walks over to Georgie's side and kisses his forehead, just like she loves him, just like she cares for him. So this is what it would be like, Georgie thinks wonderingly, amazed at the momentary bliss that floods him at her gentle touch. Then she leaves, closing the door quietly behind her. When the latch clicks closed, both cops direct their attention entirely to Georgie.

"The tip wasn't about you abusing Claudia," Marley says. "It was about her abusing you."

For a moment, Georgie can't even speak. He stares at them both. A hysterical chuckle rises in his throat, but he disguises it as a cough.

"That's ridiculous," he says finally.

Marley shrugs. "Maybe."

Carver pulls out a pad of paper from his breast pocket. "Just what is your relationship with Ms Nesbitt?" he asks, his pen poised above the paper.

"She's my girlfriend. She lives here with me," Georgie says. She's my tormentor, my torturer, he wants to say. She's my love and hate, my twisted perverted sex goddess. Don't judge her, officers. I asked her to.

(Do you think there are people judging you, Ben?

Of course there are, Dr C. Aren't you judging me? Isn't that what this is all about?)

Carver scratches down his answer on the pad.

"Does she ever hit you, Mr Gust?" Carver continues.

"Of course not," Georgie says. This time, he really does laugh, although he's not sure why. "Look at her! Sh-she couldn't hurt a spider."

The cops take a moment to think as one of their radios buzzes an encrypted message.

"There are many different ways of hurting the ones we love," Marley says quietly, with an understanding smile.

"Love?" Georgie says quietly, pretending to mull it over. "Yeah. Love . . . ."

Marley and Carver shake their heads. Clearly, the man is a goner.

"Do you have any reason to believe that Ms Nesbitt would want to hurt you, Mr Gust?" Carver asks brusquely.

"Oh really, is this necessary?" Georgie says in a brash tone. He hopes his façade is intact.

Marley smiles again, seeming to agree with Georgie at the ridiculousness of the questioning.

"It's just part of the routine," he says. "Paperwork, you know."

"Shouldn't you see a doctor?" Carver interrupts. "You look pretty sick."

Georgie readjusts the bunched-up pillow under his elbow and shrugs. "I-I feel better today than yesterday. I'll be f-fine."

The officers exchange a look when they hear his stutter.

"Sir, I think you should see a doctor," Marley says. "You don't look too great to me."

"What do you sh005eheads know about it?" Georgie cries out. Then he closes his eyes.

Marley whispers something to Carver. Georgie can't hear most of it, but the word "poison" passes his lips.

He laughs. "You two are really something. Really," he says. "You're not going to get me into the hospital. I'm fine. Everything's fine here. My girlfriend is not beating me, or torturing me, or even making me mad. Most of the time."

He laughs loudly at his own joke, but Carver and Marley will not laugh with him.

He sobers up. "In any case, you two are completely out of line here. I have no intention of charging my girlfriend with abuse, nor do I have any reason to. Now if you'd please . . ."

The officers look at each other in confusion.

" . . . get out," Georgie finishes.

They stand, but hesitate.

"Get out!" he screams.

Claudia opens the door with a bang. "What are you doing to him in here?" she demands.

"Out!" Georgie screams again.

His screams and her nagging tone follow the officers all the way out the door and to the street.

Dr C Goes Deep

"Ben," Dr C says finally, one day. For a long time she just listened as I told the story, but today . . .

"Ben," she says.

"Yeah?"

"Ben," she draws the word out, spends a long time saying my name. "Ben," she repeats, "why is the driver named Ben?"

I look at her. She is going nuts again.

"Why is anyone named anything?" I point out. "Why was I named Ben?"

She pushes her lips together.

"Is there a story there, behind your name?" she asks.

Dr C is some kind of detective, but she is always digging in the wrong direction, if you ask me.

(Parenthetical Pet Peeve) When naming a child, people who give no thought as to how name will sound with their surname. For example: Dick Hertz, Mike Hunt, etc.

"Family name," I explain. "We're all a bunch of inbred blue bloods, you know. Too many names would be tough to remember."

Her lip quivers a bit. One of these days, I will get her to smile.

"Why is the driver named Ben?" she repeats. "Is it a family name for him, too?"

"How the heck should I know?" I retort. "You don't see me or Georgie talking much to Ben, do you?"

"Maybe that's the problem," she muses.

"What?"

I swear, the woman has really lost her mind this time.

"Ben, are you Georgie's driver?"

I laugh. "Uh, no, Dr C. I haven't been driving since the robbery. You know that."

She waves me off. "No, Ben. What I'm asking, are you the vehicle, and Georgie rides around in you. That is why Ben's the driver, right?"

"I don't know, Dr C."

It is a hell of a lot more complicated than that.

Dear Diary:

Cool? Fuck Cool. I'm Awesome.

Love Can Keep Them Together

In her dream, Claudia is having dinner with the Gusts. Only instead of the ham or roasted pig on the table, this time it's Georgie who's curled up on a large serving platter, an apple shoved between his teeth.

(Parenthetical Pet Peeve) "Delicious" apples. They aren't.

His skin is still crackling, roasted to perfection. His eyes are glassy, sightless. Georgie's mother approaches with a carving knife and fork, crisscrossing their edges, sharpening one against the other. She poises over Georgie.

"I'm so glad you're not one of those vegetarians," she says, grinning horribly. "I just wanted to thank ya for taking such good care of our Geow-gie," she says and then slices downward with a flash of steel.

Georgie squeals his pain and Claudia jerks out of bed. She glances at the lump that is Georgie, his screeching still echoing between her ears.

"I am sorry," she whispers. "I am so sorry . . . ."

With a glass of wine in her hand, Claudia mopes around Georgie's bungalow. It's nothing like what she had expected.

The sterile counters are not clean because someone cares for the place and its inhabitants, someone who tenderly scrubs down the surfaces with loving consideration. No. The counters are clean because no one uses them, because the place is devoid of life. No one actually lives there.

Claudia and Georgie drift around the place like ghosts, replaying the tortures of ages past. Claudia wonders if Georgie still feels the pain, if he still gets off to it. As for her, she doesn't feel the satisfaction of torturing him anymore. Georgie is no longer every man who has hurt her, and hurting him is no longer a way to get back at every evil she has ever known. Georgie is just the man who's tangled up in her life right now, the man she can't seem to convince herself to leave. Like all the others. She loves him.

Still. She's being paid to torture him, so that's what she'll do.

Walking into the cluttered yet organized living room, Claudia kicks over a stack of Georgie's sketches. Let that be the latest blow, she thinks to herself. Now he'll have to stack it all back up. She snickers to herself. Any petty meanness can be justified, but that doesn't make it right. Claudia drains her glass of wine as she hears Georgie's alarm go off. The digital clock on the wall reads: 10:00 am. She thinks about starting a pot of coffee but, still frustrated, she opts for more booze and considers how she might torture Georgie this evening.

"Screw pain," she thinks. She is not into pain, not tonight.

That night, when Georgie walks in expecting dinner, Claudia breezes past him on her way out the door.

"Where you going?" Georgie says, confusion all over his face.

"None of your business," Claudia grins wolfishly. "Don't I get a night off every now and then?"

He can smell that she has been drinking, but then so has he. She is wearing tight jeans that show her pudgy bottom, her thick thighs. A scanty halter shows the small roll of fat at the back of her shoulders. Georgie wants to laugh at her, a little. But he thinks that maybe—just maybe—some other man might find her attractive. If he had been drinking; if she was just his type.

(I thought she was your type, Georgie? Older, unfettered . . . nice feet?)

Georgie tells that voice in his head to shut it. You live with a woman long enough, and her skin doesn't seem all that sexy anymore. In fact, it can just about make you puke.

"Sure," he grins, diabolically. "I could use a night off, too."

He flashes her a lopsided grin as she leaves, imagining her being unsettled by his cavalier attitude, then decides it's more likely that she doesn't give a shite one way or the other. Probably, she just needs a break, like she said. Maybe.

Claudia slides into the greasy, sleazy bar like she owns the place. It's been months since old Claudia has been around. For a minute everyone looks up, surprised to see her. Within seconds, the novelty of Claudia's reappearance is gone, and the crowd goes back to what they all do best—drink. Claudia fits right in; her favorite stool still bears her name.

"Gin gimlet," she orders, her green eyes glistening.

The bartender, although drunk, is not quite as gone as the other regulars. He looks at her, tilting his head slightly.

"Been a while," he says gruffly, pouring her drink.

"Yeah, guess so." She grins at him. Damn it feels good to be out again. On the prowl, Claudia thinks. Rawr.

She shifts her shoulders easily, feeling the stale bar air on her exposed skin. She can feel eyes on her, but she's not here for just any old fling.

Oh no. Claudia has a particular gentleman in mind for tonight. She has a plan, and she is sticking to it.

Of course, she started the night early in order to work up her resolve, in order to keep Georgie from sucking her into his company. After a few drinks, she plays a round or two of darts, a little pool, then bangs around the jukebox for a minute or two, catching up with the regulars. There is nothing new in their lives, luckily, nothing to catch up on except the same old shite played over and over again. And, luckily for Claudia, they are all so wasted that they can't remember what she has told them, so she tells them everything and more than everything. She tells them everything she wishes she had the nerve to do to Georgie, but can't. Then a few minutes later, one of them will stagger over to her again and say: "Hey, Claudia, how the hell you been?" and she can start it all over again.

Maybe talking about it is better than living it; she wonders if Georgie would modify the deal to make imagining new tortures, without actually doing them, a still-payable offense.

She knows the answer to that before she even begins.

Claudia sighs and puts her chin in her hands. With her elbows on the bar, she sips deeply from her fourth gin gimlet. She is starting to warm up to it. Her shoulders slouch. Her belt pulls in at her gut, cutting off circulation to her nether regions.

The door creaks open, and in walk her lucky pair.

Claudia smiles to see their faces, their arms wrapped around each other. They're so damn happy, she thinks. She knows she wouldn't hate them nearly as much if they weren't so damn happy all the time. She glowers a little, until they notice her. She arranges her face.

"Greg! Sara!" she calls. "Over here, you two!"

With intoxicated smiles, Greg and Sara float over to where Claudia waits. Maybe they are dumb, or maybe they're too trusting, or maybe Claudia never got a chance to tell them everything she thought of them. They don't seem to think that there is anything wrong with the picture of Claudia waving to them and hollering friendly greetings at the top of her lungs.

"Claudia," Sara gushes.

"Claudia," Greg belches. "How the hell have you been? We haven't seen you in ages."

"Yeah," Claudia says. "I guess because I got fired."

Sara and Greg look at her for a moment with fixed terror. Then Claudia laughs, and they both laugh with her. They are captivated by her, her wild hair, her free spirit. Her open toes beckon to them both.

"Claudia, I'm so sorry," Greg says presently. "I don't know what I was thinking, back then. It was such a terrible mistake."

Claudia grins easily. It is not Greg that she loves and hates; it is not Greg that she wants to make suffer anymore. It is Georgie—just Georgie. And for now, that means that Greg is forgiven. Sara, too. By default. Claudia puts a hand on each of their legs and leans into them, breathing her hot, ginny breath in their direction.

"That's all in the past," she insists, her vocal cords humming. Greg and Sara croon along with her.

"Oh, I'm so glad," Sara says. Her eyes shine bright. "I've missed our friendship."

Claudia wants to laugh at the woman who can call their love and hate relationship a friendship. *(Maybe you can, though. Maybe you should.)* But instead, she just smiles and keeps her features smooth. "This round's on me," she says.

The three former lovers sidle up to the bar, whispering and pointing fingers and bursting into loud laughter.

"And then my house burned down," Claudia yells finally. Greg and Sara crack up. "Can you believe it?" she goads them.

Wordlessly, with tears streaming from their eyes, they shake their heads.

"Claudia, you live such a crazy life," Sara says, giggling.

"Yeah well, it gets better," Claudia grins. "Now I'm living with the guy who burned my house down."

"Oh, you're not," Sara insists.

Greg laughs out loud. "Of course she is."

"You should come stay with us," Sara squeals. In her drunken haze, she thinks this is a good idea.

Claudia waves the woman down. "Oh, I am feeling really settled where I am. Georgie—that's his name—he's actually such a sweet man. Like an uncle, really."

Her eyes light up, almost as if she had come up with an idea on the spot. "Hey, you guys should meet him," she says. "How about tonight?"

Greg and Sara nod enthusiastically.

"I have got to meet this guy," Greg says.

"All right." Claudia smiles. "One more shot and then we're out of here."

Greg and Sara nod again, their eyelids drooping. Half an hour later, the three stagger in the dark towards the front door of Georgie's house. One of the shadowed figures giggles then stumbles into a bush.

"Sara!" One of the other shadows laughs helplessly then bends down to scoop her up.

Claudia's shadow strides purposefully up the front steps, tripping only slightly on her way. Georgie sits in his dark office with his feet on the desktop that shimmers from the light of three video cameras—cameras that he now addresses, cameras that have been set up (that have always been set up) for the single purpose of recording him and perhaps, perhaps, catching a moment of sanity.

You never know—it could work.

But at the moment, Georgie is as schizo as ever, babbling on into the night about what a poor, tortured creature he is under Claudia, how even her leaving him for a night is still a torment to him. Poor, poor Georgie. And then he hears the voices at the front door.

When he recognizes Claudia's voice among them, Georgie relaxes. But only slightly. Regardless of what he has been saying to the cameras, about how being apart from Claudia is torture in itself, he really doesn't want to face her, now or ever. He can't imagine what new torture she has cooked up for him, and he doesn't want to learn.

Georgie dives under his desk when he hears the footsteps climbing the stairs to the second floor. Just as he manages to tuck his feet in behind him, exposing his pudgy bottom to the coldness of the hard wood floor, the door slams open.

"Georgie," Claudia calls drunkenly. There is giggling behind her. "Georgie Porgie." She snorts with laughter. "Huh, where is that little muffin? My uncle-type, that is. My funny uncle."

Another explosion of laughter from the hallway, and Claudia exits, leaving the door partially open. Georgie squeezes his eyelids tight shut. He hardly dares to breathe until he hears their voices in the next room.

Then he stands and crawls to the cameras. He stands up next to the one on the left, which is positioned in such a way that he can jump behind the door if anyone comes.

"You see what I'm talking about?" he whispers into the camera. Hearing noises coming from Claudia's room, he detaches the camera from its tripod and creeps down the hallway.

"I'll sh-show you," Georgie whispers. His heart hammers in his chest.

When he gets to the doorway, he can hear Claudia moaning. He knows what is going on but can't stop himself from opening the door, anyway. It's one aspect of the part he plays, the part they play together.

The room is dark, but the moonlight glows through the single window. Claudia and her two lovers are entwined, like one massive, gyrating, screeching creature. Georgie trains the camera steadily on the beast.

"You bitch," he screeches, hardly recognizing his own voice.

The beast barely acknowledges him; it just keeps right on.

"You bitch!"

Georgie is screaming, although there is no sound . . . .

When Claudia wakes up the next morning, her unexpected doubled pay awaits her on her bedside table. Georgie is nowhere to be seen. Claudia thumbs through the cash. If the insurance doesn't come through on the house in another year or so, she will still have enough money to build a new one at this rate.

If she can make it that long. If she can stick to sleeping around and skip the cigarette burns and the S&M shite, she decides she can make it. After all, sleeping around's not that hard.

Georgie can't even look at Claudia, let alone talk to her about what happened.

He mopes up and down the aisles at the grocery store, but Margaret is nowhere to be seen. It's not her shopping day.

Georgie considers waiting around until she does show up. It will only be a day, maybe two days. The store is open 24 hours a day. Georgie could live off the free samples and produce and fresh-baked bread until Margaret shows up. Margaret will know what to do, Georgie thinks. Margaret will fuck me; she'll make Claudia look like a two-bit hooker, an over-the-hill beauty queen. Georgie knows that Margaret will never fuck him, not in a million years. But she might give him some relief, just a little relief.

Then Georgie, still moping up and down the aisles, realizes that Claudia might end up at the store, too. He has never seen her there before, but you never know. It's something new with Claudia every day, and maybe first thing on today's list is to go shopping. Georgie rockets out of the grocery store like a cat out of a bathtub.

Where does Georgie go to avoid Claudia?

To the same places he used to go. Georgie slides into place in his old haunts, the sicko-twisted sex clubs of his past, like a foot sliding into an old shoe. He walks up to his favorite, a century-old wooden house with a maze of rooms on the top floor. He sighs as his foot hits the third step—a rotted, warped piece of wood that creaks every time his foot hits it. It's as though nothing has changed.

The club is not a business on the outside, but a private residence. Nothing to see here, ma'am—just us lonely, heartbroken suckers for pain, having a friendly get-together.

"Hello, Mr Gust," says the woman who sits at the foot of the stairs. "We haven't seen you here for quite some time."

"I've been busy," Georgie says, grinning at the woman.

In these places, Georgie doesn't feel quite like the self that he presents to the rest of the world. In this house, filled with sicko-twisted perverts with their nauseating fantasies, Georgie feels quite suave. Almost normal.

"Is Samantha here?" he asks, in the mood for a good old-fashioned foot smothering.

"Hm, Samantha has a prior engagement," the woman says, consulting her clipboard. "How about Alia?"

Georgie shrugs. "Whatever," he says.

The woman shows him to a private room—a small room, with a queen-sized bed, large closet, and several mirrors.

"Alia will be in shortly," the woman says. With an artificial smile, she leaves.

Georgie sits on the bed and waits. After a few minutes, he lies on his back and stares up at the mirrored ceiling, which stares back impassively.

Georgie looks up at his own face. It's not a bad face, he thinks, although he has a hard time believing that it's really his.

Finally, the door opens again.

"Alia?" Georgie asks. He props himself up on his elbows.

"That's me," the girl says.

She is dark-skinned and petite, with bleached blonde hair or a wig—Georgie can't decide which.

"Huh," Georgie says.

Alia walks closer to him. "You wanted a foot smothering?"

"Yes . . . well, no." Georgie's thoughts are racing. "I changed my mind. Is that okay?"

Alia smiles softly. "Well, that depends on what you want me to do," she says.

"Tie me up. Cut me. Burn me. Whip me," Georgie entreats her. He can't meet her gaze. Instead, he glances over at the bedside table. Propped on it is another mirror, a small round hand mirror. Georgie's face surprises him again.

"Oh, you want it rough today, is that it?" Alia purrs. "Well, I think I can manage that, Mr Gust. Yes, indeed . . . ."

Georgie watches with detachment as Alia ties his hands with handkerchiefs to the bedposts, avoiding her eyes and his own, which, if he could stand to look in the mirror again, would beg him to stop. To come to his senses.

Claudia brought this on herself, he reminds himself. She cheated first, with those . . . those . . .

Georgie remembers the sight of the beast and anger flares hot in him. He clenches his fist and rattles the bedpost.

"Hm, someone's getting excited," Alia notes. She slowly undoes the buttons of Georgie's shirt. Then she pulls a penknife from the top drawer of the bedside table. She draws the blade gently across his chest. It is just a tickle, just a reminder of what pain could really be.

She is too soft, too gentle, this Alia. She lacks Claudia's rough edge, her true penchant for pain. She probably never gets angry, this girl . . . just uses her soft voice, the voice of reason, to keep everyone under control.

"Do you do hypnotism?" Georgie blurts out.

Alia lays a hand on his shoulder and smiles. "Afraid not."

She draws the knife a little harder now, causing a bit of a burn on his skin. She uses the sharp tip to prick at his collarbone. Georgie feels a small bit of wetness where she has been; he groans with the release that this gives him. Claudia will flow out of him as his blood leaks through fresh cuts. Maybe he will forget all about Claudia. Maybe Alia will do the trick.

"You like that, huh?" she encourages him. She scratches his neck and throat with her fingernails. "Yeah, you do."

Then she stops for a moment. She dips her fingernail into one of the small drops of blood oozing from Georgie's chest, where she pricked him. She draws a tiny, thin line across his throat.

"What is your safe word?" she asks finally.

"What?" Georgie says wonderingly. "Safe word?"

How could anything in this world be made safe?

"You know," Alia explains. "The word you say to make me stop? If things get too rough for you?"

"What?" Georgie understands now, but he is too incensed to respond properly. "Untie me," he commands her.

Biting her lip, Alia slowly complies. Georgie sits up abruptly once he is free, buttoning his shirt with rapid hands.

"I think that's enough for today," he says in a huff, as he stands.

"I'm sorry, was it something I did?" Alia asks. "Don't go. I'll do it right next time. Just tell me what I did."

Georgie turns in the doorway. "A safe word?" He scoffs at the thought. "You've got to be kidding me."

After his encounter with Alia, Georgie gets down and dirty. Only the worst of the worst will do it for him. He could not stand to sit and be "tortured" by another nice girl. He sits through innumerable foot smotherings. He is tied down, cut up, forced to crawl across hard rock crystals—all before the anonymity of strangers.

The strangers are a nice touch, Georgie thinks. They add an element of humiliation to the situation that a private room never could.

But Georgie is even less fulfilled now than he was before he met Claudia. Before Claudia, Georgie did not know what good was. Now he watches all his so-called tormentors, his fellow sufferers, and he feels nothing but contempt. These masochists do not know what it is like to have a Claudia on their chest, digging holes into their hearts. They do not know what it is like to have her in their oxygen, destroying their perfectly controlled environments. They have not woken up locked in a closet or naked in the street. They are vacationing masochists, dabbling in a pastime they do not even understand. They don't know what pain is; they don't have the slightest clue.

They are weak. Georgie has outgrown them.

By the end of the week, Georgie has had enough of the same old S&M fetish houses. He wants the big guns, something he has never seen before-something that is bound to shake him up.

He takes the recommendation of a friend (if you could call him a friend), who gives him a phone number without a name.

"Just trust me," the guy says, shaking visibly. "This is some heavy shite, here. If this doesn't shake you up, then you must be dead."

Georgie finds hope in this promise. He calls the number and is sent straight to voicemail—a lonely mechanized voice repeats the dialed number to him, then commands him to leave a message. There is the beep.

"Hey, uh . . . my name is Georgie Gust. I-I got your number from a friend of mine. Looking for something to shake me up. Looking for some heavy shite, you know. He told me you could help ". . . ." Georgie trails off. Without a name, without even knowing what the number can offer him, he doesn't have a clue.

"Can you?" he concludes lamely. "Can you? Help me, I mean. Th-thank-thank you."

An hour later, Georgie gets a text message with an address, a date, and a time.

Georgie's shiny black limo winds its way through a forest of pine trees. Up, up they climb until the trees dwindle into small, gnarled grey things, and rocks begin to jut up from the lichened earth.

The road grows increasingly narrow, the cement finally dissolving into a single-lane gravel road. The road rises high above the rocky ground then meets the towering metal doorway of a thick granite wall.

Ben gets out and presses the buzzer beside the doorway then gets back in the limousine and drives it backwards about 10 feet. The metal doorway slowly opens outward, revealing a circular plot of land surrounded by the wall.

Ben creeps forward, following the narrow dirt road that hugs the interior of the wall. In the center of the circle sits a sizeable stone cottage. Ben completes the circle while Georgie stares out the driver's side window, studying the cottage from every angle. Soon, Ben has the limo turned around and is facing the road once more, ready to drift back down the mountain. He opens the door for Georgie, who crawls out slowly and unsteadily.

Georgie strolls to the front door of the cottage. It is made of thick, dark wood and has a heavy, round, brass knocker in the center. Georgie stares at the knocker for a moment then lifts it. With a blink, he drops the knocker. It thuds hollowly when it strikes. Georgie waits, shivering a little at the coldness of the rock walls. It is

128

not long before the door creaks open, revealing a haggard woman of indeterminable age, bent at the waist in an effort to open the door. Georgie is amazed that she is capable of pulling the huge thing open at all.

"I'm G-Georgie. Georgie Gust," he says. "I'm here to, uh . . ."

"I know what you're here for," the woman says with a toothless grin. "Come in. It will only be a minute."

She gestures to a sagging chair in the corner and shuffles off to the back.

Georgie sits in the chair with a loud thump, sending a cloud of dust into the air. Georgie coughs, starts to chokes, as the particles clog his lungs.

(Parenthetical Pet Peeve) Going to work and realizing I forgot to use deodorant.

When the dust settles, Georgie looks around in alarm. The walls are dirty, covered in soot; bits of paper and clumps of dirt and pine needles are scattered across the tabletops and floor. The whole place smells like something inside the walls has died, or maybe it's the bearskin rug in front of the fireplace. Georgie wonders if the rug has ever been properly cleaned; he imagines bits of fat and meat still clinging to the underside of the fur. Bile rises in his throat as he thinks of it, and yet Georgie finds himself strangely turned on by the filth. It is strange and new—a different kind of pain, the fear of the filth that now surrounds him. He rejoices in the newness of the feeling. His penis swells.

The woman returns. She is naked, but covered in a shining film that might be—Georgie's nose twitches—lube. The woman has drowned herself in shining, slippery lubricant; it glistens from the caverns of her wrinkled skin, drips from her sagging breasts, which swing pendulum-like. Georgie can't help but stare at them, fixated. They hypnotize him. Georgie wonders if their swinging can reverse the naked sleepwalking thing that Claudia's trained his subconscious to employ.

The woman is as filthy as the cabin, if not more so. Grime clots her wrinkles and lint is trapped by the lube across her vast belly. Her forward-jutting chest tapers to a sagging, concave backside, with flesh that seems to drip from her bones like seaweed. As she reaches for Georgie, the dirt beneath her fingernails seems to grow, to stretch, reaching for him. Georgie can't move; he stands staring, transfixed, couldn't look away if his life depended on it. The woman rips the clothes from his body, tearing the buttons off his shirt, and breaking a nail—dirt still embedded beneath it—on his belt buckle.

"Whoops-a-daisy," she cackles, then whips off his belt.

Georgie is a statue, frozen. His cock stands erect in the cold mountain air. He has prepared himself for anything to happen in this place, and the fact that this old woman presents herself as lust-worthy doesn't faze him. Nothing can, not after Claudia.

Georgie can tell this old woman used to be trouble; she was a pair of double Ds who could get anything she wanted with a wink and a giggle. But time and gravity have betrayed her, have dragged her sideways and down; until now she looks more animal than human. And now—now that men no longer want her, will no longer have her, she'll have them.

Georgie is locked in her gaze. Snakelike, she slithers before him. Her arms wrap around and around him, pulling him tight to her, choking off his air. He is drawn into her flesh—the lubricated rolls and wrinkles mold around him. He can't breathe—he doesn't need to. She will breathe for both of them.

With nothing but a smile she heaves him to the rug and then swallows him whole.

Dear Diary:

Sometimes I wish I had a mother. I never knew her. Since I was a little boy. I wish I had someone who made the choice every day to put my happiness and well-being ahead of their own, to teach me the hard lessons, and to do the right thing even when he or she is not sure what the right thing is . . . . And to forgive me—and his or her self over and over again for everything wrong.

Nothing But a Brilliant, Bright Prick of Light

The rancid scent of an unwashed creature brings Georgie to his senses; he is nose-deep in the bearskin rug. Groaning, he pushes himself to his knees. He is naked, covered in lube and lint, bear fur, and dust. He vomits into the bear fur, realizes what the smell truly is, and vomits again.

The woman lies before him on the rug, illuminated by the rays of morning sunshine that dance mockingly through the grimy window. She quivers a moment, mumbles incoherently. Her hand twitches, her fingers crawl across the rug to find him. Slowly she reaches for the pile of vomit that Georgie's left (his is not the first one, of course. That is what the smell is). With a stifled yelp, Georgie leaps to his feet and runs to the front door.

The woman's hand finds the pile of vomit. "Fer chrissakes," she moans. "What the fuck is that?"

Georgie presses frantically at the door handle, shoving into the heavy wooden door with his shoulder.

"Hey, yore not leaving' so soon, are ya?" she looks up and grins. Her gaping mouth is a cavernous black hole. She will swallow him again.

With a cry and renewed vigor, Georgie shoves at the door. It won't budge. She is standing now. She is coming after him. Georgie wishes that he lifted weights, that he had the almighty strength to push open this door with a single stroke of his arm. The woman, the hag, the creature is almost upon him, her fingers, still vomit-covered, reach for him.

Georgie screams like a trapped animal. He pushes against the door again and again. It won't open. It won't open. And then . . . Then he remembers, he has to pull. He has to pull the door open. Success. The door opens easily. Light slashes through and the woman shrieks, raising a hand to her eyes as Georgie races to his limo and safety.

Ben looks up groggily as Georgie slams his palm against the door. Ben seems to be laughing at him, laughing as he unlocks the back door. The woman—whom Georgie has begun to think of as 'the creature'—appears in the doorway to the cottage, and Ben raises an eyebrow.

Ben's attitude is wasted on Georgie, who yanks the door open and collapses inside the limo with a gasp and a long, whimpering sigh.

"G-get the h-hell out of here," he commands. When Ben locks the doors and begins to roll out of the driveway, Georgie sinks into the seat. His arms and legs are buzzing, weak from exertion. He slips into blackness, into nothingness, eternity.

[Smoke Break]

When Georgie comes to, Ben is pulling in front of his house; it is noon, the sun overhead glares down, making the world too bright, too harsh. With a groan, Georgie pulls himself out of the car. Ben helps him walk inside. Claudia is not there, leaving him feeling relieved yet sad as well.

Considering what he has been through, a little reassurance would do him some good, but Claudia is not there, and neither is Margaret. The only reassurance Georgie has is himself, and he is no consolation at all. Not to anyone. Georgie crawls upstairs and into bed and falls asleep immediately.

Ben pauses for a moment in the doorway.

"Poor son of a bitch," he mutters.

When Georgie wakes again, it is nearly 5:00 am; the sun is setting, and its light gleams orange through his blinds. He rolls over, trying to convince himself that the cottage, the woman—the creature—were not real, that the whole thing was just a dream. But when he looks down at himself, at his still-slick skin, and smells the stench of bear fur and vomit, he knows that it happened.

This makes him want to break down and sob his heart out, but he can't. He can't even bring himself to cry. Eventually he gets out of bed and staggers into the bathroom. He turns the water to hot, sits on the toilet, and waits for the shower to steam then climbs in.

Claudia is still not home. Georgie putters around his house, stacking up his physics notes into neat, uncluttered piles, putting Claudia's books back in their rightful places on the bookshelves. He thinks about going back to bed, even stands in the bedroom door, staring at the rumpled mess of his blankets. But the stench of himself, of the woman—the creature—is in the sheets, so he rips them from the bed and stuffs them in the hamper and remakes the bed. Still, the stink of the old woman's cottage clings to him.

Georgie grabs the new sheets off the bed, turning his nose away from the smell. Claudia is still not home, and no matter where he goes, the smell clings to him.

These sheets, Georgie tosses into an old metal barrel he keeps stored in his shed. He dumps a canister of lighter fluid on the sheets then lights a cigarette. The smoke fills his lungs and his soul. Georgie begins to calm; the shaking in his fingers ceases. Halfway through the cigarette, Georgie grins sadly and tosses the last of the burning cigarette into the barrel. He jumps backwards as the pile of sheets explodes in a ball of flames. It's like a huge candle, Georgie thinks to himself, the biggest candle this backyard has ever seen.

Georgie lights a second cigarette, and sits on his back step to watch the fire die. Claudia comes home during Georgie's second shower. He hears the front door open and close. Please, God, he pleads. Just let her go easy on me today. He can hear as Claudia hollers his name. I'll do anything just make her go easy on me. I'll go to church . . . anything. The sound of her clomping footsteps on the stairs makes his heart skip.

I'll even pray. C'mon . . . we got a deal?

There is no answer, but . . .

"Georgie," Claudia says softly. Her voice sounds like an angel's.

Georgie peeks through the glass shower door. Through the hazy shower steam, Claudia's face glows. Her eyes are wide and luminous, a child's eyes.

"Georgie, I know you're in there," she teases. "Can I come in, too?"

"Uh, sure," he croaks. He cracks the door open an inch.

"Georgie, I missed you," Claudia purrs as she steps inside.

She is still fully clothed. Immediately, her clothes gets drenched with the hot water.

"Did you?" Georgie's voice sounds strange even to his own ears. "Where were you?"

"Ah, now. That's a secret," Claudia says, putting a finger to his lips. Slowly, she pulls her wet sweater over her head. She is wearing a white cotton bra, and her nipples poke out through the wet cloth.

Pencil erasers, Georgie thinks.

"After all, it's not like you're going to tell me where you have been?" Claudia continues.

Georgie stares at her for a minute. She gives him a secret little smile. She already knows. Maybe Ben told her. Georgie sighs.

"No," he says.

"Well, what makes you think that where I've been has been anything better?" Claudia whispers. "Maybe I really missed you, you know. Maybe I'm tired of all this. Maybe I'm just looking for a break, for a bit of relief. It's tiring keeping you happy all the time, Mr Georgie."

She laughs, but he can hardly blame her.

"I'm a little tired, myself," Georgie admits. He sets his hands on her waist. With a groan, he buries his head in her breasts, fumbling with the clasps at the back of her bra. She replaces his hands with her own nimble fingers; he sinks to his knees, clutching at her, resting his head against her soft belly.

"Claudia," he mutters softly.

Suddenly she has stepped out of her jeans—how he doesn't know. She lifts him up with her gentle hands; he finds himself hardening under her fingertips.

"How about some good old-fashioned lovemaking?" Claudia whispers, nibbling at his ear. "I think that's just the ticket."

Georgie groans and nods. He presses against her.

"The condoms," he mutters. He reaches for the shower door.

"Not so fast, Georgie Porgie!" Claudia insists. She holds the door handle firmly in place. How'd she get so much stronger than he is? Georgie wonders.

"We're doing this the good old-fashioned way," she tells him.

She takes his penis in her hand and pulls it to her. He is powerless; he is drawn inside her, an ocean in an underwater cave. It is good, he thinks, good clean fun. In a moment he erupts. Shuddering, he withdraws.

Claudia pouts, and then proceeds to feel herself up, finish herself off under the blast of the shower. She shivers, moaning, and then gasps. Her back flattens against the wall, her knees buckle.

Georgie watches as his semen drips slowly from the tangled red orgy of her pubic hair. Too slowly. No condom, his mind screams at him. Wake up, you crazy fuck. What if she gets pregnant?

At the thought of bringing a child into this world, Georgie collapses, striking his head hard on the way down, hard against the shower wall.

(Poor Georgie. So much wealth, so little else.)

Georgie wakes up again, for the fourth time that day. At least, he thinks it is still the same day. He is in his bed, in clean fresh sheets.

Claudia is stretched out beside him. For a moment, Georgie imagines that they are the happy couple, living the American Dream. Claudia rolls over and grins at him. Compared to that woman, that creature *(don't think about the creature)*, her face is smooth and beautiful. Her body is near flawless. Georgie loves her, her whole self, even the part that hurts him *(especially the part that hurts him)*. Her eyes glow as he looks into them, into her inner life.

"I love you," Georgie says. He says it out loud. He feels the words transform his soul. Everything is different now. Everything is better now.

"I know," Claudia whispers. She smiles at him; she shines with the dying sun, which sets behind her. "Do you think we made a baby?" she whispers.

Georgie feels the weakness overcome him again. His limbs go limp. But it is not so bad, this time. He can take the thought, this time. He can live with it. He turns his head at her snicker. Claudia lifts his limp hand high in the air. She drops it onto the bed. It strikes the mattress with a hollow, woody sound. Claudia rolls swiftly to her side and reaches over the side of the bed. When she comes up, she is holding a thick piece of rope in her hand.

"Stay still," she whispers, as she ties his hands together and then his feet.

Georgie would fight, if he could. No. No, he wouldn't. His arms and legs are weak bags of flesh. His mind, his heart, his soul *(his son?)* belong to Claudia now. He can't muster the will to fight her any more than he could develop the strength in his limbs.

His will is hers now.

She hefts him onto a flat, wooden dolly that lies beside the bed. There is a jump rope tied around it. To Georgie, she looks like an adorable little girl, tugging a little red wagon around the yard. She is probably just playing a game, he thinks. She hauls Georgie down the hallway and then shoves the dolly down the stairs. It bounces and bangs against the hard steps. Georgie's body is jostled and tossed. He slams hard into the banister, breaking his nose. He cries out, feeling the blood spurt; he wants to touch his face, to protect himself, but he is still tied to the dolly, falling helplessly down the stairs. He wants to stop, to cover his head, but his hands are tied behind his back.

As he strikes the downstairs landing, his shoulder takes the full force of his fall. With a snap he feels it dislocate. He screams in pain, screams again and again; he is still screaming as Claudia comes up to him, straps him more tightly onto the dolly.

"That wasn't so bad, was it?" she says brightly. Then she drags him into the back yard.

Georgie wakes up *(for the fifth time that day, if it is still the same day)* to a heavy thud then a softer pitter-patter of something striking wood above his head.

He is in a dark place—a pitch-black place. His breath shudders raggedly in and out. Georgie rolls over and onto something hard that will not budge. He tries to sit up but knocks his head on the same hard substance. He falls back, groaning, panting. Another thud, then that pattering noise echoes overhead. Georgie screams. The bitch is burying him alive.

When Georgie wakes up *(for the sixth time that day, if it is still the same day),* he is covered in pain. His body is bruised and battered, his hands and fingernails throb, and he is panting frantically. Georgie remembers that he is in a coffin. He doesn't remember where the pain came from. For a moment, he recalls a wild thrashing, a panicked horror *(don't think about it).* OK. The thud of dirt falling on top of his coffin continues relentlessly, but it's no longer the insistent noise he remembers. Rather, it is more a vibration that he can feel coming from the earth around his coffin, reverberating in the wood walls.

Georgie inhales deeply. There is not enough air, he thinks desperately. He begins to pant again. I'm going to die down here, he thinks. Fear and peace rush over him in successive waves. Death will be better, anything will be better than this, he thinks. Georgie relaxes into the dizziness that threatens to overcome him; he rides it like a pro, daring nausea to join him. It doesn't. Georgie circles the borders of a vast, dark whirlpool. The force of it lashes his mind with a cool terror. In the center is a splash of light, a tiny, brilliant white speck. Hell would be better than this, he thinks, sighing softly.

Down and down Georgie spins, down towards the beautiful speck. It beckons to him. He hears a slight giggle. He can't see himself, but he is smiling. When he reaches the light, it winks over him. It swallows him whole, and he is nothing.

Dear Diary:

To the best of my ability, to be mindful, watching everything that happens around and to involve myself with that which happens when my life journey is a part of the overall experience.

Damned if You Do

Georgie gasps and air floods his lungs. It stings and burns. The life of it rushes through his skin, setting every nerve fiber tingling. Georgie moans then coughs. He is overcome with another mighty gasp.

"Oh God, oh shite," Claudia weeps. She huddles over him, cradling his head in her lap. She wipes her mouth with the back of her hand. "I'm so sorry, I'm so sorry, Georgie!" She clasps him tightly to her. "I'm so glad you came back," she whispers.

"Wha-what?" Georgie chokes out.

Then he remembers.

"Look at you," Claudia sobs. She caresses his elbows and wrists, gently running her fingers over the bruises and open sores. "I really hurt you."

"You almost died. You did die. You were dead," she explains. "For a minute." Her eyes are wet with tears. "I had to give you CPR."

Georgie places a hand on his head and sits up. He has a headache.

She grabs him in an embrace that he is too weak to shake off.

Christ, what a day.

"I'll never do it again," Claudia sobs. "I promise. I'll never hurt you again. I love you, Georgie. I'm sorry I didn't say it before. I love you. I love you. I love you."

She bursts into fresh sobs. Georgie looks away from her disdainfully. What a spectacle this woman is. How dramatic. He holds his head with both hands.

"It's fine," he groans, in the hope that she will just be quiet. She throws her arms around him, once more.

"It's not fine," she gasps. "But I'll show you. I'll prove to you that you can trust me. I'll never hurt you again."

She begins to kiss his neck, his jaw, running her tongue along his ear lobe. Georgie's penis rises weakly to the challenge. It is tired, sure, but just maybe. Georgie grabs at Claudia's chest.

"Oh Georgie!" she cries, giving herself up to him. "Let's make love. Let's make real love, the way that normal people do. I'm so tired of hurting you."

She gasps as Georgie's penis pokes hard against her. In a

moment, she rips off her pants and straddles him on the lawn. Georgie wonders what the neighbors will think, then remembers that Claudia's one of the neighbors. He tries to hide his smile.

"Please, let's just be like a normal couple," Claudia begs, moaning as she rides him. "You wouldn't have to pay me or anything."

Georgie flips her over and mounts her from above. He pumps away inside her, willing her to shut up.

"Oh Georgie, oh Georgie!" Claudia cries. She is nearing orgasm, and so is he.

At the crucial moment, Georgie pulls out of her. Claudia gasps and moans plaintively, reaching for him. He dances out of her reach, then releases, splashing his wad over her toes.

"Mmm," Georgie hums as he finishes off the final spurt.

"Georgie," Claudia whines.

He chuckles. "How about, 'no'?" he suggests. Then he turns and leaves her, naked and yearning, on the lawn.

A few days later, Georgie and Claudia have nurtured their bruised egos and are back to business as usual. Claudia is giving Georgie small cuts on his arm with a chef's knife as she prepares dinner. There is a knock on the door. Georgie rolls down his sleeves and answers it.

"Georgie!" Margaret screeches. "I'm so glad that you're feeling better."

Georgie is bewildered. He wonders if Margaret knows about the old lady in the stone cottage or his being buried alive.

Margaret sees his confusion and greets it with a slight smile. "Is Claudia here?" she says in a low voice.

Georgie nods and opens the door wider. Margaret peeks in and sees Claudia, who waves a knife cheerfully from the kitchen.

"Oh, I've interrupted your dinner," Margaret says, her voice reflecting disappointment. "Perhaps I should come back at a better time?"

Georgie hems and haws for a moment.

"Of course not," Claudia finally yells from the kitchen. "Why don't you stay for dinner?"

"Uh, s-sure," Margaret stutters. "Just let me make a phone call."

Only a short time later, Claudia, Georgie, and Margaret all sit down before a roast chicken, frozen vegetables, and a homemade fruit salad.

"So Margaret, what have you been up to lately?" Claudia says.

Margaret proceeds to tell Claudia about her book deal and the progress she has made. Claudia nods and asks insightful, thoughtful questions, charming as can be. Meanwhile, she slips her foot under the table and applies strong pressure to Georgie's testicles.

"Ow. Oh," Georgie stifles a moan as the pain washes over him.

"Are you ok?" Margaret asks, looking at him with concern.

"Fine," Georgie squeaks. "How do you like the fruit salad?"

"Oh, it's great. Claudia, you're such a good cook," Margaret says. She smiles at them both.

"You know, I have a great idea," she continues after an awkward minute. "I was planning to go to a play with a friend of mine tonight . . . my girlfriend, actually. Would you guys like to come as well? It should be a really good show."

"Um," Georgie looks at Claudia, wondering if going to a play would interfere with whatever nastiness she has planned for him tonight. She nods imperceptibly. Public humiliation it is, Georgie thinks.

"I think that would be great," Georgie says. "We don't get out much these days. And I can't believe I still haven't met your girlfriend."

The four of them—Georgie, Margaret, Claudia, and Mandy—pull up outside the auditorium just before the play is about to begin and slide into their seats as the lights dim, jostling a few people in the process. The complaints silence as the stage lights up.

A man, dressed shabbily, walks onto the stage; a cringing, frightened-looking woman follows close behind. The man stands in the center of the stage in the halo of the spotlight.

"I thought I'd never be free of her," the man announces to the audience, sneering at the woman behind him. "Every moment of every day I would turn around, and there she'd be." He pauses.

"That's what they call love," he announces, and then spits on the stage near the woman's feet.

The audience rustles uneasily.

"And then . . . And then . . . when she told me that she'd gotten pregnant . . . ."

The woman rubs her belly, gazing on it tenderly.

"Well, I knew it had to end right then. I mean me, a father? I can't even take care of myself."

The woman looks up at him, pleading, shaking her head.

"But how to do it?" the man continues, ignoring her. "I'd tried before, and yet she always found me again, always wormed her way back into my life."

The man's face transforms into a hideous mask, with a snarling that appears to hate the world.

"There is only one way," he concludes.

"Death," the woman wails.

The stage lights drop and, when they light up again, the scene is of an exotic, Middle Eastern marketplace, filled with bright splashes of red fabric and chains of gold. The man strides onto the stage, accompanied by a different woman. Behind them follows the cringing, terrified woman–child of before.

The man and his new woman peruse the marketplace. With a grand gesture, he buys her a beautiful necklace. She protests for a moment then accepts it with glee. As she wraps it around her neck, the man steps forward.

"Even before we'd met, she was with me, following me around," he accuses, pointing a finger at the cringing woman, who tries to hide herself behind a rack of shawls.

In the next scene, the man is wandering through his neighborhood in a bathrobe, seeking the woman he bought the necklace for. The woman is nowhere to be seen. The cringing woman appears.

The man is surprised, but not unhappy.

"Hey, why not?" he figures. "It really couldn't hurt to give her a try."

The man and the woman make love in the bathroom. They eat at a fancy restaurant. They dance on the beach together. They fall in love, as people do, with pleasant dates and just enough similarities to get along, just enough differences to keep things interesting.

As the play continues, the man and the cringing woman grow close. They begin to depend on one another. They love each other, in their way, but the man is always pushing her away, and she is always clinging too tight. She wants to move in, but he needs his space. She wants to cuddle, but he has an early meeting.

He doesn't have an early meeting. He actually likes to cuddle. But the thought of actually giving in, of giving her what she wants . . . . The thought twists something deep inside of him, and he must refuse.

Soon, they are both entwined in a relationship that makes them miserable, which transforms them into creatures they no longer recognize, no longer love, but without whom they'd die.

"I love her and hate her," the man says. "I know there's someone better for me, but I'm trapped."

The woman he bought the necklace for appears from time to time. The man yearns for her; he can't get enough of her. He practically begs her to stay with him, to supplant his cringing, loving girlfriend. He buys her extravagant gifts, always greets her with a pleasant smile—a smile his girlfriend never sees. But in the end, his dream woman always escapes. Maybe she sees beyond his superficial charm, or maybe she's just too much a will-o'-the-wisp to stay too long in one place.

That is what makes her the perfect dream woman—her perfect distance. The promise that her perfection will never be marred by the machinations of the man's filthy soul. She knows that's what makes her perfect. She loves that she can ensure his yearning by constantly avoiding him. In this way, she feels the satisfaction of being loved without the responsibility.

Georgie, Claudia, and Margaret watch the play in horrible discomfort, afraid to be who they really they think they are, never completely confessing to themselves how much they can relate to the characters.

I'm not really like that, they think, all at one time or another. I'm not.

One night, the man onstage meets his dream woman at a bar. They are both there by accident, and alone. And she has already had a drink . . . or five. She is alone in a bar, as she is heartbroken after yet another failed relationship with another failed man. The perfect woman lets down her guard. She lets the man buy her a drink.

"It's been too damn long," she mutters into her tequila. She looks at the man accusingly. "You ever go three months without a lay?" she demands.

He grins. Shakes his head. Lays his hand on the small of her back.

"A gorgeous woman like you?" he says softly. "I hardly believe it."

She scoffs.

"You must be punishing yourself," he whispers. "You don't need to punish yourself."

Her hungry lips reach up to touch his. They meet, tequila churning like fire in their bellies. In moments, they are tearing each other's clothes off in her apartment. They can't even wait to move to the bedroom. He pushes her against a wall and shoves into her, hard.

She loves it.

The perfect woman likes it rough.

The next morning, racked with guilt, the dream woman confesses to the cringing girlfriend, who is five months' pregnant with the man's child.

"I didn't mean to," she begs. "I was drunk, and he was . . . I never thought we would." Her voice drops to a whisper, her face ashamed. "Please forgive me."

"Forgive you?" the girlfriend sobs. "What's to forgive? It's him— that bastard! You were single, after all. It was his choice to break my trust."

Together they wail their heartbreak.

"I've tried to leave him, so many times," the girlfriend says, shuddering, "but he always draws me back in, you know?"

The dream woman stares at her with wide eyes. "I know exactly what you mean."

In the final moment, their bond of shared grief gives way. In a fit of madness and jealousy, the cringing woman knocks the dream woman down and beats her with a thick, phallic-shaped paperweight. "He loves me," she screams. "He does. He will always love me."

Coming upon the gory scene, the man strangles his cringing girlfriend. "You killed her—my dreams and my hope," he screeches. When she is limp in his arms he tosses her corpse to the floor.

Then a hideous look floods his face. "My son," he whispers. "You killed him, too."

Sinking to his knees, he weeps. And when he stops, the man slowly climbs onto a chair and hangs himself with a piece of wire, laughing and sobbing all at once.

"Well, that was a trip!" Mandy gushes as they exit the theater. "Can you believe that? Where do they come up with this stuff?"

Georgie becomes intensely interested in a poster on the wall, while Margaret and Claudia exchange a desperate glance and then look away, embarrassed. Claudia wonders if Margaret ever would sleep with Georgie. Margaret is wondering the same thing. She hopes that Claudia doesn't believe it of her. She wonders whether Claudia would kill her, if she had reason to.

"I think the ending was a little unrealistic," Margaret says, with hollow laughter. She glances over quickly at Claudia to see if she agrees.

Claudia stares blankly, not listening. She is thinking of the cringing woman—how much she hates her.

I'm not that woman, she decides. I'm in control of this situation. I am the tormentor. Georgie's the one—he's the one who can't live without *me*. He wants *me*. He loves me. He told me so.

Claudia briefly considers getting a new job, but for some reason she can't hold onto the idea in her head for more than half a second.

"Well?" Mandy says. She looks up at both Claudia and Margaret and then searches for Georgie. "What's wrong with you guys?" she mumbles.

Claudia scrutinizes Georgie, watching as he scans the poster on the wall. She wonders how the play has affected him. How worried is he? She starts thinking about how she can drive the knife in even more deeply.

Dear Diary:

To the best of my ability, to let go of my attachments, to all circumstances, outcomes and consequences.

Hunting They Will Go

Several weeks pass. Claudia watches Georgie as he mopes around, and wonders when the time will be ripe for twisting in that knife. She takes a break from the torture, gives him time to heal—time to become complacent. She still burns him now and then and, sometimes, she brings out the whip and chains—just to keep him on his toes—but that's just child's play. Not the real deal. Not true torture. Claudia slides into a bit of a slump, weighing her jealousy against her job—and her satisfaction of destroying Georgie—against her own possible pain. They hear nothing from Margaret. Claudia hopes the play scared Margaret enough to keep her away from Georgie—forever. Finally, Claudia climbs out of the slump; she works through her reaction to the play, and when she becomes just crazy enough to go through with it, Claudia speaks.

"Georgie," Claudia says in a soft, slightly singsong tone.

Georgie looks up at her. Her eyes are wide and glimmering.

"I was talking to Margaret earlier," she begins. This is a lie, but she says it anyway. "We were thinking it would be fun for the four of us to take a trip—you, me. Margaret. Mandy. What do you think?"

It doesn't sound horrible. That's what Georgie thinks. After all, things with Claudia have been pretty nice lately. Except . . .

"Where?" he asks.

"Well, you know that cabin your parents own? Out on the lake?"

Georgie doesn't think he ever told Margaret about the cabin and this trip is probably all Claudia's idea. A nagging doubt begins to creep in.

"We were thinking," Claudia says, "that it would be a nice opportunity to get away, try something new. I mean, Georgie, you and I haven't spent one single night away from this house. Not together. Not once since I moved in."

Claudia's expression is very clear: 'No' will be an unacceptable answer. Georgie wonders how bad a trip away could be, trying hard to ignore the strong possibility that it could be very bad indeed. Very, very bad.

"Yeah, sure," he says, "sounds like fun."

Claudia squeals. "Oh, Georgie, thank you!" She gives him a hug, and proceeds to bounce around like a little girl. "Oh, it's going to be so much fun. You are not going to regret this."

Georgie thinks that he is going to regret this a great deal; he sighs and rolls his eyes. She's probably planning on skinning him alive and hanging him upside down from a tree. Yet, at this point, Georgie is beyond caring. After everything Claudia's put him through, he can't imagine her hurting any more than she already has.

And still that nagging doubt: Maybe, as they say, he hasn't seen anything yet.

They decide to leave the weekend after next even though Mandy won't be able to come. Instead, Margaret invites her friend Carl, just one more man, like Georgie, who wants desperately to fuck Margaret, and never will.

On the morning they leave, both Carl and Georgie fight to hold the limo door open for Margaret and, as they continue with the macho positioning—the huffing and puffing and kicking up dirt, Margaret goes to the other side of the limo where Ben is holding the door open for everyone. Claudia sniffs derisively and crawls in after Margaret.

"Men," she says, rolling her eyes.

"Oh, I know." Margaret giggles, lowering her voice, "That's why I prefer women, you know."

She winks. Claudia smiles awkwardly.

Georgie and Carl finally get the door open. They settle down, but not before grunting, snorting, and clearing their throats. Then Ben puts his foot to the gas pedal, and they're on their way.

Ben drops the four off at the cabin, then reverses the limo and backs down the road. Georgie watches him drive away, not sure where Ben stays and not sure he cares either.

The "cabin" is more a mansion. Rising three stories among the trees, rows of gabled windows greet the travelers. The front entrance is surrounded by a massive deck adorned with the thick trunks of two spruce trees, which form giant columns and cast shadows on the door.

Claudia pulls a roll of mints out of her purse, offers one to Georgie as they walk together towards the front entry. Georgie shrugs, and takes it, not noticing that she doesn't take one herself. He knows that when someone offers you a breath mint, you should take it.

He wonders if she's offered the breath mint because she plans on fucking him soon; the idea cheers him significantly. Sex with Claudia has not been half bad lately. He pops the white strip into his mouth, and it quickly dissolves.

For the next half hour, Georgie gives everyone a tour of the cabin, shows them to their rooms, and points out the few walking paths around the lake. He shows Carl how to start the generator, and then the two men flop down onto a soft and well-used sofa as Claudia and Margaret unpack coolers and put food in the refrigerator.

Georgie and Carl stare at each other with intense hostility for about 15 minutes until Georgie becomes distracted by a fly buzzing against the window.

"Georgie?" Margaret's voice seems to fill the room around him, echoing off the walls. "Georgie," she repeats, "are you okay?"

Georgie stares at her; her cheeks seem swollen.

"I'm fine," he answers, his voice coming from somewhere very far away.

"Be cool," Georgie thinks. "Be very very cool, cool, cool, cool." His tongue begins to feel like it's crowding his mouth, taking up too much room, crowded against the roof of his mouth. He looks over at Claudia. She looks just as evil as always. Georgie decides not to look at her anymore. Instead, he looks down at a plate full of spaghetti and wonders when it became dinnertime and when he sat down at the table and when he even moved from the living room to the dining room. He doesn't remember any of it, and he doesn't understand why his spaghetti is moving, undulating, and swirling uncontrollably on his plate.

(Parenthetical Pet Peeve) When people take food off my plate without asking.

Georgie laughs.

"There's a black hole in my spaghetti," he announces.

"What?" Carl asks peevishly, which doesn't surprise Georgie. Carl strikes him as a peevish man in general. A bit of a complainer, Georgie thinks; he watches as Carl glances at Claudia, who shrugs.

Georgie snorts. "You don't see it?" he asks, pointing at his still swirling spaghetti. "You're missing out . . ."

Margaret gets to her feet and crosses the room to Georgie's side of the table and places a hand on his forehead.

"Are you sure you're okay?" she asks. The worry in her voice is unmistakable.

"Weird," Georgie says. "I'm feeling a little weird." He looks up at her with hope, and with love shining brightly through his eyes. He pushes the love out of his eyes and into her eyes. If he does it just right, she will love him back. Georgie knows that, just as he knows that he's not sure he knows how to do anything right. And what if she doesn't love him back? What then?

A loud, rumbling thump distracts him. His spaghetti trembles in fear. An earthquake? A low-flying jet? No.

It is Claudia's fist on the table.

"Georgie—orgy orgy orgy orgy," she says. "Behave yourself for once."

"You're not my mom," he says. He sticks his tongue out at her.

Is Claudia his mom? What if Claudia is his mom? If Claudia is his mom, then he is Claudia's son. No—his mom is just a stupid, old fat lady who can't speak proper English, and has a drinking problem. That's his mom. Not Claudia. But . . . If Claudia is like his mom is (or was), then any minute now she will leave, or she will come to him crying, wearing that pink silk, lace-trimmed nightgown she bought when she was just a chubby—not fat—old lady. That nightgown that doesn't fit her, hasn't fit her in years, so tight that her breasts are always spilling out of it, taunting Georgie. Such big, untouchable breasts. Breasts he shouldn't see. Shouldn't think about.

(So don't. Don't think about them, Georgie.

Okay, he answers dutifully.)

Margaret speaks. Georgie watches her mouth move but can't hear the words she says—the words that mean she loves Georgie. Has always loved Georgie and always will love Georgie. Georgie basks in the attention, the love he feels entering every pore, setting afire every nerve. It is good to be loved by Margaret, to be treasured by such a good good person. Still, Georgie wishes he could hear what she's saying.

Claudia speaks now, too, but Georgie's not sure he cares about hearing what Claudia has to say. She loves him; Georgie knows that/senses that, but Claudia hurts him. And, as good as it feels to be loved by Margaret, that's how bad it feels to be loved by Claudia. She's a bad person. Evil even. Her face is covered in dark spots that move, swarm across her face like wasps, stinging. Georgie hopes she's allergic to bug bites and stings. Georgie hopes her throat will close and she will choke. That's what Georgie hopes.

But no. She's not choking. She's talking and laughing, covering her hand with her face.

"Claudia," Georgie says.

"Claudia," he repeats.

Claudia Claudia Claudia. I'm in love with Claudia Nesbitt? Me? In love with Claudia Nesbitt? Me, in love with the woman who hurts me? The one who tortures me? The one whose face is a mask of stinging, swarming wasps?

Georgie tries once more to call her name, but the words don't come, and he finds himself singing, sinking into the couch, the cushions. Someone throws a blanket over him. It's a scratchy blanket; its fibers irritate his arms. The blanket is nothing but scratchy fibers, and so is Georgie. In his mind, the fibers grow through the edges of the blanket and into his skin, burrowing beneath his flesh like a bot fly until Georgie is nothing but blanket, and the blanket is nothing but Georgie. He opens his eyes. They are magical, like camera eyes. (Lens?) They zoom in on the ceiling, going in for the close-up. Georgie *is* the lens. He is a convex universe made of glass. The wood grain of the ceiling flows like a river—an unmoving wooden river. Whum, whum, whum. The wood river goes nowhere. Still Georgie wants the wood to flow, to flow like water, up and out, spilling over the dam. Breaking free.

"Georgie Porgie. Georgie Porgie. Georgie Porgie!" Claudia sings. He imagines her with pigtails, like a little girl.

"How are you liking your little nappy-poo, Georgie, baby?" Claudia whispers.

Whum, whum, whum.

Margaret's face appears over the couch. She shines with the light of an angel. Claudia is little more than shadow.

"Is he any better?" someone asks.

"Not yet."

Yet, bet, debt, yeti—

"Should we call a doctor?"

"He'll be fine."

Claudia lays her hand on Margaret's wrist, encircling it with her fingers. Such a dainty wrist, that Margaret—that angel—has.

"It's just an episode," Claudia says.

Claudia—that bitch, that whore, that woman I love and hate. She created a paradise and then set it aflame. She is my world and its end, my kinky sex goddess, my creepy-crawly nemesis. She never stood a chance. I never stood a chance. We love and hate—no matter whose face she's wearing, whose heart she's tearing. I want to see her in those sling-backs; her perverted, cotton-candy blue toes peeking out to play.

A popping noise reminds Georgie to look sideways. There is a glow—a fire—and there are three people sitting around it. Georgie wants to roll over, but that would be too hard. The three pass around a glass bottle filled with a clear substance that sloshes around. They bring it to their lips, taking turns. He knows what it is. Georgie's tongue feels like a piece of felt in his mouth; he wants to move it, but can't. Clear sloshy would be a bad idea anyway. Georgie is in a good place.

Two of the people are girls, and one is a boy. The girls are laughing together. One has bright, fire-like hair. One puts her hand on the other one's leg. Georgie is angry. He remembers that he wants both girls for himself, and he can't have both. He's angry they can have each other. He watches them kiss. The bright fire-like hair glows and blends into the fire. The fire wraps around them both; walls of gorgeous flames surround them. Georgie wants to burn with them. The boy reaches out and touches them both. Georgie wants to be the boy. They all collapse together in front of the fire, and Georgie, watching, is with them, too.

Georgie walks through a doorway into a dark hall.

"Stop right there," a voice commands.

Georgie stops.

"Be careful," the voice continues evilly, seductively. "Or else. You don't want it to get you, do you?"

Georgie hears the heavy panting of some enormous creature. He freezes, terrified. "Hi, Princess," Claudia's voice whispers close to his ear. "Come on in."

Georgie tiptoes sideways to avoid the hole he knows is in the floor beside him—the monster that waits salivating, waits hoping Georgie will misstep. He creeps into the living room, now out of the hallway, where he finds Claudia kissing another woman. It's that Sara girl.

Claudia and Sara stand topless in the center of the room. Claudia is wearing her latex suit. There is a small audience beside Georgie, watching. Greg is mid-50s with long, white hair. He has a potbelly, a fuzzy navel. Georgie tics. Claudia sees Georgie's neck jerk and his eyes roll. She waves him to come closer.

"Just don't come too close—"

The creature in the dark hallway breathes heavily, drooling, just behind Georgie, waiting to devour him. The breathing revs up to a scream—a pulsing wail.

"Don't leave," Claudia shouts.

"Fuck you. I fucking love you," Georgie yells at her. "You're fucking with my mind again."

"I'm not," Claudia insists. "I'm really not. I told you I wouldn't, and I'm not."

The screaming becomes louder, and evolves into a high-pitched screech. Georgie presses his hands against his ears.

"I'm just a habit, Georgie. An addiction."

Claudia soothes him. She tapes his mouth shut and cuffs his wrists to his ankles. He is done for—captive once again. Georgie struggles to break free of his bonds. His shirt slides up and exposes his rounded belly, yet the veins on his neck do not stand out. They are nowhere near the surface. Claudia laughs. Her hair glows like fire as the flames shadow her face. It is dark. Georgie can't see—he can't see anything.

"You disgust me," Claudia whispers. She nibbles at his ear. "You're pathetic."

Georgie screams and yells at her, but his mouth is still taped shut.

"Oh. What's that, Princess?" Claudia simpers. "Are you trying to speak like a real person? Let me help you with that."

Georgie watches Sara caress Claudia's breasts as she rolls down Claudia's latex suit and exposes her fiery bush. Claudia moves away from Sara long enough to shove her shiny red sandals up against Georgie's nose. He inhales deeply and then freezes as the noise resurfaces—that screeching.

"Don't go!" Claudia commands him. His mother leers over him; a flickering candle intermittently lights her face as she clenches a carving knife and fork tightly in her fists. Flames lick at the legs of the chair. Georgie struggles, pulling against his bondage. He pleads to Claudia through the tape on his mouth, but she can't give a fuck.

She cannot care. That's what he's paying her for. Not to care. He's not paying for love. He's paying for hate, for pain, to be ground into nothingness, and waste away in a vast, dark emptiness. Claudia pulls out a condom from Georgie's wallet. She sticks her tongue out at him. She unbuttons his pants, and coughs from the smoke in the air.

Her hair is on fire, too, but it doesn't seem to bother her. Her hair. That's the source of all her power, Georgie realizes. Claudia brings her face close to his crotch and sniffs. Her face distorts, lengthens, until she's no longer human. She's a fox, a coyote. Canine. With dangerous teeth and crafty, clever intelligence. The monster begins to scream and screech, again. The smoke rises around them.

Claudia strips the latex off and stands naked before him. She tears open a condom and bites a hole in it. Laughing, she tosses it at his feet.

"You can't be safe," she snarls. "What's the point of trying, when it always comes back to this?"

Georgie strains, and screams through the tape. He tries to hide, but his penis is pulsing, trying to spring from his pants. He hates her. He wants her.

"What's that, Princess?" Claudia rips the tape off his mouth.

"Fucking whore, bitch, cunt!" Georgie screams.

Claudia laughs.

"Good," she purrs.

Claudia and Sara lie face to crotch, burying their faces between one another's legs, moaning in ecstasy. Georgie wonders if they'll let him join them.

The creature shrieks, breathing down Georgie's neck. "No, no, no," Georgie screams. He's just a little boy, a kid, not strong enough to fight back—only strong enough to know what's going on, know it's wrong, and to be terrified by it. "Leave me alone," something small and alone pleads.

But he can do nothing to stop her. Stop the pleasure. The assault. She is on top of him, riding his erect penis faster and faster. "Get me pregnant, Georgie," she demands. "Give me my fucking love child." She spits in his face.

Georgie shakes his head back and forth, protesting; his entire body shakes in protest. "Cum inside me, Georgie," she hollers. "Cum inside me, you fucking waste of a man. You prepubescent asshole." Her voice, wretched and horrible, rises and evolves into that of screaming alarm. She is evil. Wrinkled and horrible, bent and wicked. She is the crone, the hag. That creature from the forest. They blend, become one. All the women Georgie has ever known. They are one. And he fucks them all.

"Son of a crack whore, bitch, cunt," Georgie screams. And then something deep inside him releases, gives up, explodes into nothingness. He shoots his wad again and again and again. Into every woman he's ever known. For an eternity. His orgasm lasts an eternity, suspends all life around him, he is gone, brought back only by the incessant whine of Claudia's voice:

"I don't love you," she is whispering, shuddering. "I never loved you. I only want to hurt you, make you suffer. Just like you wanted. Just like you asked me. You—you're not worth it. Not worth anything but pain, and that's what I love, Georgie. Not you. Never you."

The alarm rises overhead, smoke chokes their lungs, and her hair is a vibrating nest of flame—then, pounding on the door. Someone save them!

(Poor, poor Georgie.)

Claudia's face is now peaceful and blue. Her lips open and close slightly; her eyelids are shut, calm, and dreaming. Her hair splashes purple around her head. It moves, swims; it's got a mind of its own—Claudia's hear does. Georgie gets to his feet; he wobbles, nearly trips over her. "Her hair," he thinks. Slowly, he unclenches his fingers, and feels them as blades, and they slide apart. Snip. He cuts and cuts, sliding the blades through every inch of her serpent-like hair, and douses the purple flame. "No, no, no, no, no, no, no, no—" He snips her ear, and her eyes fly wide open, and she screams. The blood seeps out, and forms puddles on the dark, wood, moonbeam-splashed floor. Georgie is screaming too, but he can't hear a sound. And, then, there is nothing; a nothing so deep there is no more room, not even for bliss.

Dear Diary:

To the best of my ability, to know that I am not the cause of others' actions.

Wake Up and Smell the Dopamine

"Georgie," a soft voice calls. His eyes flutter open. The angel stands over him. She breathes gently in his face. She is white, brilliant white, and she overcomes him.

"I'm dead," Georgie realizes. I'm dead and this is heaven.

"Why did you do it, Georgie?" the angel asks softly.

"I didn't mean to," Georgie replies groggily.

(What did I do?

You know what you did.

No. No, I don't.

If you don't know what you did, how do you know you didn't mean to?

Because I never mean anything.

No. You meant to. You know you did.

But, I didn't. You've got to believe me. I didn't mean to.

It was intentional, Georgie. You did it. You meant it.

I thought I wanted it, but I was wrong. Can't a guy be wrong?)

"Claudia," he gasps.

The angel soothes his forehead. "I don't think it's a good idea to see her right now," Margaret says.

"What?"

Margaret shakes her head in sympathy. "Don't you remember, Georgie?"

Georgie remembers the fire, their loving orgy. The fire—

"You cut off Claudia's hair," Margaret whispers. "She's furious."

Georgie laughs.

"Is that all?" he says.

Margaret looks at him sternly.

"A woman's hair is nothing to mess with," she says. "And, what did Claudia do to you, anyway?"

Margaret comes to a realization, and she bites her lip slightly. Georgie laughs again.

"You have no idea," he says. His voice is empty—terrifyingly empty. "I don't even know the worst of it—not yet, anyway."

Georgie, Claudia, Margaret, and Carl slowly climb into the limousine later that day. Georgie has a massive hangover from the drugs Claudia slipped him. Claudia, Margaret, and Carl have hangovers from their own night of revelry. Claudia needs to see a hairstylist to do something about the wreck Georgie left, and, for now, she's not speaking to him, which makes the atmosphere in the limo strained and uncomfortable. The one time he manages to get her alone she hisses at him, like a snake and, when that doesn't work, doesn't make him go away, she slaps his face.

"This, this is not what we agreed on," she snarls, gesturing to her butchered hair.

Later, Ben suppresses a smile as the group silently exits the limo. You could say he's not surprised by how things turned out. You could say that.

Georgie and Claudia drift into their separate worlds over the next few weeks. Georgie returns to his old fetishes, his sicko-twisted paid-for fantasy world. Claudia returns to Greg and Sara. Now that she has a new job, it doesn't matter if she fucks her old boss (and his wife). Actually, if she stops fucking her new boss, she might lose her job. Or get double pay. It is a toss-up, that one—

Georgie returns to the stone cottage on the mountaintop, but there is no one there. He lies on the bearskin rug, his dick limp and useless. Like a boy's. He breathes in the smell of the rug and waits for the disgust to come. He is empty. There is nothing in him anymore—no chords to strike. No emotions to feed off. His life is as boring as he always feared (knew) it would be.

Georgie returns from his empty trip to the cottage, decides he needs groceries then wanders aimlessly up and down the aisles. He's like a ghost waiting for someone to haunt. Someone to scare, to touch. Waiting for something. Anything. Nothing could be worse than this. He scans the sterile shelves crowded with prepackaged food, watches the mouth-breathers who stalk their prey—the Oreo cookies, the Ding Dongs and Twinkies—and who graze on potato chips or Fritos. Sugar or salt. Salt or sugar. The basket shudders uneasily in his hand. It is empty.

From behind he feels movement, then Margaret's voice: "Hey, Georgie." She must have snuck up on him, proving once again that Georgie's no predator; he's prey just like the Ding Dongs and Twinkies.

"Margaret." Relief quiets his poor, angry, tormented brain for one sweet second.

She stares at the floor for a moment, clutching a package of bargain bulk cereal to her chest. Georgie knows that she is thinking of the cabin, of how she saw him: the town fool, an utter idiot. Georgie knows, she's been playing it over in her mind, trying to make sense of, wondering if she saw what she knows she saw. (Everything.)

"I know that you didn't find your nanny," she says finally. She looks up at him, eyes glistening. "I know that you didn't because you're not any better. If anything, you're worse."

Georgie nods. There's no use disagreeing with her.

"So," she says, "I did some research. And the thing is, Georgie, I found her. I found her for you."

She drops her head and rummages through her purse, eventually pulling out a piece of paper. Georgie thinks about her skin as she presses the paper into his hand.

Margaret steps closer to him. She is in the small cloud of heat his body emits. Her hair smells like flowers. She looks up into his face, begging.

"Go see her, Georgie," she says. "Please. If not for me, then for yourself."

He rubs the scrap of paper between two fingers. He stares doubtfully at Margaret. She notices.

"You have to see her," Margaret says. "It's the only way."

"The only way what?" Georgie says.

Margaret looks at him reluctantly. "The only way for you to get better."

Georgie looks down at the paper. If he rubs the ink away, it will be impossible for him to find her. It will be like she never existed, like before.

He squints at Margaret. Accusing her.

"Why do you care? Whether I'm better or not, it's none of your concern."

"I'm your friend, Georgie."

He snorts at her. "You and your one-hit wonders." He glowers, face distorted. "You think a trip to the Dalai Lama, a visit to my old nanny, and a self-help book are gonna make all my problems disappear?"

Georgie holds the note up to her face. "What's next, Margaret? A magician? More doctors?" He grips the paper in both hands, threatening to tear it. "Ever think that maybe I don't want to get better, don't want to believe in all the bullshite people tell themselves to pretend they're happy? Huh, Margaret? Ever think of that?"

(Is that it, Ben? Is it that you don't even want to heal?

Is that what you call it? Healing? Hell, doc, I don't know . . .

Because if you don't, if you really don't want to get better, then why do you keep coming to see me, Ben?

I don't know, Dr C. You're the doctor. Why don't you tell me?)

Margaret's eyes are full of tears, and yet . . . Behind those tears is a fierceness Georgie's never seen. "I care about you," she finally says. "Even if you don't."

Georgie looks at the slip of paper in his hands.

"More bullshite," he mutters. "Love, healing. It's all bullshite."

"Then it's bullshite, Georgie." Margaret turns, walks away from him, leaving him to wonder if she's leaving for good, if she'll stop being his friend if he doesn't get better, if he doesn't want to get better.

"It's too hard," he wants to scream.

Dear Diary:

In general, to the best that I am able, I need to get over it, no matter what the "it" might be.

Then, Unto Them

Claudia drags herself out of her old beater of a station wagon and leans against it, staring at the dull, gray building before her. The parking lot seems to stretch in front of her like something only Escher could have imagined. Her tender breasts scream at her as they push against her bra, against the fabric of her shirt. She reaches inside the car and bends—carefully and slowly—to pick up her purse from the passenger's seat and is overcome with another wave of nausea. She retches silently, grateful nothing comes out, and then with a dogged determination staggers up the walk to the clinic. Whatever Georgie planted inside her is pure evil, as it's eating her alive, and it's got to be removed.

She has missed Georgie in some sick and twisted way. She contemplates the cottage, and also missing Greg and Sara so at least for now, she's back at the home she thinks she should call home, puttering around Georgie's house, again. A mug of warm water and lemon in her hands, she sips at it slowly, squeezing her eyes shut. She tries to pretend that it is coffee.

It is not. It never was. It never could be.

(Why doesn't she just make some coffee?

Shh, doc. Give the girl a minute, would you? She's back. I've brought her back, doc. See? I'm just not there. I am the observer now.)

And so, with Georgie away, seeing his psychiatrist, Claudia stands in front of the living room window and stares out at the view—at the narrow strip of grass between Georgie's house and the sidewalk, the carefully trimmed ficus trees, the hydrangea, and across the street is her still, burned-down house. It's an eyesore. But eventually, she knows, the insurance will come through, and she'll move back, move on, and move out. How long does she stand there, staring at the unchanging view? Finally, she gives up, moves to the kitchen, the window above the sink. A different view. One of the side street but still the same carefully trimmed ficus trees, the overgrown hydrangea. Window to window, Claudia moves, hoping for/expecting a different view, unique somehow, and when she doesn't find it, she collapses on the sofa in the living room, cradling her stomach.

She doesn't feel well and, for today, she has given up food. What's the point, after all? Claudia thinks about the how, the why, and she doesn't worry about Georgie. She worries about herself; she presses gently on her belly, trying to keep it all in. Trying to prevent anything from getting back out.

(Wait. Is she?)

She brings her hand to her mouth, belching. Oh, this isn't good. This isn't good, at all. No. She can feel the bile rising, jumps from the sofa, and runs to the bathroom. Not again. Claudia collapses against the toilet, retching again and again. There is nothing left, nothing but a little bit of lemon water. She brings that up as well. To the uninformed observer, it looks like little more than vomiting, but for those who know, who understand, it's clear that Claudia is ridding herself of every rotten thing she has ever done to Georgie—the times she humiliated him, hurt him, the time she twisted his pinky until the knuckle broke, the time she buried him . . . . What was she thinking?

Claudia sobs and hiccoughs; she belches, vomits again. She always knew it would come back to haunt her, didn't she? It was only a matter of time.

When Georgie comes home, she is standing in the hall waiting for him. The corners of her mouth are crusted with vomit; her eyes look haunted and tired. To Georgie, she looks like some ghoulish version of her older self. He stares at her, walks toward her to engulf her in his arms—she looks like she could use a hug—and steps in a splash of vomit. He is completely repulsed, can think only of getting the puke off his shoes. He steps back away from her, and again slides. Jesus. He can feel his stomach begin to heave.

(Parenthetical Pet Peeve) Shoes with 6-foot long laces that constantly keep untying themselves.

"Georgie," Claudia cries, "Are you okay? Don't fall."

She reaches for him, but Georgie withdraws. He's never been good with sick people.

"Georgie," she sobs, "Georgie, I'm pregnant."

She falls dramatically at his feet, her shoulders shaking with silent tears. Years from now, Georgie will wonder if he did the wrong thing, if there was anything he could have done to make it right, but for now all he can think is to get away from this woman—

this woman who reeks of vomit and self-loathing.

He stares at her, huddled on the floor, her arm snaking towards his feet. "Get up," he tells her.

She remains motionless, glued to the spot. Georgie glances at her, then lifts one foot, staring at the sole of his shoe, streaked with the remnants of Claudia, her vomit, and her disgrace. Her shame. He can't figure out the best way to erase that shame, without touching the vomit. He's perplexed. Maybe he'll have to wear these shoes forever.

Claudia moves, slithers toward him, tugging at his pants.

"Georgie," she whispers. "What are we going to do?"

"Is it mine?" he asks.

Claudia hangs her head.

"It isn't, is it?" he says.

She says nothing for such a long time that Georgie loses track of what he's asked, his mind drifting back to the shoe issue. These are his Hugo Boss loafers, the ones he likes to wear without socks, the ones he's had for years. The Hugo Bosses are his favorite loafers. His favorite shoes of all the shoes he's ever had in his entire life, and now they're dirty. Smeared with vomit. Ruined. Because of Claudia, who still lies unmoving at his feet.

She stares up at him, pleading. "I don't know," she finally says. "I don't know whose it is."

But Georgie, by now, has completely dismissed her and her "problem"; it's none of his concern. She's the one pregnant, not him. He's got more important problems—his shoes—and now, at last, his mind is beginning to work, beginning to solve the problem. He remembers the hose curled in the front yard, tucked neatly beneath the hydrangea. Claudia now forgotten, Georgie races back out of the house and down the stairs, pulls out the hose, then balancing perfectly on one leg and looking a bit like a flamingo, Georgie begins hosing off his shoes.

He is meticulous, methodical. He stands first on his right leg, lifts his left foot, and hoses down the sole; then he stands on his left leg and repeats the process. He is pleased that he has figured out the problem, come up with the solution. Except . . .

Except now . . . Except now that he thinks about it, how can he be sure that the vomit is only on the soles? How can he know for certain that nothing splashed on the top of his Hugo Bosses? Truth is, he can't. So he hoses off the tops then starts wondering whether anything splashed on his jeans, hoses them off as well and his shirt, while he's at it. And then, to be doubly safe, he hoses down his hair, his face, every last part of himself, until he is standing in the middle of the front yard, dripping wet.

And still . . . it's not enough. There could be vomit on the porch, on the windows, anywhere, and then, feeling like a fireman, he turns the hose on the house, washing away the stench of vomit, the chunks he knows that Claudia's left behind.

Bitch.

Finished washing his own house clean, he turns his attention to the burned-out lot where Claudia's house once stood. He aims his hose at the lot, flooding the ash, scattering it to reveal even more ash.

He thinks about Claudia's house, what it must have been like to live there, how it must have felt like for Claudia walking room to room, what it feels like now knowing she'll never have another chance to walk room to room. Not in the same house. And then he starts wondering if she's still stretched out on his hall floor. She shouldn't be. He wants her gone. She should know that, and he wonders if she does know that he wants her gone. Then he wonders—worries—that maybe she's still puking, getting his floor greasy with vomit, and he wonders if the hose will reach inside, let him clean the hall floor, the whole fucking house. Washing it clean of Claudia.

Or maybe he'll just wash her down with the hose. Hose off all those freckles, hose down all those curls. The spray would be so fast, so hard it would knock her senseless, push her back against the wall. He sees it—her body being blown apart, pieces flying—one arm in the kitchen, the other draped over the lamp in the living room; a leg in the hall, a foot on the porch. And her head . . . Her head in the attic where all heads belong. There is a precision to it.

No, Georgie thinks, that's not how it would work. She'd stay intact. There'd be no body parts flying, but the water—so hard, so fast—would dig into her, cut a hole through her belly until he could see right through. Or maybe no hole in her belly. Maybe the water would just wash away her color, her skin until she was completely translucent. A holy creature. He snickers: Claudia, holy? Claudia, clean?

The water in the hose begins to sputter and with one final spurt has run out completely. No more water. None at all. The hose is flat.

Georgie turns around. Claudia is waiting for him, her hand on the spigot.

"Well?" she asks. He walks close to her. Her eyes are still haunted, stained with tears. Her face is old and wrinkled; her chin sags, and her hair still has flecks of vomit in it. In all seriousness, who could love this woman?

"What are we going to do, Georgie?" she asks.

I don't know, I don't know, I don't know!

(I do.)

"Do whatever you want," he tells her. "I don't care."

She looks at him. Slowly, oh slowly, her eyes begin to narrow. Like mountains forming, her face becomes an angry, bitter mask.

"Fuck you, Georgie," she spits. "Fuck you hard. Right up the ass."

Her eyes glow red.

(How does she make them do that?)

"Just go fuck yourself," she says, raising her chin, daring him to hit it. "I don't need this shite."

Dear Diary:

I wish I could have the courage to abandon myself from all of my obsessions.

Claudia Moves Out

Georgie shuffles through the house, hating every wall, every window, every tile, every everything. He hates it. Everywhere he turns he sees Claudia. Here she strung him up; there she burned him with cigarette butts. Over in the chair she cut him. In the bathroom she drowned him. On the porch, she humiliated him, time and again.

Numb now, Georgie wonders how he ever thought he was bored with Claudia. With her, life was a torturous show, a jagged-toothed adventure. Without her, he is back to making thermoses of 10-shot espresso. It does nothing for him—doesn't give him jitters or clear his head, doesn't jumpstart him in any way. It's Claudia fault. Without her, nothing jumpstarts him anymore. He wants her back.

His days are endless, ceaseless. If he had the nerve, he'd end it all. Instead, he pounds coffee, smokes, does his laundry now and then, and goes shopping.

(Parenthetical Pet Peeve) Public laundromats that leave your clothes still wet after two hours of drying time.

Georgie roams the aisles of the grocery store, searching for Margaret or the perfect snack food or a two-for-one sale on cigarettes. Nothing comes of his endless searching, but Georgie— the eternal optimist—thinks maybe tomorrow or the day after, he'll walk these aisles and there in Aisle 7 will be Margaret buying the perfect snack, and she'll smile at him and tell him the store is having that two-for-one sale on cigarettes, and he better hurry before someone else buys out the entire supply.

Maybe.

It could happen. Georgie knows what people say—that truth is stranger than fiction, so he wanders the aisles, waiting for tomorrow to come, for Margaret to show, for his cigarettes to go on sale. He wanders for so long—nearly $3^1/_2$ hours—that the clerks and cashiers begin to notice him, and begin following close behind him.

Maybe I should have changed, Georgie thinks. Maybe wearing my robe to the store wasn't such a great idea. It makes him noticeable, and Georgie doesn't want to be noticeable.

"Can I help you?"

Georgie looks around, alarmed to discover that a tall, stooped man, in a crisp white shirt, red vest, and gabardine pants, was talking to him. He looks like a store manager, Georgie thinks, wondering if a store manager has any kind of legal authority.

"Excuse me," the man says again, "but are you looking for something in particular?"

The man knows Georgie's not looking for anything in particular, and Georgie knows the man—the manager—knows that Georgie knows. And still the man persists in asking. People are a mystery to Georgie. He stares into the man's face, and for the briefest of seconds, the man's face seems to melt, to morph into Claudia's, and Georgie begins to panic; he can feel the breath catch in his throat, the sweat drip down his face.

"Sir," the man asks, "Are you all right? Do you need help?"

What is it with strangers always asking if he needs help and Claudia—that bitch, that whore—never once asking? What is love if not offering help? Claudia never loved him.

"Sir," the man repeats.

Georgie blinks, deciding he's had an epiphany although he's not absolutely sure what an epiphany is.

"No," he tells the man in the vest. "I don't need help. Just tell me, is it true your cigarettes are on sale this lovely day?"

Five short minutes later, a stocky, young woman wearing a blood-spattered apron holds Georgie by one arm and the man in the vest holds the other, as together they usher him out the door. The door whooshes shut behind him, catching Georgie by the tail end of his robe, making him think—for a second—that the store wanted him back, that it truly did value its customers.

But no, not even the store wants him, and Georgie trudges home, empty-handed, where he finds the message light on blinking, winking. A mile a minute. A mile a minute, it's blinking. He presses the message button, recoils in horror at the sound of Claudia's voice echoing in the empty house.

"Hey Georgie Porgie," she purrs. "I was just thinking about you. I was at this lecture? And it was sooo boring, all I could think of was getting back home, back to my snookums. My Georgie Porgie Pumpkin Eater."

Georgie wants her voice out of his head. He blinks, wondering if the torture was all in his mind and if really Claudia is still his—all his—and she really hadn't moved out and they really hadn't broken up and that she really is just at some sort of conference, and everything is as it was, as it should have been all along. Maybe.

(The man can dream, can't he?)

Georgie doesn't want to dream. He shakes his head, clearing his thoughts, realizing the message is old, from way back when. The real message plays:

"Hi Georgie," Claudia once again purrs. "Just wanted to check in. See what's going on. See how you've been doing. What you've got planned for the holidays."

Claudia's voice rises at the end of every sentence, or rather at the end of every word. Why has he never noticed before? Where has he been? And still Claudia's voice echoes in his head.

"I know how absent I've been," she says, "and how rough it's been, but Georgie, look at it from my perspective. It's just I needed to put 100% into my own family. You understand, don't you, Georgie? Don't you?"

Georgie reels. Who is this Claudia? This self-assured family woman, this woman Georgie's never met. Then . . . Then he remembers: Claudia was pregnant. She had the baby and raised it with her lesbian lover.

His baby. His sperm-child.

But then, yet another real message plays, and Georgie realizes that . . .

(Don't think about that.)

That Georgie, the one with the baby, must have been a different Georgie, that Claudia a different Claudia. As far as this Georgie is concerned—the real Georgie—none of that ever happened.

And so Georgie—the real Georgie—listens to the real message from Margaret, the real Margaret. The only Margaret.

"Hey, Georgie, it's me," she says quietly, sounding a little scared. "I just wanted to check in with you, see if you got in touch with your nanny yet. I think it's really important. I care about you a lot, you know . . . It's just . . . Well, anyway. Just go see her. That's all."

A pause for a moment. Nothing but silence. Dead silence. Then a fast goodbye and a click.

Georgie has not heard at all from Claudia. Only Margaret. Margaret, who says she cares for him. Margaret, who wants him to get better. Claudia never wanted him to get better. Claudia just wanted to hurt him . . . make him worse. She was happy to take his money and warp him into a twisted fuck. Georgie forgets that he's the one who asked her to, that he wanted to be sick, that healthy was just too hard, too dull. He forgets all that. He just thinks, with relief, of the possibility of that happy dream couple they could have been, if only he had applied himself.

Georgie digs frantically through his closet until he finds the jeans with that slip of paper in them with the nanny's address on it. He unfolds the paper, stares at the address in amazement. The house is close. Practically in his neighborhood.

What kind of sick fuck moves into the same neighborhood where his old nanny used to torture him? Then again, his parents bought him the house. Georgie looks out the door at the front lawn for a long moment then jogs sluggishly down the steps and across the grass.

Georgie climbs out of the town car; Ben shuts the door gently behind him as he takes his first steps. The house is a two-story, gray frame house with faded blue shutters that hang crookedly aside windows that are nearly opaque from years of accumulated grime and urban air. The small, front yard is practically a jungle, overgrown and out of control, salt grass brushes Georgie's knees and the hydrangea and pyracantha tower over his head. Dead ivy hangs limp and withered from the porch railing, and climbing honeysuckle peaks from the gutter. The sound of bees buzzing and leaves decomposing fill Georgie's ears, as he walks the overgrown path to the front porch.

He sees her, furiously rocking in a bentwood rocker and glaring at him.

"So you found me, finally?" she asks. Her voice is coarse as if she's spent her life smoking unfiltered Camels, and wisps of her cottony white hair blow around her face.

"Wha-what?" Georgie stammers, wondering how she knew, how she could have recognized him after these years.

"Through all that mess in my front yard," she says, pointing a skinny arm at the front lawn, and Georgie realizes he was wrong. She doesn't recognize him. She couldn't.

Still, he finds himself asking, "Do you remember me?"

He peers at her through the dark shadows of honeysuckle trees and dead vines. How could his nanny, that woman who had such power over him as a child, had made him tremble with terror, had pinched him, tormented him, swung him from his dick, how could she have become this scrawny, pathetic old woman? Was it the ultimate justice that she, who had once towered over him, now struggles to get to her feet out of that old, creaking chair, or just a cruel twist of fate?

Georgie briefly wonders what fate has in store for him, after all that he has done.

"Remember you?" the woman cackles again, harsh ancient air escaping from her lungs. "Who in this God damn world would bother to remember a pudgy little vermin like you?"

Georgie trembles, his foot pausing in mid-air on the first step.

"Aw, 'course I remember you, Georgie Gust," the woman cackles again. "I never forget a pretty face."

Georgie shudders, as he tries to remember what he's doing here. Is he supposed to confront this old woman? Beat her? Torment her—now that she's the weak one? Or beg her . . . for what? Forgiveness?

He looks at her again, as malevolent as Claudia but in a rocking chair. Maybe she's not so weak, after all. Age isn't everything.

"Yeah, well, I was uh . . ." Georgie clears his throat. "It's just that I wanted to see how you've been."

"Fine and dandy," she says, gesturing at the decay that surrounds her. "Livin' the dream."

Georgie walks up the steps, sits down uneasily on the empty rocker next to her. She grins at him, showing a mouth missing a myriad of teeth.

"Yeah," Georgie says, falling easily into the casual drawl of her speech. "Just thinkin' about the old days, you know. Used to have a lot of fun back then."

His throat threatens to constrict and choke him on the word "fun," but he gets it out anyway.

She smiles at him, a slight question in her eyes.

"Yeah, you used to spend hours and hours here," she says finally. "Sometimes it was hard to get you to go home."

"Yeah?" Georgie feels something twist in the pit of his stomach, like he is going to blow chunks. "Yeah?" he says again.

She nods sagely then stares at him from the corner of one eye as she chomps slowly on her gums.

"That's not what I remember," he spits out finally.

A wary look crosses her face.

Georgie continues, "What I remember is that you used to torture me."

She shakes her head vehemently back and forth, but he knows that she is lying.

"What I remember," he says, "is hating every minute here. I was miserable because of you."

The skinny old woman is still shaking her head—no no no.

Georgie is relentless. "You ruined everything for me," he screams at her. "Ev-everything. Every re-relationship I've ever had is ruined because of the w-way you . . ."

Then Georgie does something he rarely does, something he has not done since boarding school.

He bursts into tears.

In that vast nothingness, that horrible numbness deep inside me, there is a churning and gnashing, ripping out my insides, crushing my bones. My rib cage.

Everything shatters and falls apart. Everything gurgles up the back of my throat, drips from my mouth. Everything.

(Ben, is that you?)

And then.

Silence. Absolute dead silence.

As Georgie grows quiet, he feels a hard, bony hand resting on his knee. He remembers that hand, how it pinched and twisted at his balls, performed unspeakable acts on him.

The woman speaks—her voice seems young, now, almost human: "I'm sorry," she says.

Georgie hiccups.

"It was horrible," she says.

Georgie nods.

"Unspeakable," she whispers.

(But there are things that must be spoken . . . isn't that right, Ben?

Ben?)

"But it wasn't all like that, you know," the woman says. Her eyes plead with him, like Claudia's. "What about your friend Marie? You two . . . You were like boyfriend and girlfriend when you were kids. So sweet to each other."

The woman's face breaks into a smile. Georgie can see that she's remembering better days. Sunny afternoons. Two kids in crisp, clean clothing running circles on the lawn, chasing after one another.

Georgie shakes his head, clearing his mind of the memory. "I don't remember that," he whispers. "Until last year, I didn't even remember you."

She grins wide. "Well, that's a blessing, isn't it?"

Georgie steps inside her rickety front door, feeling immediately ill at ease. The doorframe is crooked from years of warping from a sinking foundation; the floor rolls away beneath his feet, slightly downhill. It is dark and cool inside. Georgie waits a moment for his eyes to adjust.

"You see 'em?" the nanny's voice calls from the front porch. "They're right in there on the wall."

Georgie blinks and swivels around. An old sofa and sagging armchair rise out of the darkness, draped with gravity-warped afghan blankets and doilies, whose holes stretch like grinning mouths, their bottom lips drawn ever-closer to the floor.

Then he sees them. The pictures.

They line the wall beside the front door. Black-and-white, sepia toned—almost all of Georgie—so many of him that it goes beyond the nostalgic and slightly creepy to almost gruesome and nearly unbelievable.

(Do you believe it, Ben?

Ben?)

It's like Georgie was the only kid she ever babysat, or that he was the only one worth remembering.

And then there is the girl she mentioned—Marie. The wall is filled with pictures of her and Georgie posing in the bright sunlight, playing childish games. In one, he is lacing up her shoelaces. In another, she is riding him like a pony. The pictures flash in front of him, alternating between photo and memory . . . memory and photo.

He remembers her—the first Claudia. She stood before him in Keds and frilly pink dresses, stamping imperiously and ordering him about. Her moods were like storms across the ocean—quickly flashing in moments of terrifying manipulation, subsiding quickly once her wishes had been appeased.

He had been her slave—the first Georgie. Georgie Porgie, she'd called him. Before her, his name had been . . .

(Don't think about that, Georgie.

Ok.)

Looking at the pictures, Georgie realizes that this girl, this demanding, tiny, terrible woman, had taught him everything he knows. She was his first girlfriend, his model woman. She taught him how to love—the ups and downs of it, the grim, terrified clutching and the panicked, unreasonable, pushing away. She had taught him that love was pain and suffering . . . that it was better to hate the one you love, better to blame them for all the wretchedness they caused you.

I can do better than that, Georgie realizes suddenly. The fights, the torture—they do not have to happen. They don't have to be a part of me.

Georgie races from the house, his mind filled with the image of the happy American Dream lover he can be. He and Claudia and his son in his sunny and charming California bungalow, playing happy.

No. Being happy.

"Where you going so fast, puddin' pie?" the old woman drawls at his retreating back.

"Home," Georgie hollers, over his shoulder. "Home."

The woman cackles again, her mouth stretching into that impossible jack-o-lantern grin.

"Wouldn't be in such a hurry if I was you," she mutters. Her cackle follows Georgie all the way to the shining black limousine.

He climbs into the waiting limo and tells Ben, "Home, please."

Georgie is filled with an impossible delirium (just short of insanity). He knows he can be happy and perfect, if he just tries hard enough. He can make his own destiny. His mind rejoices. He can remake his own damn self any damn way he wants.

(Just like those new age books claim, eh Georgie-boy?)

Eh!

Ben pulls up in front of Georgie's house, tires screeching to a stop. Georgie leaps out of the car without waiting for Ben to open the door. He has no way of knowing, no reason to hope, but he knows that all his happiness is waiting for him inside. His happy dream future is only just steps away.

When Georgie flings open the door to his American Dream home, he runs headlong into a pitch-black room; thick smoke fills his nostrils, and something rough and scratchy encircles his neck. He is disoriented. Frightened. His fingers clutch at his neck, where he finds a rope—a noose actually, which is tightening around his throat. Georgie's fear escalates.

"Georgie," says her voice softly out of the darkness.

It is Claudia, his dream lover, his perfect woman. She will be nice to him if he tells her to be. She said she was tired of torturing him. She said so. He will pay her to be nice if that's what it takes. Georgie thinks dreamily of his future life as the noose tightens.

"Claudia?" he says.

Can't she see in his face that he doesn't want to play this game anymore? The rope is choking off his air supply. Georgie kicks and claws at his neck with his hands. He gurgles, trying to open his larynx to the air. He draws in a hissing stream of oxygen. Not enough. Then Georgie's mind overcomes his body's panic. She is not really killing him, after all. It is just one of those games that they are playing. She doesn't yet know that he is done with the torture game and wants to move on to something more blissful.

Ah, what the hell, Georgie thinks. One more time wouldn't hurt. For old time's sake. His gasping, bulbous, red-turned face grimaces that resembles a smile.

"What do you have to smile about?" Claudia demands from the darkness.

There is some movement on the rope as she ties it off. Then she steps into the small pool of light before him.

"What the fuck have you ever had to smile about, you freak?" she says.

Georgie finds his good humor starting to fade, as his face turns purple

"Do you see this?" She gestures to the circles beneath her eyes, her orange freckles.

"You," she says, "you did this to me. I never used to be this bad."

A sick, rattling moan escapes Georgie's lips. Spots dance before his eyes. He has heard all this before. When is she going to untie the rope? Is she going to bury him again, afterward? She stares at him in silence. For a moment, Georgie feels a stab of real fear run through him. Her eyes are haunted. Hollow. He can't see anything of the Claudia he remembers. Not in her eyes. Not in her face. The Claudia he remembers is gone.

Slowly, she smiles. Her curving lips fill his vision.

"I killed your son," Claudia whispers.

The words echo in Georgie's ears as if coming from a great distance.

"You didn't want him. You didn't care about him or about me. So I killed him."

She walks slowly to Georgie. He pulls desperately at the thick rope that rings his neck. He can't see past the fireworks exploding at the back of his eyes, but he can feel her. She touches his leg with her hand.

"I killed both of us," she whispers.

She yanks at the rope, cutting it deeper into his neck. She laughs.

"And now," she says, "I'm killing you."

Another tremendous pull and Georgie's world goes black. He can't hear her breathing. He can't feel her arms wrapped around him, or the rope around his neck.

He is nothing.

Finally. After all this time, he is nothing.

Dear Diary:

The best I can, to not create a catastrophe over anything.

Waking Up With Mr Clean

He wakes up in a world of white—a soft white glow. He tries to roll over but can't move his arms. For a moment he panics, jerking his arms frantically at his side. He can't breathe. A small cry escapes him. Then . . .

Then he understands the white room, and what it is that binds him, prevents his arms from moving.

It is a cell.

It is a straightjacket.

A man about Georgie's age taps on the small window in the door. Georgie looks up. The man smiles and opens the door.

"I see that you're up," the man says. He lifts a clipboard and props it on his forearm. "How are you doing today?"

"Wh-what?" Georgie says.

The man squints at him.

"Do you know where you are?" he asks.

Georgie shakes his head.

The man inhales deeply. "Mercyhurst Hospital?" he says. "Remember now?"

Georgie shakes his head 'no.'

"You remember me?"

Again, Georgie shakes his head.

"Dr Weinstein?" the man says. "Your psychiatrist?"

Georgie tries to shake the cobwebs from his head. "So I'm uh . . . I'm uh . . . I'm not dead?"

Dr Weinstein looks at him with a slight smile. "Alive as ever," he says. Georgie detects a slightly ironic tone, but doesn't understand it. He decides that it's nothing.

"Where's Claudia?" Georgie demands.

"Who?"

"Claudia. My girlfriend."

Dr Weinstein frowns slightly, notes something on his iPad then glances at Georgie.

"Who's Claudia?" he says.

"I told you, my girlfriend."

"You have no girlfriend."

"Red hair. Freckles," Georgie says.

"There's no one like that. Not here. And there's no Claudia."

Georgie stares at his doctor and then, as a smile spreads across Georgie's face, his arms, his neck, his entire body relaxes. No Claudia. She never existed, never hurt him. Never killed him. He breathes a sigh of relief.

And yet, at the same time . . . If she didn't exist, then . . . Then the pain of her nonexistence is almost stronger than the pain of her actual existence. If she wasn't real, then what else wasn't—*isn't*—real? No, he decides, somewhere Claudia does exist, somewhere the doctor can't find, but no—Claudia was too real not to have existed at all.

The doctor is wrong.

And then, as if the doctor can read Georgie's mind, he asks, "Do you know how long you've been here? At Mercyhurst?"

Georgie shakes his head. He doesn't want to know.

"Fifteen years," the doctor says. "Nearly half your life."

Georgie reels back, struggling to free his arms. The doctor notices.

"The trick to getting out of those," he says, motioning to the restraints, "is to stop fighting them. Stop fighting us."

Georgie's mind is blank. He can't remember fighting anyone. Ever. He is complacent, isn't he? Acquiescent. He doesn't fight.

"Do you remember what you're doing here?"

Again, Georgie's mind is blank.

"I don't mean at Mercyhurst. I mean here . . . ." This time, the doctor gestures around the room, at the cushioned walls, the small barred window. "Do you remember what you did to end up in seclusion? To end up in restraints?"

Georgie's eyes widen; he shakes his head frantically back and forth. All he can remember is Claudia. Margaret. The house in the woods. The pain. That's what he remembers.

"Well," the doctor says, turning to leave. "Why don't we give you some time to think? I'm sure once your mind clears, you'll remember."

And then the doctor, pulling a jangling ring of keys from his pocket, unlocks the door and walks out, leaving Georgie completely alone, restrained, and still unable to remember a thing.

The doctor sticks his head in the door: "It's not that bad. Really. Mercyhurst is state of the art."

State of the art, but it's still fifteen years. Fifteen years of a life

174

only imagined. He stumbles, falls to his knees. Claudia. Margaret. A dream. A dream. A dream . . . Something wets his cheeks, rolls to his chin.

Tears. Georgie is crying.

He sobs, feeling the loss and the terror rise up in him. Then it subsides. Leaving him empty. Clean. Some time passes as Georgie tries desperately to comprehend a situation that seems impossible.

Georgie gasps, pulling at his restraints, staring at the ceiling above. His personal hell. This can't be happening. This can't be real. It comes to him, then. It isn't real. This—Mercyhurst, the restraints—this is the dream. The hallucination.

He screams into the silent room: "Somebody help me. Somebody. Claudia?"

He knows she won't come.

He tries again: "I demand that all my angels, spirit guides, all of you who know me, who want to help. I demand: Touch my head so I know you're here. Wake me up from this nightmare."

Nothing happens, and once again Georgie sobs. But then . . .

He feels a hand on his head. He moves his head, trying to look, trying to see. And then Ben's face comes into view, smiling at him. Smiling at Georgie.

"You?"

Ben nods slowly.

"I can see you," Georgie says.

"Yes," Ben says.

Or is it the voice—the voice in Georgie's head—the voice that's been there always, ever since. (*Don't think about that.*)

He stares closely into Ben's face, taking in the nose, the mouth, the cheeks. "You're not bad-looking," Georgie says. "You have the face I should have had. The face I always wanted."

Ben smiles as if Georgie's said something funny. Something clever.

And then Georgie looks deeply into Ben's eyes, a mirror of the soul. His soul.

(*It's impossible to say. Neither of us turned out quite the way we thought we would.*)

"Why can I see you now?"

(*Couldn't you see me before?*)

"I don't know."

(*You don't have to talk, you know. You can just think.*)

"You're always listening, aren't you?"

(Yup.)

Georgie relaxes, staring at the blank, acoustic ceiling, thinking nothing, wanting nothing. Somewhere, even if he can't see him, somewhere Ben waits. Ben is there. Ben has always been there, always will be.

"Are we dead?" Georgie asks.

Ben gives a mental shrug. *(How should I know?)*

"You're not good for much, are you?"

(Fuck you.)

Georgie longs to pick at his fingernails, but his arms are still tightly restrained. He can't even scratch himself. He can do nothing but stare at the ceiling, turn his head and stare at a wall.

"Who are you?" Georgie finally asks. Ahhh. The million-dollar question.

(You, Georgie. I'm you. Just as you, in all your delusions, your hallucinations are me. We are one.)

Georgie wants to jump free, slam himself into the wall, but, even if could, what would be the point? What would he gain? Instead . . .

"Why is my driver named Ben?" he asks.

(Why is your driver named Ben? Or why I am your driver?)

Ben seems to be laughing. *(You never listen, do you? Dr C explained it to you hundreds of times. I drive. You ride. Simple as that. Or some such bullshite.)*

"I don't get it."

(Bullshite. I drive, but you tell me where, when. You're more than the rider, the passenger. Aren't you?)

Georgie wants to rub his eyes, clear his head. "Huh?"

(I'm not your alter ego, Georgie; you're mine.)

Georgie's mind whirls. He doesn't understand.

(You're not real. You've never been real.)

Georgie nods. Of course. That's it. He's not real. He's not the driver, not the rider. Not the passenger. He's never really been here. Not in Mercyhurst. Not with Claudia. It is a blessing. A relief.

Georgie closes his eyes, sinks slowly away. Now. Now he gets it. Farther and farther he sinks. The room fades. Ben fades. Life fades. Somewhere—far, far off in the distance—Georgie hears Ben's voice screaming:

"I want a cigarette, goddamnit. Somebody in this fucking shithole bring me a goddamn cigarette. Did you hear me? I'm Ben

Schreiber, and I want a goddamn fucking cigarette. And I want it now."

Georgie hears the voice. He smiles.

Dear Diary:

The best I can, to not overreact, no matter what. Yikes.

If you think about it, the whole world, at least my miniature world, is encompassed within the universe, this universe that we can only imagine as seemingly having no end. So with the death of Claudia, going back in time to the beginning, you can even trace the speed of light, it's an incredible phenomenon. People wondered how the damn thing was created in the first place. Back in the year 1000, men never lived long enough nor did Claudia, and they didn't travel far enough to get really beyond the town where they lived, so they could only imagine what existed beyond the hills and it's ironic because the things that existed right in front of them, they knew extremely well, every tree, every villa, every knoll of land. But they could only image what existed beyond that, and one doesn't know, we fear, ultimately. So beyond the hills, and beyond that dense primeval forest, existed fairies and sometimes demons that would rush out and destroy them, or fierce indescribable animals that would tear them apart if they ever wandered beyond their clod fields. Reality is strange. And so, I allowed Claudia to decide my imagination . . . my reality. It all began on the road.

BOOK TWO

The Road to Wakefield

Interstate 87 rolls away beneath me as the tires of Poppy's Delta '88 glide heavily over the pavement. We're doing about 75 even though the speed limit's still 65 and Pops really can't afford another speeding ticket.

The red brown and yellow leaves are falling off the autumn trees, bright colors livening up the New England countryside. It's the only countryside I've ever known, since before I can remember, since before I was born. Since before I was myself, or Georgie was himself.

My alter ego, Georgie Gust, is in the back seat, looking out the window.

His parents, Pops and Rose, are up front. (And me?)

An enormous trunk and an old, fat-tired bike are tied to the car's roof.

Wakefield's a small, blue-collar town near the New England coast that consists primarily of turn-of-the-century colonial homes, sidewalks, large grass lawns, a train station, your everyday necessity shops, a children's playground and park, a pizza place, a bike shop, a couple of restaurants, and a vintage luncheonette.

Bicyclists, joggers, pedestrians, and moped riders (Vespas mostly) line Main Street, in the center of town.

Yellow wooden arrows point toward the school grounds. They read:

WELCOME WAKEFIELD STUDENTS!

Just around the corner from the remarkable school arches and the vast school grounds is The Pen, an old, shady, rundown bar near the street corner. Homeless guys and drunks hang around outside, drinking out of brown paper bags.

Pops's car stops at a red light.

Pops fidgets in his second-hand suit and tie. He's holding the wheel tight; his head tics slightly. Pops turns to Rose, who has turned to stare at Georgie.

"They're going to love you here, honey," says Rose.

Georgie starts pulling at his clothes. He says, "Fucking cunt, fucking nigger! It's hot in here."

(Parenthetical Pet Peeve) Overheated cars, work places and other public facilities.

Then Rose says to Pops, "Aren't they, Martin?"
Pops glances at Rose. "Hmm?" he says.
"Dude," Georgie continues. "Shite, man, it's really hot."
He looks at his mother.
"Sorry," he says, and touches her nose with the tip of his finger.
She ignores him. "What I'm saying, honey, is that these kids are different. They have money. They have manners. Not like the others."
Georgie sighs. "Mo-om," he groans.
She turns to Pops. "Right, Martin?" she says.
Georgie stares out the window. He watches the lowlifes and derelicts flicking ash outside the bar.
Pops peeks in the rearview mirror. "The important thing is the Winterbourne, Georgie. Win that, my boy, and you're in."
"The most important thing is your classmates," Rose persists. "You're going make friends here. Not like that other place."
Georgie looks at her, rolling his eyes. "Going to study Nietzsche, Camus, Unamuno, Sartre," he says. "Big time. Jean-Paul Sartre even turned down his Nobel Peace Prize. Fuck, that's cool, huh?"
Pops jumps in, a little more sternly. "Hey, boy. Worry about the Winterbourne. Okay? Win the Winterbourne and you're in. In like flint."
Rose glances disapprovingly at Pops. "All I'm trying to say is . . ."
"Well, don't," Pops cuts in. "Just don't even say it."
The traffic light turns green as the Wakefield track team turns the corner and jogs past the car down Main Street. The runners wear sporty yellow jerseys; their swinging legs are perfectly in sync. They sweep past the big blue-and-gold signpost:

WAKEFIELD ACADEMY

VETUS TAMEN IUVENESCO

FOUNDED 1892

The Delta '88 stops at the administration building, pulling in next to one of the several luxury cars already parked in the parking lot.

Parents, students, and faculty crowd around the building's lawn, getting to know one another.

(Parenthetical Pet Peeve) Schools assuming that people live in a 50s sitcom and parents are always available to pop right down to the school with no notice for conferences, etc.

Georgie picks out the parents from the faculty, which is easy because the teachers don't have any kids hanging around near them. He tries to figure out which one is the dean, and then he sees her—an older woman, a teacher. Unlike the rest of the faculty, she is dressed-down, seemingly casual. Even so, she's hot enough to make any priest want to kick a hole through the stained glass windows of his chapel. (Anyway, that's what would happen, if I happened to be a priest, and I was hanging out there. If I were Georgie; if Georgie were me.)

Then a girl his own age catches his eye. Surrounded by two rough-looking jock types, she is 18 in all her glory—attractive and conservative, but slightly troubled, too. (Sometime later, she would step into the Penthouse centerfold of Georgie's life—and mine. Her breasts aren't sagging or fat, now, but puffy-nippled, pert, and pale, covered with silky cilia. They're soft, smooth, those plump belly-breasts and their dime-sized aureoles.)

Georgie jumps out of the car. He's wearing jeans, a baseball cap, t-shirt, and sport coat. Georgie takes off the dark glasses, his deep-set eyes slightly sad.

"Georgie?" Rose calls, jiggling the inside handle of the passenger side door. "Georgie, I'm stuck . . . ."

Georgie seems not to hear; he's too busy scoping out the campus. He grimaces, bobbing his head at strangers.

Rose struggles with the door. "Georgie?" she calls, sounding scared.

Finally, Rose slips her arm through the window and pulls the exterior door handle. She gasps as she straggles out of the car.

Georgie stretches one arm over his head, scratching his ear.

Rose puts her arm around him and kisses his cheek. "They're going to love you here, baby. Really," she says.

From a slight distance, the two rough-looking jocks see the exchange and start laughing. One of the girls standing nearby—he hadn't noticed her the first time—laughs along with them. The one he noticed—the troubled teen—glances at her friends, and then stares intently at Georgie. The casually dressed teacher also stares.

Dear Diary:

It is so difficult to not allow other people's behaviors to affect me in a negative way.

Settling in

Later, Wakefield students crowd the dorm, calling to each other across the hall as they check out their rooms and roommates. Georgie, lugging his trunk and bicycle, half hops, half skips down the crowded hallway, looking for his room.

Near the end of the hall, Georgie spots two geeks holding their laptops and stylus pens. Georgie sets down his trunk to rest, and the two geeks notice his over-packed steamer.

"Shite's heavy, dude. Huh?" Georgie says.

"You should have left the bike outside, dude," one advises solemnly.

The other kid adds, "It'd be lighter to carry."

Georgie blushes, gulps, and continues to drag his luggage down the crowded hallway, yelping in frustration.

Several doors down, Georgie finds his room. It's a single. He awkwardly unpacks, puts away his clothes, sets up his computer and other electronics, and finally pulls out several rolled-up posters from the overstuffed trunk: Dostoevsky, Henry Miller, Socrates, and Nietzsche, along with Edvard Munch's *The Scream*. He listens to electronica and disco while he unpacks, dancing and quivering.

Georgie tacks *The Scream* to the back of the door and begins stacking his books on the small bookshelf provided. He brought philosophy books, mostly: Albert Camus' *The Myth of Sisyphus* and Sartre's *Being and Nothingness*, along with several how-to books on writing. Soon enough, he stops dancing and pulls out an old thumb-worn French copy of Sartre's *Nausea*. I don't remember packing this, he thinks. He opens the book.

"Original. Sweet. Oh my God, it's in French," he says aloud.

A few photographs fall from between the pages.

Georgie picks up the pictures and brings them to his desk. They're family pictures from when Georgie was a small child. He's posing with his family, sitting on his father's shoulders.

Georgie is scratching his father's face off the photographs with his room key when a big grey pigeon lands on the open window above his cluttered desk. He looks at the pigeon and coos at it softly, and then feeds it potato chips from a bag in his pocket. As he leans out the window, he watches as one of the rough jock-types bursts out of the back door. The jock shouts at his cell phone as he jogs down the sidewalk, clutching a lacrosse stick and ball in his other hand.

(Parenthetical Pet Peeve) Parents who expect sports figures to be role models for their children.

"Dad. Dad. Dad. Dad! When have you ever been a father to me?" he yells. "You're always too busy helping out everyone else's kids, Dad." He stops jogging, quieting his voice. "Yeah, I know . . . okay, I'm sorry, see? Look, I got to warm up for practice . . . I'll do my best . . . I've been doing my best, Dad. Bye."

The jock hangs up, and then sees his buddy up ahead, waving a lacrosse stick. The jock with the cell phone wings the ball his way. "Yo! Heads up, Wyman!" he calls, and then sprints after his throw.

Georgie pulls his eyes back into his own, single room and flops into his bed to stare at the ceiling. Ten minutes later, he's asleep.

(And me, too. I get tired, more and more, over the years, whenever I try to make sense of everything. "Who am I? Where am I?" I ask myself. Where's Georgie Porgie? Who's Georgie and who am I? I've got to admit, I don't know, Dr C . . . Better go ask Georgie. He knows better.)

Dear Diary:

I'd wish it were easier to not allow other people's pasts to create my own present.

The birth of adult love

Students sleepwalk to their classes (but, of course, nobody's truly lucid. Not even me, or Dr C. I dream of Georgie, and Georgie's me. And Dr C knows I'm dreaming—she dreams of me. She dreams of Georgie.). Georgie wears a hat and sunglasses, riding past zombie students on his old fat-tire bike.

I see Georgie pass by me. I look up. I wake. Those students, too, glance at Georgie as he rides on. I'm nowhere while he's moving, and that's where I prefer to stay. My alarm goes off. The clock tower chimes.

Flocks of birds fly over the large campus lawn.

A bird looks Georgie in the eye. The bird sees me, sees Georgie. I'm a speck in its eye. In Georgie's eye. The bird flies away, with me a speck in it.

Back in the dorm, Georgie unpacks his ticky-tack room decorations and other bric-a-brac. He hangs his clothes neatly in the open closet.

He takes a flask from the trunk. (He remembers me—Ben—but I'm slowly drifting away into the future. It must have been me, it must have been me, made him drink. But I didn't. I really didn't. I promise, it wasn't.)

Georgie throws the flask up into the air and catches it, practicing catching it perfectly, like that, then jams the flask underneath his mattress. Like that.

He sits on the rumpled bed, pulls out his laptop, and starts writing about the idea of a woman. A perfect woman, a young woman, at her peak. She is the perfect, un-perplexed idea, his finest, first image of a beautiful woman—an alter ego. A living, colorful beauty. Georgie's One and Only. She was The One, wasn't she? (Who was she? Wasn't she—someone whispers the name again—Claudia. Claudia Nesbitt.)

Georgie describes her room, her dorm, and her school. She's there, isn't she? She's there in his version of reality, his perfect, pure, beautiful idea. He thinks that every little detail about Claudia corresponds with something so beautiful and pure and is overwhelmed to tears. Georgie falls in love instantly with the perfect idea of her.

184

(Where's she? Where's he? She's lost in his perfect, beautiful fantasy.) Light jazz creeps from the small pink radio on her desk (. . . she's lost, now, isn't she? And me, too . . . she flies away, like me, lost in this confused, perfect fantasy). Claudia's room is plastered with photos and letters and other scraps of memory—medals, awards, and decorations. There's even a blue, New York police officer's uniform, dry-cleaned and perfectly preserved in its entirety. It once belonged to a young man of 30—her father. (But her mother? Her family? Who knows? Does Claudia even have a mother? Or a family? It's all up to me, now, isn't it? Wasn't it?) Claudia's alone in her room, her shrine. She sits down to write out a letter. It opens with: "Dear Daddy, I miss you."

Dear Diary:

I wish people—including myself—wouldn't judge other people's books by their covers, yet be mindful by looking at others, without judging them.

Heidi

Where are we now? We are in Heidi's room, aren't we? Where Claudia becomes Heidi who becomes me. (But who is Georgie, if not Claudia, Heidi, or me?) A small Oriental shrine rests beneath her television set, "in memory of Tina" engraved on its base. As Heidi lights a candle above their photo together (in the photo, her sister leans on crutches), she talks on the telephone.

"Excuse me?" she says, sounding ruffled.

Heidi's place is quaint and cluttered. It's a good place, for now, she thinks. But just for now, because she loves to travel. She's currently trapped here within the boundaries of this school, this Wakefield Academy, but just for now. She teaches philosophy, but she has a medical degree. She thought she'd give teaching a shot, because her sister always wanted to be a teacher. (But her story, her life, went sour.) Heidi's a fantastic teacher (isn't she?). She's liberal, hip, radical, the Wakefield Academy ideal. But still, she tends to feel close to the students, sometimes, some of them. ("Only the special ones," she said, the special students, like Georgie, like me. But I can see the future already. I can see Heidi's future, and it's not Wakefield—it's not me.)

Her campus apartment, as it was, as it is, is filled with tangible memories of her deceased sister. A poster-sized photo of the two of them together, items that once belonged to Tina, etc. But she's distracted from her communion with her sister by another, different conversation.

"No, sir," Heidi says into the telephone. "I don't believe there should be any hesitation on your part or any unsatisfied parents this year."

Dean Winterbourne clears his throat. The sound echoes down the line.

"There was some question about a student," he points out. "A student in one of your philosophy classes."

Heidi lights another candle.

"But that boy graduated two years ago, sir."

Dear Diary:

Every mother on earth gave birth to a child, except my mother. My mother gave birth to a legend. High five for Mommy!

School blues

Georgie gets off his bike and walks, step-step-step-hop, towards the white-pillared red brick Wakefield Humanities Building. Students scurry pass him, rushing to class. Some notice his step-hop. Many decide to ignore it.

Georgie walks into Miss Heidi Berillo's classroom with his sunglasses on, his books loosely held in his arms. He picks a seat in the back, sits down, and sets his books on his desk. He checks out the other students from behind the anonymity of his dark-tinted sunglasses, pulling a baseball cap down to cover his forehead.

On the board is written:

"We agree that what is holy is loved by the gods because it is holy, and not holy because it is loved by the gods.—Socrates."

The girl he noticed yesterday, the attractive, conservative, troubled girl, rushes in, breathing heavily. She sits two rows over and a couple of seats in front of Georgie, and is quickly joined by one of the jocks—the one not named Wyman. The jock glances back over his shoulder at Georgie. He nudges the girl and snickers, but the girl ignores them both.

When Miss Heidi Berillo begins the class, Georgie drops his eyes and stares at his books, his blank notepad.

"The class requirements are all on the syllabus, as are my rules, which are very simple: No late assignments, no tardiness, and no talking out of turn. Oh, and, by the way, no sleeping. And especially no snoring."

The students whisper among themselves.

"No hats and no shades."

Georgie removes his baseball hat and dark-tinted sunglasses, as do the other boys in the room (and a few of the girls). Heidi pretends not to notice.

Finally, Miss Heidi Berillo hands out the course syllabus. After briefly describing the class format and course objectives, she gets down to important matters.

"Class, a big heads-up," she says. "Come January, Wakefield Prep will sponsor our annual open competition for the prestigious memorial prize in memory of Dean Winterbourne's late father and founding father of this, our school, the Winterbourne Memorial

Scholarship for the most outstanding senior essay. There are no guidelines or limits on subject. Any topic—philosophy, literature, science—will be accepted."

Georgie glances at the girl. He notices her slim white legs, crossed at the ankle and revealing themselves in the aisle.

"I'd like to encourage all of you to enter. Nothing ventured, nothing gained, as the old saw says. But I'll tell you more about the Winterbourne later in the semester," says Heidi.

Georgie studies the girl's feet. She's wearing open-toed shoes. Her toes are brightened by pink nail polish, half peeled.

"For now," Heidi says, "let's just get started with Ancient Philosophy."

The girl looks straight back at Georgie, right dead into his eyes. Her eyes have no expression. She nonchalantly uncrosses her legs and pulls them beneath her chair.

"And what better place to start," Heidi points to the quote on the blackboard, "than with Socrates?"

Georgie catches the girl's eyes on him again. He pretends to read his book.

By nightfall, Georgie's tired and sick of people. He studies in his bed, alone.

Through the slightly open window, he hears students passing by, joking and laughing. Paranoia does not rise in him (not like with the later Georgie). Instead, his curiosity is piqued. He goes to the slightly open window and watches the students pass by. He sees the girl.

"Think fast, Ozer!" the jock named Wyman hollers as he slings a ball. Ignoring the scantily clad female at his side, Wyman takes off through the parking lot and goes long. The jock walking next to the girl (the girl) catches the ball and slings it back, laughing. He runs after Wyman—the girl raises her hand.

"Jason!" she calls. She stops beneath Georgie's window with a sigh.

"Don't be such a poop, Claudia," the scantily clad girl hisses, catching up. Georgie perks up—did someone call his name?

"Poop yourself, Susan," Claudia says, sticking out her tongue.

"Oh yeah, real mature," Susan teases. The girls walk and talk slowly, enjoying each other, until they disappear. They disappear.

Georgie returns to his books. Finally, giving in (to me . . . to Ben?), he reaches under the thin mattress and pulls out the flask of whiskey. He gulps it down without taking a breath. So much for studying, he thinks. Pretty soon, Georgie's snoring.

The next afternoon, on Great Hill (which overlooks the Wakefield upper campus practice field) Georgie stands to watch the lacrosse team practice. Ozer and Wyman rough each other up good-naturedly on the playing field, while Claudia and Susan and several senior girls stand on the sidelines, cheering.

Georgie stares at the lacrosse field, occasionally squinting and twitching. The laughter and camaraderie of the players slowly drift up to him, as they pass him by.

At last he walks off, alone, down the tree-lined path. He shuffles along, hopping on one foot every third step.

Sometime later, Georgie is hunting for books at the Wakefield Library, researching for class. He slams a huge textbook shut and shelves it, looking down at the list in his hand for the location of the next. He hears the sound of snickering and scuffling, and looks up.

The jock Ozer approaches him slowly, accompanied by Wyman. Georgie hunches over and swivels his head back and forth. His tongue hangs out, drooling. Wyman laughs and swivels his head around, too. The two close in on Georgie, imitating his twitches and tics.

Fighting back wariness and panic, Georgie turns his back on them and walks his fingers across book spines, looking for the next on his list.

Wyman's girlfriend, Susan, laughs at the boys' antics. Claudia doesn't, Georgie notices. (And I notice, too, just like Georgie, just like I do.) Susan wears low-cut jeans that show her midriff; her hair is sticky with spray. Claudia dresses more conservatively than the other girls, knee-length skirt and a light sweater. It only makes her that much more appealing and sexy, in Georgie's dark-tinted eyes.

Ozer and Wyman stand close to him, getting in Georgie's space. They stare intensely at him, without saying a word. His face glows red and he feels the panic rising in him. He struggles and succeeds, for a moment, in stopping his twitching and tics. But time passes and the boys don't leave, and Georgie can't hold back anymore. He leaps and shudders like a deranged string-puppet. The boys laugh.

"There we go," says Ozer. "That-ta boy, G-man. Let it out. Let it all out, baby."

Wyman crosses his arms.

"Mm, Ozer, buddy," Wyman says. "Would you look at that, now."

"Mr Twitchy," he gloats.

Ozer and Wyman slap each other on the back in congratulations. Ozer turns to Georgie and sticks out his left hand.

"Good to meet you, Twitchy," Ozer says.

Georgie refuses to shake Ozer's hand, and Ozer bows and wipes his hands on his pants. Several other members of the Wakefield Boys Lacrosse Team approach Wyman and Ozer now, calling out greetings to one another, slapping hands, all smiles. They all wear matching green and gold gym sweats.

(Parenthetical Pet Peeve) As a kid in school, being the last one left when choosing sides for a team and the resentment with the other team.

As the boys head out of the library, Susan tags along with them. She's smiling, in good spirits, like she enjoyed the show. She catches Claudia standing by the checkout counter.

"You coming, C?" Susan urges.

Claudia looks down, not meeting her eyes.

"I'll catch up later," she says.

Susan giggles with the boys as they walk noisily through the library doors and out into the sunshine.

Georgie watches the Wakefield boys' easy camaraderie, fighting down frustration and envy (and hatred, don't forget hatred, too). Finally, Claudia steps up to him. She follows Georgie's gaze and sees that he's watching the boys. Georgie looks back at her, silent, waiting for her to speak first.

"That was bad ass of them," Claudia says.

"I'm used to it," Georgie says.

Claudia smirks. "It was still ass of them," she says.

Georgie shrugs.

"Do you have the text for Miss Berillo's class?" Claudia says suddenly.

"Whose? What?" Georgie stutters, confused.

"Heidi Berillo. You know, Miss Heidi Berillo? I saw you in class, you know."

Georgie flushes.

"I know you saw me, too," Claudia says.

Georgie turns away. "I found a copy a little while ago. Of the book, I mean. Did you?"

"Yes," Claudia said.

Georgie takes off through the stacks. Three days on campus, and he already has the library memorized.

"It's got a blue cover," Claudia reminds him.

Georgie, ducking around a corner, loosens up now that he's out of sight. Now that he's safe. He starts to sing. (To her, to Claudia.)

"Blue balloon! Red balloon, green balloon. Will you find my blue balloon. Red balloon, blue balloon. This balloon's for you."

He stands up and whirls around, finding Claudia standing behind him. He blushes fiercely and hands her the book.

"That was lame," Georgie apologizes. "Sorry. Sorry. Just a tune. Tune Balloon. Tooney and looney. Like a Looney tune . . . ah fuck. Whatever."

Georgie laughs nervously at himself, refusing to look Claudia in the eyes. He hears her giggling.

What's she giggling about? he wonders. Then he notices Claudia glancing down at his shirt. He looks down, too. His shirt's filthy with dust and dirt smudges from the library stacks.

"Ah, fuck," he says. "Sorry. Who cares? It's still dress code, isn't it?"

(Parenthetical Pet Peeve) Dress codes.

Claudia takes a small coin-purse from her backpack and pulls out her student photo ID. Georgie waves it away.

"What's this?" Georgie asks.

"Look." Claudia shoves the ID in front of his eyes. "It's last year's picture," she explains.

Georgie looks up.

"What do you mean?"

"I fell out of a tree. Landed flat on my face. See?"

The photograph shows Claudia smiling brightly through a puffy lip and two black eyes.

"Impressive," Georgie says with a hint of smile, but his lips quiver. "Fuckin A. What were you doing, climbing trees?"

Claudia tries to catch Georgie's gaze. She stoops lower toward him, but Georgie won't meet her eyes.

"People-watching," Claudia admits.

She turns and looks at the Wakefield boys, capering around the statue just outside the library doors like apes in a zoo. She begins to head for the door, and then glances back over her shoulder.

"My names Nesbitt, Claudia. Claudia Nesbitt," she says. "Or Claudia, to you. What is yours?"

"Georgie. Nesbitt, Claudia. Nesbitt. Georgie. Gus—Gust. Shite."

She steps up to him and shakes his hand, then arches her back and smiles.

"You've got a firm grip, Georgie Gust," she says.

"Shite." Georgie winces. "Sorry. But, it's mice to neat you, rather nice to meet you, anyway," he says nervously.

He returns her smile.

"Nice to meet you, too."

Georgie watches as Claudia walks past the turnstile. "Bye, Claudia," he whispers to himself. "Nesbitt, Claudia. Nesbitt. Claudia Nesbitt. Claudia, Claudia, Claudia, Claudia Nesbitt," he mutters.

That night, Georgie lies on his bed, studying, while the familiar noise of students shouting and laughing outside echoes in his room. The noise finally draws him to the window, but the students have already disappeared. Georgie returns to bed, tries to keep studying, but he is distracted.

He closes the book and pulls on a lightweight jacket. He goes downstairs to the lobby and out the dorm house door, his brows scowling furiously, his mind drawn inward.

Outside, on the Wakefield campus, the student noises are faint. Georgie hurries after them, following them, imitating their noise, but they're so far away that they can't see him (or I can't see them, or me). Still, snatches of conversation drift back to him.

"... The Pen ..."

"... ID?"

A short time later, Georgie stands outside The Pen, watching as crowds of students file in and out the door, rushing past him like a river of bodies. He stands there several seconds before pushing the door open. Inside, the place is smoky and jam-packed with students. Georgie approaches the bar and signals the bartender.

"Beer."

"On tap?"

Georgie nods yes.

"Beer," he says.

Dear Diary.

Right now, I don't feel so bad that so many people remember me only when they need me. In fact, I feel privileged that I am like a candle that comes to their mind when there is darkness. Nice feeling, I've got to admit. Here's hoping it will last.

The classroom

In Miss Heidi's classroom, students are goofing off. Even Claudia's goofing, holding her nose and sticking her tongue out. (At him, at Georgie.)

Heidi stands by the window, and then casually opens it. Georgie's startled by the rasping, scraping sound of metal against metal. Like fingernails on a blackboard.

Heidi tosses a piece of chalk out the open window, dusts off her hands, and walks to the front of the room.

(Parenthetical Pet Peeve) Squeaky chalk.

"True or false?" she asks. "The chalk that I just tossed out the window hit the ground."

The students look at one another, smirking and rolling their eyes.

Several students stutter out: "True, true."

"True?" asks Heidi. "How do you know?"

The chalk flies back through the window and shatters against the hard tile floor.

The students laugh.

Surprised, Heidi hurries back to the window and leans out, mouth agape.

"You dropped something, Miss B!" a student yells up from below. Georgie recognizes Ozer's voice.

"Thanks, but the two of you are late for class!" she calls back sternly.

Heidi walks around the room and looks closely at each student. She's a little imposing, at first sight—slight but straight-backed. After a long pause, she continues the lesson.

"Okay, so, assuming there are no Wymans or Ozers out there to throw the chalk back at us. True or false: The chalk I just tossed out the window hit the ground."

Claudia raises her hand. Heidi points to her. (To Claudia.)

"Yes—Claudia, is it?"

Claudia nods and snatches a quick look at Georgie. He sticks his tongue out at her, like a frog catching flies. It's a situational tic, protective camouflage. He doesn't want Claudia to see, really, or Heidi, either.

"Um, the chalk could have landed in a bush?" Claudia says.

Georgie traces the letter "C" over and over on his notebook with his pencil until it tears through the paper.

"All right. All right. All right," he says quietly.

"True," Heidi nods. "The chalk could have landed in a bush. Or a bird could have swooped down and thought it was a tasty snack."

"Bush. Bush," Georgie mutters quietly to himself. "Tasty snack. Tasty, I say. She's saying it's a good snack."

Nobody else hears him.

Some students, with knitted brows, nod at the teacher, like they're really thinking. Some only stare vacantly, or scribble in their notebooks.

Ozer and Wyman walk into the room. They take seats in the back row.

Heidi acknowledges their entrance with a frown.

"But let's assume that the chalk falls straight to the ground. Does the chalk make a hit?" Heidi asks. "Does it hit the ground?"

A few students groan and roll their eyes.

Georgie grows visibly more nervous as time ticks on. He turns a page of his notebook and completes a complex geometrical design. He starts on a sketch of an angel. Then he returns to tracing the "C."

"Dude. Fuck Wyman. Dude. Fuck Ozer. Fuckin pricks," he mutters.

Dear Diary:

It's such an empowering feeling when I forget those who have forgotten me when I really needed them, only remembering those who have made me smile and laugh when I've otherwise been down in the dumps.

Hung over

Sometime later that night, a drunken Georgie stumbles out of The Pen. His day passes before his eyes.

In the library, Georgie picks out books for his research project.

In his room, Georgie studies on his bed and writes in his journal.

In Heidi's class, students yawn and roll their eyes, not paying attention.

Georgie jerks his head up off his desk. He snaps back, cracking his neck loudly.

"Are objective truths independent of our subjectivity?" asks Heidi. "Do truths exist eternally, apart from we mortal human beings, as Socrates believed? Or are eternal truths simply situational and subjective, as the existentialists argue?"

Heidi pauses a moment, waiting for an answer.

"What do you think, class?" she asks. "Anyone? Are truths subjective or objective?"

The students look down at their books or at each other. Anywhere but at Heidi. Most of them really don't know what she's talking about. Most of them really don't care. Georgie stretches his mouth open, disguising his spasms and twitches in yawns.

"Certainly subjective," mutters Georgie. "Certainly, I say."

Heidi becomes slightly impatient.

"You don't need to be so shy," she berates the class. "This is an Introductory Philosophy class. There are no right or wrong answers, here, in this class."

She walks to the blackboard again, waiting silently for the class to answer.

Georgie looks at Claudia, who's poised to take notes. He continues to trace the "M" on his scribbled-up scratch paper. The students squirm in their seats.

"Take Miguel de Unamuno, for instance," says Heidi. "The existentialist."

Georgie looks up and grunts, recognizing Unamuno's name.

His legs get restless. He starts to twitch, slightly.

Heidi points to Unamuno's name, written in white chalk on the blackboard

(Parenthetical Pet Peeve) Fingernails scraping a chalkboard.

Beneath the name, she writes: "Basque (1864–1936)."

Georgie takes dictation from Heidi. (Or does Georgie take dictation from me? What'll it be, Dr C—Georgie, or me?

"Are we discussing Georgie's school days, now? Or yours, Ben?"

You tell me, Dr C.)

Georgie writes Unamuno's name in his scribbled-over notebook.

"Unamuno was a Spanish-born philosopher who might find himself either on the left or the right of the political, religious, and philosophical spectrums. In other words, his subjective conception of supposed objective truth could differ in different situations . . . ."

One kid drops his pencil on the floor. He grunts loudly as he reaches for it, his shaggy hair shadowing distracted eyes.

"". . . depending on when you asked him."

"Spanish born, spectrums. Subjectivity," mutters Georgie. He scribbles "S"s on his notebook.

"Which brings us back to the original question: Are truths independent of our own subjectivity?" She pauses. "Perhaps Unamuno is not the best example. Perhaps Unamuno's constantly changing subjective opinions confuse the question of objective truth. Or perhaps truth really is simply subjective. Which is it? Anyone?"

Heidi pauses significantly again, awaiting a response.

"Does anybody in this class have a subjective opinion? Or are we all waiting for objective truth to strike?"

Georgie looks around the room. He sees that nobody's willing to make eye contact with Heidi. He raises his pencil, and Heidi smiles.

"Yes. In the back. Georgie?"

Georgie blushes. He looks down at his shirt.

"I borrowed this shirt from some kid in the dorm," he says anxiously.

His distraction crystallizes a truly awkward moment. There are blank stares and bubble-gum bubbles popping all around the room.

One prissy-looking girl tags her wad of Trident underneath the desk and scoffs through her nose.

"He borrowed it?" she confirms. "Oh my God, Georgie. You're fucking psycho."

The other kids snicker and scoff, although some kids think of Georgie as normal, if a little odd. (Whatever that means, normal.)

"Sorry," Georgie says to Heidi. "I've got Tourette's Syndrome. Sorry."

"He has Tourette's?" the girl mumbles. She snorts disdainfully.

"That's fine," Heidi says. "Go on, Georgie."

"Well, the world exists independent of human subjectivity," he begins, contorting his face. His muscles tense and he stutters.

" . . . Shhh!" Georgie spits out.

The pencil-dropper barely stifles a burst of laughter.

"Mr Hendricks," Heidi says sternly, and the boy's face straightens out. "Go ahead, Georgie," she says. "Take your time."

Most of the students stare at Georgie as his body quakes. Some snicker.

Georgie's sweating. He grips his pencil so tightly that it snaps.

A few laughs echo from the back of the room.

"Yes?" Heidi urges him.

"You know . . ." Georgie stutters, his nerves enslaving his tongue. "You know. I. I. I. I . . . damn it!"

He wipes his forehead, puts his shades back on. His classmates become darkened blurs.

Heidi steps in front of Georgie. At that moment, it feels like he's only talking to her.

"Go ahead, Georgie," she says.

Georgie begins to relax under Miss Heidi Berillo's calming gaze.

"Truths are in-independent of our own subjectivity," he says, his confidence growing. "Certainly. Unamuno still could've been subjectively existential, in that he was exercising the possibilities of his individual freedom, without compromising objective truth."

Heidi's eyes widen.

"If existence precedes essence, then Unamuno was just recreating his essence as it suited him. Maybe his essence was still somehow expressing objective truth, though."

Every student stares at Georgie. They are silent. Georgie goes on.

"So, at every moment, no matter what he was asked, or what the answer was, it was true. Somehow or other."

Heidi turns to the class, which stares dumbly at Georgie. She walks to the front of the room and grins.

"Very comprehensive, Georgie," Heidi confirms. "I can tell you're reading the text with precision and understanding. Who has something to add?" she asks.

Nobody responds.

"Has anyone else done the assigned reading?" Heidi scolds.

One student sits up in his seat. He jerks a pointed chin at Heidi, his blond hair spiking upward accusingly.

"There was too much to read. Nobody could have gotten through all that."

"Apparently Mr Gust did." Heidi smiles. "Maybe he has a secret you lack, Mr Brooks?"

"I tried to read it," Hendricks replies lazily. His hair is greasy and shoulder-length, his eyes half-lidded. "But I got bored."

"How's it going to help me in the real world?" asks the prissy girl.

"Are you saying that this is not the real world, Miss Winters?"

The class snickers. Winters flushes, angrily.

"Georgie took my answer," Claudia jokes.

Claudia smiles at Georgie. (At me.)

Georgie sticks his tongue out at Claudia, and she reciprocates the gesture.

"Mr Mad Scientist," Hendricks says.

Laughter from the students resonates as the halogen lights above whiten, as though bleached.

"Yeah, Mr Twitchy," Ozer adds. Wyman laughs.

Heidi frowns.

Georgie catches Claudia looking at him. He glances down at his notebook, shredded by "M"s, and then at his broken pencil.

Claudia holds a new pencil out to him.

Georgie takes the pencil, giving her the slightest grin. His lips still quiver slightly from the panic attack, and he wipes his forehead, relieved.

Dear Diary:

I think when I question how life is treating me, I should be asking how I am treating life. Who knows? Then, I might actually get the answer I'm looking for. Anyway, onward I go, I guess, for now!

200

Talking through windows

A bell rings, and students swarm out of Heidi's classroom. Georgie takes up the rear, stepping and hopping. Heidi hurries to catch up with him.

"Georgie," she calls.

"Yes?" he turns to her.

"I just wanted to tell you how well you're doing in this class," she smiles. "You're my star pupil!"

Georgie blushes and starts to walk away.

"Hey, Georgie? You should think about the Winterbourne. Something on Unamuno would be perfect."

He nods silently, 12 times.

Dear Diary:

When does it all stop? I'm happy with it going on like this every day, even the crappy stuff.

Mr Twitchy

Georgie walks back to his dorm room from the library with a stack of books clutched in his arms. As he passes by the football field, he sees the Wakefield lacrosse team practicing. Ozer and Randy are among the players. They laugh and joke together during the drills—there's no adult in sight.

Georgie looks to the bleachers. Claudia and Susan and several other senior girls watch from the sidelines, cheering and chattering.

Georgie trips over the sidewalk, dropping a book. As he bends down to pick it up, another falls from the stack. His body quakes without his permission.

One of the players sees Georgie and points at him, mocking and laughing.

Susan turns and sees Georgie. She laughs, too. Claudia frowns at her.

"There he is!" someone calls.

"Mr Twitchy," another adds.

One of the Wakefield lacrosse players starts to imitate Georgie's odd step-step-step-hop walk.

"He looks like a fuckin' mad scientist, with that hair," says Ozer.

One player imitates the other until the entire team is hopping around the field in unison, like a troop of soldiers running some bizarre drill. One of them falls and they all crack up laughing.

Georgie, red-faced with anger and shame, tries to ignore them as he retrieves his books. But he sees when, behind the clowning players, the lacrosse coach comes onto the field. He is a man in his late 30s with a deep voice and a thick build. He watches the team for a moment, unseen by the players. Finally, he blows his whistle.

The Wakefield lacrosse team turns to its coach, abruptly sober. The coach strolls up to them, casually.

"I'm glad to see that you girls have so much energy today," he says mockingly. "Okay, everybody . . . wind sprints!"

The players moan. "Aw, come on, coach!" someone says quietly.

The coach glances over at Georgie. To his team, he says, "Line up, now, girls."

The players fall in line, and the coach puts the whistle to his lips.

"Last one across the line has to do a lap!"

202

More moans from the players. Ozer glares at Georgie.
The coach blows his whistle. The players dash.

(Parenthetical Pet Peeve) Schools assuming that kids are guilty unless they can prove they are innocent.

Georgie walks away as the team runs wind sprints behind him. Lost in his humiliation, he gets no pleasure from their punishment.

Later that day, at The Pen, Georgie tosses a near-empty bourbon glass gently out of his left hand and back into his right. He practices tossing the bourbon glass up again and back down until his grip on the glass between his fingers is perfect.

He hears voices whispering around his stool, but he does not look around and he does not speak to anyone. As far as he is concerned, he is alone.

He takes the last swig from his bourbon glass.

(Parenthetical Pet Peeve) Taking a big swig out of a can of soda, not realizing that someone just extinguished a cigarette in it.

Soothed and relaxed, he leaves a big tip under the empty glass and heads out the back door, where the streetlight floods in from the back alley.

Dear Diary:

I once heard from some old yoga instructor, something like, "The earth will rise up to greet you or you will sprout wings and fly!" I felt reassured until I thought about it!

Pushy boy

A Princeton pennant. A poster of Troy Aikman dressed as a gunslinger with footballs in his holsters. A lacrosse stick, helmet, pads, and gloves stuck neatly together with the trophy for "Wakefield Male Athlete of the Year." A photo of Ozer with his family. Piles of CDs, the stereo turned up loud. Dirty clothes piled high in a corner. A desk scattered with everything but school stuff. This is Ozer's room.

Two people are rustling beneath the covers, kissing on the bed. Ozer moans and Claudia sighs and the plastic mattress crinkles.

"No-no-no. No!"

With an effort, Claudia sits up. Ozer sits up, too. He embraces her. He kisses her again, hungry for her. She's delicate, but she keeps pushing him off.

"Not so hard, Jason. Geez."

He fondles her breast and tries to drag her back down on the bed.

"I said no!"

(Parenthetical Pet Peeve) People who can't take no for an answer.

Ozer's breath comes hard.

"Why not?" he pants.

"Because. I don't want to."

"Why?"

"Jesus, Jason. Why do we keep having this conversation?" Claudia sighs. "I'm just not ready, that's all."

"That's what you always say," Ozer scoffs. "When are you going to be ready?"

"I don't know! We used to have fun when we went out. Now this is all you ever want to do, anymore. We don't even go out."

Ozer calms down, stroking Claudia's hair.

"I care for you," he says. "A lot. And I just want us to get closer."

"If you cared for me, you would respect my feelings."

"Well, what about my feelings, Claudia?"

He kisses her neck. She arches away.

"I'm sorry, all right?" Claudia says. "I just . . . don't want to. Not now."

Ozer tries to kiss her neck. "Not now," he mumbles mockingly into her skin. "Nothing will happen. I've got protection."

"Fuck, Jason!" says Claudia. "That's not it."

"Then what the hell is it? Are you frigid, or something?"

Claudia turns away.

Ozer lets out a long, deep breath and flops back on the bed.

"Shite. I'm sorry, Claudia."

Claudia turns and snuggles against his shoulder.

"Why can't we just stay like this for a while? Like we used to? Let's just talk or something."

"That was months ago, Claudia. Things change. Come on! All the other guys are laughing at me."

"Why? Because I won't sleep with you?" Claudia draws away. "Is that all I am? Something to joke about at team meetings?"

"What are you talking about?" says Ozer. "It's just, you know."

"No, I don't know."

"I'm a man. I've got . . . needs."

She stares daggers at him and her jaw drops hard.

"Fuck your needs." She stands up and leaves. Ozer hesitates, but then stomps after her with a sigh.

Dear Diary:

Come to think of it, I'm a true warrior! Hell, I can't be beaten by anything I can laugh at.

Bar cops

Georgie stumbles out of the darkness and into the alley behind the bar, rapping to himself.

(Footnote, not at the foot: The song, "Fuck the Police" came out in '88, but this is what Georgie's rapping, from NWA—Niggaz with Attitude.

Thing is, this happened later than '88, I mean in "real" life, and every year that I push off trying to sell this goddamn book, I need to push forward the dates and the timelines within it. Besides, this stuff confuses the holy shite out of me, so you, dear reader, are not alone. Everything will turn out just fine, for all of us. You'll see.

If I actually had to keep to the truth gun to my head—I still wouldn't. Wouldn't be able to. As for the real timeline in this more-than-obvious re-telling of actual events, yes, I'm talking about creative non-fiction, I admit. Hell, it's not that hard to figure out regardless. No matter, I still wouldn't know when anything happened. Impaired thinking and inabilities to think abstractly, and the shitetiest memory, as I write this—later, later, much later—and as I attempt to recall all of this, it screws me, and unfortunately, it most likely has you feeling screwed, feeling ripped off, feeling robbed.

Accept my biggest apologies to you, the reader, for all the utter confusion, chaos, and inconsistencies here within—shite, must be driving you fucking nuts.)

(Dr C, is this likely the cause of my own time warp? Coming from an onset of a mutated gene? Dr C, of course I ask you this, being the pity-seeking, self-absorbed hypochondriac—and the guy who is still in denial about it. Could this a type of Huntington's disease? A mutation? Something fucked up on the fourth chromosome? Could you write me a script for genetic testing? Any disorder, and any rare disorder, a "disease"—I want it! Give it here. Help me label who I am. Do it through diagnosing me, as I crave, as I want, as I need. Please, you sexy thing! Even if you make it up. Even if you pretend.)

I love pretending.

So, that said, maybe we're in the 90s, but we'll call it '88, and Georgie holds his head up to the light as if it weighed 50 pounds. He steps In a discarded bag from McDonalds. He shakes it off, ignoring the cheese and mustard that stick to his shoe.

Dear Diary:

I am still a warrior! There's nothing to gossip about. I kill my illnesses! I am proud of myself! I acknowledge that and I admit that for today! I am good and I am okay! And I care, too! Today, I am my own hero!

Fuck the bar cops

"Fuckin wit' me cause I'm a teenager," he mumbles, substituting a few words with nonsense syllables. He nods. "Smoke any muthafucka that sweats me."

Holding his finger to his mouth, he blows it like the barrel of a gun. He squints, pursing his lips.

"I'm a sniper with a hell of a scope. Takin' out a cop or two, they can't cope wit' me," he raps.

A police car drives down the street and passes Georgie. It screeches to a halt halfway down the block and then backs up rapidly, lights flashing. The car jerks to a stop next to Georgie.

Two police officers jump out of the car and aggressively approach Georgie. Georgie just keeps blowing on his finger.

"You got ID, son?" one of the officers asks.

Georgie stumbles and grins idiotically at the officer. He's still singing, slightly offbeat:

"F-f-f-fuck the police."

Later, at the Police Department, Georgie sits on a straight-backed wooden bench, rapping quietly to himself. The door opens and Miss Heidi Berillo enters the room. She looks around, spots Georgie, and strides over to him.

Georgie looks meaningfully at Heidi.

"Do I love you? Do I lust for you?"

She blinks, but ignores his rapping.

"Have you been drinking, Georgie?" she demands.

"Have I been drinking?" he replies. "Have I been thinking? Don't think, drink, Georgie say . . . ."

Georgie uses Heidi's arm to pull himself to his feet.

The police officer approaches them and hands Heidi a clipboard. He indicates where she needs to sign.

Georgie and Heidi leave together, Georgie leaning hard against Heidi.

Outside, Georgie climbs into Heidi's Corvette.

She drives slowly away.

Dear Diary:

I could be deluding myself, but I believe that I have never been involved with anything for the money the credit the fame the follows nor the hits. Blah. Blah. Blah.

To the rescue

Heidi parks the Corvette in the dorm parking lot, and Georgie reaches for the door handle. He starts to get out, but Heidi stops him.

"Georgie," she says.

Georgie's still drunk.

"Bonita Applebum?" he asks.

"You need to stop this."

"Bonita Bonita Bonita. So glad to meet you."

"Georgie," she insists. "You're a smart young man. You might even be brilliant. But you've got to get your life together."

"Together or apart," he responds. "We're a team, don't you know?"

Heidi blinks back tears. Georgie opens the door and falls onto the sidewalk.

Dear Diary:

I took some time earlier this morning to acknowledge my own life, for once. In all honesty, today I celebrate what an unbelievable life I have had so far, the many blessings. Yes, even the hardships because they have served to make me stronger. Just as a gem cannot be polished without friction, nor can a life be perfected without trials.

Passed out

Claudia watches Georgie through Ozer's dorm room window.

"Heidi's down there, dropping off Georgie," Claudia says.

Ozer's sitting on the bed with his shirt off. He peeks over.

"That charity case?"

"Charity case? You mean he's on scholarship?" She pauses. "Like me?"

"No." Ozer bluffs. "He's nothing like you."

"Just because we're on scholarship doesn't mean we're charity cases."

"Believe me," Ozer says. "He's a charity case. The only reason he's even here." He sighs heavily. "Never mind."

"Never mind what?"

Ozer lies back down on the bed. "Nothing," he says.

"Tell me," Claudia demands.

Ozer sits up, imitates Georgie's twitching, and then taps his temple with his finger. "Claudia, Georgie's a retard. My father told me."

"Your father would never say something like that."

"That doesn't mean he's not a retard." Ozer shrugs. "The only reason that kid's at Wakefield is because the Board thought they needed diversity."

Claudia glares at Ozer; he laughs meanly.

"Admit a retard or two," he says. "How's that for diversity?"

Claudia turns away from him and looks out the window again. She watches as Georgie pulls himself to his feet and Heidi drives away. Georgie tries the outside door. It's locked. He checks his pockets, but pulls out nothing. Claudia considers running downstairs to let him in.

She watches as he checks out the drainpipe and starts climbing up it. When Georgie gets close to the top of the drain, the pipe starts to bend.

"No!" Claudia gasps.

"Shite!" Georgie cries as the pipe gives way. "You fuckin' bitch!"

The pipe gives out and Georgie falls, spraying rainwater everywhere.

Georgie thuds to the ground and groans.

Claudia turns on the lights. She pulls on her socks and shoes.

"Where are you going?"

"He could be hurt!"

"So?"

Claudia, in her sweats, runs out of the dorm and down to Georgie. She drops down by his side, shaking him slightly.

Ozer opens the shade, lifts the window, and hangs his head out. "The kid's a retard!" he calls out. "I told you."

Georgie lies there on his back, talking to himself. "Just one more drink, on the house, but I don't have anymore." He lifts a finger and continues in another voice, a deeper voice. "There is no more alcohol, because there is no drunk to have conception of it." He laughs hysterically, then passes out cold.

Claudia slaps Georgie across the face as hard as she can. "Wake up! Wake up!" she cries.

"Ow! Ow!" Georgie groans.

"Aw, leave him alone," Ozer says from above, still leaning out of the dorm room window.

Claudia ignores him.

Ozer waves a dismissive hand and closes the window.

The light in the room goes out.

A moment later, the same light turns on again.

"Jason Ozer!" the RA's voice screeches. "You were told lights out at 10. And chewing tobacco? That's it! You're on detention. First thing tomorrow."

Several lights from other dorm rooms flick on as students are wakened by the commotion.

Georgie opens his eyes. "Ow! Jeez! Quit hitting me!" he protests.

Claudia stops slapping him, rapidly bringing her hands to her face. The stench of alcohol on Georgie's breath is overpowering. "Come on," she says. "Get up. Get up." She tries to lift him by the arm.

Georgie mumbles dazedly. "What time is it?"

"Just past 10." Claudia helps Georgie to his feet. "You can't show up at the dorms like this."

A campus security SUV patrols nearby. Claudia freezes as the security vehicle rolls toward them, blinding with its bright headlights.

The siren bleeps. Georgie laughs when the headlights hit him.

"Shite," giggles Georgie. "Run!"

"Where?"

"Somewhere special," Georgie says. He grabs Claudia's hand, and they take off.

Georgie trips and falls, almost bringing Claudia down with him. She yanks him to his feet and they race toward the woods, hand-in-hand, yelling gleefully.

"Come on. Come on," pants Georgie.

"I'm coming."

The Wakefield woods are misty and dark. Claudia helps Georgie along. He gives an occasional hop, accompanied by the usual twitching.

"How did you get like this, Georgie?" Claudia asks. "You went to The Pen again, didn't you?"

Georgie belches and trips over a rock.

Claudia catches him. "Never mind. I don't want to know. What do you do? Run off to the college at night, get drunk, and talk philosophy with a more intellectual crowd?"

"No."

Claudia turns to Georgie, who gazes at her, dumbfounded.

"Are you coming?" she asks.

Georgie stumbles drunkenly to catch up with her. Before long, Claudia and Georgie reach the edge of a bluff.

"C-c-can't go any further," Georgie wheezes.

They sit on the cold stone, looking out over the dark valley.

"Let's not go back yet," Claudia says quietly.

Georgie nods, then the ground seems to curl up beneath him, and he sleeps.

When he wakes, the sun's coming up.

Claudia puts her hands to her face, staring in awe at the sunrise.

"Wow!" she says. "It's so beautiful."

Georgie sits up. The view from the bluff is magnificent in the morning light. The bluff drops down to sloping green hills that run alongside the blue water of the Atlantic coast for miles. The sun glares red over the water and pinks the white sand beaches.

"I've never been here before. This is amazing!" Claudia gushes.

"It's awful, huh?"

Claudia doesn't get it.

"Huh?" she scoffs. She notices a tree with the word "REBEL" carved on it.

"Awe-full," Georgie says. "Full of awe."

"Yeah," Claudia sneers. "What goes on up here, drugs?

"Yeah."

"Hm."

"This is where I come to cry," Georgie explains. "Everybody needs a place to cry."

"Yeah?"

"I'm not embarrassed," Georgie admits belligerently. "Everybody's got to cry. Sometimes even me, the Mad Scientist."

Claudia sneaks a furtive glance at Georgie, who's biting his lip. She observes Georgie's arrhythmic facial grimacing and the rapid squinting of his eyes.

"What are you looking at?" Georgie asks suspiciously.

"Nothing," Claudia says, looking away.

"Well, don't. Just don't look. Okay?"

"Okay," Claudia says. "You know, you're very sensitive. That's rare. I like it."

Georgie ignores her.

"Can I ask you something? Something personal?"

"Personal? Always," Georgie sneers. "I'm an open book. I have Tourette's. No big deal."

"Oh. No. That's cool," Claudia says, "You don't mind the . . . I don't know much about it. I just thought . . ."

Georgie's twitching stops. "No. No. It's no big deal. Trust me," he says.

While Claudia watches the sun rise over the ocean, Georgie lies back down on the ground and covers his face with his hands. "Dude, I don't want to go to the college," he moans.

"I really don't want to know," Claudia says.

Georgie lifts his head, puzzled. "Should I go to the college?" he asks.

"I don't care."

Georgie pops up onto his feet, hops with a skip and a jump over to her.

"Do you think girls would like me there?" he asks. "At the college? I could be their class clown."

"You could be that here, easy enough."

"Really?" He pauses. "Are you mad at me?"

"I don't know you well enough to be mad," Claudia says.

"Then what?"

"I just don't get you. You've got this great opportunity and you're wasting it," Claudia chides. "Getting drunk every night. Getting arrested?"

Georgie shrugs. "Yeah, I guess."

"Climbing back into the dorms. You could have hurt yourself, maybe died. It's stupid, is all. A waste."

"Every clown has his demons." Georgie looks at the rough ground.

He walks to the edge of the bluff, dismissing the whole conversation. He puts one foot over the edge, like maybe he's thinking about walking off.

"Don't," Claudia says, sharply. She runs over, grabs his arm.

Georgie smiles. "Just kidding," he says. "This time."

"That's not funny."

Dear Diary:

When I try, I commit 3% but, when I do, I commit 100%. Here's to commitment—to finishing this book I'm working on.

On the edge of something?

"I'm not laughing," Georgie says. "I wouldn't really do it. Not now. Later, maybe. After I get famous."

Claudia looks at him skeptically.

"What are you looking at me like that for? I'm going to be famous! I'm going to be a famous writer. I saw it in a dream. And rich. I saw that, too."

Claudia scowls. "You got your life so figured out, how come you can't stop drinking?"

Georgie squeezes his hands tightly against his temples. "Ah, fuck! This day. My life. It's so stupid! 5 am. I'm really screwed."

"You are what you think," Claudia intones. "Point your eyes someplace new. Somewhere good. My dad always said that."

"Said what?"

Claudia doesn't respond.

Georgie smiles warmly at her. After a moment, she returns the look.

The new day

The sun shines brightly at midday over the campus. The clock tower chimes as Georgie and Claudia walk across the main lawn, heading towards the Academic Building.

Georgie lights a fresh cigarette. He stumbles slightly, twitching, skipping, puckering his lips, and scratching himself. Claudia grins at him.

"Hey, sorry about yesterday," he says.

"It's all right. I was awake anyway."

"You should have just left me. It was my own fault." He hops.

"Yeah? But then I wouldn't have seen the bluff." She smiles.

Georgie smiles back hesitantly. "I guess I was really wasted."

"You get wasted a lot, don't you?"

"Yeah."

"Why?"

"Why?" Georgie is hesitant. "I'm not sure. I'm partly addicted, I think."

"But not really."

Georgie doesn't quite know how to answer. "Maybe I'm just trying to block out some of the more embarrassing and painful magic tricks and tics from the disorder."

"Good excuse."

Georgie sighs. "Not really. But, hell, drink allows other spirits to mingle with my own. So I'm not all by myself."

"You're never by yourself. Never. No one is."

Penny Wilder, one of the popular rich kids, a real nobody, and nobody can stand the snob, but she passes by Claudia and passes off Georgie, who sniffs, seeing Penny much less come close to Claudia. He daydreams an instant replay of Claudia's "You're never by yourself" bit, and hell knows he's wishing he were alone. With a brief shudder of self-doubt, just glad he's not Penny; in a quick daydream, he dreams of being popular, like Penny and her infamous clique, he dreams of what happens . . . if. All the while, Penny pauses for a second, smirking her familiar smug, her offensive yet attention-getting smile, repeating the only two words Georgie's ever heard her say, as if her words are expressing a judgmental opinion that she's the Queen of the school,.

(Parenthetical Pet Peeve) People who talk very slowly.

"Hi, Claudia," Penny says.

Georgie wishing he were not in school, but at the reunion, years later, when Penny's turned to the waste that most popular kids come to be. All this from two bloody words. Hi. Claudia. It seriously does him in, and Georgie has no idea why. Time stops.

Claudia's naturally quite self-assured with her simple reply, "Hi, Penny."

And that was it. Georgie completely over complicates everything—especially his own paranoid and mentally ill mind with zero resilience.

Penny, as usual, doesn't say anything to Georgie. She lifts her brows curiously and walks on and time suddenly reactivates. If Claudia only knew how and what and why Georgie thinks and feels as he does—completely alone and paranoid of people. Hell, he doesn't want to know. Some things are meant to be unknown.

"See what I mean? She thinks you're crazy to be talking to me. If she had her way, I'd always be alone."

Georgie frowns.

Claudia smiles. "That might mean something, if I cared what she thought."

"You care. It's written all over you."

"Not about her, I don't." Claudia squints at Penny's back. "Just a rich kid. She thinks she's too good for everyone."

They stop for a second. Georgie lets Claudia's comment sink in and lights another cigarette. He juggles it up and down between his fingers, getting the grip just right. Then Georgie and Claudia walk on.

"I always thought Tourette's was just about swearing and shouting and stuff like that," Claudia says.

"No, that's just the fun part," Georgie answers. "Each one of us is different. It's just a small number of us who swear."

"So you only swear when you want to?" Claudia asks.

Georgie grins. "Pretty much." Georgie grunts a couple times and wipes his nose.

(Parenthetical Pet Peeve) My nose starts running when I have no access to a tissue.

He sniffs, and then grunts again. "Mozart had Tourette's, you know, and Samuel Johnson, the writer. At least some people think they did."

"Really?"

Georgie nods. "Back then it was called The Devil's Dance. St Vitus Dance. Maybe it'll become the new trendy thing, someday. The twitches."

"Yeah, maybe. So that's why you drink? The Tourette's?"

He nods again. "That's some of it. Part of it. Fart of it. Not the heart of it."

"Do you have any friends here?" asks Claudia.

Georgie smiles and lies. "Some. Hey, what about Ozer? He's your boyfriend, right?"

"Yeah," Claudia says slowly.

"Caution, entering dangerous topic," Georgie says flippantly. He pauses. "Do you love him?"

"Love?"

Georgie hesitates. "His dad's the one who got us in here. Right?"

"Yeah. See you later."

Claudia abruptly turns and jogs up the stairs into the Academics building. Georgie finishes one last drag on his cigarette, and then follows more slowly.

Dear Diary:

I'm still writing my book, which I now wholeheartedly know for a fact I will complete. When the last letter is typed, I cannot wait to then declare to myself, quoting Cyrano de Bergerac, in French, *À la fin de l'envoi, je touché!* It's happening. I am so revved up and in the zone. I feel raw. I feel manic and bizarre. I'm going to kill this book. I'm on it, baby!

At The Pen that night

Georgie enters The Pen just as Wyman and Susan slip out. They are wrapped in each other's lips, blinded by lust. They don't even see him.

Georgie makes an uncomfortable entrance, squeezing past the lovers and spasming as he sees Ozer, who glowers at him. He slowly shuffles over to the bar and orders. He gulps down a beer and goes to the pinball machine.

Georgie, in the corner, shoves his coins into the machine and pulls the pin.

The pinball shoots down the gutter.

Georgie blinks rapidly as two college girls approach him. One, the shorter of the two, wears a Wrigley U sweatshirt, while the other hides behind glasses and a turtleneck with jeans.

"You have a girlfriend, huh?" the sweater asks.

"Lisa, he's here by himself," the turtleneck points out.

Georgie puts another coin into the machine and pulls the pin again. He won't look at them.

"No, I'm not," he says.

Ozer looks on. Georgie directs the girls' attention to Ozer with his eyes.

"He's single," he says.

The girls glance at Ozer for a second. They're not interested.

"If you had one ounce of spontaneity in you, you'd leave him and give me your phone number!" Ozer yells drunkenly.

The girls shrug him off with a wave of disgust.

"Pig," the turtleneck mutters.

Georgie finally glances at them. "Are you spontaneous?"

The sweatered Lisa turns to her friend. "Let's ask him, Jo."

Jo looks Georgie in the eyes. He's tic free.

"You ever had a threesome?" Jo asks.

Georgie answers only with a long pause.

Lisa smiles. "No strings attached," she croons.

Dear Diary:

In life, when I'm up, my friends get to know who I am. When I'm down in life, that's when I get to know who my friends are, no doubt.

Back in business

The sun rises with the morning. Birds sing. A rooster crows.

Georgie sleeps through his ringing alarm clock. Two pairs of women's panties lie across his face. When the light strikes his face he groans and rolls out of bed. He dresses, takes a small handful of medication, and hurries out the door.

Georgie stumbles into class late, obviously hung over, but with a huge grin plastered across his face. He takes off his sunglasses.

"Hello, everybody!"

There's a round of snickers and laughter from all the students except Claudia.

Heidi smiles. "Well, Mr Gust," she says. "You've decided to join us. And in such gay spirits."

Georgie smiles back. "Sort of," he says.

He sidles into his seat. The students quiet down.

Heidi begins her lecture again.

"Okay, moving right along. Today, like I told you, we've got lab, so all of you find yourself a partner."

Everybody but Georgie seems to partner up immediately. He finally stands to look around. He approaches Steven Brooks. Brooks ignores him and joins up with his swimming buddy, the feminine Kenny. He notices Elizabeth.

"Elizabeth?"

She imitates his head tics. "S-sorry, sweetie."

She approaches Hendricks. "Henny, baby!" she says.

Georgie notices another kid with a full beard of peach fuzz, who approaches Georgie with a grin, but the kid stops short when he sees a girl, Rachel, beckoning to him from behind Georgie. They partner up.

Georgie calls to Peach Fuzz. "Hey, man, what's up dude?"

Peach Fuzz looks down at Rachel's rack. He looks back to Georgie for a moment.

"Tits. Tits! Rachel, be my Valentine!"

Rachel looks at Georgie, smirks, and sidles up to Peach Fuzz.

"Well, this should be fun," she says. "Do you think we'll have to shave each other?"

"Not me. You need a shave?"

Rachel laughs.

"Hey, check out Mad Scientist," Peach Fuzz whispers.

Rachel scoffs as Peach Fuzz convulses in his chair.

Claudia, of course, quickly partnered with Eddie, who had sat beside her in Ozer's absence. Georgie's the only one left standing. He looks at Heidi from the back of the room, and then stares at his shoes.

"Georgie, are you the odd man out?" sighs Heidi.

Claudia looks at Georgie, but he won't look back at her. She stands and walks silently back to him. Some of the students break out in frantic whispers.

Heidi smiles as Claudia sits down next to Georgie.

"Eddie, I guess you're with me. Odd man out," Heidi chuckles. "Everyone got their dates?"

Georgie grins at Claudia. "Dude, you're awesome."

Claudia nods her head. "I heard you had some date last night."

Georgie smiles, slightly embarrassed. "Nah, not me."

The bell rings. The students grab their things and rush out of class, but Georgie hangs back. Claudia gives him a last look before she joins the others. He raises his hand in a slight, shy wave.

Georgie approaches Heidi at the front of the room.

"Sorry I was late again."

"It's earned you detention." Heidi smiles. "But you knew that already, didn't you?"

"It's okay. I'll just sleep. Nobody notices."

Heidi looks at Georgie, and softens. "Your essay on Sartre and Bad Faith was quite something. Impressive."

A flurry of noise in the hallway distracts Heidi. "Excuse me," she says. She shuts the door.

"Have you given any more thought to the Winterbourne? I'd encourage you to give it your best shot. You've got quite a noggin, Mr Gust."

Georgie looks up at her. "Noggin Haagen Daas." His cheek twitches. "Sorry. Poetry in my head. Lyrics."

Heidi smiles. "Listen. It's the first nice day of the season. Would you care to join me for lunch in the yard?"

Georgie jerks his head as if nodding dramatically. "Yeah, sure," he says. "I know I'm twitching, but that's a yes. God, my head's killing me."

"Yes? Okay."

Heidi grabs her bag and heads for the door, and they walk together to the yard. Around them, students wave to each other and yell, some run while others splay out on the grass, enjoying the first warm day of the year.

"Um, I have a better idea," Heidi says. "How about a short field trip?"

Dear Diary:

Jesus, sometimes the solutions to my most difficult problems are right at my damn fingertips. Shite.

Grave company

Georgie, following Heidi's lead, places small stones on the cemetery gravesites that surround them. Heidi and Georgie have a private picnic on the grass. They keep company with the Harrison Memorial, finding their own safety zones within the boundaries of the curling black iron spires of the cemetery gates.

Eating, for Georgie, is ritualistic. He lifts his sandwich to his face and smells it before biting. Then he smells it again and chews with gaping, seemingly random chomps. His elbows lift up to his ears, the left, and then the right. He squints and twitches his nose, but Heidi doesn't seem to mind. He doesn't touch his vegetables.

He looks up at his teacher.

"Why were you late today? Again," she demands.

"I was at the college, performing tics for an older crowd. The sororities love me there," he answers flippantly.

Heidi scowls. "And you're hung over."

Georgie's right leg begins to shiver. It kicks.

"Why, Georgie?"

"I don't conform. I'm a rebel."

Heidi shakes her head. "Being a rebel's the ultimate conformity. Everyone's a rebel."

"But I'm not conforming. The trick of today's youth is to rebel and conform at the same time. It's pretty hard—I'm no good at it."

"But what are you rebelling against?"

Georgie's leg shakes harder.

"Society, and whatever devil's inside me, shaking me up."

"You know, years ago they would have burned you at the stake. They would've thought you were possessed by the devil." Heidi pauses thoughtfully. "But then, they would have probably burnt me, too," she concludes.

Georgie responds with more twitching.

"What do you mean?" Georgie asks.

She grimaces. "For teaching philosophy. It was not regarded as a woman's job. I would've been labeled a witch. A rebel."

"And you would've been the devil's spawn, too, huh?"

She smiles, and continues. "At least these days, nobody's holding a gun to your head but you. Things might be as good as they're going to get, for now. Society-wise."

"I appreciate your curiosity about my condition," Georgie answers lightly. "But telling me I'll die if I don't change isn't helping. Not here. Not now."

Georgie darts away, skipping like a cripple, then runs back and dives into Heidi's arms. He cries ever so slightly.

She hugs him slowly, wrapping a tentative arm around his shoulders. Moments later, he withdraws from her with a grimace.

"Probably we should head back," he says.

Heidi and Georgie pick their way through the graveyard.

"A significant life leaves its mark on the world," Heidi says finally, looking wistfully at the gravestone inscriptions.

"What's that?" asks Georgie.

"Oh, just something an old teacher of mine used to say."

For a moment, silence.

"Have you left your mark?" Georgie asks.

Heidi sighs. "Not yet. I'm still hoping."

Georgie squints, jumping and flapping his arms.

"The more comfortable you are with who you are, the less you'll need to rebel," Heidi continues. "What do you want—for yourself?"

"I don't know what I want." His foot begins to stomp. "I just don't want to be taken over by these devils."

Heidi ignores the display. "We all have our demons," she sighs. "What sets us apart is the way we deal with them."

Georgie clucks his tongue, grunts, and sniffs disdainfully.

Dear Diary:

I took the day off and read some Tennyson poetry, all I could gather or interpret as for myself was that, it's likely better to have loved and lost than never to have loved at all. I mean, we all lose eventually; everyone gets left behind at some time— through death or other misfortune. Nonetheless, I'm back on the book now, if one could even call it a book. Ugh. Hell yes. I'm back, man. I'm fucking Batman!

There's no place like . . .

At a Wakefield diner, Ozer and Claudia share a plate of cheese fries over their Cokes. The jukebox plays twangy country love songs a little too loudly.

Ozer gestures angrily with a fry. "Dude, what the hell have you been doing with Mr Twitchy?" he demands.

"Don't call him that!"

"Georgie Porgie, then," Ozer says sarcastically.

"We're just partners. For class." Claudia folds her arms.

"Oh. Really?" Ozer looks intently at her. She glares at him.

"If you cared for me so much, you would've come to class," she sniffs. "I would've chosen you over him, if you were there."

Ozer smiles at her. "All right, then. I'll trust you. I guess I have to."

"Jesus, Jason."

"All right. All right."

Claudia finishes her soda.

"Want another?" Ozer reaches into his pocket for some change and hands it to Claudia as she nods. She takes the change and appraises it, then tucks it into her pocket.

"I think it's more—about a dollar or so."

Ozer gives her a 20. He squints hungrily at her butt as she walks from the booth.

Dear Diary:

Once again, things aren't adding up in my life, overall. I've got to start subtracting. Good for mathematics, and I suppose good for life itself, too. Fuck it.

Misery loves company

Georgie frantically throws the covers from his bed as he looks for his journal. His spasms come so quickly that they are almost invisible. He grunts his frustration and finally, giving up, he reaches under the mattress for his flask and takes a swig. He pulls on a jacket, stuffing the flask in his pocket, and leaves.

He shuffles into the woods, self-absorbed and lost in thought. His feet know the way. He lights a cigarette.

Halfway through his second cig, Georgie reaches the bluff. He stops when he sees somebody else there. It's Claudia—she's crying. She hears his footsteps and turns toward him.

"Oh. Hi," she says.

Georgie's surprised, but he manages a hello in return.

Claudia stands. "I'm sorry. I didn't think anyone would be here," she stammers. "I'll go."

"No, you don't have to. Stay," Georgie says, gesturing. "What are you doing here?"

(Parenthetical Pet Peeve) People who ask, "What are you doing here?" when they don 't really want to know what you're doing, but want to know why you are there in the first place and they don't like you being around.

Claudia shrugs. "Maybe I needed a place to cry."

"You? What do you have to cry about?"

"Plenty," she sniffs. "Believe me."

"Like what?" he insists.

"Like, maybe, pressure." She looks at him. "Oh, forget it," she says. She points to his cigarette. "Do you live off those things? I never see you without one." She wipes away her tears.

"Sort of. I guess," Georgie mumbles.

"They'll kill you."

Georgie looks at the cigarette. "I hope so."

"What? Why would you say that?"

Georgie shrugs. "Really, it's not like anyone would care."

"I would," Claudia says quietly.

The long Atlantic rollers crash in and out behind her as he stares, stock-still. She walks over next to him and soon he seems to relax.

"My parents sent me here," Georgie says out of the blue. "I hated my old school. I wanted to get away. More girls here than boys, you know. Not bad odds."

He hops to his feet, smiling.

"They called me F-Minus, all through middle school," he giggles. "That's fucked up."

"Yeah!" Claudia laughs with him.

"Shite yeah, dude!" Georgie exclaims. "Like, what is normal these days, right? What is dysfunctional? Same thing, right?"

Claudia laughs, nodding. "I'm only here because Dr Ozer, Jason's father, pulled some strings to get me a scholarship."

"Yeah, really? Small world. Dr Ozer did my mother's surgery. He pays my way, as long as I keep my grades up."

"Same here." Claudia paused a beat. "My mother's his secretary," she explained.

"Get out of town!" Georgie threw up his hands. "Is that why you go out with that dick, Jason? Pressure. That's why, isn't it?"

Claudia looks away.

"Fuckin' Ozer," Georgie scoffs.

Dear Diary:

I take a vow to never be a victim of life again. Lord, help me. No, I'm going to conqueror the shite out of it! Man, oh, man. I'm always changing. Good. I'm like a goddamn chameleon and I love it.

A good thing

Georgie and Claudia lean over the side of an old stone and wood bridge. They drop stones in the water, watching the ripples spread outward.

"I hate my parents," Georgie begins.

"My real father's dead." Claudia throws another stone.

"Lucky you."

Claudia stares at Georgie as he lights a fresh cigarette. Claudia snatches it from his mouth, throws the burnt part in the water, and pockets the filter.

Georgie does not respond.

"Don't say that," Claudia says after a pause. "I loved my dad."

"What happened to him?"

"He was a cop. A New York City cop. He had trouble sometimes. You know? With the job? With all the stuff he'd see." Claudia looks at Georgie to see if he understands. He nods. "Anyway, that's what my mom said. He'd get really depressed, and stuff."

"Like me?"

Claudia smiles sadly. "Two years ago, he was the first officer on the scene of a small plane crash," she continues quietly. "Everyone was dead. They'd died instantly."

She pauses.

"All except for this little, tiny baby. A girl. My dad tried to save her, but . . . anyway, he got, like, a medal of honor and stuff, and everyone told him how it wasn't his fault. He didn't seem too upset at the time, but he killed himself three months later."

"I still wish I was in your shoes," Georgie mumbles.

"Stop it." Claudia turns and looks him straight in the eyes. "I loved my dad. I'd give anything to have him back, Georgie. Anything."

A pregnant silence rises between them.

"Really?" Georgie says finally.

"Really. I used to be able to talk with him every night, when he was alive. Now I can talk to him when I pray, but I can't hear him answer."

"You think he hears you?" Georgie looks at her, his eyes blinking involuntarily.

"I know he hears me. I just wish I could hear him."

She gets to her feet, and Georgie follows.

"My parents never hear me. Or see me. Even though I'm right there. They've just always thought of me as the freak."

"A freak's a good thing, Georgie."

Georgie looks incredulous.

Claudia rummages through her pockets and pulls out a dime. "Know what this is?" She holds it under his nose.

Georgie examines the coin. "A dime?"

"Look at the date," Claudia commands.

Georgie looks.

"1-9-5? That can't be right . . . ."

"It was supposed to be 1956. The year my father was born." Claudia closes her fist and thrusts the coin back in her pocket. "But it's a mistake. It's what coin collectors call a freak. Because it's so different, it's actually worth something."

She smiles.

"Your dad gave that to you?"

"My mom, after he died. It was his, though."

"My dad's never given me anything." Georgie scowls at the water and throws another stone. It veers off into the brush on the side of the stream.

"Georgie . . ."

"Well, maybe that's not true. I'm a master at manipulation, you know. Maybe he did give me stuff—lots of stuff. I just don't want—" His head jerks spastically to the side. "I don't know. Sometimes I wish I could just jump ahead and be, like, 50 years old." His brow wrinkles. "What the fuck?" he mutters.

He shakes his head hard, blowing air from his lungs loudly.

"Claudia, I don't know who the hell I am!" he cries hoarsely. "I drive myself fuckin' nuts!"

"What?" Claudia puts her hand on his arm. "Georgie, are you okay?"

"Please, Claudia, please don't fuck with me, not now. You might as well just hate me. Save yourself the trouble."

Claudia remains calm, waiting for Georgie's tantrum to fade.

"You look fine from here," she says lightly. "Why should I hate you?"

"You will. It's only a matter of time."

Claudia laughs her disbelief. "Georgie, you just think entirely too much. Let go a little. It's Friday. I'd love to see you on autopilot. You know, like just acting yourself, without thinking about it."

Georgie kicks a rock from under his feet. He gets what she's saying. She sees his little smirk.

"Yeah. No pressure. Let's blow off all the pressure. You and me."

Georgie pokes Claudia on the side and she swipes at him, giggling. He skips away from her and she lunges forward; he breaks into a run.

Georgie and Claudia run together through the woods and into an open field. I'm 'free, being myself with Claudia in the bright sunlight, the spring wildflowers. Claudia picks a handful of flowers for her room, and Georgie adds to her bouquet, touching her lightly on the shoulder. She jerks away from him ever so slightly, but as the bouquet grows she minds his touch less and less. Finally her hand is so full of flowers that it can't hold anymore. The two collapse onto the soft grass.

"My dad would've been 50, this year, the end of April. Halfway to hell—that's what he called his birthday."

She pulls her knees to her chest. "I miss him so much, Georgie. I can't stand it, sometimes." She laughs without joy. "Every year, for his birthday, my mother would make him the same dinner."

"Yeah?"

"Corned beef and lime Jell-O."

Georgie shudders.

"I know, I know." Claudia laughs softly. "It's no gourmet. But he loved it, anyhow."

Georgie moves closer to Claudia. His head is next to hers, in the grass.

"And I'd give him the stupidest presents, when I was a kid. One year it was a canister of play dough."

They giggle.

"When I finally had some money of my own, I bought him a Garfield stationery set."

Claudia wipes her eyes as she laughs.

"I miss him so much. Sometimes I just can't stand it. I just want to see him so much that I want to die. To be with him."

Georgie frowns quizzically. "Huh?"

"You know? Like heaven?" she pauses and shakes her head. "How about your dad? Don't you miss seeing him? Ever?"

"Yeah. I guess so," Georgie says playfully. "Sort of."

Claudia blinks back tears.

"It doesn't make any sense," Georgie snarls suddenly. "You lose a father you love, and I'm stuck with one I hate."

"Don't say that, Georgie," Claudia insists. "I bet anything that your dad and mom love you to pieces. They just don't get you, is all."

Georgie shrugs, then smiles. He pokes Claudia again and leaps up. She jogs after him until they reach a stone wall at the edge of the field. She rushes past him.

"Come on!" She grins.

Clutching the wildflowers in one hand, Claudia scrambles atop the wall. She walks along the wall with her arms stretched out for balance. Georgie walks behind her, hopping occasionally. Claudia looks back and grins at him. Georgie reaches out and touches her leg. Surprised, she slips and loses her balance. Georgie tries to catch her, but he trips, and they both land in the mud.

Georgie tics and twitches furiously; he's terrified that she'll be mad at him. But Claudia just throws back her head and laughs. After a stunned moment of relief, Georgie joins her.

Later that afternoon, Georgie and Claudia walk through a street fair on Main Street. Georgie holds cotton candy in his right hand. Claudia has a candied apple.

"They were gated for a week, on full restriction," Georgie says. "They put hair remover in my shampoo."

"That's horrible," Claudia mutters, biting into her apple.

"I got them back, though." Georgie grins.

"What did you do?"

They halt near a fresh dill pickle stand. Georgie leans over so that his face is only inches from hers. He can smell the sweet apple on her breath.

"I put Ex-Lax in their chicken sandwiches," he says quietly.

Claudia bursts out laughing, and Georgie is only too happy to join her. After a moment, Claudia exhales and wipes her eyes. She tilts her head, smiling. "Hey, look," she says.

A troupe of mimes approaches Claudia, moving like swans gliding across a still pond. They smile with Claudia; the swans dive and scatter. A balloonist hands Claudia a balloon flower. Georgie smiles. The balloonist makes another figure. It's a monkey.

The mimes reform and pretend to be prisoners in their own cages.

The balloonist gives Georgie the monkey-shaped balloon.

"Uh, th-thanks," Georgie says. The balloonist bows and swoops after a group of Girl Scouts. The mimes follow silently behind.

All too soon, however, the day draws to a close. Georgie and Claudia walk down the street, nearing the Wakefield Campus.

"I wish we didn't have to go back," Claudia sighs peacefully. "This afternoon was so nice, so free!" She throws her hands to the sky and grins. "It's good to get away, from the pressure."

Georgie darts a glance at her and hops. "What pressure? More pressure?"

"What pressure? To be the perfect daughter. To get into a good college. To . . ." Claudia hesitates.

"What?"

Claudia looks carefully at Georgie as they round the corner where the Wakefield sign announces school grounds. "It's Ozer," she says carefully. "He wants me to sleep with him."

"Ozer," Georgie scoffs. "Why do you keep on with him?"

Claudia stares at the sidewalk in silence.

"I mean, if he keeps pressuring you," Georgie continues, trying to regain ground. "Well, you don't want to?"

Claudia nods.

"Then you shouldn't." Georgie's face transforms as every muscle convulses at once.

Claudia doesn't see.

"I don't know. I'm not ready, but he won't stop bugging me. It's all he ever talks about, anymore. We never do anything."

Georgie tries to hide a hopeful smile. "It's so simple. You don't need to impress anyone, Claudia."

Claudia nods. "It's my friends, too. They think I'm . . . they think I'm frigid."

"Are you?"

"No! I don't know. Maybe . . . maybe I just haven't found the right person, though."

"You don't owe Ozer anything," Georgie points out quietly.

"He thinks I do. He says it's normal for a boy, for a man. He says that's how guys express love."

"He's an idiot."

"Is he?" Claudia looks into Georgie's face, challenging him. "Put it another way. If you were my boyfriend, wouldn't you pressure me for sex? Wouldn't you want it? Tell me the truth!"

"Are you kidding?" Georgie stops walking. He stares at her. "I'd be . . . I'd be happy just to hold your hand. God, Claudia!"

She holds out her hand to him, her face solemn. Georgie's eyes widen. She grins. "Go on. Take it. It won't burn."

"The first time," Georgie whispers. "Nothing ever replaces the first time, right?" Hesitantly, he takes her hand. He stares at his hand, holding Claudia's like it might disappear at any moment.

"You know what?" Claudia says quietly, trying to catch his eye.

Georgie stares at their hands, feeling the warmth of her palm spread into his. "Hush," he whispers.

"I've never had sex, Georgie. Not with anyone," she whispers.

"Shite, I'm holding your hand," Georgie mutters. Only then does he look up into her face.

Her eyes are open, shining. She leans forward and kisses Georgie on the mouth. Georgie blinks rapidly and then steps closer to her. They kiss again.

Then Claudia turns, like an alarm's gone off in her head. "Shite," she mutters.

Georgie follows her gaze.

Ozer is coming down the walk, having just finished lacrosse practice.

His stick, with his helmet and other gear attached, is slung over his shoulder. He stiffens when he sees Georgie and Claudia holding hands.

Georgie self-consciously drops Claudia's hand as Ozer approaches them. Ozer's face contorts in rage.

"What are you doing with Hershey squirt?!" he yells.

"What does it look like?" she snaps at him.

Ozer looks at her clothes and at Georgie's.

"How did you get so dirty?" he demands.

"We were having sex," Claudia hisses sarcastically.

Ozer's eyes flash at Georgie, and a brilliant red flush covers his cheeks. "Well, good for you," Ozer says, his voice terrifyingly calm. "Flowers, too? Isn't that sweet." He takes Claudia's arm and jerks her away from Georgie. "Guess what? Show's over," he says.

Claudia pulls away from him. "Don't tell me what to do, Jason," she threatens.

Ozer shrugs. "You want to pick flowers with freaks, pick flowers with freaks." He turns to Georgie. "Twitchy, you are so easy to make fun of. I can't stand it!

Ozer lunges at Georgie, who backs away.

"Ahhhh!" Ozer laughs.

"Ahhhh!" Georgie repeats.

"What?" Ozer squints, wondering if Georgie's making fun of him. Georgie's silent and still.

"Hell, yeah." Ozer struts to Claudia. "Don't forget about tonight," he commands.

"I won't forget," Claudia says, her voice as cold as steel.

"See you then." Ozer spins and swaggers off down the walk.

Claudia and Georgie look at each other in amusement, rolling their eyes.

"I'm sure glad he didn't show up a second before he did," Georgie says finally.

"Oh, Georgie," Claudia sighs. Her hand twitches, but she leaves it at her side.

Dear Diary:

In the face of work-related anxiety, stress, flu, schizophrenia, dyslexia, computer crash after crash and being legally blind plain and simple, I did it! Again! I embraced the hope and the courage and I did it! Took care of the business at hand. And all simply the best I could and can. And I'm still writing, a lot of exorcising my own inner demons and angels.

Once, twice . . .

Georgie stalks the library stacks, thinking about the Winterbourne. He might just enter. He might. As he strolls slowly towards the back, he hears the sound of murmuring, of hands roving over cloth.

"Damn. Wow!" a voice says lowly. "You're good, Jason."

"Don't tell anybody, okay?" Ozer whispers.

A minute later, Georgie sees Susan trotting down the center aisle, a smug grin on her face. Georgie waits until she's almost to the door, then he follows slowly.

Georgie sets his bag down on a table and starts to stuff books into it. He watches as Wyman enters the library and Susan meets him by the door.

"Hey, baby! I'm late for class," Susan says lightly. She kisses him on the cheek. "Catch up with you later!"

Wyman takes a few steps into the room and then stops, looking down the aisles. Georgie follows his gaze. He sees Ozer approaching. Ozer holds a thick science textbook lightly in his hand.

"Hey, brother," Ozer says quietly.

Georgie twitches.

"What do you want, Ozer?" Georgie mutters. "N-not a book, huh?"

"N-not . . . n-not . . ." Ozer snorts. He looks over and finds Wyman, who is thumbing through a magazine.

"Yo, Wyman. Get over here. Wanna see something?" He grins.

Ozer brandishes the huge, heavy science book. Georgie twitches, and the zipper in his backpack gets caught in the fabric. He yanks at it impatiently with one hand, then uses the other to steady himself on the counter as a full-body shudder overcomes him.

"Yes, you drunken wastrel," Ozer hisses. "I do want a book. This fuckin' book."

He slams the book's sharp edge down on Georgie's fingers. Georgie bites back a yell as pain sears up his arm. Ozer leans in close to Georgie as he struggles to pull his hand away.

"Keep away from my girl, you little bastard, or I'll kill you," Ozer growls. "You hear me? I'll fuckin' kill you, personally. You feel that?"

Ozer leans hard on the heavy book, pressing it into Georgie's fingers. Georgie whimpers involuntarily. His eyes shoot hatred.

"You hear me?

Georgie's neck arches with pain. Ozer leans still harder on the book, grinding it into Georgie's fingers.

With an effort, Wyman pulls Ozer's hand away. Georgie snatches his hand up from under the book, holding it to his chest. His eyes scrunch with pain.

"Jesus, dude, take it easy," Wyman says. "You're gonna break his hand."

Ozer looks like it's all he can do not to jump over the table and begin pounding Georgie into a faceless nothing. Georgie wraps his arm around his backpack, not caring about the zipper, and backs slowly away.

"Come on, man. Let's get outta here," Wyman looks around pointedly. A few students who have just entered are watching the trio.

He leads Ozer away.

Ozer's face is bright red. He looks back at Georgie, whose face is also inflamed. Ozer gives Georgie the finger.

"Remember what I said!" he yells. "This isn't about you. You faggot freak."

"Faggot?" Georgie says wonderingly.

Ozer stops. He yanks his arm from Wyman's grip and stalks over to Georgie, pushing his finger into Georgie's chest.

"You! Watch your ass," he commands.

"D-don't worry, Ozer. I will."

Dear Diary:

I believe a lot of the problems in our world would disappear if more of us would decide to talk to each other rather than simply talking about everybody else. Oh well.

238

Truth, lies, and lunch

The next day, Georgie and Heidi walk down to the cemetery to enjoy their weekly lunch. Georgie smokes, as usual, with one hand. His other is shoved into the front pocket of his hooded sweater. He feels bright, animated, for some reason. He hops with a sense of purpose.

"How about we meet somewhere new for a change?" Heidi suggests as the cemetery looms into sight.

"Why?" Georgie says quickly. "I like it over there. It's hard to get away, to be alone. On campus, I mean. I like getting out, somewhere where it's quiet."

"You're a good kid, Georgie," Heidi says kindly.

"I'm a good boy, Charlie Brown," Georgie smirks.

Heidi laughs.

They enter the cemetery and quickly find a secluded grassy area, beneath some young trees. They sit. Georgie digs into his food, eating rapidly. For a while, all is silence. Then Georgie looks up from the remains of his lunch.

"You're the first adult I've ever felt I could really talk to," he says matter-of-factly. "You encourage maturity, somehow."

"Thank you." Heidi grins. "You seem especially bouncy today."

"I'm off my medication," Georgie nods three times. "I've been good lately."

Heidi's eyes open wide in surprise. "You're kidding me. The doctors approved of that?"

Georgie shrugs. "Yeah. I tapered down for a little while. And now I'm off completely. It's liberating, I think." He looks down at the grass.

"Georgie." Heidi pauses, assessing him. She sighs. "Well, maybe you really don't need them," she concedes.

"Hey, Heidi, can I ask you a question?" Georgie says suddenly.

Heidi nods.

"How come you're not married?"

"No one's ever asked me," Heidi says evenly.

"Really?"

"Really."

"I can't believe that," Georgie says.

"Believe it," Heidi responds lightly.

"But . . . but you're attractive and you've got a good job. Not to mention that you're mentally stable. And mature. All that . . ."

He stops, blushing.

Heidi smiles. "Thanks." She laughs. "But men, I think, tend to find me off-putting. That's just a two-dollar word for bossy."

"Not all men," Georgie says sullenly.

"Maybe I'm just destined to be an old maid," Heidi says lightly, seeming to study the bark of a nearby oak.

"No. Don't think that way," Georgie says. "Not unless you want to be that old maid."

Heidi's face seems overcome by relief. "Yeah, I guess I didn't really think about it that way." She grins at Georgie. "You make me feel young and alive again, Georgie. Thank you."

"Don't thank me," Georgie says earnestly. "You've done so much for me." He blushes awkwardly and digs through his backpack.

"I decided to go ahead and enter the Winterbourne," he says, pulling out a book and showing it to her. The book is Sartre's *Being and Nothingness*. "I'm writing an essay. I think I'll call it, 'On Bad Faith'."

"That's great, Georgie!" Heidi hands the book back to him. "Really. Anything I can do to help, you just let me know. Okay?

Georgie nods and returns the book to his backpack. He has to use both his hands to yank the zipper into place. As he does so, Heidi suddenly notices the swollen mess of his fingers.

She takes Georgie's wrist. "What happened to your hand, Georgie?"

Georgie tries to pull his wrist free, but Heidi holds it tight.

"I'm all right," he insists.

"Who did this?" Heidi demands.

"No one! Well, me. I slammed the window on my hand, okay? I'm all right."

Heidi looks closely at his face. "Are you telling me the truth?"

"Why wouldn't I?" Georgie shrugs.

Heidi looks at him silently. "Did you go to the nurse?"

Georgie jerks his wrist out of her grasp. "I told you, it's all right! I don't need the nurse."

Heidi takes another look at his bruised fingers.

"Here," she says quietly, pulling a cold soda from her lunch. She holds the can to his hand.

Georgie catches his breath at the cold, and then relaxes as the pain begins to numb.

"Tell me something, Heidi," he says a few minutes later. "Why do you take so much interest in me?"

Heidi looks him in the eyes. Georgie, for once, makes direct eye contact with her.

"Do you feel sorry for me?" he demands. "Because if that's why . . ."

Heidi takes a deep breath and he halts.

"At first, I admit, I was drawn to you because of your Tourette's, yes," she answers. "You interested me, intellectually, but since I've gotten to know you, my reasons changed. You remind me of someone—you remind me of myself."

"You?" You might as well mistake a slug for a horse, he thinks.

"Well, maybe I should say that you remind me of my sister. Being with you reminds me of how I used to feel when I was with her. You both talk about yourselves the same way."

Heidi wraps her arms around her knees and looks away. "She was a bright girl, and she had cerebral palsy. It wasn't a bad case, just enough to make her different. The other kids laughed at her and teased her a lot. She had no friends, she drank all the time, and she started having sex when she wasn't ready."

She stands abruptly and walks around Georgie, fingering the headstones that surround them. "Eventually she had a baby, and then went into therapy, all that. But she overdosed a few years later, and her heart stopped. Just like that."

"And you couldn't stop it?" Georgie prompted her.

"I couldn't get out of my own head. In a way, I forgot about my sister until it was too late." She turns to Georgie. "She looked up to me, you know? She'd have done whatever I told her, if I'd bothered to take notice."

"So you feel guilty," Georgie concluded. "And to make up for what happened to her, you want to save me."

"I see a lot of her in you, Georgie. You have a lot to offer the world, even though it seems like nobody notices. Maybe not even you."

"You think? Like I owe the world something because of this—" he knocks his knuckles against his head, "this gift? It's bullshite. I can't stand it. What about what I want, huh?"

Heidi trembles slightly. "We'd better head back, Georgie. Okay?"

Georgie doesn't know what to say. He plays with a fresh cigarette, but doesn't light it.

Heidi looks at her watch. "Come on, it's almost time for class."

Dear Diary:

True, I do have this condition called schizophrenia. However I feel with my entire heart, not just from a part of my conditions, which I embrace . . . living my life the best I am able. In times of suffering or elated joy, I not only feel it, I live it. I am a human being, just like anyone else. To be called crazy, insane, or simply a "bad person," I'm inclined to believe more in the act of caring. Not caring is crazier than just being called crazy.

Detention

Detention Hall is an old, silent lecture hall, with yards of empty floor space behind the built-in desks and chairs. The jerkily ticking wall clock reads 7:06 am.

Georgie lays flat-out behind the back row, on the floor, using his jacket as a pillow. His headset is on, although his eyes are closed. Classical music drifts tinny from the headphones. Some of the kids in the back row peek over at him jealously. A few slight whispers echo through the cavernous room.

The hall monitor, an elderly man named Mr Pivens, hasn't the faintest clue what Georgie's doing. He sits under the wall clock, behind a desk facing the students. He reads a newspaper as he listens to the students scratching their pencils against paper and flipping through books. Occasionally, he wipes his fingers on his green polo shirt as though to keep them clean of newspaper print. He looks down his glasses at Elizabeth Winters when she comes in late, still yawning. She's wearing pajama bottoms, a terrycloth bathrobe, and slippers. Her hair is a straw nest.

"Sorry, Mr Pivens," she says, seeming to shrink at the glances of other students at her bedclothes.

Mr Pivens doesn't even look up. "You're late," he says, turning the page. "I'll expect to see you here next week, as well."

"Shite," Elizabeth mutters under her breath.

"And the week after that, Elizabeth," he says calmly.

She sits down heavily, dropping her books loudly on the desk.

Mr Pivens raises an eyebrow, and she is silent.

Georgie smiles, although he didn't hear a word of the exchange. He's in his own world, now.

Dear Diary:

I think the child in me sees and knows. The adult only clouds the issue. When young, I believed and I was innocent; the world crowded in. Ah, to be more childlike, but either way seems to work out in the long run.

Rocks for jocks

Georgie and Claudia walk into Heidi's class together, talking and laughing. They take seats with the rest of the students, near the open window. A very slight breeze cools the overly warm room.

Heidi stands before them.

"Last week we talked about bad faith," she begins. "Bad faith, we decided, comes from reducing another person to a prescribed role. Can anybody give me an example of bad faith?"

Claudia raises her hand. Heidi points to her. "Claudia?"

"A doctor."

"Yes!" Heidi smiles. "In the case of the doctor, he or she is draped in nothing but a paper gown that confines him in an inauthentic identity. Temporarily, at least."

Heidi walks down the center row, and then sits at one of the desks.

"We all play different roles," she continues. "Some are authentic, some inauthentic. For example, I'm acting as your teacher, right now, but I'm not just a teacher. In this classroom, I play a role that doesn't fit the whole me. Therefore, I'm in bad faith."

"Huh?" Hendricks asks, looking at her like she's just cartwheeled from an alien spaceship.

Heidi grins wolfishly. "That reminds me, Hendricks. I have your test results back."

The students groan and complain as Heidi begins to hand their tests back, then begin chattering with one another, comparing scores and answers.

As Georgie turns to Claudia, a pebble flies in through the window and hits him in the back of the head.

Georgie grunts and rubs his head.

"Georgie?" Claudia looks at him, puzzled.

"Huh," he says, still rubbing his head. "Nothing." Claudia turns back to her test.

Another pebble hits Georgie in the head.

As Georgie turns toward the window to see where the pebbles have been coming from, a large rock speeds through and hits him in the eye. His glasses shatter.

With a cry of shock and pain, Georgie tumbles from his chair and grabs his face.

"Fuck! Ow!" he howls.

Heidi hurries to the window and sees Ozer and Wyman running away.

"Ozer! Wyman!" she shouts. "Stop right there!"

The boys halt and look back at her, their faces as ignorant as frogs.

"What?" Ozer asks quizzically.

"You know damn well what!" Heidi hollers. She climbs swiftly out the window and charges toward the boys.

Meanwhile, Georgie doubles up on the floor, groaning and holding his eye.

Claudia comes over to him and crouches down. "Are you okay?" she asks, trying to pry his hand from his face. "Let me see it."

Georgie resists her. "No," he mumbles.

"They can be such assholes! Georgie, let me see it."

Finally, Claudia pulls Georgie's hand off and reveals his injury. His eye has turned an angry red and is quickly swelling shut. Distraught, Claudia strokes Georgie's back and the side of his face, murmuring. Georgie puts his hand over his eye again.

"They don't even know you. They don't even fucking know you. Not like I do," Claudia says soothingly.

Georgie shoves her away and gets back on his feet. "I'm an open book, Claudia," he says loudly, not caring about the other students, who stare at him warily. "I told you that. I'm an open fuckin' book."

Georgie picks up his books and begins hurling them around the room. The other students duck beneath their desks. He grabs books off their desks and throws those as well. The pages flap wildly as the bindings boom and crack against the hard walls.

"An open book. An open fuckin' book! I told you," he screams.

He tosses his desk and then grabs pencils, notebooks, anything within his grasp. He throws everything, screaming incoherently at his fellow students. Many of them break away from their desks and run for the door. He kicks a chair across the room.

"You wanna get hurt? You wanna get fuckin' killed?" He pants heavily as the others run from the room.

Claudia stares in awe, knowing better than to speak to him but still unable to leave.

"Then leave me alone! Everyone just leave me the fuck alone!" Georgie screeches, and leaps out the window.

Out on the lawn, Heidi has Ozer and Wyman by the arms and is leading them toward the Dean's office. They watch as Georgie runs from the academic building.

"Big baby!" Ozer sneers.

"Christ, you hit him with a rock!" Wyman exclaims.

Heidi casts a worried look toward Georgie, who runs wildly to the dorms, holding his face. "Shut up and keep moving," she growls. "Both of you."

When Ozer and Wyman leave the Dean's office, Ozer looks cocky. He finds Claudia waiting for him outside.

"Hey," he smirks.

"I hope you're proud of yourself. I really hope you are," Claudia says coldly.

Before he can answer, she turns and walks away.

"They suspended me!" Ozer yells at her. "Wyman, too. We can't even play in the Knowles game."

Ozer looks at Wyman and spreads his arms, as if to say, "What did I do?" Wyman looks very much as though he'd like to punch his friend in the face.

Meanwhile, in a drunken rage, Georgie destroys his room. Blind without his eyeglasses, he kicks the trashcan and throws the ashtray and lamp, tosses his books and clothes onto the floor. He rips the drawers out of his chest and hurls them across the room.

There's a loud knocking at the door, but he ignores it. He smashes his radio against the wall. He rips the sheets off his bed and tears them apart. When everything else is gone, he beats his fists helplessly against the wall.

When the room's a wasteland, Georgie stands there, breathing heavily, sweating. He still ignores the pounding and shouting at his door.

He looks around, trying to figure out what to destroy next.

He digs a carton of cigarettes out of the mess. He empties a pack onto whatever's left of his bed.

"It's either now or never," he mutters.

Slowly, carefully, he begins shredding the cigarettes, watching the bits of tobacco sprinkle onto the floor.

"More negative thoughts I just can't afford right now," he raps.

Later that evening, Georgie comes across Claudia as she pokes around aimlessly on Main Street, looking in shop windows.

He approaches her cautiously. His eye's still a mess. He still doesn't have his glasses. At least 10 Band-Aids are taped to his hands, hiding cuts and scrapes he made in his rage.

"Hi," he says quietly.

Claudia turns away.

Georgie catches up to her. He walks erratically, stretching his groin every other step, pushing his neck out awkwardly in front of him. "I'm sorry," he says.

She keeps walking.

He follows. "I mean it. I'm sorry."

She turns on him. "You're sorry?" she accuses. "You're sorry?"

"Claudia?"

"Great! Good for you!" she rages. "What do you want me to do? Feel sorry for you?"

"Um, forgive me?" Georgie suggests.

"For what, Georgie?"

He looks at her in silence, afraid of the wrong answer.

"For yelling in class," he says finally. "For scaring you?"

She looks at him with disdain.

"You don't get it, do you?" Claudia snarls. "You didn't scare me, and I don't care that you yelled. What gets me, Georgie, is that you treated me like everyone else. You turned me into someone no different than Ozer."

"So you hate me now?" he pleads.

She stops, looks Georgie in the eye, and then walks off down the street. Georgie watches her walk away, struggling with himself not to follow. Then he turns and heads back toward the school.

When darkness falls, Georgie puts his room back together again. He's taken his glasses to a shop and had them repaired; they are stuck back on his face.

Georgie paces back and forth, sweating. He rips off his shirt. He tries to find something to do with his hands, but he can't find anything that satisfies him.

Finally, Georgie just lies in bed, staring at the ceiling. He can't sleep.

After an hour, he rises and makes a small pot of coffee. The machine funnels the last few drops of fresh brew and Georgie carries a cupful to his desk. The ashtray's gone, lost somewhere in a dim corner of his closet. A ream of fresh papers is stacked neatly in his printer.

(Parenthetical Pet Peeve) Photocopiers and printers that jam.

Georgie sits at the desk in front of his computer. He opens a writing program and begins to type.

FROM THE INSIDE:

Chapter One . . .

He deletes "From the Inside" and rewrites the title to read: "A Part of Me." Then, below it: "By Georgie Gust." He thinks again, and then begins to write:

Things really can't be as bad as they seem. The worst parts are exaggerated in the mind.

He stops writing, and then takes a long sigh.

He erases what he's written.

He shuts his eyes, thinks.

He deletes everything and starts again on an empty screen.

Dear Diary:

My main mantra in life is definitely, "Don't lose hope, no matter what."

248

Something positive

A few weeks later, Georgie and Heidi have lunch together at the cemetery. Georgie seems even more restless and on edge than usual. Heidi studies him as he twitches and exhales.

(Parenthetical Pet Peeve) "Mystery Meat" in the school cafeteria.

"You look different, Georgie," she says, musingly.
She thinks a minute, and then snaps her fingers.
"No cigarette!" she declares proudly.
"I gave them up. And I gave up drinking, too," Georgie says fiercely.
"Good for you, Georgie. I'm proud of you." Heidi smiles.
"It's tough, though. I want to tear down a wall with my bare hands, sometimes, but I fight the urge."
"You need something to take their place. Something to keep your mind occupied. Something positive."
"Like what?"
Heidi shrugs. "I know you. You'll think of something. Have you talked to Claudia lately?"
"I don't see much of her since I went crazy in class, you know, that day. Anyway, she's Ozer's girlfriend."
Georgie snorts quietly, and looks thoughtful. Later that night, he sits at his desk in front of his computer. All the lights on campus are out, except his. His shadow is hard at work.

Dear Diary:

It's so hard but how simple it could—just could—be to acknowledge that all the worry in the world could not control the future. To see that I can only be happy right now, and that there will never be a time when it is not now.

The big game

That weekend, a limousine pulls up in front of the school. The chauffeur unfolds himself from the driver's seat and opens the back door. Ozer gets out. He's holding a small duffel bag. His suspension is over, although he still can't play in the upcoming game.

Wyman and Susan stand to greet him when he steps to the curb. Claudia looks on from the entrance to the dorms. Then she turns and walks inside.

That afternoon, at the highly anticipated Wakefield vs Knowles lacrosse game, the usual hangers-on cheer riotously in the stands. Parents, girlfriends, and faculty clap and hoot as the home teams take the field. A number of students from both schools have come to watch.

Ozer and Wyman stand on the sidelines, dressed in street clothes, watching a pep squad of six chanting and waving blue and gold pom-poms in the breeze.

The game is a brutal affair and, though Wakefield fights tooth and nail, their offense is no match for Knowles' defense. Time and time again, Wakefield fans moan as their boys are sent flying off the rebound of powerful screens and tackles. With each dissatisfied grumble from the crowd, Ozer's shoulders hike up closer to his ears.

At long last, the final gun fires. The scoreboard reads: "WAKEFIELD 10; VISITOR 13." The Knowles fans cheer and rush onto the field, while dejected Wakefield players shake hands with the winners, and then walk to the sidelines.

Ozer purses his lips and Wyman's head is hung as their teammates pass them by.

"Way to go, you guys," one of them sneers.

"Yeah, thanks a lot," another says disdainfully.

The rest of the players file past in silence. A Knowles player smiles at Ozer as he marches off the field.

"Great game, bros!" he mocks.

Ozer grits his teeth. "That little prick!" he growls.

Wyman looks back and shakes his head. "Just let it go, will you?"

Georgie, of course, is utterly oblivious to the tragedy that has befallen his school's honor. Rather, he types steadily through the weekend, resting only to rub his eyes and sip at a cup of coffee.

Dear Diary:

Life is way too short to waste my time trying to convince other people that I am worthy to be loved. I think if there is a God, he made us all unique, glorious individuals, and if someone refuses to see how special I am, then I should refuse to even give them time out of my day. I should stop wasting my own precious time on the people who don't love me, and focus the spending of my time on the people who do love me. Also, that I'm sure to make time to focus on loving my own self, no matter what, since doing so will likely make it very easy for a very deserving person to love me as well. I've got to always remember that I am always loved. Hell, I might not even realize it most of the time.

A slight change of plans

Weeks pass. The snowy winter blows itself off and begins to melt into spring.

Georgie smiles as he checks off a Friday on his calendar, which indicates the month to be April.

Saturday's box says, "NO DETENTION," meaning there's a free weekend ahead.

He rubs his eyes.

Later that day, Georgie and Heidi have lunch under the shade of an oak tree near the river.

Heidi looks preoccupied. She's not really eating. "Still off the liquor and cigarettes?" she prompts.

"Yes." Georgie nods. "I've found something to replace them."

Heidi raises her brows in silence.

"My entry for the Winterbourne," Georgie explains.

"On Bad Faith? The one you were talking about last semester?" she asks hopefully.

"Kind of." Georgie looks at her from the corner of his eye, his chin jerking upward.

Heidi smiles. "Kind of? How mysterious."

Georgie blinks rapidly. "Not really. I'll let you see it when I finish. If you want."

Heidi swats him playfully on the head. "Of course I want! How's it coming?"

"A lot of it's finished already. It's hard work, but it's fun." He pauses a moment to look up at her again. "It's really pretty rewarding. All on its own."

Heidi beams, looking for the entire world like a proud mother. "I can't wait to read it. I hope I'll get an autographed copy?" she winks.

"Hand delivered," Georgie assures her solemnly.

There's a slight pause and Georgie notices her preoccupied expression. "What? What are you thinking?" he asks nervously.

"That might not be possible," she says slowly.

"Why? What do you mean?"

"I'm afraid this may be our last lunch together."

"Dude! What are you talking about?" Georgie demands.

"The school is reconsidering my tenure."

Georgie's jaw drops.

"The way that you and Claudia outperform everyone else has made people think I'm favoring the two of you."

"That's ridiculous!" Georgie says, near yelling.

"Of course it is, but it's their school, and, who knows? Maybe I have been too hard on the students." Heidi shrugs, trying out the idea.

"That's bullshite! You're the best teacher here."

"Thank you, Georgie." She smiles at him. "I appreciate that more than you know."

"Is there anything I can do?"

"Just do your best. Enter the Winterbourne." She squeezes his arm. "And win it."

When Georgie returns to his room that afternoon, he inserts his key in the door. It seems to have already been unlocked.

"That's weird," he mumbles.

He enters the room, stops, and stares. He drops his books.

His computer has been knocked over, the monitor kicked in.

"Gimme a fuckin' break!" he snarls.

Standing there, staring at the wreck, an inarticulate howl of rage rises in his throat.

His first reaction is to lash out. He looks around wildly for something to throw. He can't find anything.

Georgie starts methodically to smash his fist into the wall and then stops. He stumbles helplessly around the room, holding his head, which throbs with pain. Tears and sweat drip from his face.

He paces and walks in circles.

"Turn it around. Turn it around, just turn the whole negative thought around."

He drops to his knees at the side of the bed, hands together. He starts to pray. "God? I'm in need of a blessing, right now," he says firmly.

Georgie's twitching has almost stopped. He closes his eyes, and then takes a deep breath.

Peace seems to come over his features.

Georgie stands and begins cleaning the room.

After putting everything back in its place, Georgie gets a fresh cup of coffee. He removes a wad of chewing gum from his mouth and aims, not at the trash can near the door to his room, but at the lithograph print of Edvard Munch's *The Scream*.

"Ha! You must be the artist himself," he accuses the man in the foreground. "Not screaming, huh? But protecting yourself, from the scream of Nature."

He throws his gum and hits the "artist himself" right in his gaping mouth.

"That, my friend, is a reflex, a reaction typical of anyone struggling to keep out distressing noise, whether actual or imagined. So there. Take that!" He smirks at the poster. "Nice throw," he congratulates himself.

Georgie sits back down at his desk, in front of his sadly abused computer.

"Okay," he says, looking at the dented monitor with only the slightest hint of distress. He opens up the precious file, relieved to see that all 200 pages are still intact. He ponders the title for a moment, and then reformats it.

A Part

of Me

He stares at it and shakes his head.

Apart from Me

By Georgie Gust

He scrolls down to the last page and waits for inspiration, but it doesn't seem to come.

He creates a blank page and types:

Get out of my head.

Scrolling back, he deletes the last three words, until the page reads only:

Get out.

And nothing else. He prints the page.

Georgie rolls his eyes and stretches his fingers. He lifts his hands to his pounding head.

"Hm. Those must be what they call intrusive thoughts. You're so welcome, strangers. I am Georgie Gust, and I have Tourette's. Or maybe Tourette's has me. That's not the Word of God, they're just thoughts. Just let them roll by.

"They hate me. So fuck me, then. Okay. Okay. I fuckin' love, love, love this shite. I really do."

Georgie breathes heavily, a growl of rage starting to build.

He looks over at the door.

Stifling a false sense of calm, he grabs the page from the printer and tacks it to the gum on the Munch print.

"Get out," it screams at him. And Georgie does, slamming the door behind him.

Dear Diary:

Today, only I have the choice to be happy or unhappy. Nothing external. No past, nor future. I'm choosing happiness today!

Jump

Georgie's hunched up over his knees at the bluff, looking out to sea, ever so slightly sobbing.

Light footsteps tread behind him.

A shadow falls over his small body. He looks up. It's Heidi.

"Please, leave me alone," he mumbles.

"Are you all right?"

"Please. I'd really like to just be alone."

"That's not going to happen, Georgie." She sits beside him. "You can run all you want. But you can't run from yourself."

Georgie looks at her. "Don't you get it?"

"Everybody's got issues."

"You haven't the faintest clue."

"About the Tourette's?"

"About anything. About everything, yes. And the Tourette's. You only see what's on the outside." He twitches. "What you don't see, what you can't know, is what goes on inside." He starts crying again.

Heidi puts her arm around him.

"I'm scared. I don't know where to begin," he sobs.

Heidi wipes a tear from his eye.

"I'm everything I don't want to be," he pauses. "Shite, I don't know whether to laugh or cry. Maybe it's not even Tourette's, maybe it's me."

Heidi waits a moment and then opens her mouth to speak.

Georgie rushes on. "It all makes me so—"

Heidi grabs him by the shoulders. "Welcome to the world, Georgie! You're human! Finish with it!"

"No! Stop it! I can't!"

"Yes. It's true. You're human. You're one of us," she shakes him gently. "Deal with it. Accept it. All of it."

"Never! Nobody can!" he yells. He jumps up and runs to the edge of the bluff. He poises himself to leap from the edge.

He looks back. Heidi hasn't moved.

"Aren't you gonna stop me?"

"Let me know how it goes," she says coldly.

He stares, disbelieving.

"Go ahead, if that's what you want," she gestures for him to continue.

Georgie hesitates, teetering on the edge of the bluff.

"I'm tired of feeling sorry for you, Georgie. I'm tired of hearing you feeling sorry for yourself."

He rounds on her. "I don't feel sorry for myself. I hate myself!"

"Well, okay, then. Whatever you want to call it."

"Haven't you been listening to me? I can't take it anymore!"

"Don't hide your problem," she commands him. "Flaunt it. Laugh at it! You can't be beaten by something you laugh at."

"You don't underst—"

"I do understand," she insists, her eyes blazing. "That's what you can't accept."

"Yes, I can. I welcome it."

"Do you?"

Georgie looks out longingly over the sea.

"If I tell you that I do understand, and you believe it, then what happens to all these lies you've been telling yourself, all these years?" Heidi insists. He turns again, takes a step toward her.

"What lies?"

"How no one will ever understand you. Accept you." She pauses. "Love you," she continues quietly. "What happens then, Georgie?"

He has nothing to say.

Heidi points to the tree where Georgie has carved the word "Rebel."

"A significant life leaves its mark," she says. "What happens when you start living that significant life, Georgie? When you start admitting that people do understand? What happens then?"

Georgie watches her, his chest heaving with strain, with tears of frustration and clenched teeth. Every nerve in his body misfires.

Heidi walks away.

When Heidi begins class that afternoon, several students, including Claudia, have their heads down.

Heidi goes to the blackboard, and writes:

Friedrich Nietzsche (1844–1900)

She turns back to the class.

"Who can tell me a little about Nietzsche? What was his contribution to philosophy?"

Hendricks snorts. "He said 'God is dead'."

Claudia looks up, shocked at his initiative.

Hendricks shrugs. "Is that what you mean?"

"Y-yes," she stammers. "And what are the implications of Nietzsche's statement?"

Pause. Finally, Claudia raises her hand.

"Yes, Claudia."

"How can God be dead if He's eternal?" Claudia asks.

Georgie raises his hand.

Heidi points at him. "Georgie?"

"That's the point. Nietzsche wasn't arguing God had died, exactly, he was arguing that God never existed in the first place."

"Then what about Heaven?" Claudia asks.

A couple of students laugh.

"There is none," Georgie says lightly.

"There is so!" Claudia frowns.

Heidi interrupted. "What Georgie's getting at, Claudia, is what Nietzsche argued."

"That there's no Heaven?"

"Yes," Heidi nods.

"But what about all the people already up there?" Claudia insists.

Most of the students laugh, some uncomfortably.

Dear Diary:

I keep telling myself to always be myself, because the people that matter don't mind, and the people that mind don't matter. So, there it is!

Peacemaking

That night, Georgie sits in his room, writing.

My parents did their best trying to raise a kid like me. I'm a weirdo. A freak. I'm a real challenge. So I can't blame them if they didn't always succeed. If things didn't always work out right . . .

There's a knock on the door. Georgie opens it.

Claudia stands in the hall.

He stares silently at her.

"Can I come in?" Claudia says, shifting uneasily. "Please."

Georgie opens the door wider. She enters the room and notices he's been working at the computer.

"Oh, you're busy. I'm sorry," she says. She turns to leave; Georgie tugs her back.

"No, it's fine. Come here."

"You're writing?" She peers at the monitor. "What is it?"

"My memoirs, sort of," Georgie shrugs. "Jibber-jabber. Trying to sort things out in writing. For the Winterbourne."

"That's great."

"I'm tying it into what Heidi told us about bad faith. Remember?"

Claudia glances down at her shoes. "About lying to ourselves?" she asks quietly.

Georgie nods. "Yeah. Heidi thinks I could win."

"That's great," Claudia says sadly.

"It would pay for college, you know. All four years."

"I know."

He stares at her. "It's my dream."

"That and becoming a rich, famous writer," Claudia teases. She stands on tiptoe, kisses him, and heads towards the door.

"Wait! What's up? What do you want?"

"Nothing important. It was my dad's birthday today, I wanted to tell you."

Georgie grins. "Halfway to hell," he says.

Claudia smiles back. "You remembered."

Georgie nods.

"That was it, though. To tell you about my dad. To say hello, goodbye. Nothing important." She blows him a kiss. "Bye, Georgie."

Claudia closes the door quietly behind her. Georgie turns to his writing, smiling slightly still.

Georgie continues to work at the computer late into the evening. At one point, he stops and looks around as if he hears something distant, water crashing against rocks, he frowns. Then he returns to writing.

Dear Diary:

I don't think I am crazy. However, I do think I am creatively insane!

A twisted tree

The next morning, Georgie walks across campus to class. Students are gathered around the entrance to the academic building, talking excitedly.

Susan catches his eye and, for once, she actually looks happy to see him. She rushes up.

"Have you seen Claudia? She's gone," Susan pleads.

"Gone?" Georgie echoes.

"Gone," Susan repeats, irritated. "We can't find her."

"Can't find her?"

"What are you, deaf? I said Claudia's gone. As in, nobody knows where she is. Have you seen her?"

Georgie feels a faint dawn of understanding. He shudders.

"Last night I did."

"What time?" Susan presses.

"Eight? Nine? I don't remember."

Susan rolls her eyes in frustration and walks on. "Shite, what kind of help is that?" she mutters.

Georgie thinks. Then he turns to Susan, who's hurrying away from him. "Did anyone check the bluff?" he calls.

Susan keeps walking. She doesn't appear to hear him.

Georgie turns around and strides quickly to the woods. He hurries up the path, glancing all around for Claudia, desperately hoping to find her. When he reaches the bluff, it's completely deserted.

"Claudia!" he yells. All he hears is his own echo.

He searches every inch of the bluff, calling. On the ground at his feet, he finds the freak coin and starts to get frantic.

"Claudia?" His voice squeaks. He looks to the edge of the bluff, sees the waves rolling out to sea.

Finally, he makes himself go to the edge of the bluff and forces himself to look down.

He sees . . .

. . . Nothing.

Georgie sinks to the ground, relieved, laughing at himself for worrying, sighing with relief.

He stretches out flat on his back and cradles his hands under his head, still laughing.

That's when he sees:

Claudia.

Her crooked, bent body hangs in the bough of the tree, caught in broken branches.

Georgie screams.

Dear Diary:

Regarding some inspiring life notes and goals to myself while I'm in the zone again today. Boom. Take chances. Tell the truth. Say no. Get to know a random stranger. Tell someone I love him or her. Sing at the top of my lungs. Cry. Apologize. Tell someone what I really think. Marry the wrong person. Get divorced. Mess up. Make mistakes. Be grateful. Win. Lose. And regret nothing at fucking all!

How the shite hits the fan

Paramedics, rescue personnel, Dean Winterbourne, and Heidi stand on the bluff with Georgie.

Heidi has her arm around Georgie. His face is white and his body shakes—regularly—with shock.

Together they watch the paramedics and rescue personnel remove Claudia's body from the tree.

Georgie buries his head in Heidi's armpit.

Dean Winterbourne sees. He shakes his head at Heidi, but she only pulls Georgie closer.

Later that night, Georgie, agitated, sits in front of his computer. He writes furiously, and then deletes everything he's written.

He drums his fingers on the desktop, writes again in a flurry of fingers, and then leaps to his feet. In one fell swoop, he knocks the computer and monitor to the ground. Surprisingly, they land upright and intact.

Georgie throws himself on the bed. He balls his hands into fists and starts tugging at his hair.

"Fuck. Fuck you. Fuck me. Fuck Claudia. Fuck fuck fuck," he grits through clenched teeth.

He gets to his feet, pulls on a sweatshirt, and storms out of his room. He walks straight to The Pen, hands in his pockets and face in the shadows.

When he enters, Georgie stops first at the cigarette machine. He buys a pack and then sits down at the bar.

Ozer is already there, sitting in the back. He notices Georgie arrive, watches his every motion.

The bartender, a glass of bourbon in his hand, walks over to Georgie and sets the glass down in front of him.

"Good to see you, my man," he says cheerfully.

Georgie nods, not making eye contact. The bartender wanders off as Georgie raises the glass to his lips.

A very drunk Ozer approaches, wraps his arm around Georgie's shoulder, and starts to cry.

"Shite, Twitch, I can't fuckin' believe it," he moans. "What a waste. What a fuckin' goddamn waste."

Georgie says nothing. The glass is poised at his lips; the

unopened pack of cigarettes sits on the bar.

"I loved her. I fuckin' loved that chick."

"Her name was Claudia," Georgie says evenly.

"I know, man. I loved her."

Georgie puts his drink down.

"You didn't love her. I did. You didn't even like her," Georgie accuses. "You cheated on her with Susan. I heard you, Ozer. That day in the library, I heard you."

Ozer mutters incoherently to himself. Georgie pushes his drink away, gets off the stool, and heads towards the door.

Ozer's voice stops him. "Georgie."

Georgie turns.

"For what it's worth, man, I'm sorry. For Claudia. For your journal, your room. For fuckin' all of it."

Georgie leaves.

When Georgie returns to his dorm room, Heidi is waiting for him in the hall. His door isn't completely closed.

Heidi smiles sadly at him.

Georgie walks past her without speaking and enters his room.

Heidi follows.

Georgie looks around the room and then flops to his bed, pulling out the pack of cigarettes.

"Can I come in?" Heidi asks.

Georgie's face is stone. "You already are."

She takes another step forward, and then stops.

"I came to see how you're doing."

Georgie shrugs.

"But you weren't here, so I waited. How are you doing, Georgie?"

Georgie opens the pack of cigarettes, pulls one out.

"You want to talk about it?"

"I'm th-th-through t-talking."

He pats his pockets and looks on the night table, searching for a match. He gets off the bed, pulls open his desk drawers, and starts to dump everything on the floor.

Heidi reaches into her own pocket and tosses him a lighter.

Georgie looks surprised.

"Will that make you feel better—undoing everything you've already done?"

Georgie lights the cigarette, but he doesn't inhale.

"I went to The Pen," he says at last.

Heidi waits.

"But I didn't drink." He inhales and coughs slightly. "So I'm not undoing everything."

"Just some things?"

Georgie holds the lit cigarette still in his hand.

"How about the Winterbourne?" She indicates the computer and monitor on the floor. "Are you undoing that?"

Georgie shrugs. He says nothing.

"I wish there were something I could say, Georgie, that would make all of this somehow better. But there's nothing. I can't even tell you that you'll get over it, because you won't. I never got over my sister's death. But you go on, Georgie. That's the thing. You keep on living, and you can't afford to lose everything you've worked so hard for."

"I don't want to go on." Georgie's face scrunches up painfully, like a child's.

"I understand that."

"I loved her," he sobs.

"I know."

Georgie cries unabashedly before his teacher.

"I really did. She was the first girl I ever knew who didn't fuckin' judge me, who didn't keep looking at me like I was some sort of freak. She just let me be . . . me! You know?"

"I know."

"And now she's just . . . she's gone."

Georgie can't speak now for the sobs that have overtaken him. Heidi goes to him and wraps her arms around his shoulders. She takes the cigarette from his hand and puts it out on the desk.

When Georgie's tears finally still, he stands. Georgie picks up the computer and monitor and sets them on the desk.

"Every time I sit down to write, I freeze," he explains. "I look at the screen, and all I can see is her. All I see is Claudia. No matter what I do, I can't get her out of my head. It's so bad, I'm thinking of leaving."

"Leaving Wakefield?"

Georgie nods. "The reason I came here was so I could write and maybe win the Winterbourne and go to college. Now I don't even know if I want to go to college. I mean, a lot of writers don't even go to college."

"True, but a lot of writers do go to college. You feel like it's your fault? That you should have somehow known?"

Georgie nods.

"It's not, and you couldn't have," Heidi says.

Georgie smiles, but cautiously. He's not reassured.

"She wasn't well, Georgie."

"But she trusted me. I should've seen it coming. I should've stopped her."

"You couldn't have." Heidi pauses. "Did you know she left you a letter?"

Georgie looks at her blankly.

Heidi rummages through her purse and brings out an envelope. "They found it on her body. I told her mother that I knew you and that I'd give it to you."

She hands the envelope to Georgie, who opens it, pulls out a single piece of paper, and starts to read:

Georgie, if you're reading this, then I did it. I finally did it, finally found the courage—

Georgie looks at Heidi.

"The courage?"

Heidi nods.

—The courage to stop living the charade, stop pretending to be what I'm not. Happy. Georgie, I've been trying to get myself out of here since I was 12. Ever since my dad died. So be happy for me, okay? I'll see you. Later. On the Other Side. And remember, "Dying is an art . . . I do it exceptionally well."

Georgie glances again at Heidi.

"She quoted Plath?"

Heidi nods.

"Why?"

"She wasn't well, Georgie."

"But quoting Plath? Like she was writing a term paper or something?"

"You couldn't have done anything. She needed help, Georgie, more help than you could've given her."

Georgie gets to his feet. He slides the paper back to Heidi.

"You don't want this?" Heidi asks.

"I can't remember her that way."

Heidi nods, and then leaves.

Georgie turns back to his laptop. Soon, the shouts and laughter of students below his window drift up to his room. He doesn't notice. He types steadily, without deleting a thing. At 10 pm he goes to bed, sleeps for exactly 8 hours, and then wakes up in the morning and immediately begins typing once more.

Dear Diary:

Sadly enough, the most painful goodbyes are the ones that are left unsaid and never explained.

The Other Ending

And then there comes a bright, spring day, when all the parents, students, and faculty mill about campus, waiting for the final ceremony.

Banners hang from trees:

Congratulations! Best Wishes!

After everyone is seated, Dean Winterbourne stands at the podium.

"The Winterbourne Memorial Scholarship is one of the most prestigious awards Wakefield Academy has to bestow," he begins. "Previous recipients include students who have achieved greatness in politics, literature, and film. And this year's recipient, I am sure, will distinguish himself in whatever field he chooses to pursue. He has displayed brilliance through adversity, and triumphed over obstacles that few of us can imagine.

"And so, without further ado, I give you this year's winner of the Winterbourne Memorial Scholarship—George Gust."

Applause.

Georgie hops, skips, and jumps up to the stage. He takes his award and mumbles something into Dean Winterbourne's ear. The dean nods his assent, and Georgie takes his place at the podium.

"This has been a year unlike any other for me," Georgie says nervously. "It's been a very good year. This year I learned as much from life as I did from class, and I'm proud to accept this scholarship. However, without the presence of Claudia Nesbitt in my life—"

He pauses as murmurs from the audience interrupt him.

"I don't think I'd be standing up here today to accept this award if it wasn't for her. So I just want to say, Thank you, Claudia. Thank you for teaching me about life, about writing, and about myself."

He holds the placard above his head.

"This is for you, Claudia."

Then he grimaces intentionally.

"And, this, too."

He wraps his arm over his head and pulls his ear. The audience responds with appreciative laughter.

"And this."

He tics again. The audience claps.

"And this."

Georgie hop, hop, hop, skip, skips across stage. The audience explodes in thunderous applause.

Later, outside, students, parents, and faculty members mill about, chatting, taking pictures, and sipping punch from paper cups. Georgie stands near the water fountain, apart from everyone, clutching his diploma.

Pops and Rose approach and wrap their arms around Georgie.

He hugs them.

"That was quite an acceptance speech," Pops says.

"I was so proud," Rose cried. She hesitates a moment. "We were so proud."

Georgie's parents beam. They turn around to pour themselves a glass of punch, and pour one for Georgie, too.

Across the commons, Ozer looks on with a half-smile.

Georgie notices and lifts his hand in a half-wave.

Heidi approaches him slowly across the lawn. "Georgie?"

He looks up.

"Congratulations." She shakes his hand warmly.

Georgie smiles. "Thanks. What about you? Are you coming back next year?"

Heidi shakes her head. "No," she says.

"They let you go?"

Heidi smiles. "Let's call it a mutually agreed upon parting of ways."

"They fired you?"

Heidi pats Georgie's arm. "No, Georgie, they didn't fire me. Really, it was time for me to go."

"That's so unfair," Georgie scowls. "You're such a good teacher." He pauses. "A wonderful teacher."

Heidi squeezes his shoulder.

Pops and Rose offer Georgie his punch and put their arms around him again as Heidi smiles, her eyes glistening with tears.

Georgie hugs his parents, watching Heidi all the while.

Heidi smiles more brightly, and then cocks her head quizzically.

"Heidi, I'd like to introduce my mom and dad," Georgie says politely.

Dear Diary:

The opposite of life, love, faith, hope, and art is plain and simple: indifference. Long live my fucking art. I am not indifferent when it comes to my art!

BOOK THREE

Part I: Dr C, Meet Benjamin J Schreiber

Unfinished Intro—Buffered Off a Thought

"Ben, what are your goals in therapy?" Dr C asks.

I should have known she would ask me that. I should have guessed. It's always the first question. It's the first session, but I really can't answer her yet. (Why not? She would probably ask the next thing, and I would have to say, "Because, because".)

Because I've got a big fat gut full of hatred (Yeah, I know, I know), and all those New Age self-help audio books I've downloaded to help me cope really aren't doing shite. I guess I thought (or Dr C thought, maybe. Somebody thought.) I might be able to grab onto one of those brand-new self-help ideas and believe that we are all secretly psychically interconnected; we have an innate power of intention that creates our reality, or some such shite, and that just thinking those noble bullshite New Age thoughts would help me, heal me, make me a better, or at least give me a decent reality to start with. Better than this whole sick psych-ward bullshite I'm stuck with. This whole schizoaffective, neurotic, borderline psychotic whatever. (You call that reality?)

But the more I complain (I'm a hypocrite, I know . . . I hate complainers), and the more I bitch and moan, the more the "Divine Field" (or whatever it's called) just bounces that sick shite right back at me. Besides that, it adds anxiety, fear, and cramps—every symptom in the book. As if I didn't have enough shite to deal with, already. (But why me, Dr C? That's what I want to know.)

Dear Diary:

Today, I value myself for separating ability from inability with my unspeakable daily hallucinations, voices, paranoia, and trauma that schizophrenia presents. See? My heart does fucking speak.

Sling-backs—Out of My Deepest of Pockets

The first time I met Dr C, I just knew I was going to like her. She was wearing a pair of sling-back, open-toed, fuck-me sandals, even though she knew (she had to have known, she just had to) that I'm a foot fetishist. (Big Secret #1. So what else is news?) Plus, she had on a clingy, low-cut shirt that showed off the top of her breasts, and she kept leaning forward provocatively as she told me she was going to help me learn to love myself.

Yeah, "love myself." That's what she said. She was going to make me love myself. So, I said I didn't think it was possible to love myself (You going love me, too, Dr C? That's what I want to know). But I said if she wanted me to, what the hell, I'd give it a try. So she said yeah, she wanted. (Wanted what?) Do you think I believed her? What else could she say—that she didn't even want me to try? No psychiatrist is ever going to say that. And believe me, I know those psychos. Psychiatrists, I mean. I've been seeing them, off and on (okay, mostly on) ever since I was 12 years old. That was the year my mother decided I had ADD (The Number One Psychiatric Disorder of Choice for That Fucking Year) and she marched me off to see Dr Nora Epstein, who promptly told mother that ADD was just a fantasy disorder, and nobody really had it, not even me.

As it turned out, what I really had (so they say) was Tourette's (Big Secret #2), which was a real thrill for mother. I was the one and only kid in the county, or maybe just in the town of wherever, or at least in my middle school, anyway, to have actually been diagnosed with Tourette's, right up front. And so mother paraded me in front of her friends (and my friends, too) like some big freak show. "Show them, Benjy, baby. Show them how you twitch," she would say. Yeah, that's my mother. (You've got to love her, don't you? Because she's your mother?)

So. Dr C said she would help me love myself, and I told her I would try—to love myself, I mean. The emphasis here is on the word "try," because there are at least two real problems with Dr C teaching me to love myself. The first problem is: I can't remember ever even liking myself, even before the Tourette's. And second: I think Dr C really doesn't like me, no matter what she says. She secretly fears and dislikes me. (So what else is new?) I can tell, say, from the curl of her lip when I walk in to her office.

I might be crazy, like they say, but still, I've got an IQ over 140, and I know delusion when I see it. And I'll tell you, Dr C was just deluding herself thinking she'd ever be able to help me love, or even like, myself. Still, I'm likeable enough. Really, I'm a really nice guy, so I don't confront her. I just say, "Sure, Dr C, why not?"

And then I walk out. I go back downstairs to my limo and driver, and tell him I want to go home right away. Then, I sit there in front of the computer, iTunes playing Chubb Rock and Coldplay on a continuous loop.

I try to write.

(But what?)

Not surprisingly, I can't. I can't write.

Dear Diary:

I seem to win or lose the greatest battles in my crazy fucked-up life all within the own little lunchbox of my mind.

Retirement?

My guess is writer's block is the worst place for a writer to be. Ever. For most writers—most other writers anyway. I don't know for sure. I don't know any other writers, and I don't read them and I don't read about them. I don't need to read to be a writer. That's just the way I am. I'm a rebellious, outlaw writer: Fuck the Norm, I say. But I've got writer's block. I've had it really bad for the last year and a half. In fact, I haven't written a damn thing in that whole time. (Yeah, that's writer's block.)

Sometimes, though, when I'm in love, I'll stop writing. I know it won't last forever, and I might as well love it while it lasts. But that's not writer's block—it's lover's lock. (So am I in love? Am I? You know what I say.)

"Yeah, right. I'm in love," I say. "With myself, maybe." And I scoff. "Me? In love? Yeah, baby."

(Parenthetical Pet Peeve) Writer's block.

I think of writer's block as a pleasant break from my whole bullshite psycho routine. Only this time it's almost a full-on retirement, or something. So anyway, I'm lying there, spread out lazily on my lopsided bed, and Heidi (Big Secret #3), Heidi whispers that it's just my discontent, my malaise, my perplexity. And I listen, even if I can't quite make out what she's saying, so I know Heidi's there. And I know Georgie's out there, somewhere, too. Where the hell is he, though? Where's Georgie, baby?

I glance down at my Billy-Baloney nightlight. It's turned on, my kooky little nightlight, and it flickers when my eyes meet the little plug-in plastic lamp, like it knows something I don't. I've saved that little kiddie nightlight all these years. I don't know why; maybe because I don't like total darkness, and I don't like white light, either. I mean, I like colors—blue, red, pink—I think. But I can't think straight if the light is too bright. The see-through shades in my room are drawn; the small wooden door won't stop creaking.

And Georgie, what about Georgie? Where's Georgie?

Georgie, Georgie Gust, my alter ego. Where are you, Georgie-boy?

"The Great Perfectionist" meets "The Great Imperfection." Mr Casanova and Mr Me.

I'm calling you, Georgie-boy. I need you, Georgie. Georgie Gust. Come to me, baby.

Dear Diary:

I just learned that in Chinese, the word 'crisis' contains two characters. One represents danger and the other represents opportunity. I suppose crisis is the same thing as opportunity.

Georgie Writes Back

God, I think. I've been sending out my work for so damn long, I just can't stand it anymore. And what do I get? Rejection, rejection, and nothing but (and I can't take rejection, either)—still, I'm okay with that. I don't even know what I'm doing here, anyway. But maybe Georgie knows.

Georgie tells me to just hang in there.

Just go to sleep, now, Ben, Georgie says soothingly. In the long run, Ben, he says, you'll be fine.

That's easy for him to say. He's just a figment of my imagination, a literary device, or a delusion (who knows? I know I don't). Dr C won't even tell me who Georgie really is. And so I'm stuck here with this in-between shite, in-between diseases, in-between personalities, on the scary borders of some multiple personality disorder, or who knows? (But whatever it is, I know, I got it.)

Dear Diary:

I took some time off, not much though, and I came to realize that so many people will just forget what I said and all that I've fucking done, but they will never forget how I made them feel. That hits me hard, come to think of it. Anyway back to this book I'm cooking.

Dr C Meets Ben (A Written Account from Dr C)

I've got to say, I've never had a client like Ben Schreiber. Or should I say Benjamin J Schreiber, as he prefers to be called (he's still just Ben to me.)

The first time I met him, he was late; dressed in Armani jeans, a USC sweatshirt, Hugo Boss loafers (no socks), and an oversized blue stovepipe hat with an orange pom-pom on top. What a kooky get-up! (I can't help it. That's what I thought. What would you think if it were you?)

Okay, okay. So I reacted negatively. I admit it. Clients who show up late for their first appointment give me a bad first impression (and first impressions count!) So I prepare myself for the worst. I figure they won't be cooperative in treatment, they won't take their meds, and they won't discuss their issues. They just won't.

And besides all that, I like punctuality. Rich clients who show up late, who have limo drivers and trust funds, and see me only because they have fathers who pay to keep them out of jail, those creeps set my teeth on edge. I admit it; I'm honest. Like it or not, first impressions matter, even in therapy. Especially in therapy. And when Ben didn't even shoot for a favorable first impression, well, he just set me up to not like him. (Of course, a psychiatrist doesn't necessarily need to like her clients but it doesn't hurt. It might just even help, you know? Just maybe.)

First impressions count, and Ben made a bad impression. Being late was bad enough. But the way he entered—hopping into my office on one foot and then the other, like he was some kind of overgrown, kooky child without a care in the world—drove me crazy. (I admit it.) It's not often that a client drives his psychiatrist crazy. But Ben did that first day. Later, after I'd read his file, I felt ashamed, and maybe a little bit negligent, because Ben has Tourette's, you know. The hopping is involuntary, like the sniffing and brow-raising, and all the other twitches and tics—and dances.

And I'm also ashamed to admit that I didn't pick up on the symptoms. Ben was referred to me by the police department, and the police department hadn't sent over all the paperwork. So, that's my excuse—but still, I should be able to make an unbiased diagnosis without papers or, at the least, I should have refused to see him until the papers came through. Seeing the files might have made a difference. It still might not have been love at first sight, but at least I might have liked him better. So I confess, I admit—I let my bias against the rich and privileged get the better of me, and it showed. And I guess Ben picked up on it, too. (Yes, of course he did, I know he did.)

So Ben just sat on the couch with his legs crossed, the stovepipe hat in his lap, and smiled. He told me about how he tried to hold up the Pasadena City Bank with a cell phone. (Which is why he's in therapy. This time, anyway. It was either therapy or prison.) And then he stopped. He uncrossed his legs and then leaned forward, putting his elbows on his knees, and stared right into my face. He seemed earnest and engaged, maybe even slightly shy, and then he said: "You don't like me much, do you?"

My first instinct was to lie, to say something like: "Of course I like you, Ben." Instead, I tried to respond professionally. I smiled and said, "It's not my job either to like or dislike you, Ben. My job is to help you." And he nodded like he understood, although I couldn't tell, really, what was going on in his mind.

"It would probably be easier," he said, "if you liked me. Don't you think?"

I blushed, revealing my embarrassment. It was like Ben could read my thoughts, and I can't say that I liked it, being read like a book by some kook.

"It's okay if you don't—like me, I mean. If I were you, I wouldn't like me. Hell, sometimes I don't even like me."

By then, I had managed to get my distance and my professionalism back. I leaned forward and smiled (reassuringly, I think). And I said, "That's exactly what I am going to do, Ben. I'm going to help you love yourself." And he smiled this sad, slow smile.

Finally he looped his hands behind his neck and said, "Loving myself isn't something I know how to do. But if you want, I'll try."

So, of course, I said I wanted; he said okay.

Then he walked out.

Dear Diary:

I visited the cemetery down the street about an hour ago with some paper and a pen. I just sat there. Then I did it, I wrote down everything I don't like about myself. I ripped it up. And when I returned I burnt it. Felt fucking good, watching the burn and the blaze turn to ash. Ah.

Cutting Class

At our second session, Dr C asks me to tell her what I remember about my old school days. (What's she really after? Whatever it is, I don't want to tell her. I got this creepy feeling that Dr C's really after me.) Instead, I tell her about Georgie. (Georgie will tell her about me.)

I cut through all the crap that's happened between now and then, and I go back to my past, in search of my past, where I find Georgie hiding out. My dreams take me back to Georgie's past, too. They take me back to school. Unlike Georgie, I went to public school, even though I'm rich. Georgie went to private school. Georgie made some incredible friends there. One of them died. (And who's that, now, huh? Don't you remember, Benjy? Don't you want to remember?) One of them is dead—unlike me.

"Who's that, Ben?" Dr C wants to know. "Who's dead? Who died?" She waits, a pregnant pause. "Was it someone special? Someone very important to you?"

I ignore her, like I ignore all her bullshite questions. I just lie there on the couch, thinking about Georgie; drifting, dreaming, and free-associating about Georgie, and about her—Georgie's girl. Claudia.

Where is it? Where am I? Who am I now? Sheltered in the Quad's ivy and brick walls is a small fishpond. Its surface reflects the moonshine like clear glass, dispersing its light through the whole white-light spectrum. Georgie Gust sits on his favorite wooden bench. He's still in boarding school, posh and preppy. I'll always remember him that way; he sits there with his back straight, with good, erect posture, so he can digest everything he takes in. But I'm more of the sloucher type, the slacker type. An idler. I'm rich and spoiled—and I'm lazy.

Perplexity is my perpetually confused condition—my perpetually entangled situation. This is the kid I remember, the Georgie who's 18 and introverted, nervous. His intense slouch. His high IQ. No one can see him, but I know he's got a black eye and he's been in a couple of fights. Fighting for me—fighting for my protection. I really don't deserve him—he's a luxury item.

(Parenthetical Pet Peeve) People who think that introversion is a "bad attitude."

Georgie wears large round horn-rimmed glasses (when they're not broken) and a designer tie, lavender or yellow, or maybe orange and raspberry-blue, loosely fitting around his neck (like a noose.)

We're nonchalant, casually indifferent, Georgie and me. We're of little importance to anyone but ourselves, to anybody but me, and maybe Dr C.

We make no effort. We take no turns. It's just Georgie and me. There's nothing we really have to do, anyway.

We make excuses. We're taking excuses apart and digesting them in parts. We're fragmenting reality.

Dear Diary:

Normal people simply and completely baffle me. What's with all the body language, social cues, pettiness, and looking people in the eyes when we speak from our mouths?

Flashing Forward to Yesterday

Where am I? Who am I now? My reflection in the bathroom mirror wears some awfully feminine blouse with a black bow tie and ruffled white sleeves. This is Georgie, this is me—this time he's in the mirror, malfunctioning.

The two of us picked up an amazingly useful skill, a talent. Since we're both in our heads, in our fucked-up, full-time fantasy life, we've tried doing some fun stuff. Cool stuff with our heads, with our minds. For example, levitation—but we failed, we couldn't do it. Time travel—yes, by just putting our thoughts there, in any time we wanted. We couldn't master remote viewing, necessarily, but we were able to resonate morphologically, ourselves—this means that Georgie and I have been able to put ourselves in another place—because all of this Life shite isn't real anyway. You know, the whole notion that none of us are born, none of us ever die. Everything is infinite and eternal and circular, or maybe evolutionary. Probably all of the above. So, instead of only being able to see, or view some other place—Georgie, without a second thought, is able to place himself anywhere. The Seraphim angels alter everything else so that our presence—wherever we might be—seems natural and logical to the rest of the world—sort of like a parallel universe. This is how we escape. But Georgie will only put himself in one of two places: Long Beach, California—after all that's where Claudia is. She's still alive and well, as far as Georgie's concerned. Then there's New Mexico, the vast plateau of serenity, sometimes, where he and I can get away from the rest of the uppity fake-tits, fake-ass, fake-minded people in Los Angeles County. I just follow Georgie there—wherever he goes. The only time he'll follow me is when I go back to school. We use our immaculate imaginations to get us there—this blast to the past, of course—this inner need to go back—has a lot to do with my incomplete childhood. When I go back—back, back, back—I will sometimes make up with the bullies who used to taunt me, beat me, Mom-&-Pops-style, way back when.

Oh, Long Beach, overpopulated with those god darn fart-fetish types.

(We just have to laugh at that kind of pornography, doc—they do that shite out in the Valley. They film that shite there. Usually $1,000 a shoot—I mean the pay to the porn stars, rather, porn actors and actresses—to hell if there are any stars in porn. Everybody knows there aren't.)

Georgie and I, we pull that kind of shite right at home. A fart in the face followed by a giggle and a waving of the hand, in order to disperse the putrid smell, and responding to such a poo-toot, verbally perhaps, quietly uttering to the farter, "That was a quiet one." The receiver is taking it in as he longs for that particular hard and agitating feeling of shame, the kind of which only a good stinky fart in the face has the means. The fart, and the shame, fills an important space, the space within us where it really hurt. We can find a sense of relief—on both ends—from this kind of behavior, you might say. A relief from the physical pain as it is replaced with olfactory sabotage and humiliation.

So, yes, Georgie and I are basically bi-bisexual, that is. Still, I often think of my mother, my father, and my poor little inner child who seems to have lost his childhood because of them.

"Mommy, stop tickling me. I mean it!" I'd yell—she wouldn't stop.

My father and his emotional abuse, not to mention the sexual and financial abuse of which, these days, I don't hide the fact that I WANT PITY. Long live the Living Colorful Rich, the self-made millionaires, billionaires, fucking thrillionaires. "Ben," they say, "You're the wealthiest 30-year-old in all of New Mexico. Buy yourself a nice little jet plane, why don't you. You have the money, you know—why don't you live a little, boy?" Until the time when I actually ask for it—he, being the strict trustee of my beautiful inheritance—close to $100,000,000, replies, "Oh, Benjy, we need to talk about this, you know."

The next week, I receive a shite, little, put-it-together-yourself, model airplane. I find it crushed inside the little compact PO box.

See why I can get so angry? They'd call it a lie—those rich parents of mine. When I confront them about this stuff, they, like all other abused and abusive parents, they threaten abandonment. And I just love it.

So, in place of my own internal parent who might otherwise take care of that inner child, now that I am 30, so that he may be able to grow up again, Georgie becomes that parent. A single father. Fuck the mother, motherfucker.

New Mexico is flat and hot and dry—symbolically cold It's the perfect place to just chill and smoke the Peace Pipe. The Pagans and

Nudist Communities do their thing. We do ours. I just follow him there. I just follow Georgie. His sense of direction is better than mine.

We're staying at the Sea Port Hotel in Long Beach, California. And Georgie's current situation, as petty as it may be, has me captivated. We're in the most pressing circumstances. Something here deeply concerns me, I don't know what. So we check out, again and again, from this cheap seaside hotel, and we walk back, again and again, to our place just down the shore a ways.

Maybe there's no more sex with that woman, Georgie thinks to himself. Have I just come to that realization? Then Georgie scoffs. He's always scoffing.

Georgie and I wander home, and we watch a Jerry Springer marathon until Bobby Banks calls. Georgie forgets he has any friends, but they call him anyway. And, for sure, Bobby wouldn't be calling me in the first place, unless . . .

Were on non-com—you know, having a communication breakdown. It's a falling out—as if we didn't already have enough static already to break up the friendship. Bobby took advantage of me, fucking con artist.

Georgie picks up the line and gives Bobby the Typical American Greeting: "Hello. How are you?" etc.

I can hear Bobby's boisterous blabber even when I'm not on the phone myself. It's that loud.

"Hey, you still fucking around with that chick next door? The Long Beach Diva. That chick. Claudia, right?" Bobby finally asks.

Georgie hasn't seen his best friend Bobby since he was in boarding school, coming up 20 years ago. What a shite 20 years in-between, might I say and say again. Bobby came out to visit him there, and they've kept in touch ever since. Georgie seems to think he cares. I seem to think he wants something. The only thing I want is Georgie's girl, though. The only thing I want is Claudia.

Through the night, Claudia sleeps patiently, soundly, under her teal-colored dream-catcher, sprawled across the bed. Her slim white arms and pale legs sprawl seductively as she makes a crooked cross. Her chin presses to her chest, she's resting peacefully. But she's no more peaceful than a dead white dove—she's the amateur sex diva, her big soft breasts attest. Her breasts are heavy, like the morning dew falling on the green grass lawn outside. The same lullabies she remembers as a little girl hum from the same clock radio she keeps on her antique night table—a hypnotizing Annie Lennox ballad wafts through the stifling bedroom air and almost gets caught on the slightly-drawn, white-silk veil over her California king. (Who am I now? Am I dreaming? Am I, somehow, in Claudia's dream?)

I like to think that she's gotten fat, like Georgie (like me.) Maybe her breasts have gotten heavier, and heavier, and heavier, and now they sag, the poor things.

Georgie used to be skinny, but that was before I started to binge on the new meds.

I'm looking to understand myself, through Georgie. (You see, Dr C?

I see, Ben. Please go on.)

So, how did he get there? I meditate, not medicate, on his sordid past.

I think back to when he was posh and preppy, back to when his past might have meant something more. Really, I think, it doesn't. It most definitely does not. It never has meant anything.

I can see him with his parents, my parents, and I feel empathy for him. How could I have wronged this poor little guy? He's my own soul, so to speak, my soul-within-a-soul. It's been a long, long road. There was less traffic in the beginning, but the traffic became heavier; the road became crowded, crooked and narrow. Somehow, we got lost along the way, Georgie and me.

Dear Diary:

I'm pretty sure "normal" people are equally baffled, but better at faking it.

Long Beach: The Hub of the Warp

At our third session, what's happening now? I wonder. Dr C's picking my brain. She's trying to get inside me—wants to know more about Georgie and me. Or maybe, maybe she wants to know more about Georgie's girl and me. Georgie's girl; what's her name? Claudia. Claudia Nesbitt. (Even the name makes me shiver, sometimes, and other times I get hot, just thinking about her. Thinking about me and Georgie and Georgie's girl, Claudia. Claudia Nesbitt.) Dr C asks me what I remember about Georgie's girl, what the name Claudia Nesbitt means to me. I'm not following her. This is between Georgie and me—it's none of her business.

Where am I now? When I wake up, it's Wakefield again (isn't it?) But who, what, when am I? All I know is that time flies and the years go warping by while Georgie sleeps. He is wrapped in time's embrace. When Georgie's asleep, all he can think of is sex and satin. But he dreams about escaping, like a wild animal in some crazy human zoo; but when all the cages break open the screaming, hungry beasts stampede him like vicious predators, kicking up dirt with their hooves and claws.

He's splayed out underneath the sky, while a thousand daggers and swords fly overhead. In this hellish wonderland of waking dreams (nightmares), the circus angels sing of dirty money, poverty, court hearings, testifying monks. Never-ending canals of blood, excrement, delusion, and terror fill up my nightmare dreamscape. And I lay there with Georgie, with me, living out my fears, my mistrust, my fucking brain tumors, and who knows what else.

Dear Diary:

I just came back from my best therapy session ever. Primeval latent core emotions volcano to the surface with centeredness, tears and elation made visible via the hour-long therapy session: Priceless. I suppose I could write more about it, but then back to my book. . . . . My therapist encouraged me to talk about my thoughts and feelings and what's troubling me. I was not worried. It was not hard to open up about my feelings. I have trusted my cognitive behavioral therapist for years now. We talk about daily life, challenging traumatic issues, and music, all boiling down to mindfulness and problem-solving, often working simultaneously. My CBT therapist often helps me gain more confidence and comfort in general. And some days we reach a point where we really dig deep, and through expression of fears and inherent emotional conditioning, for example, when asked, "How would I have preferred, realistically for [such-and-such] to have happened instead?" Ah. I just had such a breakthrough, which seems to only have room to broaden its scope and range in the newly discovered primeval traumatic root. It was finally brought to the surface, after so many years. My therapist and I can only Q&A more and use today's breakthrough to enhance my quality of life in so many more areas. It was like I was an infant being parented by his adult self, being my own parent, letting the little boy in me know that this is what this means, that is what that means, and he is loved. He has me—he has and is loved by me. My therapist was only bearing witness, and prompting, encouraging and allowing me to feel safe as the little child in me learned, for example, that the raising of a hand does not mean I love you. In fact, the raising of the hand with a whack is wrong and any child will only get better and better. You always have me. Cool shite. Oh yeah!

Housekeepers Are a Blessing

Even the pack of people unloading a room from an SUV just outside his window fails to startle Georgie awake. His alarm has been snoozed, again. Georgie's half awake, half asleep, drifting somewhere between dreams and nightmares. He tries to rise, falls back, falls asleep again, and dreams.

(Parenthetical Pet Peeve) When people call me on the phone in the middle of the night, only to ask, "Are you still in bed?"

He finally wakes with white-hot sunlight in his face. He's sweating hard. He grabs his hard on. But no—he couldn't cum. Or maybe he could.

He could. He really could. He just knows he can do it. Maybe if he wasn't such a goddamn nice guy. It's his perennial problem. It's his peculiar condition, his pet pathology. He's too goddamn nice for his own good. People take advantage of him.

(Who takes advantage of you, Ben?)

Dr C wants to know. She doesn't know. She doesn't know me. It's Georgie, Georgie's girl; she's Claudia. Claudia Nesbitt. Claudia, who told him she loved him and then started fucking Sara and Sara's husband, Greg, sometimes at the same time. Who'd call Georgie afterward, or during the fucking, and tell him it was his cock she was riding, his dick filling her pussy. And she was sorry, but she just couldn't be with him, like that, ever again. Not anymore. Not like that. Not when his peculiar conditions, his pet pathologies, were so much worse than her own. Like he was fucking contagious or something.

Maybe Claudia's right. His own brand of craziness, his own peculiarities (or a better word than pathology, which reminds him of a forensic pathologist, televised), maybe really are worse than anybody else's, everybody else's.

He doesn't feel crazy, but then, maybe nobody crazy ever does. Who knows? You would have to be crazy to know, now, wouldn't you? But if you were crazy, you wouldn't know. Especially if you didn't know who you were, where you were, who's who. Who's he, anyway? I'm me! I'm him! I'm Georgie!

Finally, Georgie swings his legs out of bed and pulls on his boxers. It's his first big day on Wakefield campus, and he really must get up and get cracking, now, mustn't he? Why does he keep having these creepy little sex fantasies? Half-awake wet dreams? Why does he keep thinking about Claudia Nesbitt? It seems like she was, and is, a real person—a real human being, like Miss Heidi Berillo. But only Georgie can see how easily Claudia bruises, can see the little black-and-blue marks on her arms and ankles that confirm her reality. Georgie collects those details. He keeps her real in his mind. He remembers the scar on her anklebone, the left one, and he remembers what she told him, in bed, sitting up, her legs spread wide, letting him see all the way up her pussy.

Georgie remembers. (Doesn't he? I know I do.) Georgie remembers how impossible (fucking impossible!) it was to take his eyes off her pussy; her clipped pubic hair, the folds, the recesses. The smell. He loved that smell, loved burying his nose in her pussy, breathing her smell. No douche—no spray. Pure Claudia. Or maybe not so pure.

Georgie doesn't remember Claudia pure, or clean. He remembers the smell of her, how horny, how wet she'd get before her period, how milky, how sticky she'd be, how always her pubes would tangle, clump together, before her period, and she'd always want him to go down on her.

(Parenthetical Pet Peeve) That "time of the month."

"Clean me off," she'd say, and Georgie would.

Only before her period. Never after. Never during. Just before. She drove him crazy. (Didn't she? Or did she really, Dr C? Is Georgie crazy, or is it really just me? Georgie, Claudia, me.)

Claudia always sat with her legs spread, letting Georgie look—knew he was looking—while she told him stories. Stories about her scars. About her life. About her ankle. Claudia lifted her leg high above her head, showing Georgie her pussy, her asshole, and then she told him about her father—how abusive he was. What a drunk he was. How he threw his buck knife at her.

"Because my father is a hunter," she said, "and needs a buck knife to skin rabbits." She said if Georgie ever wanted to buy a knife, ever needed a knife, she'd go with him, because she knew all about knives. "On account of my father," she said.

Georgie wishes that Claudia said "Because of my father." He doesn't like the sloppiness of, "on account of." (She said. He said.)

But he was in love with her then, and so, of course, he didn't correct her. Besides, he remembers (she remembers) the story of the knife her father threw, and how she needed 13 stitches to close the wound.

"Can you believe it? Thirteen stitches on that little tiny bone?" she said. And, no, Georgie didn't believe it, still doesn't believe it. But Georgie was in love, and maybe still is, and it seems rude to say he thinks she's lying. To say, "Thirteen stitches are what you get for big cuts, Claudia. Not for little bitty nicks on the ankle." So he just kept his big mouth shut and let her lie. Let's her lie.

"And who's lying now, Ben?" Dr C wants to know. He ignores that, too. Georgie does. He's just thinking about Claudia again. And how much he wants her, how much he loves her, wants to fuck her, yet, he wants to love her.

And now he hates her. He fucking hates her.

He remembers her scar, her legs, and her taste (in love with Claudia. Claudia Nesbitt.) He hates her, hates her, hopes she dies, hopes he can stop being such a nice guy, a good guy. He hopes he gets the balls to kill her, drown her, electrocute her, and cut her. Something. Anything. To make her die. For himself.

"Who hates her? Who wants her?" Dr C asks. "And who died? Try to remember. Is it you? Are you awake in there now, Ben? Ben? Do you hear me, Ben?"

A knock on the door. It's a student from the next room over, checking on him, making sure he's okay. Has he been talking to himself? Maybe. Probably. His Tourette's, his bipolar, his schizoaffective disorder make it normal for him to. Georgie collects symptoms and diagnoses the way some people collect stamps, or coins, or butterflies. He has books explaining every condition he's ever had—he understands his conditions better than he does himself (or is there any difference?) Now he worries that he's talking to himself again. Really, Georgie doesn't wonder if he's going crazy—he wonders just how crazy he has become. ("How crazy is crazy, anyway? How do you know? Can you tell me, Dr C? Just how crazy is crazy, anyway? That's what I want to know.")

Dear Diary:

I had been writing another short chapter of my book but had a shite day otherwise. So I start today without the broken pieces of yesterday. Every morning I wake up is the first day of my life. I know that's deep. But hey, it has to be. And again, back to the book. Hell, I've got to give myself a breath sometimes, ah.

Restaurant Love

(Where am I? Who am I now?) I sleep. Still. Snoring and gasping in turns. Holding my breath—choking in my fucking sleep. Ben's choking, coughing up little pieces of food. The smell of wine wafts throughout his dream sensations—expensive wine, on the house. He's sleeping.

My dream takes place in the past. ("But who's past? What past?" Why don't you tell me, Dr C?)

Claudia stands outside and watches a well-dressed, elderly couple enter the Fusion Restaurant. Violin music wafts into the night air as the outside door opens, then fades, as the couple disappears inside and the door swings shut. Claudia pauses at the threshold; she enters, in step to the music.

She's shown to a seat at a table in the main dining area. She has a good view of the string quartet but she's disappointed. As she waits for the waiter, the string quartet packs up their sheet music and instruments ready to head home. Maybe she ought to leave, too. *No*, she thinks apathetically. *I need to eat something.*

A few minutes pass. Finally her waiter arrives with a bottle of the house wine. He bows slightly and offers her a glass.

She accepts the wine bottle.

"It sure is dead in here, isn't it?" she says, expressionless.

The waiter acknowledges her comment with a nod. "It might pick up later, but I doubt it."

As he finishes pouring the glass, he looks straight into Claudia's eyes and gives her a weird, college guy smirk—a grin that smacks of awkward, frustrated desire. She pretends not to see. He's dissatisfied, of course, but he shows no sign.

"I'll be back for your food order, in a minute," he says.

(I return to her, as her waiter. I come back to her in this fantasy. I'm him and he's me.)

"Do I know you from somewhere?" she asks me, quizzically smiling.

(We must've met some other time. Sometime when I was Georgie.)

Claudia is moved by Georgie's quick, subtle charm. She can enjoy him, but she can't fall in love as fast as he does. Claudia acts less impulsively toward Georgie than he'd like. She already has her sexual needs taken care of. Georgie doesn't. (And neither do I, for that matter.)

Georgie will do anything for me as long as I'm a good citizen, free and clear of drugs and booze, so long as I don't give in to temptations of substance. As long as I act like Pops wants his only son to act. So I stick to the sugar stuff and the occasional whipped cream whip-it. I'm keeping myself perfect, pure and clean, for him— for Georgie.

Georgie obsesses on people, mostly. He loses himself in a fantasy world for as long as he's obsessed with them. However long that is and however interesting they are to him. Georgie thinks about things a little too much. But still, it's a beautiful process, isn't it?

What's Georgie really like? He makes careful decisions. He's only horny when he's tired. He sweats like a pig. He works hard at sex.

"Hold me," he says. "Just hold me."

"Why?" Claudia wants to know.

It's their first official date; they're in bed together.

"Because. I've never been held before," Georgie answers. "Not like that."

But what does she think? What's Claudia feel? Claudia feels sorry for Georgie. She thinks he's an unloved hermit, so pitifully deserving. She helps him realize he can relate with others, even if they're still in high school, in Special Ed. Claudia calls herself Snicker Doodle (SD). She dubs Georgie with the out-of-place nickname "Princess," or else calls him "Corners" (referring to the dimpled corners of his mouth), or generically, "Beautiful."

(She's just naming herself with all these nicknames, I think. Probably she hands out titles to everyone she dates. They're replacement placeholders. Throwaways. Like the men she gets involved with, the men she uses. Like me. Or maybe she just gives them to the people she really loves.)

She doesn't consider herself to be Georgie's, or my own, SOB— "Subject of Bewilderment" (i.e., obsession, delusion, star model of lust and passion, bad habit.) Georgie loves her little antics and imperfections. She never says or thinks anything bad, and she doesn't seem to mind her own flaws. Life is so easy and so casual for her. ("She does, however, have a knack for fucking with people without them knowing anything about what she's doing. Doesn't she?"

"I don't know, Ben. You tell me."

"Don't fuck with me, Dr C."

"Who's fucking with you, Ben? Is it me? Georgie? Is it Claudia? Or is it really just you, Ben?"

"Okay, okay. I'll make a coerced confession. I'm going mad, I think. I don't know how to say what I want to say. The main point is that I love somebody in some strange way. Or I think I do. Call it love. Call it hatred, obsession, or madness, but I love someone. That's how I feel, as fucked up as I am. I love someone who can't love me."

"Who can't love you, Ben? Is it me? Or is it—"

"—me. And I have no greater need in the world, nothing. Just a certain requirement to remember all I am. I'm trapped within some eerie, itchy-bitchy spell, cast by somebody who can't really love me back. That somebody is me. Is that what you're looking for, Dr C?")

"Let's go and watch the sunset, Claudia."

"Yeah, sure," she says.

Leading in, leaning in, I'm hoping for a kiss. And when we get home, I smell my fingers, nervously, but I don't smell Claudia. I look in the mirror and whisper a soft hello. (To who? To whom? I wonder.) The church bells outside chime with Georgie's own song— the song he plays in his head. His psychosis starts to overcome him, the same way as last time, but different—different, but the same. This time.

(Okay, okay. I have a coughing tic, a coughing tic and a big dick. Big like a pickle. The coughing tic tickles and I like pickles. Georgie likes pickles. Claudia likes pickles.)

I wake up with the image of Georgie in my head. He's checking his mail. I've given Georgie his own PO box so he can get mail without me reading it first. Sometimes I'll send him gifts and then keep them for myself. Sometimes I pretend that we're the same person.

Georgie starts the morning with Claudia, but I stay in bed a while longer, sleeping and snoring, and thinking of her—of Claudia. We're pretty sick and tired, Georgie and I, of the same pathetic routine of morning. So Georgie decides not to shave or clip his nails.

It will all be okay, someday, sometime.

I wake up to check back on what's happened already. I'm in the kitchen making breakfast. I dump a cup of unfiltered water into a bowl of oatmeal and heat it up. I'm a microwave professional.

The washer and dryer are in the garage. Georgie finds a clean shirt in the dryer. He steps outside to put it on. He prefers dressing in public. Georgie does, he does. He climbs into his white, V-neck t-shirt, presenting himself beautifully, showing off his outstanding dance. The smooth, silky cotton polishes his waxy, college-boy skin and vintage nipples, puffy nipples, his hurly burly-boy A-cups, miniature UFOs. Bug bites. Bee stings.

(Parenthetical Pet Peeve) Seemingly deaf parents of children emit ear-splitting shrieks in public.

This peculiar collection of moments is crucial to Georgie's every day.

He hates to hang his clothes, so the dryer is constantly running. Lint piles up and the fabric softener smells like allergy.

Georgie's allergic.

He sniffs and remembers the smell of Claudia. (I cough.) We tic. We twitch. We do circus-tics, we're circus-freaky. We are just a big circus freak show, aren't we? Georgie and me.

The gray skies dull away and yesterday's rain has stopped. The dew rubs coldly against Georgie's bare feet, grounding him. He's burning a fire in his mind. Everybody's watching (aren't we?)

He's alone and invisible. He doesn't feel. He doesn't exist—he's not needed. He breathes. He thinks. But he is not. Georgie wants to say he doesn't care about this, but he does.

He wishes he could record all his thoughts and hallucinations. He wants to matter, more and more. But he's distant, far-off, aiming a spotlight down at the stage. The play goes on down there and Georgie watches unseen.

He's always the last one picked, the charity case, and the delinquent. He's just a rich kid with a big heart, and a heaping side of rage and anger, too.

He's often depressed and his moods swing in kaleidoscopic circles. The fibers in his mind vibrate and images are formed. (What images form today? The perfect, beautiful, and pure woman? Or some sinister, creepy, alter ego?)

Oh, Georgie Gust. . .

Dear Diary:

Plain and simple intermission, for once again, I've got to stop this hating myself garbage and really start to love myself for all that I am, not hating myself for what I'm not. Anyway . . . Onward bound.

Part II: From Wakefield to Rehab

Dr C Made Me Do It

Name-calling: Georgie Porgie, Mr Twitchy, Georgie, Benjy, Georgie and me, Tourette's, Borderline Personality Disorder, schizoaffective, neurotic, psychotic, blah, blah, blah.

Speaking of which, I've had two cups of coffee this morning and nothing to eat. Routine, routine, routine. Now I've got an appointment with Dr C.

I ramble way off the subject. (What is the subject? Georgie, Claudia, and me.)

Dr C just listens as I run on and on and on.

I've got another doctor's appointment today—another second opinion. (Or a third opinion? Fourth? How many opinions do I need to know I'm fucked up? I know!) Yeah, and some of these shrinks are fucked up, too. I swear. One doctor says I've got Tourette's, another says schizophrenia, and another says blah, blah, and more blah. Am I in between these diseases? I can live with that. It's cute to be an in-betweener. But who can I trust; the one on the right or the one on the left? Which am I more like? They're all puppets, Muppets, gonzo, sex-o. I'm going crazy. Going, going, gone.

(Parenthetical Pet Peeve) Cold coffee.

Two cups of coffee, and I'm all over the place. A couple of years back, I would've reacted differently, but I've changed. I skim through My Junkie Memoirs. I was such a good little kid. How did I get so fucked up? I want to swear, but I know better words. I'm choosing not to use them. I don't want to end up in hell.

(Do I, doc?

"I don't know. Do you, Ben?")

In the end, I wander and wonder.

Dear Diary:

My best friends and I—the few that I have—we have conversation that I doubt anyone else would understand. Just had one of them on the phone. I was eating a bag of chips.

What Really Happened

Dr C seems to think that dredging up the past will somehow fix my present (but are we going forward or backward? That's what I want to know.)

I'm not in therapy because Dr C wants to teach me how to like myself. (Correction: love myself. Right, Dr C?) I'm in therapy because I robbed the Pasadena City Bank. Well, no, I didn't really rob it. More like, I pretended to rob it. It was kind of a joke, really. At least, I thought it was a joke. I was high on crack at the time. On Chivas Regal, marijuana, and Klonopin, and I thought the whole goddamn thing was a fucking riot. Bankers really don't have a sense of humor; neither do cops—at least, not the cops in Pasadena.

I'd just met with my business manager about trust fund stuff. Pops was still dishing out a little cash at a time, a little scratch, here and there. I'd just learned, that day, that he'd made a $1.2 million profit on a huge position. (I couldn't tell you which one.) But the dividends they paid me were being kept, without any hold (I was told), in the Pasadena City Bank in the San Gabriel Valley. I knew then—after the meeting was over, when Ron, my manager, pulled out a few joints—I knew I needed to get that million-two in cash, run off to Vegas with a couple of Mafiosi ("Professional Baccarat Players", "Investment Managers—Gaming," they're called) and win-win-win, then die of crack smoke in my hotel room. This was one of the highest manias I'd ever gone through. ("Or that's gone through you, Ben?"

What do you mean, gone through me?

"You tell me, now, Ben.")

Anyway.

High on crack, I raced down the I-34 in my BMW, doing about 120, and then tried to take a tight turn without slowing down. The car didn't like it, and it showed. It refused to make the turn and instead went airborne, flying over the divider to the other side, landing right side up, leaving neither of us seriously hurt. It was a miracle, and I was reborn for half a minute or so. Then I slid into a blind white fury, jetted up on speed, PCP, and angel dust.

I took out some extra Klonopin 4s from my medicine collection (my drive-thru, pharmacy-in-a-glove-box) to soothe me down.

I pulled up to the mini-mall and parked.

Inside, there was this young woman, a teller. I pulled out my cell phone, leaned across the marble counter, and said in my very best gangster voice, my ego huge from the drugs:

"Listen, I don't want any problem here. I have one-point-two million bucks at this bank, and I'm a VIP customer. Want to see my driver's license?"

I pulled out my billfold.

"Check out the ZIP code: Nine-one-one-oh-one," I said. "Got it? Nine-one-one-oh-one?" I insisted. "And if I press the pound key on this, then. . ."

I waved the cell phone in her face.

(Parenthetical Pet Peeve) Handheld portable phones used in moving cars, and the erratic driving resulting from such use.

"Okay, okay, hold on a minute," she said. "I'll get you your money."

"You better be quick about it, then, babe," I told her. "I'm going outside for a smoke. I'll wait. You have the cash waiting when I get back."

But she didn't get my money. This happened to be a non-cash bank. (What the hell's a non-cash bank?) What she did instead was call the bank's CEO, who told her to call the police.

Outside, I began to see not cop cars but little pins—needle points that surrounded the two-story mini-mall. Sometime later, I found out that there had been three entire city blocks of police and sniper squads. Before I knew it, there were guns and news cameras pointing at me, all intent on capturing America's Most Stupid: Benjamin J Schreiber. That's me ("Or was it Georgie, Ben?"

Fuck you, Dr C.

"Please, Ben.")

"Get the fuck down!" I heard somebody shout.

I could feel my death right then and there. It started at my feet and crept up my shins, to my knees, and then my thighs. Later, I'd learn the feeling was a reaction to the PCP, but at the time, I was sure I'd been shot, sure I was on my way home to Jesus. (My grandmother's Jesus, that is. I've never really been much of a believer, myself.

"A believer in what, Ben?"

In anything, Dr C. Least of all, in me.)

"Down! Face down. Now!" the dots yelled.

I hit the deck. Hard. I stretched out on the pavement somewhat gingerly, since I was wearing Armani. Jesus Christ, what did they expect? Was I going to take on the Pasadena City Police with a fucking cell phone?

A cop trotted over, pointed a gun at my head, and kicked my legs together.

"Ankles crossed, hands spread! Now!" he screamed.

Now. (Now, now, now. Can't we discuss this a little later? Does it have to be now?) They were all in such a fucking hurry, I just couldn't stand it.

"Chill, dude. I'm not going anywhere," I told the air. (Or the cop. Whichever.)

Someone I never saw cuffed my ankles together, and then the cop—the one who ordered my hands to spread, Sergeant Howitzer (His real name, I swear to God.

"You swear to whom, Ben?"), yanked me to my feet.

Do you know how hard it is to stand up straight when your ankles are crossed and cuffed? I toppled into the sergeant and my head banged hard against his. It hurt like a son of a bitch. I think I yelped. (Actually, I know I did.)

The sergeant, not unkindly, pulled me upright.

"Son," he said, "you need help."

I'm pretty sure I mumbled that people had been telling me that my entire life. ("So this is not the first time, Ben?"

Just listen, huh?)

"Maybe it's time you took their advice," Sergeant Howitzer said.

Then he told me that he wasn't arresting me, just detaining me. Which made about as much sense as a non-cash bank. But what the hell, why not?

The only problem (and it was a big problem) was that detaining me included calling my Pops, who was neither amused nor un-amused. Dear old Pops was simply neutral. Like always. ("And how long have you had these feelings about your father, Ben?"

Shite. Like I always say: always.)

I talked to him at the police station. He was my one telephone call.

"Ben!" His voice boomed. "How the hell are you?"

"Well, actually. . ." I said. Then I let it drop. I wasn't really sure how I was, and I wasn't all that convinced he really wanted to know.

"Yeah, yeah, yeah," he said. "Heard all about it. Listen, son, I've told Sergeant Howitzer to get you into rehab."

Rehab?

"Call me once you get settled," Pops said. Then he hung up.

Sergeant Howitzer led me out of the station and into his car—a Chevy Malibu.

"Want my BMW?" I burst out. "I'll give it to you for $5,000. A real steal. A st-steal." I snorted hysterically.

"No, thank you," he told me politely "I already have a car."

"A piece-of-shite Chevy Malibu," I told him.

Funny thing: People—some people, even poor or middle-class people—get attached to their piece-of-shite cars, their piece-of-shite lives. Sergeant Howitzer cleared his throat once, twice, three times.

(Parenthetical Pet Peeve) The fact: Who you know is more important than what you know.

"I buy American, son," he snapped. "Always have. Always will."

"Suit yourself," I told him.

I wondered if my uncle was paying him to drag me around Pasadena, from facility to facility, looking for a place that would take me.

Every facility was full. After five consecutive rejections, you kind of lose your belief that anyone really gives one good goddamn about helping you get better; and I said so at the time.

"Look, son," Sergeant Howitzer told me. "Don't go getting all paranoid on me. Sometimes a pickle is just a pickle, and sometimes a full-up facility is just a full-up facility."

"Okay," I said. ("And you believed him, Ben?"

Like I believe you, Dr C?)

To pass the time, I rolled my eyes back up into my head and passed out. When I came to, we were in the parking lot of Valley View Hospital in Sylmar.

How many places did the Sarge have to try before he found one that would take me? Out in fucking Sylmar. ("I could tell you, if you're curious, Ben."

Just save it, doc. Tell me later.) But hey, rehab is rehab, and I am nothing if not adaptable when it comes to getting clean. Besides, my nurse Cindy was hot. She had this super-straight, ash-blonde, hair cut straight to her chin. She looked like the fucking Dutch Boy, except with major titties and a curvaceous ass.

Dear Diary:

Oh well, I guess, I'm going to lose some people in order to so-called find my fucking self. Fair enough.

Mental Ward Snuff

Who do you think I see when I walk into rehab? It's the Bureaucrat. She's your typical lunch lady—an obese white woman, weighed down by these heavy breast-rolls—whole rolls of breast-fat down her side and front. Her nametag says Betty. ("So what happened to Cindy?"

Just back off, Dr C? Okay?)

Betty shoves me into a chair next to Howitzer and checks me out. I'm grossed out. Now, I've got to admit that I'm no fucking Dutch Boy, either. But Betty—obviously, Howitzer can smell her belly-button gunk, too. We both sneak glances at her dirty clothes, the deluxe, mail order, scrub-set package: buy-one-get-one-free. She frowns at me and adjusts her smock. She's got these little happy Smurfs dancing across her boob-fat. You can smell her mold-lubricated tit-sweat, since she doesn't wash her clothes too often; once a week seems like once a day, in her book. She readjusts her collar and sticks a cinnamon Altoid in her mouth.

The Bureaucrat lets out an occasional "silent" pew-burp that she passes off as a sigh caused by the late hour. She's trimmed her moustache and plucked the hairs on her chin. She looks better than she did, she thinks, when she was young and stupid and sick herself, drinking at the community college. She'd tell all her college friends she "wanted to help people," and all her friends would admire her for it. Now nobody likes her—not the administration, and not her co-workers. ("How do you know all this, Ben? Were you checking her out?"

Just trust me, Dr C. I know psychos. And Betty, she is.

"Like me, Ben?"

You said it, doc. Not me.)

Betty's liked least by the poor sickos she takes into the ward. ("Like you, Ben?"

Come off it, doc.)

Her sternness is all mixed up with derogatory wisecracks about psychotics, and she's about as knowledgeable as the psych-ward textbooks say she should be. I imagine she's real happy in her personal life, but I can't say for sure. She's celibate, I'll say that. At least, that's how she's coming across to me. She's not sex-deprived—she's just fucking sexless. She could even be a hermaphrodite, you know, or "intersex," like they prefer to be called now. She reminds me of my mother. She's a pig in scrubs. She's America's Finest.

She rushes me through the paperwork, not even guessing that I'll read over all the papers in my bedroom. And then I'm in the psycho ward, this identity-forsaken heaven, and I'm in here to stay, until I get better, they say. Someday, when I'm better, they say, I'll get out. I'll get back to the outside world, where I can be who I am, without straitjackets and restraints. If I ever get out. If I don't lose control.

(Where I am now, I'm still here, inside. You could say I'm in Communist America. I'm still here.)

I'm lying in a cold sweat, wearing all my dirty clothes—my old, damp, partly-soiled underwear with piss-drip and loomis: the cheesy discharge from the thigh and underneath my holy scrotum— everything's sweaty, packed, shriveled within my oversized blue corduroys. My black leather belt has been confiscated by the psych-ward whores to prevent suicide. (As if I'd kill myself for Betty.

(Parenthetical Pet Peeve) Plain white men's briefs—"Tidy Whities"—Not at all sexy.

"Would you, Ben? Would you kill yourself for me?"
Give me a break would you, Dr C?)

After check-in, they stick me in this shitey triple-room with a metal bunk bed and a toilet. I'm crammed in with two other psychos like me, wearing a sweaty, yellow-stained white t-shirt beneath my favorite white cotton dress shirt. The damp shirt is cold on my skin, and I'm wrapped up in it; its buttons are loose, a couple of them broken. My one sheet-like hospital blanket is so thin it barely covers me, and when I finally drift off, I'm barely asleep. I keep double-checking to make sure I really know where I am. But whenever I check, I'm still here. Wherever that is.

The paper-flat, single pillow sure isn't what you would call fluffy or shapely—it's too flimsy to fit inside its pillowcase, but I've rolled it up, packed it with my sweatshirt, some socks, a washcloth, anything for some decent support. ("Are you looking for support, Ben? What kind of support?"

Any visible means, doc. Now lay off.) Whatever. It's not like I'm going to get any other kind of real support in here, where I'm stuck, lock-stock-and-blocked up, for real; in the psych ward.

Suddenly, the dismal fluorescent lights of the room flicker on, and my two roommates start coughing up their heavy snores. I'm aggravated, sure, but I remember not to flip my lid, lose my cool, or to show any anger, frustration, or assertion at all. Any normal reactions, I know, to the torture, neglect, and ill-care here (any drama, any drama at all) will cause the hospital techs to gather around me and lock me up in a straitjacket and restraints.

Like they did last night when I first arrived, to one of the anorexic girls, because they caught her trying to cut herself with a plastic spoon. She had sharpened it slightly, but smartly, with the sizzling heat of the external hot water pipes in her bathroom. Still, they watch her any time she has to pee, or puke or whatever. Like they watch me.

It's 5 in the morning when the lights flicker on. And I'm in a living hell, not prison, just a slightly safer version of hell. (I really hate to even write about it.

"Or talk about it, Ben?"

Even worse, Dr C, even worse.) It's a loving, beautiful, colorless hell. There are childlike crayon paintings on the walls in the activities room. And the vampire nurses take my blood every morning at 5 o'clock.

Dear Diary:

Someone just called me a crazy freak right there on the sidewalk. I just said, "Thank you." I thought nothing could throw such a person off like the proud polite crazy freak that I am. Blam.

Wax Melts

(Where are we now? What is happening this time?

"Don't write about it, Ben. Talk. Just talk.") It's noon. Another special day, just after I met Heidi—the woman from the gift shop parking lot, you know, my Heidi. Not Georgie's Heidi. I'm stuck obsessing about her, while Georgie goes on with this happy, homely life (with Claudia.) I can only imagine what they're up to. I'm all alone in the supermarket parking lot, having a daydream about the mysterious Claudia. Claudia haunts me, too, but how can I find one like her in my shite life? Georgie, I'm crawling out of my fucking skin!

(Parenthetical Pet Peeve) Able-bodied people who park in handicapped spaces.

As I enter the market, I notice a cute college coed bagging groceries. She measures me with her eye, looking like she's up to no good.

She's up to something, anyway. I pass her off as someone I might hit on, some other day (some other life.) But, of course, I'm really not interested in any chick I might hit on, let alone, actually hook up with. So. Okay, okay. She's cute, I must admit. And her nametag reads ASHLEY. Looking at Ashley, I start to daydream about Claudia again. ("So where are we now, Ben?"

Just shut up and listen, okay?)

The huge front doors of a vintage luncheonette swing open. Within, some disheveled old man makes his rounds from table to table, asking the patrons to help him out. Some patrons flip him some small change.

"Thank you. God bless you," he says.

Georgie sits alone in the corner, furtively watching the door. He watches as Claudia walks in and sits down alone a couple tables away. Georgie sees her bruised shoulder under her bra strap, and watches as the waitress brings her a cup of coffee. Then he moves over to another table to be closer to her. He wants to existential-ize her, to make her exist. He wants Claudia to be real.

She doesn't seem to mind such a forward pass-attempt from a complete stranger.

"You look familiar," Georgie says.

"You say that every time you see me," she says.

"Huh?" says Georgie.

"Hello? Hello? Anybody there?" she taunts him. "Georgie, it's me!" Claudia folds her legs. "It's Claudia," she says. "It's me! What's wrong with you, Georgie?"

Georgie's nervous.

"I don't know," he says. He sits down across from her.

His existence dulls a bit; Claudia is stealing it from him.

"Okay. You got me," he says.

She leans closer.

"I had this guy once. I was sitting on a bench in a wax museum, waiting for my friend to catch up. And this guy—this, like, total stranger—starts touching me. Fondling me, you know?"

"Fondling," Georgie says, wistfully.

"So I said, 'What do you think you're doing?'"

Georgie starts tapping his feet on the tile.

"I must have really scared him. 'I thought you weren't real,' he says."

Georgie laughs.

"I tell him, 'No, they're real all right.' We ended up dating for five years."

"Lucky him," Georgie says.

Claudia glances over casually and notices the small stiff lump in Georgie's pants.

"Do you want to sleep with me?" she asks.

"Yes," Georgie says.

"You like foreplay?"

Claudia watches Georgie smile shyly.

"Come on—let's get out of here," she says.

Georgie nods and follows her. A few minutes later, he is strolling through the canned-food aisle of a supermarket down the street. Claudia scans the shelves at eye level.

(Parenthetical Pet Peeve) Meeting someone in a narrow hallway and as I sidestep to avoid them, they move with me. I move again. So do they, blocking every move I make to get around them.

"Do you like pickles?" she asks.

"What?"

"Wake up, Georgie." Claudia snaps. "Pickles. Do you like them?"

"Yeah."

"I like the ones you can get at street fairs," Claudia says. "The full, sour-dill pickles. I can eat them by the jar."

"Me, too," says Georgie.

"So, where you from?" Claudia asks.

"Huh?" Georgie thinks. "It's complicated," he says.

"Well, what brought you here, Georgie? You on the lam—wanted by the cops?"

There's a long pause, then Claudia smiles.

"Don't tell me, see if I care."

Another moment passes.

"Seriously, why are you here?"

"I had a termite problem at home. Had to get out."

Claudia snorts. "Yeah. Me, too."

Later in the day, Georgie and Claudia undress in the Twin Lakes Motel.

Georgie accidentally bumps Claudia with an elbow in his rush. "Sorry," he says.

"Don't be. I'm just glad we met."

Claudia smiles.

"I wonder when our first argument will be."

She looks wistful.

"I wonder what it will be about," says Claudia. "I wonder if we'll have a falling out."

"Probably," Georgie decides.

"I hope not," Claudia says.

She picks out a pickle from the fresh jar of half-sour, store-brand, dill-pickle slices.

"Yeah," she says, musing. "Do you want to practice our breakup now? You want to tell each other what we really think, right this minute?"

At Claudia's prompting, Georgie starts.

"When we break up, I just want you to know that I'll be dreaming about you. Fantasizing. Even when I'm married."

"Married? You?" Claudia scoffs.

"And I'll despise you. I'll be the guy you hate that gets off to you."

Lightly, Claudia says, "You're fucking twisted."

"And you're fucking filthy, Claudia. You're a whore. You're a bitch, an easy lay."

"Ooh, you're talking dirty, Georgie. C'mon, now. Spank me," she croons.

Georgie looks at Claudia triumphantly. "Not if you want me to," he says.

Moments later, they're under the covers, making love.

"What do you want, Georgie? Huh? Little boys? Little girls? The priest himself?" She pants, grinding herself against him. "Come on, baby, tell me. What turns you on?"

"What turns you on?"

"I'm stalking you in public, teasing you with thrilling possibilities. Then I make you rape me," she purrs.

"Why?"

"Because we're both wasted, drunk, and high. That's why."

"That's sick. What do you tell yourself about yourself?"

"More fantasies," Claudia admits, pausing for a moment. "You?"

"That I'm no good."

Afterwards, Claudia relieves herself. "I'm sick. I'm dizzy."

Georgie laughs.

"Georgie, I didn't get a word you were saying," she calls from the bathroom as she washes her hands. "You were talking shite-curses, swear-words, all that gibberish. You didn't make any sense."

"I can get like that. Sorry."

Claudia looks at him so sad and alone.

"Oh," Georgie remembers. "By the way, your fee."

He pulls a wad of bills from his wallet, which sits on the nightstand.

"$4.25, right? You're from LA, Long Beach, wherever—the home of cheap sex and cheaper thrills?"

"Yeah, your 10-minute hour is up. Next time, pay me before you fuck me," Claudia demands.

"Do you want me to leave?"

She smiles, smirks, and sneers.

Georgie rolls over. "Why don't I just become your little boy toy? You need one?"

"You already are," Claudia winks. "I've got you hooked—you're already in love with me."

She looks him in the eye.

"And yes, I'll marry you." She flips her hair.

"The chances of you and me working out," Georgie says, "are as good as they'd be with anyone else."

"You have secrets. I've got secrets."

"Well, so. No wedding ring, then," says Georgie.

"No! That's silly." Claudia scoffs.

("I wish you were real.")

I come out of my fantasy and fill the shopping cart with canned tuna.

(Parenthetical Pet Peeve) Pull tabs that break off on such things as cat food, tuna, etc.

It's funny how fantasy and reality unreel separately and together. Isn't that funny?

Here's to my incredibly lonely existence.

Dear Diary:

Fuck it. I'm capable of clearing away and releasing at least some of my old feelings of self-rejection, low self-esteem, overindulgence, jealousy, and emotional instability, by relaxing my twitching fucking body for once. Releasing them, replacing them with love. As the negativity dissolves away, I can once again feel the love that is there, that has always been there, but was hidden by the feelings of the past. Screw the past. When the past calls, I don't answer. It never has anything new to say.

Part III: Getting Clean with Dr C

Pregnant With the Idea of Georgie Gust

"Who is Georgie?" Dr C asks. "If not you, Ben, then who?"

"I'm glad you asked that question," I answer. But I don't answer. (But then, I don't question the answers, either.)

You see, Dr C, it's like this: I ask myself the same question. I ask myself again and again: When was Georgie Gust first planted in my womb? Was it when I gave up my virginity, when I was fucking Kathy Friedlander in our little childhood tree house? Was he a seed of sacrifice? Was I really impregnated with Georgie, or was he born with me? Actually, I'd say, he was born years later. But was I ever Georgie's father in the first place? Or his mother? Was he ever?

I began to imagine Georgie a hell of a lot more vividly once I began writing about him—that I know. And once I started to write, Georgie became everything I didn't like about myself. So, maybe Georgie is what you might call a subconscious projection, I guess. Or maybe, a psychological double (but what does that mean?)

And there are other questions I can't answer. Like, when I'm in love (I ask you, Dr C) should I start or stop writing? Is writing my therapy? Is writing the cure-all, the end-all of my mental maladies? Or is writing really the disease, the malaise itself, the source, the cause, the root of my perplexity? And what about Georgie? What do I do about him? Is he supposed to die, in order to cure me? And what about Georgie's girl, Claudia? Why does she have to die, too? But, like me, Dr C doesn't answer.

I always imagined Georgie shooting through his mother's birth canal like a bullet. So Georgie's birth, of course, had nothing to do with me. This is probably why he's such a mystery to me. (Almost as much as I am to myself.) I mean I can't even hold my thoughts together. I'm terrible at transitions. ("Just start writing, Ben. And see what comes out."

Okay then, Dr C.)

To begin with, Georgie's parents were set up for a motel cocaine-bust.

Their cheap room is filled with smoke; the shrill fire alarm blares. Their lovemaking is hysterically passionate. And the telephone rings off the hook.

Finally, Georgie's young mother-to-be snaps into a sexual frenzy, threatening Georgie's father-to-be: "Get me pregnant!" she commands. "Just do it!"

And she slides the limp rubber from his dick.

Georgie's papa's socks are still on. The man wears a thick 70s moustache, true porno-style, right out of *Boogie Nights*.

The paid-for couple is on fire, heated in ecstasy, fucked up on a drug-induced high.

Suddenly, Pops makes that ever-so-agonizing announcement: "I'm gonna cum. I'm gonna cum!" Then he spits it out, "I'm coming!"

Just as he spurts half of Georgie through the pearly gates and into his mother's safe haven, a half dozen cops and the DEA kick down the motel room door. Talk about being in the wrong place at the wrong time. Talk about being scarred for life. And Georgie isn't even an embryo, yet.

(The invisible audience demands: We want details! Details! Details of the constricted, stressed, muscle-spermie Georgie.)

The newborn child shows early warning signs of extreme fear and emotional trauma—or maybe post-traumatic stress. He begins acting out nervous habits before he's two years old. As a youngster, he's withdrawn. He's considered an outcast. He doesn't have much self-esteem. The scared little kid is often sad and alone. Still, he's caring and thoughtful of others.

Before he's out of high school, Georgie's diagnosed with Tourette's syndrome with concomitant paranoid features, bipolar depression, schizoaffective disorder, and other bullshit psychiatric disorders. He obsesses over his bullshit afflictions, uses them as excuses for his strange, offbeat behavior when he gets high. As a result, he turns heavily to drugs. His teenage life often seems hopeless and burdensome. He sometimes dreams of suicide.

He goes to Wakefield boarding school by choice. By his early 20s, he picks up a slightly offbeat sense of humor. It helps him cope with all those bullshit psychiatric disorders.

Then, one day, this kid experiences something besides irritation, anger, or depression. He has a spiritual experience, a mystical experience. He's possessed by some ineffable sense of supernatural beauty. And so Georgie Gust enters a whole new stage in his troubled life. But this mystical experience only comes to him in short, wonderful spurts. In a year, however, this whole new growth-spurt takes him over completely.

That ecstatic teenage kid is still alive today, somewhere, inside Georgie. Inside me. ("But what about that wounded inner child, Ben? Is he still alive, too?"

Come on, doc. Lay off me. Just let me talk about Georgie, okay?

"Right, Ben.")

Flash forward to The Big One:

Georgie sits there crying. Crying his heart out. There's nothing babyish about it. In fact, it's a breakthrough to some whole new maturity. His sacred heart's bleeding. His purple pen's ink spurts and paints the page with his profound spiritual transformation.

After all his struggle and suffering, Georgie finally releases his frustration, anger, and depression. His heart and soul bleed all over the paper. For an eternity, he lives a secret metamorphosis. His ugly old life blends into something beautiful and extraordinary. He can't put words to anything—he's transfixed by something supernatural, mystical, but also somehow sexual, physical, visceral, like an orgasm. His legs and hands tremble. Everything old and ugly has changed into a positive memory. The past recreates itself while the present still exists inside him.

Something remarkable and intangible has taken over all of his senses.

This inexpressible experience, which lasts only a moment, lasts his whole life. His whole life, that is, up until now.

Everything pours out at once. It isn't an epiphany. Nobody dies. Nobody's reborn. This isn't some big tall tale, or some little fairy tale. It's real. It's genuine. It's incredible.

It's beyond what language could convey. It can only be expressed by his delirious outpouring of tears (or maybe, an outpouring of sperm—some climactic, ecstatic outburst?)

This man, who sobs with such intensity and purpose, isn't really a hero. He's just somebody I happen to know pretty well. Better than myself, maybe.

This man was once a stupid little kid, stuck in the principal's office. He's still silent and lost during the Pledge of Allegiance. He's still punished, humiliated, for not joining in with the class, the crowd. This stupid little kid is still the same rotten, out-of-shape, wannabe writer. But now he's finally completed something. (Does that sound familiar?

"I don't know, Ben. Should it? Is that stupid little kid Georgie, or you, Ben?"

Listen, Dr C, I'm talking about Georgie. Just let me talk, okay?

And, you, ladies and gentlemen of the invisible audience, assume the position.)

That's Georgie. Separate from me. That's who Georgie really is.

I'm not sure if Georgie's the result of me sobering up, or simply a figment of the world inside my head. After I'm clean for a while, the confusion swarming my head is exacerbated. My delirium and perplexity is more extreme. To this day, I don't know why.

And then the thunderstorm came. (Why are thunderstorms always female? Do thunderstorms have sex, or what?) The thunderstorm, anyway, would last more than a night or a day. She's known to Georgie and me, yours truly, Benjamin J Schreiber, as Our Private Perplexity. Claudia, that is. Claudia Nesbitt.

Claudia Nesbitt appears as she is now—ghostly and pale. She's like the Pale Horse. She's my favorite nightmare. Was it love at first sight? Sure as shite, every day. Every fucking day. Every fucking night, too.

My spine still shudders when I think of her. Her frizzy red hair, her pale skin, her sex, and her sensuality. Knowing we could've had a perfect relationship, simply because we didn't have a relationship at all, just makes me sick. It makes time stop.

I remember Georgie Gust like I remember the Shadow People, flitting before my eyes when I was getting high. Georgie makes me see someone others can't see. Someone I know very well. Someone more real than me.

His life is more interesting than mine. But, at the same time, I am this person, Georgie Gust. Georgie Gust is the feeling I get when I think of his name. The drama and chaos I find inside myself, I find in him. Georgie Gust is the clarity he shows outside me. Yet he's also a part of me. He is me. We're the same, different, but the same. It's a really fucked-up phenomenon. Does that explain me, Dr C?

I'm merely a spy, an observer, in the world of my hallucinations. But Georgie's hallucination, Claudia Nesbitt, is the woman I desire more than anything else in the world. She's the only thing left in the world I want. But who am I? What do I really know about myself? What am I, apart from Claudia or Georgie? ("When you're ready to answer those questions, Ben, you just tell me."

I'm working on it, Dr C.)

You see, I'm still stuck, still thinking about the past, Georgie's past, and thinking of myself like Georgie is me. So, I think again about why I want—I want, I want, I want! She. Georgie's girl. Claudia. Claudia Nesbitt.

God! She's really so flat, that Claudia. She's just my stereotype sex fantasy, my misogynistic wet dream. So why should I want her? Because I think she's changeable. After all, I can think what I want about her. And do what I want with her, too—in my mind's eye. So, the way I figure it, maybe if I change Claudia Nesbitt, her alterations will reflect in Heidi Berillo. ("And in you, Ben?"

And in me, Dr C.)

She's fucked up and I love her, I think.

But my very own Georgie Gust has the key to create my ultimate Perplexity through the creation of his ultimate Perplexity. Does that make sense?

Wait, what am I talking about? She's really just a stereotype character in my distorted mind. But I'm drawn to her complexity, through my loneliness. I mix and match the traits in her I want for myself. (Or is it the other way around?) I build her up like a CSI composite sketch and then get off to the final portrait.

You might as well hate me now, you see, Dr C, if you don't already. ("I don't hate you, Ben. I'm only trying to . . ."

Help me. Yeah, yeah, I've heard it all before, doc. From those other psychos.) But I'm really only trying to figure everything out. Including myself. My feelings, beliefs, and opinions are not solid matter. They keep changing. This must be the stuff of life, the stuff of perplexity.

Do what you want with me, Dr C. Everybody. Make me smile and decapitate me. Play soccer with my bloody thoughts. Tell me I'm creatively horrifying. But leave me my Georgie. Leave me my Claudia.

Voices of coprolalia set off repeated heart attacks in me. Love me. Hate me. Fuck me. Kill me. It's only a matter of time before you do, anyway. Give me a paper cut, right on my eyelid, on the corner of my mouth. I'm so lonely up here. I'm ready to die now, ready to swim into the realm of my warping mind. And now it's starting to pour outside.

(Parenthetical Pet Peeve) Paper cuts.

I feel Claudia. She watches in wonder. She looks at me the way she used to look at Georgie—with empathy, and with passion, emotion, and lust. ("And with love, Ben?"

You tell me, Dr C. You tell me.)

Dear Diary:

I think I might be considered an Outsider Artist—at least in my opinion.

What Got Me Here

I'm in the psych ward again. I've lost myself. Or they've lost me. Either way, I'm lost. I'm like the other people in the healthcare system. But I'm not in any system. I can't concentrate on anything anymore. I can't communicate, I can't see reality, and I don't want this "self" anymore. I didn't sign up for this shite. I didn't ask to be born.

I don't want challenges. I don't want to feel bad just so I can know what feeling good feels like, sometimes. That's bullshite. It's just, like, a false dichotomy, or something. We've got two eyes so we can see this depth perception, in two dimensions, but why doesn't one eye do the trick? There's two of everything. There's two of me. Or maybe even three.

Were an inflation of karmic baggage, with full-blown egos, anger and compassion, and a piece of that chaotic plane which, I say in monotone: "I fucking hate." There's really no me here, no self, and that's why I'm so mad.

Thank you, Dr C and the psych ward staff, for showing me my no-self, my non-me. There's no me, here or there, there's only this jerk-off, half-assed, half-shite particle of triple weenie, double-dick shite. (All the dicks exist for somebody to suck on. Maybe for me.) And a doubting, worried, scared, sacred something, a spirit, ME!

I hate me. I'm jealous of everybody else, because they're not me. And I'm stuck with me. I'm the nothingness they ask me to meditate on. But I don't want that nothingness. I want to be me! See?

I keep on failing at whatever I do, at what they want me to do. But I don't want any more learning experiences. I'm just solid matter. Flesh and bone and nerves—but I'm numb, here. I'm trapped. Stuck. Does anybody know what to do with me?

Is there a doctor in the house?

Take me away, Dr C.

Dear Diary:

Would I trade my co-morbid schizoaffective spectrum condition? No way. Never. Too many gifts come along with it. When "normies" banter and talk I laugh to myself on a whole other wavelength. Sometimes schizophrenia sucks but other times it is the most fascinating "reality." It keeps me on my mental toes full time. Right now in this moment, I love it! With schizophrenia alone, my severe Tourette's syndrome (only now that I'm a strong and healthy adult, I must add) remains entirely secondary. Thank God! The best part of my schizoaffective spectrum syndrome is the autism element. Other than that, the symptom called hypomania—focused, productive mild mania. Combined might someday result with my John Nash moment—a Nobel Prize. Sure.

Taking It to the Cleaners

So, yeah, the cleaning crew finally arrived at our house. Georgie's and mine, I mean.

Note to self: Is Dr C right? After only a couple of sessions? Is Georgie really nothing but my alter ego? Not a legitimate literary character, or a legitimate device? And when he dies, when I kill him off (because, after all, all literary characters must die eventually), what happens to me? Do I get bumped off, too? Do I cease to exist? And do I even care? After all, life in my humble opinion is vastly overrated. And much too long.

But as I was saying (or was it Georgie saying?), the cleaning crew finally arrived. Daydreams are hitting home runs in my head. Maybe Georgie's about to get evicted from my headspace. And if Georgie goes, if Georgie gets kicked out, what about Georgie's girl? What about Claudia?

Claudia isn't paying rent, and she's taking up all the space. Claudia's most likely hung over, or something, next door, somewhere. She's just a drag; she's just a parasite. She's just free-loading from Georgie and me. So maybe it's time Claudia got kicked out, too—maybe it's time Claudia got the boot. Time for Claudia to check out of that private bedroom in my head, and time for me to stop wasting time, wasting my life, and fantasizing about her.

It is officially afternoon. Time to wake up.

Georgie awakes entangled in a web of slack. I wake up right beside him. Claudia starts her day with cranberry juice and a muffin, eating in front of the TV. I can just see her. And Heidi? How does Heidi start her day? Cranberry juice? Tomato? We can only assume. Her blinds are still closed. Breakfast in bed has been cancelled, as far as Georgie's concerned, and he's getting angry just thinking about whatever the hell Claudia's doing. And Heidi? Heidi's probably busy with something, with someone, too. With Claudia's Greg or Sara. Maybe both. Maybe all three.

And maybe I'm just a little paranoid. I pray to know my place in this world, I pray for relief. I pray to understand, to be a better man. I think about that kind of stuff all the time, and I'm sure my Creator hears my pleas and is probably tired of all my confessions, by now.

I'm still in the bedroom, where Georgie gets down on his knees for a minute. Who's he praying to? He gives an hour to his shrink, every day. Every day, it's the same thing. He's barely awake. He's praying.

So where was Claudia last night? Claudia was somewhere else last night. She thought about Georgie often, but she was with some lady friend. That's what I think.

What I think? Hell, I'm the fucking author—that's a matter of fact. What I think. Claudia thought about Georgie all night long, too. That's what I say. That's a fact. And Claudia, she's a fact, too.

Georgie rises from his knees. He sees there's a message waiting for him on the answering machine. Similar messages will follow through the whole next year.

TUES JUNE 21 9:30 am: "Hi, Mr Gust, it's Ms Nesbitt, hi . . .I've been hibernating. I did slip out and go dancing one night. But it was only for a few hours. Anyway, I'm just working from the house for a few hours. Then I've got six clients. Anyway, I just want to say hi and thank you very much for giving me some space and some time. Mmm. I wish you were here today. All right, I'll catch up with you soon. Bye."

Georgie saves the message (he saves everything of Claudia's) and crawls into the kitchen, barely awake.

(Parenthetical Pet Peeve) An item that ceases to function the day after the warranty expires.

He opens the fridge and grabs a piece of cold, leftover pizza. There's a calendar on the freezer door. Shite, it's already November. He's been playing the same goddamn message from Claudia for five months. That's sick, that's what that is. Sick, and more than a little sad. Why in the hell can't he get over the bitch?

Back on his feet, Georgie's full of rage now that the sun shines through the window, breathing existence, and life, and light into the cold dark house. What a little addict he is! Getting agitated because of all the clutter around the house. His rage for order returns to him.

Claudia had mild OCD, but she could do the dishes and laundry just fine. She was a great little homemaker, but she was rarely there. Still, it was nice to have Claudia around the house. Georgie usually has someone else clean up for him.

Fucking housekeepers—good ones, honest ones, a whole family of them. Housekeepers are a blessing to anyone who can afford them.

Here we are, Georgie and me. Our morning routine has always been sloppy.

I look over at Georgie. He starts cursing and bitching, just like any other day, before the coffee pot even starts to brew.

Georgie's been desperate these recent months for his morning routine to bring him something new. Like a run-in with his true destiny, or a random messenger of good news. Something like that. Something new. Something good.

We look each other in the eyes, Georgie and I; it only lasts a second.

Packing to leave the house is a pathetic collection of moments. It drives Georgie fucking nuts. It drives me over the edge.

We go through the whole pocket thing: the wallet, the keys (office, home, car keys separately), pack of smokes, lighter, loose change, gum, memo pad and pen, business card holder, booger rag, and dip. Everything's always getting misplaced. Georgie stuffs his pockets and car cup-holders with whatever is handy, in a reckless hurry. He sorts them out later.

All the house drawers are cluttered with petty necessities. Still, they keep getting lost, like everything else. (And where is that Claudia, when you really need her?)

Georgie always over-packs, too. He tries not to have to leave the house too often, though. He hates to pack, and he's sick of forgetting things. He feels guilty about that. It's another problem that somebody's got to be blamed for. Like every other problem. Got a problem? Sure thing! Blame it on Georgie. Or blame it on Georgie's girl, Claudia.

He used to blame his parents. I used to blame mine. Now everything is our own fault. We don't have parents to blame, anymore. It's all our fault. Georgie's and mine.

Georgie was born as the reason and the solution for that problem. He's the one to blame. I was born as neither—for no reason. It's not my fault. It's taken us years to realize this. Especially Georgie. Things would be a whole lot simpler for me if he just realized that.

"What a great day!" Georgie declares aloud. "A fucking fantastic day!"

He stretches his arms out. He has a big smile for the moment. He has a positive outlook. But his runaway thoughts are always running, running, even if they hide out, for a second or two. No, not two. That's it, just a second. His runaway mind premeditates homicide. Then takes over.

Georgie's Wish List:

#1. "I emotionally break down and cry whenever I'm getting head. It's pathetic, but it feels so real."

#2. "I'm myself. Who else? But I still don't know myself. I'm a little confused about this."

#3. "At first, my bitching neighbor gave me the attention I crave. She saw our little affair as just perfect! Later, she failed to come through for me. I miss her, but I shouldn't. She's not worth it. Sometimes I hate her, but I'm obsessed. I can't even think my way out of her spell: Is she thinking of him? Who's him now?"

But even with these racing thoughts, Georgie's head is messed up this particular morning, anyway, all on its own. Panic and anxiety have him by the ass. He doesn't know how he might have otherwise created the rest of his day. He just dreads all the upcoming chaos and the usual necessary trivial personal exchanges with others.

Finally, #4 rolls on through:

#4: "I almost forgot. I still want to see my neighbor again. I think she's absolutely incredible."

Georgie still thinks he's justified, thinking thoughts like that. He's just horny, but he's healthy, isn't he? Still, he has these thoughts—thoughts of her. Thoughts of Claudia.

"Loving your neighbor like yourself" is fucking impossible. The "I" gets in the way. It's a self-conscious thing. Georgie's personality is a perpetual contradiction.

What was this thing with Claudia? Maybe it was love. Maybe it was lust. Who knows? He told her he loved her, didn't he? Did Georgie really mean it, at the time?

Did he really love her when she was out dancing with other people?

Was it just infatuation? Perversion? Sex addiction? Addiction to chaos? Addiction to self? All of the above? Who knows?

"Shut up. Shut up. Shut up." Georgie's ragging on himself. "You sound like your fucking Aunt Bea."

But Georgie still has a lot of questions.

"That's okay, princess," he hears Claudia say.

Georgie's spinal fluid still rushes up his neck whenever he says Claudia's full name, out loud or to himself. Her big hands become something for his third eye to see, then her toes. That Claudia, she's like some 1950s glamour goddess. She dyed her frizzy, dark brown hair that pretty, peculiar shade of red: Thanksgiving Orange, Outrageous Red.

But no matter what day Georgie wakes up, the sheer dread of putting on his prescription goggles and animating his dull world always frightens him. Reality hits hard, causing discomfort and disease. A terrible misery is born.

Then he looks at the blurry alarm clock. It's the same one he beat down the day before. The same fist he now stuffs, snugly, in his briefs, cupping his balls for a warmer night. He stays in bed for the whole Beethoven concerto.

Dear Diary:

About 30 minutes ago, my vision suddenly became extremely blurry with a following overlapping double vision effect. I was able to look at my eyes in the mirror. I didn't see any red blood. It was just odd. I recently had my eyes checked again, and yet again I do not suffer from any eye disease. Only that I'm legally blind. Also, a legally blind, dyslexic writer, of all things. My God!

A Chance Encounter: Reality?

Ben's the last in line at the convenience store across the street. He appears to be conversing with someone, but no one is speaking to him.

These people find better deals here, across the way from that 1-2-3-4-5 star hotel. Better deals on both coffee and cigarettes, Georgie announces.

"Shhh. Shut up, Georgie. Get out of my head."

Hotel gift shops are for those in a hurry and for those who don't care much for variety or value.

"I never shop there. Guests shouldn't either."

Ben gets a medium coffee and a pack of smokes, along with his change, from the clerk.

He tears open the fresh pack of smokes, juggling the medium coffee in his other hand. He steps out the door, glancing at the profile of a woman sitting on the bench outside. She is heartbreakingly beautiful.

Suddenly, Ben fumbles. He drops two quarters on the pavement.

"What are the chances of that?" she chuckles.

You're almost completely blind and deaf. Almost completely, Georgie points out.

"I know. Why?"

Because, Ben. Because. We're in the presence of a naturally beautiful older woman. It's destiny. Fate. She's the One.

"This always happens to me, especially if she's wearing open-toed shoes."

"Excuse me?" the lady murmurs.

As she is.

"I'd lose my senses completely."

As you have. As you do.

"As I am. Oh God, I hope she hasn't got the slightest imperfection of either character or . . . what's the word?"

Physique. She is just gorgeous, Ben. Isn't she? Shoot. Here she is coming 'round the mountain. Here she comes.

The lady stands, approaching cautiously. "Are you okay?" she asks.

Listen, Ben. Can you hear her? She's got that Plain Jane style, that quietly rapturous voice you crave.

Ben suddenly finds himself thrown backwards.

I wake up early for once.

By 8:30 am, I've already walked the ocean shoreline and am on my way to the convenience store to buy a cup of coffee and a pack of smokes.

It is windy. I am almost blown away. I hold onto my bright blue lampshade hat with my left hand for about a block, until I step behind the local hotel and it screens the big ocean breeze. The Sea Port Hotel is right on the water.

Some hotel guests are in line before me at the convenience store across the street. They would find better deals there on both coffee and cigarettes. Hotel gift shops are for those in a hurry and for those who don't care much for variety or value. I never shop there. Guests shouldn't either.

I get my change and tear open the fresh pack of smokes with a medium coffee in my other hand. Then I fumble the smokes, the coffee, and the change. I drop 50 cents on the pavement.

"What are the chances of that?" I hear.

I become almost completely blind and deaf. I know I am in the presence of a naturally beautiful older woman. This whole blackout/flashback kick is usual, especially if the beautiful older woman is wearing open-toed shoes. I'd lose my senses altogether if she had the slightest imperfection of either character or physique.

"What are the chances of what?" I answer. My own voice echoes strangely in the darkness of my mind.

"You were just singing 'Hotel California'," she says. "I heard you."

It must've been playing on the radio while I showered this morning. She was humming the melody, too. I shut up. I look down. She scrapes something off her heel against the steps.

"Aw! I stepped in somebody's gum," she moans.

I pull out a fresh smoke. "I think it's a Lifesaver," I tell her.

She discovers that I am right.

"But you were singing the same song as me, weren't you?" she persists.

"I don't know," I explain. "I don't remember."

And here she is. She's brought such a Perplexity into my world. My senses collect every drop of her data. Right then, the bright lights of her jewelry flashes bury themselves in the nostalgic depths of my imagination and memory.

"Well, don't be embarrassed," she suggests. "That's amazing!"

"Yeah," I say.

A vintage black Ferrari pulls out of the lot with its top down. Heidi gives it no attention. The male driver (in his 50s) probably suffers from the same premature ejaculation that the car does, backfiring.

I grunt at the thought.

"Hey, you live down the corner of the next block. You're always smoking cigarettes out front," she says.

I confess, "Yeah. Probably. Maybe."

"I waved to you the other day," she recalls, "and you just turned away."

She must have recognized the big blue hat.

"I'm really groggy in the mornings," I admit.

She smiles. "You're really anti-social."

I correct her. "Not anti-social. Non-social, maybe."

Her face lights up. She starts playing with her hair. "I was just on my way to get my nails done. I've been over at the Sea Port for the past week. God, it's this convention for work. It's so boring."

"What's your name?" I ask.

"Heidi Berillo."

Heidi has a nametag on. She must've forgotten.

"What's yours?" she asks.

"Ben Schreiber," I say, pointing to her nametag. "I was just checking to see if you were a liar."

I stick my hand out.

"You've got a firm grip, Mr Schreiber," she says. She laughs.

Later that afternoon, we are hitting it off like we've known each other for years.

"I can't believe you've never given a girl a pedicure," she scoffs.

"Really?" I reply. (I do like feet.)

I want to tell her that I am a virgin at making love to feet and toes. Hers are perfect.

Heidi's hotel room is strewn with papers and folders. And felt-tip pens. After she lights a joint, she gets a little feisty. Her hair is frizzy and red, and she is wild like my imagination. Like I imagine her imagination.

I puff away on my cigarette. I try to read what she is thinking through her huge green eyes. Which eye cries for good things? Which one doesn't?

I am simply in the moment. I become an observer of myself, observing myself. I'm not my mind. My mind just works for me. Not the other way around. I am enlightened.

For once, normal thoughts slip in, one after another. It becomes easier to focus. I'm not busy judging, analyzing, and making decisions. I am completely focused on Heidi.

I think, who's her dealer? Where's this woman from? What does she tell herself about herself?

I get the impression from Heidi's eyes that she is experiencing something profoundly empty. Somehow, she is dramatically unfulfilled. She is left with voided hope—perhaps a little like me. She looks me right in the eyes. We have a perfect moment, a true connection.

Unfortunately, it ends abruptly. I try not to pry into her life, but I am curious to know more about her. I know I'm not always the best at personal interaction. I'm not sure what is appropriate, sometimes.

She asks a lot about me, but I don't say much back. Heidi asks me about all my confusion, about what I want out of my time here on earth. Big philosophical stuff.

I tell her all of my needs are already met. I tell her I've already lived my life. "I've had enough experiences with myself. All that crap."

And I tell her about my Pops, who always worked hard and always provided my family with wealth. I tell her about my Pops, who meant the world to me.

She calls my 'I've-lived-my-life-already' bit bullshite, and takes a drag off my cigarette.

"Are you happy?" she finally asks.

"I'm not sure if happiness is what I'm really after," I say.

I tell her I am trying to actualize myself as "a writer," a concept that is still completely muddy to me. I have idealized this image of myself in my mind, over the past 10 years, but the image keeps changing. In reality, I am writing mostly in my head, right at that moment. My friends and family want me to put something on paper, to complete something, to achieve something. I don't think it matters anymore.

"Why not?" asks Heidi.

"It's like I'm too far away, in time, from when I was actively participating in things and enjoying them while they were happening."

"How old are you, Ben?"

"Thirty."

Heidi is under the veil of drugs, but she's not paranoid or tripped-out or anything. Inside Heidi, there is somebody genuine, and I can see inside her, just barely make her out. There is somebody real in there. Funny, that's always good to know.

The alarm clock radio is tuned to Billy Joel's "An Innocent Man." Heidi says she has only recently figured out her life, at age 40. I don't believe her, and I tell her so.

"I don't believe you," I say.

She says she takes things very seriously. She says that every encounter happens for a reason.

"Every situation, every consequence. Everything," she adds.

I wonder what my role in her life really is. Somehow, this woman, whom I've just met, knows me so well already. I've really missed that. People usually take very little interest in other people. But with Heidi, I feel honored and appreciated. Still, I feel like I don't really deserve the luxury.

Heidi finishes her joint and pockets the roach. She slips off her open-toed leather shoes and stretches her toes. Her light blue polish has peeled off her nails, like an adolescent girl's.

"I need a pedicure," Heidi says, smiling playfully. "Now!"

Toto's "Africa" airs next on the bedside radio: "Frightened of this thing that I've become," somebody sings. I paint her toes with New Blue toenail polish and she falls asleep.

I write a note: "Thank you. Ben."

I watch her sleep for half an hour. Then I write my home phone number below the note in my usual kiddie-print handwriting and walk out, not really knowing what else to do.

Heidi has a lecture to attend later on.

Later, I sit in my bedroom, still listening to the radio.

"Hurry, boy, she's waiting there for you."

The phone rings. The machine picks up.

Click.

"Hey, Ben, I was just thinking of you."

It's all about me now, isn't it? I can't help it.

I take a carefree stroll on the beach, remembering the best parts of growing up. They flood my mind with nostalgia. I try to remain in the present, but I am stuck in the past.

The moonshine lights up the sand, and the whitecaps, that break 20 feet out. The tide is low, the rolling is a little choppy, but the wave sounds are soothing. I remember how rich and full my life was before. Before. Before what? I wonder what went wrong. I walk along the water's edge to find some inner peace.

I have always enjoyed wandering around, not doing much. I'm comfortable in my imagination, or I'm comfortable nowhere. I think: Has love ever made one whole year of your life miserable?

I wonder if my year of misery is approaching.

It is nighttime.

I start to dream.

Heidi and I are lost in our thoughts; we take in all that surrounds us. We are walking the neighborhood sidewalks, holding hands, until we come to the beach where the whitecaps crash right at our feet. Huge seagulls with wide-open wingspans swoop in for their final feast of the day.

The next morning, the beach is empty. The sky is gray, flat and still, surreal. The gulls fly low in flocks as the long Pacific rollers wash in and out.

We revisit the past. But whose past? Oh my God! The Living Colorful Beauty is so intense. I just can't stand it.

I speak on the phone with Heidi.

"I was downstairs at one of the lectures. It was sooo boring," Heidi says.

"Boring, huh?"

"But I got several compliments on my new pedicure," she teases.

"Thank God," I say, letting out a sigh of relief.

I stand in the empty hotel room that weekend, bewildered. It had been quickly vacated—I could tell. In the bathroom, there is a wet towel lying on the floor, crumpled up from wet feet with a woman's footprints embedded. Empty single-serving soap bottles make a mess on the corner shelf. A Mexican housekeeper readies the room for its next guests.

Back at my place, I play the message player back again.

"So I thought you might like to know what a great job you did, and on such short notice, too. You were just in time for the only panel discussion I really came here for in the first place."

Her telephone had sat on the unmade bed with a box of tissues beside it.

Across the street from me is a fishing pier. A middle-aged couple walks hand in hand to the end of the pier. They stare out at the freight barges sailing into port.

There is a snack and bait stand nearby, but it hasn't opened yet.

At the base of the pier, a pay phone dangles off its hook.

There is some litter rolling around the streets. Not much, though.

"I'm meeting some cool people here, but a lot of them are really boring. This whole convention thing is really dull."

The night before, Heidi and I shared a cherry Slush Puppie on the pier. She popped a few Tylenols because, she said, her head was still throbbing slightly from all the boredom and ennui lingering over her past week at the psych conference. I declined the Tylenol. I was still awe-struck by the whirling seagulls and the shooting stars.

Only a few fishermen are out with their gear; it's still pretty early. An Asian man pulls up a small fish. The thing must be contaminated—the seawater down below is brown and slimy—but his boy grabs the bucket anyway. That small radioactive fish is a keeper.

"So, some of my friends and I wanted to hang out by the bar and talk medicine, but I was hoping we could finish our conversation from last night. I really enjoyed walking the town with you."

After the Slushie, we stopped by my place and shared a Winston. I invited her in, but she declined. We took a drive down the coast under the moon instead.

My house is empty; nobody is up yet. The whole neighborhood is still asleep. A white van drives by. A newspaper is tossed on the manicured lawn out front.

"At least before I leave tomorrow," she said. "Oh, and the weather is so much nicer out here."

Sunlight bleeds horizontally through the closed blinds in my bedroom. Pretty soon I am sound asleep.

"I was thinking about how brilliant you are," Heidi told me on the answering machine. "And, jeez, you have so much talent. People look at you and they see big things."

Expect big things. That's what she meant. Big things, little things. It doesn't matter. It's a stress I can't handle, people expecting things. Anything. Not from me. I live in my head. Alone. I buy porno, coffee, and smokes from the snack and bait shop next door, and come home. Jerk off. Alone. I'm okay with that.

The clock on Georgie's nightstand reads 10:30 am.

I wake up and glance at Georgie. I don't wake him. I crawl out of bed. The sky has cleared up a bit over the beach, and the beach is packed with kite-fliers. A dozen kites glide over the blue-fogged coast, bright with color and wonder.

The hotel room next door is clean by now. Ready for new guests.

Downstairs, a conference is just letting out. The checkout line is already out the door. Most of the guests wear nametags on their blazers. The bellboys are busier than hell.

There are dozens of fishermen on the pier. More men than fish.

"What would you do if you knew you couldn't fail?" Heidi had asked. "I love that question."

I walk the beach, having no clue how to answer.

Most of the neighborhood seems to be outdoors. Most people wear light jackets or hooded sweatshirts. They walk their dogs.

(Parenthetical Pet Peeve) Tiny white dogs with brown runny stuff around their eyes.

They walk their children. Alley cats run loose on the sidewalks, and slide underneath the cars parked on one-way streets. A few cars pass by slowly, going maybe 10 miles an hour. Pest control trucks park outside at least one house per block, it seems like.

There is hardly any crime, violence, or vandalism in this part of the city. Maybe some drugs, some domestics; you know, whatever goes down inside people's private residences—the stuff we never know about.

"Grab hold of just one project and get in there with your teeth and see what happens," she had said. "Why not? If somebody wants a story about you and you're the only one who knows it well enough, then go for it! You would do the world a favor. Hell, do it for me! I'd love to hear about all that crap, as you call it."

A small gate leads to my front door. It is a charming little pad, perfect for a loner like me.

"So what if your dad is some big, well-to-do asshole? This is your chance to shine," she coaxed. "Just go for it!"

It was really nice to have some woman cheering me on. It was the closest thing I'd ever known to true love.

Heidi mentioned that she'd found the perfect little gift in the hotel gift shop. She wanted me to call her later.

The orange sunset flashes between two buildings downtown. I sprawl out on the beach. The sun is setting earlier than usual, I think.

Why did I just leave like that? What about going back?

Somehow, I just couldn't change my mind about Heidi. Reality hit me really hard, and I was scared to go after her, like a real man.

Time stops for just a few exquisite seconds, maybe five or six, until I can't take it much longer. I am self-aware in my newly discovered growth spurt. I am happy, I guess.

I'm so happy, I start to cry—just because I am feeling good. Just because I can. Just until I need to stop.

I start to really appreciate having met Heidi. Maybe I'm still working through the obsession with Claudia.

From the beach, I head back home. I'm already starting to have conversations with Heidi in my head without her being there or being able to answer me.

How lucky she is! Is this love?

Beep.

"Hey, Ben, I was just thinking of you. I was downstairs at one of the lectures."

Beep.

"Hey, Ben, ugh . . .I'm just calling. I'm sorry. It's this stupid conference. I'm not going to go to this class I have in 10 minutes. I'm getting so sick of the same thing over and over again. I'm just in my room taking a bath. Anyway, I'm sorry to bother you. Thanks for letting me vent."

Were we just two shattered souls who ended up trying to save each other in some doomed fashion?

The door swings shut from inside the house. I never get calls. And when I do, I always miss them.

"Hello?" I answer.

"Ben?"

"You must look so beautiful in that bathtub," I say.

"That's one of the nicest things a guy has ever said to me."

Back at her place, her lovely feet await my attention. She doesn't refuse when I administer an oral foot massage while she is still in the bath.

"Right on the arches, Ben," she cries.

I love every minute of it. Her feet quiver with delight. Her toes stretch awkwardly.

"I'm . . . sick . . . I'm dizzy," she moans. "And you're incredible."

Oh, the gibberish we speak in ecstasy, moaning meaningless words.

"Sick-dizzy," she giggles intensely.

She giggles her orgasm, gibbers and moans her pleasure. I understand her, in some fucked-up way.

Afterwards, Heidi lies quietly asleep, on top of the white bed covers. She is wearing men's pajamas. I head back home.

We hadn't made love. She must think of me as the friendly type, like most other women do. But that is fine. I'm used to that.

Heidi is a little nutty, but I like that, too.

She is a mess. She is so innocently a disaster. She is the little Perplexity in my head.

I get home at 3 am. I've always loved the night, when everyone else is asleep and the world is all mine. It's quiet and dark—the perfect time for creativity.

All of a sudden, inspiration comes. Things are clearer. My ideas make more sense. I can finally start to type out, with a little passion, some interesting letters on the screen.

I'll have to begin the story from here, with me, as ridiculous as that sounds. It's been forever since I actually sat down to write again. Does this mean my writer's block has broken? Or am I just fooling myself again?

"I never meant to be such a narcissist," I cry. "I just can't get away from myself."

I've always wanted somebody like Heidi to love. But I still don't know what I need. Maybe I just need one tiny success, one simple thing. Maybe I just need something in this life that will work out in the long run. Maybe I just need to complete something, to get over some things. Maybe I just need something good to last.

God probably took delight in orchestrating me, that day. I'll call it a day of personal growth.

I never hear from Heidi or see her again.

And now my mind runs wild with quiet confusion. The little affair we had felt so soothing to the senses. I'll wake up tomorrow, thinking about today. The next day I'll wake up thinking about tomorrow.

Am I really just a perverted sex addict, like maybe I think I am? Or is this really some kind of love? (You tell me, Dr C. Please.)

Dear Diary:

I think we are all good souls, all of us, even me, even if only deep down inside.

334

The Emperor Concerto, Second Movement

He slaps the snooze button. Half hit. Half miss. It's all gross. He's sweaty and ashamed. He can't even get up. Another fucking horrible day in the life of . . . me. Georgie Gust.

And then laziness creeps in. Georgie starts hating himself. He starts to laugh.

"Snooze, damn it!" he tells the alarm clock.

He always thought a snooze was a good 9, 10 minutes. Georgie actually timed the motherfucker several times. This piece of crap mostly gives him 9 or 10 minutes of extra sleep time.

This day, that day, though, the thing can't even give him two. Cheap, damn thing.

It's 1:30 pm. Even at this hour, so far into the day, he hesitates to open the shades. He hopes it is not all dismal and gloomy outside. He's trying to picture himself somewhere out there, in the world. But he just can't picture it. Maybe if he just stays in bed someone else will open the shades, and save Georgie the trouble of discovering the day.

He closes his eyes, falling half asleep. He finds himself in a non-smoking room at the local three-star hotel. He's hotel-hopping. He needs to get away again. We always need to get away, Georgie and me, even if it's only in our head. Geographical change is the easiest fix.

Georgie opens his eyes. He can't figure out where that three-star hotel has gone. He's already forgotten—he's still at home.

The next day, our place now clean, Georgie still can't get out of his head. He thinks how much he dreads, how much he resents, the effort it takes to take another shower, brush his teeth, and clean himself up, again and again. He just did that yesterday—he shouldn't have to do it again today. Once should be enough. Once and forever. Now Georgie craves something different. He's desperate for something new. He would kill for something new. We both would. (But who?)

This particular morning, the razor burn on Georgie's neck looks like a leper's chafed jock-itch. He can't wait the couple of days for the skin on his neck to heal, but at least he won't have to spend the time and effort to shave again—and that's comforting. After all, the longer he lets his facial hair grow out, the easier it is to shave.

After all these years, Georgie still can't find the right shaving method. Currently, he's on a Panasonic electric for the first layer, then a straight edge without lotion for the second part. Back to a smaller electric beard trimmer, level one, for his goatee shadow. No lotion. No cream. No soap.

With so much nausea, angst, worry, anxiety, and despair welling up inside him, Georgie is suffocating in life. His pathetic and abused gut keeps getting filled with an extra load of explosive anxiety. It's worse than tickle torture.

He hasn't taken any risks for some time now. The rut where he's been trapped has felt so safe. He's had no view; the walls were high, the rut was deep. All Georgie could see was up and out. Up and away. (But away from what? Away where? More unanswerable questions, huh?)

Most things and events really don't have much meaning for him anymore.

Georgie needs meaning more than anything else. But meaning is exactly what Georgie hasn't got. And he probably won't get it, either.

Georgie really doesn't know what the day will bring. The only thing he knows is his sloppy routine of rituals: smoking, shiting, showering, shaving, fixing his hair, flossing, brushing his teeth, taking his meds, and organizing. He uses a ton of paper creating lists of things to do, things to accomplish, so he can feel productive. His father tells him it's important to be productive. So he tries. He really does.

He looks at the bathroom mirror with the sticker in the corner that reads:

JUST TRUST ME.

Right.

Like Georgie's going to trust any of the shitey-assed people he calls friends.

Georgie's pathetic reflection looks back at him from the empty mirror. He has this huge ego blowing up his head, like an untied condom, until it screwballs up and away. He guesses he looks all right these days. No, really. He looks good. He just doesn't know what to do about it. He's so glam rock; he's so smart. It's like he has Asperger's, or some kind of artistic autism. But he's not sick. His doctor knows that. (Doesn't she, Dr C?) He can't deal with a label like depression or stress. He feels much worse than that. He feels like shite. (Do you have a Latin name for shite, Dr C?)

When he shaves, the razor makes love to Georgie's skin. When he pees, he aims for the silent section on the toilet's water edge. Afterwards, he usually farts, shites, and pees again, while he's sitting a little too long on the toilet. Georgie melts into the quality time he takes, thinking on the porcelain tank. His thoughts are trivial. They seem important, but they're nothing he would ever act on. He is on good behavior. It's just a lot of theory.

A CD is usually skipping while Georgie's in the shower. In the shower, he strips down to his naked self. He comes into his true element. He can't see a thing without his glasses, and he can't tell you how many wristwatches he's lost because they don't have waterproofing. But that's okay. Waterproof watches are never appealing to the eye.

(Parenthetical Pet Peeve) Smudged eyeglasses.

There's no washcloth. He washes himself by hand with shampoo—not soap. Shampoo works better because Georgie is hairy, like me. But I don't wash with shampoo. I use hand-milled, organic soap from Northern California—Sunset Cedar, from a shop called Patti's Organics.

Georgie smiles in the shower because he was born a man. The shower is the one place where he's rarely sexually charged. He thinks of himself as a connoisseur, a connoisseur of filth (so soap does not appeal). Women's dirty fingernails, their smelly anal fetishes, anything nasty—her already-smoked cigarettes for the shrine, the smell of gasoline and melted hair follicles. Filth. Georgie hates dropping the soap. He hates all the bottles in the shower. They confuse him and make him think these products are really useful when he knows they're not.

(Parenthetical Pet Peeve) Long fingernails. Worse, long toenails.

He hates falling in the shower. God, what else? What else can they do to mess up his day? (What else is there to complain about?) They should have a soap dispenser that mixes soap with water, like at a car wash. It would be a time-saving convenience. It would save energy. What an idea! He should patent that, and make a million bucks. Yeah, right, Georgie.

Drying off, towels are so coarse and unfitting. Georgie gets water scars in between his toes sometimes.

(Parenthetical Pet Peeve) Hangnails.

Every day, all this, all that. Everything is still the same. Georgie doesn't change. Nothing does. Neither do I. Same shite, different day, we say. Georgie and me.

His feet are a size 12. He wears shoes all the time because his feet embarrass him. He wears blue shoes. That way, he doesn't have to think of how disgusting his own feet are.

His legs are still in shape but he wears long pants, no matter how hot the weather gets. His legs embarrass him, too. Otherwise, he is your generic, overweight pumpkin.

His plump belly sticks out over his belt. Maybe it's cute and huggie-bearish to some single sex addicts, but to hell if Georgie thinks so. He weighs in around 268. His driver's license says he's 168. The driver's license picture doesn't even look like him, but the photo came out pretty nice.

He used to be in shape. Now he just recites affirmations. Now he just tells himself he loves himself just the way he is. It's all bullshite, but it works for him.

His passport picture is pleasing. He enjoys looking at himself.

Georgie dresses up and blow-dries his hair, and then he primps and curls it. He has these highlights. He has a kind of WASPy, honk-Afro look going on. At least his hair is cool; at least his hair is always having a good day.

My hair, now my hair is dark and thick with a bit of a permanent wave. My mother always said it was my best feature. And here I always thought it was my cuddly personality.

Georgie should've picked out his clothes the night before. All his full-size shirts and comfortable pants are at the cleaners, and he doesn't fit into the 32s anymore. He went from a "large" to an "extra large" in shirts. Georgie's just started leaving the shirttails out of his pants. He used to tuck them in, neatly, and wear a belt. But no longer. Still, he'll keep the smaller stuff in the closet—the shirts and pants don't fit, but some of the clothes remind him of the past. They have a nostalgic meaning for Georgie. In Georgie's case, too, clothes make the man. (But make him what? I want to know.)

An hour later, he's finally dressed. Now for the breakfast order.

Like everything else in Georgie's world, breakfast is a chore. He washes the dishes by hand to get his mind off everything else. He can't help feeling like things are falling apart in slow motion. Doing things like that, little things, trivial things, reminds him of being hypnotized. Strolling down the supermarket aisles at midnight with the trippy supermarket music and the paradox of choice everywhere around him. In the grocery store, somehow, time feels different.

Georgie's out of orange juice, and the milk will give him gas, but milk goes best with microwave pancakes. Georgie likes his food a little cold, and he dislikes cooking. He presses the "cancel/stop" button twice on the microwave when it's down to two seconds. It's not like he's in any rush. He has all day.

(Parenthetical Pet Peeve) Fat free = taste free.

His keys are in place. He locks the door without really checking. Georgie's sick and tired of always lock-checking, lock-checking, and then remembering I forget important things after he's already out the door.

(Parenthetical Pet Peeve) If I return home, I suddenly get the feeling I didn't lock the door, then find that I did after all.

Georgie, I think, could very well be a loser, but what's that say about me? That I'd be a loser of a literary character, too? What's wrong with a whiner? A complainer? An agoraphobic with OCD? Is that me? I catch Georgie out of the corner of my eye and wonder what I've done, giving him all these issues.

He swears he's not going to check that lock—but he does, anyway, even though he's just going out for coffee and coming right back. It's not like he's going to plan his whole life, sitting at the counter, sipping his cup of Joe. It's not like he is some romantic poet at the Café Paris.

Finally, Georgie lights his first cigarette of the day—a Marlboro Light—and he worries about cancer, like everything else. And puffs away. After his first cigarette comes another cup of coffee, and then another smoke—and a couple of more smokes, after that.

He brings along his laptop computer, a pad and pen, and a couple of self-help books with the covers torn off, just in case. Just in case something strikes. He rarely uses any of these things in public. Sometimes he drives to the convenience store and sits in the parking lot. He watches people. He likes people-watching. But he doesn't like people. Go figure.

Georgie rarely looks forward to actually dealing with people. But he'll end up running into somebody every time. People get in his way, and they are unavoidable—like signs on the sidewalks, or spills in the elevator. Or sometimes Georgie gets caught in some really important check-in with somebody who really shouldn't care what's up with him. (And neither should Georgie.)

All this whining and baby shite gets him nowhere, he knows— but he just keeps bitching. He dreads being in line at the coffee shop again. He gets self-conscious and self-critical around the perfect advertisement-model-types in line ahead of him. They pretend they're holding their noses and standing clear of the stench coming off Georgie's stale, smelly sweater. It reeks of the toxic fumes of tobacco pollution. And they're all so nice and friendly, and trivial, and guarded. Now that's a challenge. Dealing with these people, I mean, without freaking out or throwing a temper tantrum.

Still, he's half asleep.

Georgie's always half asleep. No matter what I do. Except, of course, when he's thinking of Claudia. She's the only goddamn thing that really makes him feel alive.

Georgie is next in line at the coffee shop. Tabitha's working the counter, but Georgie's not paying much attention to her. He's thinking of Claudia.

What else?

Dear Diary:

I just let others say and do what they want—I just keep being me. Well, sort of.

In the Parallel Midst

I observe Georgie's behavior as he is dropped off by a limousine, in a very arresting atmosphere—a secret environment. I feel Georgie's anticipation and excitement, but we try to stay calm despite the secrecy and mystery. I finally figure out what's going on, exactly as it occurs, in this cryptic, tangential story.

On a dark desert highway, the midday sun reflects off the tinted windows of a speeding stretch limousine. The pearl-white paint of the limo muddies with the billowing clouds in the bright blue sky. Outside, in the burning desert, it's the hot, dry middle of summer. Inside the limo, it's cool. Up front, a road map is open.

From the back seat, through the sleek glass divider, I see Georgie's driver, Frank. He's focused on the long, straight road ahead. He keeps sniffing, like he has a tic, or something. Frank has been Georgie's driver for five years now. After all that time they've become really friendly—like road buddies.

Frank's passenger, Georgie Gust, is studying a face full of that New Age, self-help literature. Somebody is asking Georgie about his self-help books. (Who wants to know? Is that you, Dr C?) So, to satisfy whomever, whatever, Georgie says he's studying them to do the exact opposite of whatever they suggest to do. Georgie says doing everything upside down and backwards keeps things interesting; keeps him from getting bored.

A bright shiny pair of trendy new shoes lies on the floor of the stretch limousine. Georgie takes a deep breath, inhaling through his nose. He closes the book he's just finished: *Twelve Steps for Stupid People*. In what looks like the middle of nowhere, the white stretch limo pulls up to the iron gates of an impregnable, palatial mansion, which is surrounded with high security fences and sharp razor wire. A trio of white-uniformed security guards and police dogs check Georgie's identification cards then open the gates to let the white stretch limo through.

Georgie's checked into a private nudist colony. His purpose here, should he choose to accept it, is to find a members-only, foot fetish club within this incredibly private resort.

Passing through elegant ballrooms and elaborate security checks, he finally finds the basement ballroom where the foot fetish club awaits him to ask curious questions. He feels like he's whispering passwords in some secret code, undergoing rituals and signals in some secret initiation.

Georgie strips down in a coed restroom, keeping his eyes to himself. He shuffles along awkwardly with his head down, his hands modestly covering his genitalia. He enters the foot fetish club. Some secret admirer makes Georgie feel self-conscious, and embarrassed, but there really isn't anything wrong with Georgie attending orgies. Except that it's not the cure for whatever ails him. What Georgie really lacks, those New Age self-help books tell him, what Georgie really needs (although, of course, he isn't aware of it, at least not consciously) is his "soul's work," or his purposeful vocation in the cosmic scheme. (At least, that's what his Guardian Angel tells him. But then, who is his Guardian Angel, anyway? Is that you again, Dr C?) He doesn't have a project, hobby, job, or relationship that he can pour caring, creative energy into that would result in the respect, appreciation, and connectedness from other loving, caring people that he so truly desires. And that's what he really needs; that's what would make him better—isn't it?

Georgie and the other foot fetishists (about 50 men and women) are lying on the white marble floor, on their backs, waiting for someone or something (not sure what) to come and begin the session. Everyone is perfectly silent, holding their breath.

Finally, a loud, high-pitched siren screams, startling everybody awake, and about a hundred women enter the room. They scatter, performing barefoot massages and shoe-smothering exercises for all the club members on the floor. This orgy, club members say, is a completely safe and free arena where the foot-fetishists can be completely naked, both outside and inside, exposing themselves to each other, without shame. Georgie inhales the rank aroma of vinegar and smelly, sweaty feet, and the fetid odors seduce Georgie like a drug. He relaxes.

The out-of-body experience, the heavenly sensations, the feeling of non-existence—the sheer, ecstatic fulfillment Georgie receives from this hour-long foot-trampling—this orgiastic foot massage among his fellow foot fetishists, it feeds Georgie's best, most natural self. Among the other orgy-goers, there are ouches and moans and yelps, but Georgie seems to be at peace. He lies on the white marble floor, completely nude, with no inhibitions.

During the "coffee hour" the after party, we find Georgie alternating between daring, sympathetic, or even kind of wacky, as he chitchats with other orgy participants. Georgie's doing the best he can, working hard to make sense of his confused life. Women here seem to admire his risk-taking, his charming comments and postures, his urgent search for something to believe in. He tries to collect as many phone numbers as he can while there, and he's quite successful.

We really admire Georgie's daring, passionate intensity (don't we?) as he devotes himself to the intensely spiritual search for the painful sexual high that comes from fetishism and masochism. Some part of Georgie wants to get lost in the orgiastic swirl of fetishists and masochists, to escape into a "natural" high. Georgie's like a darshan, experiencing bliss from the mere sight and smell of his guru-like runner in the "zone," enjoying the runner's high. But there's also a part of Georgie that's self-conscious, self-aware, through the whole orgy and its aftermath.

Among the ecstatic orgy-goers, Georgie's mind sees a Rubik's Cube of interior connections, disconnections, and second thoughts—constantly shifting, constantly changing, as one feeling is ruined or replaced by another, in these perpetual couplings and un-couplings of sweaty hands and smelly feet.

Georgie's been getting off, sexually or not, on the human foot ever since childhood. It's always been an "easy-to-satisfy" pleasure, in public especially. But having advanced beyond childhood now, and finding out where the "real good" fetish houses are, Georgie's since been getting tired of his foot fetish, finding little room to expand on his fantasies. He can no longer get off so easily, as we find, even at this huge, ecstatic foot-fetishist orgy. He has trouble finishing. He has trouble reaching his climax. He needs something even more impure and unsacred, some more intriguing, elaborate, fantasy material to satisfy him.

Georgie's becoming obsessed with achieving constant, never-ending orgasms. It's a relieving distraction from being perpetually unfulfilled. He has such a voracious, addictive, and obsessive appetite that he can't imagine having anything less than total orgasmic pleasure.

Georgie's in the white stretch limo, on his way home from the foot fetish club. He's wearing shorts that reveal a pair of badly bruised knees.

"What happened to your legs?" Frank asks Georgie.

Georgie answers, "Oh, that . . . I crawled on the floor. It was covered with hard salt crystals."

Georgie asks Frank if he can sit in the front seat with him. They pull over to have a cigarette and a little heart-to-heart. Georgie tells Frank that he once had a nanny, when he was a boy, who disciplined him in sick and twisted ways when he didn't do his homework or forgot to flush the toilet. This abusive nanny hated him for his having so many privileges. She liked to see him crawl.

The whole thing strikes Frank as crazy—that somebody would actually take the time to execute all these fucked-up torture methods! He cites how the Iraqis keep prisoners in brightly lit rooms for days, subjecting them to various tortures and abuses, until the victim loses sense of self and time.

"Somebody actually sits down and thinks up this shite!" Frank fumes. "Fucking perverts. Fucking creeps."

"My old nanny used to get off to the torture stuff. She must have!" Georgie tells Frank. "Or else, why would she keep doing it to me?"

Frank agrees. He suggests that Georgie try to make something of his life. "Living well!" Frank says. "That's the best revenge!"

"Yeah," Georgie scoffs. "I'll make a mess of everything, is what I'll do."

"What do you want, Georgie, for real?" Frank asks. "You already have everything."

"One orgasm: a peak experience that will last my whole lifetime. That's what I'm really searching for. During orgasm, it's like I don't even exist. That's what I really want. Wouldn't you?"

Georgie's ravishingly starved for an everlasting orgasm, a wild rollercoaster fantasy that will show him what heaven is really like.

And since Georgie knows his goals pretty fucked up, he also keeps a much nobler goal buried deeply within him: To get married and have a family.

"By the way, how's that woman you've got a thing for? That Margaret? The helpline operator?" asks Frank.

But Georgie hasn't been in touch with Margaret lately. In fact, they've separated, still friends, for the time being.

Georgie tells Frank about his jealousy of Margaret. Her abundant life is always busy somehow. Filled with work and a sense of achievement, and even love. Georgie's life, by contrast, often feels empty, meaningless, and lonely.

When Georgie gets home, Frank drops him off in the white

stretch limo. Before Frank drives away, he flashes a brief smile. "I'll see you later," Frank says.

Dear Diary:

Biscuit, back it, rabbit, flap it.

Georgie's Home Is My Home

Georgie's living room is quaint and contemporary:

There's an overkill of every fancy modernization, every electronic doodad, and every entertainment gadget that could fit in the room. There are photos and drawings framed across the walls of all his past girlfriends, and on the bookshelves are awards, trophies, and posters from his travels. There are hardcore intellectual books—piles and piles of them—most of them in three copies. It's the same with his video and music collection.

He has way too many things. Some of his sketches and notes, left lying around, are only halfway completed. His drawings and paintings are scattered, unfinished, but still show signs of brilliance.

Then there are the graph paper drawings—intricate designs clearly drawn with some purpose. It's obvious that Georgie has a really strong mind—maybe too strong for his own good. And he has way too many projects going on—arbitrary projects, redundant and grandiose.

His past seems rich and full. But he's lost the ability to find comfort in sleep. He has nothing to look forward to. All his needs are taken care of.

The things in his house, although artistic, are placed according to obscure mathematical relationships. Everything corresponds to everything else. For example, Ben's quantum physics material is neatly clustered and labeled with the corresponding videos and books, near an MC Escher print.

The stationary bike is surrounded by trophies, workout tapes, sports magazines, and signed baseballs.

A metal ceiling fan reflects light while it's spinning, spinning slowly above the wheels of the bike.

Georgie passes by the running shower, now steaming.

Georgie daydreams in the shower, even when the soap falls. He doesn't wash his hair today. You never look your best when you're about to encounter The One, The One you've been waiting for all your life. You're never fully prepared for that. Georgie resolves never to be fully prepared.

"No sex. Love," Georgie mutters in the shower. "She must have thought of me as the friendly type. That's fine. I'm used to it. I enjoyed myself and that's all that matters. God probably took delight in watching his orchestration of me that day. I'll call it personal growth. I'll never see or hear from Claudia ever again.

"My mind ran wild with quiet confusion. It felt so soothing to the senses. I could wake up tomorrow, thinking about that day, the next day about today. While I'm in love, I stop writing, for the most part. I know it won't last forever. I'm in love. I scoff at the thought. Me? In love? In love with Claudia? Me? In love with Claudia."

Radiation Babies: One of Them is Georgie Gust.

Georgie thinks: Yet she drags off my cigarettes so seductively.

Dear Diary:

Today I'm deciding that my life is my own. No apologies or excuses. So, all day I've just been writing a lot, masturbating more, and seldom cumming, too . . . Ha.

Cumming Too

In my home office, at my New Mexico ranch (or is it our home office?), several home video cameras record me in this cramped space, all from different angles.

I set the last camera up, and then sit down at my desk. I'm slightly on edge, nervous and scratching myself silly-like. I speak to the cameras. Holding a set of remote controls, one for each camera, I often fumble.

"You can see me close up," I say. "Real close."

With the remotes, I zoom a couple of cameras in.

"I'm here," I say, "stuck inside this little home office."

I roll one of the cameras around to capture the yard outside the window.

"Outside, it's scorching hot. I can barely breathe out there. Hell, I can barely breathe in here."

Dear Diary:

I sure am schizophrenic, which is to say that I suffer from schizophrenia, also known as "split-mind disease," even though this label has caused a lot of confusion with multiple personality disorder, which is not the same thing. The symptoms are common, yet you won't find two schizophrenics who are alike. This illness affects us all differently. As far as I can tell, I'm a schizophrenic with paranoid tendencies and extreme social anxiety. Author Sylvia Plath described the mental chaos as existing within the eye of the tornado—still and practically void, while everything else is ripped, ridded, and devastated all around you. This, I can agree with.

Don't Be Afraid To Let Them Show

Georgie takes my shirt off; a black t-shirt that has "Bitch," written on the front in thick, white letters. It's drenched with sweat. He wrings it out, dripping, right on the floor.

Georgie rinses his hands and returns. He takes one of the cameras off of its tripod and shoots from his hands. So he can shoot me. But I'm halfway crawling out of my skin—only halfway, though. Everything is stuck at the surface, where the "I" in my reality meets the "we."

"God," I say. "Right, Georgie?"

"What?" he says.

"Fucking yuck," I say.

"Ben, how are you feeling?"

"Itchy," I tell him. "My whole body itches."

(Parenthetical Pet Peeve) Backs always itch where and when I can't reach to scratch.

He watches me scratch myself.

"Where?" he asks, "Where do you itch, Ben?"

I show him where, and more itches surface. Light dandruff seems to sprinkle on the floor. Not just head-dandruff. Whole-body dandruff.

"Ankles," I say, "inside my elbows and under my knees. My groin. Crotch."

More dandruff sprinkles like dust-motes in the sunlit air. "Hey, what is that stuff?" Georgie says. "Scurf? Scruff? Err, what?"

He zooms in with the camera on the dropping flakes.

"I'm telling you, okay?" I say. "Scabs. Flakes." I go on and on about it. "You know? The stuff is, like, growing on me."

"More like you're scratching it off," Georgie says.

Suddenly, I lighten up. "Ve-ery funny," I say with a slight laugh. "You know, I call them creepy-crawlies." I pause.

After giving it some thought I say, "Here, man, take a look at this." I expose the gunk underneath my fingernails. "Scrunge. Scroties."

Georgie backs off and lowers the camera. "No, thanks," he says. "I'd rather not."

"I'm fucking grossed out. I'm just so . . . dirty. You know?"

"Then take a shower, Ben!" Georgie says sardonically. "You're being way too hard on yourself."

"But I'm just so scruffy," I scoff. "So yucky."

"Ben, come on, partner. Old buddy."

Dear Diary:

I'm manic today, so I'm to journal all my stream-of-thought today. So how's your day so far? Etch-a-Sketch-on-Acid-Stream-of-Thought—Over—and—Over—Pseu-Pseu-Pseudonym—Boo. I need to write fiction. More fiction. I need to write. I NEED MY WRISTBAND. And man-oh-man, brand new newbian, my new psych meds adjustment—whoa! It's goodies. Almost better than purple Pez! Tics, be nice now. Again, I let my freak flag shine with my mentally ill mind and unsurpassed resiliency. And treating people as they are, so they remain that way. Treating them as though they are already what they can be and I help them become what they are capable of becoming. It is what it is and was what it was. Moving onward. I'm an ever-evolving process myself, of consciousness, itself. Make it and makeshift it. Prototype it! Grab it. Snag it. Life is short; making it my best day forever and always—always—always myself. It is possible to not be myself, so I'll be me with the occasional pen name. Ah. And a la fin de l'envoi, je touché. But not quite yet—The book—the book—and a bathroom break.

Office Bathroom

I'm still complaining when Georgie leads me into the shower.

"What are these ultraviolet-blue boils about to burst on my thighs? I can't even close my legs right!"

Dear Diary:

If I was a girl I'd want my name to be Mo' Niique! Random thought, totally worth putting on paper.

In The Shower—Water Off

"Might pop the boils, huh?"

"Yeah, man!" I exclaim. I turn to Georgie. "Is it hep?" I say, excited by the possibility, "or what?"

"Hep?" Georgie echoes. "No. Why? Do you want it to be?"

I think harder as Georgie helps me take off the rest of my clothes. I can see, and even smell, my skin. It's sporadically yellowed.

"Is it AIDS?" I ask, just to annoy him.

But Georgie isn't annoyed. "No, Ben," he tells me, "No. Really. It's not uncommon for a diabetic, like you, to have these. These . . ."

I feel a lecture coming, so I break in. "I know. I know. The lesions."

"You, Ben. You can get these lesions, as you call them."

"In a way, yes, in a way I want AIDS. I want even cancer."

"That's stupid. Why?"

"So," I say, "so I can go through more illness, so I can overcome anything, maybe everything. I'm sort of rebelling or conforming against something—or for something. I don't know." I shrug.

"Pretty hard to do both at once, though." Georgie turns the shower on.

I yelp.

He flushes the toilet and I yelp louder.

(Parenthetical Pet Peeve) People who flush the toilet when I'm taking a shower.

Later that afternoon, I watch the trees outside losing their leaves. But the wilderness, the trees—everything is closing in on me.

The tall trees block most of the mountains in the distance.

I try to step out of my own little world at home or in my head—but I'm all alone, shivering, with only a towel wrapped around me.

Georgie shows up again. He steps closer to me. I have some Cyndi Lauper song playing in my head. I think it's called "True Colors," and it's stuck on repeat. She's singing some crazy lyric about feeling small in this crazy world. I feel like I'm wrapped in a blanket of blood-orange, warm-orange, actually, pure fucking orange.

"Come on, Ben." Georgie says. "No daydreaming. Not now. Come on back inside."

"Wait, I'm still freezing," I whine.

I walk around on the pathway towards the river. I guess I must look agitated. I guess I must look that way because I still am. Agitated, that is. I am the agitation. I must be choosing, I must be manifesting, those New Age books say, this agitation. My "Divine Force" must be doing it this very moment. I'm manifesting the agitation of my infestation.

Then I get this thought, an instant of bliss, where I'm a lesbian, a woman. I'm in this coming-of-age film where my wife tells me how beautiful I am. I tell her the same thing, too. "You're so beautiful," I say. The film is a small art-house epic with a limited audience and, of course, the critics kill it. Still, I'm in love, privately, with the woman I want—who I want to be. My lesbian wife smiles and I see Georgie is right behind me, zooming in with the handheld camera like he thinks I'm thinking this shite up. Like I'm choosing, like I'm manifesting this shite. He's busily capturing all of my announced irritations as I continue to blurt them out. And now my daydream is over.

I'm still scratching myself furiously. Bugs and mosquitoes swarm over me.

"See, Georgie? Look." I say. "Mosquitoes. Clit-nibbling." I say. "It's like a tic."

Georgie drops his gaze, looking around the viewfinder.

"Clit-nibbles? That's a good one. You mean they're biting you," he says, eyes zooming through the lens.

"My arms," I say, "My face. My ankles. A bee's nest. Mosquitoes and wasps. There's too many fucking bugs out here."

"Like I said," Georgie says. "Come back inside now."

"Fine," I say. "I'm coming."

"You can't run, Ben. You can't hide." Georgie says, "From anything. Can you?"

As we walk back, I can't even respond.

"See? You're stuck" Georgie smiles encouragingly. "Now come on back inside."

There's a long pause as we keep on walking. Georgie puts his arm around me. "Why not give us a tour of the house?" he says. "Will you, Ben?"

I'm barefoot, wearing my robe, still talking to Georgie's camera. I jump around the house, giving the tour of all its shortcomings and issues, like it's me. Like I'm on "This Old House," or something.

"Well," I say, "the walls are concrete, cinderblock, 70s stuff. Outside. Dirt, no grass-infested with goatheads and foxtails. The goatheads, they jam into my bare feet like sharp crystal glass."

"You're stinky, dirty, overgrown, hairy, scarred, bare feet," Georgie prompts. "Just look at you, Ben."

"I know. I have to pull the suckers off, each little fucking goathead, one by one, and the dogs keep bringing them in, too."

I let the three dogs in. Outside, the courtyard is adorned with colorless landscaping and a few empty fountains. Why don't I remember any of this? It's always been ugly, just plain ugly out there. After peeking, I turn my inside-out back inside.

"Jeez," I'm thinking. "It's like, 120 goddamn degrees out there. The humidity is up to nearly 40%. So much for getting out of New York. So much for getting out of California and moving out here, huh? Out here to Albuquerque, where the weather is always just gorgeous. Where everything is beautiful."

I start feeling doubtful.

"So much for this suffocating morsel of love, living in this living hell. So much for this poor, mortal morsel of a person I call myself. Whoever myself is."

"Eloquent," Georgie says. "That's very eloquent, Ben."

I look at him, showing him my sorrow, and smile. "Okay. Cut," I say.

Dear Diary:

One thing I can't define? Time. I can waste it, use it, abuse it, and kill it. Blah. But I don't think anybody can define it. Cool shite, feeling the runner's high in the writing zone. I can handle the mania. So it's sure worth the depression, when it comes.

354

History of Sex

It's nighttime, the dead of night. Sometime in the past. I'm in our guesthouse. (And I guess you ought to know: Our guesthouse was once New Mexico's nastiest crack den. Still is, in my mind. Yeah, it still is in my mind.)

The phone keeps ringing and ringing. The dim bulb light flickers, lighting up the cramped living room piled knee-high with dirty clothes, abandoned pizza boxes, crushed beer cans, half-eaten chocolate bars, everything a pig leaves behind after months of just letting it lie.

I stumble through this mess, with a crack pipe in my mouth. I'm searching for the phone. And the phone just keeps on ringing.

The Troupe (a troupe of zombies) jerk spasmodically out of the walls. The Nameless Movie Director, a slick guy in his 30s, carrying a megaphone; The Fit and Slim Jogger, a really sleek dude in his 20s wearing an Olympic jogging outfit; The Successful Stockbroker, a flashy dresser in his 40s in Armani with Hugo Boss kicks; and The Poor Homeless Guy, who's old-aged or ageless, dressed in ratty clothes filthier than the mess in our crack den. All of them surround me, spasming and jerking, shuddering and twitching.

And from somewhere, Georgie appears. Or maybe from nowhere. Georgie says I don't even notice how creepy they are, these crackhead dudes. But I do. I really do.

Georgie says those crackheads watch me, when I'm not watching. Like now. They copy me when I rummage through my pile of clothes, discovering an old closed umbrella. (Why an umbrella? Who knows? Not me.)

(Parenthetical Pet Peeve) If I leave my umbrella in the car on a cloudy day, it will rain. If I bring it with me, it won't.

And then the phone stops ringing.

Dear Diary:

I don't know what my dream is, so I think about what I want my life to feel like. Then write it out. Thus living it. Living the life, baby!

Umbrella Makes Me Spread My Wings

I pick up the umbrella and examine it intently. It's one of those cheap umbrellas that will snap, break, tear, and tatter away with the slightest gust of wind. A Georgie Gust of wind, for example. (Are you there, Georgie?) Funny. I never use an umbrella, so somebody—some other crackhead—must've left it here while making a delivery of cheese or crack or whatever I was into at the time. I don't remember somehow, but I must've been in the rain. It must have been sometime. I can't remember. (The time is now.)

The zombies copy me. They pick up their own closed umbrellas and examine them intently. Their umbrellas are the expensive kind with elegant, cane-like handles, looped, curled at the end, sort of mobster style. Real gangsters, not gangstas. You know—classy.

Thunder booms. Lightning crackles. The room glows. Rain begins to pour.

I open my umbrella, but it's shredded, and I'm instantly drenched in the downpour.

The zombies open their umbrellas, which are not shredded. They look at their umbrellas. They look at me. They look at themselves. They seem somewhat confused.

I take the crack pipe out of my mouth. Drippy rainwater pools up in the bowl so I can't light it. (So much for the umbrella, huh?)

I dump out the water, try lighting the pipe. Then I notice the zombies again. I hold my crack pipe up in their direction, like I'm asking them for a light, without really asking. You know? (The zombies know.)

The zombies back off.

And the rain stops.

The phone starts ringing again.

I'm not wet anymore, but I'm not carrying the shredded umbrella, either. I still have the unlit crack pipe in my mouth. I'm still looking for a light. I'm still searching for the phone.

I crawl over piles of dirty clothes, across discarded boxes of pizza. I creep over all of the garbage.

The zombies, also not carrying umbrellas anymore, follow me. They creep after me, searching.

And the phone keeps ringing.

I pick up a crushed pizza box and shake it, hard. Something

rattles around inside. I don't know what.

The zombies pick up their pizza boxes and shake them, too.

I open the pizza box, exposing a crumpled pack of cigarettes. I pull out a cigarette from the pack. I light it up and take a deep drag.

The zombies do likewise. They talk to themselves like this is some goddamn party. Wine glasses pop up in their hands.

With a lit cigarette still stuck in my fingers, I smile at them. I pick up a half empty beer bottle with cigarette butts floating around inside it, and I raise it in their direction, like I'm toasting them.

"Here's to you, zombies," I say. "Fuck you, anyway!"

Then I down the beer, butts and all. And to me, this foul brew tastes good. Tastes something, anyway.

The Director, Jogger, and Stockbroker watch me, shaking their heads in disapproval, like I'm some kind of second-class citizen or something. Maybe even a transvestite, maybe a queer, maybe something even creepier. Hell, I'm better than all you zombies! I want to say.

The Homeless Guy downs his beer, too. He belches happily. He nods at me like he likes me.

"Thanks, brother," he says.

I stretch out on the mound of dirty clothes and pizza boxes and close my eyes. I'm trying to get some shuteye. I try to tell myself I'm dreaming all this, like it's all some kind of sweet dream.

The Homeless Guy stretches out, like me, and shuts his eyes, too. He starts snoring, like he's having sweet dreams too.

The Director, Jogger, and Stockbroker keep staring at me disapprovingly.

I take a deep breath like I'm falling asleep, and drop my cigarette. The Homeless Guy drops his butt, too.

The phone stops ringing. Time passes.

I open my eyes. The whole room is on fire. But at least The Homeless Guy and the other zombies are gone. I must have burnt them out, I think.

Somehow, I have the lit cigarette stuck back in my hand again, but I don't care about the burning room anymore.

I watch the fire get bigger and bigger, and then watch it shrink and die out, for no reason. From nowhere, out of the fire, steps Georgie Gust. He's in his 30s, Georgie is. And he's my alter ego— that's my Georgie. He's sitting there on a pile of dirty clothes.

Georgie has the crack pipe in his hand.

"I thought you quit," he says.

Georgie scolds me like I'm his alter ego, or something.

"Crack?" I say. Then I glance nonchalantly at the cigarette in my hand.

"They will kill you, you know," I hear.

I take a dark, deep drag.

"Emphysema," Georgie says, "Cancer. Heart disease."

I flick the lit cigarette in Georgie's direction, like a big gummy booger. It splats onto the carpet.

"Tsk, tsk," Georgie says.

He just stands there, brushing off his clothes, even though no cigarette butts even landed on him.

"Real mature there, Ben," I say to myself. (You see, I'm Georgie, too, and Georgie Porgie's me. We're really close, Mr Georgie and me. Sometimes we don't even know who's who.)

"Just burn down whatever you don't like," I say to Georgie. "Why don't you? Starting with me." I keep on staring at Georgie for a long time. Finally, I say, "It's Kelly."

"What? Who?" Georgie replies, incredulous. "Your wife?"

"My wife. Sure, all of us remember, from the get-go. Kelly is my wife, and my future wife, too. We're lost in time and space. Kelly's the one woman I haven't let in on my secret obsession with you, Georgie, and your obsession with Claudia. I've been keeping everything from her and have never been honest with, her, with Kelly. I blame you, Georgie. She needs to know. "

"After all the confusion ends, Ben, if it does, well, I want to get her back, but you deserve her more, I'll admit it."

"But I am Ben and Ben needs Kelly the most. Ben will battle by any means, Georgie; you don't need this cracked-up confusion. You've got Claudia already. Ever since you stopped at the silly store. And look where you are now. Take a look at Kelly and what you've done to her. And look, because that's what you've done to me, too."

Kelly, an emaciated, skin-and-bones, apron-wearing, rolling-pin-carrying Housewife Zombie in her 30s, twitches and jerks into view.

Georgie takes a closer look. "That's not your wife," he says. "That's not Kelly."

The Housewife Zombie from the 1950s twitches and jerks out of sight; she's replaced by Conservative Zombie Wife (a Grace Kelly clone), wearing a straight skirt that ends well below her knees, an angora sweater with a clip, and sensible flat shoes.

"And that's not your wife, either," says Georgie. "You can't fool me."

Conservative Zombie Wife spasms and jerks out of sight. She's replaced by The "Real" Kelly—still a zombie, but kind of sexy, wearing a tight t-shirt and jeans.

I stare at her for several seconds, "Oh, Kelly, my wife to be, my Living Colorful Beauty. I do. I remember."

"She doesn't get me," I say.

"Ahh," Georgie says. "I get it, Ben. It's the old line. It's my wife—she doesn't understand me. Right?"

Kelly flashes a "Yeah, sure," kind of look at Georgie.

"It's not me," he says. "It's him. Blame it on him."

Kelly flashes the same kind of "Yeah, sure," look at me.

"She doesn't get my . . ." I say, "she doesn't get my obsession. You know." I pause significantly. "She doesn't get my Claudia."

Claudia Nesbitt, the Real Zombie Pin-Up Poster-Girl for the eroticism of homeliness—old, chubby, bespectacled, pimpled, chunky, and brutal. Besides that, a vampire undulates lasciviously into view.

I sigh in rapt appreciation.

Kelly lifts an eyebrow.

The phone starts ringing again.

Claudia notices Kelly. She hisses, baring her fangs.

Kelly flips Claudia off with a stiff "fuck you" finger and twitches and jerks out of sight.

Claudia watches me as I look for the phone. Still undulating, she comes closer and closer.

Stepping between us, Georgie blocks her path.

She stops dead. Claudia's dead, I tell myself, get used to it.

I throw clothes from one pile to the other. I throw pizza boxes from one end of the room to the other while Georgie and I talk.

"She gets jealous," I say.

Georgie is still keeping an eye on Claudia.

"Who? Kelly?" he says.

"Yeah. Kelly," I say, "She's my grill. She grills me, see?"

The Stockbroker wheels a grill into sight and douses charcoal fluid on it. I briefly see myself spinning on the rotisserie.

Georgie frowns at him disapprovingly.

The Stockbroker wheels the grill away.

I can still hear the phone ringing, but it seems quieter now.

"Constantly," I say.

I shrug.

The Housewife Zombie shows up again. She shakes the rolling pin menacingly, first at me, then at Claudia.

"That doesn't sound like the Kelly I know," says Georgie.

The Housewife Zombie disappears. The "Real" Zombie Kelly shows up again, looking slightly miffed, but maybe also somewhat amused.

"And all she is," I say. "All Claudia is . . . was . . . ever will be . . . is an obsession. You know? She's just a figment of my imagination."

Claudia frowns, begins to fade out.

I finger my crotch.

"And a goddamn good one, too," I say.

Claudia wavers back into sight.

Kelly fingers her own crotch.

"And what is Kelly?" asks Georgie, "Chopped?"

The Movie Director shows up again, carrying a meat cleaver.

Claudia's image gets clearer.

"No," Georgie says to the Movie Director. "Just say no."

The Director disappears.

"There is . . . was . . . will never be anyone like Claudia," I admit.

Now Claudia is crystal clear. She's right there in front of me.

And I'm just about masturbating.

Kelly imitates me.

"Fuck me," she says, but tauntingly.

Claudia wavers.

The phone gets louder.

The Movie Director shows up again and starts fondling Kelly. She fondles him back, but she keeps looking at me, like she doesn't give two shites about him. Trying to make me jealous, or something.

When I get real again, I stop fingering myself.

Claudia fades out.

"There's no one like Kelly," Georgie says. "Right, Ben?"

The ringing phone keeps getting louder.

"If you don't watch out, Ben, she'll leave you. You know that, Ben," Georgie says. "Just like Claudia."

I look distracted. Annoyed, even.

And that's when Georgie disappears.

I keep looking for the damn phone. It blares unbearably.

Like before, I throw everything from one side of the room to the other.

The phone blares and hollers.

I'm holding my ears.

"Goddamn phone!" I shout.

The ringing phone turns into police sirens.

The zombies—all of them, including Kelly—climb out of the pile of garbage. Georgie's there, but this time he's a zombie, too.

One by one, they slip simple black suits over their costumes, then clip guns and police batons on each other.

I shriek (not necessarily out loud, though) in terror as the zombies turn on me. The zombies want to eat me. I'm nothing but zombie bait.

I race away. Over the clothes. Over the pizza boxes. Over the whole mess.

I'm outside, now, somewhere in Albuquerque. I race through an alleyway lined with metal garbage cans and dumpsters.

Every time I pass a garbage can, it clatters noisily down and starts rolling towards me, forcing me to jump over it.

Every time I pass a dumpster, one of the zombies pops up and points a police baton at me.

I'm terrified. I keep racing away, panting and sweating.

I fall down. I faint. I blink out.

I wake up back at the crack pad, just like before. I have a crack pipe in my mouth, and I'm lying on a pile of old dirty clothes.

I'm alone.

The phone rings. Not so noisily.

A toilet flushes in the background.

Georgie walks into the room. He glances at me and nudges me with his foot.

I roll over on my side. The phone is underneath me.

Georgie picks up the receiver.

"This is Ben," Georgie answers. "I'm not here. Leave a message."

The dial tone fades and fades.

Blackout.

Dear Diary:

If I was rich, I wouldn't be greedy. I'd donate half of my riches to the needy. But I am a diagnosed schizophrenic. But I'm ill, chill,

361

cool—ill. Not mentally ill. Well, in a way. Artistically ill, like Van Gogh, among others.

Part IV: Dr C Meets Mr Clean

Mr Clean

Excerpts from Ben's secret diary:

It is always late September, always Indian summer, when the air is always really crisp and clear, the red, brown, and yellow leaves are always changing, and the bright summer light is always fading away. It's never winter, it's never spring, never summer. It's always fall, always September 1987, when those creepy builders are tearing up our old house. I'm shut up inside and I can't even get away from the fucking noise and smells. I always want to go outside and ride my bike. But my mother says, "It's too cold to go outside, Ben." And so all day long there's this whine of electric drills and power saws, a shrill, high-pitched screeching noise, and the sweet–sour smell of freshly sawn wood attacking my nose, my ears, and my eyes.

I'm 11 years old—just a little squirt. Not even big enough to be the big jerk I'll turn out to be. But, yeah, it's me—Benjamin J Schreiber. Only I'm called Benjy, now, mostly. I'm living with mother and Pops in suburban New York, three doors down from New Jersey. My mother rags at me daily in that same whiney, high-pitched voice: "We are not from New Jersey," she says. "We are not like those Jersey people."

My mother is really clear about that. It's the one thing that she is ever really clear about. We are not from New Jersey. She says that only niggers, spics, and white trash live in New Jersey. And so, mother says, we're definitely not from New Jersey.

"Okay, mother," I say, to get her off my back. "We're not from New Jersey. Now can I go outside and ride my bike?"

The whole truth is that I don't care where I'm from, really. I just want to go outside, where the sycamore and maple leaves are changing. I just want to go outside, where the whole world is on fire with blazing colors. The leaves flame red and gold and the sky is a brilliant, vivid blue, a Georgia O'Keefe kind of blue. I just want to go outside and ride my bike, but my mother says it's too cold out.

"It's too cold to ride your bike, Benjy," mother says. "You'll get sick. You have to stay inside, with me." And I have to listen to her, because she's my mother. But I know she's lying. I can see it in her face. I can see the way her eyes shift away from me when she tells me—her lips purse tight, "No, Benjy. It's too cold. You'll catch your death." Or maybe, mother, my death will catch me?

My mother doesn't want to let me go outside because my Pops is divorcing her and she can't take the thought of being alone, not even for a little while. That's the real story, behind her bullshite lies. But she doesn't have the guts to tell me. And I know it.

Our family is so unhealthy that I can feel it, taste it, and see it. It's like being sick, or tired, or dead—though I don't know, really, what dead people are like. Or even really sick people. I only know something is sick, or tired, or dead in my family now that Pops is leaving. For my mother, I'm the uncle and son, maybe even the husband and son she never had (and now will never have.) How can I be all of those things for her, anyway? I'm just a kid, just 11 years old. Yeah, that's me, Benjamin J Schreiber. Only you can call me Benjy, mother.

My mother never says she's lonely—not to me, anyway—but she tells her friends. Especially Rita. She talks to her friends like I'm not really there, even when I'm right there in the room. She talks to Rita Morita, Rita with the short hair and long, painted nails. Rita comes over Tuesday and Thursday afternoons to play canasta and drink gin and tonic. My mother tells her, "I can't take it, Rita. I just can't take being alone like this."

"Now, now," Rita says and pats my mom's hand until she starts crying (my mother, that is). My mother says she's not going to make it and what is she going to do? Meanwhile, Rita polishes off her third cocktail and pours herself another.

And that's why I can't go outside—because it's not Tuesday or Thursday, and Rita's not there to keep my mother company, and because my three-year-old sister is too little to be company. So I have to be there for mother, and be her Little Man, even though she knows, and I know, that I can't give her what she really needs.

So, instead of going out, I kneel on the nubby white couch, resting my chin against the back cushion and stare out the window. Instead of riding my bike, like I really want, I have to listen to Mike Nova, the contractor, who's sitting at the piano in our living room (my mother's living room I guess, not mine—so white and stark and modern as it is. Blindingly white). I listen to Mike Nova droning on in his whiney voice, just like those electric drills and power saws screeching in the background, trying to woo my mother into getting more bang for her buck. But he's just trying to talk her into expanding the renovation into a complete remodel.

Which she does. Eventually. Mike transforms a simple remodel job into something more like a whole second home built over the skeleton of our old house.

This demolition job, this so-called renovation, this complete remodel, it will be my mother's final fall fling. It is her last big double dip into my father's money, because after this, they'll split the money.

All I know is that my Pops is never around anymore, and I can't handle that, either. It's like a big empty spot, and that sick, tired, dead feeling fills our old new house. Pops told me early this morning he would be home tonight, but he's not. And he's not home the next day, either. So, I spend the whole day in my own secret loneliness, my sick, tired, dead feeling—like a winter weariness. I sit staring out the window at the blazing trees and the red, brown, and gold leaves, waiting to see a bald albino jogger I call Mr Clean.

Mr Clean runs past our home every day. Same time, same place. Though he looks old and big and strong to me, he can't be more than 20. He's still young, even if he's old to me. And he has that sleek look like a big hungry cat, like a big cat stalking prey. He just runs, every day, no matter what the weather is like. He runs around the whole block, the whole town, with his white t-shirt never showing any sweat, and his white mailman shorts pumping, and a big silver cross necklace bobbing to the beat of some old, sick song in my head. He never stops. It doesn't matter if it's Christmas, New Year's, or any other holiday. He runs every day, all day long.

Still, no one else in my family has ever seen him. Not Rita, either. Maybe he's not even real. How the hell should I know? All I know is that I've seen him, and now I can't stop seeing and seeing him, in my memories and dreams.

But late that day in September of 1987, I think of him like a White Porcelain Stallion, like the white clay figurines on my mother's shelf. Maybe he's really sick, I think. Maybe he's terminally ill, or maybe he's just fake sick, like my mother, sometimes. Maybe he has nothing else to do except run his whole day, run his whole life away. Even at night, I watch him from my bedroom window and I know he'll be there, eventually. Someday, he'll be there for me. "Just wait," I say. "Maybe that's him now."

Here he comes now, Mr Clean. Here comes Mr Clean.

Dear Diary:

I just heard from my psychiatrist and apparently there are a few more people in my life who I've just now been told are hallucinations and that I am their hallucination. It's messing with my head because that's what my novel is about—to me, at least—with the same concept. I am pretty sure this will be night number four without sleep. My book has become synchronistic with my life, which is why I started writing it in the first place, which I understand seems odd, but once again I'm questioning my own physical real existence. This autism spectrum stuff—or whatever it is—for real—It's crazy, man. I want to stay awake, sleeping without dreaming and dreaming without sleeping for the rest of my life with all of these mental maladies. It's the most fascinating "existence"—so to speak—ever known to any human being, literally. Oh my goodness it's amazing and entirely 100% synchronistic.

366

Dr C Meets Mr Clean

So, this is my writing therapy, huh? My writing-as-therapy. That's what Dr C says, anyway. ("Write it out, Ben," she says. "Write it out of your system.") So Dr C agrees with Kelly. "It's probably a good idea," she says, "to write out some of the grosser stuff—the obscene stuff, the violent and sexual stuff; write all of that first. Get it out of you."

Yesterday, Dr C asked me what, specifically, I was talking about with her that I wasn't willing to write about. So I explained it to her: "For one thing, like the way my stepmother was in bed, and how salty her pussy tastes."

How about that, Dr C? Is that what you want me to write?

Dr C looks a little cautious, worried even.

"Yes, I would like you to write that stuff down," she says. ""Whether it's true or not."

Okay, then. Just write the stuff, she says, whether it's true-to-life or just another one of my childish sex fantasies. She tells me how much she hates the stuff Hollywood is coming out with nowadays, and how she's not somebody who cares much for any story arc, or any continuous through-line, or any happy wedding endings. Stuff like that—the "real" stuff—even depressing plots make her feel better entertained and better brained, she says. Watching those is time well spent.

Like when she's psycho-tapping my sick brain. Like now.

I agree with Dr C.

I say, "Dude, man, I know."

Like with Kelly, my maybe wife-to-be, my Living Colorful Beauty.

When I'm with Kelly, I feel like just being myself all morning, not getting up or getting going, or anything. But Kelly drags me out of bed and into the "Morning Routine." She has this strong desire to "help" me, to make me stronger. She wants to get the old "me" back. She wants her true partner back, she says. But it really comes down to her frustration with the world in general, not "me." I don't believe her, what she says. I think it's me.

I think she gets mad at me—the old me, new me, or whatever. I tell her she's just pissed off at me. And she says, "Not mad, just frustrated."

And I say, "Same thing, babe—you know what I mean. Mad or

frustrated or pissed off, it's basically the same thing."

I'm really trying my best just to get up with her, get in the shower, take my meds, and take an active role in our mornings. I try not to just lie there on the couch all morning just thinking and feeling and getting shite straight, when she's all active and productive-like, flitting around. Unlike me, who wants to just lie with my smokeless tobacco lodged in my lower lip. But it's hard, really fucking hard. For me, anyway.

It's a good thing Kelly and I have in-home care coming now. We get more attention from them now than we did last week, when the in-care people first came to the house. Initially, they came to distill all of Kelly's worries and insecurities. Of course, they could really only quell some, not all, of Kelly's insecurities and worries. There's so many of them. In fact, though, I admit, she's been a real trooper with me.

I have no clue how difficult her living with me has been. I haven't got a fucking clue how unending the stress and frustration must be for her. I see it takes a toll on her, though. She won't really talk about that shite. But, for the most part, she's catering to my every need because my health is important to her, just like her health is. We just might find some peace and some kind of happiness, whether together or apart, in the long run. We just might. Hey, stranger things have happened.

Like Georgie always says, "In the long run, it will all be fine." Georgie comes and goes, but he's always a part of me, more than just a spare part. He's like a Seraphim, you know, a guardian angel. Like maybe Michael, Gabriel, even Lucifer before he fell (maybe even after). I haven't figured out all that much about him. About Georgie, I mean.

Sometimes, though, he shows up in my life like the Devil, the Bad Angel, instilling chaos, fucking with my electronics, and scaring the cats off. You know, that sort of poltergeist shite. Other times, he's Seraphim, the good angel—he's my savior, my caretaker. He watches out for me and takes care of me when I need it most.

Other than that, though, he's just a part of me, Georgie is. We move ahead, we back step. Still, Georgie and I stick together. He's always there, somewhere in the foreground, when I expose my confessions, my sins, my fetishes, even scat and incest—all that bull. I know it can get pretty bad, pretty crazy, and pretty sick. Maybe I selfishly hand my insecurities to Georgie. He's more like the passive type, see, he's a passive observer, and I observe and judge him. But since he's stickier than I am (Yeah, he's sticky and jelly-like, blob-like, but fresh, not foreign), I have an easier time dumping my symptoms and pathologies onto him. It's almost like he doesn't mind taking on my worst, you know? Almost like the dude actually likes it.

Sometimes we fight about things—usually when I'm off my psychotropic medication for a period of time. Or when I just get so fed up with my life that wanting to attempt a fucking crime seems like a good idea. During those times, I just dissociate because I'm overwhelmed, and I start fantasizing with Georgie, letting go. Well, I have hardly any social life at this point, anyway, and no "real world" experiences. So, yeah, I'm pretty much bound to whatever place I'm in and whomever I'm with.

I guess those New Age books would say that Divine Intervention determines the places I am in at the moment. And the people I'm with show up partly because I give everybody else all the control over my life that I can. I'm trying to sell my life, giving money away; for example, lots of money, fucking lots, to anyone who might trade it for my sanity, tranquility, fulfilled hope, lessened fears. Selling it for some kind of love. Whatever love is.

My family is fucking crazy (the whole extended and nuclear family, I mean). They are the Living Colorful Rich. They have all kinds of issues with erratic boundaries (sexual boundaries) and emotional neglect. The same kind of stuff you hear from everybody else in America—like on talk shows and late-night radio, that kind of stuff. It's a sick country, sometimes, isn't it? You know, they have a really high rate of medical cures in Third World countries, and families there tend to hold together better. I live a couple of hours from Mexico, basically just north of the border. That must be a good sign, I guess.

I'll never get that fucking family to feel my love—and I sure can't feel their love for me. Love is like the Satanic cult I'm disengaged from. But I still crave the way they would forgive me for being myself if I worshipped them. So they swing around the metal can of sulfur smoke, and they say they love me, all my life. They navigate my angels and demons. They revive me. They pick me up and string me along if I love them. I say, fuck them.

I say that because I did. Fuck them, I mean. But I hope I don't bring any of that shite up again. Most of that crazy stuff I need to keep to myself, just so I have some secrets left for myself. So I can feel like I have something left that's me, like, all mine. I've done the incest gig. I've fucking been there, too. Where haven't I fucking been?

I won't read anything they send me, and I never answer the phone anymore anyway, especially if it's Pops. Still, my father is trying to buy this house so I can live here, rent-free. He wants to buy my dream house, I guess—he's already bought my other dreams, and so has my stepmother, Gladys. Why not this one, too? Gladys started a small publishing company when she found out that I wanted to get into one myself. And Pops, he started funding films and film festivals, stuff like that, when he learned I wanted a film career. They said I'd never have to work and I shouldn't work, even if I wanted to.

So why should I? I mean, why should I sweat and piss for chicken-scratch at some bullshite, sub-minimum wage job? Or sell my sorry ass on the cheap side streets, when Gladys and Pops already supply everything I need, free and clear. The only question is: Why do Gladys and Pops pick up my tabs, and support me in my squalor and luxury when, as far as I can see, they don't even like me (let alone, love me?)

But now I know why. It's because they want to buy and sell me out, cheap and easy. So they can control me. They want to kidnap me and knock me out and fly me on their private jet to some mental institution lock-up, and put me in long-term rehab even though I've been sober for over five years now. And I ask you, Dr C, is that any way for a wholesome, loving father and a swinging, sexy stepmother to treat their sweet, loving stepson and first-born male child—even if he's a big fuck-up, like me? I tell you, doc, it's all upside down and backwards. It's all fucked up. But the transgression is lovely, don't you think?

So what will I do now? I'm going to go read what I've just jotted down for Kelly to see. Maybe she'll tell me that I'm on the right track again, writing my big blockbuster classic novel, *Living Colorful Beauty*. Maybe she'll be the sweet, sexy muse I need to help me over my writer's block. Get me to spill out sperm and words on the sweat- and blood-stained writing paper, like I did back when Claudia and Georgie were making it together for me.

But Kelly is in another one of her "frustrated" moods. She must've just gotten another crappy e-mail from someone in my family—Gladys, I bet. Instead of going to bug her, I have a smoke just outside her office. Her windows are open, and I can hear her on the phone with one of her lawyer friends asking about my father and my trust fund. I know she feels insecure and really thinks she deserves long-term benefits, and my family's trust and appreciation too, for putting up with me. All that shite. But I'll tell you, she isn't going to get any of that shite from Ben's family—the fuckers.

Kelly needs to cum, I think. But she hasn't let me near her coot in a long while. I feel like jerking off to one of the titty pics I have of the late, transgressive writer, Kathy Acker. She kind of reminds me of Claudia. But Claudia is tall—maybe 5 foot 10—and Kathy Acker can't touch Claudia's tits-n-ass. Still, I just love jerking one once in a while for Kathy Acker, even with her double mastectomy and stretch marks. She's nice, I'll say. I like nice. I can deal with nice. Good fantasy. Good feeling. Nice.

Jerking off like that, I train my hand for war. I'm all for pointing my finger at myself and feeling everybody else get fucked. My heart seems to have gone straying off, somewhere, maybe into a delicate obsession with Georgie's girl, Claudia. Whoever she is. Whatever she is, for me.

Everything started back when we were invincible, Georgie and Claudia and I, back when we were young, when we were kids, when we were curious. We had nothing good enough to last. We had nothing to really hang onto, but we had each other, Georgie and Claudia, Kelly and I, didn't we? Or that's what Georgie tells Claudia, anyway.

I wonder if Kelly knows about all the longing I've felt, just to, just to . . . be alone. Just to exist. To be . . . just to be anything, even nothing. Sixth grade was an acid trip straight out of a summer movie, or something. And somehow, the trip never stopped.

Dear Diary:

I endeavor to stay busy while melancholia, "sadness," and literally black bile: mental, physical and emotional symptoms of depression and despondency deepen. There's still an inherent resilient warrior and activist in me, inspecting in mediation that such feelings subsist as one and the same. Feelings are always valid. They can be trusted.

Second Skins

I used to get so mad at school.
The teachers who taught me just were not cool.
The Beatles

"Class," Mrs Petite says, "today is our first day of sex education." We snicker. We're in sixth grade. Of course we snicker.

Mrs Petite frowns. The worry-lines across her forehead deepen. Her voice is clipped, terse. "Before we begin, everyone in this class will be required to say aloud the following words without any laughter: Sex. Penis. Vagina. Breasts."

"Say, Sex," she tells us.

"Sex," we say.

"Okay, class. Very good. Georgie, that was especially good."

From Mrs Petite, I hear for the first time the words I've come to know, so well, as an adult. I never even crack a smile as I go on.

"Penis. Vagina. Breasts."

Dick. Pussy. Tits. Cock. Cunt. Noonies.

Twenty years later, the word "breasts" still whistles through my teeth as I struggle to make it plural.

"Breast-ts-ts-ts," I say. And I'm back in sixth grade.

"Always use a condom," Mrs Petite says.

"Always use a condom," The class repeats every word in unison.

I'll never forget: Always use a condom.

Dear Diary:

The best feeling occurs during the times I realize I can be completely happy without the people I thought I needed the most.

A Man Ahead of His Time

I collected my first porn when I was nine. I pilfered it from my father's closet. My Pops had nothing but triple-X stuff, real hardcore, crotch-shot porn. Nothing nice. Nothing tame. No *Playboy*, no *Penthouse*—straight to *Taboo* and *Cherry Poppers*—a sticky, dog-eared copy of *Anal Amateurs*.

At 10 I was determined to buy my first X-rated magazine all by myself, using some of the Christmas money I'd saved up from my Aunt Beatrice.

So, one day, I ditched recess and the whole elementary school thing. Instead of playing Kickball or Asses Up with the other kids, I rode my BMX to the Quik Fix on Maple and Fourth. Stepping inside, I saw that the place was basically empty, and nobody too scary was working at the counter. It turns out to be Randy, some 19-year-old kid, with acne scars and an "I don't give a shite" pose. He's the most promising for me of all the employees I've ever seen there.

"Hey man," I say, looking around. "Cool."

I tell him I'm 18 and I'm there to buy a magazine.

(Parenthetical Pet Peeve) Using size six models in magazines and plus size catalogs.

"*Hustler*," I tell him.

"Yeah, right," he says.

His breath hits my face. It's rank, sick, stinking of coffee and cigarettes. So I pull back.

"Tell you what," Randy says, a smug smile on his face. "If you can reach *Hustler*, you can buy it."

I can't reach *Hustler*, but I can easily reach *Genesis*, and it's mine—just like Randy promised. I pay for it, I roll it up, I stick it down the front pocket of my jeans, and I pedal back to school just in time to march inside with the rest, post-recess.

Dear Diary:

Gay love exists in over 1,500 species. Gay hate exists in only 1. Is that so? I think so.

Boy Scout Brothel

A year later, the three of us (Lonnie, Andrew, and I), we organize a sex club, a little kiddy brothel. We set up inside the built-by-Boy-Scouts tree house in Lonnie's backyard. We play tame, safe games there, like Truth or Dare and Spin the Bottle. Then we play nasty, kinky games. We try to get the girls to act out the scenes from our forbidden magazines and videotapes.

Several girls (our age and younger) let us finger-fuck them. They make us taste their bubble-gum cum off of our dipping fingers. We call it "hitting third base." Then we hit second next. We take first last. We like going backwards like that—starting at third, working our way back to something tame. Once you've "made out" with a girl, you're officially "going out."

We have a pee-pail up there, and we watch Kathy Friedlander, the girl I'm going out with, pee sweet-n-easy. Then she wants to watch me. I had asparagus for dinner, probably every night for the last two weeks, for that matter. So, I gladly take Kathy in private to the bathroom downstairs, near the garage. I sit down to pee. I know the asparagus will make my pee smell funny. But Kathy isn't too thrilled.

(Parenthetical Pet Peeve) Men's poor bathroom "aim."

"No," Kathy says. "Don't make pee-pee sitting down. Stand up, so I can see."

I tell her I can't see crap when she's sitting down, squatting over the flower pot, up in the tree house. But hell, I stand up anyway—I'm a gentleman. And pretty soon, I've lost all fear of my semi-public pee. We make out and end up fucking through high school, but we don't tell a soul because she's not a popular girl and I'm a fucking computer geek, Math League contestant, and teacher's pet. It's like we're adults trapped in our little-kid costumes, acting out our early childhood sex-kicks, our little kiddy child porn roles, for whatever creeps and pervs and child molesters might be watching in the invisible audience.

And it all started out, like I told you, at our little wilderness in our secluded clubhouse where porno was preferred to pussy footing. I did other things those years too—stuff for school and sports and shite. I was a multi-talented individual. You know?

I look back fondly on those times when we were all invincible. Our fathers, brothers, and cousins never knew where their stacks of *Playboy* and *Penthouse* disappeared to. Or maybe they knew, but didn't care. Or maybe they knew and, well, you know. We knew exactly how to access them. We just borrowed them like we were at the library, and the clubhouse stayed full of variety and bulk material.

And latex condoms, too. We kept it safe. We kept it real. As real as big-time, grown-up adults playing at little kiddy sex can ever be.

When I'm in seventh grade, my father drops a box of non-lubed rubbers on my bed. I think he's discovered our little sex club in the backyard and he's encouraging me. He isn't, though. He's just covering up for himself. In case I get in trouble, maybe.

"Always use a condom, Georgie. Double up if you have to," Pops reminds me, so candidly. "I left a lifetime supply in your bedroom. They're pretty self-explanatory."

"Huh?" I say, embarrassed.

"Your business is your business," he says. "Just use them and use them well."

"Don't worry, Pops, I will."

"No babies, and none of that hokey-pokey stuff, ya hear?"

"Of course, Pops. I know."

I open a couple samples of the latex condoms along with *Webster's Dictionary*. I know we can have a better supply for the tree house at our fingertips, but I decide to keep these for myself. It's time for research.

I check the dictionary.

La-tex: a milky liquid or usually white sap in certain plants, such as the poinsettia

Con·dom: a thin sheath, usually of rubber

I enjoy feeling the complete covering of my private part. That smooth, baby-soft sheath is just like heaven to me. It reminds me of those stress squeezer balls you find in novelty gift shops. Or whatever substance it is that fills the inside of that elastic-y action figure, Stretch Armstrong.

As an adult, I pleasure myself with latex wrapped around me— snug, warm, wet with saliva. There's no mess to clean up when I'm through.

As Real As

That's right, I think, as the saliva of other women and their vaginal juices complement my less frequent sexual experiences, later on in my 30s. That's the way to do it. And I invite any woman who has a fetish for latex herself to share that desire with me. Her looks don't matter all that much. Something can always be done about that. I have a lot to cover up myself. And what I need is a partner with enough dignity to hide her flaws as I do, with a second skin. I have issues in my adult life, like a real fear of getting somebody pregnant. I fear big responsibilities, since I was never brought up with any. Responsibilities, I mean.

Looking back, all my sexual preferences seem to have been selected with such divinity and such a sense of appropriateness. Maybe the "Divine Force" was watching out for me there, too. I go for older women who already have kids or can't have kids or don't mind the balloon. It's even better if they prefer it. I go for a clean woman, a safe woman, someone who doesn't make demands or ask for commitments. But a wild party is always welcome, especially if she makes the first move and happens to live right next door. I really go for women with issues.

Women like Claudia, who loves latex not on her lover—only on herself.

Claudia Nesbitt must have been the daughter of a 1960s feminist who taught her to hate men. And somehow I was just the man to fulfill her hate. So, when Claudia and me got together, it was a marriage made in hell for the both of us, I guess.

Whatever else, she sure wanted men like me to suffer, and she used her limited charms to lure the bottom-feeding, desperate, love-starved men of our culture (men like me) into her web. Regardless of how susceptible I was to her seductive temptations, Claudia cast me as a victim of conspiracy in her own private persecution fantasy—her perverted sadomasochistic sex play.

(So what happened, Dr C? How did I ever get into this mess? I was such a good little kid. Really.

"If you got yourself into it, Ben . . ."

Yeah, I know. I ought to be able . . .

"To get out of it."

So I'm trying, already. I'm trying.)

So you see, Dr C, how I overcome Claudia's sinister man-trap is what matters the most to me. And when I'm freed from her at last, and I've discovered the real me by discovering the real her . . . .

("Will you be free, then, Ben? Or just caught in another trap? A sinister man-trap of your own device?"

Well, I don't know. At least it'll be my own trap then, huh, Dr C?)

But getting back to Claudia and me: Claudia had a thrilling personality, always upbeat and perky. She spoke in short sentences. She got right to the point. Her otherwise pale face was always decorated with glitter, like an adolescent princess, and her arms were covered with the "Temporary Tattoos" of Lucky Charms' marshmallows.

Claudia lived for Harley Davidsons. She never owned one, but she dated guys who did. But then, she dated a lot of guys. Her favorite summer vacation pastime was Six Flags Magic Mountain, or Six Flags Over Texas, or Six Flags Over Georgia. Mostly though, it was Magic Mountain. Vintage wooden roller coasters satisfied her lust for things fast and chaotic. So did her men—and that led to her dangerous affairs, not just with men, but with women, too. Strippers, hookers, bikers, dykes—and then the drugs-hard liquor, pot laced with angel dust, and the occasional visit to King Arthur's Strip Club in the San Fernando Valley, with the older women who swooned over her. That was Claudia's wild life, away from Georgie and me.

She never paid for a thing. She only had herself to offer, and her package always seemed plentiful. Those naturally luscious lips that others would pay thousands to own didn't need surgery, and her oversized, natural pear-shaped breasts, which I could make out only by the stretch and pull of the second skins that covered them, were perfect, just like they were. There was always some sweet mama or sugar daddy to pick up Claudia's tab. And when Claudia rode double, the ride was always free.

(Parenthetical Pet Peeve) People who are obsessed with knowing whose fault something is, instead of working to find a solution.

When she lived across the street, her original handwritten diaries detailing her adult sex life were placed open on the living room coffee table. A jumbled collection of toys, costumes, and a wardrobe of textiles were stationed throughout the rest of her house. Her favorite pornographic apparel was a blue latex jumpsuit with fluorescent-green latex boots, along with a matching two-inch thick green belt with an orange buckle, black gloves, and a black cloak. It spelled C-O-V-E-R M-E U-P. All of me.

Claudia was the type of naughty next-door neighbor you find in your favorite wet dream. She had a slightly sagging ass, but it sagged in just the right sexy way, like a real woman's. I stared at it when she stepped out for the mail in her terrycloth bathrobe and her wet, just-washed hair. She'd answer the doorbell in skimpy latex lingerie, sometimes a smooth rubber bra or sometimes just with black electrical tape crisscrossing her relaxed, puffy nipples. She sucked fire out of the mailman's breath any time there was a special delivery that wouldn't fit in her mailbox. She illuminated temptation like a big neon sign.

Otherwise, Claudia was always pretty quiet and subdued—a secret control freak. The way I see it, doc, her visual cues and her visible charms provoked the subconscious mind's ability to make fantasies perfect. She'd fall asleep in her first-story bedroom with the blinds open, a nightlight on the wall, and glow in the dark stickers of the stars and planets on the ceiling.

She lived alone and often woke up for a midnight snack. I watched her from my place—through the windows, through the walls. Her refrigerator was covered with pictures of herself all shot by herself—in some pictures she was sticking her tongue out, in others she just showed off her paint-covered feet, or maybe an obscure angle of what I figured was her vast beige areola. The cockpits of her nipples had wrinkles and folds that became geometrically complex when she was aroused, even slightly.

Unfortunately, what I got were only snapshots, just pictures of the real thing—never the thing itself.

What could she be hiding? I often wondered. She was never seen in her naked element. But she was mine. She was all mine, I say—and she'll be mine, all mine, again someday. But then again, maybe she never was really mine at all.

Anybody who experiences Claudia loves to hate her, unless they enjoy self-deception. She's a manipulative she-devil in disguise. She is a Mrs Jekyll inside a Dr Hyde. Her Jekyll-side bursts out when she slithers into that second skin, which covers up her all-too-sinful sexual nature and her prize-winning ethics. But whatever she wears, she doesn't fool me. Not anymore.

Claudia is drenched with forbidden qualities and secret temptations. But as the puny, pathetic, desperate, wimpy horn-dog across the street from her, I was attracted to Ms Nesbitt because I could piece together from each piece of her puzzle, things I once enjoyed or things I could never have (the forbidden kinds of things I just didn't have the balls for.) And Claudia was the best piece of all—the puzzle piece that put it all together. And besides, we both had a thing for fabric—certain kinds of fabric.

Claudia seemed, at least at first, the complete antithesis of my mother, who was strict and abusive, both at once. Since my mother learned things the hard way, by force, so would I. She, like my schoolteachers, taught me to be faithful, to practice safe sex, not to be gay or sexually ambiguous, and to be normal. (Whatever the hell normal means.)

"Act like a human being," my mother would yell at me. "Ya look like a damn zombie half the time, Georgie. Fuckin' smile! Be excited."

"You're obsessed with sex! Don't dwell on sex," she'd constantly demand, slapping me across the face or screaming over the telephone.

She'd already found out about our sex club in the tree house by the time I left home for boarding school.

"Don't do drugs. Don't drink. Don't cheat. Don't pretend. Don't worry about everything all the time," she commanded me.

What did she expect? What did she want from me? An angel? A virgin? Whatever she wanted, it sure wasn't me.

(And what did Claudia want from me? I'm still trying to figure that one out, Dr C.)

Partway through my college years at NYU, I started to see a shrink. My first shrink was a proper sweater-wearing old lady doctor who gave me the creeps. If possible, she was even more controlling and critical of me than my mother was. Dr Jenny Danielson. That was her name. Dr Jenny was certain that I had a lot of letting-go to do. She said that I wore a mask over my face. Literally—that my goatee and mirrored shades were a disguise. She'd tell me, "Take those sunglasses off and shave your beard. Let us see the real you."

But I never showed her.

(Parenthetical Pet Peeve) Patting around on the rug looking for a lost pair of glasses. Worse, hearing a "crunch" while looking for them.

Claudia, on the other hand, was a perfect match for me. We were two doomed, tortured souls. She had many relationships, gay and straight, even with married men and married women. She said she questioned her affairs sometimes, but since they made her feel good, she held onto them. Claudia did drugs. I didn't. I had a problem with drugs and quit. Claudia didn't think she had a problem with much of anything. And she never quit. I had to run 5 miles a day to just barely keep in shape. Claudia didn't have to work out, and still she maintained a perfect body. She was poor and I was rich, and so I thought maybe I could spoil her unlike anyone else—but no.

Claudia practiced unsafe sex. I preferred rubbers. She was 40. I was 30. She was a ball of chaos. And I have this rage for order. She was a big bundle of contradictions. She was a marriage counselor who had never been married, a parenting educator who never had kids, and a rehab counselor who never quit. She was a walking oxymoron.

But what bothers me most about Claudia Nesbitt is that after she lured me in the first time, any time after that, when I'd call her or want to see her, or fuck her with a rubber, I'd have to wait a lot longer than my cock could bear. I just kept on getting let down. I wasn't allowed to make out with her in the middle of our street because her sugar daddy or her sweet mama might show up any minute and blow her whole setup. So she'd swap spit with married men right there on the sidewalk by my kitchen window, but she'd rarely lock lips with me. She said she couldn't love me. She was just using me, and I knew it. But when she did use me, when I told myself she really did use me and made myself believe it—those rare moments were holy and divine.

To put it simply, Claudia Nesbitt was, and is, a no-win situation for me, or anybody. But when she climbed into her latex gear and refused any rubber with me, she was simply incredible. I couldn't, I can't, get her out of my mind. I lost my dignity for her. I became sensually (or sexually) obsessed with her. And I was always dying to see her naked. You could say, I guess Dr C, that as a masochist I was in the perfect relationship. I loved everything about her, but I could never have a healthy relationship with her. Everything was strained and stretched to the breaking point. And as I became obsessed with the agony she caused in me, my character deteriorated. I became a much less dignified person as time went on. I lost all self-respect.

I started to not even like myself much. As if I ever really liked myself, from the get-go, anyway.

The last night we were intimate, about a month after the time we'd last been together, we proved to be inseparable—until our second skins came off and we had to really look at each other stripped naked as we were. As we weren't—and this is how it began:

Just when I think I've had enough torture and emotional abuse from Claudia Nesbitt, I discover a small handwritten note by my front porch.

Georgie:

Find your costume and just show up. Your unexpected entrance last month was morning bliss—until today. Having not seen you in some time, my affection toward you has cooled to mere fondness. I'm becoming indifferent. I don't want that. We've been separated from each other far too often even though you live right next door. I want to see you again, Georgie. Tonight.

I gasp, chewing a bite out of one of the homemade oatmeal cookies she's left with the letter. I continue reading:

As you know, Georgie, my house was robbed last week. I have no erotic products left in any of my closets. Some pervert must have ripped off my skins and toys. But I've changed since then. Come over and see for yourself. I'm sorry for otherwise completely amputating myself from your life. I didn't have time. But now I must have you. I require your services, tonight. Come to me, Georgie.

XXX,

Claudia.

Immediately, I grab an orange jail jumpsuit from last Halloween (I was an escaped convict at the big party) and I storm over to her place with the cloth and cuffs in my hands. I have a box of rubbers clenched between my teeth as I run across the street. I am in such a hurry for love, lust, and submission that I leave the keys to the handcuffs in the bedroom closet, along with my unmentionables (I'm not sure we'll need the keys, anyway.)

I don't know what to expect. Do I hope to see Claudia in the flesh?

The door slams shut behind me.

"No condom tonight, baby boy!" Claudia's voice calls out from the bathroom. "Throw them in the fireplace before I come out."

I keep a couple in my pocket and drop the box into the blaze. Claudia steps out, fully nude, to watch the sizzling cardboard disappear in the blazing fire.

"The fire that keeps your house warm might eventually burn it down," Claudia says seductively.

I gaze at her pale flesh.

"You've changed," I say. "You're perfect. You're even more perfect than you were before."

"I'm doing the best that I can," she sings quietly in her best Beatles' imitation.

There are no drugs, no other lovers present, no tattoos, no secret diaries, no makeup—not even any jewelry.

Finally, Claudia is nude, completely nude—completely naked before me. She has not the slightest blemish on her skin to ponder. There should be celestial music playing to the gentle beats of her all-natural angelic presence.

No sooner does this idea come to my mind than she turns on the CD player.

It must be one of her Beatles' days, I think.

"Woman, I know you understand, the little child inside of the man," they sing.

John Lennon

The window shades are closed. We're sharing a private wilderness.

Claudia lights a few beeswax candles and pushes the coffee table over to the side of the living room. Cautiously, she bends over and covers her eyes. She spreads herself wide open, gaping for me. The abstract pulp of her pussy is tucked snug beneath her dark pubic Hitler 's tache.

What the hell is this woman thinking?

I pause, spellbound, mesmerized, and stupefied. Claudia starts dripping ever so slightly onto the hard wooden floor.

I've been erect for about 5 minutes. I roll down my shorts. I decide to secretly double up, fearing the worst.

Watching her loose lips dangle like the beads of a pearl necklace, loose, free, and liberated, I enter my covered key into her flesh machine, the forbidden gates of a hell I've never seen before.

The smell of perfume pervades the room. The sound of moist suction has the fibers in my mind vibrating until any sense of control is lost.

(Parenthetical Pet Peeve) When people wear perfume or cologne which smells like Raid. Worse, when such perfume makes me sneeze. Even worse is when the "Smelly One" walks by and I can actually taste the fragrance.

"Harder," she cries.
I fuck her harder.
"Deeper," she says. "Don't stop, Georgie!"
The condoms are on, but she doesn't seem to notice.
"I'm so wet," she cries again. "I'm so wet because of you."
More fleshy friction makes the slurpy, slushy noises of a sensual circus. I reach around and index her erect little clit.
"The clit is so important, so-o-o sensitive," Claudia moans. "Put your spit on it, hurry."
I reach around and underneath. I rub her swell in small circles with two fingers, then three. I massage her pronounced outer labia back and forth as it twitches. She's throbbing quicker than the beats to John and Yoko's *Double Fantasy* album, which is still on repeat—track ten: "Woman." The taste of grapes dipped in corn syrup, that's all I can think about.
I'm about to erupt, but I hold it as long as I can.
"I'm so close, Georgie," Claudia reveals. "I love you, baby. I fucking love you."
Suddenly, at the point of no return, both of my rubbers snap open at once. We hear a light, defeated, clicking sound. The first break is followed immediately by the second. My sperm explodes through to her pussy-haven, unable to withstand the bliss.
Claudia's personality shifts instantly. She becomes her old self so easily. "Oh, great." She sighs.
I extricate myself from her and squint down at the floor.
"I think something popped," she says. It seems like she's glad it's happened. "I think you doubled up on the pleasure I asked you to get rid of."
I can't say a word. I'm shattered in a million pieces. All my dignity is lost. Claudia is the missing piece.
"Are you on the pill, Claudia? Please say yes."
She shakes her head no, and smiles slightly.
I remember the time I told her I never wanted to see her again.
She kisses her fingertip and brings it to my lips.
"I'm not letting you go that easily."

I still want her, of course. If I had the choice at that moment never to see her again or to marry her, I would marry her, no questions asked. I am just so sure she is the woman of my dreams.

"I'll be raising my baby with another woman," Claudia says.

"What about me?" I argue.

"I never really loved you, not like that, but I know you've fantasized about this for some time. Admit it. You enjoyed yourself."

"You're crazy!" I holler.

I have been obsessed with her. I admit it. Now, in an instant, I know I've been wrong about her, all along. She isn't the woman of my dreams. It's the idea of her that fascinates me. Not the Claudia in the flesh, but the Claudia in my mind.

For me, Claudia was The Idea made flesh—an Idol, an Icon—a Living Colorful Beauty, a more-than-incredible phenomenon. And now the perfect, pure, beautiful woman I idolized becomes all-too-human, all-too-real, for me.

Likewise, the real me emerges the following week. I am ready to be an adult for once in my life, I tell myself. I am ready to have some responsibility. I try to convince myself I'd be the perfect father for Claudia's baby. I would have someone to love, my own kid. We'd raise a child together, Claudia and me. And I would face the brutal consequences and heart-wrenching fears of my self-exposure. I need to grow up, fast. That's for sure.

My moment of clarity comes when Claudia and I meet for coffee in town that week. When we meet, Claudia uses the longest sentences she's ever used, with me—or anybody. She talks on and on about nothing. Until she finally gets to the point.

"I can't have kids, Georgie."

Gulp.

"My tubes are tied," Claudia says, "I just wanted you to be honest with me. I like you. I fucking love you. I do, Georgie. I don't want to be such a crazy girl anymore. I just want simplicity."

And then it strikes me—I know she's lying. There's just no way that she loves me. Maybe she's always been lying to me.

I never knew what a wake-up call was until this afternoon, over a particularly strong cappuccino. The blend is just as sweet, seductive, addictive, stale, pungent, and dark as the person I used to be and the person Claudia Nesbitt would always be. (In my mind, anyway.)

All that time, I was trying to be safe, and doubling up meant security to me. And Claudia blew the whole thing in one climactic moment of self-exposure and embarrassment, ridicule and humiliation.

I moved out of town a few months later and never saw Claudia Nesbitt again. She fucked me, and she fucked with my head. She fucked me up, bad—still, I loved her. I still love her in my own twisted way. She won't really ever change. And maybe neither will I.

Wait a minute! Who am I kidding? The affair I had with Claudia caused unbearable confusion in me. Especially looking back on the things that might have happened, what might have been. Claudia took everything worthwhile out of the past 30 years—my whole lifetime—and I blame her for scrambling my self-esteem.

I'm in a stupid metamorphosis. Shite, I've exposed myself to you now, haven't I, Dr C? And finally, now, you can hate me for it. Like I said you would. And by the time the demons overcome us, you will know for sure that we, that Georgie's, disintegrated more than you might have imagined. By the end, when you're still wandering and wondering, What has happened to you, Ben? Something terrifying and blissful will have happened to Georgie—a daydream will have been fulfilled for him, a reward will have come true for Georgie and for no one else.

To the fans of Georgie Gust: We love you. You're our heroes.

Dear Diary:

I wish people would speak for me, and others who cannot. Someone, like myself, who's often so defenseless or just not able to communicate effectively; ugh, I just wish that other people could speak up and speak out when I need help. So I continue writing with the occasional cigarette break.

Love Beyond Dignity

I wake up bombarded with the same leftover intrusive thoughts and obsessions from yesterday. I shudder to think what today might bring. My alarm clock rings after I've stared at the ceiling for 10 minutes. I'm still in bed. I let the alarm clock ring. Its tiny pendulum knocks back and forth against the bell, but the chimes get slower and slower, as the batteries inside start to wear out. I stretch my arms and curl my toes. My eyes are crusty with sleep and my mouth is dry.

Finally, I get up and head to the sink. The bathroom light burns out as soon as I flip the switch. Noon sunlight squeezes through the two small window blinds to my left. I douse my face with cold water. I twitch.

I sit on the can and drain myself. I remember the nightmares I had just minutes ago. They kept me in bed, overtime. I tried to beat them off, but they finally won me over. I can't remember the details, but I dreamt of another world. Someplace I've never been before.

In that dream world, I could feel that what this world considers happiness and joy was actually considered pure misery there. All my senses and perceptions existed as their own contradictions. I was with my best friends, drinking, laughing, and playing, but I could see myself as I was dreaming, and I was aware that I was dishonest and selfish and not deserving of love. All the pleasures of this world, in my dream life, seemed wrong and false. I tried to make them seem true and real, but could not.

I still have a belly full of angst and suffering, now I've woken up.

I think of my life now. My real life. Am I a selfish, antisocial narcissist now? I ask myself. Am I delusional? Are my senses intact? Is everything all right?

I think of lost love. I think of the loss of my childhood and the loss of my life. I guess you could say this is a form of depression. It's hard to accept that I've turned out for the worse. I used to be such a good little kid—happy, bright, and full of life and vigor. I had dignity, I think.

I head upstairs to my office and start dosing up on Joe. I think of what love without dignity means to me. I've been stuck on this thought for a couple of weeks now, ever since I saw that Nicolas

Roeg film, *Bad Timing*. In that flick, Art Garfunkel and Theresa Russell play two tortured souls, stuck in a dark and disturbing sexual obsession. Not long after I saw that flick, I checked out Roman Polanski's outrageous *Bitter Moon*, another study of the dark side of love. I knew I wasn't alone when I saw those films.

I knew that I wasn't really all that disturbed—not any more than normal.

Stendhal's book, *Love* (*De L'amour*), sits on my desk. Stendhal's notes on the unfortunate unbalances and nuances of love have me chilled. Even centuries ago, I know other people were subjected to bad health, sickness, even death, because someone wouldn't give back their love—it's in all the stories and books.

What has caused this imbalance in me, in men? And why do I think anybody should care?

My misery continues Wednesday at 9:55 am.

Just back from the drugstore, I play Georgie's answering machine at home.

Beep: "Good morning, Mr Gust, Miss Nesbitt calling. Hi . . . I don't want to completely abandon our friendship, so I thought I'd give you a call. I almost called you last night when I was running around, cleaning and doing laundry and stuff. But I was kind of on . . . I was kind of in . . . the zone, and I didn't want to break up the zone. You know? Anyway, I just wanted to call and say hello. Just to check in with you to see how you've been and what's going on with you and what you're going to do for the holidays. I'm probably going to go back east. Anyway, I just wanted to stay in touch, and apologize for amputating myself from your life. It's just, it's just been really . . . I needed to put 100% into my family, and I'm glad I'm the type of person who can do that with her family. So, anyway, all right sweetie. Have a beautiful day. I actually just got back from a little morning walk, and oh, it's just gorgeous. So that's it." I can hear her beau's motorcycle starting up in the background. "I'll just catch up with you one of these days. Bye."

I don't hear from her again until that Thursday at 7:31 am.

Beep: "Good morning, Mr Gust. Ms Nesbitt here. Just had two seconds and wanted to say good morning and have a beautiful day. I'm always running off and around and about and just wanted to say hello since I'm not the best at returning calls. Take care. I'll catch up with you later. Bye."

Dear Diary:

The greatest advantage of speaking the truth is that I don't have to remember what I said.

388

Therapy

To Whom It May Concern:

It doesn't work to say, "Georgie, don't dwell on it." I've got an illness, and I hope you can understand that. It hurts me when you tell me what to think or how to feel, because I really can't help thinking or feeling. I think that's why we've never had a real, healthy relationship all these years. This is not a heart attack. It's just a sudden realization.

I've been reading up on mental disorders and trying to identify with whatever I can. Part of me says I should just get out of the house, get a regular job, and make friends. But that's easier said than done. And there are medical explanations for my inability to make decisions and stick to them. A lot of things relate back to past events or situations where I was hurt or taken advantage of, and fear of betrayal and abandonment and feelings of low self-worth and shame and guilt still overwhelm me.

I'm unable to just let go. And it takes me years to give up any obsession. I turn inward, giving myself up to my imagination and fantasy. (What else am I going to do, right?) I just can't take the excess of stimuli from the real environment. (Reality? Is that reality?). It's overbearing. It devours me. There's a whole spectrum of issues I've been dealt that I can't deal with or deal out.

I continue on my path, looking for meaning and self-discovery.

With Lost Love and Lust—and Daydreams,

Georgie Gust

Dear Diary:

I definitely believe in both all that I fear and all that I want. Onward bound heroically through this perpetual seven-hour long anxiety attack. I'm still here, learning and seeking, resilient and alone in the entire enterprise.

Mother's Naked Friend

For the past three months, I've seen Dr C every Monday and Wednesday, promptly at 3:30 pm. I like seeing her on the half hour, rather than the hour. It's odd. Unique. Peculiar. Good word—peculiar.

I like that I'm peculiar. "In fact," I say, "I've elevated peculiarity into an art form from the way I dress to what I eat to whom I choose to have sex with."

The older the better. That is why Dr C, even with her sling-back, open-toed, fuck-me sandals and electric blue toenails, doesn't turn me on. She's just too young. As far as I'm concerned, a woman under 40 is still half-formed, still immature.

"Let's talk about your fascination with older women, Ben." Dr C puts on her professional bedside manner. "When did it first begin?"

Well now, Dr C let me tell you. My fascination with older women started early, right around the time my parents got divorced. Right about the time, in fact, when I saw Darlene Krokus naked.

Apart from Rita Morita, Darlene was my mother's one and only New Jersey friend. She was around all the time after Pops left. She was there for dinner and canasta, and she was there from 3 to 5 every Thursday afternoon, immediately after my mother's weekly Weight Watchers meeting.

My mother was a Weight Watchers failure. Not only did she not lose weight, she actually gained weight on the program. Ostensibly, my mother gained weight because of a glandular problem. But in reality she gained weight due to Darlene's love of hot fudge brownie sundaes topped with whipped cream, nuts, and maraschino cherries.

Even at age 12, I knew that nobody could lose weight eating hot fudge brownie sundaes. But Darlene had mother convinced these were special "negative calorie" sundaes that would actually burn calories and help her lose weight. Like exercise, but more delicious.

Mother was never too bright, and after Pops left, she believed whatever she wanted to believe, no matter how asinine. She refused to see the connection between the food she crammed down her throat and the big black number—that magical number—that rolled up on the bathroom scale. Up and down, down and up. And then: Up, up, up.

Mother was a pretty big woman back then. She's even bigger now, I guess, but she was still hefty back then. And with Darlene's help, she got even more so. Darlene, unlike mother and mom's other friend, Debbie Sedgewick, was a Weight Watcher's success. She was always fit and trim and she got fitter and trimmer, despite all those sundaes. Both mother and Debbie idolized her. They wanted to be just like her, and they would do anything Darlene told them to do—which included eating "negative calorie" sundaes and playing racquetball at the Tenth Street Gym.

The thing was, my mother never exercised. Never. Even getting out of bed in the morning was too strenuous for my mother on most days. If she'd had her way, she'd have had assistants to roll her straight from her bed to the kitchen on a gurney. They'd serve her her coffee and her Pop Tarts, and then they would roll her on down to the living room, plop her straight down on her overstuffed chair, and switch on her omnipresent TV.

But when Darlene was around, my mother was a completely different woman. She got motivated to at least pretend that she really knew how to exercise. But she never did. In reality, mother never once played racquetball—she always found an excuse not to. One week she had gout. Another week she had a goiter. And once, for an entire month, she had a pernicious anemia that left her light-headed and much too weak to do anything but stay in the house. (I have a sneaking suspicion that mother is the reason I have trouble with hypochondria.) And when she ran out of diseases, my mother relied on me, and my persistent "mystery disorder," to keep her off the court.

Which is how I ended up seeing Darlene Krokus naked.

My mother had already used up her gout and her goiter excuses. And she hadn't yet discovered the pernicious anemia excuse. So mother dragged me along to explain why she really couldn't play for yet another week (and maybe another after that.)

A tanned and toned Darlene, dressed in white shorts and matching knit shirt, met us in the lobby of the Tenth Street Gym. Darlene kissed the air on either side of my mother's face. And then she ruffled my hair.

"Oh, Rose," Darlene trilled. "He's getting soooo biiig."

I blushed appropriately and scuffed my toes against the tiled floor.

"And sooooo handsome," she said.

"He's still a handful, though," mother said. "In fact, Dar, that's why I really have to sit this one out. Benjy got himself kicked out of school again." Mother rolled her eyes. "The twitches and tics, you know," she said. "They just don't understand them at school."

"Oh, poor Benjy," Darlene said.

I blushed.

My mother massaged the base of my neck, like she really loved me, or something. And she told Darlene she'd meet up with her after racquetball.

Darlene beamed. "Absolutely, Rose," she said.

My mother marched me off to the women's locker room, so she could weigh herself.

Okay, now. Nearly 20 years later, I still have to wonder about my mother's motivation. I was 12. I really didn't need to be with her every minute, and I certainly didn't need to be in the women's locker room. But she's my mother—a woman I'm still trying to figure out.

When I was 12, I was sure her motivation was to humiliate me. And so I fought back—maybe I couldn't keep her from parading me and my Tourette's out in front of her friends, and maybe I couldn't keep her from dragging me into the women's locker room, but I could keep her from weighing herself in private. In fact, I delighted in keeping her from weighing herself.

My mother's weight has always been a carefully guarded secret. On her driver's license, she admits to 150, which she hasn't weighed since *she* was 12.

My mother, still gripping my neck, pulled me with her into the locker room. Then she pushed me down on the bench, and told me not to move.

"Sure," I said.

I promptly grimaced at her. The grimace is one of my favorite tics, and one I can always perform on command.

"And stop doing that," she told me.

"Okay," I said.

I blinked, wrapped my right arm over my head, and scratched my left ear.

My mother hurried away.

I waited half a second, and then snuck off after her.

I ducked in between the rows of benches and lockers, intent on finding out how much my mother really weighed. It was something I was always trying to do, even back at the house. I'd pretend I had horrible explosive diarrhea and was just about to let loose unless she let me into the bathroom with her. Right then, at that precise moment.

Once, I actually pushed open the door and burst in on her and her secret scale. I tried to sneak a peek at it but my mother shrieked, jumped off the scale, and all I saw was the needle bouncing back and forth, forth and back. Up and down. Up and down. Up, up, up.

So, that day in the locker room, I was really bent on discovering what my mother weighed. In fact, I was so intent and focused I almost, but not quite (not quite by a long shot actually,) failed to realize that Darlene Krokus, in all her naked beauty, was standing directly in front of me—completely nude.

I turned a corner, and came upon her. Darlene Krokus, breasts and pubes uncovered. She was magnificent.

Her breasts, they were gorgeous! Flat, with dark prominent nipples. They took my breath away and made my dingdong go straight up, made my little general stand at attention. I loved them. I wanted to put my 12-year-old hands all over them. I wanted to fondle them, molest them. Do unspeakable, secret things to them. Yet, as wonderful as those breasts were, they couldn't compare with her hairy snatch. Her juicy pubes. Her perfect V-shaped patch. It made my mouth water. So I just stood there gawking at Darlene, who stood naked, talking to fat Debbie Sedgewick.

Finally, Darlene must have felt my presence, because she turned, caught my eye with hers and smiled. Seductively. Invitingly. Then glanced at the bulge in my pants.

"Enjoying the show?" she asked.

Then she pulled her clothes on, oh so exquisitely, methodically, torturously slowly, all the while staring straight at me.

What a glorious four months that woman gave me—four months of unmitigated masturbatory pleasure.

When I finish my tale, Dr C doesn't say anything. She just kind of wrinkles up her mouth, shows her crooked tooth, and raises her eyebrows. She drives me crazy, sometimes, wondering what she's thinking.

So I tell her more about Georgie. My thing for older women is something Georgie shares. Age is so relevant in Georgie's sex life— he's fascinated with age. It is, of course, one of the only things we share because, like I say, Dr C, Georgie's really not me. He doesn't even look like me. I look like a rock star, a young David Bowie or Simon Le Bon. I'm hot. I wear Hugo Boss loafers, no socks. Armani jeans. So I'd rather be who I am than be who Georgie is, even if Georgie's me.

Every day, all day long, Georgie does nothing. He doesn't change, doesn't move—nothing changes or moves in Georgie's world. Whereas for me, I'm right with the next big thing—and I'm not hung up on that early childhood sex thing, like Georgie is. Believe me, Dr C.

Would I lie to you?

Dear Diary:

I tend to believe that when people love, they love even when their loved one might not be all that lovable.

Mother's Lava Soap

So. Like I say, when my mother wasn't parading me out in front of her friends, making me twitch on command, she was yelling at me for being a smart ass, or for having Tourette's, or whatever else pained her spirit that day. She was grooming my life, prepping me for borderline personality disorder—if only I'd known what that meant back then.

What were my symptoms? Well, I'll tell you about symptoms.

I feel an exaggerated emptiness now, a drive to fill my private void, and I act out a whole disturbed cycle of emotions. Somewhere deep inside I must still be this traumatized, wounded little kid. The wounded little kid Mother made me because I can still recall the slightest detail of her domination over me, and I'm afraid.

"You think just because you've got some sort of fuckin' disorder, that I'm gonna let ya talk to me like that?" she'd shriek.

And then she'd swat me on top of the head with a rolled-up newspaper. Like I was some kind of two-legged mutt.

I hated my mother growing up. I know that's probably a horrible thing to admit. But I really just couldn't cope with the woman. I had Tourette's. It made me swear. I couldn't help it—I couldn't fucking help it, I swear. But she didn't seem to really care. And when she wasn't swatting me with the newspaper, she was washing my mouth out with soap. And, yes, I know lots of mothers wash their kids' mouths out with soap, but my mother washed mine with Lava Soap.

Even now, 20 years later, I still taste pumice when I swear.

Now I'm in therapy again, dredging up the past, looking for answers, and I wonder if all that pumice somehow got me thinking about women's feet and if that's what left me with such a peculiar fetish. My foot fetish.

Dr C says that a foot fetish isn't peculiar and is quite the opposite—common in men like me. Especially men like me.

"Like me?" I ask, looking away from her, at some silly calendar on the wall.

She stammers, stutters, catching herself. As I turn my eyeballs back at her, a ribbon of saliva drips from the corner of her mouth. For a minute, she looks so goddamn imperfect, it's all I can do not to throw her on the ground and fucking attack her right there in the psych ward office.

But then she clears her throat and smiles. She slurps the spittle back into her mouth.

"Men like you, Ben," she says. "Men with self-esteem problems."

Self-esteem problems? Self-esteem problems? Yeah, right. I know. I have self-esteem problems, which is probably the reason I love feet. Please step on me, I say, and my self-esteem.

No fucking duh.

Dear Diary:

Here's to trying just one more time.

Waste: Notes on Ben's Novel

I'm frustrated with having so damn much to say about something so simple. The words in my head have turned into tossed salad. The real problem involves my year-long obsession with Claudia—or Heidi—or maybe both of them. Maybe it was the love at first sight between Heidi and me that made me admit what was happening between Georgie and Claudia. Maybe it made me face my obsession and my perplexity and the trouble they've caused me. Things have really gotten blown out of proportion.

Claudia was my dream woman. Even though we split up she still haunts me, like a real flesh-and-blood person. She infests my otherwise incredibly lonely and desperate existence with her specter. When Claudia came into my life and our love was born, I decided to sober up. I wanted to become a better person, just in case I ever saw her again. But instead of lifting the fog and confusion from my mind, life without alcohol and drugs has only added to my perplexity. I blame my overwhelming mental derangement on my incomplete love affair with Claudia.

Meanwhile, my desire to succeed in life (to succeed in a better life than this one) takes second place to her. To Claudia. Besides, I already have everything I need. I have one desire left: the desire for Claudia and me to make it, full-time. But since she's not there anymore, all sorts of fantasies, both haunting and exhilarating, have taken up residence in my dreadful little mind. Like right now, I'm possessed by the fantasy of sinking.

I'm writing this pastiche in the present tense, but it's all happened at different times. What I'm writing about, I mean. I can't think. I leave my existence behind. The light is dim. Everything is quiet. The sky is gray, flat, and still. The rain falls without a pause, in absolute silence. Watching the clock, I wait for tomorrow. I throw my pack of cigarettes away. I'm no brilliant demagogue. I'm an aberration, a misconception—a miscreant.

These antidepressants really don't do shite. My vision is getting murdered; I'm going blind-like, finally. Forever. My sense of sight is diseased, as it were. Seeing Claudia was just like seeing the devil, face to face. It's nighttime, now. It's time to get to sleep. But I stay up and write. About Claudia. And my imagination is on fire.

I think I see Claudia everywhere, but I can't have her. Oh God,

I'm just a waste of sperm and egg! What has gotten into me? Lord, God, hear our prayer! And Claudia? I'm sick of you. And Heidi? Humph! I've tried, I've tried; God knows how I've tried. But I've failed to get what I always wished for. I twitch. I tic. I take a tack and prick my skin just to feel something. But I know nothing I feel can be put into words. Everything is stuck in my thoughts, like all I feel is somehow kept secret, even from me. So I lie, of course. Just listen to me mumble, like a mouth full of marbles! "Claudia! Claudia. Claudia. What a shitey mess. I'm not even Irish. Just look at the mess I've made."

I'm still alive, but that's about it. I need to finish what Claudia and I started, on the miraculous day I made my pathetic little trip to the convenience store and had my first encounter with her. Everything's a little dreamy, though. Dreams really aren't any more significant than our everyday thoughts, I guess—maybe even less so. Still, I think the same things every day, the same damn repetitive things. But these things I think still confuse me. My dreams don't confuse me like my thoughts do.

Georgie and Claudia muddle up the atmosphere.

"I love you," Georgie tells Claudia, just as he dissolves into a deep, deep slumber.

Maybe there really will be no more sex with that woman, Georgie thinks to himself. Have I just realized that?

I watch Georgie scoff. He switches off the bathroom light, leaving only the light that crawls beneath the bathroom door. A whole parade of creepy people hover over his head. They all wear halos.

"They must be watching over me, like guardian angels. They're looking after me. That's it," Georgie decides. He steps out in his terrycloth robe. "I've got to get back home, but I don't want to go."

Checkout is at noon.

At 2 pm., Georgie's back home. He's spent the whole night at the local cheap hotel because geographical change is the easiest quick-fix solution. Georgie's kicked back in his reading chair facing the white wall in his bedroom. He's thinking about the strange episode at the cheap hotel. He stands up and pulls the window shade down. Who is possessing whom? he thinks. What's going on here?

A little while later, Bobby Banks calls him up. Georgie's forgotten he has friends. It's a typical American greeting: "Hello. What are you up to?" etc.

"Hey, you still fucking around with that chick next door?" Bobby finally asks. "That chick Claudia, right?"

I'm fast asleep in dreamland. Georgie's alarm clock's silent on the nightstand, batteries removed.

Georgie and Claudia keep getting caught up in my endless attempt to complicate things, somehow. Because that's what my mind does. Or maybe that's what Georgie's mind does. What's the difference? I don't even know.

I feel like a minor character in a bad B-movie. I'm nothing but a poorly written slob in some really shitey, crap-stinking network-produced "Movie of the Week." I'm so fed up and tired of myself. I'm finished. I'm through. I'm all washed up.

"Keep trudging along, buddy. You're not going to die anytime soon. So quit-cher-bitchin!" I hear Georgie yell.

I yell back at him.

"Fuck, yeah! Georgie."

The doctors advised me last week about the importance of always taking my meds.

I want to get off them. But I remember how I miss my sanity when I'm off them. I'm a psych case, aren't I? Ben J Schreiber, psycho freak, that's me. I am such a stereotype—a nothing. Nothing exciting, nothing important—maybe I'm not getting prepped for anything, after all.

I'm in my new home in LA (I finally moved here from Manhattan, after Pasadena) but the "sober hallucination" of Georgie Gust is more frighteningly vivid than ever before. Pretty soon, I bet our new neighbor, Claudia Nesbitt, will take up residence in Georgie's mind. I can sense her secret existence. She's beautiful, whether you want to believe it or not. Fuck that, dude. She's perfect.

But Claudia's a chaotic woman. The whole idea of her excites me and my imagination goes wild. She still does it for me to this day. I'm still going crazy for her.

Georgie's affair with Claudia has shattered the whole heart and soul of the desperate, lonely man who just wanted to replace Heidi with Claudia.

Jump inside one of our heads for about 5 minutes. There's never a dull moment up here. Go ahead. Jump right in.

Thank you.

To the reader, looking back, with love . . .

Ben.

Dear Diary:

I count my night by its stars—not shadows; to count my life with smiles, not tears . . . and my thoughts trail off. My train of thought has definitely left the station but my writing, my craft, my art, my industry saves me—it's still all right here and now. And moves on, manically.

Family Reunion

Some minor details: Georgie used to wear these huge, round, horn-rimmed glasses until he lost them. He ended up getting a pair of wire-rimmed, round, Lennon specs pretty soon afterwards. He grew his hair long and wore a goatee at that time. He cut that crap out by the time his pet Perplexity intruded on his little lack of a life, though.

He had a lot going for him, back then. He still tries to stand out. In fact, he's wearing a pink and aqua blue button-down shirt today. But then again, Georgie hasn't left the house yet to show it off—to let the ladies think he's lovely. Instead of writing and thinking this, he really could be whistling some silly tune and walking down the street outside. He maybe could be meeting up with somebody new, a complete stranger, while still being out there.

He looks in the mirror. The brightly colored sides of his flashy designer blouse are drenched with armpit sweat. He looks good and long, ignoring the damp. He gets manicures and pedicures. He curls his hair and uses a blow dryer, too. He even waxes his eyebrows. He's turning into such a girl! Maybe it's a DNA thing. Maybe he has, like, extra X-chromosomes.

They say some XXY boys develop into men, even though they have two X-chromosomes. Maybe Georgie had a cord transfusion with some chick's blood when he was still a baby. Maybe that's why he's so sick and feels so strange—or maybe not. How do I know?

After all, he's straight and sober. His history is straightforward.

The summer sun screams with pure energy. Georgie's nervous twitches and tics pop along to some simple song just skipping in his head. He dances to that pop song with rhythm and complexity. He jerks his head. He tells people he can't help it, he's sorry.

He'll be hooking up with the extended family for a little reunion back in the Hamptons pretty soon. Okay, so the family reunion is in a smaller, poorer section of the area in the narrow streets where staff members of the glitzy estates live—somewhere near the real Hamptons. But it's basically the same thing.

Part of him still lives in the cult of luxury. But he's still very much desperately alone. (Kindly refrain from jealousy, if you're the jealous type. You can trade your life in, if you want, before the end. It just might take a while.

PS. Don't trade it. Believe me. It's really not worth it.)

Before the holiday, Georgie's been getting some long-awaited phone calls from a couple of people who would be at the reunion. Like his cousins and step cousins, and second cousins, all just checking in ahead of time. Checking out the pre-reunion stats to see what they're up against. Who disappeared? Who has died? Knowing as much as possible about the other family members beforehand is of vital importance to the feuding clan.

After the party, the cousins and aunties and great uncles will probably gossip about what they've seen.

"Georgie's gained some weight since the last family reunion," they will say. "He's getting fat," they will really say.

Most people just tell him he looks different. They won't mention what they really notice—that his looks have changed for the worse. His fat ass and creepy love handles look feminine. Somehow, rolls have jammed onto a scared man–child. Georgie answers these check-in phone calls, the few of them that come through, with a friendly air of being there for them. He tries to ask the interrogators about their shitey little days.

They all seem to have some kind of life. They've got things going on, events and circumstances to check into, trials and trivia, and all that crap—all for some main purpose, all to move everybody along with the tide. To go with the flow, you know? They have actual connections with real people, collaborative connections, and positive directions. What does Georgie have? A big fat ass and creepy love handles. And a lot of shite he's just not dealing with.

Georgie's set up some plan to tell them nonchalantly that he has some good things going on in his life, some things he's working on, some promising endeavors. He has things in the works. He keeps busy with work and stuff.

But by the time he gets cued in, Georgie always ends up kicking himself in the face. He starts describing, in great detail, all his newfound weaknesses, all the new addictions and additions that popped up since he and whoever last spoke. And then he'll end up telling them the truth, the way he sees things, from down there in his head. Wherever his head is.

He really believes that somebody, just out of the blue, might someday actually understand him and even make him happy. But inside Georgie there are no smiles. Without words, he's desperately begging somebody from the inner family circle—the one that controls it all, who is loved, to turn on some secret switch in the invisible boardroom that will turn the tables around again for him. That will make him feel good. He will even love himself again then. He still wants to feel some new and positive things, good things that will last for the better. But that switch was never even there to begin with.

The relatives finish their slightly disguised interrogations and end up not calling Georgie back for another year, even if Georgie makes the effort to connect. His calls are neither accepted nor returned. That's why Labor Day weekend is always a dismal time, every year, for Georgie Gust.

Still sitting down, Georgie lights another cigarette. He thinks about when and where he lost that edge he used to have, when he was on top of his game. When he was a winner.

He used to dance and play with all these new ideas and thoughts. He used to be able to see the beauty in things, for example. But his gifted creativity, his selfish back tickling—those things he had finally lost touch with. There's only nostalgia left from those more innocent times.

His younger self is still attractive to him. Back then it was a safety zone. A sanctuary, a refuge, but, of course, it was also a lie. Lies are usually very attractive. Georgie's blue balls hurt like a small weight's sitting on his scrotum. Georgie's blue balls are a constant pain. And, even worse, the stress and anxiety shows up on his skin. He has these herpes-like fever blisters on the corners of his mouth and on his lips. And his genitals will be a whole other story. The strong heat outside sure doesn't help.

(Parenthetical Pet Peeve) People who leave their children in a hot car on a summer day.

Georgie always hated the heat. He keeps the A/C on high, even in the car with the windows open. He has a second air-conditioning unit installed in his master bathroom, just to keep blowing the cold air out. Georgie's bedroom has two of them, and his bedroom is small.

(Parenthetical Pet Peeve) When people leave their dogs in a hot car on a summer day. Do them a favor. Leave them at home.

He is going to bed for the night around 3 in the morning. He lights up his last smoke and broods on the upcoming family event. He's really just making a big deal out of nothing. Then he gets his second wind.

He'll probably make a couple of jokes about turning gay or something, just to cover up his embarrassment and fear. He'll try to get inside their thoughts, to know what they're thinking. I know it's all okay anyway, they will think, he thinks. I still like him, they will think. So what if he's without a woman?

Georgie knows there's no such thing as true uniqueness, or anything like that.

Finally, the events of the day replay in Georgie's head. They'll end up becoming part of the dreams he will have afterwards. But the nightmare will have a more profound effect on him. He always hates to suffocate in fires, and drown in two inches of water, and burn in the house while the firemen just watch and let it all happen, even if it's all just happening in a dream.

Dear Diary:

O Meds! O Docs! Of the symptoms of these recurring. Of the Consumers of the Providers. Of hospitals fill'd with the ill. Of my meds forever reproaching my meds (for who more foolish than my doctor, and who more sane?). Of symptoms that vainly crave the meds. Of the doctors and meds mean. Of the struggle ever so-called crazy'd. Of the poor results of all meds. Of the plotting paranoia and sordid symptoms, I see imaginary people 'round me. Of the voices and useless vocalizations of my speech—with rest, my symptoms intertwined. The question, O meds! So sad, the side effects. What good amid these meds, these docs, these mental maladies. O meds, O boy? My medical mental take on Walt Whitman. Blip. Blam. Boom.

First Date with Perplexity

I imagine what it was like, our first date. It's foggy outside and I'm real anxious, until Claudia takes shape and she finally exists. I'm hungry. I'm thirsty. Where and when does this date take place? I ask myself. Georgie answers all my questions.

(Don't look at her) Georgie says. (Tell her your flaws, your fears, and your needs.

Make sure she's aware of your high-maintenance personality.)

"Shhhh! Quiet!" I say.

Finally, Georgie does the date for me. He always gets what I want.

Georgie and Claudia are at The Fusion Restaurant.

They order a sushi dinner for two. They get a table for four.

Their first public date begins with his light knock at her front door.

Tap-tap.

Do we hallucinate noise? I ask myself, and knock again, twice.

That is all the noise Georgie has the balls to make.

There's no doorbell.

Tap-tap.

The door is already open a crack.

Georgie steps back a bit. He waits for an answer.

"Coming!" he hears.

Claudia sounds like an aristocrat answering a peasant in some old period piece film.

"Let's go," Georgie calls out, impolitely.

She pretends she's surprised to see him.

"Princess!" Georgie calls her. "I'm just kidding."

They walk together up their street to the commercial district where all the shops and restaurants are. Georgie holds her left hand. He sticks to her left side so he can grab her with his right hand, if she lets him. But Snicker Doodle wants Georgie on the other side.

(Parenthetical Pet Peeve) Using an umbrella when walking into a store and having to carry that wet, dripping stick as you shop.

"I was battered over the head with a wine bottle from that side," she reveals. "And I still have this fear. Could we just switch sides?"

"Okay, baby."

Georgie doesn't know if she's pulling his chain or not. But he feels a strong desire to see her naked at this point. He requires strong proof that her past history with other men ended through their fault and not hers. Georgie wants to see the damage done. Including any and all scars.

He could just decide she is a liar. But he doesn't know what she's lying about. Maybe she's a chick with a dick, a witch, a bitch—a prick-tease with a disease. He can't say for sure.

Will he end up lying to her, too?

"I have schizophrenia," he declares.

His Perplexity doesn't mind.

She tells Georgie she's a social worker.

"My mind plays tricks on me, sometimes," Georgie throws out.

"It does? So does mine."

The score's even. Georgie 0, Claudia 0.

The new couple eats dinner, and then heads back to Snicker Doodle's little sanctuary down the street. On the way back, Georgie remembers that she offered to pay half the supper bill—he wouldn't hear of it. He thinks that he should have let her pay the whole thing, but it's too late for that.

Before saying their goodnights, Georgie and Claudia stand by the front door to her place.

"I don't want . . . I don't want to fuck you, Georgie. Just so you know. I don't want to fuck you," says Claudia.

"May I touch your breasts?"

"No, not yet. Thanks for asking, though."

"Thank you."

"No, thank you."

"No, thank you."

Dear Diary:

Former awkward moment: When someone in a public place would mutter, "disability, mental illness, Tourette's," or "crazy," and all eyes would fall on me. Way different story these days—I revel in such occasions now, even look forward to moments as such. Bring out some charm and it's all good.

From The Inside

Georgie jerks off, and then writes another shitey poem. The Nervous Narcissist listens in. His teeth sparkle as he hears his alter ego speak to him.

I'm alone. But I'm not bored. It's over now. We're done and through. These things we used to do.

Claudia looks Georgie in the eyes, breathing that same sick-dizzy, sad-puppy, bulldozing, THIS IS THE END look you would expect just before a breakup. Georgie wishes she could see for herself just how pathetically she is coming off. If she only knew how unattractively her true California girlishness reflects off her face, he thinks. It's all so clichéd, so stereotypical. Georgie has a burning urge to slap that girl, hard. But what Snicker Doodle wants is unclear. Even at age 40. She's still fucking around with several people at the same time.

Georgie wonders if she is ever miserable. He's pissed off, thinking she has never been burned, herself. He quit smoking again, but he still wants to light up—right now. I'll smoke later, he tells himself, I'll have just one more cigarette, somewhere, sometime. He bites his teeth.

"Was Claudia ever miserable, even slightly, ever?"

His Perplexity might eventually get hooked up with a 70-year-old, wrinkled sugar-daddy that she could butcher and eat alive, some Newport Beach land developer with a terminal heartbeat and lots of money. He would end up married to his mistress, the Great Bitch-Love, Claudia, somewhere undercover, a little discreetly. He would croak in bed beside her, long before she started to feel the age upon her. Then she'd get the estate–she'd work it out that way.

Georgie, get your gun.

The old man could leave Snicker Doodle with next to nothing except a free ticket to the funeral. But that won't happen. Not with Claudia—her luck is always too good. Georgie feels like a stalker, because he is a stalker. He's a fucking mess. He is mentally tortured, by Claudia, by himself.

Dear Diary:

Even when worst of things occur in life, its "reason" could simply be reminding us we're human and thus have human feelings, emotions, and experiences.

408

The Slow Fade-Out

MON JUNE 27 10:29 pm: "Hey Georgie. It's about 10:30. Anyway, I'm just going to stop working and go to bed. I don't even know when you called me. Anyway, the fiscal year ends. You know, of course, this week. There's a big push to get reports in, and charts and paperwork and audits and everything. Done. So. Anyway. So. That's where I'm kind of focusing. And then after Friday—well, that should be nice. I should have a break. Anyway. I hope things are good with you. And that's it. I'll catch up with you later. Hopefully you're having beautiful dreams right now. And. I guess good morning as well. Because it will probably be morning when you get this. Mmm. Bye."

Sleep deprivation.

You just want the next day to come soon after getting a full night's rest. That's all you want—a new beginning. And I need a short story. What I really need is a high-concept, great story piece— a script to a film that would attract a good soundtrack. The script, a page-turner; the film, a tear-jerker; the audience, truly involved. But what could the story be? I need to find this story. Is it a mix of what I have now? Or a brand new idea using what I've learned from what I've got? Could I write it fast? Could I pound it out, like putty? What are the themes? In what order? Love. Buddies. Friendship. Obsession. Moving on. Identity. Adventures: at least three big themes—death, loneliness, despair.

Philosophy. Intelligence. Generation X. Affluence. The Honda Generation.

Dear Diary:

I'm not to blame for my illness, but I am responsible for my health. Mental illness, to me, should be considered a third party. Not the core of the individual. I am not to blame for my mental health condition, but many of my actions are influenced in part, due to my mental illnesses.

End of November

I wanted to give her the finger. I wanted to shoot her a real big FUCK YOU—but what about me? I kept planning what I was going to do the next time I saw her next door. Maybe I'd get a real goodbye, at least. For the past week, she'd been parking her car right near my back door. Right near the garage, near the office at home, near the kitchen. The doors I always use to get from here to there, when I'm dosing up on caffeine and sugar, my mind screaming.

You're still in love with her! Admit it—you're still in love with her.

Where was Georgie when I needed him most? She was alone, and I ran and fell into her arms. Hopelessly, pathetically, profoundly, in one long since over expired love epic. The epic love affair of the century still rests within my heart. My poor, butchered, tormented, tortured heart—my wrecked, strong, very weak, and still tired heart. With its thumping beats overlapping in a sound prairie, a thunderstorm of bolts crashing, scissors chopping, teeth clenching recklessly. Letting havoc rip out of my soul, giving into all the temptations Georgie could ever bear for the rest of his life.

Yesterday.

Today started as fucked up as it ended—a good day? Yeah, it was good. This whole time I've been trying to understand myself, and to be understood by others. I was just a closet pervert. Now I'm a public pervert. So is Georgie. And he can still function in a normal daily life scenario—at least, as normal as things can be for now. I need to exercise my mind. I need to get some more things out. I need to have sex with my mind until my mind has an orgasm and splashes all over everything. And spills its sweet love once stored inside.

Yeah, I fucked it. Ah, yes, it had very little to do with this morning or tonight, with today. It started last night. It started a few weeks ago. It started when Georgie started trying to get rid of his Perplexity and have sex with somebody else just so she wouldn't be THE LAST ONE.

Georgie lights a cigarette and starts puffing. He's on his tenth shot of espresso today and just starting to get down to the nitty-gritty. His phone has been ringing off the hook all morning.

Her Last Words:

"You know what? I just don't have the time to give you." Claudia says with withering disdain. "I just don't."

Dear Diary:

Regarding responsibility for my actions, with or without mental illness—but as a human being, and to recall Eleanor Roosevelt's famed, "In the long run, we shape our lives, and we shape ourselves. The process never ends until we die. And the choices we make are ultimately our own responsibility."

Claudia, Heidi . . . My Perplexity

I took it all in, stuffed it deep inside, real hard. Within a few minutes, I headed to the garage. My shadow followed me there.

"Georgie," I said. "Get in the fucking car, you fucking bitch!"

Georgie started swimming into focus. Just so I could believe he really was there. He was still the same hotshot hallucination of my misperceptions. He's a spitting image of my big fat ass and my big fat head and my really bad fucking breath.

He's just as big an asshole as I ever was. Except he did nothing wrong and I blamed myself for everything. I never learned the right way to deal with conflict. Once the excitement of any new relationship faded away, any conflict naturally dragged me into a fear of uncertainty where I'd simply call that relationship quits.

I catch myself in this awareness. I'm aware of this awareness. And I'm about to burn the bridge with myself on it. With Georgie still there, I pop the CD changer on in the car. I've already fired up the German gas-guzzling ignition. The key in the hole chimes like the cash register followed by Pink Floyd's "Wish You Were Here." I put the speakers on hi-fi and strap up, and smoke the rear wheels out of the garage.

Georgie and I are silent and stern-eyed as I run the stop sign at the corner.

Can you tell heaven from hell?
Blue skies from pain?
Pink Floyd

At the first red light a sudden agonizing realization comes to me—every light we hit will turn red before we hit it. So I stop the car then and there, shut the engine off, and lock the keys inside. Georgie gets out and I follow. He knows what I'm up to better than I do myself. But I take my anger out on Georgie, anyway.

(Parenthetical Pet Peeve) People who remain stopped several seconds after the light.

"Have you lost it completely?" Georgie asks.

I force myself out with a hint of spit and scat.

Georgie opens the passenger door and slips back inside the car. He shows me the key he has dangling from his fingertips and starts to laugh.

Your heroes for ghosts.
Pink Floyd

I grab the key from him and insert it back in the driver's-side lock and lock myself out. I catch myself firing up in even more of a road rage and make a cool entrance into the coupe again. Confusion is overwhelming. I'm having another spell. Another episode. Fuck.

We drive up the coast about a mile or so where I find my new home. I sign the lease that day and move in the next. I call the garbage haulers to take everything in the old house, figuring I'll tell the landlord, "I'm out of there," whenever I get around to it. I just want to get away from all the lousy sex and bad women and bad people I've had no clue how to relate to at the old house. So I found this full service apartment building I'll probably collapse and croak in, where I'll be free to be completely alone, haunted only by fears and regret.

For the next month, I keep seeing Claudia everywhere I go, everywhere! She comes up with different identities, in different scenarios. She's driving different cars, romancing different people, even speaking through other people's voices. For the love of God, these women are all Claudia! I swear!

Georgie gets another saleswoman to move in with him the very first day they meet. He's buying a new bed. She's selling it. It breaks; they fall apart. Then they fall into bed together. They have some kind of strange schizophrenia where you know you have it, but you're not allowed to be told you have it. It's like, the opposite of schizophrenia. Or something. The doctors tell Georgie and me that all the chaos is normal. We're completely trapped, whether alone or together. And somehow, that's supposed to cure me.

I look in the mirror and see myself at last, not just the reflections (and reactions) of everybody else.

Dear Diary:

A person can only offer as much love as he or she has found within themselves, however one might argue that we learn to love ourselves more fully by loving others. And again, I try, one last time. Hell, I commit my literary crime.

More from Waste: A Novel by Benjamin J Schreiber.

I felt generally on edge, a bit anxious, a bit nonexistent. I felt nervous, paranoid, and urgent, unlike yesterday. But still, I bore up under it all somehow. I finished another day, even with the recurring theme of "death" in the first person, in my head, every minute. The whispering voices have dissipated, but perceptual hallucinations are still present.

Looking at Heidi's (Yes Heidi's, I know. I realize now it is Heidi's, not Claudia's) place next door, the whole emotional situation became extremely awkward for me. And besides, they wanted to switch my meds. Fuck, are they bending my mind back together? Have I taken the right pill? No, I've been off my fucking meds for five days, now. I'm thinking half asleep, the writer's block, it seems—it seems to have lifted. It's gone. I think I'm okay, in a way. I try, I try, and I try.

I try to find things out about her, about Heidi, that are impure, detestable, and inferior. But still, I'm wrong to judge her. I don't deserve to judge her. That's what I tell myself. But I do, I do! I judge her—I judge Heidi. And I want to yell at her, scream at her, beat the crap out of her in public, but I can't. I just can't. I wasn't brought up that way.

Claudia and I couldn't just be fuck-buddies. Of course, I talked my head off trying to talk her into it. I wanted her that bad, really bad. So bad it hurt. Yet, I couldn't even come with her at the end. I was jealous, she said, of her "abundant life." Fuck it. Fuck her. Fuck everything. It's all Claudia's fault.

The way that Heidi can balance such chaos astounds me, even with her career. How does she do it? I remember her diatribe about the "forbidden love affairs" that attract her, that she questions, that still make her feel good. We were on a date, when she discoursed with such disdain. I'd taken her out to dinner to be with me and she blabbered about all the other guys she dated and fucked. That's not fair. Shite, I'm through with her.

"Oh, Ben, you're learning."

"It's over!"

You said it to her.

She simply said, "Okay."

Legend has it that OK stands for zero killed.

Dear Diary:

Schizophrenia, alogia, and apathy can osculate my tuckus. I'm built for this impedimenta.

Ben and Pops

Georgie looks down at us from above, somewhere, someplace. He must not have been fully integrated into the life with me, or with Ben, the genius. Georgie was not needed, and I was not the full-fledged narcissist in need of another self. Or at least, I wasn't. Not yet. I was still young, before sixth grade. I'd recently been armed with the popular labels: Attention Deficit Disorder and Tourette's. And mother was on vacation, on a cruise, with my sister Lenore, of course.

"You always ruin every vacation we take together, Ben," I'd hear whenever they'd leave the front door, and me, for a Carnival Cruise, American Princess, etc.

Later, I'd drift away from them. From sis and mom, I mean. Mother would tell me, "It would be really nice to have you back in the family."

I'd take her remarks as: "You should be back with us."

What she probably meant was:

1) "I won't cop to anything! It's all yer own fault."

2) "I know I can't have ya back. I'm sorry, sorry—but no!"

3) "Yer an out-of-control brat and I hate ya."

Something like that.

God, that woman still makes me angry. I love her, I hate her, and I really don't want her to leave. Life with mother was always borderline this, crisis-after-crisis that.

Georgie could feel the living colorful beauty of the immaculate synthesis. It's just a byproduct, the flip side of fear. Dr C calls it the immaculate built-up split inside me—a synthesis and a split?

Afterwards, Georgie would need to take in everything Dr C said. He would need to swallow and deal with it. Maybe he would end up in a tap dancing class, instead.

Tap-and-dance to the beats of Bologna.

He was looking over at me. My Pops was. I was eating a pizza and staring at the television set, with the occasional glance over at my father. We were alone together. Father had nuked up some microwave popcorn. They would have just started to pre-install microwave units into the newer condos in America, and we were in a condo, only an hour's drive away (an hour's drive, Lord) from the small ski village of Sandy, Utah. This boy's vacation away from home happened before Pops broke the bank, so we were all a lot more modest than we are today.

It was a father–son trip. We flew by plane in coach, into Salt Lake City, and we did a lot of driving with the radio on, making memory-building music. The windy snow was crystallizing on the drifted boughs of the trees. There were snowy white pines and even red cedar. There were young deer running loose in the nearby state parks. The purest sensation of adolescent nostalgia (before the fact) was already causing tiny shivers in my spine. It was making my thin, little, boy-arms shiver. Or maybe it was the snow?

Snowed in as we were, I was stuck with my father. We were watching a rented copy of *Raising Arizona* on VHS, just after the BetaMaxes became obsolete—I can't remember when. Most of the best parts of growing up have dulled in my mind, and any magic has finally been quelled.

That first Saturday night, my Pops and I took a soak in the outdoor jacuzzi. The steam was rising up and over the wall thermometer, which said the temperature was 20 degrees, maybe 15. Like I said, I don't remember all that well.

All I know is, I fell asleep on the couch that night, and we hit a couple of slopes on Sunday. Pops took me to the top of the steepest black diamond slopes. I was challenged to race down, with Pops right behind me, even without the agility I had as a kid.

Pops wiped out at the bottom. I wiped out, too. We stood up shaking off snow, and started laughing.

We had fun while it lasted. I knew I'd have to go back home to mother, eventually. Pops left mother shortly after.

I'd never have another father–son experience quite like it. I guess that's why it means so much to me now. As faded as the memory is—it was. It isn't—the one & only.

Dear Diary:

Hey, not to spoil the ending, but everything is going to be OK!

Alter-Ego Claudia: Georgie's Nightmare at Noon

Since the new medication regimen seems to be working and the writer's block seems to be done, I feel rushed. That's strange, isn't it? I'm not used to being rushed. So, Georgie spends a whole day de-Claudia-izing his otherwise crappy little house. His living room is now the small front room studio where he just sits around without any furniture. He lets the monotony take control of him, wishing for the next day to begin and this current day to end.

Georgie is dilly-dallying on this whole business of finding a new place to live. Starting early in the morning, getting up early for once, he cleans out his house completely. The whole idea of Claudia is surgically removed through the subliminal process of thought-stopping. All the enlarged photographs and framed letters and handwritten notes have been locked inside a storage unit in the next town. His collection of vintage Pez dispensers, vanilla-scented candles, and novelty gifts are now locked away inside the hell of Georgie's mind. The candles he got for his birthday have been kept like new for too long He . Now they're all being burned.

Get your gun, Georgie. Georgie, get your gun. As if there ever was any gun. Go ahead, Georgie. Load it with love. Shoot your fucking dick off, if you want.

But "Not tonight, Georgie," is what she says, over and over again.

She's fucking around with him, he thinks.

Here comes the heat.

The hot light from the bleeding sun sucks into the camera. We're inside the dark studio, with all that's left of Georgie's old pad, somewhere in Los Angeles. The blinds are closed. The sunlight bleeds through them horizontally. Georgie is 30 years old. He's shivering, scruffy-faced, and cold. He holds a can of mace. There are lines of coke drawn on the floor beside him. He suffocates in smoke by the shut-up door. These flickering, lit candles surround him; the lights are dim. Ten ashtrays are occupied with smoldering cigarettes and joints. They give off whole loaves of white dope smoke into the still stifling air.

Georgie's wrapped in a blanket. He's self-aware.

The Brit-Invasion pop music of your choice is muffled but loud. Alternative music follows.

Georgie's a one-man crowd.

There's the blasting static of a radio dial turning. These are the inarticulate sounds of Georgie's head. He is burning. He's drenched in sweat. For the first time, he's in debt. He can barely suck in a breath of clean fresh air, much less this filthy, shut-up cloud.

Women's panties with their rank sex odor and an array of sex toys are scattered on the floor. There's more—her notes, her gifts, and her dead flowers. Seconds pass like hours. Georgie clenches a cup of water and nearly drowns in it. He chokes and likes the sound of it, drowning.

They're at the beach. Georgie's wrapped in satin bed sheets. The moonlight illuminates them.

She's 40, 41. She never gave her real age to anyone. Georgie and she are posing for pictures, all happy and shite. He's got a cigarette lit. He thinks the long beach is a huge public ashtray.

They run around on the sand, playfully screaming. Georgie remembers this as he tells it to me. Claudia dips her big feet in the white, foamy, chilly water. Georgie smiles at the sight of her bare feet. He tries to lick her ankle, but she dunks his face in the water, dismissing his affection.

Often she refuses his advances, even while in bed. He wonders if she would ignore him if they were wed.

His head is bobbing in and out of the water as she pushes him down. He spits out sand. He is almost drowning.

Claudia laughs with mischief. She takes Georgie's hand.

We're in the middle of an empty parking lot, near Claudia's piece of shite, '91 Honda. The CD player is on high. There's more music.

Georgie and Claudia dance together with a big "Discount Clearance Store" banner in the background, like total suburbia—a suburban idyll.

The fire alarm is blaring high. We're back in the studio where Georgie's beating himself up.

"Somebody save me!"

At the door to an apartment across the street, a woman's voice cries.

"Come in."

Georgie, blowing bubble gum, opens the door only to find Claudia kissing another woman. It's that Sara chick, Claudia's alcoholic lesbian lover, mystery woman of misery, now in the flesh. I can't see her. She must not be real either. Claudia looks her over.

Her eyes widen majestically.

"Georgie! Hi, princess!"

She hallucinates Sara, Georgie hallucinates Claudia, and I hallucinate Georgie. Claudia and Sara stand topless in the center of the room—Claudia's in latex gear.

There's a small audience witnessing. Greg is 55 with long white hair, a puff-belly, a fuzzy navel, and a wedding band. He's an oaf. He's with his wife, Sara who's 25, skinny, and boney. She can't help looking innocent. She's wearing a gold cross like a lucky charm. They watch lesbian make-out scenes like stiffs sitting side by side, their hands folded in their laps. They don't flinch a muscle.

Georgie tics. Claudia sees his neck jerk and his eyes roll. She waves him to come closer.

"Just don't come too close."

Georgie swallows his chewing gum. He can't take his eyes off the fantasy woman he's concocted in his mind. She kicks off her pumps and calls him on.

"Tell me a little more about yourself, Georgie," she says. "I want to get to know you better."

Georgie grabs one of her shoes. He smells the vinegary sponge of the soles. Greg and his wife smirk at each other.

Embarrassed and ashamed, Georgie starts to run away.

"Don't leave!" Claudia shouts. Georgie freezes. Then her voice softens. "I want to introduce you, Georgie."

Georgie hesitates.

"Fuck you. I fucking love you. You're fucking with my mind again."

"I'm not fucking with your mind," Claudia says. "Damn it, Georgie! I told you I wouldn't do that. I told you!"

The fire alarm next door is still firing off.

Claudia dashes out her front door and into Georgie's studio.

Georgie is still sitting in the middle of the room. The fire alarm is louder. We hear Claudia perfectly, however. Georgie looks up.

She explains, "I'm just a habit, Georgie. An addiction—but I've got my life together. It's all figured out!"

Georgie's heard that before.

His eyes are desperate, ready to give up completely. He knows all of this is only a figment of his imagination.

His imagination is mine.

She tapes his mouth shut and cuffs his wrists to his ankles. His chest sticks out. Georgie fails to restrain her. He's a captive.

We're at a sushi restaurant in town. Georgie and Claudia are having dinner together. Georgie hands her a pink rose. They walk hand in hand, together on the sidewalk in the center of town. She kisses him. He pinches her ass.

Claudia continues explaining herself in the studio.

"Georgie, I was only using you when it was convenient for me. I'm a woman, Georgie. I'm from another planet. I never even told you that I loved you, did I? God! What's wrong with you?"

Suddenly, Claudia can't breathe right.

They start fighting physically too, now. Georgie does his best to defend himself while still caught up in the chains. He looks like a wounded rocking horse. Claudia finds this amusing.

"Georgie, you're fighting! Look at you go. Let go!"

Georgie makes muffled sounds.

Claudia mimics him.

"Stop! Stop! What are you trying to say, baby?"

She puts a stranglehold on him. She kisses him hard while he tries to hold back. Claudia pulls out a rubber from Georgie's back pocket. She licks the tape over his mouth.

Georgie squeaks.

She undoes his pants, coughing from the smoke in the air. She puts her face up close to his sex.

"Just don't touch my breasts. Don't even ask." Then she realizes. "Oh, you can't anyway. Fine!"

She undoes her bottom and tosses the condom away. It seems like everything's in slow motion for a second.

Georgie is still locked up and suffocating.

Claudia sees he's trying to say something. She undoes the tape on his mouth.

He's out of breath.

"You fucking whore bitch cunt!"

Claudia laughs.

"Good," she says. And she tapes him back up.

"I'm a social worker," Claudia mocks.

Everything is still and quiet for a moment.

"Now, get me pregnant! I want to abuse you, just like you wanted it. I love it. I don't love you."

She's fucking Georgie, fucking raping him. She rips off the tape from his lips.

Georgie yells, "Get off! Get off!"

"I am. I'm getting off. I have complete control, now. Cum inside me, Georgie! Cum inside me, slut!"

The phone rings. Police officers are pounding at the door. Somebody else must have called them—probably Rocky, the feminine florist who lives next door. Georgie cums hard, unloading himself deep inside her, hating it, feeling shattered and corrupted.

Another day, Claudia and Georgie are making out on the sofa. Before the day he raged mad and the shite really hit the fan.

Georgie says, "I love you."

"Thanks," he hears.

Georgie is on the phone with Claudia.

"I have 30 of your messages saved on my voicemail!" says Claudia. "I like listening to them on my way to work. Wherever I go, I get to smile."

She's on her way to the car. It's parked outside. She forgets exactly where.

Georgie is watering his lawn.

(Parenthetical Pet Peeve) People who think 7 am is a fine time to cut the grass.

He tries to break up with her before it's too late. But Claudia suspects his weakness. She smiles with squinted eyebrows.

"I'm not letting you go that easily," she says.

Back in the studio, Georgie's entirely wiped out.

Claudia unlocks and un-tapes him. She leaves, without showing the slightest expression.

Georgie blurts out, "It never ends!"

Claudia looks back.

"I'll call you," she says.

She shuts the door behind her.

Georgie knows she won't call.

The smell of wine and weed evaporate off Claudia's deep beauty. She sneaks back into the studio, coming up behind Georgie, holding a camouflage shotgun. She blows his head to shreds with 10 explosive shots.

"Get out of your head, you sick fucking twist!" Claudia screams. "Love is a lie. Don't you know anything?"

Georgie sees red, and then black.]

Dear Diary:

I may lose the people I love and the things I have. But no matter what happens, I never lose myself.

Easy Steps to a Perfect Pedicure (Déjà Vu)

I take just one of the pills, and I remember Georgie. I remember when I moved out West, in the last week of October. I remember it differently, still fuzzy, still a little surreal. Shite, Pasadena and all of Los Angeles County were blisteringly hot, and I was working up an uncomfortable sweat. I heard screaming and yelling. It was Halloween, and Claudia, who lived across the street, had just broken up with her girlfriend. Her lover flew out the door as Claudia chased her down the sidewalk.

All the little kids, in their G-rated costumes, were excited to see the upcoming catfight. Some looked frightened as their parents and chaperones shielded them from danger.

I watched from my front window. Claudia slapped her ex right across the face, and the bitch went down. It took only one shot from Claudia and the ex was lying on the ground slurring something obscene like, "Dicksucker!"

The kids in our little yuppie town, just bordering the San Marino mansions, were eager for my "dollar bills instead of candy" setup at the front door. Claudia watched with a bottle of wine after her lover finally took off for good.

Within a couple of minutes, she looked at her watch and twitched. Dashing from her front patio, she came to mine. The children scattered as I smiled nervously at my new neighbor. She was prancing, wide-eyed, pursing her lips like she had something stuck on the tip of her tongue. And she wanted to tell me (what did she want to tell me?) Her face was still covered with red lipstick kisses. She leaned over my front fence.

"Come here, little boy. Come here."

I stepped in closer.

"Hi," I said.

"Hi, neighbor. I'm Claudia. I know we haven't met yet—but, well, you probably just saw. Yeah, my girlfriend and I were on pretty thin ice together."

"Yeah. Sorry to know that," I explained.

She looked me in the eyes.

I looked down at her bare feet. Her big pale feet. Her perfect, long, little toes; her adolescent-pink nail polish, halfway scraped off. She was about 40 or so. Her hair was crazy red. Her personality was wild, intoxicating, like my imagination. After all, she saw me looking down at her floor-floaters and took me out of my pathetic, horny little spell. I felt close to her, but I was interrupted by her soft voice. It was sweet and a little raspy.

"I forgot. There's this Halloween party I'm going to be late to, up in Hawthorne. I need my nails done, and my girlfriend, well my ex I guess, was going to do my feet."

A teepee started to build in my pants.

"What are you going as?"

"A hooker."

My balls started to scream for a bucket of ice. I repeated what she said in my head a couple of times in disbelief.

Claudia was a bombshell.

Paula Cole's erotic music played softly on Claudia's cheap little CD player. "Feeling Love" was the tune, and we were surrounded by lit candles—mostly vanilla-scented. I wore a light blue dress shirt with a loose tie and ripped denims.

Claudia was completely naked.

"I can't believe you've never given a girl a pedicure."

"Believe it. I'm a virgin, Claudia." I was solemn.

She sat on her toilet bowl. I held her foot in my lap. My cock was feeling really left out, but I liked feeling this agony, at least for the moment. This woman didn't even know my name. She looked down at me. We were still complete strangers, and I thought she was a lesbian. I questioned whether or not my boner was a bad thing. Were we being sensual? Good God damn! You bet we were!

Claudia handed me a bright red container of Tiger Balm.

(Parenthetical Pet Peeve) Child-proof containers that turn out to be adult-proof.

She asked me not to put my fingers in between her toes, because she was really ticklish, see? So I just closed my eyes and massaged her feet for a couple of minutes, which passed slowly like they were hours.

"Mmm. That's so relaxing. It tingles. It's warm," she moaned.

I removed her old pink nail polish with store-brand nail polish remover. Claudia said I was a quick learner.

I was then instructed to fill a tub of warm water, so I did. And then I added some salts with a vanilla-scented foot soak. She soaked her feet for about 5 minutes until she fell asleep. I didn't want to wake her. So I removed her beautiful, clean, pasty-white feet from the warm water and patted them. I greased the palms of my hands with a hefty dose of body lotion she'd stolen from some hotel. Then I started to massage her feet from the toes down to her heels. Her feet twitched a little. She shivered. My eyes were closed, just like hers.

(*Parenthetical Pet Peeve*) Bending over and splitting my pants in public.

She had pumice stones laid out by the sink. I was familiar with what they did from watching pedicures in beauty parlors. So I dabbed some more lotion on the stones and very gently buffed the areas I felt still needed softening. There weren't many. By the time I had finished, her feet were cotton-soft. I kissed them, hoping she wouldn't wake up. A sad smile passed across her face. I passed it off as part of a dream she was having. She was a Di Vinci angel. She was heavenly and peaceful. I wanted her to be mine.

I dabbed more lotion on her feet, covered them in large plastic baggies, wrapped warm towels around her feet, and let them sit for 15 minutes. She woke up.

"Well done. Well done, mister." She smiled. "Would you bring me a glass of that red wine from the kitchen?" she asked me in the most pleasant of voices.

After I returned with her wine, she lit a joint and took a few seductive hits from it. She offered me a drag with a languid gesture. I nodded in the negative.

"Good boy," Claudia said.

Removing the baggies, I massaged the remainder of the lotion into her feet. Then I buffed her toenails furiously, starting to have a little fun. My boner softened a bit. We laughed together.

"What color would you like?" I asked.

"What do you think? What would look good on me? Say, if you could have my toes?"

And up went my groin stick again. Pre-cum was leaking out. I could feel it. I touched it for a second, and she busted me.

"What are you doing?"

She laughed.

"Nothing."

I carefully painted her nails with a base coat, separating her toes with cotton balls. When they dried, I colored her toenails with two coats of "Hooker Blue." I was in a hurry to leave so I could go back home and jerk off as fast as I could. I was sweaty with guilt, shame, and frustration.

"Neighbor, wait!" she called as I rushed to go.

"I have to go. Sorry."

"But I'm late for the party," she exclaimed.

I stopped in my tracks.

"I want to congratulate you on what a great job you did on my pedicure! And on such short notice, too."

I smiled, still horny as all hell.

"Now it's your turn."

My face shot back that, "Am I in a dream?" look.

She had me sit on the same toilet seat. And she sat herself on the floor where I had sat. She stayed perfectly naked and told me to get naked with her.

(Parenthetical Pet Peeve) Pay toilets.

I undressed slowly and sat down in front of her with my huge boner at attention.

"This has become your night after all. I need to thank you, neighbor. I need to welcome you to the neighborhood. What's your name, anyway?" she asked.

"Georgie. No, Ben."

"You silly thing! Make up your mind."

"Just call me Ben."

"You're young."

"I'm 30, but I admire older women. Mature women. Women older than me," I confessed.

"And you like feet?" she asked respectfully.

Before I could say anything, her freshly pedicured feet crept up my thigh and gently rubbed my balls and shaft. I felt queasy, sick, dizzy, in heaven, in agony. I could see right into her crotch. Her shaved pussy was dripping wet. Her vagina looked so lonely.

Within a minute, I couldn't take it any longer.

"Claudia, you have to make me cum!" I demanded. "Fast. Please. Make me cum. I promise I won't ever ask you again in such a selfish hurry. Please?"

Her feet began to stroke my erect cock up and down. It was tall, proud, rising toward my face. All my boiling love-sap was about to explode.

"Do you want to cum in my mouth?" Claudia asked.

"On your feet. Just like that. Don't stop. Don't stop," I begged.

"Are you close?"

And before I could answer, I splashed her feet with my white nut.

Claudia masturbated her clit in a restless fury and squirted all over the work I'd done on her feet. I rubbed it in with my big hands, massaging what was left of her new feet.

We nodded out together.

The next morning, Halloween was over. We had to get up, get out of the bathroom, and get off to work. I skipped showering that morning—the leftover aroma of sex on my skin was my private souvenir.

I knew that I wanted to see this woman again and again, in Long Beach. Strangely, I knew I would strike up a relationship with Heidi Berillo in Long Beach, and we'd both be involved in catastrophic love affairs beyond our dignities, beyond our distance. I knew I had a solid premise for the big novel: a living, colorful beauty, and a local borderline personality. Or would that be two personalities? Or three? Or four?

A parallel universe. A universal reflection of personality itself. Oh Lord, hear our prayer.

I'm making it, fucking making it, man.

Swimming back to the surface or, at least, back to doc.

Dear Diary:

I'm trying again, to enjoy my own life without comparing it with that of others.

Rehab and Mother

Dr C hangs on my every word when I talk about the robbery and rehab. I know she doesn't want to get hung up on every word, but the thing is, she can't resist a story of mayhem and criminality. No one can. You learn when you're a writer that violence, criminal behavior, sex, and drugs—all of it, any of it—sells. And that's all I'm doing—selling Dr C a story and hoping she buys it.

"Does that mean you're dishonest?" Dr C asks.

I think—I pretend to think—and shake my head no.

"Not dishonest," I say. "Not exactly. No. I wouldn't say that."

"Then what would you say, Ben?"

I think—I pretend to think—and say, "Now, well . . . I'm not exactly sure. What would you say, Dr C?"

Dr C smiles, but says nothing.

Of course, what else could she do?

She wants me to jump in. She wants me to fill the silence with my own thoughts, my own impressions. I sink into the chair. I refuse to play that game. Several seconds pass. Several long, silent seconds. Finally:

"Did I tell you my mother visited me in rehab?" I ask.

Silently, Dr C shakes her head no.

"Want me to tell you about it?" I ask.

"If that's what you want," Dr C says.

Typical psychiatric bullshite.

"Well now, Dr C, if I didn't want to tell you about my mother visiting, I wouldn't have brought it up in the first place would I?"

"You sound angry, Ben. Are you angry?"

"Not me. Uh-uh. No sir. Anger is a waste. Why get angry? Be happy."

I laugh.

Dr C does not join in.

I sigh and begin my newest story: My mother and her short, tight, curly hair, and her grotesque, out-of-shape obese body. This is my greatest fear—that one day I'll wake up looking just like her, and then I'll have to kill myself.

Dr C smiles sardonically. Then she asks if Georgie is patterned more on myself or on my mother.

It's a stupid question and one I refuse to answer.

Then Dr C asks if I enjoyed my mother's visit. I laugh. Could anyone enjoy a visit with my mother? My mother has one of those East Coast voices, loud and nasal—she's always clearing her throat—and if I didn't know better, I'd swear she has Tourette's. She's an Episcopalian. However, with her talent for guilt, I always suspected she was a closet Catholic.

"Interesting," Dr C says.

"What?" I ask.

"All of it," she says, then smiles enigmatically.

Christ, I hate enigmatic smiles.

I continue. My mother was a firm believer in regular church attendance. She even required that I become an altar boy. Why she went to church, or what she thought she gained, was never clear to me. She certainly didn't learn to love in church, at least not in any New Testament way. No, not my mother—my mother was quick to hit (spare the rod, spoil the child, the Good Book says), and she brought that up when she visited me at Valley View.

She sat on the side chair in my room, her fleshy legs crossed primly at the ankle, and cried.

"I just don't know what I did wrong, Benjy. Tell me. I'm a reasonable woman. What did I do?"

"And what did you tell her?" Dr C asks.

I think about that. I don't pretend to think, I do think. And, what the hell? I don't remember. I've never remembered any of the things I've told my mother, only the things she's told me.

"And what are the things she's told you?" Dr C asks.

"Stand up straight. Don't slouch. Be normal. Stop ticcing like that."

"It must've been hard to do all those things."

It must've been, but I don't remember. I don't remember any of the things I did. Did I obey? Rebel? Why can't I remember? Why can't I fucking remember?

Dr C reaches for my hand. I pull back.

"Psychiatrists who touch their patients are suspect in my book. Sorry."

I get to my feet.

"Well, Dr C," I tell her.

My voice is rich, cultured, and melodious—everything Dr C is not.

"Well," I repeat. "Same time Tuesday?"

She nods.
And I leave. I'm so out of there.

Dear Diary:

Every day may not be good, but there is something good in every day.

End the Violence

My mother was always stressed. Always. Because she had this thing for talking in extremes, being in extremes. She was always mad, never good.

At the dinner table, mother, sis, and me:

"Shut up and eat yer peas, before I give you a fuckin' beatin' yull never forget."

She bullied me and my Pops, my sister and me. She even bullied the poor little dog, "Punkin," a tiny, black and gray Shih Tzu adopted from the county fair. Punkin would eat her shite, with wafts of steam coming off it, in the dead of our suburban winters. In turn, she'd be maliciously tortured by my mother. Mother would say, "Bad dog, Punkin, bad dog," and whack the living daylights out of her. As Punkin aged, she became more and more skittish. And mother would tell me how skittish I was becoming. And we'd yell. Yes, typical American Family yelling fights.

"Where do you think you're going?" mother would ask.

"Boarding school."

"Where?"

"Boarding school."

"Hmm, where again?"

"Boarding school, mother. Pops said it was okay. I've waited for this. Let me go. I just want to go."

After each time I answered, "Boarding school," I got her fat, whacking hand across my pale and stubbly teenaged face. There was blood coming out of my nose and ears.

"Where?"

"Boarding school."

Whack!

"Where?"

"Fuck you!"

Whack!

Mother wore no wedding ring, just a white gold, six-carat diamond ring that chipped at my ear and only-to-cherish teen sideburns. Well, the left one anyway.

"Where?"

Until finally I yelped, "Fuck you, momma-bitch, fucking Wakefield Academy in New England, cunt rag!"

Then I swung one huge pounding punch down onto her nose which, click, snap, broke and bled. And mother never hit me again.

I carried all my familial baggage through college and through every broken relationship. I was broken-hearted from being a fucking Pinto, Honky, Worthless, Piece-of-Shite who needed a new mother.

That's what love means to me.

Mother was obsessed with the family and our secrets—the love-making and the beatings, all the things that'll keep my novel off the bestseller list. I've taken my hits and stings with an "I'm the victim, and fuck you, Dr Phil." The whole family scene was just plain bad.

Mother had knickknacks around the house: porcelain elephants, and collectibles. She was artistic by nature, although nothing ever took off for her, and she couldn't read (like me). The two of us together might have gotten through one regular book in our lives and that would be mostly her—no, maybe me. I don't know.

She burned food. She was a Little League mom. She loved me but didn't know how to show it. My mother was obsessed with sex. She liked to appliqué life-size, anatomically correct penises on my sister's Cabbage Patch Dolls and on one of my own. The penises wouldn't have been all that bad if she had done the same thing with an occasional vulva or pudendum now and then, but she didn't. It was just penises.

She was obsessed—with my penis as well. She liked to play what she called "groineology," where she'd grab me high on the thigh, right on the groin, and dig in as hard and tight as she could, her blood-red nails leaving imprints on my skin.

"Groineology, Bennie," she'd say, laughing all the while.

"Kiss me on the lips," she'd demand, even when I was 25.

"Turn yourself into your father, and into me," she commanded. And as the victim of my own mom and dad, when they Mother-Dearested me, I now collect all the movie memorabilia.

Oh, and she hit me. Did I mention how much she hit me?

My grandmother's, my father's mother's, last words to me were, "Oh yeah . . . Rose. Boy, Benjamin, the way she used to hit you." And she died peacefully that night in her bedroom, at 99.

Georgie tells me to watch Dr Phil. And now it's Dr Phil's voice in my head, telling me to let go and fucking give me a break, you lousy, lazy, beautiful little baby.

Please, Dr C. Seek help soon.

Dear Diary:

Overall, I'm too positive to be doubtful, too optimistic to be fearful and too determined to be defeated.

Second Skins with Footnotes

Dr C asks, "You've mentioned Heidi before, Ben. Why don't you tell me more about her?"

"Heidi's my obsession. My Perplexity. She's the woman who changed my life—and not in a good way. She brings back Georgie, who hasn't been around since Mrs Petite. Claudia is Georgie's Heidi."

As an adult, I pleasure myself with the latex wrapped around me, snug, warm, wet with saliva. There's no mess to clean up when I'm through.

All this time, I've been trying to be safe and doubling up meant security to me. I move out of town a few months later. I never see Claudia Nesbitt again. She fucked me, and she fucked with my head. I loved her in my own twisted way. She wouldn't really ever change. Who was I kidding—myself, maybe?

I see her everywhere. Claudia, Ashley, and everyone, everywhere. She's the essence of every woman I come into contact with. She never ends, like one mirror reflected in another.

Talk about an obsessive–compulsive personality. This fantasy world in my head, in my heart, it's becoming my reality. I just can't seem to get over her, over Claudia. And I only met her once.

"Am I turning into psycho-boy?"

Where's the simplicity I once knew? How might I regain that?

"This all too, shall pass," I hear. "You'll be just fine in the long run."

Dear Diary:

As for myself, autism is my superpower!

Benevolent Georgie

There is a genuine goodness to Georgie, as unsacred and as unwholesome as he might otherwise be. Yes, he does see beauty in every woman. He gives away his money, he's religious in the truest sense of the word, and he holds people in the highest regard. Is it I who have the racial tics, then? Am I the one who lets people cut in line? No, it's Georgie. He holds the door open for everyone, even for 10 minutes, as they all pile out at rush hour. It's Georgie who carries packages. On his way to Dr C's, Georgie buys food for the homeless and hands it out, carefully deciding by their homely looks who gets what. Georgie forgives everyone, more or less, even when they don't deserve forgiveness.

The sun beats down on Georgie's arms as he walks through Rainbow Park on the corner of Seventh and Cherry. It's an urban park, not in the best neighborhood. There's trash on the sidewalks that surround it and stores with boarded-up windows, and the bums and the down-and-outers, who stand on the corners and panhandle for change and food. Whenever Georgie remembers he stops at the Carl's Jr up the street and buys Western Bacon Cheeseburgers, chicken strips, and crisscross-cut fries. Then he hands them out to the beggars who line the street. And whenever he has the time, he picks up at least two pieces of trash to throw away.

(Parenthetical Pet Peeve) Animals digging through the trash.

Sometimes he buys Kentucky Fried Chicken instead of Carl's Jr, and sometimes he picks up three pieces of trash instead of two. He likes to pick up trash because it makes him feel like an environmentalist. Like he's contributing in some way. Once, by mistake, he picked up a baby's soiled diaper and it grossed him out so bad that he couldn't pick up trash for a month.

Across the street from the park is the 7–11, and kitty-corner is the Shell station where Georgie buys his blue raspberry Slush Puppie—the best drink he's ever had in his life. It tastes like frozen cherry Kool Aid, except it's carbonated slightly. Georgie drinks his Slush Puppie, and it's better than any orgasm, any bright sunny day. Otherwise, he could be in heaven. The original Slush Puppie is that good. It's the best thing he's had, ever since he can remember.

(Parenthetical Pet Peeve)

How the nutritional value of any given food is usually inversely proportional to how good it tastes.

Georgie feels good. It's a Wednesday, and he likes Wednesdays because that's when he sees Dr C, same as Ben: from 3:30 to 4:30 pm. He likes Dr C. He thinks she's kind and he likes that she sees him (and me) on the half hour. It's different. It makes Georgie feel special, noticed.

Georgie knows that Dr C doesn't believe he exists. She thinks he's only a figment of Ben's imagination, or worse, a symptom of his pathology. But that's okay. Georgie doesn't mind. He knows he's real, and that's all that matters. At least for Georgie.

And Georgie knows all about Ben, even if Ben doesn't know all about Georgie. Georgie knows how Ben thinks of nothing but Heidi and then puts it all on Georgie. Ben says it's Georgie who's the character, Georgie who's the literary device (what a joke! A man can't be a device!), Georgie who can't get over Claudia. And so on. Georgie knows better, though. It is Ben who can't get over Claudia.

Ben, when he thinks of the real Georgie at all, thinks of Georgie from the past. He remembers Georgie in sex class, in the tree house. He doesn't think of Georgie in the present at all. The Georgie who buys DVDs on female masturbation, who works to understand a woman's body, who sometimes wants nothing more than his partner's orgasm.

Ben dismisses Georgie, which sometimes hurts Georgie's feelings. But not today. Not when the sun is shining and the breeze is cool and he gets to see Dr C in . . . Georgie checks his watch. In another 2 hours.

He takes a seat on the bench nearest the swings, where he always sits, and watches a young mother push a little blond-haired boy, maybe three or four, higher and higher into the air. The little boy screams in delight.

The problem, the all-consuming sadness and despair, for Georgie (and me, too) stems, he knows, from his own mother. A woman Georgie's memory can't access. Ben has him locked out. Nobody gets to know Ben's mother.

Nobody.

Georgie's ultimate goal is to be like Mozart on his deathbed.

There's Mozart, dying, with Salieri reminding him he's a genius and that he, Salieri, will finish off the great masterworks of his life. Meanwhile, Mozart slowly dissolves in his insanity.

Georgie Bartholomew Gust: May he rest in peace.

Dear Diary:

Finding friends with the same mental disorder as myself: priceless!

Part V: St Valentine's Day Massacre

Journal. . .

Diary, Journal, Self, Whomever, Whatever. . . . Maybe Dr C.

"So how are you doing today, Ben?" Dr C asks. Like she really wants to know. "With the therapy, I mean."

What am I supposed to tell her? Whatever I tell her, she really doesn't want to know, but here goes nothing.

Look, I really cannot tolerate the current symptoms I'm experiencing. They drag me in and out. It's taking me a long while to even get anything down on paper here. But I put out the best effort I could ever make. And I'm fighting for my life.

My head is a constant firecracker. My tongue curls up and wisps out through my puckering lips. My mouth is contorted, pushing out the skin under my mustache and beard. My head snaps back and forth rapidly, with extreme force, with every incoming fragment of thought, any slightest bit of self-awareness. Usually, the head will jerk to a singular, asymmetrical beat, but un-rhythmically to a POUND after POUND, POUND-POUND, with varying intensity. The thoughts want desperately to escape.

All I can still think about are my stories, my work. I don't want down time, free-time, or Georgie-time. My work is required all the time, every time, period.

I must keep my voice low. Others, all around, hear me. They are suspicious and they spy on me. Earlier, cars were beeping at me. People on the streets and in the parking lots were snickering about me, in those same whispers I hear at night, when I'm alone. But they look away before I can see who they are. They're real, and it's tempting to know them, especially if they have a cell phone or are with another person. They might want to call the cops because they're suspicious, though.

Cars back off when they're behind me, or at my side, at a red light. Sometimes the passengers cover their faces, like what they're saying is secret. When the traffic moves faster, other cars lay on their horns honking at me two, three times, until I think I've run somebody off the road. I look back and the racket has stopped. People always yell at me, but this isn't typical. Police sirens and helicopter noises come and go when I shift into second or third gear. The energy is high, and these noises dissipate no sooner than they've started. Some of them last two, maybe three, seconds.

(Parenthetical Pet Peeve) People who lean on the horn the second the light changes.

Some of the whispers return when I make it to my first destination. Dropping off my landlord's check in Seal Beach is a 15-minute drive. The ladies from the hair salon are snickering about me. I hear, "He's the one," leak from their twitching mouths, quietly. Then they walk back inside. I write a note to the landlord and keep my cool.

My head snaps back again. I can't focus on the red lights, but I handled the whole trip better today than yesterday. I didn't sit through whole cycles of them, red–green–yellow, and back to red again. I could barely drive back, with my head snapping and my eyes rolling, and my hands coming off the steering wheel and into some finger-stretching, waving-like gesture. The music really wasn't helping much, either.

I've been so confused that I forget how to turn on my video camera, make coffee, or find keys (it took me 3 hours this morning to find my car keys.) The medication I took an hour ago is making me feel dizzy. My head tics are still there. I still feel a little high. I really can't drive now or even go outside. I can't open any windows or blinds. I've got to choose what phone calls to take, if any. I might start craving the hallucinations that usually come in higher doses of whatever-it's-called, this medication shite, these meds—I miss them.

Half an hour later, I'm fucking stoned on this shite. I need help, an aide, a live-in, something. I can't function as a person, currently. I'm really scared, but the paranoia (I can't believe it) is either different or less. Or something. I don't know what. I don't want anyone to see me. What I'm feeling must definitely show in my face, my hands, and my body. I'm not sure exactly how. I'd be scared to know.

The doctor will call me soon, I guess. I'm not sure if I'm explaining these symptoms right. I get so utterly confused. I'm losing my mind. I can't think of any treatment that would help. Hell, the treatment makes it worse. Is this terminal? Will this get worse? What is it, really? A sickness? A disease? A pathology? Or what?

I still need to make my mark somehow on the world. My friends can't show up for me. I don't dare tell them of my misery. I can't tell whether I'm up or down.

No. Let's try harder.

Let's say:

I'm just as okay as the New Age people say I am. I'm as okay as Dr C wants me to be. I plod along. I trudge along. I dictate my own misery. But, by the name of God, there's a reason for this drudgery.

I'm ready to start the day, again (I hope). I wake up on my own again, before my seven-hour alarm. This whole situation has to be a repetitive routine. Like the same old nightmares I experienced again last night, or rather, this morning.

The Tourette's in my neck and throat keeps getting worse. I'm making a valid attempt to write as much as I can stand, hoping that maybe some of these night terrors and the morbid confusions of the day will finally dissipate. So far, it's not happening, though.

Yesterday was horrendous. The night before, Georgie put on a dream patch fuelled with nicotine. He's armed with one every night during sleep so he can dream—vividly and lucidly dream. He's more lucid when he has the classical radio station on, or even the television—anything to actually flash the dream images and nightmare scenarios at him.

The night before last, he dreamed his best friend, Bobby Banks, was getting married to some big pop star. The dream caused an extremely uncomfortable angst, and Georgie's imagination was wounded. He knew his best friend Bobby Banks was a faithful man, and that brought on the angst. I've become a faithful man, I think, in my recovery. Still, I feel almost abandoned by my best friend.

Claudia is promiscuous, slutty, and, besides, she's a compulsive liar. She signifies the perplexity and confusion, not of my heart, but of my perception. After all, other people don't see things the same way I do. This morning's dreamscape caused the same feeling of suffocation. For whatever reason, I'm not able to make my mark on this world. I can't even leave my neighbor. I'm trying to grow stronger, but I can't take the unbearable pressure. But it's something so tiny. A woman who is as bisexually needy as a straight man craves pussy. But does she need me? Does she need to? Claudia couldn't even kiss me when I stopped by to give her the greeting cards for her new apartment, because Sara was nearby.

"No. No. We can't kiss here. It's just not right," Claudia said.

That's why I left her the last time. That's why I'm addicted to this woman. I've got nowhere else to go. How can I escape her? Am I really a damaged person?

I want to say, "You fucking lush. You fucking dyke. You fuck with my mind, in my nightmares—I want to kill myself, just because you exist. I hate myself because of you. Huh? Would other guys put up with this? Where are they now, then? It's been over a year and you're just a waste of my time. No, I really don't love you."

"You make me want to sleep with you again and again," she says.

I vomit on her face and on her chest, and she says the same thing. She wants me to sleep with her, because of the mess I'm in.

"Get a life," she echoes. "Get a life, Georgie-boo. I'll see you again soon."

What lies deep in her past? I'll never know. She's just a character of my experience—what a bitter, sharp, stinging pinch. It really hurts—it makes me tic. I pucker my lips and "click." I need out, but I still feel I need to make my mark on her first. This is the most important thing to me. Discovering myself, so I can make my mark artistically. Every day I collect the moments and shove them inside. I store them until I'm about to burst. But I don't. There is maybe a good reason for this. I could be a very new soul, so to speak—an infinite soul. I consider these metaphysical questions for a moment. But I'm really much more interested in making sure Claudia has a really shite day.

"I'm having a shite day," she'd confess every Wednesday, for reasons I'll never know.

Her internal turmoil doesn't manifest itself outside. I feel this same old feeling. It's déjà vu all over again.

I love her. I hate her. I'm jealous too, because she can balance such a fucking crazy life so nonchalantly. How can I be a better person? I can't make myself a better person, but that's exactly what I crave when I'm writing. So perhaps I'm still learning, only the hard way, again. I need this shitey relationship—it's a part of my secret plan. It's the Divine Force manifesting in my life. Yeah, right.

I come closer to finding myself the more I write, think, and cry. I drain myself through these outlets, letting the thoughts seep out a little—sharing them or giving them away. Or maybe I'm draining myself emotionally when I cry in the shower with music, alone, softly with fear. I try to hone in, to get closer to the truth about me, to know myself, not in my superficial pretentiousness, but genuinely—my true self. Then maybe I'll have a better relationship with the world, with the social and familial climates I'm so uncomfortable with now. Then the rest of them can all fall back into their own places. I really feel like that. It's all really just a matter of time and sticking with it, never giving up, never.

I puff away on my cigarette. I find out that I'm crazy. I realize what it takes to be a king is more than I'll ever know. I know what tools I'll need to make my mark. It gets a little clearer the more I feed the solitude with the things I know. I'm so limited by my excuses, my medical maladies, my in-born genetic deficiencies from the baggage of abuse, neglect, and life—I'm ruined forever, and it's none of my fault. I want to leave this world and come back with something remote and profound, a message or call—I want to change the universal thought.

I've got to keep in constant contact with the doctor today. I cancelled the trip to San Francisco. I'm as stressed as I was as a teen.

Let me lose my mind so I can get over this. Someone, God, please help me. Don't let me go yet. I know I still take it all too seriously. I know no other way.

Dear Diary:

I don't think I give myself enough credit.

A Valentine Reminder

It's Valentine's Day.

I get out of the house and into my car. It's a little hatchback I've had practically forever. I barely drive it, but sometimes I just need to get out of the house. It's damn lonely being single sometimes, especially on this special holiday.

So I celebrate myself. I sing. And I ponder the what-could-have-been of Claudia, back from Wakefield. I don't give that composite sketch of her enough time obsessing on her, after all. I figure I owe her.

I drive down the Pacific coast. Traffic is safer there than on the LA freeways. But I get bored before long and head back home. I'm a little sad, a little wimpy, and pathetic.

I remember my last break-up. It was back in college. Claudia went elsewhere, but back when I was immature, impulsive, and horny. I didn't break up with that Claudia—she broke up with me. She fucking died on me, mother-fucker, man. What a cop out. I brought her back to life with the help of my Georgie Porgie, my pal. I owe him. He's good to me. That surely takes the cake. Valentine's Day memories? Not at all.

I hardly ever answer the phone. That's what voicemail is for. I remember I was in a pissy mood all morning. Claudia owed me a call. I shut the ringer off.

"Hey, it's Claudia. It's Friday, and it's around 5 o'clock or so, I think. I'm home. I'm going to be home the next couple of hours so if you get this in time, give me a call. I'm sorry I didn't call last night but you can call me today."

I opened a fresh pack of smokes and lit up. I gripped the portable phone and dialed back, wishing she'd answer. I remember thinking about her kitchen.

She lived a couple of hours away. I used to take the train to see her. She was a fucking animal. So was I. We were sex-a-holics.

After our initial blind date, I brought Claudia back home with me. When she spoke openly of her frustration with menopause, my roommate knew that something was slightly off with Claudia and me.

"Isn't she a little old for you?" he suggested, unaware that some people never age when you're one of us, the very few of us left.

But my roommate was a little weird himself. He liked his girls young, real young-all-too-fucking young. Fucking pedophile, I thought.

Claudia had stretch marks. For some odd reason, they attracted me. She had those old-lady nipples. She couldn't have kids and she was loyal. No rubbers were ever needed.

The phone rang once. "Hello?" she answered.

"Hi."

"How are you?"

"Great."

"Good."

Claudia and me, we are Typical Americans—sophisticated, eloquent, articulate.

"So, what's happening?" I asked Claudia.

"Oh, I'm just eating."

(Parenthetical Pet Peeve) Heating up a cup of microwave soup and the container flips, spilling its contents.

"Some vegetable soup, some tea . . . I just wanted to talk, if you had time," she said candidly.

Then she broke up with me. And it wasn't even because of my age.

"I don't want to put the blame on you," she said. "It's not something you'd be able to solve. You need someone more attractive and around your age, and very, very into you."

"No regrets. No hard feelings," I told her.

There was a long silence. No one tried to break it for several moments.

"So, do you have another man in your life now?" I asked politely.

"No. The thing is—that's surprising. There always has to be someone and you assume that if I'm not with you, then there must be someone else. I'm just really independent."

Another long, uncomfortable pause.

"What went wrong?" I asked her. "Were you uncomfortable with me?"

"No. I don't necessarily . . . I mean, I'll tell you this, but I think I'm a really low maintenance person, so maybe it's just my particular perspective. But I think you're kind of high maintenance. You need to know from me, always, that everything is all right. You have a constant need for reassurance. But I think of how you were so honest with me and that was so important to me. You always asked how I was feeling, too—you weren't selfish or anything. I just can't deal with that. I just can't take care of you."

"What should I work on? I mean, I'm probably not going to change."

"No," she said, "don't change! Again, there's your need for reassurance. Listen, I'm pretty free-ended. I hope you're not lonely."

I immediately changed the topic.

I love The Talk women engage in if you request an analysis of What Really Happened. You can find out all of your weak points and your strengths, even before you cease to ever lay eyes on her again—just as she's becoming your ex. So you learn more about how the other species relates to you during the break-up than in any point during the relationship. You learn not just what a dick you really are, but how your ignobility and unworthiness have actually become apparent. Because of The Talk, I get a clearer picture of who I am, and what a piece of work I can be for women to deal with.

But nothing has ever stopped me from pursuing love, whether it's true love or not. I keep trudging right along, even through the worst storms. There's some huge void in my life I've got to fill, somehow. And I have got to figure some things out.

Valentine's Day is over now. There's always some promise for next year.

Maybe by then I'll feel a little different.

Dear Diary:

Maybe I'm the Rush Limbaugh version of myself today, writing and reviewing my work. Maybe it's the two hours of sleep I got last night. The voices, the schizophrenia I've got, or that my heart has actually been touched, way deep. Maybe that's why I'm even on this computer right now at all. I'm human—Angel. Demon. Human. (ADHD!) Let D be for the Dichotomy. I live amongst everybody else, with our collective overall human condition. I lose the fear and the paranoia, and just write—right now . . .writing . . . Until I die.

446

Funeral

I fantasize my own petty little funeral. I lie in the overpriced coffin, fully insulated, wondering what all the live ones are up to—and the dead ones, too. Maybe I'm just a little angry. I cried myself to sleep last night, like a little baby, like a loser. While I'm lying there, I hear all the women I've ever been with speaking their minds. They comment on what kind of lover I was.

It's Judgment Day.

"He was fine; I mean, he was all right. He was really sweet and really cute."

"He was really funny."

"There were so many times we'd have these intense conversations, all this philosophy stuff, and he would just go off and get . . . totally crazy, you know? And I'd just sit there, completely confused, and start crying."

"I never knew completely what was going on in his head. I think that's what I loved about him the most, though—his complexity. I couldn't get bored with him easily."

I think of all the other broken hearts that bled on this earth. They had so much passion, but their lives were probably dull. Still, they had this passion. The passion welled up inside of them right until the end.

There's so much brilliance scattered throughout the history of mankind: works of art, philosophical diatribes, subtle moments of supreme happiness, legendary artifacts buried in basements, epic beauty, manuscripts hidden in the trash—all that stuff. I try to feel important, despite all of it. I'm surrounded by nature. I'm not even sure what it is I'm still looking for.

The women continue whispering over my grave.

"I was always curious to see what would happen next."

I hear music, a Bach death march versus Led Zeppelin, divided by Culture Club. I try to translate all that I hear into a personal love story, but all I want to do is die.

My funeral is held at a crack house.

The women in my dream shared moments of true happiness with me—they shared my life. They're now merely delusions.

"Was there really anybody even there?"

I gasp.

I try to stay alive. Keep the faith.

I'm out at the bar late, giving in to temptation.

"You've worried me these last 24 hours."

She stayed with me when my car overheated in the rain. I want to remember this. Remember her.

"Move on."

"Change, reduce the bad stuff, the rage, the blaming, the spoiled boyishness, the lying, the violent thoughts."

I tried to change before it was too late. I did. But I failed to commit, and I couldn't follow through.

She slid my hand away the moment I made her cum with my fingers. I made love with a live person. I was in the moment. The moment is gone.

I lied. They lied.

I broke up with another woman this morning. Melanie.

I had no self-respect for the last time, at last. It was finally over. All the chaos, all the madness—it was all over.

I remember tearing up when the two of us made love for the first time. I thought no one else would know.

Melanie was The One.

During the procession, traffic is a mess. Fear sinks in.

"Am I still alive?"

I can't tell. I seem to have separated from myself. I question the news helicopters, hovering above me. I've become a complete narcissist, delusional. I'm stuck in myself. Still, I feel like something is incomplete. Claudia. I remember Claudia more than anyone.

(Parenthetical Pet Peeve) Gridlock. Worse: gridlock when on your way to work. The worst: gridlock when on the way to the hospital.

The choppers fly like locusts, weaving back and forth, taking out everyone on the freeway with machine guns and rocket launchers. I'm the only one to escape. The whole city is a parking lot, a massacre, a graveyard. I'm lost. The whispers still linger in my head.

"I welcomed you into my home, felt drawn to you and your loneliness."

I held hands with her for the first time. It's never felt the same again—nothing has. I'll never forget the feelings. I felt cheated, but I wasn't.

"I don't think that either of us used the other."

"It was a warm and loving exchange between two shattered souls."

"I'll save you, you save me."

I pray to be corrected. I'm meeting myself now for the first time, thanks to those who once fulfilled my life.

"You're a very intense man, and I am much too delicate to deal with all of you."

"When will you be ready?" I asked.

Memories I've saved throughout the years have such a profound impact on me. I think, Who am I? Who was I? (Who was he?)

"It's been almost three weeks since I've seen you, and I hope you were able to maintain your goal. I must say, however, that your absence from the bar is a positive sign."

(Parenthetical Pet Peeve) Drunks. Worse: loud, obnoxious drunks. The worst: loud, obnoxious drunks driving cars.

"You ran like a madman to the drugstore to get me an aspirin when I had that extraordinary headache."

"You opened up and cried your pain to me. You made me laugh."

"You were loving to my animals, and you didn't complain when Candy and Lolly's fur made you all stuffed up."

"You ate my Thanksgiving dinner. You asked for seconds."

"You said, Thank you."

"You held me. You held my hand when we walked. You gave that bum two dollars for bringing back my necklace when it fell off."

"You cleaned your bathrooms before I came over."

"You said to me, 'You were the most beautiful in that bathtub.'"

And it was all so lovely. There's beauty in conflict, too. In despair, everything takes on a new meaning.

"But you are so many harsh and unforgiving things."

"Part of growing up is taking responsibility for what you do. Stop blaming everybody else. It's hard enough to be a parent to somebody without issues. Yours did the best they could. Now it's your job to do the best you can."

"So, take care."

"I miss you."

"I just wanted to hear your voice."

"Whenever you need me."

"You respected me when I asked you not to call, and you didn't."

"Nobody's holding a gun to your head but you."

"Might you find the love and strength inside yourself, the love that I have witnessed and have been grateful to receive. Might you learn to understand yourself and take control of your life in a loving, healthy way. And, like I said, make some goddamn changes, positive changes."

"I am leaving you."

"You have hurt me profoundly."

"Verbal abuse, alcohol, yelling, gambling, harsh criticisms, humiliation, disdain."

"On your good days, you were definitely more affectionate than usual."

"You opened doors for me. You said things like, 'This is your night.'"

"You are the only person I know who truly made me feel like a woman. Nobody else has yet."

"I have confidence in myself from you."

"You made me feel more miserable than happy."

"Do this. Do that."

"You called me bitch, even when we were most intimately together."

"You farted on me. I couldn't believe it!"

"But inside, you're a sensitive and tender gentleman. Where did that man go?"

"I just hope that the pain, sorrow, and bitterness will eventually fade away."

Very important detail: I didn't know what I was doing! Blind ambition captivated my every thought and action. I dissolved. I made my dwelling in solitude. I acquired, personally, what I was able. My character remains the same. Strange and bizarre thinking, mental disturbances, caused my mind to suffocate. I withdrew from reality the best way I knew how.

I'm still addicted to Melanie. I love this woman who can't love me. Melanie has a lot of baggage. Melanie's a lot like me. I thought she would be all right with me, being like me. I guess I've changed a little. So, what did she have to say about us?

"We're two different people. But I'm not going anywhere."

I'm doing my best just to forget about her all day long. I begin with some kind of ending. But I require detail and important facts, and truths that elicit positive emotions.

I think about how love can't always be rushed. Love at first sight, true love. They're lies (but I'm attracted to them). I dive into a bag of chips and buy some smokes and a small lighter at the counter. I pay with my check card. Caffeine, smokes, Slush Puppies, dreams of purple Pez—they're a little hard to find these days. A little like happiness. Like love.

In the end, I wonder what all that really means. I want these echoes to make me a better man. I'm not alone, after all. I'm still here. I move on the best I can. Things get a little better during these short mental detours. We change. I change. I celebrate. I sing. I improve myself, somehow. It's all like a broken-hearted jubilee.

I'm out of milk and sugar, and the coffee is almost done brewing. It's damn past one in the morning, and I require amplification. The supermarket is open late, really late. I've got to head over there now.

(Parenthetical Pet Peeve) Supermarkets that require me to buy $10 worth of groceries before I can use their coupons.

Maybe I'll pick out some point-of-purchase items from the display by the checkout line—a pack of chewing gum

(Parenthetical Pet Peeve) Chewing gum or a packet of triple-A batteries to store in the freezer, or something.

Georgie needs a light bulb over his desk.
I need a nightlight to plug into the bathroom wall.
I need to write another list.
What else? Another set of scattered thoughts.

(Parenthetical Pet Peeve) Can openers that leave a small sliver of the can still uncut.

My living room is quaint and contemporary.

There's an overabundance of every fancy little modernization, every known electronic doodad, every conceivable entertainment gadget that can fit in a room without cluttering it.

There are photos and drawings framed across the walls and on the bookshelves, representing my past. Past girlfriends, awards, trophies, posters from my travels.

There are loads of hardcore intellectual books—just piles and piles of them—most of them in three copies. It's the same with my video and music collection.

I have too many things, and I've got too many copies of my things. Some of the sketches and notes lying around are only halfway completed. My drawings and paintings are scattered, hardly complete, but brilliant.

The graph paper diagrams have been drawn with some purpose but with no implications, resembling intricate patent designs and blueprints.

It's obvious I have a strong mind—maybe too strong for my own good. And I have too many projects going on, arbitrary projects, redundant and grandiose.

My past seems rich and full. I've lost that richness and fullness lately, finding comfort only in sleep and in having nothing to look forward to. All my needs are taken care of.

The things in my house, although artistic, are mathematically arranged and, somehow, everything corresponds to everything else. Quantum physics material, videos and books, are neatly clustered and labeled beneath an MC Escher print.

(So as not to confuse myself, it's simple, in as much as the confusion is the clarity. The clarity is the confusion, Doc, it's frightening because it scares me too and I admit I oftentimes ask myself why. My bike, and the trophies, sports stuff, and so on, the home within my home, thus additional confusion, in this home. It elicits a very visual view, voilà, into my space, MySpace, my home, my wife, I mean my life both of which and whom also confuse me and thus everyone. If I were the therapist: voilà, I did; I used to have some sort of life. Perhaps it is gone. Surely it's gone, I used to travel the world. I was awarded in sports, but no longer. I'm now alone with a continuum of collections I've saved to remember, not use. Maybe it's trauma of PTSD, posttraumatic stress disorder, fuck. Maybe it's my own version of Proust's diatribing his epic words, remembering the things, things of the past; at least I think, fuck, now I have thought in the past tense, that I used to have a damn life. You've never been to my home, or any of them, might I add. So, I'll exhibit some sort of visual tour of my sense of home within the rooms. What about the world within my miniature world? What about the suffocation within my surroundings? Blah. Boring. The matrices of my old spinning fan refracts light on to something else that is similar, in some way, metaphor after metaphor, it's the best way to describe it, or anything for that matter. My home, on its own, elicits my obsession with everything, and for my own compulsions for creativity: compulsions, creativity and confusion, and yes, even where and how all lights shine under the shade. I am meticulous about having 3 copies of everything, 3-3-3, you see? And that he is super organized, so as in a movie, one of my lamps is a vintage film or stage play sort of spotlight. The lamp, the spotlight, it shines its light onto a pile of DVDs, and my movie collections, films I have produced, and maybe I never produced anything, I just don't know. My batch of brilliant sketches remains unfinished and incomplete—people so many times say that I am too smart for my own good—that there is "someone in there," inside me—an undiscovered brilliant Tesla kind of multi-rounded physicist, inventor. Ha, all of this is common with all my whatever— "illnesses," as all of you shrinks, I'm sorry, but you have all dropped on me. Labeled me, and why? To understand? Who in his or her right mind can be understood? I don't even want to be understood. I like, I fucking love, the mystery of me. I seem to create this effect—this so-called side effect, ha, of super organization and, ah, my so-called, self-dubbed brilliant mind? I don't give a damn. I'm now just a nothing of a mere creature living in some dreamland. Possibly none of this is, nor was, true to begin with. Delusion. Delusion. Delusion. Fuck it. Yeah, screw it, okay? None of it happened, like fucking fiction, fear of non-fiction—my all telling entire tale, my Alibiography, my entire novel—this one—is a literal collection of facts, of myself. I'm a documentarian of my whole life, minute-by-minute, moment-by-moment —momentum.

In short, all of my trophies relate to the bike-racing awards, because I always wanted to do something, anything, athletics, and I never have, Doc. It was and is all—all of it—and all in all, in the past. You know as much as I, that I am stuck in the past, and ramble with my mouth full. Fuck, here's some self-therapy, my alibi —my defense, my mechanism. I bought the things in my life from someone else's life, so fuck me for it, but all at thrift store after thrift store—I'm poor. I've created not only a false past but also another person's past; perhaps theirs was false too, why else would they sell their stuff? It's anonymous. And I love anonymous living, other people's lives therefore everyone else's pasts, because everything takes place in the past. Someone else's life? Ah, Doc, come on, I wish you could see where and how I live. It's the same.

Picturesque pictures of the place. There, so I lied, so go right ahead, Doc, and diagnose me with yet another distortion. Perhaps present me with a proper pathetic pathological liar problem. Go right ahead. We can probably laugh about it all later. My whole life, the people and places within it, my life story—mine-mine-mine, all within my rationalized reality—is just a pastiche of composite sketches—the whole fucking thing—everything. I never wanted to be everything. What I want is to be someone. (So, biscuit, back it, rabbit, and flap it. Gadget, badge it, bag it—boom!)

The stationary bike has trophy-lined shelves alongside it, along with workout tapes and sports magazines and signed baseballs.

A spinning metal fan refracting light blows air at a ceiling fan, which spins slowly above the wheels of the bike that spin slowly at the metal fan. I pass by the running shower, now steaming.

I daydream in the shower, not minding when the soap slips. I don't wash my hair today. After all, you never look your best when you're about to encounter the one you've been waiting for all this your life. You're never fully prepared. And neither am I. Neither is anyone.

"No sex. Just love," I mumble to myself. She must think of me as the friendly type. That's fine. I'm used to it.

I enjoyed myself. That's all that matters. God probably delights in orchestrating me now. I'll chalk it up to personal growth. I'll never hear from Heidi or see her ever again. My mind runs wild with quiet confusion—it feels so soothing to the senses.

I'll wake up tomorrow, thinking about today, and the next day I'll think about today. And while I'm in love, I'll stop writing for the most part. I know it won't last forever. I'm in love—I scoff at the thought. I love all this scoffing business. I'm closed-captioned, projecting in H-D.

Dear Diary:

I am sleep deprived, should I be writing anything until you get sleep? Of course I should. Of course I should write more, sleep less. I'm a wise man, after all. A wise ass, like I always say; a narcissist.

454

The Narcissist

Let me lose my mind. And let me find it. Fuck it—I'm going out for a walk on the beach. It's only a block away. The voices in my head are raging today. They're calling me a winner. Do I believe them?

I've already done enough damage in this lifetime, and I've paid for it. In triplicate—but I'm okay. It's the others I'm worried about. It's all the chaos out there. I remember breaking up with her twice, that little princess, that unthinkable seductress, my Perplexity.

I have to vent a little. I just learned what June Gloom meant last week, after hearing Claudia talk about it. I've lived out here for five years. (Is that even a West Coast term? Ol' Gloom-n-Doom?)

What is it that I want? I have no idea how far I'm going to walk. Am I really after happiness?

The city built this pathway on the beach to encourage exercise. It's nice. The rain fell last night without a break, but it calmed down to a slight drizzle this morning. I look at my watch. I wait for time to pass. I wonder how far I'm going to walk. This walking is good. What else is? Is that important to me? I think I'm a pretty giving guy, but, hey! I admit, there's a narcissist in there, too. I wonder if that's common. Hell, in humans, anything is common. God, I'm getting blisters already. I wish I didn't smoke.

I collapse on the beach and close my eyes. If I'm ever going to get to the point, I'll have to keep going over it and over it, again and again, until I reach perfection.

That's where I'm stuck.

Claudia, everybody, Claudia, Claudia! Claudia. What's the next big thing? Who will be the next big death? What about the next big technology, the next fad, or the next killer drug?

I suck down another cigarette. I can't smoke in my office. This aristocratic little shithole office I often call my Think Tank is stifling me. I said I was frustrated. So what?

I'm dying. The way I see it, I only have 15 more days to live—my death is already scheduled somewhere between the 15th and the 25th of December this year. I definitely won't see the next year when it comes. (If it comes.) I won't even leave my 20s. I won't see, hear, taste, smell, or touch again. I won't remember or experience anything other than this. Hell, I won't even exist.

I have to write all this stuff down before it's too late. I don't know why I waited so long, anyway—I guess I just didn't know any better.

It has to be about me now, doesn't it? I can feel it—the nausea, phlegm-coughing, anxiety, paranoia, loneliness, bitterness, and nostalgia. I start to laugh hysterically at my own demise. It lasts for an hour, a fraction of my life.

I knew I'd have an early death, since I was a kid, in fact.

Now I'm not even sure if my life was worth it.

Or if my death will be meaningful.

Or what.

Dear Diary:

I have the confidence to jump into the unknown. If I have a hard time landing on my feet, those around will catch me. I sure as hell hope they would!

The Orange Button

I check into another hotel. I should've signed up for points when I first started staying here. But it would probably be just another hassle, another scam—I really can't stand all the junk mail that comes with membership. I get so confused with all the sign-up forms, too. Maybe I'll sign up later. I'll ask at the front desk before I leave. The front desk clerk knows me, and my "situation." I come and I go pretty often. My stays lack consistency, but who cares? I just need to get away again. I need a change of scenery. (But even there, the same ghosts haunt me.)

I'm addicted to change, even if it means coming back to something I've already done, somewhere I've already been. As long as it means I'll be switching gears, I'm happy. I'm in the same room I had before. The little orange button on the remote that says ORDER in thin black letters is a good friend by now. I remove the top bedspread. I put toilet paper on the porcelain tank and try to make the tanning lotion look like it has never been used. I take down a washcloth and start fantasizing.

That's why I come back here.

Everything is at my disposal.

I find myself drawing naked pictures for hours, staying up late at night, pushing myself to the edge of insomnia. I'm half-awake, I'm half-baked, but I'm clean. I long ago lost the consistency, charm, and nonchalance of my youth. I perfected it, and it shattered right before my eyes. I was in my mid-20s, somewhere. Now I make a small effort to regain a sense of self-discipline. It's tough to get back into the swing of things. All my routines have shut down.

Can the paradoxes of life be worked out through some utilitarian calculus? Why didn't I get that far in school? Instead of history, they should have taught me how to be happy.

Is this what being an adult is like for others? It's impossible to know—no one would tell me the truth, and I couldn't tell it to them, either.

I need a home, a home base, a starting point—a life lesson.

I write in haste, racing the conclusion. I'm worried and paranoid. I don't want to be filmed, but there are spy cams everywhere.

Through the spy camera's eye, I can see my funeral from above, like in a dream with some friends who might show up for it. I'm outside myself, but still in-self. There's a lot of 80s music, a dance, Bach's *Toccata and Fugue in D Minor*. I make a cameo on a video screen and tell everybody how much it hurts to die. I send them my greetings and let them know I'm watching them from the other (dead) side. I prepared for this, sort of.

People put things in my coffin—a cell phone, letters, pornography, and paraphernalia. Then they raid my house. They take keepsakes to remember me by, or just to have. Afterwards, they ask what really happened to me.

I died without a will because I had too much else to do. My lack of will leaves everyone angry and betrayed. It's an open coffin, and my eyes are open. The paramedics caught me in the nude and didn't leave me a tip.

My heart was bleeding. I said no pictures.

Everyone will promptly forget my life and times. (Who knew it, anyway?) I'll live on only in the hearts of others. They will make me immortal—but who cares about immortality? Not me. My consciousness is gone, and I've left all my worries behind.

Dead, I dwell in some other dimension, maybe even the fifth. I like the fifth—it welcomes me back whenever I revisit. I haven't been back in a while, not since the CJ Webb Bank incident. Two guardian angels comfort me, and so I walk around the Earth like everyone else. I'm really dead though, whether it looks like it or not. Sometimes, I question whether I ever even existed. Then all my memories start over again. If I have memories, I must have existed.

Okay, okay. So I'm rambling again. Dr C just listens. I don't feel anything. I can't seem to shut my mouth.

I still can't find my house keys. I don't like the idea of a hide-a-key—I was already robbed once. It took me awhile to recover. My house is a mess, anyway. That's why I'm always trying to get away—fast. I like it here at the hotel. Everything is at my fingertips. Everything is fast. The service, the food, the women—just like fast times.

Love, though—love can't always be rushed. I've seen examples of how fast things destroy people and put them in debt. It's a modern concept.

I'm thankful I have some money and a rich family. There's nothing like saving a relationship with your parents. What am I going to do with all this damn time, though?

Dear Diary:

My obsessions are a state of mind, so I make them good.

Broken-hearted Jubilee

Enough was enough.

Enough coffee and cigarettes, enough drugs, sugar, weight gain, hard liquor, beer—enough sex and self for me, for a while—enough habits and addictions, fears and phobias, money and resentment. Enough everything.

Thinking too little about the consequences, I took a drive up to Fat Anne's palatial tent in Palos Verdes, just to say, "Listen, baby, I'm through. I'm finished." This Fat Anne wasn't Anne the Bartender from way back whenever, in my old drinking days back in Manhattan. This Fat Anne was my good friend, the quirky little alternative pagan that she was. My little starlet song-bird.

I wanted to tell her face-to-face, since she knew me better than I knew myself, that I'd been diagnosed with something. It could've been anything, a little in-between disease, some kind of "otherwise not specified" junk, and she showed the most compassion and sympathy of anyone I knew at the time.

This Fat Anne was a woman confident in her obesity. She was assertive and feministic, a neo-fashion slut. She was just another Lane Bryant eBay-bidder. I met her at the local Tourette's support group. She was a lesbian, and her tics were top-notch. She had a better finger-stretch than my retarded little wing and a "head-banger blast" that far exceeded my Beethoven. We shared a common madness—we were both attacked by a constant flow of imps. But still, Fat Anne was destined to disappoint me too, in the long run.

As I was leaving her pad, she looked at me darkly and said, "Georgie, you know what? You're selfish, more than you realize, and I don't want to be your friend anymore. Anyway, thanks for stopping by. It saved me from writing you an e-mail."

Amber Sirkus called my cell as I drove back home. I refused to take her call, so she left a voice message.

"Did you get the bad news from Anne yet? Call me back. You never call me. Bye."

Fat Anne was my best friend. She was one of those temporary friends I'd take for everything I could get until the bridge between us broke. I gave her things, too. Like my heart, like rent money but, all sappiness aside, I'd be better off just admitting the worst in me.

And Fat Anne knew it.

I dreamed last night that I was at a benefit dinner with four women I was sexually involved with. Then, this Princess, a mysteriously recurring dream character known to me only as Lisette, approached and said, "Could you sleep with me? Or do you want to stay here with them?"

The others in the ballroom looked at me. I looked at the others at my table. They smoked their cigarettes and sipped sake.

I replied to Lisette with disdain. "Yeah, I'd like to stay with them," I said.

Lisette was acting like me, the way I acted in Claudia's real life. I was always checking to see if Claudia would fuck me, just one more time, and then one more time after that. I knew she couldn't love me. What an ass! I can't stand myself.

At home, my bed is broken from all the bouncing it has done with whoever would do it with me—it sure wasn't Claudia's fault.

I start to cry, letting out the little angst-ridden baby inside me. Crying is the best therapy.

How silly of me, trying to find a love that would last.

I woke up, suffering from an excess of emotion and exaggerated sensitivity to everything wrong. (In my mind, in my fat, bloated stomach.) My sense of self and my sick, desperate attraction to taboo and sex define me. My expectations are inflated. I'm self-indulgent.

What do I need? Those New Agers tell me to overcome my selfishness through self-discipline. To know life by knowing, really knowing, myself.

I look to Georgie Gust for that. He's more myself than I am.

I spend another night at the hotel, grateful for the cold air of the room. The heat, dampness, and darkness of home—my private hell—have suffocated me inside a self I can hardly bear. There's no need to sympathize with me, however. I feed on this solitude. I revel in it. I know little of anything else. My racing thoughts are tied up in knots. The depression and angst, the schizoaffective, mind-losing, self-deprecating, self-induced hell of my head, the hallucinations and hypocrisy, leave just room enough for me to get to be a better man.

These are only thoughts. They're not the Word of God or anything, so I don't worry. I light another cigarette and listen to the neighbors drinking beer outside.

What a smooth intro.

I broke up with Melanie last night. Our obsession lasted only two weeks—then our passion for each other cooled down to mere indifference.

On a good note, I got to sleep all day and received no phone calls.

I'm pathetic. You might as well hate me, but I need this outlet. Mock me, anger me, and put me to shame.

Until then.

Dear Diary:

Of course I talk to myself. Often, I need expert advice.

Dialogue with Self (After the Funeral)

Georgie, Georgie, Georgie—when did you first realize that you don't really matter?

That I don't really matter? When I first realized that if you only live once, you only die once.

There's a difference?

Yes. To live life to the fullest is to appreciate life—to make babies and babes, and to trust others. To live life fully is to love, to work hard and play hard, to take advantage of every moment.

And you don't really believe in all that stuff?

Well, you know that saying—"Life's a bitch and then you die."

But there are a lot of good things in life, too. A lot of good, sweet things. A lot of sweetness to suck out of life's sour bitterness.

Of course, you take advantage of the good times and make them happen. You create those scenarios.

Yes.

But what about love? The pornographic puzzle? Where will I find love? At the bar? At work? No. I don't work. I don't have to. I don't want to. I just want to find love.

Maybe you should work.

What?

Work, maybe you should.

And be judged worthless? Work for money and be paid like shite? And then be treated like a baby treats a dirty diaper?

(Parenthetical Pet Peeve) People who throw used diapers on the ground after changing their baby in public.

The getting paid part shouldn't mean a thing to you. You already have a lot of money.

But I have no friends.

Meet them at work.

Work?

You could volunteer.

Charity? I'm so selfish. And nobody's ever helped me.

That's not true.

I've always paid for help, paid for friends, paid for hookers. I've always paid for everything. My sole means of support is money. Sometimes I just want my life to end—sometimes, now, or soon. I'm sick. Sick. Sick—and tired. I mean, I'm just holding out to see if things get any better on their own, without me having to do anything.

Why don't you just get out of your self for once?

But my self doesn't even know how to take care of itself! How can I leave my self all alone?

Faith?

Fuck faith. You think with faith that shite will be less smelly? It's always going to be shitey. I mean smelly, rancid.

Why must you always bring up excrement, Georgie?

Because that's what I think of myself—I think I'm shite. I think shite is funny. And it happens—like me. I like to be treated like shite. Ugly women turn me on.

Good one, Georgie.

They are my possibilities.

What are your probabilities?

I have many moods: invisibleness, despair, morbid melancholy, mystical terror, 18th-century angst. And that dull, somber depression you read about in 19th century Russian novels. Moods. I go through many mood swings. And that means there's always the possibility that anything can happen.

But probably?

Not.

Interesting. But what if you could change things?

Believe me, I can't.

You can't change things to your liking?

Right. I've been trying that, ever since the start of thing . . . the start of things and me. Things have been there, ever since the start of me.

Change your self! Change the things around you, if you can. But remember the serenity prayer—remember not to think too much, too hard. Don't be too hard on yourself. And above all, don't be so hard on me. You really do need me. Oh yeah. And respect your thoughts. Have you got that now? Is that perfectly clear? Good.

Don't worry. Other people are hard on me anyway, so I don't need to be.

That's only the way you perceive it.

But that's why I don't really matter. I just chatter. And clutter. It makes me sadder. See, my thoughts don't really matter now, do they?

Have you ever been butt-fucked? Wholesomely used?

No.

Honestly?

Yes.

Is your mind racing and wandering now?

Yes.

Do you feel alone and invisible now?

Yes.

That must be my fault.

But why do you think I care to ask? About you?

Because you are me.

But you're not thinking my thoughts. I'm thinking yours, but my dialogue is mine. It's independent of you. So I don't need to worry about censoring and editing my thoughts. Or do I?

The things in my head are nothing especially unusual or of any vital importance, are they?

They're unique to you. When you think for yourself, for example. Like you are now. But I still see what you're saying. Being noticed and recognized is important. Striving for personal achievement, if nobody else knows about it, really is pretty worthless.

Unless you're invisible and alone.

Loneliness doesn't have to bring despair. In all those old photos of you, you're smiling all the time, whether you're alone or with other people. And the "you" in those photos is an independent idea. You're just a cause with and without a reason—and with a reason, all the same. It's sort of existential, isn't it?

They're just images of you—like the pictures in your imagination. So you might as well enjoy them. Smile. Laugh at them. Laugh at you, for God's sake.

Yes. I know. Generally speaking, I'd say I should look for my self-worth and not fight against it. It's got to be in there somewhere, anyway. Right?

If you can imagine it.

And I can. I know I can. But you . . . your life used to be so full. And now you're so easily hurt.

Maybe I'm a case of what they call "hopeless romanticism." My mind is starting to scatter. I'm losing my touch. I'm losing my grip. I'm sorry. I don't drink anymore. I only smoke.

Everything is becoming a cliché. My life especially—I'm becoming just words, just writing. All that's left of me is a metaphor.

What matters most—my past—is disappearing! It's depressing, isn't it?

Calm down . . . calm down, Georgie. Tell me, what do you want?

I want to be able to spend more of my money and affluence—to make more of it—to create with it. I want to have enough motivation to connect with another woman on a loving and sexual level. That's what is most important to me. I've never been in love. Mutual love. Reciprocated love. I've been addicted—addicted to the lie of love—but that's all.

Do you love yourself?

Hell yes and hell no. It depends on my mood and whom I'm with and what's going on around me.

What about right now?

Now is just not important. Only the past is.

What if the now is important? And what if the future is, too— both of them—then what?

What, are they important then? No—because I don't know.

If you could choose to make them important, would you?

Yes.

Why?

For others.

So. What you do is not entirely selfish, then?

It really is, though. What I do for others, I do for me.

You sound so ridiculous.

No. I sound brilliant!

You like that about yourself, don't you? You think that you really are brilliant.

(Parenthetical Pet Peeve) Blind conformity.

I like that I don't have to conform to public knowledge or even leave my house to figure out most of The Big Puzzle. It makes me different. I do, however, hate having to be a philosopher—because the answer to everything is so simple. Because there is no answer— there are only questions. Everything is constantly in question, and from new questions, new answers are formed—new theories. The answer is: there is no end to ideas. Our imagination is somehow infinite.

All right. Then, let's talk about love. If you want love then your next lover, the next one coming, she must be different, but still like you. Is that correct?

No. Not like me. She really has to like me. That's all—if she ever comes.

And love you?

I will love her. I guarantee it.

Are you thinking again of excrement?

You got it!

Focus.

No!

Does that bother you?

No. But I wish it did. It's a part of my condition.

Okay.

Okay? No, it's not okay.

Right. Your thoughts are not the Word of God, to quote yourself.

Right. And I stole that from somewhere, anyway. There's nothing original here.

What is original? Billions of people have existed and not existed already. Of course there are no original thoughts left. Human imagination has been experienced in all its fullness. And it will keep being that way for a while, too—too full. It's impossible to articulate all the thoughts you think. Some you just need to keep to yourself. Especially when the mind is working at top speed.

But, all in all, I just can't figure myself out. There's this woman.

If you can't figure yourself out, try figuring somebody else out for a change! There's so much else to worry about, there's no need to worry about yourself all the time.

How am I supposed to make time for more figuring out in my life?

I think you're scared.

Of course I am.

Because you don't know what might happen if you stop thinking about yourself?

It has got to be better than this, this fucked-up life.

Well. If nothing I say will help, why don't you just wait until your next mood swing?

No, wait—come back. Come back! That sucks. We're not finished yet. You're abandoning me? I'm abandoning myself?

If I stop thinking of me, will I still exist?

Halloween

Georgie's brain starts to process thoughts again.

Strange images are formed. Strange voices whisper to him.

"Is happiness what you're really striving for?"

"Do you even know what you want?"

"The ultimate goal is freedom."

"The Desert Island Disco."

"Activities and relationships to pick and choose from."

"Are you in love?"

"Do you really know what you need?"

"What makes you feel good?"

"Do you smile sometimes because it's ethical?"

"Your thoughts are full of the things you loathe. But are these things a part of your life?"

"You're a lifetime member of society. You're also a lifetime member of a gym."

"You have a gift. You are a talented individual. You owe it to the world. You owe it to the world and to yourself to share your talent."

People are telling him this kind of crap all the time.

"Everything seems so melodramatic."

"You're more than stressed out."

"You don't have depression."

"You feel worse than shite."

"It's only the symptoms of anxiety. It's all in your head."

"You think you have too many memories, and consider them symptoms of despair. Everything your memory collects is buried in the depths of nostalgia."

"Your life seems like an insipid gathering of heaped-up time."

"Others try to tell you you're fine. You think they are fucking with you."

"You always knew you were different. So did everyone else."

"You take medication. You used to call it medicine. Your meds might need adjustment. It's okay now to tell people what drugs you're really on."

"You reveal yourself in déjà vu, so it all ends abruptly."

"You have a few good friends. Most good people do. All of them fail to be there for you when you need them most. They make you who you are, in all your fullness."

"They called you an old soul. You consider being brand new."

"You're constantly trying to change your life. You spend most of the time only talking about the changes you want to make."

"You fail to make a full commitment to anything and follow through 100%."

"Conform to a little popularity. Read the latest bestseller. Make sure it's a self-help book. Do the exercises they suggest. Create your day. It's that simple."

"You analyze everything. You should be dating somebody else."

"You give and take too much. Try moderation."

"You complain about big corporations and the government. You continue to pay them because you have to."

"You leave your past behind. It starts creeping back in again already."

"You think you live in a fairy tale."

"You think life is clichéd."

"You don't really think you will ever die."

"You might start thinking about everything soon, something concrete, something hard, something personal. I'm not talking about you."

Does this crap really ever stop?

Dear Diary:

Today, I release any feelings of self-rejection.

The New Way to Feed Solitude

In the end, I wonder what all of this really means.

Maybe this man is a hero. He's stuck in the misery of self. He didn't mean for it to happen like this. It's not his fault. Really.

He's confused—he doesn't have a stable self. He doesn't have any real identity. He just wants his own version of who he is. It doesn't really matter what the others think, he thinks—in the long run.

His attempts to find a new way to feed his solitude and also feed a desire to find something of his own. But the desire needs to be in control of the man, not the man in control of the desire. He just wants solitude. He just wants to be left alone.

But loneliness doesn't permit the expression of emotions—the emotions just build up inside. Dark emotions rise to the surface— jealousy and hatred. He craves a resolution to his internal quest of self, his facing of self-alone. The mechanism to grab hold of this missing self would need to come from something that's already there.

His affection for self-knowledge can instinctively be turned around to express thoughtful affection towards another person. But he is ruled only by narcissistic desire.

At first, he couldn't even see others as the unique beings they really were. Others were only an opportunity to release his negative feelings. A vacuum grew in the place where real communication should happen. By relaxing, taking things slow, and teasing himself—not expecting much—he finally gained time for his sensuality to grow, producing all the best connections to happiness. He hinted at things more than once, certain things. Some things hinted at themselves. He couldn't contain them. His mind was near collapse.

His nostalgia, his ideas of the past make up for everything in the moment and beyond. He can finally release it and let it go for good. What already happened has happened. The possibilities for the future are filled with meaning and substance.

What was probable becomes possible.

And in this new discovery, he realizes that everything is genuine—everything. What really happened, what was imagined, what was perceived and experienced, everything. They define who this man finds himself to be. He's as imperfect, as selfish, as selfless, as loving, as probable, and as possible as anybody else—as everybody else.

He becomes this man—this affectionate, sympathetic, genuine individual—for other people.

We jump to conclusions. We criticize. And we move on.

We're doing the best we can.

You're not alone.

Like I said in the beginning, you're doing just fine.

Dear Diary:

Today, I feel open-hearted, kind and compassionate, for once.

Is This A New Beginning?

The self-proclaimed narcissist and introvert, the author, finally has a realistic idea. Skittish horse that he is, he returns from the restroom.

(Parenthetical Pet Peeve) "Air dry" machines instead of paper towels in public restrooms.

He takes his seat by the window in the front row. They still haven't announced takeoff yet. He has a clear plastic cup of diluted OJ and a bottle of water. He downs them fast. He thinks, How lucky I am to be sitting in first class. It was a free upgrade, since his original flight never made it to the airport. There were mechanical problems.

A strange woman takes the aisle seat. "Hi! You don't have to move. Don't worry—don't move. I'm fine in the aisle."

"I prefer to be the one who moves out of the way for any bathroom-goers—I've got a big bladder, myself," Georgie says. "I just thought no one else was coming at this point."

"Don't worry about it. If you have to go, I'll move."

Don't worry about it? At least she isn't some stinky old man. He looks at his overgrown fingernails, and puts his hand out.

"My name is Georgie."

"Hi Georgie. I'm Maggie Fox."

She shakes his hand. "You've got a firm grip, Georgie."

"Yeah. I love to fly."

"Well, we've only got an hour or so. It's not so bad."

"No, not bad at all."

And so a simple man is born. His name is Georgie Gust. He's an hallucination. He's all that I am today, for now, forever, for whatever reason. He's what we're after—sometimes an overload of stimuli from the environment just gets in the way.

What if he keeps in touch with this woman after the flight? (What is Georgie thinking?) What if he gets her number and actually tries to pick her up?

The flight hasn't started, and already Georgie's mind is racing. The events of the past year bombard him with an urgent pressure. So he just sits there, thinking. He remembers how pathetic everything has been since he became an adult. He remembers the transition he felt within himself when he transformed from an asshole little kid into a guilty and responsible abuser of waste.

It's so easy to make fun of this guy! Now he really doesn't feel like going home, ever.

Maggie is already buried in the current issue of *People Weekly*. The attendants collect the pre-flight drinks and announce the takeoff procedures. Georgie looks out the window.

We fly on, even through the storms, and we're fine, he thinks. Everything is okay. We're here now, and everything's cool.

I never thought anything good would last, but I'm holding onto this. I can't slow down my pathetic little life, just to think about things. I don't have time to regroup and analyze. I was caught up in a stupefying sexual obsession and a mind-bending paralysis!

It was fun while it lasted, though.

Perplexity is that awareness you have at the worst moment of any mental suicide attempt, when everything's confused and at times too heavy. I'm experiencing it right now.

"Just slow down, and take it easy," I hear. Who's talking? Georgie—or Dr C? "Stop thinking. Just stop. Feel the blood run through your hands, your feet—your body. That's what matters. Now, get dressed and get out of here."

I'm awake and I step outside. The sunrise is magnificent. The sand on the beach absorbs the bright light as it intensifies, turning pink. I glance back for a moment and remember Georgie. I think of all the excuses I made just to get over someone I thought was the perfect match for me. It was a big mistake, but completely necessary. She was a nice woman, but we weren't made for each other.

So what? I'm alone, now and again. And it's all right now.

"Who is this voice you keep talking about?" Claudia asked over dinner one night.

"They're just thoughts," I told her.

I think of Georgie. He can really be overbearing, sometimes.

Dear Claudia,

I know the voice is really my own. I'm sorry it didn't work out between us. The rest is history.

Yours truly,

Benjamin J Schreiber . . .

. . . Georgie Gust

Dear Diary:

Right now, my self-esteem is strong, stronger than usual and strange but true.

Part VI: Rest in Peace

Support This Troupe

"So what do you want to talk about today, Ben?" asks Dr C.
"Nothing," I say. Only I don't really say it.
The two of us are alone in the room for now.
Does Dr C hear it, anyway?
"You look sad today."
I shrug.
"Anything going on?" asks Dr C.
I shake my head.
Silence.
Georgie appears through my light tears.
"Tell her," he says. "Tell her about."
The clock ticks.
I decide to say something. Even if it's wrong.
"Well, did I tell you about the jogger?"
Georgie shoots darts in my eyes. Not that! he silently screams.
"What jogger? You mean . . . ?" Dr C nods. "The one who ran every day—Christmas, New Year's? The one who always wore the same clothes, no matter what the weather? The one who ran every day, all day, past your mother's house, and only you saw him?"

(Parenthetical Pet Peeve) Choosing a two-piece outfit or shoes in the store, only to find that the sizes don't match.

Georgie sinks back into despair.
I nod.
"What about him?" Dr C asks.
Nothing about him, Georgie interrupts.
Dr C doesn't hear anything. There's more silence.
Silence.
Silence.
But Georgie won't let the whole hour be quiet. Silence is just too awful.
"Did you want to talk about the jogger?" Dr C nudges.
"Not really," I say.
There's a long pause.
Finally, I say, "I always thought he was doing my mother."

"That he was her lover?"

"No, doc, just doing her."

"That's interesting."

"Not really."

Georgie wants to scream: Ask her why! Why is it interesting?

I shift in my chair. I cross and uncross my legs. Finally, I ask, "Why?"

Dr C's eyebrows rise just slightly.

"Why is it interesting?"

I nod.

Dr C hesitates.

Silence.

The silences are killing Georgie. Without noise, he might not exist. Make it stop! he screams.

"Well," says Dr C, "If I'm remembering correctly, didn't you tell me that the jogger was young? A college student, maybe, I think you said?"

I nod. "So what?" I say.

"Well, considering her age at the time," continues Dr C, "That would have made the jogger young enough to be her son?"

I nod again. But I say nothing.

"And didn't you tell me that he ran silently? That nobody in the neighborhood even knew his name? That you were the only one in your whole family that ever even saw him?"

I nod. Still, I say nothing.

Finally, Georgie (or me) can't stand the silence any longer. "I called him Mr Clean," I say.

Dr C's face pales. "Hmmm. That's interesting, Ben." Dr C says without conviction. "That's very interesting to me."

"What? Mr Clean?" I ask. "It's just a name—it's a bathroom cleaner. You know, like the big bald guy with the earring. Who cleans like a white tornado, or something?"

"No, Ben. Not just the name." Dr C swallows a frog in her throat, or a toad, or something. "The whole thing—your mother and the jogger and you, and the fact that only you see them. Now, that's interesting."

Dear Diary:

Oh hell. I love and respect myself. Why not? Maybe I just think too much. Who knows? The past keeps crawling up on me, so I just keep writing.

Demons

There are demons in Ben's bedroom. Demons that make his dresser snap, crackle, and pop when he's trying to sleep at night.

He lies alone in his bed, in his solitary bedroom, and he tries to sleep. But he can't—because of the demons. He tosses and turns beneath the silver and brown brocade bedspread, and wonders how long he has before the demons take over completely.

When he first moved into his new apartment, the demons only played in the living room. But when they got bored of the living room, the demons played in his office, too. They'd make his computer shut down and start up again in the middle of the night, when nobody was there. Ben would be lying in bed, just trying to sleep, and the chime of the computer starting up and shutting down would wake him up, like some crazy alarm clock that only rings when you don't want it to—or like a wake-up call you don't want to take.

The demon computer got so terrible that Ben finally unplugged it before going to sleep, just to throw the demons off track. And that should have taken care of the problem, Ben thinks. But it didn't stop the demons. The computer still came on and shut down, all by itself.

Then the demons moved into the bathroom. They made the lights flash on and off without flipping the switches, and they made the shower run hot and cold without turning on the faucet. Some people (not Ben, though, not Georgie) would've taken all this demonic activity as a sinister signal, a satanic eviction notice, or at least a slightly unsubtle excuse to look for another apartment. All Ben did (all Ben could do) was buy crystals and sage from the psychic shop down the street and start looking online for an exorcist.

Finally, he found a New Age exorcist who was ready to take the job (for a modest fee, of course). A Reverend Jezebel S Constanza, Exorcism Specialist. Reverend Constanza drove up from La Jolla, took one look at how Ben lived, and tripled the usual market price of exorcism. So Ben spent $3,000 for Reverend Constanza to sprinkle sage around the baseboards, place crystals in the northeast corners of all the rooms, and tell Ben he needed his aura cleansed. Which she would be happy to do for another $3,000.

Ben was slightly disgruntled at the price. After all, it was just a routine exorcism—an everyday demon-cleansing. But he paid anyway, even though he knew the mark-up wouldn't have occurred if he lived in a two-floor walk-up over on Seventh Avenue. But living where he did, in a high-rent district overlooking the Pacific, Reverend Constanza thought she could take him. She thought she could both jack up the price and feed his paranoia. (And she was right.) Still, the whole pitiful scam made Ben mad. Especially since, if anything, the demons were even worse than ever, afterwards.

And they still are. Ben lies in bed, late at night, trying to get some sleep. And instead of counting sheep, Ben watches the ceiling fan above his bed spin on and off by itself. He listens to the TV sputter as if electricity coursed through it and only static spat out. It wouldn't be so bad, Ben thinks, if I wasn't so alone—so goddamn fucking alone—day in, day out—day in, night out. If I could have someone else here, dealing with these demons with me. But Ben's alone with his demons. Not like Georgie, who is out every night with different women.

(Parenthetical Pet Peeve) Power outages.

Georgie, it seems, has dedicated himself to the purpose of getting over Claudia. Georgie, it seems lately, is absolutely manic about overcoming her—but not Ben. Ben, it seems, can't do much of anything at all except lie in bed, awake, in the middle of the goddamn night, and listen to the demons who have overtaken his world.

Or at least repossessed his electronics.

Dear Diary:

I successfully released some—actually many—feelings of self-rejection today. Until next time . . . .

Georgie and Dr C

At the next session, only Georgie shows up. (Does Dr C even ask where Ben is? Does she even notice who is missing? Probably not.)

Georgie's frantic. He paces. He can't sit still, or even just lie quietly on the couch. He's going out of his fucking mind, crawling out of his damn skin.

Dr C just watches him, curiously. Who is he, Ben, when he isn't Ben? she wonders. Where is he, Ben, when he isn't Ben? Hell, she knows—she has to know, after all these sessions! But Georgie can't stand to be watched. He avoids her eyes. He swallows continuously. He sniffs, tics, and hops.

"You look agitated," she tells him.

"Agitated?" Georgie jumps. "Me? Agitated?"

He looks like a visitor from another world—that's how Georgie looks.

"Can you just sit still?" she asks. "Or lie down on the couch?"

Because he's so passive, so submissive, so suggestible, Georgie sits down right away on Dr C's couch. But he immediately pops back up again.

"No," he says. "I can't."

Dr C smiles. "What's going on?" she asks. "Why are you so agitated?"

"Agitated? Me?" Georgie repeats. "Why do you ask? Why, nothing is going on! Or else, everything is going on. How can I answer a question like that? I can't! I really can't decide. I can't decide what's going on, what isn't going on—how can I decide? I can't fucking decide," he whimpers. "Just don't ask me questions like that, okay? Questions I can't answer."

(Parenthetical Pet Peeve) People who laugh at or ridicule people or things they don't understand instead of asking questions and learning something.

Finally, Georgie stops ranting. And Dr C lets the silence follow.

Finally, there's only silence.

And silence again.

The silence is fucking killing Georgie. It makes his head throb. He needs a temple massage, badly—or a foot rub. He needs somebody to touch him, to stroke him, and to break the silence. He needs somebody to love him.

He needs somebody to love—to truly love. Not like all the women (How many have there been?) sucking his dick, his balls, and his ass, fucking him, and getting themselves off on him. He needs somebody, finally, who really loves him. Somebody who can see beyond what he pretends to be and what they pretend he is— somebody who will really touch his soul. That's what he really needs. And that's what he'll never have.

The passing thought, the depressing realization, spirals him downward. I need my meds, he thinks. Where are his meds when he needs them? At home, he thinks. That's where. But if they were here, he would take them—he sees himself swallowing pill after pill, bottle after bottle.

Peace. He needs peace.

Dear Diary:

I feel emotionally centered and balanced today, overall.

Mother Ghost

Ben shares his bedroom with the resident demons. The lights flicker on and off, the TV set goes on and off, on and off, like a strobe light—all by itself. Ben's not doing it. Ben's not making it happen. And he just can't take it. And even worse, his Mother/Angel/Older Woman (Claudia? Heidi? Claudia?) comes to him at night. She pushes the hair off his forehead and strokes his hand.

"You need to move, baby," she says.

Ben groans. He rolls over on his side.

"I'm not going anywhere."

The older woman climbs into bed with him. She strokes his back and tickles him.

"You need to move, baby."

Ben climbs out of bed.

The Older Woman—his mother, his angel, his lover—is just an illusion. A hallucination. In other words, she's not real. And the whispering voices in his head—her voice, so soothing, so insistent—they aren't real, either. (Are they, Dr C? Tell me they're not, Dr C.)

He brushes his teeth. He stares at his reflection in the mirror. His hair is dirty, and he could use a shave. He ducks his head, spits into the sink, and straightens up again. His angel, his mother, his lover is standing there behind him—she's smiling into the mirror at him.

"This house isn't good for you, baby," she says.

How is he supposed to listen to an illusion? Better to listen to his Perplexity. He tries to just ignore her. But it isn't easy.

She pokes the back of his head. Hard. She tells him: "I am not an illusion."

He continues the attempt to ignore her.

"You're not going to be able to ignore me forever," she says.

Maybe not forever, Ben thinks, but for as long as I need to.

"And how long is that going to be?" his illusion asks.

How the hell is he supposed to get the voices out of his head when they can read his every thought? When they know what he's thinking even before he does?

"Not every voice," she says. "Just me. And trust me, Benjy, you need to move out of this house."

She pauses for dramatic effect.

"It's haunted." The demon mother snickers. "I know. Because I'm haunting it."

He knew it. He knew it all along. The fucking place really is haunted.

"With demons?" he asks.

"With memories," she tells him.

He would rather have demons.

"Who wouldn't?" she says. "Memories are so much harder to get rid of."

Ben twitches and tics, bobbing his head to the right and then the left and then forward. He raises his right eyebrow and grimaces.

"You don't like memories, do you, baby?"

You're just an illusion! Only a hallucination! Georgie silently screams. *I don't have to listen to you, because you're not real.*

Still twitching and ticcing madly, he heads into the kitchen for an energy drink. His illusion follows right behind, tsk-tsking the entire way.

"Caffeine," she says, "is the absolute worst thing for tic-in'."

"I know that," Ben says, sniffing. He sniffs so hard that he seriously worries, for a second, that his brains will leak right out of his ears.

"Stupid, stupid, stupid," his illusion says.

"Shut up," Ben tells her.

But she ignores him. "First," she says, "ya don't have brains. Ya have a brain. And it won't leak out yer ears from sniffin'. The only way it'll leak out is if ya decide to shoot yourself in the head. Then it'll leak out, that's for sure. Out yer ears, out yer nose—do ya wanna try?"

His illusion is even crazier than he is! It figures, doesn't it? John Nash gets a CIA operative for his illusion; Ben gets a cross between Carol Kane and Sandra Bernhardt, neither of whom appeal to him sexually, and neither are the least bit emotionally stable.

His illusion, dressed in white gossamer, appears directly in front of him. Is she some kind of succubus, or incubus, or whatever? Which one is which? He can't remember.

She clears her throat. "What I said," she says, "is: Would ya like to try?"

Okay, okay, okay—now he knows she's an illusion. Now he knows she is not real. Which means that he's on dangerous ground. The more you talk to an illusion, a hallucination, the stronger it becomes. And still he can't help himself. Shut up! Just shut up! he tries to tell himself. But the words are out of his mouth before he's had a chance to think.

"Try what?" he asks.

His illusion, his gossamer mother–angel hands him a blue steel, white grip .38 special. "Blowin' yer head off," she says. "Watchin' yer brain leak out yer nose and ears. Ya wanna try it, Ben? Ya really wanna?"

She presses the gun into his hands. "Nobody'll know," she says. "Yer all alone. Who's to know?"

She is the devil. She's a demon, Ben tells himself. He's got to stop talking to her. He's got to stop listening to her—or she'll catch him in her spell, and she will kill him. So Ben backs away from the apparition, letting the gun slip from his hands down to the floor. His angel/demon/mother picks it up. She presses the sleek, cold blue steel grip back into his hands again—and smiles at him.

He just now notices her crooked teeth. They're yellow and snaggled, sharp-edged. Her crooked teeth scare him. He shudders. He fights the urge to hop—first on his left foot, then on his right. First left, then right. Like reading left to right. Left to right. He's going to hop; he's going to tic. He's got to. He's going to.

The teeth, the breath—they're his mother's—and that's his mother's lipstick smeared on the enamel. His mother scares him. She's always scared him. But somehow, he just can't get rid of her. He just can't get away from her.

He wants to go home. But he is home. There's nowhere left to go. Why not? Why not pick up the gun? Wasn't it his mother who always said to him:

"Benjy, if ya wanna check out, now, remembah: Check out fast. No drugs. No hangin' yerself. Ya jump, Benj—from the 32nd floor. An yull never live to tell about it." Then she laughs. She screeches. She cackles.

And Ben knows now—his mother was a witch. She had these long, pointed fingers. Her nails were always filed sharp, like claws; they were always grabbing at him, digging into his flesh.

Is she really dead? Ben wants to know, or only living dead? Ben prays: *Oh Lord, please hear my prayer. Kill her, Lord. Kill her so I don't have to. Please, Lord. Don't make me kill my own mother.*

And then Ben flashes back to another memory of his mother:

They're in the Hamptons. It's 1987, and Ben is 11 years old. Mom has gotten heavier, this year she's up to 250 pounds, at least. She wears this massive, red-striped bathing suit with a white gossamer cover-up. She floats, bounces, and galumphs into his bedroom, night after night. She's crying. Always crying.

"Ya don' know what it's like, Benjy. Ya really don' know what it's like—when yer husband decides ta leave ya."

He loves his mother. He really doesn't want to see her cry. He will do whatever she needs to get her to stop crying. Stop crying.

He sits up in bed. The blankets slip from his skinny, naked, 11-year-old chest. His mother is sprawled at the end of the bed, sobbing.

"He's leavin' me, Benjy," she moans. "He's leavin' me. I just know."

"Mother, don't cry," he begs. "Please don't cry. Please."

She creeps him out. She makes him shudder—but she is his mother. She buries her head in her hands. She sobs; he sees her giant bosom heaving.

She sobs and heaves. And Ben watches. He watches the sleeves of her nightgown slip off her bare shoulders, exposing the top of her breast, the massive brown areola. He doesn't know what to do. He can't remember ever seeing her breasts before. He wants her to cover them back up, but she's crying, crying—and she won't stop.

"What'll I do, Benjy?" she pleads. "Where will I go?"

He hates to hear his mother cry. It's worse than hearing his sister cry, and almost as bad as hearing his father cry. Mothers shouldn't cry, he thinks. They should be happy. Happy always.

"He's the only man I ever loved, Benjy," she whimpers. "What'm I gonna do?"

Ben doesn't know what she's going to do next. He just wishes she'd cover her breasts; he doesn't want to see them. He shouldn't have to see them. They're gross and too big—and scary. My mother's breasts are scary.

"And the only man who ever touched me," she moans, "like that. Oh, Benjy."

Ben thinks about his father touching his mother. He thinks about the porn mags and all those exposed pussies—those wide-open pussies. And he thinks about his father touching his mother . . . like that, there. He thinks about his father fucking his mother. And putting that . . . there. It's gross. Oh God, it's gross. Ben knows it's gross, but he is still getting a hard-on. He can feel it tenting his pajama bottoms. He wishes his mother would leave. Just go away. Go away, mother.

Instead, she flops to her stomach across the bed. Her hand rests on Ben's thigh. Her fingers are cold, her nails sharp. Ben can feel them scratching, tattooing his skin. Groineology. They're massaging his legs, working their way up—they're moving toward his balls, his dick—his shaft. Oh God she's touching . . . that. He groans.

Ben tries to move away, but his mother's hand holds him tight. She begins to stroke him.

"Your father," she says, "was the only man who ever touched me." Her voice drops. "Sexually, I mean."

Ben wants his mother to stop, but he's paralyzed. It's like he's turned to stone—he can't talk. He can't move. Not even when his mother slithers up his body. Not even when his mother's naked breasts smash against his bare chest. Not even when she kisses his neck and drags her tongue across his bare skin, and slides her mouth down his chest, to his belly, to his cock. Not even when she takes him in her mouth and begins sucking on him. And not even when, a few seconds later, he cums with a spasm and a shudder that shakes his entire body, leaving him ashamed and humiliated, wishing he was dead.

Even then, Ben can't say a word. He can't even move a muscle. It's like he's dead-invisible. He's floating high above the world. He watches his mother discreetly cough into her hand and deposit the prepubescent cum she's sucked from him onto her fingers.

"Oh, my," she says, tugging the straps of her nightgown back over her shoulders. "Oh my."

And Ben, still floating high above the whole world, doesn't know why she's saying, Oh my, oh my—like that. He doesn't know why she keeps repeating herself. He doesn't know why she won't leave and go back to her own room.

She slides off the bed. She readjusts her nightgown. She flips her hair behind her ears.

"Benjy," she says. "What we did right now—I don't want you thinking there was anything wrong with that. I was just giving you a bit of relief. Okay, honey?"

Ben still can't talk.

"The thing is, though, baby . . ." his mother stops. She bites her lips, lowers her brow—still searching, Ben thinks, for just the right word. His mother's like that. She always wants exactly the right word.

"So, okay," she finally says. "The thing is, some people—your father included—don't always understand how things are between mothers and sons. So, I'm not saying don't tell anyone. I'm just saying you probably should be kind of careful about who you do tell—because I know you, Benjy. And I know how you never want anyone to . . . disapprove of you." His mother waits, then adds, "Or be mad."

(Parenthetical Pet Peeve) People who start a conversation with, "I don't mean this the wrong way, but . . ." or "I'm telling you for your own good."

Ben says nothing. His stomach is in knots, remembering how it feels, when people disapprove of you, when somebody is mad at you—when nobody is happy with him.

"Or not even talk to you anymore."

Ben can't take it. He starts crying.

"For God's sake, Benjy, lighten up," his mother says. Then she takes his nose between her fingers and twists. Affectionately. But it hurts.

Ben's tears fall harder.

His mother, her nightgown slipping from her shoulder again, bounces out of the room.

"Lighten up, baby. Life is just too fucking short to go through it all hang-dog. Know what I'm saying?"

And then she's gone.

The room is quiet and Ben can't stop thinking about her. Mother. I did that with my mother, or she did that to me.

He thinks about how his mother goes to every single one of his Little League games, and he thinks about how she bakes chocolate brownies from scratch, and makes fudge sundaes with vanilla ice cream and hot fudge sauce. He remembers how on his ninth birthday she took him and three of his friends to McDonald's, and then over to Coney Island, even though she said that nothing but niggers and spics ever went to Coney Island these days. He remembers how his mother, when she bandages his knees, kisses them with her mouth open, to suck out the germs, slathers them with medicine, and then sticks colored Band Aids all over them. She's a good mother, Ben thinks. A mother who loves me—a mother who takes good care of me. She doesn't smack me around like my buddy Luke's mother. I'm lucky, Ben thinks. I have a mother who loves me like that.

Finally, Ben falls asleep, still thinking about how his mother loves him and how his father is leaving them both.

Dear Diary:

Tough writing session today, but I remain centered and balanced. I do miss the beach though. I used to go there a lot to feel centered. Water seems to ground me.

To The Shore

Somewhere back in Long Beach, Dr C stands outside the front door of her psychiatry office. She watches a big yellow taxi pull away and notes with a sigh that she's just missed it. And she's just glad, for once, that she's missed it.

Her wide-open eyes focus farther, like a dilating telescope, on the back seat of the disappearing taxi. And she thinks she sees that she has succeeded in something, in whatever primal therapy she had to offer. *Or maybe,* she thinks, *Ben and Georgie (and Claudia, too) have succeeded in whatever goals they might have had for their strange life journey together, and I was just along for the ride.* She smiles. The strangely familiar passenger in the back seat wears an oversized black hat with a pom-pom on top. She stares after him, but he doesn't look back.

Dr C still remembers the Benjamin J Schreiber who walked into her office that day (skipped, hopped and jumped into my office), but in a wholly different light.

I really wondered what we might discover behind that creepy demeanor and the kooky costumes. So I wandered and wondered, and poked and probed, into the black holes and blind spots behind the masks—and I kept on wondering until we reached the goal, I guess (whatever the goal is.)

And so, Ben J Schreiber, say "Hello" and "Goodbye" to Georgie B Gust—and give my best to Claudia Nesbitt.

Dear Diary:

I'm not usually that political, but I have been thinking a lot lately that we are making it through this world together, while it's about time we all turn the page. When all human beings and living creatures are given equality and freedom, it'll inspire our doing right whether or not we are able to make ourselves feel something we do not feel. We can make ourselves do right in spite of our feelings. Whether it be red signs, or not, on social media platforms, plus signs, or equal signs, with so many people increasing support of all human rights, it can and will inspire many others to take more action—small changes, regarding any form of discrimination. I, too, would rather see any equality signs and images supporting love itself, than pictures of angry animals and ironic self-shots, today. Of course there's a time for everything, as I see it. It's "we, the people" who create change. Same sex marriage seems at the forefront currently, and gay, lesbian, bisexual, metrosexual, transgender or not, so many people seem to be stepping up even more, lately. From here, I believe we will all enjoy a freedom that too many do not currently have.

Part VII: Postscriptum

Meanwhile, Back At Ben's New Mexico Ranch . . . .

The cleaning crew could've arrived at any minute, but I still lay there, holding my Living, Colorful Beauty, just letting go. The memories of my life would be lost and forgotten, otherwise. So, despite everybody, despite Claudia and Kelly and Granny and Uncle Martin, and despite the musing Gladys and the amusing Claudia, the many-faced muse she's been for me, I still sit here in the house in Albuquerque, New Mexico, writing my brains out and worrying myself with my own death.

Beautiful sagas of alternative songs resonate through the empty room. As the New Age-ers might say, this room has been attuned to my mindful awareness of self. In other words: It's got "me" written all over it. It's got semen on the cement walls, like a dirty old motel room, and vaginal membranes from some psych ward panties I collected off some slut, some crazy bitch I picked up—but aside from that . . .

Dear Diary:

I suppose I do stir up controversy. The hermit I may indeed be. I do enjoy provoking disagreement and even disapproval, even in public and online, for sure. My approaches to life and art, though a paradox, I consider myself an anti-artist who has this burning urge to create and add to creation, which I believe, defines art alongside self-expression. It's this effect of dichotomy. I seem to provoke disagreement and disapproval.

Ben J Schreiber

I send my short story to one of the editors, by e-mail, fast. It's a true story from the other day. I think it will read as a commercially viable something or other. I wish Kelly would understand.

I pray now, and I go to sleep. Women and angels, they hover over me silently and quietly. I'm fucking loving it. Loving it, yeah.

Dear Diary:

Ideas seem to be pulled right from my pockets and all the while, there's already too much creation as it is, and has been for a while now. I just add to it, in stockpiles, for that's the only way. Here's an idea, rather a self-diagnosis, in that I seem to "suffer" from this dynamic of narcissism with no self-esteem, since low or high levels would be artificial: either one has self-esteem or one does not. So why not add to my comorbid diagnoses . . . I "suffer," and laugh, suffering from this gosh darn Savant syndrome. . . .

Checking the Mail

It's early morning; too early for anyone to be up, yet—not even 9 am. I stumble out of bed, grab my glasses, pull on a robe, and head down 16 floors to the mailboxes.

It's Tuesday, and I always have mail on Tuesdays (left over mail from Monday.) I never check the mail on Monday. Maybe there will be something from my publisher, who keeps sending back everything I write, usually with these cute, coy, cryptic little notes.

And there, in the back of the mailbox, jammed between a circular from Amazon.com and one for "Wanted: Largest Collection of Adult DVDs!!!" is the letter from William & William Publishing. I tear it open in the hallway; Cary's letter flutters to the floor. I bend, pick it up, and I damn near give myself a hernia. (I'm putting on weight these days, going from 160 to 190 and then bouncing way up to a diabetic 265, all in the space of six and a half months. I think I'm dying. Hell, I don't think—I know.)

Cary's letter is not encouraging:

In a strange way, your short story, "Second Skins," makes sense—following the truth of what really happened, I guess, since our coffee marathon in LA, when you tried to explain everything.

You're quite a handful, Ben. Otherwise, the stuff you've been sending in recently has been point-blank twisted and unnatural, but somehow, it makes sense. It's hard to try to think of this as fiction. Even for someone who doesn't know Benjamin Schreiber, it's going to sound autobiographical. The biggest problem I see with the story is that it casts Georgie as the hero, when he isn't even a plausible anti-hero.

That's the problem with Cary Banks. She wants me to be either a hero or an anti-hero. When, of course, I'm neither.

Instead of writing back, I sit at home and obsess and wonder why I can't get anything published. People tell me I'm the next Bukowski or Burroughs, which means nothing to me. I write what I write, I fill it with cheap sex; what I know, what I'm good at, and wait for the go-ahead. I'm still waiting for the contract.

So far, I've been waiting a year and a half. That's 43 chapters, 92,322 words, mostly about Heidi and me or, maybe, I should say, mostly about Georgie's Claudia.

Dr C said in our second session that I have a problem with

obsessive thinking.

"No shite, Sherlock!" I blurted back to her. "What else is new?"

She also said that Georgie's not a real character; that he's nothing but an alter ego stuffed with all the funky feelings I refuse to feel. And when I get healthy, Georgie will die an appropriate death. And then, maybe I can move on with my life.

But whoever said I wanted to move on? Where would I be moving to, anyway?

Dear Diary:

I suppose to "suffer" from demonstrating this horrifically profound and prodigious capacity or these inherent abilities within this otherwise schizophrenic and affective spectrum, to reach far in excess of what would be considered normal? I mean it's one of the more pleasant aspects of such a complex handicap. I learn to love it, laugh at it, when I can, and just taking pride in it. It's not like it's going to harm me or anybody else, and if I do stir someone up, it's on him or her. I tend to move ahead, even through the storms . . . This might be off topic but I love scoffing, especially when the word "scoff" is subtitled in a brilliant foreign film. Those are the best. Ah, how random it is, how it all comes in, all the hypomanic thoughts and schizophrenic voices, all at once; I think my train of thought has left the station again, at this point. So I have a cigarette and write more and more. I'm the Energizer Bunny.

On Kelly

I got another e-mail from Kelly. I think she likes me—yeah, me? Give me a fucking break, already. Still, I wish she'd send a picture—something to add to my private collection.

Dear Ben:

Your "novel" (if that's what it is) is fascinating work, with its gritty, impersonal sex. It tears my heart in two. That much is very nicely done.

The problem though, as I see it, is that your reader cannot possibly follow your train of thought all the way through the 400-odd pages of Living Colorful Beauty. It's too disjointed. You don't want to lose the reader, do you? You want them to feel for you and cry for you and bleed for you, and work through the whole mess with you, right?

So: How about adding a through-line, just to lead your reader by the hand through whatever story you have to tell. Does that make sense?

Oh, and, by the way—the quote includes one on one, just like you asked. Best of luck with this incredible project—let me know how else I can help.

Sincerely,

Kelly

About Kelly: I love this whole business she has of saying, "Does that make sense?" She's my editor. But she's dominant. I want to be her servant, her slave boy, her boy toy, her big beef on the hoof. She must have a habit of asking if that "makes sense." I can hear it in my mind, just like she is speaking it to me. I can tell where she's at—and her little quirks like that really get me going. But on the novel—what's she saying about the novel?

I think about it over a coffee mug filled with espresso. Ten minutes have passed. Still nothing.

Yeah, Kelly's okay. She's cool with my disjointed prose style and my kinky sex parts, anyway. She's a hell of a lot better than Kevin at "Gold Hand," who writes:

Mr Schreiber:

First off, no, not the "Trish" piece. Too clichéd. Perhaps the main storyline is rooted like this: The romantically doomed neighbors, Georgie and Claudia, are an attractive couple who, having rushed their passion in each other from the very beginning, split up. They're both inflicted with a low sense of self-worth as their actions show.

Blah, blah, blah; yap yap yap. Just self-important editorial hackwork. You can tell he doesn't really get it.

Coming up next: When I Broke Up With "The Real Claudia": Heidi.

Dear Diary:

I have many people in my life—some come and some go—and I call the few people I trust, my notorious "realty mediators."

Another Living Colorful Beauty?

I just wrote you a letter, Kelly. It's real garbage. It's an attempt to write you a letter, but it came across really bitter and angry. I meant it to be genuine and friendly but, once again, it obsesses on the negatives and on my pathetic self and my giving up, so to speak— my possessing you. It lets you know that I want to be left alone to rot it out. (*Rotting It Out*. A good new title for *Living, Colorful Beauty*, don't you think? I just can't stand that I see myself in you. It's ugly and scary. Or, at least, it scares me.)

I've left the letter on the kitchen counter, along with your mail and mine. There are my diabetes prescriptions and my poster from mail order. (You may open it for a look. It's small, but it's a good quality frame-able poster. And it says how I'm feeling lately: FUCK YOU, YOU FUCKING FUCK). The new paper (100 sheets) is on your desk, and my new t-shirts are hanging in my bedroom closet, the one closest to the entry, in case you are interested. I don't like the "I haven't escaped, they gave me a day pass" one, anymore. (I'll keep it for the house.) But you should try to read, if you feel up to it, the aqua blue one with the psychedelic insignia on it. It says "Fuck You," kind of in code. Sorry, don't take it personally. Sometimes I just say, "Fuck you," to everything and everybody.

It's just my stuff, you understand.

I'm still angry and I have a little energy left.

I meant what I said in the letter about your distance and my inferiority. I'm losing myself and losing you. This isn't some emotional intimacy we're getting involved in. It's all my flaws and faults we're getting involved in—my twitches and tics and the schizophrenia. I am killing you, more than I could ever kill myself. I just can't help it—it's just me. You must be a wreck. My letter was meant to be apologetic, to acknowledge my regression and my false sense of self-worth (you could call it depression). I'm not saying it's worse than that.

It's like (forgive the choo-choo-train metaphor) I'm dragging along the whole freight train of these personalities, these identities, the reactions of others—and this philosophy, which just shrank up to fit me earlier in life than it did for most people (who will live to an older age than I will). Anyway (back on the train), once the train runs along the tracks, the caboose moves forward, but is always looking back (like in my journals from the Claudia intermission: "RLB"—Reader, Looking Back.) The caboose doesn't really contribute any power, not like the engine in the front; the caboose isn't really necessary (like me.) And surely cabooses like me stay at the tail-end of society, hanging out with damaged freight (the old worn-out body), seeming silly and out of place beside the cars that make up the majority or essence of the train.

You could just uncouple and nobody would notice (or care) as life goes on without you. The train will still stop and go, hold itself together, and function terrifically either way. But eventually, without you, it will run out of energy; grind to a stop. (Or, otherwise, die.)

Ben . . .

Dearest Ben,
There's absolutely no reason to apologize for anything. I think you're pretty awesome. You're the hugest and most adored part of me that I can imagine.

Kelly

Dear Diary:

Instead of spending time after time over-editing my work—given my first drafts are literally my best, exterminating all rational thought—as for my current piece, I'm definitely going to leave all the written pieces on the floor, leaving them be as they are then move the hell on. It will all turn out just fucking fine. I just know it. I can bicker with my editors later, and dance my attendance at the opera house when all is done. I always wanted to see *Don Giovanni* live on stage. Anyway, I'm on a real roll today. Rolling up my sleeves and on the go.

Back To the Heat

Dear Kelly,

I'm so sorry in advance for coming across as bitter. You'll see why I'm bitter after a few minutes reading. But as for Living, Colorful Beauty—well, looking over your critique, haven't I left enough room in this novel for reader interpretation? Who is my reader? Didn't I leave any place for the readers of this, my greatest work to date, to come up with judgments, images, and emotions of their own? Have I simply chosen certain fragments of this anguished life? And, yes, haven't I done a real good job of getting into the depressing, yet fascinating, train-wreck mentalities of both Georgie and myself? But is that all I've done? Is that all I can do? I guess so. I'm pretty sure about that.

I question this work now.

The whimper, the bang—it's not really over yet, is it? Tell me it's not over yet!

You're telling me that I should keep combing the hair out of this piece, that it's still "not good enough" (for whom?). I've got to spend another year polishing and writing and working on new additions and editions, alack, alas! I don't know. I know I haven't put enough provocative scenery into it, much less incorporated any real action and dialogue, or any depth—I know, yeah! Praise the Lord for no depth, by the way! I know you still wish you might feel some more empathy for the characters in my life, as part of the Living, Colorful Beauty. You are my living colorful beauty, honey. But as you read this, can't you feel anything more than, "Oh, okay, I see—he's just another Chuck Palahniuk wannabe. Ooh, he's the next fucking Bukowski, or fucking Kathy Acker—as in lust as I am with Kathy Acker!"

Am I to be just some creative writing clone with a knock-off novel whose ramblings sometimes resonate—in your crotch; in your heart—and to call this book (I'm sorry, something happened yesterday, and I'm hurt and, um, spent), to call this novel, if that's what it is, "unfinished business?"

What the hell is this? You think that I, as the writer, the narcissist, the fucking cupcake lover, whatever the hell I am—you say I just have a lot of imagination and a witty eye for detail, experimental structure, and I'll add: peace of mind? Random *thoughts? (This is my aunt. This is sex with a condom. This is Vanilla Sky with Tom Cruise. This is fucking tops, baby!) Hey, listen up now! This stuff is about hope, I thought—hope for everything that was unclear before, hope that things would come to fruition and become real, tangible, loving, and peaceful; things, like us, like we want to be. And, without hope, so what?*

Okay, if you want to get all edit-y on me (I'm sorry, baby, I'm trying to get to the point. Please bear with me here), here's another non sequitur: Our fucking dogs are fucking barking again at the demons in the fucking house. We need to fucking soundproof the office.

Okay, I've had enough. I'm just babbling and ranting, now, I know.

I'm really trying to be level-headed and nice, here. It's nice. Okay, Kelly, baby?

This is your brain on drugs, like this is what I found in my frustrating venture out there in the outside world, all on my own, yesterday when I walked out by myself. I walked all the way to our usual psychic advisor—the one we've been seeing since we moved out here in the desert together. And this is nothing about those silly tapes. (The psychic, just so future readers know, was Sabrina. But Sabrina wasn't there, and Sister Clara was filling in for her. Sister Clara was down the street at the "New Age Shoppe," as usual. But I wasn't prepared for the strange, creepy things and awful demons that would follow me there.)

And just so you know, Kelly, I do love you, you Lady to Love, and I want you. I want you so badly. Do I have you, Kelly—like I want? Do I, really? Kelly, I know we are both still new at all this, this whole being-lovers-and-living-together gig. And I admit to my obsession and that I'm dependent on you, just as I'm dependent on my fucking family. They're still staring at me. But I'm happy, you see? Sister Clara (you probably don't remember, but we met her at the meditations we go to—she was there the first night, I think, the first night we attended, when we met that massage therapist who said she could help with the Tourette's stuff. Anyway, Clara was sort of off to the side with the Shoppe owner, Evelyn), she's probably in her early 50s, has this straight, shoulder-length, gray hair, a huge Celtic cross pendant, and dresses in the Southwestern New Age style, you know, a poncho and pagan shoes with huge buckles. Silver and stone rings galore on unpainted fingers, nails kind of like yours—a little long and natural looking. (Do you remember her? Do you remember Clara?)

So I step inside, asking for Sabrina. I'm extremely out of breath, since the long walk to the New Age Shoppe was exhausting—what is it, a mile or so? The Shoppe keepers ask me if I'm all right, because I'm strangely red-faced and unsure of myself. Of course, I tell them it's my allergies, although I'm sure that isn't true. The Shoppe women and the owner, specifically, you know, they look rather inquisitive—strangely so—and they ask where you are and I tell them you're home working on your own book, as you are, and I add that you're excited because it looks like you'll probably be showcased in the New Yorker in a few months. Finally, one by one, the New Age Shoppe keepers inform me that Clara (who we both barely know, or at least I barely know her) wants to see me in private. And somehow, I feel a sense of disillusionment.

The owner, Evelyn (she's that larger, older lady who always talks about her son) escorts me to the back room and into one of the smaller psychic chambers off to the side, and Clara's seated there in front of me. I sit down in a chair, like I'm her client, or something. And I'm, like, totally wondering what's going on (you see, when I'm with the New Age-ers, I even start to talk like them!) So I ask her, "Hey, Clara. What is happening?"

Mid-stroke of the pen, Kelly walks in. Something about her seems slightly unreal—she wears angelic clothing, a bridal veil. She stands in the doorway, apart from me. "Hey! Let me read you something I wrote this morning. Okay?" Her voice seems to echo just the slightest bit.

I nod.

"You are the sweetest man alive, and I thank God every day that you have come into my life." She reads from a scrap of paper held in her hand. "Thank you for the flowers, the orchids, the bonsai tree, and the ficus. They are so alive—like our relationship. I love you very, very much."

I look at her. "I want to hold your hand, even if it's just for the one second. If you don't give up on me, then I hope you'll do nothing different, except just help me realize how bad I am, because I need to really surrender to that," I say in a rush. "I see me in you, and I can't stand it. What should I do? Should I let myself die, Kelly? I don't want to die."

If I die, who would I be? Would I have to be me?

What about Georgie?
(What about Claudia?)

Dear Diary:

All that I am is the result of what I have thought. My mind is everything. What I think, I become.

Fortune

I step inside the small booth finding psychic, Sister Clara, waiting for me already. I sit across from her, like I'm a client or something.

"Hey, Clara. What is happening?" I say.

Sister Clara removes a tiny Mead spiral binder from a small paper bag at her side. She lays it on the flimsy, cloth-covered reading table between her and me.

"Ben, I am aware that we've never really been properly introduced," she begins, her voice quiet and soothing. "And what I have to say to you is rather private and personal. In fact, it's very private and personal. It's about you, Ben. And it touches the most intimate, secret, and most painful parts of your life. But, to put it simply," she coughs, "I was in the middle of a meditation and I started writing down, drawing what I saw. And what I saw were things about you, Ben—things from your subconscious mind, or maybe from your present and past lives; your previous reincarnations and your karmic chains—and I couldn't bear to let this go by without witness."

I blink. "Really?"

I'm still not impressed, fairly certain that Sister Clara is just trying to hype me up for paid readings. Until she opens the first page of her little red notebook; Clara flips the pages of the notebook to a leaf covered in some sketches of various feminine figures interacting with a small male baby.

"This is you, Ben. Not Georgie, not Benjy. This is you and your grandmother, Ben—your real grandmother. Not your mother, not your aunt. This is your real, biological grandmother."

I could see what Clara had drawn: a precious little boy, an infant boy with a little penis, too! And the grandmother was holding the little boy, me the baby, by the dick—and only by the fucking dick. This woman, my own grandmother, was torturing me! But how could Sister Clara get this from my subconscious mind, or whatever—how could I have remembered it?

What the fuck? I thought. And then Clara started flipping through the filled-in pages—a whole notebook of sick and demented art, of me and my grandmother, and then me together with my aunt and then my teachers from nursery school. Even the nanny from Trinidad, who was supposed to be taking care of me when I was at home—separately, they're all performing very disturbing acts of violence and aggression on my innocent infantile genitals.

In one of them, a nurse of some kind (dark-complexioned) performs medical procedures on my skin, in the private areas—medicating, stitching, and bandaging my bottom and my little baby cock.

I'm in shock. I can't think. I just keep staring at that notebook and its sick and demented pictures. And I wonder what the fuck has been happening in my subconscious mind, since those earliest of years, since my sex life began (rape!), and what that has to do with who (or what?) I am now.

"To put it crudely, Ben, this one is cosmetic surgery," she explains. "Just a cover-up job, so that you wouldn't know later on what they did to you in your earliest childhood. You might have a subconscious memory now and then, but you wouldn't know what to do with it. Until, finally, I picked up the impressions and pictures in your subconscious mind."

Sister Clara hands the small Mead spiral notebook to me. I leave the New Age Shoppe without another word, choking up and sobbing, as if staggering from a heavy blow.

Large metal keys and bells that hang from the swinging door jingle as the door closes behind me.

I walk slowly home, clutching the notebook to my chest. When my lungs threaten to end me, I stop for a broken moment. I can strangely, somehow, still manage to breathe in and out. Finally, somehow, still manage to really breathe.

"Ah, God. Just let me catch my breath."

My head clears as I keep on walking.

"You should see this thing, Kelly," I say to myself. "This fucking notebook, this fucking picture book that Sister Clara showed me, and the fucking pictures she drew of my grandmother and my nanny and all those crazy women, doing those sick and demented things to me when I was just a helpless little baby. It tells me things I never would've known about myself, things I never would've wanted to know. It tells me why I'm such a fucked-up human being, why I am what I am.

"Why I can't function like a normal human being. Why I can't love myself, or anybody else. That's what they meant, all those psychos and doctors and cops, when they said I needed help and told me I better take it—and I didn't want help. I really didn't want to know.

"But now I know what I am and why I needed the help. Now I know what happened to me back then, when I was just a baby in my grandmother's house—but I still don't even know.

"What do I have there, down below? Is it even a natural cock? I mean, a natural penis? What is it—is it me? I still don't get it now, do I? Do I?"

And I dissolve into tears so hard that I can't think anymore. Choked up and sobbing. Crying like a baby. I kick away the dirt at my feet, but I can't kick it well enough, or hard enough, to make it better.

I'm almost home, now. I only have whatever dignity is left in me. I only have the dignity of who or what I am, and whatever I might be, left there inside me. That my poor, pathetic, hopeless self, that pitiful, abused past—I am only and just that. I'm just me.

And even that's nothing but a fiction, nothing but a lie I invent to disguise my past and hide.

Oh, God (or someone, something.) Please.

Give me the courage just to be me.

When I finally stumble back to the house, there's no car in the driveway.

"Your car? No car. I thought you were already home by now, baby," I mutter.

I check my pockets and groaningly kneel and peer beneath the doormat. No keys. The sun is hot now, I can scarcely breathe. I pound with both fists on the door.

"Kelly! Let me in!" I cry, as though she's really there. All I hear is the dogs whining and barking at my strangely familiar voice.

"I know we started out pretty rough here, Kelly," I plead. "I knew my family would never approve of us, not even if we got married. But I'm waiting for you, baby. It's just like you said: The stuff we write, the shite we say, we make it real—we manifest ourselves in the world."

I hear what I've said—I cease banging. The dogs are quiet now.

"I can hear the dogs still barking. Kelly. Kelly!"

There's no answer. Everything's completely silent and empty—a pin could drop. I scuff my shoes on the dirt and gravel of the driveway.

"Sit, Ben, sit. So you can digest everything," I command.

I sit on the hard rocky driveway.

"I just want to live. And if that means carrying on these stupid, superficial relationships with family and friends, then so be it.

"Please, God, just let me live."

Dear Diary:

I believe that it is better to tell the truth than a lie. I believe it is better to be free than to be a slave. And I believe it is better to know than to be ignorant.

506

Inside

Outside are the noises of twilight—crickets and coyotes, and dogs.

I sit before a long line of cameras, still set up to record, just like before, with Georgie. I speak.

"I'm still here in the psych ward. No, I mean, in my home with the cinderblocks and cement and stuff. With my electronic bracelets and monitors. I haven't been able to escape yet, but they give me day passes and things. But I'm home—I'm still at home, you see.

I stand, flinching, and cover the camera lenses, one at a time, until they see nothing but blackness. I sigh, and continue to speak.

"At least I'm not alone. After all, they still might need to establish the cause of death." I point accusingly at the cameras. They don't see. "It's there—in these things, in the tapes. If they ever bother to look for it."

I stand up and gather together my papers, my keys, and a notebook from the desk.

"I can feel it. I really can," I say for the benefit of the cameras. "We're all getting older and wiser. And sometimes, you just have to listen to the sounds of your life—the profound silence that resides somewhere inside you—somewhere in the emptiness. The deep remarkable hollow-sounding thing."

I light a cigarette and take a puff, then set it down on the ashtray leaving it to burn.

"But I can't see the sounds anymore, obviously. I can only feel the colors. And they're brilliant and alive. They're living beautiful colors."

I turn to go. I speak to the doorway and my voice echoes through the empty house.

"As for tonight, I'm going to go get groceries and fertilizer for the lawn outside. And I can't forget the firewood, finally. We can build a beautiful fire tonight. Maybe we'll find the living, colorful beauty inside."

The cigarette drops off of the ashtray and onto the desk. Then it rolls off onto the carpeted floor. (It must have.) I don't see.

"It's okay, now. All that is past me now, I hope. I just have to hold onto this—this present, this unbroken moment. And who or what I am now—I just might have found my self, at last.

"We'll just have to see about that, Kelly and me. We'll just have to see."

I leave.

Dear Diary:

I think it's about time now that I take a break from you, at least for the time being. I've got to get back to the other writing at hand. I suppose I'll write back in you upon completion of my book. I'm going to create a few more sections and let it go. Alas! —Ben.

BOOK FOUR

Soliloquy (for Dr C)

It is 3:10 am. This chill night air really makes my skin crawl. It's so quiet here that it gives me the creeps. I ought to be in bed, I guess, catching a few Zs. But the twitches and tics just keep me awake and these meds I'm strung out on won't let me sleep.

I haven't slept in three days. But hey! I'm not complaining. At least I'm out of rehab and I can get back to my writing; my cryptic transsexual writing. My creepy secret wet dreams—my perplexity, my perversity—*The Secret Sex Diaries of Benjamin J Schreiber*.

Yeah, that's me. Benjamin J Schreiber. Or at least I think that's me. (But does Dr C think that's me? That's what I want to know.) See, Dr C? I'm writing again just like you told me to. Writing therapy, shite! Does this feel like therapy—does it look like therapy? Does it read like therapy? Tell it to the doc! Not me. I'm not buying it.

But the doc buys it. Dr C that is. She's the latest psycho brain-picker in a long, long line of shrinks my dear old dad and stepmom have hired to try to make me cop to the crazy rap. Yeah, dear old dad and mom—they slap me into rehab and expect me to come out as some kind of wholesome, normal, healthy human being—or something. Huh! Just think. Me! Benjamin J Schreiber? Like I ever was some kind of wholesome, healthy, normal human being—or something. Imagine that if you can. (I know I can't. And if I can't, it'll never happen.)

It's like I tried to tell the doc. "Doc," I said, "it's like I have these sleazy snuff flicks, these schizophrenic sex-and-drug skits, these skuzzy blue movies playing in my mind all of the time. Sleeping or waking, on the street or at home, whatever, wherever, it doesn't matter. I have these schizophrenic sex fantasies and psychotic porn movies playing in my mind—and Georgie Gust. He's in them. And Claudia Nesbitt, she's in them. And sometimes I'm in them. Sometimes that Dr C, she's in them too. And sometimes, creepy people I don't even know are in my dreams and somehow I just can't make them stop. (You know what I mean, doc?)

Yeah, right. That Doc C—she knows, doesn't she? She sees those schizophrenic porn flicks and psycho blue movies playing in my mind, or somebody's mind anyway, somebody just like me. But she isn't talking. She just keeps asking me these sneaky questions trying to poke around in my mind and pick my brains. Trying to get inside my brain and see what makes me twitch and tic like I do—like she's trying to cure me. I don't even know if I want to be cured. (You've got to want to be cured, Ben, Dr C tells me. Otherwise, it just won't work.)

But I'm not buying that, either. Believe me. I know these psychos—I know these shrinks. They're crazier than me, and that's saying something. They're a bunch of loonies and freaks, creeps and perverts. And I'm not letting any shrink poke around in my secret sex fantasies and stick her fingers into my sleazy pornographic dreams and try to take them away from me—or maybe get me stuck back in rehab again. For life. So I keep that Dr C at a safe distance. You know what I mean? I keep her at arm's length, and I don't tell her anything that isn't good for her, don't say anything that she doesn't need to know. Which is nothing at all, if you ask me.

But at least that Dr C got me over my writing block. I've got to give her that. She cured me of my writer's block. If you can call it cured. So now I can write, write, and write. I can write my brains out (or my crap out, whatever). I can finally write whatever shite I want straight from the schizophrenic subconscious, from the psycho-porno underworld. Just me and my psycho sidekick and schizophrenic alter ego, Georgie Gust (that's me)—and, of course, Georgie's lifelong porno-chic obsession and freaky cheeky perplexity, Claudia Nesbitt. Claudia Nesbitt; my kinky sex goddess; my creepy, peeping nemesis; the number one love-and-hate object of my whole twisted love and sex life. (Keep writing, Ben, Dr C says. Just keep writing.)

At least this way, if Dr C catches me writing this crap and busts me to my ex-wife for alimony or something, I can always say, "Hey, that isn't really me! It's just Georgie and Claudia, see?" Georgie Gust and Claudia Nesbitt, who keep stalking me and haunting me and making me write this crap. Who keep acting out these schizophrenic blue movie skits and creepy porno-flick wet dreams that keep running through my mind. Because, see, I was supposed to be cured. I was supposed to be clean. I was supposed to be off this sex, drugs, and porn obsession I picked up somewhere along the way. And I swore (honest to God!) that I wouldn't go back again. (Of course I'd say anything, just so they'd let me out of rehab.)

Well, now, here I am. Sure as shite! Benjamin J Schreiber! I'm back for another schizophrenic blue movie and sleazy sex-and-drugs flick. Along with Georgie Gust—my creepy schizo-sidekick, and kinky sex partner in Perplexity and perversity—and Claudia Nesbitt, our freaky sex goddess and sado-bondage mistress. Yeah, and all these other freaks and loonies too—all these other creeps and pervs, those other schizophrenic bitches and ho-ho-ho's. They're real. Or aren't they? Don't ask me. (And don't search me, either.)

All I know is that I keep on having these schizo-fantasies, these psycho-porno interludes or whatever. So I write them down in my secret sex diaries and let Dr C try to figure out what they're all about: what's real and what not—what's me and what's Georgie. And what is this thing we have (Georgie and me) with that Claudia Nesbitt?

What a freaky threesome we'd be now, wouldn't we, Dr C? What a kinky hook-up for the creeps and pervs' wet dreams, you see—just Georgie Gust, Claudia Nesbitt, and me.

Benjamin J Schreiber and a cast of millions out there in the invisible studio audience—we're all ready for another freaky blue movie skit and schizo-psycho episode in: *The Secret Sex Diaries of Benjamin J Schreiber*.

Dear Diary:

I am confined but only by the walls I build myself.

Part I: A Day in the Life of Georgie Gust

A screaming alarm clock on the nightstand reads 9:00 am.

Georgie lies in bed under the sleep-rumpled covers, his bare feet sticking out the bottom. He's wearing long pajama pants without a shirt. He rolls over, slapping the snooze button, and the alarm clock stops squawking—for the moment, anyway.

Several hours later, the squawking alarm clock on the nightstand now reads 2:00 pm. Georgie finally rolls over and cuts off the alarm. Groggily, strung out and hung over, he struggles out of bed.

Georgie waddles into the kitchen in his old worn-out bathrobe. He rubs his eyes. He looks around the kitchen. It's a wreck. Dirty dishes are piled high in the sink, trash is scattered across the counters and on the floor. In other words, it's a typical morning in a typical day in the secret life of Georgie Gust.

He looks down at the stove and sees a cold leftover grilled cheese sandwich in a frying pan with only one bite taken. Georgie takes a big shaky bite of last night's reality-sandwich and tries to gag it down.

Georgie has a marker board up on the refrigerator with a "To Do List" stuck to it. The only thing the list says is: "GET CIGARETTES." The scribbled note has a checkmark by it.

(Parenthetical Pet Peeve) Pens that run out of ink when writing down something important.

Georgie glances at the telephone and answering machine. The red light is blinking. Georgie lifts a pack of cigarettes from the counter and reluctantly presses the "Play Message" button. He takes a step back to listen.

The first voice is feminine but firm. "Good morning, Georgie. It's Patty at the bank. Your account is overdrawn again. Can you plea—"

Georgie hits the delete button. The machine moves on.

"This is a courtesy call from Visa. You have an overdue balance of four thousand, nine—"

Georgie hits the delete button again. The machine continues to play.

"This is a message from Publisher's Clearing House letting you know that you are now out of the running for the ten million doll—"

Georgie hits the delete button. The machine keeps playing.

"Hey, Georgie. It's your moth—"

Georgie hits delete. The machine starts to play another message but Georgie hits the delete button again and again until there are no messages left.

Georgie takes a cigarette out of the pack and puts it in his mouth. He doesn't light it yet. The cigarette dangles loosely from his lips as he walks over to the constantly heating coffee pot that is still half-filled with old coffee. He takes a dirty coffee mug out of the sink and inspects it.

It doesn't look too bad, he thinks, just a little scraggy around the edges.

He shrugs his shoulders.

Fuck it, he thinks. Just give me the coffee and I'm out of here.

Georgie pours the two-day-old coffee into the mug. He takes a sip. It's so hot it burns his tongue. Georgie drops the mug on the kitchen floor and coffee spills everywhere as it shatters.

Georgie just stares at the spilt coffee and walks into the bathroom.

On the can, Georgie looks at the silver toilet paper dispenser. The roll is empty. His bleary worn-out face is also blank and empty.

(Parenthetical Pet Peeve) Unknowingly dragging toilet paper stuck to your shoe.

He steps in the shower, talking to himself.

The soap drops, thudding as it strikes the porcelain tub.

Georgie bends. He slips and falls.

"God damn," he moans.

What a way to start the day, eh?

Georgie tries to start anew in the kitchen. He lines up 10 espresso cups on the counter, each filled with black tar. He pours a sugar shaker along the line of cups, running back and forth between them, an unlit cigarette dangling from his lips.

Georgie pours each cup into a large thermos. Then he walks out of the kitchen, stepping right into the spilled coffee and porcelain shards. Coffee splashes up over his feet, but Georgie doesn't notice.

After downing half the thermos, Georgie steps into the bathroom. He turns on the hot water in the shower and just lets it run. Steam fills the air, moistening his lungs.

After a few minutes, Georgie lights his cigarette and sits down on the toilet. He picks up a three-month-old copy of *Newsweek*. He thumbs through it, scans a few words, scopes a few pictures, and then throws it down.

The radio plays "A Day in the Life," by the Beatles.

Eventually, Georgie gets dressed and walks out the front door into the white sunlit street. He stands out on the front patio, smoking a cigarette and drinking a beer. A couple of his neighbors are outside their houses too. It's a ritzy suburban subdivision somewhere in Los Angeles County.

A well-dressed woman is walking, pushing a baby carriage. She waves to Georgie's neighbor. The well-groomed neighbor casually waves back.

The well-dressed woman walks by Georgie. Georgie sheepishly raises his hand and waves. The well-dressed woman walks right past him like he doesn't exist. A few minutes later, another well-groomed couple comes walking up the street. They, too, march right past Georgie like he doesn't exist. (Like, maybe, he doesn't, even?)

Georgie takes another pull off his beer.

Although superficially nobody notices Georgie, the neighbors are really watching everything that happens at Georgie's place. There are quite a few of them actually, snooping and peeping behind the closed blinds and shuttered windows. Mostly they're the housewives stuck at home with their toddlers while their husbands are at work.

And then there's Deb and Kristen, Plain Jane lesbian lovers, both 35 years old, who live across the street. Deb is the butch dike. Kristen is the feminine balancer. They walk, hand in hand, to the front yard of their next-door neighbor, Robyn, chatting about their neighbors. (We wonder [Don't we?]: whom are they talking about? Could they be talking about Georgie and Claudia?)

"She's the perfect housewife," Deb sniffs. "She does the shopping, she does the laundry, and she does the dishes. All she does is wait on him."

"Don't underestimate her, Deb," Kristen snipes. "All she really wants is his money, his inheritance. He's worth millions."

"What about the sex?" Deb asks. "Do they still have sex, do you think? After all these years, it's got to be good."

"After all those years, it better be good," Kristen jokes.

They snicker.

The two approach Robyn's yard. She's sunbathing with her three-year-old toddler, who plays with squeaky toys in a playpen.

Robyn, who's pregnant and in her 30s, reads a tabloid on a chaise longue; she's a blondish, girl-next-door type, with a deep voice and frizzy red hair underneath her blonde highlights. While sunbathing, she covers herself against the sun in any way that she can.

Kristen and Deb scope her out, saying hello.

"Hi, Robyn," Kristen chirps. She turns to the toddler and starts babbling baby talk. "Hiya, baby boy. Wugga wugga wugga." She pinches the boy's cheeks.

(Parenthetical Pet Peeve) People who speak in a high-pitched tone.

"You know, Kristen, Deb," Robyn says. "You're probably right." It's immediately clear that she's been following their conversation. "But I do bet it gets boring after a while," she concludes.

"I think she's one of those 'quiet criminals'," Deb whispers. "I think she's a real freak."

"How so?" Kristen wants to know.

"I don't know. It's just the two of them." Deb smirks. "They bring the weirdest people over; one leaves and then the other leaves. They never go out together. And besides, they're so anti-social."

"So what's wrong with that?" Kristen asks. "He comes home one day like he's just won the lottery. He's got a new car, he re-does the house, and she picks out the colors. What more can a woman want? Nobody's perfect, you know."

"They're probably swingers," Robyn guesses. "They're probably wife-swappers."

"What's that supposed to mean?" Kristen asks nervously. "So what?"

"I think she swings both ways," Deb snickers.

"So what, Deb?" Kristen asks.

"Yeah, so what?" Robyn snickers. "So do I."

Kristen rolls her eyes. "Yeah, right," she says.

(Parenthetical Pet Peeve) That anyone thinks the President's sex life is any of his or her business.

Georgie walks through the house, drinking the last of the espresso from his thermos. He lights a cigarette and gulps down of the final, cold shot for fast, Fast, FAST relief.

And Georgie sees that the day is nice. There are white, pillowing, slow-moving clouds, blue sky, and bright sun.

"Shite," Georgie grunts. "Not another beautiful day."

He twitches and tics his discomfort.

Georgie walks out onto the second-floor patio. He looks down below. The hardworking landscapers have their power-blowers on high.

A police helicopter flies overhead, loud, Loud, LOUD—a cigarette boat screams by in the distance.

Fire truck sirens whine.

Georgie's face shudders. His arms jerk up from his sides. In a moment of panic, Georgie escapes downstairs. He climbs into his car and blasts out of the driveway.

Georgie arrives at his office around 3:15 pm. He's only 6 or so hours late. In the messy trashed-out office there's a desk, with a computer and papers strewn everywhere. His inbox is piled as high with papers as the sink in Georgie's kitchen is piled with dishes.

Georgie stares at the landscape of his desk for a long time. Finally, he glances at an empty picture frame on the wall. There's nothing in it except the blank wall. Georgie alternates his attention between the desk and the wall.

This goes on for some time.

Finally, Georgie reaches for another cigarette. He notices it's his last one.

When Georgie gets home, he looks at the marker board and erases the check mark by "GET CIGARETTES." Then he picks up a marker and rechecks it.

[Smoke Break]

The next day, Georgie walks down the street singing "A Day in the Life," by the Beatles.

At the same time, an anonymous New Age-type woman, about 40, professionally dressed and wearing open-toed high-heeled shoes, also walks down the street. She's singing the same song as Georgie: The Beatles' "A Day in the Life."

The New Age woman sings the verses only just after Georgie

does, like she's imitating him, only with some slight time-lapse delay. After the New Age woman has finished the first verse, Georgie starts in on the chorus. After Georgie's finished, the New Age woman starts in on the chorus.

Georgie and the New Age woman both turn the same corner at the same time, singing the same song. They run right into each other. Georgie hears that she's singing and immediately stops, like he's embarrassed or something. Somehow he just knows (we just know) that the New Age woman is Claudia Nesbitt.

But he's not going to admit he knows, is he? (Of course he isn't, and neither am I.)

"Were you just singing that Beatles song, too?" the woman asks.

"I, I'm not sure," Georgie stammers.

"Yeah, you were," Claudia says. "I just know it, that Beatles song, from the *White Album*. Or, I mean, *Sgt Pepper*."

"Yeah, yeah, yeah." Georgie sounds excited. "It's . . ."

Georgie searches his memory for the name of the song, but still draws a blank.

"A Day in the Life," Claudia smiles.

"That's it!" Georgie gushes.

Georgie smiles for the first time all day.

Claudia lights a cigarette.

"Do you happen to have another of those?" Georgie asks. "By any chance?"

Claudia hands Georgie one of her Virginia Slims.

Georgie looks sheepishly at the woman's face. He notices her frizzy red hair, her bright green eyes. Almost immediately, his shy eyes dart from her face to the brightly painted toes in her open-toed shoes.

Georgie can't take his eyes off of her stunningly painted toenails and stylish feet. He looks at Claudia like a guy who's having a one-way conversation with a pair of huge tits. Georgie tries to look Claudia in the eyes, but he just keeps looking down at her feet.

Claudia looks down to see what Georgie's looking at and finally notices she's stepped in something sticky.

"Ah, damn it!" Claudia curses politely. "I stepped in somebody's gum."

"I think it's a Lifesaver," Georgie says helpfully.

Georgie playfully knocks the Lifesaver off her heel with his foot. He gives a shy grin as the New Age woman with frizzy red hair and green eyes inspects her brightly painted toes and open-toed high-heeled shoes. Georgie notices a wedding band on her finger, but that just excites him even more.

"So, do you . . . ?" Georgie begins excitedly. "Or don't you . . . ?"

Georgie and Claudia carry on a conversation, their lips moving and smiling.

They are both obviously into each other. They keep laughing and talking excitedly. A few times, Georgie points to Claudia's brightly painted feet, and she giggles girlishly in response.

Claudia lights Georgie's cigarette.

They decide to check into a motel.

[Smoke Break]

In the motel, Claudia sits on the couch while Georgie's sitting on the coffee table. He licks the stylish arch of Claudia's right foot while she croons to Moby's "Everloving," which plays over the tinny radio.

Suddenly, in the entrancing midst of this passionate, romantic seduction scene and delirious foot-fetishist's fantasy, reality blinks out.

The whole scene changes.

Dear Diary:

Fuck it, as for my being happy? I can only be happy now, and that there will never be a time when it is not now. So, el-blam-o!

Part II: Another Day in the Secret Life of Georgie Gust

The motel room is empty. In the bathroom, a towel has been thrown out on the floor; it's crumpled up from wet feet. There are wet footprints on the bathroom floor and empty single-serving soap bottles on the corner shelf.

The housekeeper, Mary, gets the room ready for the next guests.

The telephone sits on the unmade bed. There's a half-used box of tissues beside it.

Georgie stands in the corner of his well-groomed yard, watering the closely clipped grass with a green garden hose. He smiles and waves to a neighbor passing by on the street.

The neighbor, well dressed, ignores Georgie—of course.

From inside the house, the phone rings twice. Claudia's voice echoes quietly from the answering machine:

"Hey there, Georgie," she says. "I was just thinking of you."

[Smoke Break]

The blue moonshine lights up the white sand beach and the white-capped breakers. The tide is low. The whispering wave-rollers are quiet and gentle.

Walking alone near the water's edge is a party of one, cigarette in mouth—a slightly disheveled, paunchy, middle-aged man. (Who is this guy?)

It's Georgie, of course. But he looks slightly out of shape. Why does he look so bedraggled, so downtrodden? What's happened to change the Georgie Gust we know and love (don't we?) into this disheveled, haggard stranger we scarcely know?

Still, even though Georgie looks pretty scruffy, like he's been slacking, maybe drinking and doping, sinking into a dissolute life of drunkenness and dissipation—he still has that drug-addict sexiness some girls really go nuts for.

Although he's lost in thought, he's still taking in everything around him. The whitecaps crash louder and the screaming gulls come storming in for a meal.

Early the next morning, the white sand beach is empty. The sky is gray, flat, and still. The screaming gulls fly low in flocks.

The Pacific rollers wash in and out, whispering with a mysterious voice.

Out of nowhere, Claudia's voice appears on Georgie's voicemail.

"I was downstairs at one of the lectures," Claudia's voice murmurs. "It's so boring, but I got several compliments on my new pedicure."

We're revisiting the past again, aren't we? We're back in The Early Days of Claudia Nesbitt and Georgie Gust. (Right?)

Can't we ever escape the past?

Claudia's raspy, husky voice echoes on Georgie's voicemail:

"So I thought maybe you might like to know what a great job you did. And on such short notice, too. What a swell guy you are."

[Smoke Break]

The old wooden pier juts out into the immense blue ocean. A middle-aged couple walks hand-in-hand toward the end of the pier. They stare quietly out at the barges coming in. There's a snack-and-bait stand to their left; it is still closed at this early morning hour. The receiver of an old black payphone dangles off its hook. Scrap litter blows in the wind.

Out of nowhere, Claudia's husky, sexy voice appears on Georgie's voicemail:

"I'm meeting some cool people here," she tells him. "But a lot of them are really lame. This whole convention is really boring."

Only a few fishermen are out with their fishing gear. It's still very early in the morning.

An Asian man pulls up a small fish that dangles on fishing line. His small son grabs the white bait bucket.

Out of nowhere, Claudia's smoky, sexy voice appears on Georgie's voicemail:

"So, you see, some of my new friends wanted to hang out by the bar and talk medicine. But I was hoping we could finish our conversation?"

A delivery van drives past. Somebody tosses a newspaper on Georgie's well-groomed front lawn. There's a big pile of old rolled-up newspapers on the closely clipped lawn.

Out of nowhere, Claudia's chirpy, worn-out voice appears on Georgie's voicemail:

"The weather's so much nicer out here. We should at least get together before I leave tomorrow."

[Smoke Break]

Bright red sunlight bleeds through the closed window blinds. Georgie's sprawled on the bed with his eyes squeezed shut, passed out, sound asleep.

Out of nowhere, Claudia's cheerful encouraging voice appears on Georgie's voicemail:

"I was thinking about how brilliant you are," she says. "And, yikes, you have so much talent. People look at you and they see big things."

The silent alarm clock on the nightstand reads 10:30 am.

Out on the beach that afternoon, the sky has cleared up a bit. The white sand beach is packed with kite-fliers. A dozen kites glide along the windy coastline full of living color and wonderful beauty. On the old wooden pier there are dozens of fishermen. In fact, there are more men than fish.

At the hotel across the road, a professional healthcare conference is just letting out. Conference guests come swarming out of the emptying motel lobby. The checkout line is backed up out the door. The professional conference guests still wearing official nametags check out of the hotel, one by one, two by two, and three by three.

The well-dressed bellboys are busy trying to handle two or four bags each. The flustered guests press tips into the bellboys' hands and hop into waiting cabs.

[Smoke Break]

Georgie's three-story suburban penthouse is really quite modest. So are most of the three-story houses in this suburban neighborhood.

Out of nowhere, Claudia's boisterous, challenging voice appears on Georgie's voicemail:

"What would you do if you knew you couldn't fail?" she asks. "What would you do if you knew you couldn't fail?" she repeats. "I just love that question."

In this modest suburban neighborhood, the neighbors wear light jackets when they walk their dogs. A few stray house cats prowl the sidewalks. A small crowd of early-morning walkers chat and gossip on the sunny corner near lines of sporty new cars parked on the white sunlit street. It seems like a friendly neighborhood. (Doesn't it?)

Out of nowhere, Claudia's gritty, deep-throated voice appears on Georgie's voicemail:

"Grab hold of just one project and get in there with your teeth and see what happens," she challenges him. "Even if you don't really have to, to make a living. Why not? What have you got to lose?"

Georgie's slightly pretentious suburban house is on a sunny street corner. It's the biggest house on the whole block. It's also got an ocean view. It takes up two full lots, what with the three-story house and the modest guesthouse over the three-car garage.

Out of nowhere, Claudia's shrilling, encouraging voice appears on Georgie's voicemail:

"Somebody wants to tell a story about you and you're the only one who knows it well enough!" she cheers him on. "Go for it!" she says.

The front yard is a small grassy area with exotic landscaping, a patio, and a white board fence. The house is made of brick, of course.

Out of nowhere, Claudia's hard-bitten, satiric voice appears on Georgie's voicemail:

"You'd do the world a favor. Hell—do it for me!" she barks. "I'd love to hear about all the shite you've been through."

A small gate leads to the front door of his charming and desirable home. The house is a little big for just one person— especially a lonely guy like Georgie.

Out of nowhere, Claudia's mawkish, jeering voice appears on Georgie's voicemail:

"So what if your dad is some big well-to-do public figure or whatever?" she mocks. "This is your chance to shine." she applauds. "Just go for it!"

She pauses.

"Oh, just . . .wait a minute . . . ."

At Georgie's plush suburban home, the Mexican housekeeping staff arrives in a black Ford Excursion. The boss, a fortyish Hispanic male hipster named Sanchez, wears a ponytail—his son, Rueben, who's about 21 years old, is dressed as a Mexican gangster. The female assistant is an Anglo who's sweet and polite and wears glasses. But, oddly enough, she speaks no English at all.

Out of nowhere, Claudia's saccharine, girlish voice appears on

Georgie's voicemail:

"I have a sweet little gift I found in the gift shop down here," she purrs. "It's the perfect little gift. Just for you, Georgie."

The Excursion Park is on the shady side of the house near the three-car garage.

Out of nowhere, Claudia's middle-aged, tired voice appears on Georgie's voicemail:

"Anyway, my number should've popped up on your phone," she says, ringing off. "Just let me know what happens."

The crew unloads the cleaning supplies.

[Smoke Break]

The silent alarm clock on the nightstand reads: 12:00 pm.

Georgie's a little bit heavier and maybe too tall. Otherwise, he's a handsome young man (we think.) He lies in the sleep-rumpled bed, looking beat.

Crumpled-up piles of slick pornographic magazines, and a tiny video player that rolls a Triple-X show, surround Georgie. But Georgie's not really watching. (Is he?)

Georgie's feet hang out of the slightly yellowish sheets. His socks dangle limply over the nightstand. Georgie wears long pajama pants without a shirt, revealing his stressed-out little jelly-belly.

He sits up in bed and leans over. He peeks out the bedroom window through the shuttered venetian blinds and sees the cleaning crew unlocking the back door, about to come inside. He starts to panic.

"Shite." Georgie says. "They're here."

He gets up out of bed, agitated. He finds his wire-rimmed glasses on the nightstand and puts them on, but immediately he notices they're smudged. He wipes them clean as best he can with his pajama pants.

Georgie spots the clock and turns its face away, mumbling jumbled pseudo-garble to himself. He rechecks the time with his watch and two other alarm clocks in out-of-reach places.

He decides that it's officially afternoon.

He twists open the blinds. White sunlight beams through the horizontal bars.

Behind the closet door, an old white hotel bathrobe hangs.

Georgie wraps himself up in the robe and folds his arms, wishing he could find the waist tie.

He opens his bedroom door but the Mexican housekeeper beats him to it.

Georgie has no choice but to say something. "Hi," Georgie says.

The woman smiles at him. "Hola," she says, and steps into the bedroom.

She's only slightly embarrassed. The woman has obviously run into Georgie before on other occasions, when he was in even worse shape than now. She speaks in Spanish and signs to Georgie that she'll come back at a better time. She sashays away down the living room hallway.

Mary, the Mexican housekeeper, returns to the kitchen where Rueben is prepping the dishes and unloading the dishwasher. Without taking orders, Mary swipes up a mop and starts scrubbing the tile floors.

(Parenthetical Pet Peeve) Having to wash the dishes before putting them in the dishwasher.

The boss, Sanchez, starts the coffee machine.

The three talk to each other in Spanish. Rueben switches on the small clock radio that's mounted by the kitchen sink. Mariachi music swarms through the air, thick with the scent of soap.

Strung out and hung over, Georgie stumbles in and grabs a pack of smokes. He ducks out, mumbling, and then strolls through the still-disorganized living room. It's a disaster.

Georgie turns to the front door to smoke on the porch. But before he gets there he stops for a moment, turning back to the disheveled bathroom. With the unlit cigarette still propped in his mouth, Georgie starts the shower water running on hot. Then he walks through the door and sits heavily on the porch steps.

Georgie tries to light his cigarette but the lighter only flashes and sparks without catching flame. He takes a fresh matchbook off the patio table and lights the whole matchbook. With the matchbook flaring wildly, he finally lights Claudia's Ultra-Slim 120.

On the white concrete sidewalk in front of Georgie's plush suburban home, Georgie's well-dressed neighbor walks a small baby. The man's dressed appropriately for the cool day, wearing a light windbreaker and thick jeans.

"Nice day, isn't it?" the neighbor says. "For something, anyway."

He waves cheerfully to Georgie.

Georgie still isn't dressed yet. He's still wearing his old heavy bathrobe.

Georgie turns his back to the white concrete sidewalk and faces the house. His reflection in the front window stares back at him vacantly. He's a little embarrassed. He's really not the social type.

A delivery boy enters through the small front gate. He pulls Georgie's paper from the stack and hands it to him, with a new delivery menu from Ling's China Garden.

Georgie nods. "Thanks."

While Georgie still stands smoking in the front yard, Deb and Kristen, holding hands, approach Georgie's corner yard with their dog.

One of them starts to wave hello, but Georgie has already put out his cigarette and headed back inside where the bathroom is bellowing steam.

Georgie powers up the DVD player that is mounted outside the bathroom door. The 1001 Living Dead Strings start playing their *Greatest Hits of Great Dead Teenage Vampire Lovers*. Now there's music, Georgie thinks.

(Parenthetical Pet Peeve) "Science projects" in the refrigerator: in other words, rotten leftovers.

The Mexican houseboy, Rueben, fits a stack of DVDs onto Georgie's CD tower shelves. He returns to the kitchen fridge, checking off the first item from the list:

Things That Need To Be Done:

#1) PUT DVDs AND CDs INTO PILES.

#2) SWITCH FURNITURE AROUND

#3) COLOR-COORDINATE CLOSETS

Georgie slouches through the crowded living room, staring at the lists of things to do written on little pieces of scrap paper that are stacked on his coffee table.

In Georgie's New Age living room there's a sheer overkill of every little-known fancy gizmo and cheap modernized gimmick, every cutting-edge electronic doodad and trendy entertainment gadget that could possibly fit into a single room. But somehow, the room's still neat and organized.

There are 8x10-inch glossy photos and brightly colored drawings framed and tacked up along the walls. And on the bookshelves there's certificates displaying Georgie's distant past: awards, trophies, and graduation records. Pictures of old girlfriends.

There are piles and piles of hardcore intellectual books stacked in piles of three hardcover copies each. The video and music collection also exists in triplicate.

He has too many things, and too many copies of his things. Some of Georgie's sketches and notes, peeking out of folders and from behind books, are only half finished. His drawings and paintings are scattered randomly on the hard surfaces of the room. They're hardly done, but still brilliant.

Graph paper diagrams seem drawn with purpose but with no immediate implications—along with intricate patent designs and obscure blueprints.

It's obvious that Georgie has a strong, inventive mind—maybe even too strong for his own good. He has too many projects going on for one slothful slacker dude. Arbitrary projects; redundant and grandiose projects; stupid, trivial projects; but still, too many—way too many.

Compared to his present, Georgie's past seems distinctly rich and full to him now. Somehow he seems to have lost that richness and fullness (that living, colorful beauty). Now he finds comfort only in his troubled sleep. He has nothing to look forward to, now. Now, all his needs are taken care of.

The things in his house, although artistically placed, are almost mathematically arranged. Somehow everything corresponds to everything else.

Georgie's quantum physics textbooks are neatly clustered and labeled with the corresponding videos and books, near an MC Escher print.

The stationary bike has athletic trophies stationed near it, along with workout tapes and sports magazines and signed baseballs.

A spinning metal fan refracting light blows up at a ceiling fan. The ceiling fan spins slowly above the wheels of the bike that refract light from the metal fan.

Georgie passes by the still-running shower on his way to the kitchen. At the kitchen entrance, Sanchez holds out a smoking cup of coffee for Georgie. Georgie takes the coffee cup and carries it outside through the kitchen door.

On the back patio, Georgie smokes a butt and slugs down his

coffee in small shots. He bobs his head to the beat of his own secret song.

Georgie's house phone rings through the big open house.

He ignores it, taking another drag off his cigarette.

Now his cell phone rings, a distant chiming. He throws his cigarette down and runs into the house to find it. Then he remembers he's left the cell phone outside, but he returns too late.

He sets the cell phone on the patio staircase, fidgeting with it.

Finally, Georgie steps into the hot shower and sighs—too late. He takes his soaked wristwatch off and sets it near his glasses on the steamy toilet seat.

We hear the soap drop.

Georgie slips and falls inside the shower.

"God damn it," he mutters.

The CD player starts skipping.

The vacuum cleaner sucks up the area rug outside the bathroom door.

Georgie turns off the hot water. He peeks out of the shower for a dry towel but there are none. There are only a couple of washcloths and a roll of toilet paper.

He glances at the hair dryer but decides to dry himself with the washcloths and toilet paper instead.

He's miserable. He's pitiful. He's better than you or me.

He's our Georgie!

So what else is new?

[Smoke Break]

After drying himself off, Georgie sits on the can. Now there's no toilet paper, either.

He starts up the shower again.

Meanwhile, the Mexican cleaning crew is taking their lunch break in the kitchen.

Mary carries a pile of dirty clothes out back.

The digital microwave clock reads: 2:00 pm.

Georgie turns on a light switch in the living room but the bulb is burnt out. He keeps on, not noticing. He opens all the sun blinds throughout the whole living area and lets the white sunlight burst in.

Still wearing his old white motel bathrobe, he searches for clean clothes in his closet and the laundry room, but they're all being washed. In exasperation, Georgie tries on a few old shirts and pants from his younger days, but they're all too small. He decides to wear them anyway.

Now that he's finally showered and dressed, Georgie starts looking for something slightly interesting to do. Hell, anything to do. He starts rearranging the things in his messed-up bedroom.

He walks out back still wearing his too-small clothes.

(Parenthetical Pet Peeve) If they have it in my size, I won't like it. If I like it, they won't have it in my size. If I like it and they have it in my size, it will cost too much.

He removes an outfit from the laundry basket: shirt, sweat pants, socks, and shoes. They're all very colorful and bright. Too colorful and bright, he thinks, and too clean, too.

He slaps on a funky blue hat with his wild, colorful, basket-wrinkled outfit.

To make himself even sexier, Georgie sprays aerosol deodorant all over his already-clothed body. He brushes his yellowish, coffee and cigarette stained teeth.

(Parenthetical Pet Peeve) Getting deodorant stains on my clothes.

He reads the bathroom mirror, which has a handmade label that reads:
"JUST TRUST ME!"
Would you trust this man to sell you a used car? he thinks, or to sell you a used life? Staring himself in the eyes, he shudders. Not me, he thinks.

He shaves (first with an electric, then with a straight-edged razor) without shaving lotion, although 10 different brands of lotion are squatting on his vanity counter.

He cleans a different pair of bifocal, wire-rimmed glasses and heads back to the living room that is still bright with daylight. The Mexican housekeeping crew is finally cleaning and organizing the mess. In the spirit of hospitality, Georgie joins them.

He starts switching the pictures on the wall, rearranging the furniture, putting a few minutes' time into shuffling and restacking his scattered notes and half-finished drawings.

He arranges the books in a different order.

He contemplates a crack in a glass picture frame on his wall.

The room was fine the way it was, he thinks. Now I'll just trip over everything at night when I sleepwalk.

Finally, Georgie leaves the rest of the living room remodeling to the Mexican cleaning crew.

The hell with it, he thinks. Let them deal with it. That's what we pay them for, isn't it—to clean up after us?

Georgie checks inside the fridge looking for something to eat. He sniffs the milk and tries to make himself drink it, but he can't gag it down. Finally, he decides that it's sour and he pours it down the drain. There's nothing much else in there, he thinks. Nothing edible, I mean.

The freezer's loaded with microwavable TV dinners.

(Parenthetical Pet Peeve) People who put empty containers back in the fridge or freezer.

Georgie grabs a cup from the dishwasher and fills it from the empty sink. He drinks it and washes the cup by hand, and then puts it back into the dishwasher.

Georgie puts some Whizzo! frozen pancakes in the microwave.

He sets the timer for 2 minutes and pushes the "START" button.

The microwave spits and hums ominously.

While waiting for his Whizzo! pancakes to explode, Georgie fantasizes washing and scrubbing in slow motion—an entirely overfilled sink of dishes, pots, and glasses. It's a soothing, romantic wish-fulfillment fantasy.

(Parenthetical Pet Peeve) When guests rinse out a glass then put it in the sink, instead of putting it in the dishwasher when there's no extra effort involved.

Of course it's nothing I'd ever act on, he thinks. It's just a fantasy.

When the timer's down to two seconds, Georgie presses the "CANCEL/STOP" button twice for no apparent reason.

It's not like he's in a rush, is it?

Don't answer that, he thinks.

Dear Diary:

Bloody hell, I'm going to just leave all the broken pieces I've been trying to analyze and over-analyze, and move the hell on. Live the life. Live the fucking dream life!

Part III: Living the American Dream

Georgie and Claudia have an enormous three-story McMansion in the sprawling suburbs of Los Angeles. They're having the McMansion remodeled this year, turning it into their American Dream—a model home.

In the background, the home restoration is in progress. Sharp staccato hammering, shrill high-pitched drilling, and raspy sawing noises echo throughout the house.

Although it's already afternoon, Georgie is in the kitchen performing his morning rituals. We still can't make out his face to see which Georgie this might be.

"She really wasn't into me then," Georgie muses. He's mulling over his past—his love life with Claudia. "I knew I wasn't good enough for her. I only wanted to better myself so I could have her. But that was a long time ago. Things are different now—time has passed and now I've changed."

Georgie scarfs down a handful of breakfast cereal.

"I really couldn't go on that way," he mumbles through wads of softened cereal. "I couldn't live, knowing everything about my life at any given moment. Knowing that I loved a woman who couldn't really love me. I'd be living a lie. And I just couldn't live with myself as a lie—or with Claudia, either."

Georgie looks out the big picture window across the vast acres of well-manicured shrubbery and well-groomed suburban lawns. There's a swimming pool, a tennis court, and a series of lawn chairs beneath white sun umbrellas in his front yard.

As Georgie continues to muse, a half dozen fluorescent green tennis balls shoot out of a serving machine. They bobble and roll aimlessly on the green pavement.

Beneath the white umbrellas, Claudia, in white tennis dress, and Marco, her secret lover (the Mexican lawn-boy), are oblivious.

"I think I'm a love addict," Georgie whispers to himself. He twists the blinds shut.

A strange man peeps through the kitchen window, bending the blinds with his fingers. This, too, is a different Georgie. (Do we know who he is? He's snooping and peeping on his own secret fantasies. He's butting in on his philandering fantasy wife Claudia. A little mystery and intrigue surrounding the breaking of the marital taboo piques his prurient interests.)

"You know that feeling you get when you hold a girl's hand for the first time?" Georgie addresses Claudia, although she doesn't know it. "Well, I don't feel that anymore. Not with you. Not with anyone."

Finally Georgie frees the stuck window shade and closes it.

The construction workers are hard at work restoring the enormous three-story McMansion where Georgie and Claudia live. The kitchen's a mess; kitchen tiles and plumbing parts are scattered everywhere.

An old-fashioned refrigerator is being hauled out by two young men in work harnesses. Georgie cuts ahead of them, hurrying from the back of the kitchen to the foyer at the front of the house.

A man working on scaffolding over the front door drops his orange hardhat by accident. It barely misses Georgie's head as he darts beneath a ladder. Georgie doesn't notice. He studies himself in the vanity mirror by the front door.

He's handsome because he's rich and he's built like a Hollywood idiot. He picks a piece of lint off his collar and runs out hastily, grabbing a leather garment bag by the door and a set of unmarked keys from the coat rack.

He leaves his brown leather briefcase behind at the door-but only for a moment.

Georgie's hands are full. He wipes his forehead.

What am I doing here? he wonders, How did I get here?

Where am I going now?

Who am I, really?

[Smoke Break]

Georgie and Claudia's chauffeur, Charley, is short on time as he charges toward their elegant BMW coupe, two large suitcases clutched in his fists. The American Dream Couple are planning their dream vacation.

Claudia's wearing a white-and-red summer outfit with a big floppy hat. She swishes across the well-manicured lawn toward the elegant BMW coupe.

"Georgie longs for me," she whispers to herself. "I'm everything for him."

But the metallic shine of the brand new German sports coupe somehow dulls Georgie's existence. Impassively, he runs his eyes over the vehicle from front to back. Even the whitewall tires gleam. The back license plate reads: "WEAPON."

Claudia's not impressed.

"He's just a little bit pretentious," she confides to Charley. Charley pretends not to notice.

Reaching inside the coupe, Georgie opens the electric trunk. He drops his garment bag inside and manually shuts the trunk with a slam. The trunk jams shut.

Georgie grunts and rolls his eyes—abruptly the whole scene changes.

Georgie and Claudia stand before the decorative pond at their college campus. (Uh-oh—what's this?) A young Georgie opens a jewelry box with a huge diamond engagement ring for a young Claudia. He's on his knees making a marriage proposal. Claudia's playing hard to get but Georgie's persuasive—or at least he's persistent.

"This is why you should marry me," he says.

He flashes the huge glittering rock before Claudia's cold green eyes.

But Claudia's still not impressed.

"You mean because of the size of that thing?" she smirks. She takes the ring from him. "I'd like to put it on." She pauses. "Myself."

Georgie's quick with his response. "So," he says. "Is that a yes?"

Claudia brushes him off with a slight languid gesture. "Let's just enjoy what we've got together, right this moment," she smiles at him, her teeth blinding. "Like I said to you before, Georgie. It's just so—it's just so good. So perfect just the way it is."

She pauses again.

"Please don't spoil it," she pleads, admiring the rock.

Finally Georgie gets the trunk closed. He opens the door for Claudia and she slips into the plush back seat. Charley revs the gas and the elegant BMW sports coupe pulls away, nearly leaving Georgie behind as he hops in the swinging open door.

Claudia is whispering to herself.

Another weirdo finally caught up with the times, she thinks. He had so much potential! He never really saw things through, though—it's so unfortunate—for both of us.

She remembers their honeymoon, a perfect white boat on an

endless blue ocean. At first, it was all so romantic. We went sailing to Catalina Island. We honeymooned in Paris. We went mountain biking in the Mohave.

Her memory disappears like a glittering soap bubble that pops.

She sighs.

"And then it stopped," she says out loud.

From the back seat of the sleek sporty BMW coupe, Georgie waves to one of their young, attractive female neighbors who is jogging by in pink Puma sweats. Claudia watches with vague disgust. She's not jealous. She's only distantly fascinated and slightly appalled by Georgie's sometimes prurient, voyeuristic, masochistic interest in other women.

Is he mentally stiff she wonders? Or am I? He always was a dork. And you know what they say: Once a dork, forever a dork. But I married him didn't I? Is this what marriage is really like?

Real.

Just to see if she can get to him, Claudia pulls up her shirt and flashes her bare breasts at Georgie.

But Georgie just grins and licks his finger.

Claudia shivers and laughs.

Of course, there were other reasons, she reminds herself. He's hung like a bull. But he hardly uses it properly—hardly properly.

Georgie senses Claudia's disaffection but doesn't let it disturb his self-esteem.

As long as the wife's still a little interested, he thinks. That's all that really matters at home right now. This is really what marriage is like, like they say—only mutual self-interest with a hint of disgust and loathing.

I don't really believe it, though.

As we know, Georgie has many quirks. For example, he sports a nervous facial tic, especially when he's trying to make Claudia exasperated with him—as he is—as she is.

He flaunts his nervous twitches and tics, she thinks disgustedly. He thinks they add to his character.

Affecting nonchalance, Georgie tries to light a cigarillo with flimsy book matches, one by one. But the matchbook runs out before he can get the cigarillo to smoke. He tosses the matches away in obvious frustration. Despite his sophisticated exterior, he's a failure.

Sometimes I hate being me, he thinks.

Claudia sees through his flimsy façade.

He tries to cope with all his problems, sexually, she thinks. But he's so, so insecure, insensitive, like a child, with his pretty little toys. Claudia smiles, remembering the closet in their bedroom filled to the brim with pornography and sex toys.

I think he loves me, she thinks. I think I love him. I think I do. I think he thinks I love him. But do I really?

Georgie scowls at his shoes.

I think she loves me, he thinks. I think I love her. I think she thinks I love her. But do I really?

What a work of art! What a piece of work she is! She's as beautiful as she is stupid. I don't know why it's all such a love/hate thing with her. Do I love her? Or do I?

In Georgie's mind, Claudia prances in slow motion though a mysterious dream landscape composed of all his childish sex fantasies and adolescent wet dreams. She's a ballerina, a diva, but also a whore, a cock-queen.

She's all woman, he thinks; she's all women.

Georgie sighs.

There might as well be music, he thinks. Playing to the beat of her life.

And lo! There is music billowing and wafting around her, a medley of Top 40 hits from the 1001 Living Dead Strings playing *Famous Romantic Vampire Teenage Love Songs You'll Always Wish You Could Forget.*

Georgie's fascinated and bemused, uplifted and swept away by Claudia's beauty.

She's *The Portrait of Modern Woman*, he thinks. And the *Sexiest Thing since the Venus de Milo*, and besides, we've been into S&M, kinky sex, and other voyeuristic tricks ever since college days. She especially likes age-regression fantasies. I'm into spanking and sadism, sometimes. Or is it masochism?

At Georgie's words, the whole scene changes.

In the murky black-light depths of this infernal den of sin and iniquity, Claudia's photographic image is blended into Georgie's kinky sex fantasy of her. She's a nasty dominatrix in black latex, alone in an S&M club, wielding the whip over her slavish worshipper.

Georgie's sucking on her toes, to her orgasmic pleasure.

The fantasy abruptly ends.

Back at the house, it's a new day, post vacation. Georgie watches as Claudia bounces toward him from the yard. She's prancing like a female unicorn in heat, dancing, like a pole dancer to the beat. She's Claudia, the lascivious redhead with the fiery green eyes.

Claudia's smile is pearl white and big-toothed, seductive but slightly creepy. She removes her crumpled baseball cap revealing more of her perfect outer beauty. Her ponytail slides out from the cap and swings wild and free; the wild streak of platinum highlights in her frizzy red hair reflects the brilliant sunlight over the suburban landscape.

Georgie sees the smoldering wildfire in her frizzy hair and wild eyes and becomes enflamed once again with her beauty.

She colors her hair as if it's really greying, he thinks. But she'll always be a living colorful beauty to me.

Georgie notices a smoldering fire-starter in Claudia's hands. His curiosity is piqued.

"Where'd you get that?" he asks.

"Marco gave it to me," she confesses. "He enflames me, as you, Georgie, do not."

She lights Georgie's cigarillo with her wildly flaring fire-stick. Georgie tries to look sophisticated, debonair, but starts coughing and hacking spastically. Besides, she's singed his eyebrows off.

Claudia interrupts a carefree game of tennis to intrude on the husband? Georgie thinks. What could she want? Is she a housebreaker and a heartbreaker, or just another simple country girl gone wild?

"Between you and me, everyone on our block wants to be like Claudia," Georgie mutters. "Wild and free, swept up in the living colorful beauty of the moment. But most of them just smoke a lot of pot, surrounded by clouds of grey. It drives me fucking nuts. What do they think they are, Aborigines or something?"

Georgie waits a few seconds while the silence and suspense build. Finally he deadpans:

"Wake up, people. It's the 21st century."

Dear Diary:

Yes, I am the direct result of what I fucking think. My mind is everything! So, sure as hell, what I think I become, and I am. I am that!

Part IV: The End of a Dream?

Georgie Gust and Claudia Nesbitt's swank suburban McMansion in the New Age yuppie subdivision has become even more bloated and gargantuan with additional posh residential wings, and elaborate landscape gardens sprouting and growing as if magically, organically, from the original three-story house.

But inside Georgie and Claudia's luxurious palatial estate, all is not well. In fact, Georgie and Claudia are having their first big spat, their first big tiff, their first big lover's quarrel—and the first cracks are appearing in the impregnable edifice of their passionate love affair and romantic dream marriage.

"That was Ismael on the phone," Georgie casually announces. "I've got to leave for Las Vegas sooner than planned. In fact, I have to go right now."

Flinging herself on a sofa, Claudia whines in her pathetic, sappy way, as if she's crushed by Georgie's offhand announcement.

"Why can't I go with you to Vegas?" Claudia pleads. "You know I've always wanted to go there but you never take me! You never take me anywhere!"

It's obvious that Georgie really doesn't care. While Claudia whines and weeps, he casually wipes a water spot off the well-polished chair with his finger.

Claudia sees that Georgie's oblivious to her pleas. She becomes abruptly calm. "Georgie?" she says.

Still Georgie says nothing. He won't even look at her.

"You see, everyone," Claudia laughs bitterly. "Georgie's the strong, silent type. He talks with his hands a lot, when he won't talk with his mouth. He has big hands." Claudia laughs again, somewhat hysterically. "Like one, like the other."

"What are you talking about, Claudia?" Georgie says, "Sweetheart, how many times do I have to tell you—it's a business trip, that's all. It'll be boring. I'll take you with me to Vegas another time, I promise. I'm sorry, babe. But, you know, it's a last-minute call."

Claudia pouts. "But you know, dear," she says. "I get so lonely whenever you go out of town."

Georgie scoffs. "Come on, Claudia," he chides. "You're a big girl, now. You don't need to pretend that you need me around. You've got plenty of toys to play with around the house. I'll only be gone a couple days, you know?"

Georgie's already packed and ready to go. His suitcases have already been stowed in the coupe. So he strides down the front walk toward the car without paying much attention to Claudia, who tails along behind him.

As Claudia strides up alongside Georgie, she wraps her slim arms around him and strokes her sleek supple figure seductively against him. She even shows him a slight hint of her black G-string panties and lacy push-up bra.

"Please, baby. Take me with you," she whispers. "I'll wear that sexy black negligee you bought me. And I'll let you . . . You know . . . ."

Still, Georgie's all business. Impatient with Claudia's obvious attempts at seduction, he detaches her grip from his arm and briskly checks his Rolex. "Come on, come on, Claudia," Georgie clucks pettishly. "I've got a flight to catch. I'm already 15 minutes late and you know I really can't miss this flight."

Georgie gives Claudia a quick peck on the cheek and strides toward the car. He smiles because even though he knows he's being a cad, he also knows it's perfectly ethical for him to do so.

"I'll take you up on that negligee offer when I get back." Georgie attempts a sexy grin that just seems creepy. "Okay, princess?"

Slipping out of Claudia's grasp, Georgie quickly slides into the car. He slams the door shut and backs out of the driveway, leaving Claudia petrified with fear, rejection, and shame. She swings her tennis racket back and forth, chewing her lips.

For a couple moments, Claudia savors the hatred that boils in her. Then she bolts inside the suburban penthouse door, dropping her high-strung tennis racket somewhere in her tawdry forgotten past.

Sweeping into the bedroom, Claudia slams the door and throws herself on the bed.

Her bedroom is pretentious, decorated in prime Beverly Hills-style luxury. Everything is white-and-red color-coordinated, even the trim on her pillows. She sits on her bed to make a phone call.

"Amanda, it's me," she says. "Claudia."

"Claudia, hi!" Amanda chirps delightedly. "What's up?"

"Oh, nothing," Claudia dully responds. "Georgie just left for a business trip to Las Vegas. I need to get out of this place."

There's only silence on Amanda's end but Claudia babbles on.

"Do you want to go out for dinner? I've been thinking about that new Thai place, corner of Sunset and . . ."

Claudia trails off.

A steak knife is carving meat in a plush, contemporary dining room. Amanda is thirtyish with plump but sensible thighs. She's setting out serving dishes and silverware for two on a candlelit table, clenching her portable phone between her neck and shoulder.

"Oh, Claudia, I'm so sorry," Amanda croons. "I just can't. I've got this date planned for tonight. And, well, as a matter of fact . . ."

A strong man's arms caress Amanda's bare legs.

Claudia's slightly desperate. "Oh, I see." she says. "Well, what about later tonight?" She pauses. "I really miss you, Amanda." She plunges on a little too eagerly. "I really need somebody to talk to. You're my best friend, and . . ."

"I miss you too, princess," Amanda says gently. "But I can't play tonight."

Amanda pushes the man's hands away from her waist. She feels slightly guilty about giving Claudia the brush-off. But what else can she say?

"I have plans, you know? And . . . stop it, Stevie! Anyway, I think this is going to be an all-nighter. Know what I mean?"

Claudia's sullen, silent.

Amanda knows she's hurt. "Sorry, baby," she apologizes. "But I'll call you tomorrow. Okay?"

Claudia's eyes fall in disappointment. "Sure," she says. "See you later, babe."

She hangs up the phone slowly and starts rubbing her arms with a blank expression on her face. Bitter tears well up in her downcast eyes. "What a lucky lady she is." She bites her lip. "Damn her."

Claudia stares at the elaborately framed, gold-tinged wedding photo on the dresser. Georgie and me, we really were the American Dream couple, weren't we? she thinks bitterly. Oh yes, we were—or I thought we were, anyway.

She leans forward and with a single swoop of her arm, knocks the heavy gilt frame to the floor.

[Smoke Break]

In the St Mary Magdalene Drive-Thru Chapel of Our Lady of Immaculate Deception in San Luis Obispo, California, Georgie Gust and Claudia Nesbitt, the American Dream Couple, exchange their vows. The white-robed transvestite priest is waving some horrible smelling patchouli incense over them and reciting some New Age horseshite.

Georgie's a ghastly, pale-faced corpse and Claudia's vaguely in shock as they gaze at one another, faking connubial bliss. Finally, their wide-open eyes meet; their white-lipped mouths say I do, but no words come out.

The white-robed priest says, "You may kiss the bride."

Stevie and Amanda swoon toward each other's lips in Amanda's immaculately set dining room. As she falls toward Stevie, Amanda notices that she didn't quite put the phone on the hook. The dial tone whines.

She bends over and hangs up the phone. Stevie reaches for her throat.

Amanda giggles with a sexual undertone. She's still under the spell of Stevie's tender caresses. She moans.

A swarthy, hairy hand strokes her bare chest, fondling her gold cross necklace.

In Claudia's suite, the bath water runs. Claudia lets the bubble bath soap slip through her languid fingers. She drops her sexy red bathrobe with the ruffled sleeves and reveals her black lacy lingerie. She broods sulkily as the soapy water fills up the bathtub, softly stroking her smooth belly.

In Amanda's penthouse kitchen, Stevie pops the cork on a bottle of champagne. Cabaret music plays softly on vinyl as white champagne bubbles spurt and gush from the chilled bottle.

Amanda laughs. "I want to be a bad girl tonight. Do you want to be my bad boy, Stevie?"

"Ready and willing, babe." Stevie smiles. "But do you think you're really ready for me? Are you ready for your all-nighter?

Amanda feigns shyness, still playing coy. "Maybe," she says. "What are you going to do for me?"

Stevie doesn't answer, at least not in words. But he moans, ever so softly against her.

Pushing back against the stove, Amanda whispers, "Yes, oh yes. Oh, baby." Her slender hands are locked into silver handcuffs behind her back.

She turns around toward Stevie and presses her slim body against his, breathing seductively and moaning harder. Their shadows cast forbidden movements on the dimly lit ceiling as the orchestra rises to a crescendo.

The small bell chimes as a well-dressed couple makes their way through the dusky entrance of some romantic nightspot. Claudia's seated at a candlelit table, eating dinner alone.

A white-and-black suited waiter approaches her table with a chilled bottle of red wine wrapped in a towel. He speaks to her graciously with a slight French accent.

"Would Madame wish another glass?"

Claudia samples the wine. Then she lifts her wineglass, which sparkles with the restaurant's many candles, and smiles at the well-dressed waiter.

The smiling waiter fills her wineglass and walks back toward the kitchen.

A handsome male twosome is escorted to the window booth opposite Claudia. One of them is darkly tanned, rather tall, and prematurely bald, but still handsome. He wears a flashy suit and brightly colored tie and speaks with a thick New York accent.

The tall man takes a seat with his male escort. The escort is blond and a business assistant type. He's also a sharp dresser, but his sleeves are rolled up like he's ready for business. He takes the seat opposite the tall dark man.

The two dump stacks of office paper on the table and immediately start talking serious business. Still, the blond has a slight air of passion in his voice when he converses with his dashing accomplice.

"So, I start tripping on this whole thing," he says, "about having all this potential, the best education, enough money to live comfortably, and then having little or no drive. It's like I'm waiting for an opportunity that might never come—you know, like I'll end up never living up to my full potential, or something. It's like a Generation X thing. Right?"

During their intense conversation the very tall man uses a lot of flamboyant hand gestures when he talks. He has big hands—a little like Georgie.

"Well, our parents, you know?" the dark man butts in, taking off on a digression. "All the baby boomers, they're all about to retire. You don't think they're scared shiteless to hand down their companies to us? And they should be, if you ask me. We live in this cult of luxury even if we don't have any money or any success. We spend money but we don't want to have to work for it. For us, the focus is the luxury, not the work. Other people, like our yuppie parents, for example, settle for the middle ground more easily. But, you know, it's the risk-takers, the big risk-takers, who get successful, who live up to their potential. People like you and me, John."

Their waitress, a flashy brunette named Shannon, dances over to the booth. She's bubbly and animated, but she's wearing a fake smile. Standing hipshot in front of them she momentarily blocks Claudia's view of the two men. The two men don't even notice Claudia.

"Hi! How are you this evening?" the flashily dressed waitress asks. "My name's Shannon. I'll be serving you tonight."

The tall, dark man lifts an eyebrow and checks her out. "Shannon?" he asks. "Or Shawna?"

"Shannon," Shannon repeats.

"Shannon," the man says suavely, like he'll remember.

"Yeah. You got it." She smiles. "Say, can I interest you gentlemen in a cold beer, iced tea, two-for-one margaritas?"

For some reason, Shannon's ingratiating manner really sets John off.

"A beer? Two-for-one margaritas?" he snorts. "What is this, a nuclear bomb? You don't want to have to call the cops on me now, do you?"

Unfazed by John's outburst, Shannon keeps smiling brightly. She looks sideways at the dark man, who tries to cover for John's irrelevant tangent.

"You've got to understand," he explains. "John here is an alcoholic. He's recently divorced. And besides, he's single, too."

John breaks into a smile.

"Guilty on all counts," he says. "I am. I admit it."

(Parenthetical Pet Peeve) The fact that OJ did it; we all know it.

Shannon smiles suggestively.

"So am I," she says.

"I'm okay," the dark man concludes. "How's about a dry

martini?"

"Oh, right!" Shannon blurts.

"What about you, John?"

A slightly more relaxed John looks up at his waitress.

"I'll take a Coke," he says.

The tall man looks amusedly at John.

"We don't have Coke, sir," Shannon starts to reply. "But is . . ."

John interrupts her with a wave. "It really doesn't matter," he says. "Just bring me a glass of water."

Shannon smiles again, eager to please. "Still a good choice!" she smirks.

Still, John's unresponsive. "Uh huh," he says.

Shannon bends over and whispers breathily into John's ear. "Tone it down some, okay?" she pleads. "I liked you all right until you started talking." She smiles again. "I'm willing to give you a second chance though."

Shannon walks away. She smiles at Claudia and then checks on the next table in her section.

The two men pretend to continue their slightly off-the-wall conversation. But the tall dark man is ticked off.

"What the fuck?" he says. "What was that all about?" His hands begin to fly and dance.

At the next table, Claudia's amused. She sips her wine as she watches him.

"That did not just happen. You're ridiculous, Johnny boy. You better shut up while you're ahead, you get me?"

A busy busboy brings sweaty glasses of chill ice water for the two men. The schmoozing twosome continues to converse and harangue each other excitedly.

Meanwhile, a temporary waitress who's filling in for Shannon follows up with the twosome's real drinks.

"Shannon likes you," the temp says to John. "She's a little bit embarrassed by your friend, but she likes you. Shannon's an awesome chick. Don't mess it up, chuck."

After dropping off their drinks, the temporary waitress scurries out of sight.

A few minutes later, the dark man's flamboyant hand gestures knock his ice-cold drink onto Claudia's lovely legs. The vermouth and gin splash over her perfect pedicure. Claudia's skirt's so short that she freezes up. She catches her breath.

"Oh!" she gasps.

The man jumps up immediately.

"Ah Jeez, I'm sorry, miss," he says. "I just . . ."

"I just knew this was going to happen," Claudia snaps. "The way you kept flailing your hands around like that."

(Parenthetical Pet Peeve) Spilling food on my clothes while I eat—out.

Claudia mimics the man, flapping her arms and waving her hands exaggeratedly. He rushes over to Claudia with his dinner napkin. He bends down to wipe the spilled gin and vermouth off her feet. But before he applies the napkin Claudia stands up in righteous agitation.

"Don't you dare!" she spits. "Don't you dare touch my . . ."

The man suddenly notices that this chick sounds strangely familiar.

"What?" he says, dazed. "Who?"

The man looks more closely at Claudia's frizzy red hair, her heart-shaped face, her green eyes—somehow, he seems to recognize her.

"I'm sorry," he repeats. "Excuse me, miss, but I—"

Claudia cuts him off again. She's a little weird-ed out, too. "Excuse me, sir. But if my feet are bothering you—"

As the dark-haired man and Claudia stand staring at each other, their eyes lock in a self-hypnotic trance.

"Excuse me again, miss," the man breaks the spell. "But is your name Claudia, by any chance?"

Claudia nods, speechless.

The man points to himself. "Remember me?" he asks. "I'm Sir Tony. Sir Tony Halldale."

Finally, Claudia snaps out of it. "Sir Tony?" she gasps. "Sir Tony Halldale?"

"At your service, Miss."

Sir Tony jumps to his feet and grabs Claudia's table with his big red hands. Claudia's green eyes widen.

"Hey, wow! Claudia! It really is you, isn't it?" Sir Tony beams. "After all dese years—it's really great ta see ya. Shite! You look fantastic! A little grape juice here and there maybe, eh, but still!"

Claudia laughs. "Thanks, Tony. And so do you. Look fantastic, I mean." Claudia quips. "The, uh, sideburns weren't your strongest feature."

Sidestepping Claudia's jibes, Sir Tony makes an obscure private joke.

"And so. The peach was peeled and here we are."

Of course, Claudia doesn't get it. "What? The peach?"

Sir Tony grasps Claudia's warm hands in a cool handshake and then realizes how impersonal the gesture seems. He moves closer.

"Well, well, well! Remember? 'Claudia the Crazy'?"

Again, the private joke's lost on Claudia. But she's desperate enough to play along and she laughs.

"A handshake instead of a kiss?" Sir Tony deadpans. "Here! Let me give you a hug!"

Claudia sways toward Sir Tony's embrace, his all-encompassing hands. "Oh Tony," she says. "It's really good to feel you."

Claudia knows she's a little too melodramatic, almost maudlin, almost mawkish. And besides, she's got a bad case of the giggles. As Sir Tony clasps her shapely figure to him, she starts to crack up.

But Sir Tony only sees Claudia's beautiful smile. Their warm hands caress one another—Sir Tony's swarthy, hirsute, dark; Claudia's slim, small, and white in his big palm.

"I don't mean to butt in, but . . ." Sir Tony hems and haws. "Do you mind if I join you?"

Claudia casts a sympathetic look at John, who's shifting uncomfortably in his seat.

"But, Tony," she says, "what about your friend?"

"Who, him? Forget about him," Sir Tony blurts out. "Johnny and I were just talking business. But we're done talking business. In fact, John was just about ta leave, weren't you, John? He's got, like, a very important date. Right, John?"

John smiles slightly sheepishly and pushes back his chair. "Yeah, sure thing, Tony," he says. "I'll catch you tomorrow."

"Right-o, John-boy," Sir Tony bluffs. "And, hey, let me know how your date works out!"

John hurriedly puts all the official papers back in his briefcase and gestures at the passing waiter. "Oh, waiter!" he calls. "Check, please."

The waitress, Shannon, comes swishing past, writing her phone number on a napkin. She presses the napkin into John's hand as he slips her the tip.

"I get off in 10 minutes," she whispers.

John winks at Sir Tony and walks briskly away.

Sir Tony takes the seat closest to Claudia. He's already forgotten John.

"So," he smirks, "alone at last."

He pulls his chair closer to Claudia's.

"I forgot to ask you. Are you expecting anyone?"

With a flippant gesture, Claudia waves off the question. "Just my husband," she says. Then she rushes on. "You know, Tony, you never used to ask to cut in back when we were in school. You just plopped down right beside me."

Sir Tony is only slightly abashed. "Back then, I was stupid, immature, impulsive, and . . . horny."

Claudia smiles at his sophomoric humor. It reminds her of the good old days, before Georgie and her. She laughs. "I'm just kidding, Tony," she says. "My husband isn't coming."

Sir Tony cracks a big smile. "Well, well! That's even better! For you and me, anyway!"

He pauses. "After all, you know what they say! Two's company."

Claudia smirks. "Tony," she says, "you really haven't changed, have you? You're still the same old Tony."

"Well, I mean," Sir Tony blusters. "You could be expecting your boyfriend, or something, and . . ."

Again, Claudia cuts him off. "Relax, Tony," she says. "I'm not expecting anybody."

"But is anybody expecting you?" Tony wisecracks. "I mean, like, do you have to be home by midnight, or you to turn into a pumpkin or something?"

"Jeez, Tony, relax! You're still the cautious one, I see."

"Cautious, but still alive. After all these wives." This time, the tactlessness of Sir Tony's joke surprises even himself. "Wow, babe," he apologizes. "That really was lame. My apologies."

"You don't have to apologize, Tony." Claudia's smiling, supportive. "That really was funny. You're a funny guy, Tony."

They stare at each other silently for several awkward moments, their faces slightly tense, their hands shy, nervous, their eager eyes.

Finally, Sir Tony breaks the rapt silence. "You know," he says. "It's been a long time, Claudia."

"Yeah, I know, Tony." Claudia pauses. "You left for New York that summer."

"Yeah, well," Sir Tony shoots back. "My dad died, you know."

"You hated your dad."

"Yeah, I did," he admits. "But after he was gone, you know, all the memories . . . and, well, anyway. I decided I liked everything about him. It was all part of the nostalgia."

"But you left me, Tony."

"Yeah, well . . ." Sir Tony trails off.

"Mmm," Claudia muses. "And then what?"

"You may not remember, but . . ." Sir Tony flashes back to his early college years as a J-school nerd. "I went up to Ithaca. I majored in Journalism."

Claudia, remembering, starts to feel strong again. "You know, Tony, you really make yourself sound like a creep." She takes a sip of wine, keeping her eyes on Sir Tony. "You've got to say it like you believe it. You've got to say it like you were proud. It's got to feel good to say it, like that. I went to Ithaca and majored in Journalism."

Sir Tony laughs. He's slipping into his TV anchorman persona. "It really does sound a little pompous, doesn't it?" he confesses. "But, okay. Ready? Are we on the air? Here goes: And so, after Claudia jilted me, I went up to Ithaca and majored in Journalism."

Claudia's surprised to feel the change in herself and Sir Tony. "Yes! Yes!" she cries. She's so excited that she claps her hands together.

Sir Tony is now transformed into a full-fledged TV personality.

(Parenthetical Pet Peeve) Ed McMahan saying "Amurrican," instead of "American" on his "American Family Publishers" sweepstakes commercials.

"I was the Big Man on Campus in my J-school class. And I'll tell you, folks, there's nothing like being a legacy at Ithaca.'"

Claudia pretends she's impressed. "Wow. Ithaca."

Sir Tony nods.

"Anyway." Claudia's mood shifts again. "All my friends left town that summer. Everyone left except me."

"I remember," Sir Tony sympathizes. "And then, right after school ended, your twin brother was in that bike accident."

"Jimmy. Yeah." Now Claudia gets serious. "I stayed with him in the hospital night and day for two weeks. Then I spent another six weeks with him, in bed at home."

Sir Tony pulls his chair closer. "You two were really close," he says. "How's he doing these days?"

"He made a miraculous recovery." Claudia smiles. "He's fine now—he's married, he has three children and a great job. He's really—" But Claudia breaks off, catching herself in mid-sentence.

"Well . . . ," she says. "Then again, I think maybe now he's doing volunteer work. Helping the homeless or something."

"Whadda ya mean?" Sir Tony slips back into his accent. "Why, dat's great news! Dat's really great!"

Slightly flustered, Claudia changes the subject. "Speaking of great news," she says. "I see you've done pretty well for yourself. I hadn't seen you in, oh, decades! And then, one day, I'm watching the five o'clock TV news, and suddenly, bang! There you are, big as life."

Claudia picks up a teaspoon and holds it in front of her mouth like a microphone.

"Good evening," Claudia says, in character. She's doing a pitch-perfect Sir Tony Halldale impersonation. "This is Sir Tony Halldale for the National News Tonight."

Sir Tony and Claudia laugh together.

"You know, Claudia, it's just the breaks," Sir Tony says. "I got a lucky break, is all. The old anchor called in sick and they needed somebody right away. So they looked at me and said, 'Let's give this bum a break.'"

Claudia briefly touches Sir Tony's hand. "So were you just . . . lucky?"

"Sure." Sir Tony strokes her hand. "They grabbed me, put a mike in my hand, a camera in my face, and said, 'Talk.' So I just started talking, and like they say: The rest is history."

Sir Tony and Claudia smile and gaze into each other's eyes.

"So. Enough about me," Sir Tony changes the conversation as a five-piece jazz band begins its evening set. "What've you been up to?" he asks.

Claudia pauses for several seconds before answering. "Well, I'm married," she says. "Yes. Married. To this wonderful guy, Georgie Gust."

Claudia feels a slight twinge of guilt at baring her marriage to Sir Tony. But she plunges on. "We've been married for 10 years. We have a wonderful mansion and a big estate out in the suburbs. Georgie's a self-made financial manager for his own company—Georgie Gust Enterprises."

Now Sir Tony shifts uncomfortably in his seat. She sounds pretentious, he thinks. But he doesn't say anything out loud. Instead he says, "He must be a really rich guy then, huh Claudia?"

"Yeah, I guess so, Tony." Then Claudia lies. "And a great husband, too."

"I'm terrible with commitment," Sir Tony confesses. "You have any kids?"

Abruptly, Claudia turns serious. "No," she says. "I can't have any. We've tried everything."

"I don't mean to pry, but," Sir Tony says, "is it really you, Claudia? Or . . ."

Sir Tony and Claudia's eyes lock. She seems distracted, distraught.

"Oh my God!" Claudia suddenly blurts. "Wow! For a second there, I just had this really strange déjà vu! But I didn't know who the third person was . . . . " Claudia trails off.

Sir Tony is a little confused, but also amused. "Third person?" he says.

"Yeah, Georgie!" Claudia gushes. "It's weird, the déjà vu gets so intense it's like I have to share. I have to admit I'm having it, or it's really like overkill."

Finally, Claudia realizes that Sir Tony is not sharing her excitement and calms down. "It's really overwhelming, though," she says. "You know, Tony?"

"Yeah, yeah. But relax." Sir Tony strokes Claudia's arm. "Don't blow the whole thing by talking about it. Just try to keep it going and keep it between us—just between you and me. Don't blow it by telling it to everybody in the joint. Don't get too excited. And if it works out."

On impulse, Claudia reaches over and taps Sir Tony on his nose.

"We're exploring other avenues now. Maybe adoption." Claudia smiles into Tony's eyes. "What about you?" she asks. "Are you married?"

Several glasses of wine later, Sir Tony Halldale and Claudia Nesbitt are still wrapped in an intimate tête à tête. Sir Tony is still carrying on his half-hearted seduction of Claudia.

"I thought you knew, Claudia." Sir Tony feigns embarrassment. "My third wife left me a month ago."

"Oh, I'm so sorry." Claudia feigns sympathy. "Do you mind if I ask what happened?"

"Absolutely, I thought you'd never ask." Sir Tony plays the wounded innocent. "She and some guy got together and together . . . and, well, you know the rest."

Although Claudia's secretly pleased, she pretends sympathy. "I, I'm sorry," she says. "Really, Tony."

"You are? You really are? Why should you be?" Sir Tony seems slightly too eager for sympathy. But maybe it's just the wine. "It's okay. Really. It doesn't hurt so much, now. I guess I shouldn't have taken so many trips out of town. But, then again, it sure as fuck was worth it."

Sir Tony and Claudia abruptly realize it's getting late. Sir Tony looks around for a waitress, but the place is empty.

"Where's the damn waitress?" Sir Tony curses. "Damn waitresses are never there when you need them." Sir Tony checks the dining floor again but there's no waitress in sight. "I could sure use a good stiff drink, right about now," he mumbles. "Guessing it must be last call."

Sir Tony changes the subject. "So, Claudia, tell me. Why are you here alone?" Sir Tony is probing for her weaknesses. "Where's Georgie, your husband? It's Georgie, right?"

"My husband's out of town on business." Claudia keeps up the façade. "He went to the trade show in Las Vegas. He'll be back in a couple of days."

She touches Sir Tony's nose again and smiles. But Sir Tony is still suspicious. "Are you sure, Claudia?" he says. "You wouldn't bullshite me, would you?"

Finally, a waiter (who might be Georgie's secret body-double) approaches their table. When the waiter talks, his voice echoes through the restaurant, as if it was a hollow shell. But still, Georgie's voice doesn't ring any bells for Claudia.

"All through with your plate, Madame?" the waiter asks.

Claudia's plate is wiped clean. For some reason, she has a big appetite tonight.

"What do you think?" Claudia says, trying to act superior. "Does it look like it?"

Georgie picks up her plate, and then Sir Tony's.

"Oh, and, waiter," Sir Tony says. "Would you bring me a dry martini? Uhh, and make it very dry, okay?"

Without waiting, Claudia butts in. "I'll have the same," she says.

"Two dry martinis, very dry," the waiter disguised as Georgie (or is it Georgie disguised as a waiter?) repeats. "Coming right up. I'll bring them right away."

Georgie the waiter walks away.

"So." Claudia leans closer. "What brings you here to LA?"

Sir Tony shrugs. "Oh, it's no big deal, Claudia," he says. "They're giving me the key to the city. You know, hometown boy makes good, the same old story."

"At least in this case," Claudia smirks, "the story has a good male lead."

Sir Tony smiles.

"It makes good copy, anyway."

The band strikes up another old standard.

Sir Tony perks up. "Listen, Claudia," he says. "You hear that?"

But Claudia doesn't pick up her cue. "What?" she says. "Is it . . .?"

"That song." Sir Tony winks. "Don't you remember?"

Claudia pricks up her ears and smiles. Slowly, she starts to sway to the beat.

The old sentimental song brightens Claudia's green eyes.

Sir Tony notices her big teary eyes and smiles. Suavely, he reaches for Claudia's hand. It's already in his lap. "Do you want to dance?

"What?" Claudia pulls away. "Here? No."

"Sure. Why not?" Sir Tony coaxes. "Come on, Claudia. Let's dance."

But Claudia still hangs back.

"After all," Sir Tony continues, "we haven't seen each other for a long time. And, besides, I'll be leaving tomorrow. Come on, Claudia, for old time's sake."

Finally, Claudia gives in. "Oh, all right," she sighs.

Sir Tony pulls back her chair and helps Claudia up from her seat. He's being chivalrous, and Claudia likes being wooed.

The Second American Dream Couple dance in the aisle. The off-duty waiters, waitresses, and kitchen staff crowd the doorways, watching and smiling.

As she swoons into Sir Tony's arms, Claudia's bright green eyes close. She remembers the last time, in 1988. The old sweet song continues

[Smoke Break]

The Wakefield High School gymnasium is glittering and glowing on Senior Prom night. Sir Tony and Claudia are the Prom King and Prom Queen, dancing to the same sweet old song.

A brightly-colored banner reads, "Wakefield Senior Prom, 1988: Living the Dream." The basketball court is filled with wholesome, well-groomed teens dancing to a five-piece lounge band, live. A well-dressed, pretty Wakefield coed is crooning.

A dateless Georgie sits behind the limelight, watching.

The old sweet song ends.

Sir Tony and Claudia keep on dancing.

Sir Tony kisses Claudia's cheek. She smiles dreamily.

Sir Tony escorts Claudia back to her seat and sits down beside her. He lifts his martini glass for a toast.

"Here's to, uhh . . ." He pauses. "What'll we say? Renewed acquaintances?"

Claudia smiles, lifts her wineglass, and raises it to his.

"Sure, Tony. Whatever you say." She clinks her wineglass with his. "To renewed acquaintances."

They both take deep drafts of their cocktails.

"Last call!" the bartender hollers.

After closing time, Claudia and Sir Tony stand outside the restaurant.

Sir Tony offers Claudia a handful of peppermints. Claudia pops a few into her mouth.

It starts to rain lightly.

"Oh, darn!" Claudia says. "I didn't know it was raining."

(Parenthetical Pet Peeve) Wearing glasses in the rain.

"Well, it wasn't raining inside," Sir Tony says discreetly. "Where are you parked?"

Claudia points toward a big black BMW coupe. "Over there," she says. "On the other side of that BMW."

"Wait here a minute," Sir Tony says. "Don't go anywhere."

Sir Tony dashes back into the restaurant and then returns with a big plastic-covered menu. He covers both of their heads with the menu.

"C'mon, babe. Let's go," he says. "We can dodge the raindrops."

As they briskly walk across the parking lot, Claudia clings to Sir Tony's arm.

"That was awfully resourceful of you," she says. "Opening my umbrella, I mean."

Sir Tony puts his arm around Claudia. "Come on," he says. "You don't want to get wet, do you?"

Sir Tony walks Claudia to her car. It is a brand new white Volvo. As they come closer, they see that one of her tires is flat as a rail.

"Ahhh, God!" Claudia blurts out. "I don't believe this! These are brand new tires!"

Once again, Sir Tony becomes her knight in shining armor. "Don't worry, Claudia," he says. "I'll change it for you."

"That's sweet of you," Claudia whispers. "But it's raining, Sir Tony. You'll be soaked."

Sir Tony brushes off Claudia's reservations. "I don't mind, Claudia. I'm already wet. See?" He shows her his damp pant legs and shirtsleeves.

"I'm wet already," Sir Tony repeats. "That's what she said, see?" Sir Tony winks at Claudia with a childish smirk.

She shakes her head and smiles. "You haven't changed much since junior high school," she says. "You know, I'll just call AAA. Somebody will come out. They'll have it fixed in no time." She pulls her cell phone out of her purse and begins to dial.

(Parenthetical Pet Peeve) No matter what I need in my handbag, it will be at the bottom, buried under all other contents.

Sir Tony quickly snatches the cell phone out of her hand. "Claudia, listen to me. It's the weekend, it's raining, and it could take hours for a truck to get here." Sir Tony locks her gaze with his. "Why don't I just give you a ride home? You can have the flat fixed in the morning." He gently takes the cell phone away from Claudia.

Claudia's eyes are glazed, her speech slurred. She's having trouble walking. "Yeah. I guess you're right, Tony," she says. "And, besides, I'm beginning to feel those martinis—I probably shouldn't drive. I usually only drink wine, you know."

As they begin to walk to Sir Tony's car, Claudia stumbles.

Sir Tony catches her, picks her up, and carries her in his arms. "You're right, Claudia," he says. "Maybe you did have one too many."

As they walk, Claudia looks at him with a suggestive gleam in her eyes. She nestles her head against his chest.

Sir Tony leans over and kisses Claudia on the mouth.

She returns his kiss, embracing his neck.

That old sweet song just goes on and on.

[Smoke Break]

Sir Tony slides in behind the wheel and switches the windshield wipers on high. The slight rain spatters on the windshield and puddles the black rain-slick streets.

As Sir Tony and Claudia approach Georgie and Claudia's swanky, three-story McMansion, Claudia leans over to give directions.

"It's the third house on the right," she says. "The one that's all lit up, like—"

Sir Tony butts in. "Like Claudia Nesbitt?" he smirks.

"Yeah," Claudia giggles. "I guess so."

In the pitch blackness of 3:10 am, Georgie and Claudia's American Dream Home shudders and huddles beneath the rain. The spotlights make ghostly shadows in the fog. (Somewhere, Georgie Gust is boarding an airplane in the same persistent rain.)

Upon some inscrutable signal from Claudia's fingertips, the white garage door of the three-car garage opens. A shiny new black Cadillac pulls into the driveway and parks in the garage, still dripping from the black night rain.

Sir Tony parks the big black Cadillac in Georgie's parking spot and turns off the ignition. Smiling, he turns to Claudia. But Claudia has her head down.

"Claudia," Sir Tony says, a little too brashly. "I just want to say thanks for a wonderful, wonderful class reunion."

But Claudia keeps her frizzy red head down and her green eyes turned away. "Yeah, I . . ." Claudia's voice trails off. "Thank you for the ride home."

Finally, she looks up.

Sir Tony puts his arm over the seat and leans in for a kiss. Impulsively, Claudia puts both arms around him. She pulls him closer. They rub noses. She smiles. Sir Tony's bright black eyes hypnotize her with a serpent's longing.

"It's so late!" Claudia gushes. "I know you have somewhere you have to be, don't you, Tony?"

"I've got nowhere to go, except . . .," Sir Tony blushes, "here, with you."

"Oh, Tony! You're so sweet." Claudia presses his hand. "Do you want to come inside?"

"I'd love to," Sir Tony says.

On invisible signals, the white garage door slowly closes behind them.

Outside, the black night rain keeps falling.

[Smoke Break]

White sunlight bursts in the plush, well-upholstered bedroom of Claudia Gust. From the bedside table, Claudia speed-dials someone on the pushbutton telephone. While waiting for a response, she paces the floor, obviously distraught, flustered, and slightly unnerved, almost hysterical.

Claudia's beautiful face floods with tears, her black mascara running down in streaks. She's barefoot in a white terrycloth robe.

On the other line, somebody sleepily picks up the phone.

"Hello?" Amanda yawns, still half asleep. "Who is it?"

"Amanda!" Claudia blurts out. "It's me! Claudia!"

Slightly hung over, Amanda mutters under her breath: "Shite."

"Thank God you're home!" Claudia frantically hisses, "You've got to come over right away, please!"

Amanda can tell from Claudia's voice that something's seriously wrong. "Claudia, what's going on?" she asks. She's fully awake now.

"Listen, Amanda!" Claudia whispers. "I can't explain right now. Just believe me—you've got to come over, right now. Please! And hurry!"

"Okay, okay." Amanda sighs. "I'll be right there."

Abruptly, Claudia hangs up. Still flustered, she rubs her slim arms nervously as she paces the deeply carpeted floor.

"Oh. My. God," she says. "I can't believe this is happening to me."

Finally, she stops and stares out the bedroom window. White sunlight breaks across the unkempt lawn, which is still wet from the black night rain.

"What am I going to do now?" she whispers to nobody in particular. And, of course, nobody answers.

Distraught and shell-shocked, Claudia starts to sob. Black tears roll down her ravaged face.

Black rain out of a clear blue sky.

[Smoke Break]

Amanda is still in bed with her beau. He's sprawled, face down, his face flat against the pillow. A few raindrops still fall outside the bedroom window.

"Who was that, honey?" a sleepy male voice asks. "Somebody I know?"

"It's Claudia," Amanda answers. "She sounds really upset. Like something's seriously wrong."

"Well," the male voice asks without getting up. "Did she say what it was?

"No. She didn't say." Amanda sits up in bed. "She just said she needed me right away." She pauses. "She was crying," Amanda says.

"Oh, okay." the male voice mumbles. "Why don't you go check it out?"

"Yeah. Okay," Amanda says. "I guess I have to."

Amanda puts her feet on the floor and stands up unsteadily. She heads for the cluttered closet and tries to find something decent to wear.

The male voice mumbles something into the pillow, still not getting up. "While you're in there," he says. "Get my overnight bag out, will you?"

Amanda takes out a black garment bag and lays it on the bed.

Finally, Stevie sits up in bed and turns his head. Surprisingly, he looks remarkably like Sir Tony Halldale, but 20 years younger and not prematurely bald.

"Thanks," he says. "Amanda . . . ."

"Oh, how sweet!" she exclaims. "You remembered!" She crawls onto the bed and snuggles up on his back and neck.

He grunts.

"I really don't want you to leave." Amanda sighs. "Can't you stay just a few more hours?"

The swarthy, black-haired man shakes his handsome head. "Sorry, babe," he says. "You know I can't. If my wife ever found out about you and me, she'd . . ." Stevie leaves the sentence dangling.

"But Stevie, you know it's my birthday." Amanda tries not to whine. "You can't leave. Don't leave me alone on my birthday."

"Ohhh, shite," Stevie groans.

"I'll do whatever you want me to do."

It's exactly the kind of offer that gets Amanda in trouble. Fortunately, Stevie's too polite to take her up on it. (Isn't he?)

"It's your birthday," he says. "It really should be the other way around."

Amanda's grateful for his consideration, but still desperate to keep him with her. "It doesn't matter," she says. "I need you."

Stevie pauses. "You'll do anything?" he asks, laughingly.

"Yes," Amanda says. "Anything."

Stevie sits up in bed. "You know what I've been asking for." Stevie smirks. "Are you willing?"

Amanda briefly ponders his proposal. "Okay," she says. "I'll do it. Just don't leave me."

Stevie laughs mischievously. "It's a deal," he says.

Squirming back into bed, Amanda starts passionately kissing him. Playfully, he spanks her ass. "Now, go see what's bugging Claudia," he says.

Amanda salutes him. "Aye aye, sir."

She slips on a terrycloth bathrobe and slippers on her way out of the room. Stevie laughs to see her stumbling out the door, half-dressed and half-cocked.

"And hurry back!" he calls.

[Smoke Break]

Outside, black thunderclouds and windy rain have closed in again.

At Georgie and Claudia's American Dream home, Claudia, looking into the small vanity mirror on her dresser, wipes away her black tears and tries to repair her ravaged face. Then she opens a drawer, rifles through a few pieces of stray lingerie, and finds a .38 caliber handgun. Gingerly, she picks it up.

She wipes her mouth, pushes back her hair, and raises the weapon slowly to her face. She looks directly into the barrel curling her finger around the trigger.

Outside black thunder crashes.

White lightning flashes.

Inside, the bedroom lights flicker on and off.

The gun drops from a startled Claudia's grip.

She peeks out at the crashing rain showers and heaves a deep sigh of relief. She picks the gun up carefully and puts it back into the dresser drawer.

Claudia rummages through seductive clothing and finds an unopened pack of ultra-long cigarettes and a lighter. Taking the old, stale cigarettes out of the still-wrapped case, she leaves the drawer open.

Claudia holds the unopened cigarette pack in her shivering hands. She takes a deep breath and opens the package. She takes out a cigarette and with her shaking hands places it between her lips.

She flicks the lighter but it only makes a small shower of sparks. Frustrated, she throws the lighter on the floor.

Claudia leaves the room with the old, stale cigarette still dangling from her lips. She stalks into the kitchen and frantically searches through the clutter in the cabinets, drawers, and counters. At the gas range, she turns one of the burners on high. She pulls back her hair, leans in, and lights her loaded cigarette with the gaslight flame.

She turns off the burner, steps back, and takes a deep, long drag. Her eyes roll up into her forehead as she inhales; she feels a relaxing, smoke-filled release.

After taking a few more drags on the cigarette, Claudia sits on the kitchen counter and opens the drawer beneath her. She pulls out a small porcelain saucer. Claudia flicks cigarette ash into the delicate piece.

Immediately, there's a sharp knock at the door.

"Amanda!" Claudia whispers to herself.

She darts out of the kitchen in haste.

In the white, high-ceilinged foyer, Claudia unlocks the front door. Without waiting, she swings the big, white wood door open.

"Amanda!" Claudia says. "I'm so glad you could come!"

Outside, it's still raining. Grey sheets of rain obscure the street, making it difficult for Claudia to see exactly what's on her stoop.

Before her is a chubby little redheaded, freckle-faced boy who holds an umbrella over his head with one hand and a box of chocolates in the other.

"Hi! I'm Banana," he says.

There's long pause as Claudia tries to understand the strange apparition that's appeared on her doorstep. But Banana keeps talking, oblivious to stormy thundershowers and black rainfall.

"I'm selling Boy Scout candy to help support my Sixth Grade class fieldtrip to Disney World. We've been saving box tops and coupons all year to help pay for the trip."

Claudia is still in shock. She really doesn't know what to say

"Would you like to buy some candy?" Banana asks. "They're only a dollar each."

Faced with Banana's cheerful cherubic demeanor, Claudia just stands numb, dumbfounded. She has no response. Instead of smiling, she turns deathly pale. Her black tears fall with the sputtering raindrops.

Finally, Banana tries another tack.

"You've been crying?" he asks. "What happened?"

But there's still no response from Claudia. Shivering, she only shakes her head and moans, "Oh, Banana."

Although he doesn't know what's happening, Banana takes the hint. "Maybe I should come back some other time," he says.

Claudia, still shivering, nods and closes the door.

With the heavy wooden door closed behind her, Claudia leans against the doorjamb and lets the shivering contortions play over her face. Suddenly she comes unwound with an awful, wretched scream.

While Claudia's still silently screaming, the doorbell rings again.

Claudia perks up, turns around, and opens the door.

This time, it's Amanda. She looks messy, like she just got out of bed, and is completely soaked with rain. She's more than a little pissed-off. "Claudia, what the hell's happened to you?" she blurts out.

Claudia starts to sob.

Amanda slips inside and shuts the door behind her. She soothes the troubled Claudia by patting her back and stroking her hair. After being upset, Amanda turns apologetic

"I'm sorry, Claudia," she says. "I didn't mean to be a bitch, whatever it is, I'm sorry."

But Claudia only cries harder. "Oh, Amanda, I'm finished. I'm through!" she says, "I fucked up. I mean, I really fucked up, this time."

"It's okay, honey," Amanda says. "Come on, now. You can tell me. What is it? What's happening?"

Claudia's crying fit finally runs out of steam. She slowly lowers herself onto the floor.

In her exhausted condition, she stares at the wedding pictures of the American Dream Couple on the wall until everything finally blurs and fades out.

Then she heaves another big sigh and stands up. Pulling herself together, she looks directly into Amanda's eyes.

"Oh, God, Amanda!" Claudia says. "Georgie's going to kill me!"

"For what, Claudia?" Amanda asks. "You still haven't told me."

In answer, Claudia says, "Follow me."

"Where?"

Claudia doesn't respond. Instead, she hurries up the stairs. She doesn't even look back to see if Amanda's behind her. Confused and upset, Amanda follows.

Claudia halts at the entrance to her bedroom on the second floor hall, and Amanda runs up behind her. The two stare at the white-and-red canopy that drapes over Claudia's bed. Convulsively, Claudia sobs again. She can't look.

There's somebody in the bed. Curiously, Amanda walks in to take a closer look. All she can see is an older man's premature-balding head peeping out from under the bedcovers.

Amanda's only a little shocked. So Georgie's lost a little peach-fuzz off the old toupée, she thinks. What's the big deal? She shrugs her shoulders and spreads her hands, palm-up, like she's still a little confused.

"Claudia, baby," she says. "I thought you said Georgie was out of town."

Claudia shakes her head. "Yeah. That's right, Amanda. He is out of town."

Amanda's still confused. "Well, so what?" she says. "Who's this, then?"

Amanda sees that Claudia's about to lose it again and immediately cuts her off.

"Claudia, shut up!" she shouts. "Just don't say anything! Just don't tell me, just shut up, already!"

Amanda walks up to the anonymous gentleman under the plush bedcovers. She lifts the rumpled bedclothes and peeks over at his face.

She gasps.

"Oh my God! Claudia!" Amanda shrieks. "It's that creepy TV news guy from Channel 43! That Sir Tony What's-his-face!"

Now it's Amanda's turn to be slightly hysterical.

"What's he doing in your bed?" Amanda demands. "Or maybe I should ask: What are you doing with that creep in your marriage bed? You should get him up and out of here before Georgie gets home!"

Claudia breaks down again. "I wish I could, Amanda. I really wish I could," she says. "But I can't."

Amanda shakes her head. "What do you mean, you can't?" she says. "Just tell him to leave. If he doesn't want to leave, just kick his ass out of here!"

Amanda steps over to Claudia, who's still standing by the door. She takes her by the shoulders and starts to shake her vigorously. "Listen, sweetheart—you've got to tell me. What's this creep doing in your bed? Where'd he come from? Where's he going? And where's Georgie? Do you even know?" she asks. "Do you at least know, or even suspect, what he'll . . . I mean, does he know anything about this, or . . .?"

Amanda whispers, pointing to the sleeping celebrity.

"This TV news creep. This Sir Tony Halldale, is he the real thing?" she wants to know. "Or is he just some kind of stupid mistake?"

Still, Claudia doesn't answer.

Amanda thinks the worst for a moment. "Or, oh, I get it!" Amanda says. "Did this guy try to rape? Oh, no. No!"

Finally, Claudia snaps out of it, and, crazily, bitterly, laughs. "Rape me?" she asks. "Oh, no. God, no! Of course not." Claudia shakes her head. "That's not the problem," she says. "The problem is I just can't wake him up!"

"For God's sake, Claudia!" Amanda asks. "Why not?"

"Because," Claudia pauses, "he's dead." Claudia burst into tears again.

"What did you just say?" Amanda demands. "You mean that TV news creep, that Sir Tony What's-his-face, that creep is dead? Like, really dead? And not just playing dead, or whatever? Oh. My. God! Claudia!"

Amanda leans heavily into the wall, eyeing the bed warily. "Oh my God!" she says again. "I am so not ready for this. You know, Claudia, that today's my birthday?"

Claudia covers Sir Tony's head with the bedspread again and walks over to sit with Amanda on the floor at the foot of the bed. They hang their heads in their laps.

Claudia starts rubbing her arms. They're both having an attack of bad nerves.

"Did you . . . did you kill him, Claudia?" Amanda asks,

suspiciously. "Please don't say you did. Because if you killed him, Claudia . . ." Amanda leaves the innuendo dangling.

Claudia shakes her head again. "No," she says. "No. No. No. I didn't kill him, Amanda. I swear."

"Then how'd he wind up dead?" Amanda demands. "For God's sake, Claudia! I mean, like, how'd it happen?" Amanda puts her arms around Claudia, but Claudia just keeps rubbing her arms.

"I swear to you, Amanda. I don't know. I really just don't know," she says. "All I know is last night we—we accidentally made love. It just happened. Then we fell asleep. And when I woke up, he didn't. He didn't wake up, I mean. I shook him and I slapped him. I said, 'Wake up! Wake up! Wake up!' But he didn't."

Claudia shakes herself awake again. "This is so totally unreal! Like some kind of bad dream, or something!"

"Yeah," Amanda sneers. "But, like, whose bad dream is it, Claudia? It's not my bad dream."

But Claudia's off on her own private tangent. "What I want to know is . . ." She pauses. "What am I going to do, now, Amanda?"

Amanda stands up and walks toward Claudia again. "I don't know, baby. I don't know," Amanda confesses. "All I know is that I'd like to get out of this room though . . . pretty soon. Like, right now. You with me?"

Like all catastrophic crash witnesses and tragic victims, Claudia and Amanda would so much like to just pick themselves up, brush themselves off, walk away from the crime scene, and never look back. But it isn't so simple, is it?

(We're not going to let them get out of it that easily, are we?)

Of course not.

Suffering another attack of shivers and jitters, Claudia whips out another ultra-slim cigarette. Amanda looks vaguely surprised.

"Hey!" she says. "Claudia! You started smoking again?"

Claudia shrugs, lights up, and takes a drag.

"I'm going to die anyway," she says. "When Georgie gets home."

"Oh, Claudia, that's no excuse! You promised! You swore! You said you'd never, ever . . ." Amanda's husky voice trails off. "Can I have one?" she begs.

The phone rings.

[Smoke Break]

562

Georgie Gust, in the grungy back seat of a cheap East LA cab, is speeding away from the Los Angeles airport.

Georgie is on his cell phone. While he talks, the cabdriver watches his suspicious tics and twitches with squinty eyes in the rear-view mirror.

"Hey Claudia, sweetheart," Georgie gushes. "It's me, Georgie."

[Smoke Break]

Her black-rimmed eyeballs rolling in a silent movie scream, Claudia looks daggers at Amanda. They're both sucking down their ultra-slim cigarettes like kids with popsicles.

"Oh, hi, Georgie!" Claudia chirps. "Honey, what's up?" Claudia nervously taps Amanda, gritting her teeth.

"Hey! Are you okay, baby?" Georgie asks. He sounds worried. "You don't sound too good. You sick or something?"

Still shivering slightly, Amanda shakes her head, slashing an invisible knife, hand across her throat, mouthing silent words to Claudia. Just get rid of him she's saying. Do what you have to do. Claudia tries to ignore her.

"Oh, no, hon. I'm all right, really." she says, trying to sound convincing. "I just have a slight headache. I'll be okay."

Claudia changes the subject. "But what about you? Are you all right?" she asks. "How is Vegas? How's the trade show? Are you having a good time?"

In the black-and-white cab, Georgie smiles, the cabdriver's eyes narrow.

"Pretty good," Georgie says. "But I missed you."

Georgie squirms in his sagging passenger's seat. He's slightly aroused, thinking of Claudia. He's wishing he was already home, with Claudia in the plush bedroom, watching her slowly strip for him from her elegant black satin dinner-clothes down to her sexy lingerie. Down to her shapely, blue nail-polished feet, her pretty, slightly misshapen toes.

"So, I left a day early," Georgie says. "I'm in a cab. I'll be home in 15. And I bought you something special that you're really going to love. See you soon, babe."

Claudia's petrified, paralyzed, in rigor mortis.

"Oh. And, hey, Claudia   " Georgie pauses for the suspense, "don't forget what you promised me."

Claudia is silently screaming, half-alive, half-dead.

"What you said about that sexy lingerie."

The white-and-black cabdriver watches Georgie smile.

"I've been waiting."

[Smoke Break]

Downstairs in the kitchen, Claudia vomits on Amanda's feet.

"This is it, Amanda," Claudia coughs. "He's coming."

Amanda joins in on the gag, pouring hers on the side.

"Oh. My. God." She spits. "He's coming? Claudia, he's going to kill you."

"You, too," Claudia reminds her. "He'll be here any minute."

Without warning, Amanda experiences a brief moment of sanity. "It's no use. He's going to find out sooner or later anyway. Give it up, Claudia," she says. "Just call the police."

Claudia spins. "Are you crazy?" she screams. "I'd kill myself before I let Georgie get something like this on me, he'd never let me forget! He'd torture me with it for the rest of my life."

Claudia pants, staring at her friend with wild eyes. "Seriously, Amanda. I'd rather be dead than—"

"Oh, shut up, Claudia. You would not," Amanda snaps. "You'd do anything to stay alive and get this corpse off your back, and still cheat on Georgie, too."

Obviously, Amanda knows Claudia.

"Well," Claudia protests. "It was a good line, anyway."

They both light another ultra-slim cigarette. They wave the pungent smoke over the puke.

Finally, Claudia finds resolution.

"Come on, Amanda!" she shouts. "We've got to do something!"

Barefoot and in bathrobes, their hair a mess, Claudia and Amanda run up the stairs.

Downstairs, the doorbell rings.

Claudia and Amanda freeze.

They tiptoe back down and watch, horrified, as the big brass doorknob slowly turns. The white front door slowly opens and Georgie walks inside, closing his umbrella.

"Honey! It's me!" he shouts. "I'm home!"

Claudia and Amanda are still petrified, mortified, and incapable of saying a word.

"Hi, Claudia!" Georgie bursts out. "Aren't you glad to see me?"

Claudia tries to fake a big, sexy smile. Her whole body's frozen. She feels somewhat like a cryogenically preserved corpse.

Still in bathrobe and slippers, Amanda stands behind Claudia, her big blue eyes shooting darts at Georgie.

Just get rid of him, she's still thinking. I don't care what you have to do.

Feigning warmth, Claudia hugs Georgie tightly. Beaming with satisfaction, Georgie smiles at Amanda. He feels perfect love toward all women.

Sneering, Amanda gives him the finger.

"And, you know, dear," Georgie chatters on, "the whole way from the airport, the freeway was wide open. Absolutely no traffic."

"Oh, really?" Claudia says. Over Georgie's shoulder, she's waving Amanda up the stairs.

"It's like the whole world was bringing me home to you" he pauses, waxing poetic.

"Or, anyway," he says. "The East LA freeway was."

Amanda rolls her eyes and gags silently. "That's so nice," Amanda says. "You're so, so . . ."

For once, words fail her. She looks at Georgie with knives in her eyes, and then bolts for the door.

Claudia breaks away from Georgie and charges toward Amanda.

"Where are you going?" she demands. "You can't leave now."

But Amanda wins the doorway. At the threshold, she turns around triumphantly. "I can't?" she sneers. "Just watch." Before she leaves, she tosses a match into the disjointed hallucination of Claudia's burning house.

"I forgot," Amanda says. "I left a fire burning in my fireplace. You can't be too careful, you know." She looks straight at Georgie. Then she flings the zinger. "You shouldn't play with fire, you know." She pauses. "The fire that warms you can be the same fire that burns your house down. If you're not careful."

All three stand stupefied, paralyzed, mortified, for a brief moment. Finally, Amanda says, "Or whatever."

After a moment, Georgie's nose twitches. Despite his passion for Claudia, he looks around distracted. He sniffs.

"What's that smell?" he says.

Embarrassed, Claudia looks away.

Amanda reaches for the doorknob.

They all hear the upstairs toilet flush.

Amanda stops dead in her tracks. She and Claudia stare at one another, wide-eyed.

"Claudia, dear?" Georgie asks. "Who's that upstairs?"

Claudia's speechless. So is Amanda. Georgie doesn't get it.

(But the joke's really on him, isn't it?)

"Claudia, darling?" Georgie asks again. "Who's upstairs in our bathroom?"

Claudia's still stupefied, tongue-tied, gagged, and bound. So is Amanda. And Georgie still doesn't get it.

With a brisk, predatory leap, Georgie wrenches open a nearby closet and pulls out a sawed-off shotgun.

Claudia and Amanda are scared shiteless.

Stalking upstairs, Georgie is cautious brandishing the sawed-off shotgun in his arms. As he peers suspiciously over the foyer, the upstairs bedroom door slowly creaks open.

Sir Tony Halldale walks out. He's totally nude, except for the cocktail napkin he's clutching over his flaccid manhood. He's still half asleep and half hung over like a walking zombie.

Claudia and Amanda gasp. It's as if Sir Tony's been miraculously resurrected from the dead.

Sir Tony's still groggy. He is oblivious to the man with the shotgun that stands in the swanky second-story hallway. He's just looking for his old high school sweetheart and long-lost love, Claudia Nesbitt.

"Claudia?" he calls.

Without sobbing, Claudia hides her face in her hands.

And Georgie? Of course, Georgie's enraged. Georgie's fuming! He stomps back down the stairs, throwing away the sawed-off shotgun in disgust. He starts stalking Claudia, instead. He figures that shooting is too good for her. He'll strangle her, with his bare hands.

"Claudia, dearest?" he snorts. "Who the fuck is that?"

Sir Tony peers downstairs at the Three Musketeers: Claudia, Georgie, and Amanda. He's still befuddled, bewildered, baffled.

"Claudia?" Sir Tony sniffs. "Who are these people?"

Stepping between Sir Tony and Georgie, Amanda finally answers:

"Sir Tony Halldale, I'd like you to meet Claudia's husband, Georgie Gust. Georgie Gust, I'd like you to meet Claudia's old high school boyfriend and romantic lover-boy, the Channel 43 TV anchorman, Sir Tony Halldale."

"Pleased to meet you," Sir Tony blusters. "Charmed, I'm sure."

"Shut up!" Georgie screams hysterically. "You! Just shut up!"

"But Georgie, dear," Claudia murmurs. "I can—"

"Just shut up!" Georgie shouts.

"Claudia, I—" Sir Tony starts to say.

"You! I told you!" Georgie shrieks. "Just! Shut! Up!"

Sir Tony, Georgie, and Amanda look at Claudia.

"Claudia," Georgie says.

"Yeah, Claudia," Amanda says.

"Uh, Claudia?" Sir Tony says.

Outside, the brake pads of a delivery truck screech.

"Oh, no." Claudia says. "It happened again." Sheepishly, Claudia tries to smile.

Sir Tony and Amanda look at Georgie.

Georgie looks down. His shoes are planted in puke.

All we can hear is a fury of gagging and vomiting, until the doorbell rings.

Dear Diary:

I believe that it is better to tell the truth than a lie. I believe it is better to be free than to be a slave. And I believe it is better to know than to be ignorant.

Part V: The Crack-Up

After Georgie discovers Claudia's half-hearted affair with Sir Tony Halldale, Georgie and Claudia's American Dream marriage is on the rocks. And as Georgie and Claudia's American Dream marriage cracks up, their posh New Age Suburban Yuppie McMansion also starts to disintegrate.

Remember the previously well-manicured lawns and groomed shrubbery, the swanky, silvery dining rooms and upholstered, posh living rooms? You can't help but take a certain prurient interest and voyeuristic satisfaction watching the whole elaborate dream fall apart.

In slow motion, in time-lapse photography, we watch Georgie's and Claudia's dream house splinter and crack. Cracks and chinks appear in the superficial brickwork veneer and simulated wood-grain siding. The white concrete sidewalks and black asphalt driveway start to break up like they've been hit with an LA earthquake. Shaggy, overgrown shrubbery and frayed, ragged grass grow over the white-pillared front porch. Dirty dishes pile up in the kitchen sink, dust settles over the plush upholstery and shag carpets, and elegant telephones ring in the empty rooms and abandoned closets.

Nobody answers.

(What's the question?)

Is anybody home?

Georgie, maybe.

Claudia's gone.

[Smoke Break]

A black-and-white cab pulls up to the shaggy, grassy curb in front of Georgie's McMansion. The blue-uniformed driver takes a suitcase out the trunk and slams it shut. Then he scuttles to the cab door.

With a single arm gesture, he flings the back door open. A shapely, slightly older woman with frizzy red hair steps out. The blue-uniformed driver slams the door shut and accepts a small gratuity from the shapely red-haired woman. He tips his cap.

The driver scuttles back to the front seat and jumps in. The cab drives away.

Out of boredom, Claudia dances around the white concrete sidewalk and across the scraggly, un-mowed front lawn. She strikes a pose here and there, like she's playing for the invisible video camera. It's like she's practicing for a ballet recital, having nothing better to do. (But we know, don't we? She's dancing for us.)

Inside the swank three-story Dream House, Georgie's private phone rings. He takes the call. Absentmindedly, he looks out the front door and sees a shapely, red-haired woman standing on the front walk.

"Hey, mom!" Georgie blurts out. "Great to hear from you!"

Georgie looks down at the nail polish bottle in his hand.

"Great!" he enthuses. "Everything's just great!"

But suddenly, Georgie sees Claudia prancing and dancing on the shaggy front lawn outside the big picture window and abruptly cuts off the conversation.

"Listen, mom. Something's come up," he says. "I have to go. I'll call you later."

Later that evening, Georgie and Claudia's slightly decrepit, three-story McMansion is lit up like an airport.

Claudia's astonished. Even in decay, the Georgie and Claudia's American Dream McMansion is so much swankier, posher, and larger than her wildest memories.

"This is our house?!" she gasps.

Georgie blurts out an irrelevant comment. "My Pops died," he says, deadpan. "A couple years ago. While you were away."

Claudia's immediately downcast and saddened by the news.

"I'm so sorry," she says. "Really."

Georgie shrugs. "You know, me—" he starts to say. But he changes his mind. "He left me a lot," is all he manages. "Shite, Claudia!"

Swinging wildly between extremes, Georgie's mood changes again. "I have my own private airplane!" he blurts. "A $68 million fucking jet airplane!"

Of course, Claudia's mood swings, too. "I'm so glad for you," she says. "Really."

They're a couple of real swingers, aren't they?

Georgie Gust and Claudia Nesbitt.

[Smoke Break]

The next day, Georgie and Claudia sit at a rusty lawn table in the slightly overgrown back yard of their enormous three-story McMansion.

"Why did you come back, Claudia?" Georgie wants to know. "It wasn't, like, me, was it?"

"I just wanted to come back home," Claudia answers. "To visit the past. In search of—oh, I don't know."

She changes the subject.

"How has your Tourette's been?" she asks. "Are you taking your meds?"

"Fucking awful!" Georgie says. "Can't you tell? The fucking meds. . . " He trails off.

"Are you still drinking lots of coffee?" Claudia asks. "It's not good for your Tourette's, you know." Claudia pauses before making a calculatedly tactless remark. "You're not the easiest person to live with, anyway."

But Georgie still doesn't get it. He's off on another tangent.

"God, Claudia!" he bursts out. "It's been, like, what? Ten, eleven years?"

"Since what?" Claudia asks.

"Since you . . ." Georgie trails off. "You know."

Claudia changes the subject. "You may not believe this, but I missed the shite out of you, Georgie."

"What do you mean, you missed me?" Georgie shouts. "You at least have to meet me! I broke up with you, like, five, six times!"

Claudia shrugs and waves her hands. "Yeah, well," she says. "That was a long time ago."

"And besides that," Georgie rants. "You cheated on me with that, that creepy TV news guy, that Sir Tiny What's-his—"

"Sir Tony Halldale," she sniffs. "And he isn't—"

But Georgie keeps ranting. "And then you cheated on me with another woman!" He shakes his head and mutters: "A fucking beautiful woman."

But Claudia only scoffs. "Beautiful, yeah. She was beautiful." She's amused. "I told you that right from the beginning, Georgie."

"Oh, yeah. You told me. And then you lied to me. You said it was a platonic, friendship thing. No sex. That's what you said."

"Yeah, I said that." Claudia smirks. "I said lots of things. But things change, Georgie."

"I was completely honest and open with you!" Georgie accuses.

"And you wouldn't even have a threesome with me."

Finally, Claudia laughs out loud. "Listen to you!" she snorts. "She was a lesbian, Georgie! She only liked women."

"So what? God!" Georgie mocks. "Can't I like women, too?"

"Can we go inside, Georgie?" Claudia asks. "I'm really cold."

"You can say that again," Georgie mumbles.

"I'm really cold," Claudia says.

In the slightly decayed, dusty living room, Claudia and Georgie are kissing on the white-and-red plush-upholstered sofa.

Georgie starts getting romantic. "Come back to me, Claudia," he says. "You know I love you."

But again, Claudia only scoffs. "Thanks for the offer, Georgie-Boo," she says. "Maybe I'll think about it."

[Smoke Break]

Days later, Georgie is in the slightly cluttered, messy den, playing back telephone messages while Claudia listens.

"You see how much I love you, Claudia?" he says. "I have at least 30 of your messages saved on my voicemail."

But Claudia's not interested in replaying the past. "This place is a mess!" she says. "Don't you ever throw anything out?" She stomps out.

Georgie continues to play back Claudia's old telephone messages, when a strangely familiar voice abruptly blurts out:

"You think I'm gone, Georgie. But I'm not," she says. "You won't get rid of me that easily. You think you can, but you can't."

A burst of static blasts from the answering machine—and then the strangely familiar voice blurts out:

"You'll never forget me, Georgie. No matter how hard you try."

[Smoke Break]

Amidst the rusty lawn furniture and ragged, overgrown grass, Georgie and Claudia dine on the patio beneath a sagging white-and-red umbrella. Music plays softly from the car stereo, which is tuned to the Golden Oldies station. Claudia's put on her old white-and-red summer dress and floppy hat, and has dyed her hair summer blonde. In this current incarnation, she's the epitome of the blonde bombshell, while Georgie's the dark and handsome stranger.

There's something strangely ritualized and excessively formal about their speech and manners, as if they're simply repeating old scenes from their distant past.

Finally, Georgie stands and holds out a hand to Claudia. In their empty driveway, Georgie and Claudia dance to the same old sweet song that plays on the coupe's speakers. Georgie and Claudia are specters, ghosts in some old black-and-white silent movie, as they dance on, and that old sweet song slowly fades away.

As the western sun slowly sets behind them, Georgie and Claudia dance on to disco music from the BMW's car stereo. The stereo is playing the feverish, pulse-thumping disco beat of some great '80s classics, "Stayin' Alive," "Night Fever."

Claudia grooves like a natural, her hips swaying and thrusting with the heavy beat, but Georgie's still Georgie. Although trying to be suave, debonair, romantic, he can't help coming off as clumsy, slow-footed, heavy-handed.

As they dance together in front of their enormous three-story McMansion, white mist slowly rises from the concrete, and swirls around their feet. The old blue moon is a glittering disco ball overhead.

Georgie sweeps Claudia off her feet and whispers: "I love you, Claudia. Come back to me."

"Ouch!" Claudia says. "You're standing on my toe!"

"I'll do whatever you want. Just let me kiss your feet!"

"Oh, Georgie, please! Don't grovel." She titters.

Later that night in the big white-and-red canopy bed, Georgie and Claudia lie together, exhausted. Panting. Sweaty.

Claudia's only slightly relieved, still a little frustrated. "Oh, Georgie, you make me queasy!" she says. "I'm sick, dizzy."

Georgie laughs. "It was good for me, too," he says.

"Georgie," Claudia says, getting serious. "I didn't understand a word you were saying, when we were . . . you know. You just started spewing out obscenities and swear words, cursing, all that gibberish. You didn't make any sense, Georgie."

Georgie's apologetic but still laughing. "I can get like that, sometimes. Sorry."

Abruptly, his mood swings. "By the way," he says tersely. "You forgot your fee." He pulls a fistful of bills from the cluttered nightstand. "It's $4.25, right?" he sneers. "You're from East LA, right, home of cheap sex and cheaper thrills?"

Laughing, Claudia plays along, brusquely pulling on her clothes.

"Yeah," she smirks. "Your 10-minute hour is up, sir. But remember: Next time, pay me before you fuck me. Or you won't be getting any."

"Here" Georgie throws the handful of bills on the bed. "Keep the change, sweetheart."

Claudia stands and stuffs the bills into her brassiere. "You're a real big spender," she coos. "Do you want me to leave? Right now?"

Georgie gets on his knees and grovels. "Don't leave me," he whines. "Why don't I just become your little boy toy? You need that, don't you?"

"You already are," Claudia shoots back. "Since we kissed on the beach, and you fucked me, I've got you hooked. You're already in love with me."

Georgie sighs. "You're my one and only. My soul-mate."

Claudia simpers. "You're my sugar daddy, my lover boy, my Romeo. And yes, I'll marry you."

Unexpectedly, Georgie stands up, brushes himself off, and gets serious. "You know, Claudia," he says, "the chances of us working out together, married, are as good as they'd be with anyone else."

Claudia laughs. "We're made for each other, Georgie-boy." She pauses. "You've got secrets, I've got secrets. And we've both got problems, big problems."

"So?" Georgie mopes. "The marriage is off, no wedding ring, then, huh?"

"No!" Claudia sneers. "That's just a silly tradition."

Georgie grins. "You know, Claudia," he says, "sometimes I almost wish you were real."

She laughs and then falls back into the big white-and-red poster bed, tired of the game. Georgie snuggles up to her; trying to rekindle the sparks of their old flame, but Claudia is too chilly.

"Umm, Claudia? May I please touch your breasts?"

"Not tonight, Georgie," Claudia says over her cold shoulder. "Thanks for asking, though."

Georgie rolls over to sulk.

[Smoke Break]

The next morning, Georgie is rummaging in the fridge for milk.

Across the messy kitchen, Claudia whispers, "Hey, Georgie, look."

But at the moment, Georgie's got his head stuck up the fridge. "Just a minute, sweetheart," he calls. "I'm busy."

With her sultry, silky voice, Claudia whispers again, "Georgie? Oh Georgie-girl."

Behind Georgie's back, Claudia drops her top. "I need you to tell me, Georgie," she purrs. "Is one of my tits bigger than the other?"

Finally, Georgie turns his head. His jaw nearly drops. "Jesus, Claudia," he says.

"Well?" she demands.

"Hell, I don't know," Georgie mutters.

He turns and runs up the stairs, diving into Claudia's white-and-red bedroom. Sitting on the bed beside the cluttered nightstand, he hits the speed dial on the telephone.

"Mom, she won't have sex with me," Georgie complains. "I don't know what the hell's going on. I don't know what the hell's wrong with me?"

Georgie's mother's voice echoes like a diva's across a colossal studio amphitheater.

"It's dat Claudia, Geow-gie. I always told ya. She's just usin' ya fer what she can get outta ya! Ya gotta get rid o' her, Geow-gie. Ya know she's not right for ya—I always said so."

Georgie whimpers and pulls the phone away from his head.

"Ya gotta get out mow-ah," his mother insists. "Find yourself a nice goy-il, who'll take care o' ya, and give ya some adorable little kids. I always told ya, Geow-gie, didn't I?"

Georgie holds the phone at arm's length and waits silently, patiently, for Mumsie's mother-and-son sex talk to just stop.

Finally, he just sets the phone down on the nightstand and goes back downstairs.

Well, here we are again, folks, aren't we? Yes, it's Another Day in the Secret Life of Georgie Gust. Only this time, Georgie's not alone. He's still trying to sort out his complicated love/hate relationship with Mrs Georgie Gust, Ms Claudia Nesbitt.

In his white terrycloth bathrobe, Georgie peers down at his coffee, like a psychic reading tea leaves. As he peers, he whispers absent-mindedly to himself: "Stale. Dark. Sweet. Addictive. Strong."

He slowly lifts the thermos closer to his lips, inch by inch. Then, at the last second, he backs off. Finally, he just pours the whole thing down the drain. He watches it slide out of sight with longing.

In a self-mortifying fit of thwarted outrage, he grabs a pack of his favorite smokes. Gnashing his teeth and baring his claws, he rips the pack to shreds. Next, he grabs the carton out of the freezer. Growling and foaming at the mouth, he starts tearing up the carton.

When his schizophrenic fit of self-abasement and pious abnegation is finished, he finally pauses to look out the window and think. His self-conscious mind's gone blank, but in his collective subconscious he hears a strangely familiar voice whispering.

"I don't think you really miss me, Georgie-boy. I think the only thing you really miss is the sex."

Even alone, Georgie finds himself repeating and replaying the same old stupid, tired scenes, saying the same old stupid words, over and over again.

"You didn't miss me, Claudia. I broke up with you like, five times."

This time, Claudia's response is slightly different. (But how can that be, if she's just a memory?)

"But you always came back for more, didn't you?" Claudia repeats. "And then you wanted to marry me."

"Who wanted to marry who?" Georgie asks Claudia (Or whomever.) "I wanted to marry you?"

"Don't you remember, Georgie?" Claudia whispers. "You bought me that enormous diamond."

Georgie changes the subject. "Let me ask you again, Claudia. How do you think our marriage would work out if we ever got married? And see what answer you come up with, now that we've been married."

"Well, the marriage might be hell," she says, "but the sex would be great!"

[Smoke Break]

Claudia is taking a walk with her old friend and neighbor, Sara, indeed, Greg's old Sara. She's pushing a stroller with Claudia. On the curbside, Georgie is taking out the garbage that Sara reminds him of and what Claudia might really be—just garbage. He pointedly tries to ignore all of his neighbors. But Claudia won't be ignored. Never.

"Georgie! I'm so glad you came out," she says. "I wanted to introduce you."

Georgie snifts. "What's that smell?"

Claudia's miffed. "It's really none of your business," she says.

"But I've been drinking wine and smoking pot. With Sara."

But what about Greg? What about us, Claudia? This is crazy as fuck, man!

Claudia and Sara impassively look Georgie over. "Please not in front of our diminutive, our little one."

(Parenthetical Pet Peeve) "Natural" childbirth ranking right down there with "natural" dentistry.

"Oh, and Georgie," Claudia says. "This is my wife now, remember Sara? She completes my sentences. She completes my life. As you, Georgie, do not."

"Greg didn't either, as you can see, Georgie," adds Sara.

They walk on. The new threesome.

[Smoke Break]

Upstairs in the old master bedroom of the slightly decrepit McMansion, Georgie spies on Claudia and Sara, who have bunked up in the guesthouse.

Across the scruffy unkempt lawn they spy on him back through the blinds of the guesthouse window. At the exact same moment, all three shut the blinds. But Georgie can't stay away from the window for long.

Slipping silently into the master bedroom, Claudia sneaks up behind Georgie and puts a gun to his head. Georgie's still occupied with the guesthouse and doesn't notice until-the ear-splitting sound of 10 explosive pistol shots, their echoes slowly fading in the black night.

[Smoke Break]

Claudia charges out the guesthouse door and bursts in Georgie's front door.

A silent fire alarm is screaming.

We still hear Claudia perfectly, though. Just like she's standing right in front of us.

A strangely familiar voice says: "I'm just a habit, Georgie. An addiction. I don't need you anymore, see? I've got my life together. I've got it all figured out. And what about you, Georgie-boo?"

Georgie's eyes are desperate, scared, haunted. He's ready to give up. Is he really dying, already?

576

Slipping up behind him, Claudia tapes his mouth shut and cuffs his wrists to his ankles.

In the old master bedroom Georgie seduces Claudia's bare feet with his mouth. Bending over the languidly reclining Claudia, Georgie makes an awkward, lumpish figure. He can't find his balance. He falls to his knees. His hands are still cuffed behind his back.

Claudia demands a pedicure, but Georgie, salivating, is incapable of submitting. Stroking her arms and waving her shapely bare feet before his nose, Claudia teases him as the silently screaming alarm clock on the nightstand passes 4 full hours.

Finally, she rips the tape off his mouth and watches him squirm and wriggle against his bonds.

Frustrated and enraged, defiant and abject, Georgie begs. "Come on, Claudia. You can't leave me like this."

Impulsively, Claudia gives in. She undoes his cuffs. "You're right, Georgie," she says. "We've got to give our marriage more time to mature. We can work things out, can't we? If we only try."

Georgie starts to cry.

In his mind, Georgie is still in cuffs, his mouth taped shut. The Black Magna Dominatrix, Claudia, stands over him, shaking her whip and chains.

"Georgie, you fool!" she taunts him. "Of course I was just using you whenever it was convenient for me. I was just trying to make you my slave. Just look at me! Do I look like some submissive, whining bitch? I'm the perfectly empowered, dominant woman! I'm the super-woman! And I never even told you I loved you, not once! It was all in your head, Georgie-boo!" She scoffs. "God! Get a life, or something, will you?"

Suddenly, Claudia coughs. She can't seem to breathe right. Something's stuck in her throat. She spits it out and turns to Georgie, stronger than ever.

Writhing and groveling in his bondage, Georgie tries to fight her physically, with little effect other than a feeling of puny ridiculousness.

Claudia only laughs. "Georgie! You pitiful little worm!" she says. "You're fighting!"

Georgie's voice is stifled, muffled, "Stop! Stop!" he cries.

Claudia mimics him. "Thnop! Thnop!" she snorts.

She takes a stranglehold on Georgie's cock, kissing him while he's holding back. She pulls out a rubber and snaps it against his thigh. Then she makes him kiss her ass. Slowly, suggestively, she undoes his pants, coughing and hacking asthmatically, bringing her face closer and closer to his groin.

But when Georgie starts to respond, she snaps at him. "Don't touch my breasts!" she commands. "Don't even ask."

Slowly, seductively, she undoes her bikini bottom.

Still writhing in a slow motion striptease, she tosses the condom away.

"Now, Georgie," she whispers. "Get me pregnant."

Georgie's still bound and gagged, struggling and suffocating.

"No!" he shouts. "You bitch!"

"Thno!" Claudia mocks. "Nyu bith!"

Claudia lowers herself onto him, taking him inside her. "Georgie, you fool!" she coos. "I'm a social worker! I'm only here to help you."

"Get off!" Georgie screams. "Get off!"

Claudia's now perfectly calm, cool, collected.

"Oh, Georgie. You see, I am." She towers above him. "I am getting off. And now I have complete control over you."

Suddenly, the telephone rings. Strong fists pound on the door.

Georgie shudders and explodes inside her.

Claudia smirks. "And now, you've gotten me pregnant! You'll never be free from me, again! As long as you live." Claudia thrusts her face close to his, whispering into his still twisting and writhing features. "Don't you understand, Georgie?" she whispers. "I only want to abuse you. I love abusing you. Because, you see, I really don't love you. In fact, I think I really hate you now."

"Fire Department!" stout, authoritarian voices shout. "Police! Open up!"

(Parenthetical Pet Peeve) Door-to-door evangelizing.

The sturdy white front door comes crashing down.

Still chafing his wrists and pacing back and forth, Georgie's wiped out.

"It never ends!" he sobs.

Claudia walks out, casting a last look over her cold shoulder.

"I'll call you," she says.

And then she walks out forever.

[Smoke Break]

The silently screaming alarm clock reads: 10:00 am.

On the other side of the wall, we hear the sounds of a man and woman having sex.

The old master bedroom is decorated with erotic artwork.

The anonymous man's feet hang out of the sleep-rumpled bedcovers.

The old master bedroom sounds hollow now, and there's the ripping, tearing sound of fabric being hit, repeatedly, over and over again.

In the white-and-red canopy bed, Georgie's under the rumpled bedcovers jerking off with his laptop on his chest. He's watching porn with his headphones on and he's still thinking of Claudia.

The silently screaming alarm clock reads 10:15 am.

Georgie is still jerking off.

The silent alarm clock reads 10:44 am.

Georgie's tired and sweaty. He tries one last time.

By his side, the clock face turns ahead to 10:45 am.

There's a big sigh as Georgie gives up.

"This is pathetic," he says.

That night, Georgie is still in bed with his laptop. But now Claudia's beside him.

"Stop working," she nags. "Put the computer away, Georgie. Just go to sleep."

Georgie shuts the laptop up.

"Thank you, dearest," he says. "You know how much I love you."

"I love you, too," she says. "Do you want to have sex?"

"Claudia? Sweetheart?" Georgie asks. "Is that you?"

In a black silk negligee and sexy undies, Claudia slowly leans toward him.

With a snarl, Georgie puts a gun to her head.

[Smoke Break]

In the old master bedroom, Claudia suddenly wakes up, startled, sweating.

There's no one else around. Georgie's gone.

She pulls out a dildo from under the sheets. She drops it on the floor.

She sighs with exhausted relief

"Ah, fuck," she curses. "I'm really a sick bitch."

[Smoke Break]

It's a scorching hot and dry Southern California day outside some desolate, anonymous motel room somewhere, in a sleazy little beach town, in the off-season.

In the anonymous motel room, the cheap ragged blinds are closed. The white sun bleeds horizontally into the dusky studio motel set, making black and white shadows like bars in the stifling and stuffy air.

Georgie's shivering, suffocating in smoke, but he's still wrapped up in a blanket. His face is drenched with sweat. He can barely suck in a stale breath of fresh air.

Women's panties and assorted dildos are scattered on the floor. Georgie surveys the wreckage: her notes, her gifts, and dead flowers, a bucket of water.

The silent fire alarm finally screeches on. And with it, Georgie is also set off.

"Kill me! Kill me!" he screams "Fuck you! Fuck me! Fuck the world! I want off!"

Georgie dunks his head in the bucket of water, gasping for breath.

He sits on the bed, panting. Slowly, Georgie removes a .44-caliber revolver from a black leather bag and starts to play with it. He plays the 1950s Hollywood cowboy, twirling the big ugly revolver around his trigger finger, pretending to shoot over his shoulder.

Then nonchalantly he puts the barrel of the gun inside his mouth and aims upward towards the top of his head. After a moment, he takes the gun out of his mouth.

"The biggest mistake people make in killing themselves," Georgie explains matter-of-factly, "is not shooting straight."

He squints, as if reading the old broken script from invisible cue cards.

"Don't aim for the back of the throat, you'll just blow your neck out. Aim straight for the roof of the mouth. That's where the brains are."

He wraps his lips around the gun and pulls the trigger.

The hammer clicks harmlessly.

Exhausted, Georgie sits down hard on the old broken-down sofa. He lays his head back and shuts his eyes, laying one hand over the gun, which sits still on his lap.

580

Through the walls, Georgie hears a couple arguing, pots and pans banging, furniture sliding across the floor. And then a little girl cries, "Mommy! Mommy!"

Still half-asleep, Georgie hollers through the wall. "Shut up, little girl!"

A man's distant voice shouts, "You fucking bitch!"

The dull thud of a body hitting the floor, the little girl sobs, "Mommy!"

Wearily, Georgie gets to his feet still carrying the gun.

He crosses the room and puts his ear against the wall.

Silence.

Dear Diary:

I can't challenge myself to deal with—the "what is" and not the "what is not."

Part VI: The Flashback

Georgie reclines with a half-smoked cigarette on the closely clipped front lawn of his modest, three-story suburban home in an anonymous subdivision. All too soon, the smoke runs out.

Georgie groans as he rises to his feet.

He walks down the deserted beachside street along the windy shorefront, near a flashily lit convenience store.

Sluggishly, slump-shouldered, he slouches through the swinging glass doors and into the air-conditioned store. He walks through like a zombie, like a rat in a familiar maze grabbing exactly what he wants.

Georgie pays the pretty sales clerk for a pack of smokes and a snack. She smiles.

"Have a nice day!" she chirps.

Georgie grunts, turns, and leaves.

On the waterfront Georgie strides home with his trembling hands full, trying to smoke a cigarette and eat a burrito at the same time. Suddenly, he's struck with a wild idea. He juggles the burrito and the cigarette, pulls a memo notebook from his back pocket, and scribbles:

"WRITE DOWN ALL THE THINGS I WANT TO DO WITH MY LIFE. START WITH TODAY."

Then he draws a flashing light bulb (for inspiration, get it?), which he turns into a fat lady bending over, seen from behind.

Satisfied, he shuts the book and walks on.

He starts humming the song he heard playing when he was in the shower. He passes another sleazy, fleabag motel and keeps singing to himself: "Such a lovely place . . . such a lovely space . . . ."

Out of nowhere, a strangely familiar woman's voice starts humming the melody.

Georgie and Claudia make a cute meet. (Don't you think?) Like some cute teenage surfer couple in some wholesome, 50s beach movie, they're both singing.

"We are all prisoners here, of our own device . . . ."

Abruptly, Georgie stops singing, but Claudia keeps right on. "Livin' it up at the Hotel California."

She's not embarrassed. She's not shy. (She's singing for us, isn't she?) And when she sees Georgie watching, she only sings louder.

"Such a lovely place, such a lovely place, such a lovely space."

Georgie looks down at her shapely, well-manicured feet.

Suddenly, Claudia stops singing too.

He's looking at her brightly colored, bluish-painted toenails.

As he walks past her she finally speaks to him.

"What are the chances of that?" she asks.

Georgie stops staring at her feet and briefly looks into her eyes.

"Huh?" he asks. "Of what?"

Claudia smirks.

"You were just singing 'The Hotel California,' weren't you?"

Georgie's too befuddled and embarrassed to answer.

"I don't know," he stammers. "I don't remember."

Claudia laughs.

"Well, don't be embarrassed! You don't need to be shy with me. That's amazing, isn't it? I mean, like, the coincidence—us both singing the same song at the same time, like that?"

Finally, Georgie lightens up and laughs a little.

"Yeah, that was weird." he admits. "You were singing 'Hotel California,' too, weren't you?"

Intrigued by his mysterious shyness Claudia tries to draw Georgie into a conversation.

"Hey, you live just down the corner of the next block, don't you?" she says.

She pauses like she's just remembering something—she doesn't know what.

"Oh, hell!! I know who you are!" Claudia snorts. "I know where I know you from!"

"Yeah?" Georgie says. "Where?"

"You're the guy who's always out there on the front lawn, smoking a cig. Right?"

But Georgie is still staring at her feet.

"Yeah, maybe," he confesses. "I guess."

Georgie's evasive, noncommittal. But Claudia picks up on his shyness and confusion.

"Hi. Hey!" she says. "You really are anti-social, aren't you?"

Politely, Georgie corrects her.

"Not anti social," he says, "Just non-social, maybe."

Georgie's still being evasive, but Claudia doesn't push the issue. Instead, she simply acts supportive, compassionate, caring.

"Wow!" she gushes. "That's amazing! I just had this flash, like, you know, déjà vu or something. I had this flash like we've met before, in another life, or something, maybe?"

Still, Georgie says nothing. He can't think of anything to say, and he can't escape the feeling that he's stuck in some old, bad dream. So Claudia picks up the slack, all by herself.

"Anyway, I was just on my way to get my nails done," she says. "I've been over at the Sea Port for the past week."

She pauses, then confides.

"It's this professional pedicurists' convention I have to go to for work. It's so damned boring!"

Finally, Georgie breaks his stupefied, tongue-tied reserve and blurts out:

"What's your name? If you don't mind me asking."

"I'm Claudia," Claudia smiles. "Claudia Nesbitt."

"That's nice," Georgie flashes back. "Or, I guess that's nice, huh?"

"Yeah, I guess." Claudia laughs. "What's yours?"

"I'm Georgie," Georgie agrees. "Georgie Gust, or, at least, I think I am. That's who I was the last time I checked."

They shake hands, firmly. Georgie's grip is strong, but Claudia's is stronger.

"You've got a firm grip there, Mr Gust," Claudia laughs. "Would you like to arm wrestle?"

Georgie apologizes.

"Sorry," he says. "I didn't want to hurt you."

Georgie looks down again at Claudia's open-toed feet. Claudia's hooker-blue toenail polish is peeling off intriguingly. It looks slutty, Georgie thinks. But sweet, like sex candy.

[Smoke Break]

There are doctor's papers, notes, and conference binders strewn around the cluttered bedroom area of the cheap motel room.

Georgie's giving Claudia the pedicure she always wanted in the brightly lit bathroom. He's using "New Blue" nail polish, Claudia's pick. Claudia basks in Georgie's rapt attention.

"I really can't believe you've never given a girl a pedicure before," she says. "You're just so . . . so good at it!"

Georgie basks in Claudia's praise. "Really?" he says.

He buffs furiously on the last bluish layer, laughing at himself for being so strung out behind the whole foot-polishing routine. But it's turning him on, sexually, at the same time.

It's making Georgie horny, Claudia, too.

[Smoke Break]

As sunset fades over the white sand beaches Georgie walks home still excited by this afternoon's meeting with: The Love of My Life, the Number #1, The One and Only, Great Love. My soul mate, Claudia Nesbitt.

Just as he gets home the phone rings. He rushes inside.

When he picks up the phone, he's already missed the call.

He pushes the "MESSAGE" button.

Out of nowhere, Claudia's silky, languorous voice fills the empty room.

"Hey Georgie," she purrs. "I was just thinking of you. I was downstairs at one of the lectures. It's sooo boring. I wish I were with you, instead. Doing . . ." she pauses suggestively, "you know."

Georgie's swept up and possessed by the fragrant memory of Claudia's shapely feet, blue toenail polish, and the fragrant smell of her foot-sweat wafting to his nose.

Almost immediately another message comes in, clashing with the previously recorded message.

Out of nowhere, Claudia's choked-up, sobbing voice fills the empty room. She's very distressed, nearly in tears.

"Hey, Georgie," she says. "It's me again. Claudia. Hey. Ugh. I'm just calling . . . I'm just calling because . . . I'm sorry. I'm just so bored at this stupid conference. I'm not going to go to this class I have in 10 minutes. I'm getting so sick of listening to the same thing over and over again. I'm just in my room, taking a bubble bath. Anyway, I'm sorry to bother you. Thanks for letting me vent."

Almost immediately the phone rings again.

Georgie picks up the phone.

"Hello?"

"Georgie?"

"You must look beautiful in that bubble bath."

(Parenthetical Pet Peeve) Image consultants.

"Oh, Georgie. That's the nicest thing anyone's ever said to me."

And she really means it, too.

"Seriously, Georgie," she says. "That is one of the nicest things a guy has ever said to me. You just don't know . . . the things guys say, when they . . . you know."

Through the swirling mists of the motel bathroom, Georgie massages Claudia's feet. He makes wild, passionate love, orally to her fetidly smelly feet.

She moans in ecstasy. "Oh, please." she pleads. "Don't stop. Do me right on the arches."

Georgie is in ecstasy as her feet quiver with delight.

[Smoke Break]

Georgie and Claudia wake up together both still fully clothed. Georgie smiles into Claudia's eyes. She immediately falls back to sleep.

Gently, Georgie caresses her hair and her feet. For a few brief moments, he watches her sleep, still oblivious. Then he leaves, quietly, without waking her up.

As the cheap motel room door closes, we see the blue nail polish bottles strewn across the cluttered nightstand. Beneath them, Georgie's left a note that reads, simply:

"Thank you.
GEORGIE"

[Smoke Break]

Georgie comes home with a Styrofoam cup of coffee in his hand. As he steps onto the front porch, he tells himself he's really ready for the day. He opens his mailbox and shuffles through a few bills. Then he unlocks the front door and steps inside the empty house.

The house is still a mess, with dirty dishes and clothes lying haphazardly throughout the kitchen and the living room. Quickly Georgie picks up the dirty clothes, cleans a few dishes, and sets his house in order before he finally sits down to write the first installment of *The Secret Love and Death of Georgie Gust and Claudia Nesbitt*.

I'll have to begin the story with me, as ridiculous as that sounds, he thinks. It's been forever since I actually sat down to write.

He starts writing:

By the end I knew I'd succeeded. It was just one of those things.

586

I enjoyed myself and left. That's all that mattered.

God probably took delight in watching his orchestration of me that day.

I guess I'll just chalk it up to "personal growth."

The next day, things were even better.

I'll probably never hear from her or see her again—or, maybe not for a week at least, anyway.

He turns on "Hotel California" on the CD player and keeps typing through the whole day without distraction, looping the one song over and over again.

Out of nowhere, Claudia's brisk business-like voice breaks into the quiet room.

"Hi, Georgie," she says.

Dear Diary:

I learn to be quiet. To shut the fuck up, learning to be silent more and more, and loving, because if my silence does not love it will make me insensitive, which I certainly am at times. I don't mean to. And then my silence is that of a cemetery—dull and dead. It will not be a silence that can celebrate, sing, dance, and bloom in a thousand and one flowers. And love is only possible if you are fearless. Maybe I am the man who is afraid and perhaps cannot love.

Part VII: The Fantasy, I

The blue full moon lights up Georgie and Claudia on the white sand beach. They're a happy-go-lucky fun couple, all perfectly white-toothed smiles and sleepy, bedroom looks, like they're posing for cheap promotional brochures for some ritzy beachside resort or sweaty tourist spa, somewhere in Southern California.

Georgie and Claudia chase each other playfully around the big white sandlot. Claudia dips her feet in the white-foamed seawater as she sits at the edge. Georgie tries to lick Claudia's wet, gritty feet, but Claudia girlishly grinds his face into the salty tidewater, using her perfectly manicured, stylish feet to hold his head down. Georgie's hair bobs up and down with the rising and falling waves as Claudia laughs.

As the sun sets, Georgie and Claudia dance in the empty beach parking lot near their sporty gull-winged car. The car's CD player is set on high volume, playing 80s disco music with a pulsing, throbbing beat, but slightly shrill, unnervingly tinny through the metal speakers.

In the background, a silent fire alarm wails—abruptly, the whole scene changes.

[Smoke Break]

Wildly flinging and throwing himself around the crowded studio, Georgie is playfully beating himself up, imagining that he's Claudia.

"Help!" he shouts, mocking himself. "Somebody save me! Help!"

He's completely alone in the studio. (Except of course, for us.)

Georgie keeps screaming.

Still nobody answers—the whole scene changes.

[Smoke Break]

Georgie timidly knocks at the half-open door to Claudia's pad. He's got an invitation, but he still doesn't know what to expect. And, of course, he's shivering, nervous, excited.

Claudia greets Georgie at the door in sweet dishabille.

"Come in," Claudia purrs in her husky, low voice. "We've been expecting you, Georgie."

We? Georgie wonders. But he doesn't keep wondering long.

Georgie pushes the door open and finds Claudia kissing . . . another woman. Georgie's surprised to see that it's Claudia's friend Amanda (But, where's Stevie?)

Both Claudia and Amanda are topless. Claudia wears sleek, black latex tights.

A middle-aged couple observes the festivities—a white-haired man in his 50s and his distinctly younger wife, in her 20s, and all of wide-eyed innocence, watch stiffly, sitting side by side.

Sultrily, seductively, Claudia welcomes Georgie to her den of sin.

"Tell me a little bit more about yourself, Georgie," Claudia vamps. "I really want to get to know you."

Somehow, Claudia seems to have sprouted sharp, pointed teeth and blood drips from her bright red lips.

Georgie immediately turns to run away. He tries to open the front door but the lock jams. He shakes the handle rapidly expecting Claudia to sink her fangs into his neck at any moment.

Claudia changes again, becoming a sweet sex kitten, coy and playful. Her whiskers twitch.

(Parenthetical Pet Peeve) Small dogs who hump my legs.

"Oh, Georgie," Claudia purrs. "Please don't leave. I want to introduce you to my favorite sex toy and lesbian lover, Amanda."

Amanda simpers and preens for Georgie. But Georgie, out of nowhere, starts screaming:

"You're fucking with my mind! Both of you! Bitches!"

"I'm not fucking with your mind," Claudia snaps back. "Damn it! I told you I wouldn't do that, I told you! Don't you believe me?"

Georgie writhes and grovels on the floor, a nervous wreck—somewhere in the background a silent fire alarm goes off.

Georgie pounds his fists on the floor and screams, and the fire alarm keeps on wailing—inexplicably the whole scene changes.

At a trendy yuppie coffeehouse in the same big city, Georgie and Claudia sit on the fashionable terrace sipping coffee and relaxing with smokes. With the three-fold stimulation of coffee, cigarettes, and Claudia, Georgie waxes poetic.

"The morning cup of coffee," Georgie rapturously enthuses, "has a subtle exhilaration about it, which the happy influence of the afternoon or late night cup of tea cannot equal. The pungent fragrance, the piquant aroma, the racing pulse—the rumbling bowels."

Claudia agrees.

"It's true," she says. "A splash of coffee in the morning really gets me going. You know, sitting here, like right now? I feel so romantic and free. I feel free to be me."

Georgie changes the subject.

"You know, dearest, when I got that money from the savings and loan trust fund, I suddenly felt . . . trapped."

Claudia agrees. "Yes, dear," she says. "I know just what you mean."

Georgie ignores her. He's caught up in his financial woes.

"You know though, sweetheart," he continues. "If I did accomplish the whole financial coup at the bank, it's only to the good. It's all . . . good . . . it's mainly because I was driven by the need to know whether I could accomplish something I wasn't sure I had the capacity to do. Like, pull off a big financial scam. I was trying to get over, you know, the self-doubt thing. My impeccable morals were totally out of the picture."

Claudia laughs shrilly. "Business first, then ethics, right?" Claudia smiles. "Oh, Georgie. You're such a card."

Georgie sulks and nods self-importantly.

"Yes, I suppose you're right, dear." He takes a sip of his triple-strength latte. "Yeah, I guess I am."

Claudia keeps preening and grooming him.

"Besides," she murmurs. "Morality's mostly a matter of geography. And look where we are . . . what city is this, Georgie? Do you remember?"

Still Georgie ignores her.

"I know, dear." Georgie makes a flippant gesture. "It's all very nice . . . nice, yeah. But, you know, something's still missing."

Claudia's baffled. She raises her high-arched eyebrows.

"Missing?" she asks.

Georgie pauses a few seconds, exhaling cigarette smoke from both nostrils. Finally he turns and looks at Claudia as if he's just remembered she's there.

"You know, dear," Georgie continues, "at times, I think I'm overly rebellious. I just really don't want to miss this opportunity to rebel, you know."

Claudia's eyes widen. She nods. "Yes, dear, I know. I understand perfectly."

She pauses before expressing her disagreement.

"But if you think about it, Georgie, darling." She smiles. "Every act of rebellion expresses some sort of nostalgia for innocence. Doesn't it? At heart?"

Georgie's surprised to hear Claudia dabbling in profundities. He sips his triple latte and continues. "But people, kids our age" Georgie frowns sagely. "We all have the same problem."

Claudia falls back into her supporting role. "What problem is that, dear?" she says. "I guess I just don't understand."

Georgie settles comfortably into his superior role. "The problem is, Claudia," he lectures, "how to rebel and how to conform at the same time. Look at how we're solving the problem. You and me, we defy our parents and run away and get ourselves in trouble. And then—"

Claudia gently cuts in. "And then we smile," she says.

Georgie frowns and nods. "Yes. But without any reason," he says. "Without any reason."

Claudia basks in Georgie's approval. "Yes, of course, dear." She pauses. "But that's what gives the smile its charm."

Georgie changes the subject. "Listen, Claudia," Georgie gets serious. "If I told you I was going to make a realistic decision, you would immediately think I'd decided to do something bad. Am I right?"

Claudia squirms. "I'd base it on your past history," she equivocates. "Realistic or not."

She pauses. Then she smiles. "But reality, my dear. Reality is something we'll rise above. My Georgie told me that once upon a time. Long ago."

Georgie nods, content in his wisdom to let Claudia recite his own profound aphorisms for him.

"As a youth, you learn." Claudia recites. "As you get older, you start to understand."

(Parenthetical Pet Peeve) The older I get, the faster time passes.

Finally, Georgie cuts in.

"But in our youth" he says, "we know everything. Old people just believe everything. There's a big difference, Claudia."

Chastened, Claudia casts down her eyes.

"We must shock old people out of their minds," Georgie

continues. "Generally, we're the ones who keep them up to date."

Claudia frowns, confused and troubled. "I don't know, Georgie. But," she wonders, "well, if we're so smart . . . so what?"

Claudia plunges on.

"I mean, we know everything don't we? But what about our money and our future . . .? What's the plan? Where are we headed next? What's our destiny now that we're always running away?"

Georgie's slightly nonplussed, but he doesn't show it. "Well now, Claudia" he says, "let's just not look too far ahead. That, I think, would be a mistake. A big mistake."

Claudia's relieved. "Okay, then," she says. "Let's just tackle one thing at a time."

Georgie's gratified by her submission.

"Yeah, right," he says. "We'll just have to learn the rules of the game. But we have to stay low-key for a while . . . until we make our big move."

"But that means," Claudia adds, "that we'll have to play the game better than anyone else."

Suddenly, Georgie's stricken by remorse. "Man!" Georgie abruptly shouts. "I'm starting to feel real guilty about the whole bank-job thing. I don't know why. It just struck me."

Claudia bites the nail on her middle finger hesitantly. Is Georgie going to start getting moral or something? she wonders. Finally, she reminds him:

"There may be responsible people but never guilty people. My Georgie told me that too, long ago, in another country."

But Georgie's still serious. "No. Seriously, Claudia." He grimaces. "I think we have a problem. I really think, morally, we should give the money back. I'm just too nervous. I'm afraid I'm going to blow it, or something."

Georgie lights another cigarette but on the wrong end.

Claudia sips her coffee.

"Calm down please, Georgie," she cautions. "Don't lose your head now."

Now it's Claudia's turn to be smug, wise, superior. "We have to continue on a path. Our guiding path has to be clear to us at all times. Our path's not far away, it's right here. We have a car right here. We have money. Lots of money! We have everything we need. What else is there?"

Now Georgie's relieved. He knows Claudia's behind him 100%.

She's with him, heart and soul. He feels he can bare his soul to her, just this once.

"I know we've just met, but . . . ." He pauses. "Claudia, I like you. You fascinate me."

"I like you too, Georgie," Claudia murmurs.

"Lovers," Georgie pronounces, "on the other hand, know just what they want and not what they need. We really don't need this money. Because you and me, Claudia, we've got each other. We want wealth but right now we really only have each other."

Claudia agrees.

"We do. I've got you, Georgie." She pauses. "And you've got me. I guess you could say that we're fortunate in that sense."

Georgie waxes poetic again. "You see, Claudia," Georgie proclaims. "America is like a whole big apple pie, set out on the counter somewhere, right smack dab in the middle of 10 billion starving people. We thought we were the greatest nation on earth. But, somewhere, we made a mistake. We violated the law, the law of God. And, depending on when you do it, and whether you get away with it, you can't defy the laws of God without paying the consequences, sooner or later."

"Yes. Oh, Georgie. You are so very right."

Claudia flashes and glows with Georgie's wisdom. But abruptly, Claudia's mood darkens.

"You know, Georgie," she cautions, "we probably have more ability than will power. There's no limit to how complicated things can get when one thing leads to another."

Claudia wants Georgie to save her, to protect her, to be her big strong man. She wants him to be there for her. "You're right," she faces facts. "We could go to prison if we don't hide out for the rest of our lives. The cops are after us. And, like, we don't even react to them. Like it really doesn't even matter."

Claudia pauses, her high-arched eyebrows furrowed with thought.

"What do prisons do, anyway?" she asks seriously. "They don't rehabilitate criminals, they don't protect us. What the hell do they do, anyway? They make criminals. Don't they?"

"They make you think," Georgie answers, turning hard-bitten. "They make you think about the big questions. Who you are, why you're here, how the hell you got here. And especially, how the hell you're going to get out."

"You just sit in a cell somewhere with a bunch of other criminals and brood over the nature of things, I guess," Claudia muses. But suddenly she has a change of heart.

"Let's turn ourselves in, Georgie! Should we?" She doesn't wait for an answer. "But secretly, we'll give the money back. Right? We never had a plan anyway. What were we going to do? Just go and get married too young, move into a condo by the beach and grow old and tired of each other? Go on spending money on things we really don't need? We'd be the All-American retired couple."

Georgie nods. "Sort of," he says.

Claudia grabs his arm and starts dragging him across the parking lot. "Come on, Georgie!" she shouts.

Georgie, reluctantly, lets himself be dragged toward the getaway car. "Okay," he mutters.

"Come on, Georgie!" Claudia repeats. "We'll be clean! We'll be free! But, more than that, we'll be happy!"

"Let's put the whole bag of loot, all fifty thousand bucks, in the Salvation Army bin in the parking lot," Georgie whispers. "We'll help others and ourselves. Whatever."

Georgie ponders briefly, almost reconsiders, and then stands resolved.

"We'll be broke. We'll be crooks. But at least we'll be off the hook." Georgie strikes a noble pose. "People have got to help each other. Don't they? It's nature's law."

The couple pays their check with some of the money from their bag of loot. They leave a big tip. Then they walk over to the Salvation Army bin in the parking area and toss the whole bag of money inside.

They jump in the getaway car and squeal out of the parking lot. Moments later, Georgie and Claudia are driving along the eight-lane freeway.

(*Parenthetical Pet Peeve*) No matter how late at night, no matter how far out I am in the country, there's always a car coming to make me wait when I want to turn left, there are cars waiting to turn left, there are cars coming from the left when the right side is clear. When the right side is clear, there are cars coming from the left.

"I'm taking you to the airport, babe," Georgie speaks loudly over the roar of the freeway. "You should go back home. Just leave me here."

Claudia looks at him in surprise. "What? What are you going to do?"

"Damn it, Claudia! My head's like a frigging prison. All I can get out are words."

Georgie turns to Claudia with a stricken look. "I need some private space away from . . . from us. I need time to think about things. Don't worry, though, we'll meet up again. When I find a safe hideout, I'll send for you. We'll get wasted together on my 21st birthday."

As the sleek sporty getaway car speeds down the freeway, the whole scene changes once again.

In an enormous crowded airport somewhere in the same big city, Claudia's about to board her flight. Georgie's holding her hand and looking sincerely into her eyes.

Claudia's giving him mixed messages, he thinks.

"We'll write?" she asks. "We'll keep in touch?"

Georgie shrugs. "No. That's too risky," he says. "Just meet me. When the time's right, we'll make a fresh start. We won't rob anyone. We'll just talk, and go to college together or something, if you want. No strings attached. It'll be perfect again, Claudia. Like it was. You'll see."

Claudia's still confused, ambivalent, noncommittal.

"I don't want to take the Baccalaureate exam again," she complains. "I already failed it once. I want to start all over again, from the beginning. I want to make a fresh start."

Georgie shakes his head. "This time, we'll be victors together. You and me." He nods. "Just wait and see."

Claudia seems unsure. "Wow," she says. "I can't believe I've grown so close to you, you bad boy. You're a bad boy, Georgie. Do you know that?"

"Bad boys can grow up to be good men," Georgie insists. "You wait and see, I'll be a man when you return. Things will be better."

Claudia starts crying. "No. Really, you're perfect, Georgie. Please don't change. I love you just the way you are."

Georgie's apologetic. "I'm sorry, Claudia. It was a foolish bank robbery. The whole thing was really pretty funny."

He pats her hand and kisses her cheek. "You better give them your ticket and get on board, now. You don't want to miss your flight."

Claudia can't tear herself away from him. "I'm already going to miss my flight." She sniffs. "Why was it funny? The robbery, I mean you can tell me."

"It was a non-cash bank!" Georgie laughs. "That's why. I pranked you, babe."

Claudia's suddenly miffed again. "What?!" she says.

Georgie laughs again. "I couldn't even take out my own money. Isn't that funny?"

Finally, Claudia smiles. "That was really stupid, lover boy. Really stupid."

Georgie's slightly abashed but unrepentant. "I guess some things are meant to happen that way. Some things just don't go according to plan . . . and besides, I didn't know, either. It was my first time."

But Claudia only scolds him. "Bad boy! You're a bad boy, Georgie Gust!"

They kiss.

"I didn't know how to tell you," he mutters.

"I enjoyed our conversation, though." she smiles.

Georgie smiles with her. "I'm an idiot," he says.

"A complete idiot," she agrees.

Georgie watches as Claudia walks through the flight-tunnel toward the airplane. She disappears.

Georgie walks back to his car. He's talking to himself again.

We had fun while it lasted. She never came back to America. I told her she might not like it here after Paris, and Brussels, and Rome. After all the dizziness and excitement of that sophisticated jet-set life, after the whirl and glitter of the stylish fashionable chic, she might never come back to America. She might never come back . . . to me.

Dear Diary:

I've never made a mistake. Ha! So here's to trying something new for a change! Maybe then I can make my mistake by fucking it all up in my own deluded fantasy—my desolate and futile life.

Part VIII: The Fantasy, II

In some completely different big city, Georgie and Claudia are completely different people. This Claudia wears a stunning blue turtleneck, a long blue skirt, and blue-rimmed glasses. Her stylish chic clothes and faux European accent are quietly rapturous. Georgie wears a blue pinstripe suit and an outlandish paisley tie that doesn't quite cover his bulging paunch. Georgie's slightly graying but Claudia still has the flaming frizzy red hair and svelte hourglass figure of her misspent youth.

Georgie rides up alone to his swank inner-city penthouse apartment, carrying a small bonsai tree and a bag of chocolate kisses.

(Parenthetical Pet Peeve) Vending machines that take your money, but won't give you anything and won't give your money back either.

At the 33rd floor the elevator stops. The elevator door opens and Claudia gets in.

"It's just like déjà vu all over again, isn't it?" Georgie suavely strikes up a conversation. "I believe we've met before, haven't we, somewhere—perhaps in Paris? Prague? Schenectady?"

Claudia smiles but doesn't answer. She's obviously struggling for words.

"Haven't I seen you somewhere before?" Georgie goes on. "Maybe on the Riviera? Rio? Or in my dreams, perhaps?"

Georgie's the epitome of the sophisticated debonair playboy.

"What's your sign?" he asks slyly. "I'm a Gemini. You must be . . . " Georgie smiles mysteriously, "No, don't tell me. Let me guess."

"To answer your questions," the Francophone Claudia smiles again, "I am, obviously, how you say, a French girl. Je parle francais, tout court. A . . . and, the English, it is, for me . . . how you say? Tres difficile?"

"So," Georgie deftly picks up Claudia's cues, "what part of France are you from? St Louis, Cincinnati, Notre Dame? Or, maybe, Quiche Lorraine?"

Fortunately, Claudia completely fails to catch his drift

"I have been in your United States for five months now," she says, obviously excited to have a sophisticated gentleman like Georgie to talk to among so many swarming, sweaty, belching barbarians. "I love your summer weather. To swim. I, love to stay . . . how you say . . . in shape? But me, I am just . . . what do you call that? I just love the chocolate. Your Hershey Kisses." She grins widely.

(Parenthetical Pet Peeve) Vending machines that won't accept my money at all. Worse, when the item I chose in the vending machine gets hung up and doesn't fall to where I can get it out of the machine.

"Simply ravishing to meet you," Georgie kisses her hand. His eyes fall to her brightly painted toes and stylish feet.

"Who does your toes?" Georgie gushes. "I just love your pedicure! Can I have your phone number? Or, am I being too forward?"

"Oh, you Americans!" Claudia simpers. "You are so naïf! But so so charming."

Claudia's mannerisms and accent shift to a slightly sinister Zsa Zsa Gabor, as she hands Georgie a slip of paper.

"Here you are, dahlink—my cahrd. Please call my agent. Perhaps, ve can arrangch, a-rendezvous?

"Oh. My. God." Georgie falls to his knees. "You are too, too kind. Perhaps I might kiss your feet?"

"Please to make arrangechmingks vit my agent?"

Finally, Georgie snaps out of his wild reverie. Resuming his sophisticated, suave manner, he elegantly requests Claudia's home address and phone number. She scribbles something on a business card and presses it into his hand. Immediately, the elevator door opens at the 66th floor and Claudia walks hurriedly away down the romantically lit penthouse corridor.

Georgie dazedly scans the business card. It reads:

"P.S. I don't know why you want my home address, but here it is. For some strange reason, I trust you. I believe in fate. Call me.

CLAUDIA."

Georgie's already missed his floor. The elevator door slams shut and the elevator rumbles and rattles downward again.

[Smoke Break]

On their first date, Georgie and Claudia drive onto the Interstate southbound, into New Jersey. Georgie wants to show this elegant French mademoiselle The Real America and The Real Americans who populate it, right here in Passaic, Hoboken, Parsippany, and Patterson. And Claudia's eager to impress this well-dressed, mysterious man-about-town who epitomizes for her The American Dream, which she too heartily believes in. The statuesque French torch singer with the spiky hairdo and sculptured robes, who sings the glittering promise of freedom, liberty, and equality (banality, mediocrity).

Claudia now looks slightly younger. With her sophisticated, elegant clothes and heavy pancake makeup, she resembles a Lauren Bacall, a Katherine Hepburn. Georgie can't get enough.

As he drives, Claudia leans back in the reclining passenger seat staring out the black-tinted window. She rests her head on a throw pillow and resumes speaking her fractured French.

"Zeorgie, dahlink," Claudia purrs. "You are so very, how you say . . . recherché? You are supposed to be a good American host, you know . . . like our Jerry Lewis, your movie star . . . but instead, I come here and you rob the bank, you kill someone, maybe . . . and we are always on the run! Where's the America I see in the movies? Where is what you call . . . the American Dream?"

Georgie's wearing a 50s gangster get-up: snap brim fedora, dark suit, and dark tie. He sneers at Claudia under his low hat brim and smokes incessantly. But when he speaks, his voice is surprisingly calm, bland, and matter-of-fact, like a TV newsman.

"Well, you know, the government, the government controls our movies, Claudia. The government is into organized crime. The government is organized crime. And the government, well, the government looks out for its own. Why, just look at that financial bail-out racket, the colossal national debt . . . and who services the national debt? You know, I think it's easier to commit robbery in the US by setting up a big bank rather than holding up a bank clerk. People give liberally to big corporations and big financial institutions . . . the bigger the better."

Georgie's non-descript, flat-toned voice trails off.

Claudia laughs a very dry, French laugh.

"You are so very funny, my little one! In France, it is very different. France is the country where the money, it falls apart. How you say? Poof! Oh, the French, Georgie the French! We are so . . . je ne sais quoi, you know?"

"Yeah, I know about the French," Georgie deadpans. "You can't trust the franc, and you can't tear the toilet paper."

While Georgie shakes his head, Claudia just keeps on laughing, almost hysterically.

Finally, Georgie cuts her off. "But, seriously, Claudia, you know," he says. "There's always been something fishy about the French."

Abruptly, Claudia stops laughing and becomes sophisticated, languid, and blasé once more.

"Oui, my little one. You are so right." She waves a slim black arm. "Where I come from, it so, so . . . I hate it. Everyone, they complain all the time. About everything. Nothing."

Georgie nods. "Thank God it's not like that, here in America . . . or not yet, anyway. In America, we still have seasons—four of them—and all in the right order. But, France, now, France? There's no winter in France, no summer, and here in America, we have morals. There are no morals in France, either, are there?"

Shooting a quick look at Claudia, Georgie realizes that he might have offended her Francophile sentiments and Parisian sensibility.

"Apart from that, though," he continues before she can answer, "I think it's a fine country. La France, and a fine people, too. DeGaulle, and Marianne, and, who's it? Mendes-France. Pierre Mendès France. Yes, the French."

He pauses, diplomatically, seeking words to express his profound admiration and eternal ardor for the Fourth Republic.

"They gave us The Statue of Liberty, you know," he says. "And Louisiana! Where would we be without Louisiana?"

But Claudia doesn't answer. She's still seductively daydreaming of Parisian cafes and street scenes.

"Mais oui," she murmurs. "Paris is the café of Europe."

At the word café, Georgie immediately snaps awake. His black-rimmed eyeballs pop open, and he grips the steering wheel with white knuckles.

"Oh, God, yes!" he snorts. "Paris! The cafés! The coffee!"

The Francophone, Claudia, shares his passion for bon vivant. She blushes. "Oui!" she says. "We must stop for coffee, non?"

Taking a deep drag on his cigarette and letting the smoke curl out his nose, Georgie pulls himself together again. Now he's perfectly cool, calm, in control.

"Perfect," he says. "It's still morning, sweetheart. It's morning in

America, and there's a little place I know, just around here, where we can get a good black cup o' Joe, my little French kumquat."

Claudia swoons. "You are so suave . . . so romantique!"

[Smoke Break]

After their drive, Georgie sits in his briskly-upholstered, crowded office.

Computers, monitors, and electronics fill this elaborate office space. It's fit for a pin-striped, bow-tie-wearing, traditional pipe smoker—a Great Tycoon or CEO . . . . But Georgie's dressed down, sporty, casual, as he sits handwriting a passionate letter. He's still slightly dazed from his fatal meeting with the mysterious, exotic Claudia Nesbitt. So, even though he's in his usual office routine, he can't really make himself work.

"I prefer snail mail," Georgie's whispering to himself, as if talking to Claudia. "There's something more meaningful about the whole act of writing to someone special. Taking out the pen, feeling the handmade paper, personalizing the print, smudging the fingerprints, sticking the stamp and licking the envelope . . . . "

Georgie shivers with scarcely suppressed excitement.

"I like the whole idea that Claudia and I are taking our sweet time getting to know one another. We're keeping the pace of our little romantic affair discreetly slow, what with the mail and me . . . . There's nothing I want less than another doomed relationship that flies on too fast, but this thing with Claudia . . . it's something special. Meaningful. Real . . . . I can just feel it."

The enormous wooden door to Georgie's office abruptly swings open.

On the front of the door, there's an elaborately embossed sign:
GEORGIE GUST ENTERPRISES
Georgie Gust: CEO.
And below that, a print-out:
Long-Term Investor in a Short-Term World

In steps Ismael Marks, Georgie's male secretary. He's around 35 years old, flustered, disheveled, with messy hair and a loose tie. He's sweating profusely and his sleeves are rolled up. He brusquely storms in, oblivious to Georgie's romantic passion.

"Georgie!" Marks shouts. "All hell's broken loose on the floor—Intercoastal's taking a dive! It's a $2 stock now. What'll we do?

We're ruined!"

Georgie's perfectly calm, cool, collected, although slightly peeved.

"How many times have I told you, Ismael?" Georgie's lip curls with his withering scorn. "Knock first."

"Sorry, sir," Marks answers. "But—"

Georgie cuts him off.

"Marks, I bought that stock at 50 cents," Georgie speaks clearly, as if talking to a lunatic or idiot. "Whatever I do, I'll make a killing . . . now get lost. Can't you see I'm in the middle of something really important?"

After his bewilderment wears off, Ismael Marks sees the shy smile behind Georgie's witheringly curled lips.

"What's this?" Marks asks, gathering courage. "Another one of your peculiar obsessions? Another of your curious perplexities? Whatever happened to the online dating . . . you must've made the moves on a pen pal . . . Is she hot? Is this . . . a hook-up?"

Three other associates in Georgie Gust Enterprises (sometimes called "the guys"), stylish young men in their early 20s, approach the door. Their eyes widen with jealousy and curiosity. When Georgie notices the peepers peering through his door, he discreetly covers his love-letter. With an imperious gesture, he chases them out of the office.

"Guys, get lost."

But the guys don't scare easily.

"Oooooo-o-o-oh, Mr Romantic . . . ." they chorus. "Dream Boy . . .the Poet . . .a modern Casanova . . . ."

Georgie slams the enormous wooden door on his not-so-secret admirers. He tries to pick up writing his romantic billet-doux, but he can't recapture the passionate mood of before . . . .

Somewhere outside the office door, several different alarm clocks ring indistinctly. The whole scene changes once again . . . .

Dear Diary:

I'm angry again. So, fuck it, I'm going to be exactly who I am. Shite, my secret misery, my existential crisis, and whatnot. I always am exactly who I am. So what now? Ah, with my breath after breath.

Part IX: The Secret Love and Death of Claudia Nesbitt and Georgie Gust

In Georgie's current fantasy, he and Claudia's New Age Yuppie McMansion has blown out of proportion. It is now the size of a bustling metropolitan airport or the heavily fortified presidential palace of some scarcely populated underdeveloped country.

Wait. Let's not exaggerate. It's only Georgie and Claudia's American Dream Palace. It's not Versailles, the Taj Mahal, or Wal-Mart. In fact, it's probably only a little larger than some central European fiefdoms or central American banana republics.

Beside the Olympic swimming pool, Georgie reclines on a hammock in freshly laundered sweats and a matching headband, reading a letter to himself. On the front lawn, Claudia is giving a press conference interview to a whole corps of rapt, adamant reporters.

"As far as my most intriguing quality, hmmm . . ." she ponders the question profoundly, pursing her pretty lips and furrowing her brow. "I guess I'd have to say it is my unending ability to smile outwardly even if my heart is being broken."

Inscrutably, Georgie smiles.

Surveying the well-maintained grounds of his enormous estate, Georgie jogs along a tree-lined path with several servants scurrying along beside him trying to keep up. Among them, a scantily clad Claudia trots along resplendent in bikini top and tight shorts.

"And I just wanted to say, Georgie, thank you, thank you for the bonsai tree and the bag of kisses. I don't know how I can ever thank you enough."

Georgie waves a limp-wristed hand, as if to say, "It's nothing". And Claudia's panting, panting just to keep up.

On the scarcely used tennis courts, Georgie swings his high-strung racket and volleys green tennis balls from a serving machine. Dozens of fluorescent green tennis balls bobble on the green pavement. On the other side of the net, Claudia stretches and practices her serve, waiting to be beaten again by Georgie's blazing game.

"And I enjoy the outdoors, too. Especially when I'm challenged by a brisk, invigorating game of tennis," Claudia's voice echoes across the court. "I think it would be a pleasant way to meet each other for the first time."

Claudia Nesbitt is a natural beauty, set against the plush, ornamental gardens and bosky tree-lined vistas of her and Georgie's Dream House. She is in green silk evening dress and Georgie is in a white-tailed tux and black tie. They take a romantic stroll together, holding hands. They flash big smiles, prancing and dancing with playful, sexy energy.

Before them glistens an enormous goldfish pond with white-foamed fountains, tumbling waterfalls, and a wide pathway where the white-shafted sunlight bleeds through the old white oak and black elm trees. Sweeping her off her feet, Georgie picks Claudia up and carries her away. Dashingly, he brings her to the goldfish pond and pretends to throw her in.

Swept away, Claudia wraps her arms around his neck and smiles into his eyes.

"Oh, Georgie," she whispers. "Marry me."

Georgie pulls an oversized jewelry case out of his white tuxedo pocket. He flashes a 50-carat diamond engagement ring before Claudia's dazed eyes. On his knees, he removes the brilliantly gleaming engagement ring and tries to put it on Claudia's faintly glowing and slim ring finger.

"No, dear. I insist. You go first," he says. "Repeat after me: Through sickness and health. Through richer or poorer. For better or worse. Through whatever crap the whole world chucks at us. I love you, Claudia Nesbitt."

Claudia's speechless with adoration.

"Well, I guess—I love you, too, Georgie Gust." She falls into his arms. "Or whatever." she says.

They kiss.

[Smoke Break]

It's Georgie and Claudia's honeymoon night—the blithering consummation of their sacred marriage, the blighted blush of their wild love affair, the perfect night of passion and betrayal to seal the pact of their connubial bliss. In the elegant master bedroom with the big white-and-red canopy bed, the white fluorescent lights are still on. Georgie Gust and Claudia Nesbitt make passionate love together, softly, gently, and slowly, building to the torrid peak of their erotic lovemaking:

The perfect pedicure.

With his lips Georgie massages the slim, white arches of Claudia's feet. His enflamed tongue passes up her legs to her calves, to her thighs, then back down to her feet and toes, which shine with a perfect dark red polish.

Claudia writhes and moans with unspeakable pleasure.

"Oh, Georgie, Georgie, Georgie," she finally gasps. "I can't believe you've never given a girl a pedicure. You did such a beautiful job. A perfect job. How can I ever thank you?"

Beside himself with ecstasy, Georgie looks up shyly as Claudia slips off her gossamer chemise and push-up bra.

"I'll tell you later," he answers dazedly. "Lights on or off?"

The American Dream Couple gaze deeply into each other's eyes. With a single breath, a single heart, a single tongue, speaking together, they say . . .

"Off."

Breaking down in hysterical laughter, they roll down to the bed together.

Blissfully laughing, forever after.

On the white sand beach, beneath the blue full moon, Georgie and Claudia's excruciatingly passionate lovemaking continues with a brisk skinny-dipping romp, and feverish roll among the beach-blankets.

At the San Clemente Town Center and Shopping Emporium, the enormous black asphalt parking lot is empty except for one black Jeep.

(Parenthetical Pet Peeve) After waiting patiently for someone to back out of a parking space, some moron comes around from the other side and zips into it before I can.

The driver's side door of the Jeep is open. Claudia and Georgie sway slowly to the wafting music, their perfect bodies sculpting and molding together in romantic passion.

[Smoke Break]

On the white sand beach, beneath the sultry white sun, Claudia and Georgie still in their elegant wedding attire, walk playfully along the windswept shore. They're waving digital cameras and flashing candid camera pictures back and forth at each other. They're laughing and happy, so much in love.

On the old deserted fishing pier, Georgie and Claudia stroll leisurely along the boardwalk. Wearing her black silk wedding dress, Claudia tosses silver coins into the splashing water. Bemused, Georgie stands silently, admiringly, behind her.

"Oh, Georgie!" Claudia gushes, "you don't know—how I've dreamed! How I've waited for this! Our honeymoon! Oh, Georgie-Porgie. I want us to stay this close together forever! Let's not drift too far away, Georgie. Please?"

Profoundly sensing Claudia's deepest desires, Georgie attempts to comfort and console her, to soothe the passionate heartache within her secret soul.

"Tonight," he whispers huskily, "is your night again, Claudia darling." Georgie takes her in his strong, flabby arms. "Whatever you wish for, Claudia dearest. Whatever you dream for, I will do for you. Your wish, your dream, is my command."

It's exactly the kind of offer that always gets Georgie in trouble.

"Well, now that you mention it, Georgie darling," Claudia says. "Since you offered—you know I really wanted to see that Tony Krishna play, at the Screaming Angel Theater of the Absurd. But you said it was sold out?"

"It was sold out," Georgie deadpans, tongue-in-cheek. "But for you, Claudia . . ."

"Oh, Georgie," Claudia swoons. "You're just so—so . . ."

"Irresistible?" Georgie smirks.

Later that night at the Screaming Angel Theater, Georgie and Claudia sit in their own invisible studio audience, watching themselves. It's as if they're alone in the theater, in the center seats, the only spectators in their own private psychodrama.

Georgie slips his arm around Claudia. She snuggles closer.

"You see, Claudia darling," Georgie whispers breathily in her ear. "The whole play is sold out. I bought all the tickets they had. And they're all playing—just for us."

"Oh Georgie, baby," Claudia whispers back. "You're—perfect."

She kisses him.

But Georgie's too wrapped up in the spectacle on stage to respond.

"Shhhh!" he hushes Claudia. "It's starting."

(Parenthetical Pet Peeve) High prices of refreshments at movie theaters. Worse, having to go to the bathroom at the movies during an exciting part of the film.

On the theater stage, the surrealist psychodrama has just begun. An old couple tromp on stage—two men, married, gay. They sit to eat an invisible meal with real forks, knives and spoons, and soon their son, Georgie, joins them.

"Uncle Ben," the son says. "Them people out there in the invisible studio audience prob'ly think, jes fr'm the way we're sittin' here, that yer both my daddies. I mean, Uncle Ben, yer Georgie the First. And Uncle Eric, yer Georgie the Second. Er sumpin' . . ., er maybe, Dad, you could be Georgie Number Two."

All three Georgies laugh hysterically. Walking off, Uncle Ben and Eric hold hands while the son watches. In the rollicking humor and action-packed excitement, Eric forgets his line. He stutters: "Uh, yeah . . . ."

For some inexplicable reason, Uncle Ben finds this hilarious. He can barely control his laughter. "If ya'all'll excuse me," he says, trying to hold back his snorts and hollers, "I seem t've forgotten mah lines, too. If ya'all'll just lemme crib from the script, ah'll be fine, from the next scene on. Ah promise!"

Georgie and Claudia are wide-eyed, stupefied, baffled, uncomprehending. The theater falls silent. Strange, hollow sounds echo through the amphitheater, like whispers and screams heard in dreams. The two hear Eric's scuffling footsteps as he walks off stage. Eric snowballs into a hysterical laughing frenzy as he tries to reenter the stage. He's laughing his ass off, really hard, until finally he collapses, writhing and wriggling on the invisible stage. It's totally gut-busting!

Several minutes pass. The invisible studio audience squirms and twitches in their invisible seats. Still, Eric can't stop himself from laughing—and neither can the two spectators, Georgie Gust and Claudia Nesbitt. He's the funniest thing Claudia and Georgie have ever seen in their lives! He just keeps laughing and laughing! Now Uncle Ben and the kid get in on the hilarity, just like Claudia and Georgie. The whole invisible studio audience is cracking up! This guy's pathetically comedic—he just can't get enough of himself!

[Smoke Break]

The two self-satisfied spectators, Claudia and Georgie, leave the theater a few hours later still uproariously laughing. As they step outside the invisible theater doors, Claudia suddenly realizes something. "Oh! My purse!" she shouts.

(Parenthetical Pet Peeve) My change purse opens itself, dumping change inside my handbag.

But Georgie (Our Georgie, the Original Georgie, the Real Georgie, Georgie # 1, 2, 3, 4) is perfectly calm, unflustered, unruffled.
"Wait here," his stern manly voice commands. "I'll be right back."
With a skip and a jump, he darts back into the theater. Obediently, the delectable, desirable Claudia waits patiently outside. As Georgie hastily makes his way back out of the theater, he holds up her purse, showing that it's safe. Supremely serene, beautiful, beatified, Claudia smiles.
But some fatal shadow of disaster makes Georgie cry out. "Hey!!!" he shouts, "Watch out!!!"
As they stand near the white-shadowed street, a sinister black car comes crashing across the curb and hits Claudia from behind. There's a terrible scream.
The black birds that were watching fly away.
Three weeks later, Georgie is devastated by the unforeseeable tragedy but still trying to display a stoic courage (for Claudia's sake.) He's visiting Claudia in San Clemente Memorial Hospital, anxiously awaiting the white-suited doctor's post-op prognosis. As he paces the waiting room floor, chain-smoking cigarettes and searching the white-veiled doctor's eyes for clues, he wonders:
Will the supremely desirable, delectable Claudia Nesbitt ever awaken from her sleepless coma to dazzle the watching, waiting world with her eternal beauty once again?
Finally the white-coated doctors deliver their verdict: Claudia Nesbitt is fully handicapped. She's awake, alive, and breathing, but almost completely paralyzed—everything but her arms and her bust, from the neck up. Her once supple shapely torso and slim legs (including, tragically, her feet) fail to respond to her whispered commands.
"I'm so sorry, Georgie," Claudia sobs. "No more pedicures."
Georgie, struggling not to break down completely, takes her

delicate hands in his strong grip.

"It's . . . it's. . . ." he whispers, "quadriplegia."

"No, Georgie," one of the white-veiled doctors corrects him. "Quadriplegia means all four limbs. What Claudia has is only paraplegia; that is, two limbs."

"Thank you, doc," Georgie sniffles. "I'd forgotten my Latin suffixes."

But before the white-coated doctor can elucidate Latin prefixes, Claudia Nesbitt's bell-like singsong voice breaks into their whispered conversation.

"You don't need to deal with this," she proclaims fighting back tears. "Georgie, don't sacrifice your life for me. Go ahead, Georgie— pretend I'm dead. Marry Clio. I'll be fine." Overcome by emotion, Claudia smiles beneath her tears.

Sobbing himself, Georgie thinks furiously, She always said she could smile through anything.

Addressing Claudia again, Georgie swears his love. "Baby, I'll stay with you forever," he vows. "I already told you that, Claudia, my love."

Georgie and Claudia lock lips in a passionate but platonic kiss.

[Smoke Break]

Georgie sobs in a highly arched cathedral, kneeling down in a front row pew with scintillating shafts of multicolored light falling on him from the stained glass windows.

The black-robed minister steps in to console him, offering a private communion. A prostrate Georgie accepts the proffered wafer on his extended tongue.

In the fleshpots and dives of the big city, Georgie's sorely tempted by strong drink and the lascivious women who come on to him, testing his devotion to the bedridden Claudia. Giving in to a brief moment of temptation, he steps up to the glittering bar and sees his slightly haggard, wan face in the full-sized mirror.

The bartender is wiping the counter with a white towel. "What'll it be, Mac?" he proposes. "Straight? No chaser? On the rocks?"

A sexy, well-endowed brunette who is similar in superficial appearance to the sublime Claudia Nesbitt approaches Georgie at the bar. "Will you buy me a drink, too?" She rubs up against him. "Handsome."

In a supreme act of strength and will, Georgie refuses both the strong drink and the lascivious woman with apparent ease and shyly eyes the door, looking for a way out.

"I gotta go," he mutters to the disappointed diva. "Sorry. Maybe next time."

But we all know, now (Don't we?), there's never a next time.

[Smoke Break]

After an incredibly long, agonizing year of painful therapy and massage treatment, Claudia Nesbitt recovers from her tragic accident enough to start performing her private toilette and making brief forays outside the San Clemente Memorial Hospital.

So Georgie, encouraged and heartened by Claudia's progress, swears to resurrect her from her bedridden convalescence and finally release her from her captive hospital room.

The white-coated doctors and physical therapists are skeptical. But Georgie and Claudia's love is strong. And eventually (we know, don't we?) love overcomes all barriers. Love heals all wounds.

Love conquers all.

[Smoke Break]

Claudia, wobbling slightly but still standing on her own two feet, enters the physical therapy room of the San Clemente Memorial Hospital convalescent ward using her miracle prosthetics. Her devoted, obedient Georgie is watching *Ten Years* on the flickering TV.

A discarded newspaper is scattered on the well-worn sofa beside him.

Quickly rising and throwing down his Modern Maturity, Georgie gets up from the couch. Passionately, he kisses Claudia on the cheek.

"Good morning, Angel," he smiles.

But he's surprised and stunned when Claudia playfully takes exception to her affectionate pet name.

"Princess, dummy!" she banters. "I'm not an angel, yet. Okay?"

Georgie controls his temper, although he's still stinging from the rebuke. "Whatever you say, pet," he apologizes, contrite. "But I didn't forget. Today's your birthday."

"Oh, Georgie," Claudia gushes. "You remembered!"

"I'm taking you out on the boat today," he continues. "Then we'll check out your new prosthetics, and tonight I'll make passionate love with my wife. Yes, you, Claudia. I'm offering one thousand kisses as a birthday gift. You just have to tell me where you'd like them.

Despite her prostheses and paraplegia, Claudia still smiles, infinitely seductive, yet innocently sweet.

[Smoke Break]

Alone on the open sea, Georgie pilots the sleek streamlined speedboat at full roar, the white-foamed wake crashing and plunging behind the propellers. Alone, he's lost in thought. He's a man on a mission screaming over the deep-throated engine's dull roar, his splattering tears mixing with the splashes of seawater from the bay. The windshield wipers thrash the falling droplets.

When he pulls up to the dock, however, Georgie's face is calm and smooth. With perfect solicitude and supreme devotion, Georgie helps the handicapped Claudia down into the hold. His divine love is evident in every gesture and move he makes.

The prosthetic Claudia is self-assured, confident, and ready to seize the day and make the world her oyster once again.

"Georgie, honey," she says. "I want to go out on that boogie board thingee."

Georgie's proud of her recovery as the proof of his love and their strength, and is pleased to see the fully recovered Claudia taking on the challenges of their future life together. "Whatever you say, pet," he beams. "This is your day, baby. I'm just here to give you everything you want, my angel."

Sardonically, Claudia laughs. "You forgot again, dummy!" she scolds. "I'm your princess! Remember? I like it so much better when you call me princess!"

Georgie smiles. They stop, frozen in passion. Georgie and Claudia kiss.

But then she breaks away, laughing. "Come on!" she shoves him playfully. "It's my birthday! Let's boogie board."

He laughingly agrees and ties off the board, gingerly helping her down the ladder to the water. Then he runs to the wheel of the sleek, streamlined speedboat and looks back at her over his shoulder.

Basking in Georgie's gaze, Claudia's excited—almost child-like. In a shrill voice, she calls out, "Okay! I'm ready. Let's go!"

Casting a wistful look over his shoulder, Georgie calls back: "You ready back there? I'll go slow."

"Full speed ahead, Captain!" Claudia cries.

He slowly accelerates, checking behind him with each increase in speed. As the sleek, streamlined speedboat reaches full steam, Claudia gives Georgie a big thumbs up.

"Faster! Faster!" she shouts. "I want to feel the sea-wind in my hair!"

Still, Georgie is careful, maybe overly cautious. "Not yet," he cries. "Wait until we're further out."

The white-capped inlet between the bay and the sea stretches before them.

The sleek, streamlined speedboat, with Claudia trailing behind, reaches the open sea. Claudia clings tightly to the boogie board, her numb legs dragging along behind her.

Captain Georgie steers the bucking and plunging speedboat through the white capped inlet. Behind him, completely inaudible above the roar of the high-speed motor and the crashing waves, Claudia cries out, "I just love this summer weather!"

The white blonde-haired mermaid Claudia, all smiles, cries out again, still unheard above the screaming outboard motor noise and wave-roar. "You know I just love to swim."

On the plunging and bucking boogie board, Claudia slowly loses her grip. Slowly, silently, she slides off the slippery board, sinking down into the chill, fathomless waters.

Above the thundering waves and the roaring motors, Georgie can't hear her shrill girlish voice crying out her last words:

"I love to stay in shape. I believe in fate!"

On the high-arched poop deck, Captain Georgie still steers the boat dead ahead, oblivious to the tragedy and disaster in his wake. The throaty roar of the magnificent twin outboard engines fills his mind with power and speed.

Claudia struggles to take a few teeth clenching gasps above the surging seawater. She futilely tries to grab onto the board, but it slowly slips away. She gasps feebly and then goes down for the third time.

I'd have to say it's my unending ability to smile, she thinks.

With wild sea spray in his eyes, Captain Georgie casts a last look back behind the boat. He sees the plunging boogie board bouncing upside down in the white-capped wake.

Thank you, Georgie-boo-boo, for the bonsai tree and the bag of chocolate kisses, he remembers her voice.

Silently, with a wide open mouth and bulging eyeballs, Georgie screams a silent scream of agony and despair.

Captain Georgie yanks the keys out of the ignition. He checks for life preservers, life jackets, and then freezes as a slowly dawning realization strikes him.

"Shite," he curses. "I don't even know how to swim."

"Oh, Claudia, oh, Claudia, oh Claudia—don't do this to me, Claudia! Not now. Not forever. How can I go on living with myself knowing?"

I'd have to say, it's my unending ability to smile, she thinks, breathing seawater, A pleasant way to meet each other for the first time.

[Smoke Break]

On the white-capped beach, the bereaved Georgie takes a long, self-torturing walk. Every step he takes in the slippery wet sand is staggering, agonizing.

[Smoke Break]

On the bucking and plunging speedboat, Captain Georgie rides hard into the stormy night. He's trying to get over the tragic death of his ex-wife. He's moving on the best he can.

[Smoke Break]

At Georgie Gust Enterprises, the guys' faces are all downcast, drooping, glum. Balefully glaring around the morose staff-room, Georgie suspiciously stares them down.

There's a long uncomfortable silence.

Finally, Georgie speaks.

"Well, come on guys! Get out there and trade!" he hollers. "Intercoastal's at 24.50. Why don't you dump half at a quarter?"

There's an answering silence from the guys. Georgie has to bluster and bluff to break their sluggish spell.

"Snap out of it, guys!" he shouts. "Now get out there and hit the floor!"

Slightly embarrassed, Ismael Marks approaches Georgie.

"Georgie," he asks sympathetically, shyly. "Are you all right?"

Staring Marks down, Georgie smiles a frozen white-toothed smile. "See this smile, Marks?" Georgie boasts. "It's a skill I've learned. It gets me through times when the going gets tough. I just smile in the face of tragedy and disaster and the whole world has to smile with me. Whether it wants to or not."

With these inspirational words, Georgie claps Ismael on the back.

"Listen, Marks," he says. "Things are fine. Now, we've got to get the energy reports finished by the end of the day. So let's get on with it, huh?"

Ismael Marks reluctantly shuffles out of Georgie's enormous office, sneaking a glance back for one last look.

On the big wooden office desk there's a gold-framed wedding photo of Georgie Gust and Claudia Nesbitt, both happy as all hell.

Dear Diary:

I realize I can—yes, I can experience peace of mind, a sense of purpose and meaning with mental illness or not. Writing out the transgression does help, enormously.

Part X: Down and Out with Georgie Gust

It's an old, dingy, broken-down luncheonette on some big city downtown street. White fluorescent lights beat down on the chipped Formica countertops and the swiveling lunch-counter stools.

Through the big picture window, we see the half dozen regular customers and a few walk-ins slouched and hunched over half-eaten plates and steamy coffee cups. A waitress in a white-and-red dress and beehive hairdo stands waiting, taking orders.

A young man clumsily bundled up in a green duffel coat, slacks, and utility boots walks past the luncheonette entrance, smoking a pipe. He stops, thinks about going in, and then shrugs and turns away.

An old beat-up domestic car drives past the young man and toots the horn jauntily. Someone inside waves. The young man waves back. He doesn't even notice the scruffy, dirty old bum who elbows past him and makes for the luncheonette door.

Georgie's now a disheveled old homeless man wearing an unbuttoned, olive green, Vietnam Veteran's jacket and Salvation Army shoes. He's filthy and disgusting but he still has a confident self-assured step.

Without hesitating, Georgie opens the entrance door to the luncheonette.

Two middle-aged women shoot dirty looks at Georgie as they brush past him on their way out.

Georgie walks in without noticing them and slouches over to the counter, watching a couple in the corner with the shadows of his eyes.

The man is in his early 20s. He's slick, handsome, athletic, and bored. He's wearing a college sweatshirt. The girl is slightly older, but still pretty. She's coed-cute, but still insecure. A couple of large shopping bags sit next to her on the booth-seat.

"Travis, I'm talking to you!" Ashley grimly purses her lips. "Wake up! What the hell's wrong with you?"

But Travis scarcely notices.

"Huh? Nothing," he slurs. "Nothing's the matter with me."

"Are you coming with me to Julie's party?" Ashley looks worried.

"It's tonight!"

Travis shrugs.

"Ashley," Travis starts to say, "you know—"

But Ashley cuts him off.

"Who's more important?" she demands pettishly. "Me or your friends? We were invited to Julie's party two weeks ago!"

"But, Ashley," Travis starts to say again. "I promised—"

But again Ashley cuts him off. "You promised me!" she shrilly pouts.

Bored, Georgie turns his head to the man sitting next to him at the counter, Mr Wilton.

Georgie knows that Mr Wilton is Mr Wilton because he's one of the regulars. Dressed in a 1950s-style grey flannel three-piece suit, Mr Wilton reads *The Wall Street Journal* over lunch every day. After scanning the stock prices, he stuffs the paper in his brown leather briefcase that sits on the booster seat next to him, and lifts up a packet of official-looking papers.

Mr Wilton mumbles some garbled pseudo-cursing. He gets tense when Georgie turns his face to him, like Georgie's butting into something he has going with the waitress or something.

The whole rest of the counter is empty.

Although she's a completely different person, it's obvious that the waitress is Claudia. She pours Georgie a steaming cup of black coffee. Unlike the thirtyish New Age Claudia or the elder Francophone Claudia, this Claudia is slightly plain looking, plain speaking, monotonous, dull, and distinctly unoriginal. (She's a waitress in a greasy-spoon café! What'd you expect—Brigitte Bardot?)

"How are we doing, huh?" Claudia asks. "Cold enough for you?"

"What do you want me to do, predict the weather?" Georgie snaps back, although he's not really being unfriendly. He's just a bit surly all the time now, on account of something. "I can't do anything about it!"

"That's right." Claudia agrees, placating him. "You can't."

"Everybody talks about the weather," Georgie complains. He leaves the sentence dangling.

After Georgie's outburst, Mr Wilton slides over one seat to avoid any more contact with the bum. He knocks over his coffee cup in the process.

"Damn it!" Mr Wilton curses. "Spilled the damn coffee!"

Claudia comes over with a not-too-clean-looking rag. She wipes up the mess. "Mr Wilton, you ought to be more careful," Claudia scolds gently.

"Dammit!" Mr Wilton curses. "It's all over my mortgage papers."

"I'll get you a fresh cup," Claudia soothes his wrath. "It's no big deal."

She fills a fresh new cup of coffee for Mr Wilton. She's the matchmaker, the peacemaker, the go-betweener. She's the woman in waiting who greets men at the door and serves their manly needs and sends them back into the cold, cruel world again—a little warmer and a little less peeved. Usually.

While Claudia clucks in sympathy and pours another cup of coffee, the big glass door swings open and two young kids enter. Georgie slowly turns his head to examine them. Well-groomed and dressed conservatively, but still looking slightly depressed, the two mope their way inside. One of them walks with an old-fashioned black cane. Georgie knows them, too. The one with the cane is Adam and the other is John.

The two pause at the first booth, but decide to sit next to Georgie at the lunch counter.

Claudia notices they're looking sort of down and beat. "Hey, boys," she greets them. "Aren't you going to sit at your regular table?"

"It's just not the same," John tries to smile. "Since . . ."

"I know. It seems like only yesterday." Claudia commiserates. "I remember . . . ."

Adam chokes back tears. He stands up.

"I'll be right back," he says to John, not looking at anyone.

Adam limps to the back of the diner toward the restrooms.

Without missing a beat, Claudia switches her services to John. "There's fresh coffee today," she says. "It's nice and hot."

The white-and-red smiling waitress turns to pour the boys some coffee.

Georgie slides over a seat to sit next to Mr Wilton again.

"Rough day huh, bud?" he whispers.

Mr Wilton is taken aback. "Excuse me?" he says. "Were you talking to me? Why don't you mind your own business, Mac? And I'll take care of mine,"

"Don't knock yourself out, buddy," Georgie snorts. "Ever hear the phrase 'Don't work too hard?' If you keep on worrying like that, you'll never get anything done."

Mr Wilton becomes ruffled and defensive. He seems to grow a little in his jacket. "Hey, I work like this all the time!" He snorts. "Twelve hours a day, six days a week. And in a year, that's like—let's see. . .twelve times six times fifty-four, that's . . ."

(Parenthetical Pet Peeve) When eight hours at work pass by much slower than eight hours at home.

Mr Wilton looks to Claudia for validation in his calculations. But all he gets is a smirk and a blank stare.

"What is this? Grand Central Station?" he objects. "Can't a guy even get a simple cup of coffee here without some lowlife, some deadbeat, some . . . some stumblebum getting in my face?"

Mr Wilton pokes Georgie with his pointed finger.

"Hey, bud-a-roo," Georgie protests. "You better think twice before you put me down. Look, see there? Right there in your hand? Three fingers pointed back at yourself, see?"

Mr Wilton checks his distemper and decides to loosen up a bit. "Ah, so. What is this now?" he jokes. "Fortune cookies for breakfast?"

"Yup," Georgie grins. "The kitchen was empty. Except for us smart cookies."

Warming up to Georgie's friendliness, Mr Wilton transforms apoplexy to apology. "Sorry, bud," he says. "I didn't mean to snap at you. It's just—business hasn't been so great lately."

Georgie shrugs. "Don't sweat it," he says. "I don't worry about it."

Georgie changes the subject. "So what line of work are you in?" he asks jovially.

Mr Wilton grimaces. "I'm working hard or hardly working," Mr Wilton bluffs. "That's what all the girls used to ask me before I got married."

He slaps Georgie on the back. "But hell, after I was married it was different. The women, they had to know what size my bank roll was, because I run the biggest bank in town." Mr Wilton guffaws and chokes on his own joke.

Georgie slaps him on the back until he stops coughing. Then Georgie picks up Mr Wilton's BMW key chain and twirls it around his finger. "Well," he starts to say. "You don't seem to be doing too ba—"

But Mr Wilson cuts him off. "Yeah, you could say I'm doing alright. Okay?" He snorts again. "As good as anyone else these days."

Georgie laughs inappropriately. "Okay, Mr W. Here's another fortune cookie for you: 'You should work to live, not live to work.' Ya know?"

"Yeah, you know, I always say 'You have to stop and smell the roses,'" Mr W blusters. "I mean, what's the point of planting roses if you never take the time to smell them?"

Georgie beams inscrutably. "Simple, huh? But sweet." he says. "Just like a fortune cookie in your tea leaves."

Mr Wilton takes a serious turn. "It's like they say, son. It's all about reaping the fruits of your labor—or they used to say that, anyway. But when do I get my fruits, huh? Tell me that."

Before Georgie can snap back another sweet little fortune cookie of immortal wisdom, Mr Wilton's huge cell-phone rings.

"Excuse me," he nods apologetically. "I gotta take this phone call." Without getting up, Mr Wilton takes the call.

"Connie, I won't be coming in," Mr Wilton says. "No, not today. Why don't you reschedule—just reschedule everything. No, not tomorrow, either. I'll tell you what, how about I call you. Don't call me." Mr Wilton shuts down the phone.

Georgie beams approval. "See, Mr Wilton?" Georgie says. "Don't you feel so much better now?"

Mr Wilton smiles. "Ya know, Mr . . . What's your name?" he says. "You really made my day."

Georgie smiles satisfaction. "Don't mention it," he says. "And I really do sound like a fortune cookie, huh?"

Finally, Adam returns to the counter.

"You okay?" John asks. "You all right now, bud?"

Adam shrugs. "I'm still alive," he says. "I guess."

John pokes and prods him playfully. "Hey, come on, man!" he ribs Adam. "Enjoy your java. Get an edge."

But Adam stays distinctly surly. "I'm already stoned," he says. "I've got my edge. Go get your own, buddy boy."

Meanwhile, Ashley is still probing for Travis' reactions. It's like trying to find the pulse in a prune Danish.

"What's your problem, Travis?" Ashley pleads. "Why are you like this?"

"What are you talking about? Like what?" Travis sneers. "Hey, I woke up and went shopping with you, didn't I? What more do you want?"

(Parenthetical Pet Peeve) Hot dogs, 10 to a pack. Buns, 8 to a pack.

"What more do I want? What more do I want?" Ashley rants. "You know damn well what I want! I'm sick of your stupid jokes and your surly attitude. You always act like I'm, just, sooo not important to you!"

Travis sits up to make a big speech.

"Listen," he starts to say. But before he can continue, Travis forgets whatever he was going to say. "Whatever, Ashley." he concludes.

Since Claudia's behind the counter picking up dirty dishes, it's up to Georgie to be Mr Hospitality. So he tugs on John's slumped shoulder.

"Sorry for interrupting, but . . ." he smiles knowingly. "Lousy moods seem to be contagious today. I'm getting yours. Do you mind if I butt in?"

Glad to be distracted, Adam and John give Georgie their undivided attention.

"Where's Josh?" Georgie asks. "If you don't mind my asking."

"Josh is dead, man," Adam deadpans.

"Oh. I'm really sorry to hear that, bro." Georgie says, sympathetically. "But hey, ya know—I know the feeling."

"Hey, man," John says. "You weren't even there."

"And you're not dead," Adam follows up. "So just buzz off."

But Georgie's not bugged. And he doesn't buzz. "You think I haven't been there?" he shoots back. "You think I haven't done that?"

John and Adam stare darts into Georgie's red eyes. But still Georgie's not bugged.

"It's just, guys—I've seen too many kids go down too soon," he sighs. "I cope by remembering the good times. You guys really had some great times together—don't throw away the good times. Don't let those memories die, either.

Adam and John stare at Georgie with obvious hostility.

"Hey, man! He was our best friend, man!" John says. "Of course we had good times with him."

"That's just what I mean!" Georgie cheers. "Keep those alive! Keep the good times alive!"

Abruptly, Adam breaks down, distraught. "Oh. My. God." he confesses. "It really was all my fault. The car skidded. There was black ice on the street. I couldn't stop."

"Don't take it out on yourself, man! Don't blame yourself!" Georgie blurts. "How can it be your fault? Shite happens! And shite like that happens to everyone! Everyone. So just think about it."

As Georgie, John, and Adam try to work out their deep grief and mourning for their beloved lost friend, Travis and Ashley are working up to a serious domestic episode.

Ashley's stifled frustration and silent rage intensify. She points her well-manicured finger at the sulking Travis, still angry as all hell at his neglect and indifference.

"What do you mean, 'whatever,' Travis?" she rants on. "Don't give me that self-pitying garbage! For two years, I've been dealing with your selfishness and I'm sick and tired of it! You hear me? I'm sick and tired of it!"

But Travis, of course, is still indifferent. "Ashley," he sighs half-heartedly, "just relax. You're making a scene, you know?"

"Making a scene! Making a scene!" Ashley shouts. "I'll make a scene for you! Just you try to stop me!" She jumps to her feet, blown up twice life-size with rage, and glares down at the incredible shrinking Travis. "You know, Travis," she says with withering scorn, "You're the most self-centered and shallow person I've ever known!"

Without flinching, Travis rests his arms on the back of the slick plastic booth. "What about your old boyfriend?" Travis smirks. "What's his name?"

Finally Ashley cracks. "That's it. That's it!" she shouts. "I've had it! We're finished!"

"Like, whatever, babe." Travis shrugs.

Enraged, Ashley dumps her plate into Travis' lap. He ducks as chicken and gravy spatter across his jeans and onto the vinyl of the seat and the hard tile floor. Ashley grabs her full shopping bags and storms toward the big glass door. But she trips on the floor mat and nearly falls before making her exit.

Always the Good Samaritan, Georgie ("Mr Hospitality") Gust reaches for some napkins on the counter and gallops over to Travis, helping him clean up the mess in his lap.

"Thanks, dude," Travis says. "That chick is, like, crazy man."

Georgie takes a seat beside Travis. "You really don't give a damn about her, do you?"

Travis smirks, sarcastically. "What a brilliant observation," he says.

Georgie nods. "Hey, when I was your age I didn't care about a thing, and I had everything going for me. And now look at me! I'm down and out! I'm a deadbeat—a bum!"

Travis sneers. "So now you're going to tell me how looking back, you had this flashback or something and you saw, like, how you should have done things different, huh?

"Not exactly."

Georgie stays calm. He's a shining beacon and quiet center of wisdom and wit amidst the chaos and confusion of the luncheonette.

Travis scoffs.

"I got drafted," Georgie begins.

Travis begins to take interest. "You mean you were sent to Vietnam or something?"

Georgie continues speaking in his calm, passionless voice. "Two weeks later, I was getting my head shaved, grabbing my ankles, baring my butt, and hauling a brand new rifle around. Suddenly, I had to care. I had no choice."

Travis perks up. "Yeah?" he says.

"I left my girl, my home town, everything. I was stuck out in the jungle. And ten thousand little guys in black pajamas were trying to kill me. It was crazy. I had to start all over again from scratch when I got back home. It was tough putting the pieces back together."

Georgie pauses, waiting for his harsh life lessons to sink in. Travis is silent, absorbing the message. Georgie continues.

"We've all been through a lot. There's a lot of shite coming down and when it hits the fan, you have to do whatever you can to get by. You know, we need to get through it, whatever way we can. I want to learn to live through everything I can take, everything I can handle, just so I know I can take it. Hopefully, I'll even enjoy it, too."

Georgie's used up his whole stock of platitudes and aphorisms from *The Collected Wisdom and Wit of Georgie Gust*. Yet, he goes on.

"So." Georgie looks Travis in the eye. "What gets you up in the morning, guy?"

Travis sticks out his hand. "My name's Travis," he says. "I don't know, exactly. How about you?"

"Well, if you haven't figured it out yet," Georgie recommends, "don't sweat it." Georgie relaxes again. "You're still young, Travis." Georgie smiles. "You probably hear that all the time, right? Don't you? That you're young?"

Travis smiles back like he knows exactly where Georgie is going with this. "Mmm hmmm . . ." he hums, nodding excitedly.

"So, are you going to try and tell me you never felt anything for Ashley? Not ever? What about in the beginning, when you guys first met?"

Travis yawns. "Shite. You know, I was just so intimidated by her. She's older and smarter. I felt stupid, clumsy, like a kid. I couldn't, I couldn't . . . I don't know the word."

"Deliver," Georgie finishes for him.

Travis abruptly gets up out of his seat and slides a 10 under the water glass. "Hey man, I gotta go," he says. "Nice meeting you though."

Georgie butts in before the young man can bolt out the door. "Like I said," he says, "you're still young, bud. Don't make the mistakes I made—don't throw your life away. Go call her. Tell her you're sorry. Tell her exactly how you honestly feel. And see what happens. You really can't lose. It's a win–win situation—you'd just be doing the right thing."

"Yeah thanks, man." Travis is obviously smitten with gratitude. "But I really gotta go." Travis sticks out his hand again.

Georgie clasps his palm in the death-grip of the Brotherhood of Flawed Men and slaps Travis on the back. "Don't mention it," Georgie says. "If you ever need anything . . . ."

"Right on. Thanks," Travis says, "but I didn't quite catch—"

Georgie cuts him off. "It's Joe," he says.

"Right on." Travis repeats.

Georgie and Travis do another Brotherhood handshake. Travis can't quite break Georgie's strong grip.

Finally, Travis slaps Georgie on the back and breaks free. "Catch ya later, bro." he says, and heads out of the café.

Watching Travis leave Georgie shakes his head and mutters to himself. "Stupid kid. You know I was like that, too—once."

With Travis out of his sight, Georgie approaches Claudia at the cash register.

(Parenthetical Pet Peeve) Store clerks who ignore kids waiting in line to wait on adults who came in later than the kids.

Claudia peers shyly at Georgie. She won't meet his eyes. "So," she says, "you fixed that, huh?"

"Hey, babe," Georgie says. "I'm finished with that coffee now." Georgie slaps a $5 bill on the white Formica countertop. "Could I ask you a favor?" he continues.

Claudia smiles. "Depends on what it is," she says. "Name it."

"Next time," Georgie wisecracks. "I'd like it black as hell."

Georgie smiles at Mr Wilton, who has moved on to this month's copy of *Sports Illustrated*. He has his smiling face stuck in a chocolate ice cream sundae topped with a fudge brownie and whipped cream, lost in a brave new world that was once much sadder and darker.

"Strong as life," Georgie emphasizes.

On the other side of the lunch counter, Adam and John are holding their guts, laughing as ice cream drips down their knuckles from the cones they grip tightly in their hands.

"Strong as death," Georgie repeats.

Just then, Travis walks back into the luncheonette. He's clutching two quarters in his sweaty palm and trying to remember an important phone number. "Do you have a pay phone?" he asks Claudia.

Claudia tosses her frizzy red hair toward the back room. "In the back," she says. "By the restrooms."

Georgie smiles again. "Sweet as love," he whispers seductively.

Claudia gives him a sidelong look with her bright green eyes. "Hmm," she says, "Just like a cup o' Joe."

Georgie sets down his mug and abruptly the whole scene changes.

[Smoke Break]

Once again, Georgie is dressed in smart and professional business attire. He walks up the crowded street with a brown paper bag in his hands. The brown paper bag is just big enough to hold a small revolver.

He stops in front of Dave's Gun Shop, which squats beneath the bright glow of a revolver in neon. Absentmindedly, Georgie drops a set of keys and a bottle of Prozac on the white concrete sidewalk. They bounce slightly and then rest against the toe of his right shoe.

From somewhere, a single electric guitar note resonates.

Georgie bends over and picks up the keys and the bottle. He opens the Prozac bottle, removes two pills, and swallows them down. He puts the keys back in his pocket.

Georgie walks on, still absent-minded.

The whole scene changes.

[Smoke Break]

Georgie is riding the bus. He's sitting in an aisle seat. Sitting beside him is another Claudia, a completely new Claudia. This woman is sympathetic, maternal, and middle-aged, wearing inexpensive Wal-Mart variety clothing.

Out of nowhere, Georgie starts talking. "Do you like buses?" he asks. "I mean, city buses. Like this?"

Claudia of the Wal-Mart wardrobe smiles sympathetically at Georgie, but says nothing.

Encouraged, despite her silence, to carry on his one-way conversation, Georgie continues. "I like buses. I like their smell. All those diesel fumes, they really get my heart pumping."

Georgie pauses in his monologue. Then he strikes out in a completely different direction. "Not that I need to ride a bus." Georgie sniffs. "Not with my money."

Wal-Mart Claudia smiles disbelievingly, condescendingly, at him. Uh-huh, sure. You have money, she thinks.

Georgie notices Claudia rolling her eyes and blusters back. "Really. I'm worth millions. Twenty-five million, in fact." Georgie pauses again. "But it's in trust. You know about trusts?"

The Wal-Mart Claudia stares out the window, imagining that the conversation will end if she stops paying attention to it.

But Georgie goes on anyway. "I didn't think so," he smugly remarks. "Most poor people don't."

Georgie glances across the aisle at another woman. This woman is a stunning blonde in her early 20s. But she's not Claudia. She's not even close to Claudia.

Floundering slightly in his own verbiage, Georgie tries to bring the conversation back to the original subject.

(Parenthetical Pet Peeve) Confused shoppers who block store aisles while they make up their minds.

"But I was talking about buses," he addresses the Wal-Mart Claudia. "Wasn't I?"

The Claudia of the Wal-Mart wardrobe glances back at him, friendly again. Talking about buses is something she's suddenly happy to do, even if Georgie does all the talking.

"The thing is," Georgie says, "I really like buses. I really do. Buses make me feel like I live in a big city."

"You mean," the Wal-Mart Claudia speaks for the first time, "you don't live here?"

"I mean a real city," Georgie emphasizes. "You know, with skyscrapers and subways and garbage in the street."

Claudia looks confused.

But Georgie plunges on. "You know, like New York." Georgie is displaying his sophistication. "Or London. Or Brussels, even."

Claudia tries desperately to keep up. "I didn't know Brussels even had garbage."

Georgie smirks. "Every city has garbage," he says. "Especially big cities."

"Yes," Claudia admits. "I guess that's true."

Distracted, Georgie glances away from Claudia to seek the sleek stylish blonde across the aisle. He stares intently at her until finally she feels his stare. She glares back at him and angrily clutches her purse to her chest.

Georgie chuckles. "She thinks I want her money." Georgie laughs. "Me . . . Mr Georgie Baby!" Georgie shakes his head. "Stupidity like that," he shrugs. "I used to get so mad."

The Wal-Mart Claudia stands up and clutches the handgrips.

"But not anymore," Georgie adds, somewhat pleadingly.

"Sorry, mister," Claudia apologizes. "This is my stop."

Georgie stares uncomprehendingly. He keeps talking to himself. "I really don't get mad about anything anymore," Georgie tries to convince himself. "Or hardly anything, anyway."

"Umm, mister?" Claudia is becoming peevish. "I need to get off."

Still Georgie stares at her blankly.

"Could you let me out, mister?" she almost begs. She's pushing against Georgie's shoulders and knees as he continues his self-obsessed soliloquy.

"You see?" she says. "There it is—Wal-Mart. That's my stop."

The Great Shrine of Middle American Democracy beacons through the smog and debris of its vast black asphalt parking lot, as other passengers stand up in the aisles, getting ready to disembark. The Claudia of the Wal-Marts is becoming increasingly desperate, almost ready to break down in a flurried confusion of cheap hairspray and sticky deodorant, shedding blood, sweat, and tears.

After a slight pause she says pleadingly, "Please?"

Georgie stands up and lets her into the aisle. She hurries up the bus and disembarks at the crowded bus stop beneath the enormous sign.

Georgie sits back down again. He's left alone for several seconds mumbling to himself.

"They used to call me a madman," Georgie grumbles. "A madman. I'm not a madman."

The young blonde woman across the aisle glances around the crowded bus as other Wal-Mart passengers get on, looking for an empty seat far away from the crazy, mumbling man.

A nattily dressed older gentleman carrying a newspaper approaches Georgie. He looks questioningly at the seat next to Georgie. "Is that seat taken?" he asks.

"I'm not a madman," Georgie repeats. "Really. I'm not."

"I really don't give a damn what you are, mister," the older man says. "I just want the seat."

Grudgingly, Georgie stands up and gives the older man the window seat. "I'm not mad." Georgie keeps mumbling. "Really."

"Good," the older man says. "I'm glad for you, mister." He opens his newspaper and begins to read.

"Madman," Georgie goes on. "It's an outdated term, anyway."

The older man tries to ignore him.

"The same with 'lunatic'," Georgie adds. "It's completely out of date."

The nattily dressed older man continues to ignore Georgie. The stylish blonde woman glances even more nervously at him.

"We prefer 'mentally ill'," Georgie informs them both. "Or maybe schizophrenic."

Georgie pauses. "Or how about," he adds, "nuts."

The nattily dressed older man nods at his newspaper, trying to convince Georgie he's not even listening to this one-way conversation.

Georgie chuckles. "People used to be really mean to me," he says, "but not anymore."

The nattily dressed older man sighs and gets to his feet.

"Oh, is this your stop?" Georgie asks.

The older man doesn't answer. He just pushes past Georgie.

Georgie slides over to the window seat. "Now people are kind to me." Georgie's talking to the window, which doesn't respond. "Like my nephew, for example. He's only seven and already he understands bra sizes."

(Parenthetical Pet Peeve) Bra straps that pop.

A fat lady with a plethora of bulky packages sits down next to Georgie.

"I didn't understand bra sizes until I was married," Georgie explains to the fat lady. "And then my wife explained to me what it meant to be a 36C."

"You mind scooting over a bit, buddy?" the fat lady asks. "I'm kind of crowded here."

Georgie looks at her for a long, long time. Finally, he says, "That's because you're kind of fat."

"And you're kind of rude," the fat lady snaps back. "So move the fuck over and shut up."

Georgie slides over until he's taking up only half a seat. "I used to think I was invisible," Georgie confides. "But now . . ."

But the fat lady cuts Georgie off. "You always talk to yourself?" she blurts.

Georgie's unperturbed. "Only when no one else will listen," he says.

The fat lady shakes her head in disapproval.

"You see," he confesses. "I see a shrink. He's a bona fide, certified member of the American Psychiatric Association."

The fat lady shrugs. "So what?"

"You see, lady? People who see a shrink," Georgie explains, "They're allowed to talk to themselves."

"Not in public," the lady strongly objects. "It's annoying is what it is."

"I beg your pardon," Georgie says, "but you're annoying too."

The fat lady rolls her eyes.

"You're just lucky I don't get mad at people anymore," Georgie adds. "Because if I still got mad at people—boy, oh boy, would you ever be in trouble."

But the fat lady stares him down and Georgie slowly shrinks away to nothing. He doesn't say a word until he gets off at the office of his clinical psychiatrist.

At the psycho's office, the older heavy-set psychiatrist, Dr Scheisskopf, sits trying to listen with open ears to Georgie's diatribes and rants. As usual, Georgie completely fails to make eye contact with the doctor. He has no facial expression, no emotional affect, and a completely flat voice, yet he speaks very distinctly and brightly—almost autistically.

There is a long silence as Georgie runs out of steam. When Georgie doesn't start talking again, the psychiatrist tries to break the ice.

"So you took the bus today huh, Georgie?" he asks. He's feigning interest, trying to get Georgie to talk. "How was that, Georgie?"

Georgie stares blankly without responding.

"Am I right?" the psychiatrist goes on. "That's what you said, isn't it? You took the bus?"

Georgie shrugs, his face expressionless, his eyes empty. "If I said so, then yes," he answers. "It must be true. You must be right."

Trying to pick up on Georgie's response, the psychiatrist keeps prodding and probing. "You rode the bus then," he observes. "And how did it go?"

But Georgie still looks blank.

"The bus ride, I mean," the psychiatrist adds. "How did it go?"

Georgie shrugs again still blank and empty, expressionless. "It went all right I guess," he admits. "I'm here now, aren't I?"

"Yes, you are, Georgie," the psychiatrist prompts. "Are you glad to be here?"

Again, Georgie shrugs. "Just as well here as anywhere else," he says. "And if I weren't here, I'd be somewhere else. Wouldn't I?"

The psychiatrist has to submit to Georgie's unimpeachable logic. "Yes. That's right, Georgie. You would." he says. "But what I wanted to know was if anything unusual happened along the way."

Georgie furrows his brow and purses his lips before indifferently answering. "No. I can't say that anything unusual happened," he finally admits. "What usually happens on the bus? I get on the bus. I get off the bus."

Georgie pauses. "I talked to some people," he says.

The psychiatrist thinks, *Now, we're getting somewhere, maybe.* "You talked to some people, Georgie?" he repeats. "That's unusual, isn't it?"

Georgie shrugs again. "I don't know. I guess so," he confesses. "I told them that I like buses even though I don't really have to ride them, and even though I have a trust and I could buy a bus if I wanted. I told them all that." Georgie's flat emotionless voice trails off.

The psychiatrist pushes his lead. "So you talked to people," he says. "And how did people respond to that?"

Thinking of the blonde woman and the fat woman, Georgie starts to become slightly animated, almost interested. For some reason, he's already forgotten about Claudia with the Wal-Mart wardrobe.

"There was this one woman," he says. "She thought I wanted to steal her money so she tried to protect herself like this . . . ." With a certain genius for imitation, Georgie mimics the pretty blonde woman clutching her purse to her chest. "She was funny," Georgie says without laughing. "I laughed at her."

After a brief pause Georgie tells about the fat woman, too. "And there was this big fat lady who sat next to me. She told me to move over," he mimics her settling herself in the seat and making him move over. "Like I was crowding her. Like I was taking up two seats. She was real funny, too."

Still, the psychiatrist doesn't say anything. He's trying to silently prompt Georgie to talk, which Georgie finally does.

"I told her it was a good thing I don't get mad at people anymore," he says, with a slight hint of anger. "Boy, oh boy," he says. "That's what I said. Boy, oh boy."

After getting what he was after, the psychiatrist finally breaks his silence. "Were you mad at her, Georgie?" he prompts. "Did you threaten her?"

But Georgie shrugs off the psychiatrist's question and continues his monologue.

"I went to Wakefield, I told her," he says. "Harvard, too, after my NYU undergrad—she said she didn't care. I said, maybe she should care, huh? People are so stupid."

Georgie abruptly stops talking and leaves the phrase dangling.

The psychiatrist keeps silent again waiting for Georgie to talk.

Georgie finally does. "And you know what else I told her?" he says. "You know what else, doc?"

"No. What, Georgie?" the psychiatrist raises an eyebrow. "What did you tell her?"

"I told her that the more I learned, the more I became conscious of the ridiculousness of human nature. That's what I told her. The ridiculousness of human nature and the sheer absurdity of it all."

The psychiatrist is obviously disappointed. He's set a trap but Georgie somehow didn't step in it.

"So you didn't threaten her, Georgie?" he prompts. "You didn't try to scare her? Or make her afraid of you?"

Already bored, Georgie looks at his wristwatch. "What time you got, doc?" he asks "Is this almost over?"

The psychiatrist relaxes, convinced he won't get anything incriminating out of Georgie this time. (Oh, well. Better luck next time huh, doc?) "It's over whenever you like Georgie," he says calmly. "You're the boss here. Remember?"

There's a long pause. The big white wall clock above the couch ticks on.

Finally Georgie offers another off-the-wall observation. "It just seems like, I told her, all my years at Wakefield, and all my years at Harvard, existed for the simple purpose of proving to me that I was an utterly absurd person, no different from any other absurd person. No different from her or anybody else—because we're all absurd people, see?"

The old overweight psychiatrist looks at the white-faced, expressionless wall clock. *Oh God,* he thinks. *Now he's turning into a philosopher on me, huh?* But still he plays along. "And how do you feel about that, Georgie?" he asks. "Does that make you feel sad? Depressed? Anxious?"

Georgie laughs sardonically without amusement. "I think you know how I feel about that, doctor," he answers. "It doesn't make me feel depressed or suicidal, or anything. But sometimes I wonder—is that all there is? You know?"

The older heavyset psychiatrist feigns interest, but he's really thinking of something else, a thousand other things. Just waiting for Georgie to talk himself out. Of course, eventually he does.

"You know, doc," Georgie goes on. "I've never been much of what you might call a joiner. I'm more of a loner, doctor, and the idea that I may be no different than anybody else, no less absurd than anybody else. Well, it tickles me. It makes me . . ."

Georgie lets the thought go unfinished. He gets slowly to his feet. "Let's just say," he says, "it's been a bitter pill to swallow. I like that, though. It's been the bitterest of pills. Not like those meds you give me, doc."

Georgie puts on his coat, bundles up, and stuffs some leftover bags into his pocket. "It makes me laugh, doc," he says. "It makes me feel clear and calm, and empty—and I like that. And I also like the fact," Georgie goes on, "that I no longer feel angry. I get mad sometimes, sure. Like I did with the fat lady on the bus today. But when I think how stupid and absurd, and comical everything is—I just laugh and I'm okay again."

Still, the older psychiatrist can't resist taking a few jabs at Georgie's exposed psyche, just to see what kind of reactions he'll get.

"And you don't have trouble with your neighbors anymore?" he asks. "Like you did before?"

But Georgie is gone. Empty and blank again. "Neighbors?" he asks. "What neighbors?"

"You know," the psychiatrists prompts, "The ones who fight?"

Still Georgie stays expressionless, his slightly overweight face a smiling, leering, tragicomic mask.

"The ones who keep you up at night?" the older psychiatrist goes on. "Who you hear slapping and beating each other through the wall?"

Still, Georgie says nothing.

"You're no longer having trouble with them?"

Indifferently, Georgie shakes his head slowly.

The bored psychiatrist finally gives up.

"Good," he says. "Next week then? Same time? Same place?"

"Yes," Georgie repeats. "Same time. Same place."

Georgie is already gone. As he opens the door he stops, and then turns back. "Or better yet," he says. "I'll call. I'll call to confirm. How's that?"

The psychiatrist has already dismissed his patient. "That'll be fine, Georgie," he says. "You just call and let me know."

As Georgie shuffles out the door the psychiatrist calls after him, "Next week then, Georgie."

The psychiatrist mumbles to himself, "A clear case of Asperger's Syndrome—with complications, of course."

Underneath his notes, the psychiatrist writes:

ASPERGER'S.
(With?!)
And then he continues:
PATIENT NAME: GEORGIE GUST
VERY BRIGHT. MISINTERPRETS FIGURES OF SPEECH AND/OR SOCIAL CUES. SEVERAL PSYCHOSOCIAL STRESSORS. FLAT AFFECT & VOICE. LACK OF MOTIVATION. SUICIDAL IDEATION.
And beneath that:
Prognosis: Interminable Analysis.
No hope for cure.

Dear Diary:

It works!

Part XI: Epilog: The Waxworks

With Claudia Nesbitt tragically dead, the bereaved Georgie crushed, devastated, without reason to go on living, decides to sink his whole inheritance into a colossal project: an enormous wax museum containing surrealistic waxwork mannequins of classical heroes, and immortal figures of ancient and modern history. Georgie's secret plan is to immortalize Claudia by making her into a Greek goddess or Romanesque empress, a Byzantine queen or Hollywood sex goddess—Helen of Troy, Cleopatra, the Venus de Milo, Claudia of Monroe—whose statuesque sculpture, breathtakingly captured in perfectly life-like wax, will live forever in the bemused and astonished minds of contemporary women and men.

To fulfill this rapturous fantasy and romantic dream, Georgie must find a still-living woman to serve as the perfect waxwork model for the immortal Claudia. Although he has found a highly skilled waxwork sculptor (Amos "Famous" Daedalus) whose craft in fashioning supple wax into divine human forms almost matches Claudia's perfect beauty, the sculptor cannot work without a suitable true-to-life model. And there Georgie's grandiose project and glorious dream stews and stymies for want of a second beauty to equal the one and only, the incomparable, the true—Claudia Nesbitt.

Strolling down the crowded city street, Georgie Gust swaggers and struts through the shuffling crowds with a big lollipop stuck in his mouth. (It's a daylong sucker, and so is he. There's one born every day. And it's Georgie's day to be.)

Georgie pauses on the white concrete sidewalk to contemplate the enormous edifice (an old abandoned waterfront warehouse with smashed windows and a broken-down roof) that soon will be unveiled as:

GEORGIE GUST'S ONE & ONLY ORIGINAL, CLASSICAL, WAX MUSEUM!

The shuffling crowd around him has no comprehension of his grandiose project and glorious dream. They only push, shove, and elbow him out of the way.

"Hey, Mac!" it sneers. "What's the matter with you?"

"You stupid or something?"

"Get out of the way, huh?"

Georgie continues to slurp his daylong sucker, oblivious to the barbarians and philistines around him.

Although he's in the same sophisticated elegant clothes as before, he's much heavier. In fact, he's become rather portly and almost fat. In Georgie Gust's perpetually bemused mind, Claudia Nesbitt is still as perfectly statuesque, as eternally beautiful, and as immortally youthful as she was in the golden days of their secret love.

A broadside poster next to the museum door shows a brightly colored, glossy picture of several wax figures. Including Claudia looking supremely beautiful—incomparably sexy, yet untouchable—in death as in life.

Crashing through the museum's workroom door, Georgie enters to find his faithful assistant, Amos, hard at work on his immortal project.

Engrossed in his sculptural work, "Famous Amos" looks up to see The Boss in a distinctly un-Georgian state of distraction.

Stupefied, mesmerized, and bemused, Georgie peers around the cluttered workroom as if he's never been here before; as if he is seeing these works of classic heroes and ancient deities for the first time.

As Georgie dawdles and gawks, Amos works among several wax figures in various stages of disfiguration and defacement, deconstruction and disrepair.

There's a sway-backed, bow-legged figure vaguely reminiscent of Roy Rogers or Gene Autry, whose cowboy-hatted head is melted, making him The Wild, Wild West's greatest disfigured cowpoke or zombie lawman.

Beside it is a conservatively dressed feminine figure, vaguely reminiscent of a very young 1960s-esque Queen Elizabeth, with a smiling face that is chipped and gouged, and makes her Great Britain's first defaced maiden queen or living dead monarch.

Snapping out of his stupefaction and distraction, Georgie finally pulls up a chair and sits down. He looks impatiently at his wristwatch. "You got 5 minutes, Amos," Georgie snaps. "Convince me this Hall of the Unknowns thing is the way to go. Make me believe it's the next big thing."

Amos drops his work and wipes his hands. He shuffles his feet on the dusty floor as he hems and haws for a few seconds before answering. "Think about it, Georgie," Amos says. "Who really wants to see another waxwork Tom Mix?"

Georgie's eyes widen as he does a double-take of the disfigured cowpoke. "That's Roy Rogers," he says. "I think."

"Or a baby Queen Elizabeth the 93rd," Amos goes on, "when they can see themselves, their family, their friends and next door neighbors captured in immortal wax?"

The cherubic Amos' face is faintly illuminated and numinously haloed by his immortal conception. But Georgie still looks unconvinced. So "Famous Amos" winds up his pitch.

"It's not just my idea, Georgie," Amos coaxes. "It's a really old idea. It goes back to the Greeks, Romans, and the Christian Middle Ages when artists made dolls in the images of their monarchs, heirs, and their family, friends, and neighbors. It was for admirers to worship and adore—or maybe just to stick pins into. Of course, some things have changed since then and maybe some people have changed, too. But one thing doesn't change and that's the eternal human need to desecrate, defile, and downright hate whatever they once worshipped, adored, and loved.

[Smoke Break]

"Georgie Gust's One & Only Original, Classical, Wax Museum!!! will serve the profoundly spiritual need for the contemporary populace. The only difference is that we make our suckers and dummies perfectly life-like, life-sized, and realistic. The better to worship and adore, and the better to stick pins into, too. And, of course, we charge them to see them, and we charge them to worship them, and we charge them to stick pins in them, too—or to stick pins in themselves, as the case may be."

[Smoke Break]

With furrowed brow and pursed lips, Georgie still looks unconvinced.

"I'm telling you, Georgie," Amos cajoles, "it's the biggest pitch since PT Barnum's Three-Ring Big Top Circus! It's the biggest spiel since Jenny Lind, the Swinging Soprano Songstress! It's a surefire winner! As The Man once said, 'You'll never go broke trading on the American public's need to stick pins in celebrities.' And besides,"

Amos concludes, "it really can't be any worse than what we're doing now, can it?"

Spent by his impassioned spiel, Amos swabs the sweat from his brow and goes back to working on the cowboy. Abruptly, in a fit of pique and faced with Georgie's yawning indifference, he throws his tools down on the waxy floor.

"Just listen to me for a minute, Georgie! Dammit!" Amos bluffs. "Do you know how many times I've fixed this guy after someone decided to deface him?"

Georgie just shrugs and sighs. "No, Amos. Tell me. How many times have you fixed him?"

Amos starts to count, moving his lips and using his fingers like an elementary school student learning mathematics, but finally gives up. "A lot!" the exasperated Amos blurts out. "That's how many! And we don't even know who he is!"

Still breathing heavily, Amos pauses as he tries to keep his cool and pull himself together.

"He's just some big cowboy creep." Amos spits out bitterly. "At least if we put in some humble, homely local people from Sheltered Cove, we'd know who they were—and so would they."

Giving in to Amos' enthusiasm, Georgie finally laughs. "If anybody really wants to know, huh?" Georgie scoffs. "Which I doubt."

Famous Amos turns back toward him, sensing an opening. "Just think of it, Georgie," Amos wheedles. "We start small: one or two small town celebrities—just to see how it goes."

Hesitating and cautious, Georgie thinks it over.

"And once it catches on . . . ." Amos leaves the sentence dangling.

"I'm not sure, Amos." Georgie is still dubious. "Maybe if we dress them up a bit. You know, give them different clothes, different noses, and different heads?"

"I'm telling you, Georgie." Amos slaps Georgie's back. "This is going to be big—really big. It's The Next Big Thing."

Finally, Georgie nods. "Okay, Amos. We'll give it a try," he grimly agrees. "But I'll tell you, buddy, this better work out. Because if it doesn't . . ."

Georgie waits to let the threat sink in.

"Your ass is waxed."

[Smoke Break]

The swank three-story suburban McMansion in Sheltered Cove, New Jersey, is dimly lit as it usually is. Georgie Gust dreams for days on end; he's sprawled on the living room sofa, drinking beer and munching junk food while his current dream wife, in his dream life, is Clio. She performs domestic chores in their beautiful, very modern kitchen. The dream connects Georgie's thumb and forefinger into a circle, making it A-OK.

He watches *Jeopardy* on television. A smiling Alex Trebek is waiting for a successful contestant to select another $10,000 question.

"I'll take Greek Mythology for $300, Alex."

The sweaty contestant looks slightly nervous and on edge as his finger taps the buzzer. Alex reads the cue card:

"Hesiod referred to them as the nine daughters of Zeus and Mnemosyne."

The invisible video camera pans across the three contestants as their faces go totally blank.

Georgie Gust blasts them with his withering scorn. "God! What idiots!" he scoffs. "'Who are the Muses, Alex?'" he mocks.

Then suddenly, Georgie pauses. "I used to think Clio was my muse," he mutters. "Because of her name."

Another pause. "I met her at State. When was it? Back in the golden age of . . ."

[Smoke Break]

A slightly more well-groomed and younger (but still awkward-looking) Georgie sits at a big wooden table. Books are strewn around him. He holds one book in front of his face, pretending to read.

Instead of reading, he's actually staring across the room at a slightly more statuesque, younger, and prettier Clio, who's intently reading a book and chewing on a yellow pencil.

"Yes, that's her," Georgie muses. "Clio, just as she was when I first fell in love with her."

"I just loved the way she chewed on that pencil and how she left little bite marks all over it. Little love-nips. Now, Clio still chews pencils. But . . ."

"Now, I don't really love it all that much."

[Smoke Break]

At the same big wooden table in the University library, Georgie and Clio are talking. Both are smiling, laughing, and shuffling books and papers with their distracted hands.

Georgie, the campus hot shot, is practicing his technique and working his lines. "So," he smiles suggestively. "Your name is Clio, huh?"

The shy and demure Clio nods pettishly as she whispers, "Yes . . . ."

Picking up the subtle cues, Georgie goes on. "I've never met a Clio before," he says. "Sounds like an astrological sign. Sort of."

Clio giggles.

"Seriously, though," the suave Georgie pushes on. "Where did you get a name like that? A Greek goddess or a household detergent, or something?"

Clio laughs awkwardly. "My parents are Classics' scholars," she says. "They love the Greeks." She pauses, as if she is exposing her deepest secrets. "You think Clio is a funny name?" she says. "You should meet my brother. They named him Hermes."

Georgie clucks sympathetically. "I bet the other kids gave him hell on the playground."

Clio nods, looking dreamily away. "They still do."

[Smoke Break]

Georgie is still sitting on the overstuffed couch, still staring at *Jeopardy* on the enormous, 205-inch TV screen.

Slamming the door to the three-car garage, Clio walks in carrying bags of groceries. "Georgie? Are you busy?" she calls. "Could you give me a hand, please?"

Sluggishly, Georgie gets up from the couch.

Glancing at the TV, Clio notices that Georgie is watching *Jeopardy*. "Georgie?" she clucks critically. "You're watching *Jeopardy*, again?"

Shrugging off Clio's tone, Georgie takes the bulging shopping bags from her. "This is a new one, honey. Not a re-run." Georgie keeps watching the TV set behind Clio's back. "They ran the 'Greek Mythology' category again."

Clio ignores Georgie's excuses. "There are more groceries in the car," she says, "if you can tear yourself away from the TV."

Georgie grabs a couple of grocery bags and follows Clio into the kitchen.

"Sure thing, honey," Georgie says. "Glad to help out."

Clio is still slightly peevish. "It's just . . ." she pauses. "I thought you knew Mom and Dad were coming over. I thought you'd be cleaning and tidying up. Whatever."

Georgie sets the grocery bags on the counter. He doesn't react to Clio's innuendoes.

Clio pushes her point. "You did remember, didn't you?" she asks.

Georgie walks out of the kitchen. "I don't understand why they're always over here," he mutters. "Your mom and dad, I mean."

Clio snaps back. "They're not always over here, Georgie," she says. "You're exaggerating again."

"What is it?" Georgie mocks. "They can't afford to feed themselves? Is that it?"

Clio's takes up the defense. "They're old," she says quietly, "and frail."

"Yeah, maybe," Georgie concedes. "But they can sure pack in the groceries, huh?"

"Georgie." Clio warns, "They're my parents."

"Yeah, yeah. Okay, honey." Georgie sighs. "I'll try to be good."

Later that evening Georgie, Clio, and her parents, June and Leopold, are sitting around at the big wooden dining room table that is piled high with food.

Clio's parents are old, yeah—but they sure are not frail. In many ways, they look stronger, huskier, and healthier than Georgie, who's looking a little peaked.

Leopold is a stocky and muscular specimen. While Georgie watches Leopold stuff fried chicken and potato salad down his gullet, he checks out Leopold's stylish "No Whining" t-shirt and tattered designer jeans.

June is a stringy and vegan-thin woman with long, unkempt, gray hair and no make-up. She wears only natural fibers and picks at a full plate of food.

"Clio, honey?" she asks "Is this chicken free-range?"

Catching Clio's eye, Georgie raises an eyebrow. Clio ignores him.

Suspiciously, Clio's mother puts a tiny forkful of food in her mouth and chews tentatively, like she's afraid the chicken will bite back.

Meanwhile, Leopold is eating heartily. "Georgie-boy!" he booms out. "How's that shop of yours coming along, GW?"

Clio rolls her eyes. "It's a wax museum, Daddy," she says. "I told you."

Leopold shrugs and waves his hands. "Sweat shop, wax museum," he gripes. "Same thing."

Georgie wants to impress Leopold. "We're expanding," he says calmly, glancing at his father-in-law's waist.

Clio rolls her eyes. "Don't call him GW, Daddy," she scolds. "His name is Georgie. I told you."

Leopold shrugs and waves his hands again. "Georgie, Porgie, Pudding and Pie," he says. "Georgie, GP, GW—same thing."

Across from Leopold, Clio's mother reaches her skinny fingers into her mouth and plucks out some half-chewed chicken. She smiles apologetically, but Clio is not amused.

"Mother!" Clio tsks.

Leopold ignores them both. "You don't mind if I call you GW, do you?" he asks Georgie.

June blurts out, "I'm sorry," she says. "But you know I eat only free-range."

Georgie, ignoring Leopold, butts in. "And organic," he observes drolly.

Smug and self-satisfied, June beams back at Georgie. "See? See?" she says to Clio. "Your husband remembers."

Meanwhile, Leopold continues to pester Georgie. "What kind of money are you making, now" he asks tactfully, "that you can afford to expand?"

Clio rolls her eyes again. "Dad-dy," she whines.

Leopold brushes her off. "He doesn't mind," he says. He playfully punches Georgie's shoulder. "Do you, GW?" he says.

[Smoke Break]

After the Great Free-Range Chicken Dinner Massacre is over, Clio washes a sink full of dirty dishes while Georgie dries.

"That wasn't so bad," Clio casually observes. "Was it?"

"Compared to what?" Georgie asks incredulously. "World War II? The Battle of the Bulge?"

"Hon-ney!" Clio sing songs. "It really wasn't."

Georgie finishes drying a big stack of dinner plates and hangs the damp towel on the refrigerator door handle. Clio nervously observes, watching and waiting.

Finally, she bursts out, "Well, say something, Georgie! Don't just stand there."

"You feel like taking a walk?" Georgie asks.

Clio frowns and shakes her head vigorously. "No!"

Shrugging her off, Georgie walks out of the kitchen. He rummages through the cluttered hall closet for his summer weight jacket, slips it on, and shuts the front door on his way out.

Slightly distracted, shoulders stooped in his thin jacket, Georgie walks past the brightly lit and bustling Tully's Diner. Through the big plated-glass windows he notices Claudia, the waitress, flirting with the customers in her short skirt and low-cut blouse.

Bemused, he stares at her.

[Smoke Break]

As before, "Famous Amos" works amidst the clutter and ruin of the workroom.

This time, however, the workroom is even more cluttered than usual. There are several bulletin boards and a display board, each filled with bristling clippings of black-and-white photographs from the local Sheltered Cove newspapers: *The Sheltered Cove Sentinel*, *The Sheltered Cove Gazette*, and *The Sheltered Cove Observer*.

In the newspapers, there is an array of pictures of the swarthy and handsome young Mayor Greene and the whole Sheltered Cove Police Department in full dress uniform. Also, the Sheltered Cove Fire Department in partial undress, with trucks and hoses, and the Sheltered Cove Elementary School complete with the principal, teachers, and students.

Of course, there's a picture of the frizzy-haired, hipshot Claudia in a white cap and waitress skirt, working at Tully's. She's smiling and laughing as she carries an enormous tray full of heaping plates.

Behind his big wooden desk, Georgie shuffles through piled stacks of mail. Despite his well-dressed and elegant demeanor, he looks worried.

(We know just what he's worried about. Don't we?)

[Smoke Break]

In the white-carpeted living room of Georgie and Clio Gust's white-pillared, classical and elegant McMansion in Sheltered Cove, New Jersey, Clio works at her computer. She's talking on the phone and laughing all the while.

The big white wooden front door swings open and Georgie walks in, as he slams the door behind him. He briskly strides into the living room, still looking distracted and worried.

A guilty expression flashes over Clio's face. She hurriedly hangs up the phone and smiles weakly at Georgie. "You're home early," she says.

Without looking at Clio, Georgie glances at his watch. He shrugs as if he hadn't even noticed the time. Clio notices his furrowed brow.

"Anything wrong?" she asks.

Georgie doesn't answer.

[Smoke Break]

Two hours later, Georgie slouches on the overstuffed couch and stares blankly at the TV.

Swishily and silently, Clio, dressed in a black silk evening dress, sweeps into the room.

Abruptly shaken out of his distraction and worry, Georgie looks up and whistles. "Woo-woo! Clio!" he says. "Aren't you fancy?"

Like a classic ballerina, Clio swirls and twirls before Georgie's eyes, then finally whirls to a stop in a perfectly poised relevé. "You like it?" she whispers. "It's for you."

Georgie beams. "You look terrific, honey!" he says. "What's the occasion?"

Clio blushes. "No occasion," she murmurs. "Just a night out with the girls. That's all."

A shadow seems to pass across Clio's face, but Georgie is too amused to notice.

"Looks like quite a night!" he blurts. "Where are you girls going?"

Defensively, Clio feigns hurt at Georgie's distrust. "I don't ask you where you're going when you go out."

Georgie holds his hands up in mock surrender. "Just making conversation, Clio," he says. "Nothing to get upset about."

Clio smiles. "I know. I know," she says. "I just feel a little guilty, maybe. That's all, you know. Just getting out with the girls. It's been a while." She heads towards the door.

"Are you going to be out late?" Georgie asks.

She turns back, looking annoyed again.

"I don't ask you . . ." she starts to say, and then leaves the sentence dangling.

"I know, I know," Georgie repeats mockingly. "You don't ask me when I'm getting home."

She stares at him, still looking annoyed.

"Should I wait up?" Georgie asks.

"No." Clio answers. "Don't wait up."

After a microwave dinner on the couch, Georgie walks past Tully's Diner. Through the big, plated glass window he glances into the white-lit and busy restaurant. In her white waitress cap, low-cut blouse, and short skirt, Claudia is laughing.

Shivering slightly in his thin jacket, Georgie stares longingly at her.

That night, in the white-and-red canopy bed, Georgie is fast asleep.

Still wearing her black silk evening dress, Clio tiptoes into the white-carpeted bedroom and undresses silently. She slips into bed beside him and rests her head on his chest.

[Smoke Break]

Amos Daedalus sits at his workbench, cradling the disembodied head of a statuesque wax figure on his lap, as he carefully positions a platinum blonde wig on the bald pate.

There are noises at the warehouse door, as if somebody was trying to open it, but the door is stuck shut.

"Famous Amos" looks up just as the big wooden door crashes open and Georgie flies into the room.

Amos, amused, watches Georgie slowly pick himself up off the floor. "Jesus, Georgie," he says. "You about gave me a fucking heart attack, you know?"

Georgie carefully brushes off his stylish clothes, trying to look dignified. "I just stopped by for a minute," he says, looking at his watch. "I just thought I'd see how The Hall of the Unknowns is going."

Without getting up, Amos turns the platinum-wigged and waxen head on his lap toward Georgie. It is a generic mannequin's head—it could be anybody.

Seeing Amos' expectant look, Georgie reacts with befuddlement and confusion.

"It's Claudia," Amos says.

Georgie does a comic double-take. "Claudia?" he says doubtfully. "You mean—from Tully's Diner? That Claudia?"

Seeing Georgie's scornful look, Amos reacts with defensiveness and hurt. "She's not done yet." he whines. "I still have to get the nose correct."

In Claudia's presence, Georgie is more calm and quiet than usual. "But Amos," he says gently. "It doesn't look anything like her."

Dashed, downcast, and defeated, Amos still faces up to Georgie's criticism. "Yeah, okay," he says. "Maybe it doesn't right now. But it will. I swear to God, it will."

"Yeah?" Georgie says. "You swear?"

Amos' lip quivers slightly. He nods.

Georgie holds out his hand. "Okay, Amos," he says. "Give her to me."

Cradling the waxen bust in his strong hands, Georgie carefully examines the mannequin's head. "This isn't Claudia," he says. "Claudia has those fiery green eyes, that frizzy red hair, and an unusual bone structure. Those perfectly sculpted . . ." Georgie leaves the sentence dangling.

Slowly and thoughtfully he gives the platinum-wigged, waxen head back to Amos.

Amos takes the false Claudia by the hair and holds her up like Perseus with a laughing Medusa.

"So, Amos. Where did you get this bogus Claudia?" Georgie asks. "Did she ever even model for you?"

Slightly embarrassed, Amos shakes his head.

Georgie is baffled. "Then how did you ever get this Claudia?"

Amos points to the newspaper pictures tacked to the bulletin board.

Striding over to the nearest bulletin board, Georgie looks over the clipped-out newspaper pictures. He finally pulls the black-and-white photograph of Claudia, the waitress, off the board.

"Jeez, Amos!" he scoffs. "No wonder! This doesn't look a thing like her, either."

With his bare hands, Georgie rips up the false image of Claudia Nesbitt and disdainfully hands the shredded picture back to Amos. "You'll never capture the true Claudia that way, Amos," he says.

"You need to get her to sit for you."

Amos only scuffles his feet and shakes his head. "No. Huh-uh. No way." he says. "That modeling thing never works. Not with waxworks. Not for me. I'm telling you, Georgie, models, when they're not professional, always move—and when the model moves, the wax melts."

Georgie ponders this profound artistic truism for several minutes before responding. "Well then, Amos," he finally says, "if she won't sit still for you, you can at least take her picture. Close up. As close as you can get."

Pulling away suddenly, Amos shudders, like maybe he's afraid to get too close to his work. "Georgie, man!" he says. "I'm an artist! Not some kind of trick photographer!"

Georgie flashes Amos a withering look. "Amos," he says calmly. "You promised me. You swore to me."

Before Georgie can finish his sentence, Amos cuts him off. "Okay, okay," he says, "I'll take her fucking picture."

[Smoke Break]

Sometime later, Georgie Gust leaves The One & Only Original, Classical, Wax Museum!!! His faithful, loyal, and trusted accountant, Richard, is with him.

At the doorway, they talk confidentially and repeatedly nod to each other. Finally, they shake hands and then go their separate ways.

Georgie locks the big wooden door with one of many keys on his giant key ring.

In the bustling and crowded Tully's Diner, Georgie and Clio sit at an intimate table in the farthest corner of the restaurant. Empty plates and half-full glasses of soda litter the small table.

(Parenthetical Pet Peeve) Opening a can of soda that has been shaken up.

They're in the middle of a difficult conversation. Clio's grilling Georgie about Georgie Gust's One & Only Original, Classical, Wax Museum!!!

"But, Georgie. Really," she protests. "How is this wax museum ever going to make money?"

"Clio, honey," Georgie soothes her, "can't you at least listen to

646

me?"

Clio feigns a long-suffering patience. "I am, Georgie," she says. "But . . ."

Without paying the slightest attention to their petty spat, Claudia the waitress sidles over. Imperturbably, she starts clearing their plates. "How you kids doing?" she asks, offhandedly. "Want anything else?"

Trying to put on a false face, Clio smiles grimly. She gently kicks Georgie under the table.

Georgie takes the hint. "Just the check," he says.

Claudia, of course, pretends to not notice the ill-feeling that surrounds their table like a foul stench. "You got it," is all she says. She rips the check from the pad and smiles at Georgie. "Thanks for coming in," she says. "Come back and see us, okay?"

Distractedly, Georgie watches Claudia sashay off as she swishes her hips.

Clio watches Georgie's eyes. After a terse silence, she finally bursts out, "You know, Georgie, I have never liked that waitress."

Still distracted, Georgie stares at the check. "Huh? What?" he says. "Why not? What's wrong with her?"

Clio sniffs. "Well," she says, "she's cheap, for one thing."

Still staring at the check, Georgie doesn't respond.

Clio tries to break Georgie out of Claudia's spell. "Well, Georgie," she sniffs. "Did she at least get the check right?"

Without looking up, Georgie says, "Hmmm?"

The bottom of the check reads:

Your Server: #9.

Claudia Nesbitt.

[Smoke Break]

Later that week, Georgie and Clio Gust are sitting at the same intimate table at Tully's Diner—it's honestly just a poorly lit table off in a dark corner. Of course, they're having the same secretive, festering, and seething marital difficulties that they both stubbornly, and futilely, pretend to ignore.

In the dismal illumination, they begin to peruse the oversized sticky-looking menus. As they sit brooding silently behind their menus, Claudia the waitress sidles over and stands waiting with her pencil and order pad in hand.

Behind his sticky menu, Georgie smiles shyly up at her.

Behind her greasy menu, Clio looks disenchanted, peevish, and bored. She notices Georgie's infatuation with Claudia and she's obviously not amused.

Claudia is serenely wrapped in her distant beauty, with her white waitress cap, and her shocking red hair sticking out in every direction like a frizzy halo.

"Morning, afternoon, or evening, folks," she wisecracks. "We serve breakfast anytime at Tully's Diner. So, what would you like to drink? Coffee? Tea? Soda? Postum?"

Clio tries to smiles at Georgie through his sticky menu, with no success. She glances sideways at Claudia as she orders. "Iced tea for me," she says. "Do you have herbal?"

Claudia smirks and smacks her Juicy Fruit. "Sorry, hon," she says. "Nothing but Lipton's. And no decaf, either."

Clio frowns slightly. "Well, then," she says. "How about lemonade?"

Claudia, scratching her head with her pencil, doesn't answer. Instead, she turns to Georgie.

Basking in Claudia's beauty, Georgie's quick to speak. "I'll have a chocolate malted." Georgie puts down his menu and briefly turns to Clio. "Clio?" he says, not meeting her eyes.

The conspiratorial silence and sexual buzz between Claudia and Georgie is undeniable, palpable. From her dark corner, Clio mutters annoyed, martyred. "Just water."

"Okay," Claudia says. "One chocolate malted and one water, coming up!"

Swinging her hips, Claudia starts to walk away.

Before she's out of earshot, Clio calls out: "With lemon."

Although she obviously catches Clio's order, Claudia doesn't turn around. She just waves a hand in acknowledgment. "You got it," she says, still not looking back.

Clio, disgusted, shakes her head.

Georgie picks up Clio's disgust but doesn't admit it. Instead, he changes the subject. "So," Georgie still won't meet Clio's eyes, "how's that promotion going, honey?"

Clio reels back as if Georgie has slapped her. "Georgie! It's not a promotion!" she snaps. "You know I work for myself, right?"

Georgie's indifferent, unperturbed: "I know that, Clio," he says calmly.

648

Clio rolls her eyes in exasperation.

Georgie recognizes the familiar gesture and backs off slightly. "Okay, Clio," Georgie says. "How about we start again? I say I'm sorry. You say that you forgive me, and then we'll be even. Okay?"

Clio, in a huff, says nothing.

"Please, Clio," Georgie pleads.

Georgie obviously doesn't want to be embarrassed before Claudia—but Clio wants to make him squirm.

There is a long silence.

Finally, Clio breaks down. "It's all right, Georgie," she says in her martyred voice. "I don't mind. You can't even keep track of what I do or who I am. Really, I don't mind if you ignore me. You'd rather pay attention to that . . . that . . . !"

Claudia swishes back. She swings her waitress tray casually in front of their faces as she sets the chocolate malted in front of Georgie. Then she puts a sweaty glass of ice water, without lemon, in front of Clio.

Clio, of course, can't help but notice. Still, she says nothing. Claudia sashays away again, serenely indifferent.

Clio fumes. "It figures," she says. "I just knew she'd do that."

Georgie looks quizzical as if he hadn't noticed.

"The lemon?" Clio says. "Really, I just knew she'd forget."

Georgie feigns concern: "Well, so what, honey?" he says. "Why didn't you say something?"

Clio sniffs. "It doesn't matter."

Pretending to want to make the evening with Clio work, Georgie tries one more time.

"Okay, Clio," he says. "Just tell me about the big account you landed today, then." He pauses. "Please?" he says.

While Georgie and Clio are still snorting and sniffing at each other, Claudia comes swishing back carrying a small bowl of lemon slices. She makes a dramatizing display of setting the bowl in front of Clio. "Silly me!" she singsongs in a sweet musical voice, "I forgot."

Clio accepts the offered bowl petulantly and ungratefully. "Oh, thanks so much!" she says, dripping sarcasm.

Naturally, Claudia is sublimely indifferent and coolly distant. "You two ready to order?" she asks.

Frowning and pursing her lips, Clio rolls her eyes and picks up the menu.

Behind his menu Georgie smiles at the imperturbable Claudia.

Claudia pretends not to notice.

Several hours later, Clio and Georgie sit in the half-empty diner at the same small table in their dismal, poorly lit corner. They're subdued, restrained, but obviously still fighting. Plates of untouched food sit on the table between them. The crushed ice has melted in Clio's glass.

"I just don't understand, Georgie," Clio continues, "why you never remember anything I say. I told you weeks ago about the *Times* account and how, if I got it, I'd be copyeditor for this entire area. Not just Sheltered Cove but the whole greater metropolitan area, too. The entire northern part of the state! You still just don't give a damn!"

Georgie feigns interest most unsuccessfully. "I remembered," he says. "I took you out to dinner to celebrate. Didn't I?"

Clio stares at the ceiling. She's frustrated, unhappy, and angry.

While scattered customers slouch toward the checkout counter Claudia swishes over to Georgie and Clio to see if they're ready for the check. "Okay," she says. "That's two meatloaf specials with succotash and gravy and a small desert bowl. Can I get you kids anything else?"

Perking up in Claudia's presence, Georgie smiles and shakes his head. Clio turns her face away as she tries to snub the imperturbable Claudia.

Claudia simply drops the check on the table and walks away.

Frustrated, exasperated and fed up, Clio jumps to her feet. "That's it, Georgie! I'm walking home," she says. "I'll see you when you get home. If you get home."

As Clio huffs out, Georgie sits silently and watches her leave for several long seconds. When Clio sweeps through the big glass door, Claudia swings back toward the dark corner table. He takes out his wallet and pays her with a $50 bill.

"You can keep the change," he says. "I'll see you next time."

But Georgie doesn't get up to leave—and Claudia hangs around.

"She's some lady, huh?" she says, jerking her frizzy redhead toward the swinging glass door. "Is she your wife?"

Georgie nods. "Yeah, I guess so," he says. "At least, we've been married seven years."

(Parenthetical Pet Peeve) The idea of giving the bride away, like a bag of old clothes.

"Well, you know, mister," Claudia says, "forgive me for saying so, but she seems a little—harsh, maybe?"

Georgie shyly glances up at the statuesque and beautified Claudia. His slightly haggard and unshaven face is a curious mixture of gratitude and guilt.

"Yeah," he says. "That's my wife, all right."

Claudia smirks sympathetically.

Later that night in their enormous master bedroom, Georgie and Clio lay in bed. Clio is sleeping and snoring softly with her bristly back turned. Georgie is still wide awake as he stares at the ceiling.

The silently screaming clock on the nightstand says: 3:10 am.

Georgie lies there and fantasizes.

At Georgie Gust's One & Only Original, Classical, Wax Museum!!! Georgie sits on the cluttered workbench, bemused and entranced as he stares at the statuesque waxen head of Claudia the Waitress. The whole workroom is dimly and sadly suffused with a sepulchral green twilight. The mannequins, even Claudia the Waitress, look slightly ghoulish.

Georgie stares at Claudia—at her pallid and waxen face. Then he turns his own face toward her and smiles.

For a brief and fleeting second he almost believes she is smiling back.

For a few seconds more he stares at her shapely, waxen breasts. Then, blushing deeply, he averts his eyes.

[Smoke Break]

A slightly slimmer, younger, and more handsome Georgie, nattily dressed in a blue pinstripe suit and flashy tie, walks by Tully's Diner. He impulsively walks over to the big plated glass windows and peers in.

Claudia the waitress dances from table to table, breezily taking orders and flinging down full, heaping plates of steamy cheeseburgers and drooling meatloaf specials before the smiling, laughing customers. She's still sporting her white waitress cap and frizzy red hair, but she's exchanged her ordinary, humdrum waitress uniform for a breathtakingly sexy, belly-dancing costume.

(Parenthetical Pet Peeve) Dogs who drool on me.

For a few minutes, Georgie simply watches her and laughs. He then suavely glides over to the swinging door, throws it open and steps inside.

The whole diner sparkles and flashes. Soft music plays in the background. Glasses clink. Customers eat and drink and laugh merrily.

Wanting to join the crowd, Georgie sits down at a spotless table with white linen tablecloth, crystal wineglasses, and sterling silverware.

Without missing a beat in her swirling, dancing waitress routine, Claudia swoops over to him. She sets down an elegantly upholstered menu with a monogrammed leather cover embossed in gold letters. Then she stands transfixed in the brilliant white fluorescent lights awaiting his order.

"What'll it be, mister?" she asks in a scintillating and golden voice. "Cheeseburger and fries? Possibly the meatloaf special?"

"You're beautiful," Georgie says.

"I know," Claudia beams back. "That's what all the guys say."

"You're immortal," Georgie adds. "You're divine."

"Yeah, that's right." Claudia chews her Juicy Fruit gum. "I wouldn't have it any other way. So, what are you having?"

With his sophisticated, debonair, playboy manner, and irresistibly sexy smile, Georgie winks and says, "You."

Claudia the waitress laughs melodiously.

After a brief epiphany Georgie drops his sophisticated, playboy manner and suave style, and steps back into some version of reality. "Just kidding, my pet," he says. "Bring me the usual."

Claudia the waitress smiles knowingly. "The usual, huh?" she says. "You mean, The Works?"

Georgie smiles back.

Immediately, Claudia swirls, twirls, pirouettes, and dances balleretically away. She reappears instantly with a silver platter filled with an assortment of gourmet foods and wine—foie gras, escargot, and exotic cheeses. Claudia hovers over him and feeds him bits and morsels of tasty delicacies—harem girl-style. Georgie swoons back in his chair and starts eating voluptuously.

Somewhere outside this brilliantly glittering soap bubble of seductive and sybaritic fantasy, somebody sneezes and sniffles with post-nasal drip.

(Parenthetical Pet Peeve) Sneezing.

The boorish, anonymous somebody sneezes and sniffles again.

Snapping out of his self-hypnotic fantasy, Georgie scowls, frowns, and harrumphs.

The sophisticated and elegant restaurant immediately fades away.

[Smoke Break]

Now, Georgie, in shabby overcoat and grungy ragged pants, is standing on the scruffy sidewalk in front of Tully's Diner.

A decrepit old homeless man stands next to him sneezing, sniffling, and wiping his nose on the empty sleeve of an old ragged coat.

[Smoke Break]

In Georgie Gust's One & Only Original, Classical, Wax Museum!!! Georgie is, as usual, hard at work as he gets ready for the Spectacular Grand Opening Celebration and Gala Wax-Warming! that is scheduled for just a few weeks away.

He sits at the workbench holding a headless Claudia the Waitress in his arms. The white fluorescent lighting is perfect—the strikingly life-like mannequins appear to pulse and glow.

Holding Claudia in his arms, Georgie can't take his eyes off of her breasts—her perfect, inviting, and delectable breasts.

But then Georgie looks up at where her perfectly sculpted head should be. There's nothing there.

Quietly, Georgie mutters to himself, "No head."

Suddenly, and with a horrendous crashing sound, Amos breaks through the front door and falls face first onto the workroom floor.

With Amos' unexpected entry, Georgie is rudely shaken out of his worshipful reverie. "What the fuck, man?!" he shouts. "Didn't I tell you? Always knock first!"

From the dusty workshop floor, Amos looks up at Georgie and slowly gets up. "Huh? Georgie?" he spits out, still somewhat confused. "What are you doing here at this hour?"

Amos spies Claudia Nesbitt on Georgie's lap. "And with Claudia the Waitress, too, huh?"

Georgie sets the statuesque and headless Claudia-mannequin down and glares at Amos. But he's still too stunned and embarrassed to come up with a quick comeback. Amos takes advantage of Georgie's silence to make up.

"Hey, man," he says, "I'm sorry if I scared you. I've been having a problem with that freaking lock all day."

Finally getting his bravado back, Georgie blurts out, "So you just break the fucking door down?"

As Sheltered Cove's greatest wax sculptor, Amos isn't famous for thinking fast on his feet. "Well," he says. "Yeah."

Amos deftly maneuvers the conversation away from the broken door and nods at the mannequin in Georgie's arms. "What do you think of her?" he asks Georgie. "She doesn't have a head yet, but I'm working on it. I'm working her head and I'm going to make it purr-fect."

Georgie is caught off guard by Amos' quick-change act. "Perfect?" he asks. "How?"

"What do you mean, how?" Amos parries. "I'll tell you, Georgie."

"I mean," Georgie counters, "do you have a picture of Claudia or something? Or maybe . . ." he shudders, "a death mask?"

Amos scoffs. "What you talking about?" he snorts. "Picture? I don't need a picture!" He gestures at Claudia the Waitress. "How can you forget a face like that?" he asks.

Still slightly off guard, Georgie looks at the defaced and headless figure, then back at Amos. "Like what? Like this?" he snorts. "This Claudia doesn't even have a face!"

Still, Amos keeps up his bluff. "Shucks, Georgie," he scoffs again. "I remember what she looks like."

"Okay, then, Amos," Georgie smirks. "If you remember Claudia Nesbitt so well, then what color eyes does the woman have, huh?"

Still, Amos tries to fake Georgie out. "Blonde hair, blue eyes," he says. "All blondes have blue eyes, you know?"

Georgie stares at Amos until the embarrassed sculptor drops his gaze.

"She's a red head, Amos. Jesus, you have no clue." And now it's Georgie's turn to scoff. "Hey, you need a photo of Claudia to work from, or else—"

But before Georgie can make any other stellar suggestions, Amos cuts him off. "Fine, man! I'll work from a photograph!" he blurts out. "So hook me up with a photo!"

"Me?!?!" Georgie sputters, caught off guard by the unexpected twist.

"Yeah, you!"

(Who else?)

[Smoke Break]

The stylish and elegant Georgie walks past Tully's Diner and glances inside. He stops when he sees Claudia swooping gracefully from table to table.

She seems even prettier than Georgie remembers—even prettier than he fantasizes and dreams about. He stands there for several seconds, just staring at her.

[Smoke Break]

In still another version of this obsessively repeated scene, Georgie walks past Tully's Diner and abruptly stops.

It is the evening hour between late lunch and early dinner specials. He spots Claudia the Waitress sitting at the counter alone. From the inside pocket of his blue pinstripe suit, he removes his camera phone.

He just keeps staring at Claudia until, as if sensing his presence (his breath, his eyes, his voice), she slowly turns.

Georgie pretends to talk on the phone. There's a silent click.

Claudia instinctively sneezes.

Georgie ducks his head and walks away.

[Smoke Break]

In still another repetition of this obsessively repeated scene (Is it a nightmare? Obsession? Psychosis?), Georgie walks past Tully's Diner and abruptly stops.

There's no Claudia there.

Georgie keeps walking.

In still another repetition of this obsessive scene (All right already! We get the picture!), Georgie walks past Tully's Diner and abruptly stops.

He scans the smiling and laughing crowds and the hustling, bustling waitresses for a long time. Finally, he sees Claudia waiting on tables as she smiles and laughs with some regular customers. In a split-second flash, Georgie aims the camera-phone through the big plated glass window and shoots his masterpiece.

Swept up in his obsession, he continues to stare at Claudia with a strange mixture of desire and repulsion. He's torn between the obsessive drive to flee immediately and the intensely consuming desire to fling himself at her feet.

Finally, he walks over to the big glass, swinging door.

The door swings open. Satisfied customers exit.

Bemused, consumed, and dazed, Georgie flees.

[Smoke Break]

Amidst the wreckage and rubble of his cluttered sculptor's workshop, Amos unveils the completed Claudia figure.

Georgie does a tragic double-take. He's immediately stunned, shocked, and horrified. The statuesque and waxen effigy of Claudia the Waitress looks like she's about to sneeze.

Georgie is appalled, aghast, and disgusted.

"What the fuck!" he bellows. "She looks like she's about to sneeze!"

"Famous Amos" sighs and shrugs. "Yeah, well," he says, "it's realistic. You snapped the pictures and I gave it my best shot. You should have taken more photos and maybe I'd get her, like, you know—smiling or something."

Georgie struggles not to snarl and leap at Amos' throat. "Amos. Listen," he says. "We don't have enough money to be—"

But before Georgie starts screaming, Amos cuts him off. "To be what?" he scoffs. "Craftsman-like? Artistic? Aesthetic, maybe?"

"To be fucking around, Amos!" Georgie screams.

Amos only snorts. "Fucking around?" He sniffs. "Freaking fucking around?!" He repeats, "Who? Me? You brought me the world's shitetiest photograph to work from, Georgie, first of all. Like maybe you took it through a big plated glass window or something! And then you didn't—"

"I didn't what?" Georgie snaps. "What didn't I do, Amos?"

Amos slacks off slightly. "You didn't ask her, that's what!" he scoffs. "Like, you didn't have the freaking balls to ask her to even model, pose, or vogue, or whatever. Or . . . or . . . or, even fucking smile, Georgie! I mean, fuck, man!"

Now it's Georgie's turn to cut Amos off. "Fuck that, Amos!" he shouts. "Fuck this, man! Fuck that, man! Fuck—fuck you, man!"

Taking a wild swing, Georgie kicks some junk on the cluttered floor. He's obviously losing it. A waxen head imbeds itself on his pointy-toed shoe.

656

Amos shakes his head in disbelief.

Georgie tries to shake off the disfigured head.

There's a long and stupefied silence.

Finally, Georgie sputters, "J . . . j . . . just—fuck it, Amos."

Amos pats him on the back and smiles sympathetically. "Don't worry, Georgie," he says. "I'll work it out, man."

The disfigured head falls off Georgie's foot; Georgie stops sputtering.

Amos smiles sardonically.

"And, Georgie?" he says

"What?!" Georgie shouts.

"Sorry, man."

[Smoke Break]

Several days later, nothing has really changed. Georgie is still standing next to the cluttered workbench. The white fluorescent lighting is dim, slightly garish, and slightly ghoulish.

The statuesque sculpture of Claudia the Waitress seems vaguely greenish, slightly cheesy, and maybe half dead (or half alive?). Her white-toothed, half open mouth looks harsh and biting. Her glittering green eyes are cold and hard.

Somewhere between nightmare and dream, Georgie hears Claudia (What Claudia? Which Claudia?) call to him in a soft, seductive, and siren-like whisper.

"Photograph me, Georgie," she whispers. "Picture me. Print me. Capture me and keep me in your memory. I just love, love, lo-ove pictures. Take more pictures of me. Please, please, please, Georgie-boo-boo! I can never get enough pictures of me! More, more, more pictures."

Snapping out of his reverie, Georgie slowly exhales. He holds his hand to his heart with a slight shiver like he's having a coronary—or something.

Georgie Gust is not a profoundly religious man, usually—but at this moment he crosses himself and whispers, "Jesus. Jesus freaking Christ."

He shakes his head as he walks out of the workshop and leaves behind only silence, darkness, and the faintly creepy sound of slowly melting wax. In the stifling gloom, black mascara runs like black tears down Claudia the Waitress' perfectly waxen face.

In the black asphalt parking lot outside, Georgie finds his piece of crap Toyota Tercel parked in the white semi-circle of the silent streetlights. As he reaches into his pocket, he drops his car keys and, bending to pick them up, discovers a large piece of red linen slowly floating down to the black asphalt parking lot.

Bemusedly, he picks up the scrap of linen and slowly picks up the keys.

Indecisively, he casts a furtive look back at the brooding and silent building. Then he looks back at his jingling car keys.

He thinks about going back in.

Then he thinks about his car keys.

Back and forth, and back and forth.

Until, finally, in the sweaty waxwork workshop, Georgie stands next to the cluttered workbench. The white fluorescent lighting is soft and slightly pink. He is alone with the sculptured mannequins of "The Hall of the Unknowns," and especially with the statuesque figure of Claudia the Waitress.

With a sweeping and magisterial gesture, he pastes the frizzy red cloth from the black asphalt parking lot back where it obviously belongs—on Claudia the Waitress' pubic patch.

Georgie catches his breath. Claudia Nesbitt stands in front of him. She's perfectly beautiful and perfectly naked—all women and all woman. Her perfectly pursed red lips seem moist and damp—almost kissable, almost edible. They're slightly parted revealing the tiny gap between her two front teeth.

Her perfectly smooth and supple skin is flawless, life-like, and dewy, as if the perfectly sculpted wax had in fact become immortal flesh—or maybe something more than flesh. Her superbly sculpted breasts are plump, firm and round, and her nipples are erect. They long to be stroked, touched—suckled.

For several eternities, Georgie, Pygmalion-like, feasts his eyes on this immortal creation. This perfectly beautiful woman—this woman without flaw and without sin: Claudia the Waitress. Claudia Nesbitt. The one and only, the eternal—she is the immortal.

Finally, Georgie drops his eyes again to her frizzy red pubic patch—so silky, so full, so almost kissable—almost edible. The clump of frizzy red hair falls off again.

Georgie starts to snicker and snort. He finally laughs out loud. "I always fall for dames who don't have their shite together," he sputters as he addresses the mannequin. "You know what, baby?

You really have to get yourself together."

Georgie laughs uproariously at his own joke.

[Smoke Break]

Later on, "Famous Amos" is busily working on Claudia the Waitress mannequin. He's sculpting and molding her statuesque body just after having removed her disembodied and defaced head.

As for Claudia (whatever Claudia, whichever Claudia, whoever Claudia might be), Claudia is still headless. The patch of pubic hair falls off once again.

Amos snickers and mumbles to himself (or to whatever Claudia he worships), "Ah, fuck, man, come on now, baby, don't be so bitchy." He casts a cold eye where Claudia's head would be if she had one. "Claudia!" he screams. "Quit dropping your tangles or I'll get the idea that you want to be waxed!" Like Georgie, Amos laughs uproariously at his own joke. "Ha ha ha, he he," he chortles. "Get it? Waxed. Down there, I mean."

Getting up off his knees, Amos stands with the frizzy pubic hair in his hand.

Also like Georgie, Amos' bad humor sometimes runs to the obscene—the scatological. "All right, Claudia baby," he darkly threatens. "I have to go to the bathroom now while nobody is looking. So, why don't you just turn your head away?"

Amos takes another look at Claudia the Waitress and starts chortling uproariously again. Then he drops to his knees to remove a few frizzy shreds of Claudia's leftover pubic hair. It's not exactly clear what he's doing. Maybe he's just twitching around.

Whatever he's doing gives him some enormous sense of satisfaction.

"There ya go, Claudia, honey," he nods. "You're officially in modern times now, baby."

As Amos enters the bathroom he stares blankly towards the workroom and whispers, "Boy, when you gotta go, you gotta go, huh?"

After his business, Amos holds Claudia the Waitress' disfigured and eyeless head in his lap while he strings her frizzy red hair in the sweaty workshop. He painstakingly dresses the decapitated mannequin in her white-and-red waitress uniform. Fussily, he leaves the top buttons undone just a bit to show just a slight hint of cleavage.

He puts the perfectly coiffed and smiling head on the impeccably dressed body and stands back to admire his handiwork. She looks almost too perfect. Yet, somehow, less inspired than the real thing.

"Famous Amos" glances over at the 8x10" brightly colored and glossy pinup calendar on the wall and rips a statuesque page off the frontispiece.

Only four days until opening.

At Georgie Gust's One & Only Original, Classical, Wax Museum!!! Georgie sits on the cluttered workbench as "Famous Amos" shows off the Claudia the Waitress mannequin.

Finally, Georgie is a rapt admirer—a true believer.

"Jesus, Amos," he rhapsodizes. "She's beautiful! She's perfectly sculpted. Perfectly life-like!"

Amos only chortles as he fingers the statuesque Claudia's perfectly life-like breasts. "She's better than life-like, Georgie-boo," he snorts. "Believe me. I know."

Georgie blushes. He tries to change the subject. "What do we do with the old, sneezing head?"

"Famous Amos" plays the proud father. "Save it. Save it, man!" he blusters. "Never throw your art away. Never. You never know when you might want it or even need it again. Like, when we become famous."

Amos flies off on another hysterical outburst of uproarious laughter. Georgie tries to calm Amos down but only sets off another delirious outburst.

"Okay already, Amos," Georgie drones. "It wasn't that funny."

Georgie looks at the 8x10" waxwork, pinup calendar. "We open, you know, in like, three days?"

Abruptly, Amos stops snickering and becomes nervous. "No-o-o!" he moans. "You gotta be kidding! Three days? Oh, crap." Amos finally trails off.

"And I have the in-laws here tonight," Georgie adds. "So I won't be much help."

"Crap!" Amos curses. "Which one is worse—your in-laws or my wife?"

It's still not exactly clear what Amos means by these cryptic words. Whatever he means, Amos' dejection leaves Georgie feeling defeated, put-upon, and downtrodden.

"Whatever, man," Georgie says, walking out of the old, broken-down front door.

"Georgie?" Amos calls.

But Georgie's gone.

[Smoke Break]

Georgie walks the black midnight streets, stoop-shouldered with his hands shoved in his pockets. On the festive occasion of the Grand Opening!!! of Georgie Gust's One & Only Original, Classical, Wax Museum!!!, he imagines everything going up in flames—the old, broken-down warehouse burning down to wreckage and ashes. All of those perfectly sculpted mannequins and beautifully molded figurines melted down into splattered puddles and shapeless blobs. The tragedies of death spoken of in the opening passages still haunt him in bright flashes and sinister shadows.

As he walks broodingly huddled and crookedly hunched into himself, Georgie Gust starts muttering. His slight psychotic edge is almost bordering on crazy.

Georgie Gust, looping back on himself, walks slowly by his One & Only Original, Classical, Wax Museum!!!, trying to sense all that he can from its cold metal doors and the smell of sewage from the empty street. A rat scatters into the alleyway. Georgie takes everything in. It all seems to be dead—dead and defeated.

(Parenthetical Pet Peeve) Coming upon double doors and one of them is always locked.

An old crooked lamppost on the corner emits a static buzz as the white-lighted headlamp blows out. Without Claudia or Clio to comfort and console him, Georgie is completely alone now—and in the dark.

As he snoops around the back alley, Georgie sees Claudia the Waitress' perfectly sculpted and waxen head lolling and rolling around in the gutter, near the huge waste bins. Without quite knowing what is happening, and feeling too dejected and disturbed to rescue Claudia's decapitated head, Georgie simply observes the shapely head roll like some crippled and half-dead thing, until it comes to a complete stop.

[Smoke Break]

In still another version of this strangely familiar scene, Georgie and Clio are sitting at a small and dark table in Tully's Diner, quietly bickering.

Clio is disturbed by Georgie's erratic behavior and wild mood swings, whereas Georgie is bothered by Clio's snooping into his business and her parents' constant intrusions into their private life.

"What's wrong with you, Georgie?" Clio whines and nags. "What are you talking about; you're 'not so bad?' You're really, like, crazy sometimes."

Georgie snorts. "You have the audacity to call me crazy?" he rants. "Your parents, sometimes, you know—they just about drive me crazy!"

Clio frowns, defensive and apologetic, but still she continues to accuse. "I know my parents are difficult for you," she admits. "But, come on. What are you trying to say?"

"I'm just saying . . . ." He shrugs. "The visit wasn't bad, I guess."

Clio nods as she begins to feel vindicated. "I know," she says. "It was good—a good visit."

"Yeah, right," Georgie concedes. "It wasn't bad, I guess . . . ."

Immediately Clio picks up on Georgie's unspoken words. "What are you saying, Georgie? Really?" She doesn't wait for an answer. "You're saying it wasn't good, aren't you?"

Georgie rolls his eyes. "I didn't say that. No," he repeats. "Don't put words in my mouth, Clio."

Clio isn't really listening. "That hurts my feelings," she goes on, "because you're basically saying that you don't like my parents."

Georgie rolls his eyes again. "When did I say that?" he asks. "When did I ever say that?"

Just as Clio is about to respond, Claudia the waitress switches over to their small corner table and adopts her statuesque waitress pose: she crosses her arms beneath her breasts and juts her hips out to one side. She's chewing bubble gum, as usual, and blows small bubbles with her mouth.

As Clio's about to speak, a bubblegum bubble pops loudly.

Claudia giggles. "Excuse me," she says. "I just—bubbled!"

Clio rolls her eyes. "God, Georgie!" she starts out, but she leaves the sentence dangling.

As Georgie looks up at Claudia the waitress, it's like she can read the slightly pornographic fantasies and sexual daydreams unraveling in his head. She knows how he wants to plead guilty to them (To her. To Claudia.) Instead, he chooses to just ask, "Could I have another cup of coffee? If you're not too busy?"

Claudia the waitress just stares down at him as she continues to chomp her bubble gum.

"Please?" Georgie pleads.

Insecure, unsure, and not knowing where he stands with Claudia, Georgie appeals to Clio, but he gets no support from his wife.

Instead, Clio appeals to Claudia. She jerks her head toward Georgie. "He's not being very nice today," she says primly. "Is he?"

Claudia is supremely indifferent. "What?" she says.

Clio repeats herself. "I said, 'He's not being very nice today. Is he?'"

Georgie looks down as he attempts to hide his slowly reddening cheeks.

Suddenly and spontaneously, Claudia blurts out, "I like him!"

Clio's taken aback. She reacts as if she'd been slapped. "What?" she snaps. "You what?"

Claudia is imperturbable. She gestures toward Georgie. "Him," she says. "I like him. I don't like people who aren't nice." With that, she sashays away.

Georgie wants to say, "See?" But he keeps quiet.

Clio bursts out, "Well, you're not! You're not, you know?"

"Not what?" Georgie asks, feigning innocence.

"You're not nice!" Clio blurts.

Now Georgie is taken aback. "No? I'm not so bad," he protests.

Sullenly and silently, Clio seethes.

While Georgie and Clio keep up their embattled silence, Claudia swings back with a full pot of coffee for Georgie. As she pours, she keeps up her banter. "Wow. It's black, huh?" she adds. "See what I mean? It's good Joe today—strong and feisty."

Perking up, Georgie glances at Clio and makes his delivery to Claudia. "Like you, huh?" he says, blushing brightly. "Uh, like black coffee. The coffee's not bad today, either."

Claudia the waitress pretends to be flattered. "Awww," she whines, somewhat mocking. "Thanks for the compliment. I'll pass it on to the boys in the kitchen."

Still, Georgie feels he's made his point. He smirks to Clio, "See? She knows." he jerks his head at Claudia. "I can be nice."

Despite herself, Claudia cracks a slight smile. "Oh, yeah," she says as she sidles away. "You're not bad."

This is the highest praise Georgie has received all day.

In still another strangely familiar scene, Georgie and Clio are nibbling on their food while the regular customers, at many of the other tables, have already left. Only one other table besides Georgie and Clio's is still occupied. It's complete with a boisterous group set on ribaldry later in the evening.

Claudia the waitress wears her white-and-red Tully's t-shirt without an apron while she helps the busboys clear some of the dirty tables. In a sudden fit (that's not as spontaneous as it seems) she pulls her still-clean white shirt up over her nose and mouth and sneezes loudly: "Aaaa. . .CHOO!"

Then she sneezes again—and again—and again.

Georgie, only slightly embarrassed, raises his voice and calls toward her. "Bless you!"

The other table hushes, and for a moment everyone is silent.

In the diner, the busboys, waitresses, and kitchen help all have their eyes set on Georgie—even the drunk and loud party at the back table.

Claudia the waitress turns toward Georgie. "What?" she asks.

"I said, 'Bless you,'" Georgie repeats. "It's allergy season."

For a brief and passing moment, Claudia the waitress turns bad. "Yeah. It's allergy season," she scoffs. "It seemed to start right when you walked in." Then she stomps off.

With a slight jerk, Georgie turns toward the wall beside him. He's suddenly fixated on a local eatery award encased in thin plastic and dated for 1978.

Clio snaps her fingers to break Georgie's spell. "Georgie! Georgie!" she cries. "Wake up!"

Georgie, still transfixed, mutters quietly. "We open tomorrow."

[Smoke Break]

As the day of the Grand Opening!!! of Georgie Gust's One & Only Original, Classical, Wax Museum!!! approaches, "Famous Amos" nervously rearranges the various sculpted heads and waxen torsos of the five or six mannequins in "The Hall of the Unknowns" gallery. This gallery is the most spectacular, the most beautiful, and the most perfect—mostly because Claudia the Waitress, or Claudia Nesbitt, is showcased in it. After switching the figures around several times, and experimenting with several different arrangements, Amos can't quite seem to get the perfect tableau that he's searching for. He keeps trying, anyway.

Meanwhile, the invisible video camera outside the old, broken-down warehouse picks up Georgie Gust in his three-piece suit and flashy tie, as he tries to open the jammed front door.

"Hey, Amos!" Georgie cries out. "The door is jammed again! Dammit, Amos! Where's Amos? Amos!"

Finally, Amos rushes over to the big door. "Hold on a sec!" he shouts. "I'll get it."

Georgie is impetuous and impatient. "Come on, Amos!" he shouts again. "We open tomorrow! Hurry up. Now, please!"

Amos nervously searches his pockets as he fiddles with the keys, and wipes sweat from his forehead all at the same time. "One minute!" he calls. "I'm coming!"

Georgie, of course, can't hear him. "What?" he cries again. "What did you say?"

Amos continues to fumble the keys. "Hold on a sec," he mutters. "I'll be there in a sec!"

Georgie bangs on the door and shouts, "A-a-mo-o-os!"

Inside the sweaty waxwork workshop, a big florescent light bulb on the ceiling blows out and crashes to the floor.

Still Amos fiddles and dawdles. "Wait!" he calls again. Finally, Amos starts to laugh. "Wait! Wait! Wait!" he gasps hysterically. "I never thought I'd have Georgie Gust and Claudia Nesbitt waiting on me," he whispers, snickering.

With a sudden jerk, he gets the door opened.

Sophisticatedly and elegantly dressed in a blue pinstripe suit and flashy tie, Georgie enters the warehouse still looking at his watch. He's sweaty, nervous and obviously pressed for time.

Amos greets him boisterously. "Hey there, big buddy!" Amos smiles. "What's happening?"

Georgie is in no mood for pleasantries. "We open tomorrow is what!" he shouts. "What's going on here?"

Under pressure, Amos seems slightly fragile, cracked, and nearly hysterical. "Ha-haaa!" he screeches, "What's going on is we open tomorrow! Yes. Yes! Yes!"

Georgie rolls his eyes. "Amos," he says as he strives to be compassionate, patient, and kind.

Amos digs around in the filing cabinets, but whatever he's looking for remains hidden. "Come here," he coaxes. "Come here, buddy."

Still searching for the unknown and hidden something, Amos takes Georgie into the Men's restroom located in the back of the dusty and cluttered workshop.

It's a true Men's room complete with urinal and tank; its masculine with the scent and sight of Thine Unflushed Porcelain Throne, testosterone-inspired literature, and 8x10" glossy pinup calendars plastered from wall to floor.

For some inexplicable reason, Amos pulls an old dog-eared issue of *Star* magazine from the pile of old supermarket tabloids, and thumb-worn pornography, that drape over the white porcelain toilet.

Amos starts flipping through the pages. Georgie is restless.

"Sit!" Amos orders.

As he plops down on the white toilet seat, Georgie rolls his eyes. He still says nothing and waits for Amos to speak.

"Look. Look. Look," Amos says, flashing the dog-eared pages. "What do you see?"

Georgie shrugs. "I don't know. People, I guess." The dim light bulb flickers in the restroom. "Okay, I get it. I see celebrities."

Amos only shakes his head to indicate that Georgie is still clueless.

"Yeah, okay, Amos," Georgie says. "They're good photographs, right? Voilà!"

Amos nods. "Yeah, right," he says. "Good photographs—candid photographs." He flips to another page. "Aww, look at Britney yawning! So sleepy, and fucking yawning!" he enthuses. "And look how interesting that is. She's on a freaking talk show yawning! The fans just eat it up."

Georgie is still baffled. "So you're making fun of me," he asks. "Right?"

Amos shakes his head. "No, idiot," he scoffs. "The point is—it works. We can do the same thing and make money from it. Just like freaking Britney and fucking Oprah do."

Even at this final moment, Georgie is still skeptical. "Yeah, but," he says. "We're talking about Unknowns. Not celebrities."

Amos gloats. "Yeah, man," he says. "We're talking about Unknowns. We're talking about creating something to know about them—like they're celebrities. We make it so people want to know it. We get people talking."

Georgie remains dubious. "How?" he asks

Amos smirks. "By creating a little controversy."

Slowly, the whole sleazy scam starts to dawn on Georgie, although it doesn't make him any less skeptical. "Oh man, Amos," he moans. "I don't know."

Amos soothes him. "Listen, Georgie," he says. "It's like you say— we don't have the money to putz around. So we need to work with what we have."

In the midst of Amos' pitch, Clio walks in on them. She's even more doubtful than Georgie. She looks back and forth between the two men. In disbelief, she sighs. "Whatever it is," she says, "I don't even want to know. The two of you . . ."

Despite his own doubt, Georgie tries to reassure her. "No, Clio," he says. "You really do want to know."

Amos seconds the motion. "Yeah, Clio," he says. "It's all good stuff."

Trying to be friendly, warm, and intimate, he steps closer, but Clio instinctively backs off.

"Hey, Clio," Amos soothes her. "Sorry I kept him so late. I need to go fuck up some faces." As Amos walks away, he continues to chant. "Thank you, Georgie. Thank you! For whatever, man. Whatever, wherever, whoever—just, thank you, man."

Wanting to make up with Clio, Georgie sticks out his hand, but Clio pulls him up short.

Georgie hems and haws, "I'll tell you when we get home," he offers.

Clio looks Georgie right smack dead in the eye as she replies. "It better be good, Georgie. It better be good."

Dear Diary:

I take what I want and leave the rest . . . or however that saying goes.

Part XII: Coda: Benjamin J Schreiber Writes to Dr C

So you see, Dr C, it's like I have these schizophrenic blue-movie skits, and sleazy hardcore video clips, flashing through my nightmares and daydreams all the time—night and day, and day and night. It's not like I'm making them happen. It's not like I'm writing the script. It's not like I'm the director or producer, or anything—it's more like, I'm just another spectator or bystander out there in the invisible studio audience, watching the skits and clips flash past. Or maybe I'm the invisible cameraman behind the invisible video camera, just rolling along and shooting the pictures, and watching and waiting for whatever happens next. I can't switch the channel, or change the script, or rewrite the scene, or even make the whole stupid thing just stop!

You see, Dr C, it's like those schizophrenic blue-movie skits and sleazy hardcore video clips just keep playing over and over again, in some kind of continuous tape-loop or endless cinematic flashback. They're stuck on instant replay, or whatever—and sometimes the same scuzzy characters show up and the same crazy scenes keep playing, like it's déjà vu all over again, you know? Like there's Georgie Gust, okay? There's that Claudia Nesbitt—and there are maybe three or four other characters who keep showing up in different bodies or different egos, even though I know they're really just the same creepy people. They're the same creeps and perverts, the same suckers and chumps, the same bitches and yo-ho-hos—I already know—and they're always stuck in some kind of perpetual jilted lover's quarrel, or some self-destructive and abusive relationship. It's like they just can't get out of the same stupid trap, or get away from wherever they are—or even just make the whole world stop.

So sometimes, you know, doc—sometimes I think that maybe they're trying to tell me something. Maybe they're sending me messages and beaming me signals through my daydreams, my fantasies, my nightmares, and my wet dreams. Maybe, someday, it'll add up to some kind of message or moral or something—like in those old-time movies and old-fashioned radio plays—or, maybe, like those fairy-stories, folktales and myths. But you know, they just don't fit together; those schizophrenic blue-movie scripts and hardcore porno clips—they just don't fit together, no matter how I try to write them down, or how I try to play them out, or how I try to shuffle them and juggle them into some kind of storyline or movie plot. And then the whole stupid thing falls apart like some jump-cut, film splice flick or cut-up video clip that didn't really work—and it won't get taped up, or glued down, or somehow stick together again—ever. No matter what I do.

So then, you know Dr C, the only thing I can think is that maybe the whole world is crazy, and maybe I've gone crazy too—and the whole world's getting crazier and crazier, every day, and in every way. Or like that Georgie Gust says to his shrink, somewhere in this whole crazy mess: in all his NYU undergrad, and Harvard graduate education, and all that Wakefield prep-school jazz, and all of that psychology, those humanities, that literature and art—it just makes him think how ridiculous he really is and how absurd everyone else is, too. It makes him think how the whole world is just wacko when you get right down to it. The whole world is stupid, and meaningless and empty. And then I think, well, if the whole world really is absurd, and everybody else is just as ridiculous as me, then why bother to write, or paint, or do anything? Why bother to make movies, or tell stories, or even get out of bed for that matter? Why even bother to go on living?

You know what I mean, doc?

Dear Diary:

What's done is done. What's gone is gone. One of my life's lessons is to always move on. Getting over my first love, dealing with the heartbreak, dealing with all the death and erosion, and dealing with life itself. It's fine to look back and think of fond memories, but I think if I keep moving forward, I will, indeed, live a much happier life, plain and fucking simple.

Codex: Doctor C Writes Back to Benjamin J Schreiber

Yes, Ben. I know exactly what you mean. You should know, too, that it's not just you. Many other people sometimes feel like the whole world is crazy, and that they're crazy, too. A lot of people think the whole world is ridiculous and pointless, and that their entire life is just as meaningless and absurd. Some people feel like everything is falling apart around them and they don't want to go on living. And, they don't have any kind of cosmic glue, or spiritual super goop, that'll stick it all together and make the whole world work for them so they can just go plugging along. Maybe they just don't have what it takes to make the whole world stop being ridiculous, and meaningless, and stupid, and absurd and make their whole life seem worth living again, too.

But, you know, Ben, maybe you're right. Maybe those schizophrenic blue-movie skits and sleazy hardcore porn-flicks (as you call them) are trying to tell you something. Maybe they really are like fairytales or folktales, or old-time movies or old-fashioned myths with some kind of message or moral hidden somewhere inside them—like fortune cookies. Maybe they're sending messages from your deeper self and beaming signals from your subconscious mind, your libido, or your ID ego (or whatever you want to call it), or even from the whole collective subconscious of the human race.

The message they're sending you, as far as I can see, Ben, the moral they're trying to tell you, is really pretty simple. Despite all the self-destructive, abusive things and all the hateful, hurtful things Georgie and Claudia (and everybody else) do to each other, and despite the absurdity, ludicrousness, and ridiculousness of it all, the message or moral they're sending is really pretty simple and pretty straightforward, you know? The message or moral of the whole story, as I see it, Ben, is this:

They're trying to show you what it's like to get stuck in hell, and know that you're stuck in hell, and still not be able to find the way out, when all along, Ben, the way out is right there in front of you. All you have to do is look for it—all you have to do is want to get out. You can raise yourself out of hell, you can make a new life for yourself, and you can make the whole world over again, Ben, whenever you want to—and all you have to do is want to.

Because, you see, Ben, in this crazy, mixed-up, stupid, and absurd world, everybody needs somebody or something to make everything whole. It's to save them from the absurdity and meaninglessness, the ridiculousness and stupidity, of their existence. For some people, that somebody or something is a person, a spiritual teacher or holy man, a great lover or secret soul mate who makes their whole life complete and becomes the entire world for them. For other people, that somebody or something is a spiritual teaching or religious doctrine, a secret philosophy or work of art, that makes the whole world speak to them and convinces them they can live forever.

Georgie Gust and Claudia Nesbitt, as you see them, Ben, are people who want to find the whole world in a significant other, and build a whole world around that other person, to save themselves from the stupidity and absurdity of their empty, meaningless lives. Of course, Georgie and Claudia's struggle to discover the whole world in each other, and build a world around themselves, are tragically doomed to disappointment and failure because neither one of them can really fulfill the other's fantasies and dreams. Neither can carry the whole weight of the world they're building together.

Because neither Georgie nor Claudia can really accept the stupidity and ridiculousness of their significant other, or the absurdity and emptiness of their great fantasy, they get caught and trapped in their self-destructive and abusive relationship. They're stuck in a self-perpetuating cycle of hateful and hurtful acts, and they just keep repeating the same self-destructive actions, and playing the same stupid scenes, and somehow they just can't break the cycle or get out of the loop, or take a deep breath and tell themselves to just stop!

Georgie Gust and "Famous Amos" Daedalus on the other hand, are people who build a whole world around a creative delusion or a life-changing illusion and try to transform the stupidity, absurdity, emptiness, and meaninglessness of worldly human existence into an immortal sculpture or an eternal work of art. The problem is that the world they want to create, to save everything from absurdity and meaninglessness, and save themselves from stupidity and ridiculousness and emptiness—the "Hall of the Unknowns" in Georgie Gust's One & Only Original, Classical, Wax Museum!!!— can't really support their spiritual aspirations and artistic illusions.

So, their statuesque, classical sculptures and waxen talking heads of self-important small-town celebrities, and unknown street people finally become just as stupid, absurd, meaningless, and ridiculous as the world they're trying to escape.

So as much as everybody, just like you, Ben, needs somebody, or something, to make the world whole for them and save them from the their solitary, empty lives, it's also important to remember that no single person in the whole world can support your whole, solitary, empty existence. They can't make the world whole for you if you can't do it yourself. The world is what we make it, and so the whole world is only as we allow it to be, as we make it to be, as we name it to be. If it's what we make it, then we can make the whole world over, and make ourselves over, too—but only if we want to. Otherwise, the whole world really is just as absurd and stupid, just as empty, and meaningless and ridiculous as we think it is.

Also, Ben, it's important not to take those eternal works of art, or immortal waxen sculptures, those great passionate love affairs, or our secret soul mates too seriously—or to take yourself too seriously, either—which is maybe the only real message or moral that Georgie Gust and Claudia Nesbitt, Sir Tony Halldale, and "Famous Amos", Stevie and Mary, and all the others are trying to teach you, Ben. Their only real purpose, meaning, or reason for existence as far as anybody can say for sure, is to teach you how to laugh.

Does that make sense to you, Ben? Or am I getting too moral? You know, you can make me stop, too—or you can make me do whatever you want me to do. Can't you? If you really want to or have the will to do it because you, after all, are the author—which is as close to "the gods" (or God) as we get in this stupid, absurd, meaningless, empty universe. And whatever you do, Ben, it's all up to you.

So, Ben, no matter how bad things get, no matter how stupid and ridiculous and absurd the whole world seems, even if the whole world goes crazy—remember, Ben, don't forget to laugh.

Appendix: Final Q & A Session between Benjamin J Schreiber and Dr C

Well, okay then, Dr C. If you're so smart, and you think you know everything, let me ask you a question: What does Georgie Gust really want?

That's a simple question, Ben. I can give you a simple answer. You see, Georgie Gust, like countless other American men of his psychological profile, weight, age, and character type, simply wants to find a perfect and flawless, beautiful and untouched, pure woman whom he can worship and adore while writhing and groveling at her feet. Someone he can love with his entire soul while she treats him like dirt.

You mean like Claudia Nesbitt, doc?

Or maybe it's like Georgie Gust's idea of Claudia Nesbitt. You see, Ben, because no actual sweating, breathing, menstruating woman could ever possibly hope to live up to Georgie Gust's supreme stereotype and highly repressed sexual fantasy of his ideal woman, Georgie Gust is subconsciously obsessed, and compulsively driven, by the unspeakable need to desecrate, defile, and compel the perfectly beautiful woman—to submit to his self-punishing, psychological abuse, and sometimes to actual physical torture, so that he can feel superior to her and make her what he wants her to be. You see, Ben, just like you, Georgie Gust . . .

Whoa, whoa, now! Wait a minute there, doc; let's not get personal. I've got another question for you.

Okay, Ben. Go ahead. Shoot.

What I want to know is this, doc—if you're such a psycho-guru and know-it-all shrink, and have such keen insight into the male character, why don't you tell me: What does "Famous Amos" Daedalus really want?

That's another simple question, Ben. I can give you a simple answer—in a nutshell. You see, Ben, like countless other sexually repressed, emotionally frustrated, and secretly homosexual American men, "Famous Amos" simply wants to create his own supremely idealized stereotype, and subconscious sexual fantasy, of the perfect woman who will embody his sublimated and spiritual ideal, and still submit to his disgusting, pornographic fantasies.

(Parenthetical Pet Peeve) Men who wouldn't date anything else but a gorgeous woman even if they look like Jabba the Hutt.

Wait a minute! Okay. Yeah, I get it, doc. So you'd say, doc, that because Amos can't ever really find some perfectly beautiful woman, or flawlessly pure babe to live up to his sublimated sexual fantasies or spiritual ideal, or whatever—then he tries to make a perfectly beautiful, flawlessly pure and ideal woman by carving her out of wax and making her into a department store window display, or wax museum mannequin, or something?

You got it, Ben. However, not even a perfectly beautiful display window mannequin or flawlessly pure wax museum sculpture can ever hope to live up to Amos' perfectly sublimated stereotype and highly repressed sexual fantasy. Amos, like Georgie Gust, is subconsciously obsessed and compulsively driven by the unspeakable need to desecrate and defile, to debase and mortify— even his own supremely beautiful stereotypes and flawlessly pure images of the department store mannequin or the wax museum sculpture.

To shite on her, you might say, eh, Dr C?

Right, Ben. So, like Georgie Gust, and maybe like you, Ben, he can prove to himself how superior he is to those mere sweating, breathing, and menstruating mortal women. He can then reign supreme as the sublime creator-god, and highly spiritualized wax sculpture artist, within his own private universe and fantasy world of the wax museum.

Well, you know, doc—I have to admit you have a point, there. It seems like you know Georgie Gust and "Famous Amos" pretty well, now, don't you?

You know them, too, Ben—even if you don't want to admit it.

Hey now, knock it off, doc! It's nothing personal, you see?

Sorry, Ben. I'll be good now.

Good enough. Because you see, doc, I have one more question for you. What I want to know, doc, is this: What does Claudia Nesbitt really want?

Well now, Ben, that's a little more difficult, isn't it? But you know, Ben, despite the fact that Claudia Nesbitt is a pretty complicated character (and maybe she isn't just one woman, but an amalgamation of a bunch of women—all lumped together into one), I really think I can give you a fairly simple answer to that question.

Okay, doc—go ahead, shoot. But watch where you're pointing that thing, will you?

You see, Ben, Claudia Nesbitt, like Georgie Gust, like "Famous Amos," and maybe even like you, Ben . . .

Aw, c'mon! Get off it, doc!

. . . like everybody else in the whole human world, Ben, Claudia Nesbitt really just wants to be loved. Loved wholly and completely, for who she is as a real, live, sweating, breathing, and menstruating woman. Complete with her flaws and imperfections, complaints and complexes, with all her cruelty and perversity, her craziness and insecurity—and despite the fact that she really is something of . . .

A bitch! Isn't she, doc? I mean, she's . . .

. . . a difficult woman to live with. Just like we all are.

Even me, doc?

Women and men—even you, Ben.

But nobody can ever really give us the complete and unconditional love we want, huh, doc? Except maybe our mothers . . .

So, we get stuck in these self-destructive, abusive relationships and failed marriages. We do hateful, hurtful things to each other and just repeat the same stupid psychodramas over and over again.

Like Georgie Gust and Claudia Nesbitt?

Right, Ben.

So do you really think, doc . . .?

Think what, Ben?

We could just snicker and chortle and snort.

And chuckle and snigger . . . .

And laugh our way out of it?

And smile through our tears . . .

And the whole thing would just disappear?

And the whole world would be a paradise—a heaven on earth.

And we'd all be perfectly beautiful and perfectly sane human beings?

It'd be worth a try, wouldn't it?

Okay, doc. Here it goes . . .

One, two, three. . .

Ha, ha, ha. . .

And he, he. . .

BOOK FIVE

Glad You're Not Me

Contract

I will engage only in nudity or erotic content that is portrayed in a normal, healthy, positive, non-violent, and consensual manner, and relates only to normal, healthy sexual desires. I will not engage in nudity or erotic content that is portrayed in an unhealthy, violent, painful, non-consensual, morbid, shameful, sick, degrading, prurient or patently offensive manner, or that doesn't otherwise relate to normal, healthy sexual desires. I will only engage in conduct that I find fulfilling; I will not engage in conduct that I do not enjoy or do not find fulfilling.

Signed,

Jonathan Harnisch

Mentally Ill Artist

I'm a mentally ill artist.

I made a video about that—a three-part 'talking-head' kind of documentary all about having schizoaffective disorder and the symptoms and what it was like coping with it every day. A pretty good video. Illuminating.

And then some mental health organization in Portland, who hadn't even watched the video, told me I wasn't really a mentally ill artist; rather, I was an artist diagnosed with a mental illness.

Yeah?

Well, as Bette Midler used to say, "Fuck 'em if they can't take a joke."

Sleep Dep

I haven't been able to get a good night's sleep since I was 12. My wife tells me I fight sleep, whatever that means. Sleep deprivation. Sleep dep. Insomnia nearly every night.

I just know that for the past two weeks, I've averaged 3–4 hours a night. Not enough. I get kind of crazy without enough sleep. I start hearing voices, imagining things. Kind of like being off the meds I get because I'm a mentally ill artist.

Like I said, "Fuck 'em if they can't take a joke."

Poetrusic Praise

My friend from my Long Beach days, Myriam Gurba, a fellow Touretter, just had another book published—*Wish You Were Me.* It's so good and I want to write her in all my manicky, sleep-depped mood:

This is an extension of my manically induced, but absolutely necessary Facebook note I just wrote. Your latest publication: *Wish You Were Me.* What can I say? My Dear Friend, as—ass—I am indebted to you, but me, first—first—1st—first—for me, as usual, yes, ME, for I haven't changed that much, since I retired from Being Your Santa. Other than needing sleep (symptom of schizoaffective-insomnia), overall, I'm finally stable; new med removed the voices and the ha-Lucy's, which I call my real friends, the hallucinations. Lucy is just one of them, ha!—and most the Sz (schizophrenia) symptoms. I'm much better these days and coming on 10 years clean. Married still, awesome, I see you are too. Fuck yes. Miss "us," know what I'm saying? But don't miss 2006. It was a turning point where I lost EVERYTHING, and my family took over, and I just continued to slide. Slide slide slide. Down down down. But I hit bottom, got diagnosed finally, and redefined my values. Am about to crash from this rapid cycle, but still I'm reading your chapbook, over & over, it is purring, per, purr-perf-PERFECT. My wife cried, at the Santa part. Me, too. Too much. You have such luxurious powers over my flitting and fleeting emotional dysregulation. For so many reasons—from our friendship, to hanging out, to that one tranny story in the Beamer (I still have it).

Never Follow An Outline

Negate the outline. Wander the reader astray, do not attempt to care for the reader, kill the reader. Kill him or her. Do not mention any Borderline Personality Disorder, perhaps only implying one. No, the schizoaffective nullifies it.

Rape the neighbor, the character in my head is sublime, her pornographic nipples sting my lips; her lavish cunt stinks.

Imagine punishment, embed it in the reader's mind, and confuse her. Write it as if to My Future Wife, Natalie, maybe Claudia. No let's keep things on the real tip. Q-tip. Bet me and let me spend 10 years on it and dump all the anger inside, out there. I'll serial publish a ton of stuff—yeah! If I can keep my shite together enough to then defragment it all, and do my own Gurba-induced Tourette's thing. She can do hers—her Tourette's thing. Readers, take it all in. I, Jonathan Harnisch, man of mystery and with tits and titillation I try to fuck a thrilling tranny, getting sky high on speed first. Without doubt, no doubt, to do everything you despise and all that I feel contempt for, for I secretly loathe my self, the suave Sir Jonathan. Hate getting personal or public, or pubic. Say, I'll say "Fuck" as often as you might and I can. Fuck, I'm the author. We narcissists tend have low or no self-esteem.

Ode to Granny the Trannny: Nurse Natalie

Tourettic, schizoaffective anger, and puke; only words come out.

I was eating chocolate-covered almonds in bed last night. When I awoke, I thought I pooped in the bed because I fell asleep before I finished eating. I'm a bad, bad boy, but that's perfect . . . you're a bad, bad girl.

It's 5:00 am. No sleep, two days, three nights:

I'm really a good person. I think of Mysterious Mr Bleeker. I write to My Future Wife.

He loves you, My Future Wife. He just doesn't know how to show it.

He's angry and unfocused. And, yes, he is still aware of his relationship with you, My Future Wife.

He declares, "Here's to Modern Woman!" So here's to Modern Woman at Her best. . . .

White trash princess, hanging halo, suspended above.

I become Mysterious Mr Bleeker.

Natalie, I kiss her soft fatty belly, putting kisses there. Mother of three, not yet a divorcee. I suck on her second extra-long toe. It pleases me.

She walks, chest thrust out. Proud-breasted. I fantasize about our wedding day and that Natalie's boobs are big.

Her husband beat her, an uncle molested her, and now, I love her.

I'll date her, with all her baggage 'cause I ain't perfect either, girl. Natalie, sweet Natty, how I'd love to tongue thee. You say you like the "finger in the butt" trick. My index will turn brown for you.

You're shy. So am I.

You say you love me.

I say, "Kill me! Eat me! Suck me dry!" I love you, too but I want to give you an all-inclusive makeover. Like that TV show, *X-treme Makeover*, where they give you $200,000 worth of plastic surgery and you're unrecognizable, my dear.

I'll dress you up like a little boy and pretend I'm Jesse Friedman. Hell, his case still elicits enormous media attention for leapfrog, baby, leaping the fuckin' frog—exonerate Jesse, for his wrongful accusation, discredited psychology, they say. Gurbz and I watched *Capturing the Friedmans* on DVD. LOL. At least we did. At least I did.

Talk about ME. Only me. I deliver, baby. "Gracias, grassy ass," as Gurbz would say, so hey.

Throw me in jail, baby. Make me The Homewrecker of the Year! I'm worse than Angelina Jolie. I'll fuckin' take anyone, including women with lots of babies. But your tubes are tied, baby. I'd untie them with my teeth if I could and give myself a vasectomy with a grapefruit spoon. I'd first give us a thousand babies, for you and me, a thousand baby-cakes. A MILLION SCREAMING, WHINING BABIES for us to clean up after and for you, they'll suckle at your white, milky teat.

Give me your motherly skim latte, you nut job, I beg you. With your pussy juice, I'll make a caramel macchiato. I'll get high off your sweet Hershey ass, you sexy thing. I'm sick over you. I want to throw up all my love on you. If you ever bleach your asshole, I'll have you arrested. So give me that brown eye, you three-eyed-brown-eye boo boo. You make me a rectal philosopher!

Allow me to spoil you rotten and play mind games with you.

"You start."

"I will shove my fist in you, grab you by the entrails, and turn you inside out, red and slick and juicy."

"I'll buy you a glass dildo and you can pretend you're a slut while I give you. . . drumroll . . . your first orgasm. I want to eat tuna out of your pussy. Mix in some mayo and make myself a salad."

"I'd rather be fishing. Wanna cum?"

"On your boat ride? Yes. I'll sail away with you, like the Toto song."

Carry me off into the blue sky with its cloudless heavens with your tender caresses and charming rank vinegar-smelling toes. But first, let me shave your head and buy you a wig intended for a chemo survivor, you poor thing. I'll be in the bathtub, shaving my legs. Then I'll shave my balls with a straightedge and cut it a li'l, just so I can see you during the day at the doc's office and have you stitch me up. My poor bathtub will be clogged with my bloody leg hair. I'll have to call a plumber who will also find my feminine products clogging the pipes.

Friend, Lady, Baby, Countrywoman, lend me your ass. And your rears. I mean ears. Ear lobes. Lobe. Frontal lobe. Lobotomy. I need one.

Natalie, please, suck my brain out of my ear! My face hones in. Make your pussy SNEEZE!

"Ah-choo!"

My pussy needs to quit smoking. I think it has emphysema. It's an angry woman's face SCREAMING with swollen tonsils. AHHGLGLGHHH!

Next time you French kiss me, remove the offending masses, those tonsils that swell and block the passage of semen down my throat. Let me love you for once. Let me feed you lies. Let me lace them with arsenic, a pretty tasting poison that will make your tongue dance and your eyes dilate. I'll make pee-pee in your butt, then you make pee-pee in my mouth, then I turn that into the pee-pee that will go into your . . . ya know. The pee-pee look like Gatorade but doesn't taste like it. It tastes metallic.

Golden showers. Roman showers (throw up, yuck!) Red Showers. Brown showers. (Shitey.)

I'll cook you a Thanksgiving feast of feces and frankfurters. I'll sex you up so high that my temperature rises to fever level. I'll do the cooking in my rectum after I take my thermometer out. I'll buy the cookbook, first. When we're good and full, stuffed with shite and weenies, Wesley Willis will come over and have a threesome with us, serenading us with his big dick melodies.

We'll attend a Freemason's Meeting. We can all have an orgy out in front of the boys in turn for secrets and magic lights. They will dance around in their funny hats, speaking in their silly language, letting us in on the "big secret" daddy Bush and little Bush both know. We'll get all your ex-husbands and all of my ex-girlfriends together and we can circle-jerk around them. Rape me, Natalie. Eat me, digest me, and we will become one.

Mock me, anger me, shame me, but love yourself, you tormented, pale child. Before you can say you love me.

Chew on this . . . It's my big toe nail. Chew on this . . . It's my hair, lots of it, and lots of fucking plucked hair . . . tricky, trichotillomania. Tug on this grapevine hanging off my asshole. They're called hemorrhoids. Be gentle though, it kind of hurts. It's tender to the touch. Put your tongue to it. Bathe it in your motherly saliva . . . it's a new kind of sex, hemorrhoid-philia. Worship me. Capture my raisins in a glass jar and save my small but many growths in a secret place. Make ritualistic prayers unto them.

Invent a new kind of religion, a religion of my secretions and tumors and cancerous cells, those that are my offspring, me multiplying, inside you . . . in your barren womb.

Obsess on my medical records you have a copy of. Want me to get sicker and sicker. Want me to have one billion diagnoses of psychotically bizarre, buffalo shite diseases . . . crazy stampeding manias of unknown schizo-typical dysfunctions. I require you. Punch me in the face, screw out my eyeballs. Suck on them like a couple of cough drops.

I dreamt you'd have elephant pussy. I've got a silly Dumbo pussy. Her gray-leather lips, their broad wingspan helps me fly. I fly away.

Can you whistle out of your ass? Just pretend you ate something sour and blow a doodie right out of the park. Gross.

I ate too many vegetables to just give a whistle. The blow will be more of a yodel, to be heard on the Alpine slopes. Smell my ass, if you get anything out of me. I will give you a million dollars covered in shite if you love me. Give me an orgasm so that I faint and die and my dry bones start to quiver with such delight. The Big "O" lasts for a century.

I want to wake up in Satan's arms in the seventh ring of hell that Dante spoke of . . . I want to be suckled by Satan himself, at his left breast. Force me into a woman's body. Turn me into a flaming tranny. Hate me. And torture me. Especially my little acorns. I want to be a tranny whore working Santa Monica Boulevard and I will give all my money to the Tourette's charity.

Clamp my boy nipples. Tie them to the bathroom door at Jack In The Box and SLAM the door shut. Start cheering when you hear me yell. I hope you do it so hard my nipples pop off and I lose so much blood that I die and you revive me by holding a Jumbo Jack under my nose. I'll douche you with a fire hose, if you want. I want a fire hose in every orifice along with a fucking regular garden hose so that I can contrast water pressure.

Remove my pubic hair with a burning torch. Keep your pubic hair the way it is, please. Tickle the fungal infection between my toes with the feather of a rabid pigeon. Chop my head off while I sleep. Look me in my glassy eyes as you kick my decapitation around the room, laughing, cheering more and more. Let a little gassy out for a quick intermission. Play soccer with my bloody thoughts. If you have any questions, please see above.

Fuckin' bury me in the river, my entire—everything. Whatever. Finish me.

Okay, I'm finished.

P.S. Tear my fingernails off, all the way, the skin underneath is soft, like a flat boil. Slice off my eyelids with a rusted razor blade so I can see everything. Tell me you love me at last. Give me a death sentence. Drug me up so that I'm so delirious that I jump up and land flat on my face. Take a lit cigar and melt my eyeballs. Make me a victim of massacre.

Cremate me and eat my ashes.

Why I Fucking Write

My goal: To attain an ounce, a moment of seemingly impossible peace of mind, through complete honesty and self-love, by any means necessary.

As I sit here in complete solitude—

To Dance with "Crazy."

This is live TV. I'm on the air. Live and real deal. It's the only way I can see it happening. And that, my friends is my "bluff" face. However it comes out. I can't bluff the truth. I just can't. Not these days. No way at all.

"Can I see the complete absurdity yet pure 'possession' that this illness has on me?"

Silence.

"Come to think of it, my mind is the problem. The disease."

Remain Silent.

Indeed, those are just thought patterns. Thoughts—that's it. Not the Word of God we're talking about.

But, wait; my mind plays tricks on me. I might not be able to trick schizophrenia, but I can play with my mind. Let me give it a shot. Let me try to laugh.

OK, I cannot.

For now, as I cry my eyes out.

Inner Child

There is something about being loved and protected by a parent (or guardian) knowing that I can be loved for who I am, not what I can do, or might one day become. Unfortunately it's not usually like this in every single situation. From time to time, my parents made mistakes during my childhood. Possibly I was the mistake, or unwanted. But I don't know. I had every material thing that I could have ever wanted, but there was still something missing, as if I felt distanced from my parents, or misunderstood, in the ways that they treated me. At times, I had felt completely loved and accepted by my parents, but for one reason or another, they were unable to care for me, provide for me, in some ways that would have been very important.

Sometimes I feel like I am trying to make up for the experiences in life that were absent when I was a child.

Who the Hell Am I Now?

Envision a blend of a mentally ill mind with unsurpassed resilience and fiery intellect and your result would be the brilliant me.

Manic-toned scripts with parallel lives, masochistic tendencies in sexual escapades, and disturbing clarities embellished with addiction, fetish, lust, and love, are just a taste of themes found in my *Glad You Don't Live My Life*. Conversely, my award-winning films capture the ironies of life, love, self-acceptance, tragedy, and fantasy. I would have otherwise wanted to create art that evokes laughter and shock, elation, and sadness, but overall forces you to step back and question your own version of reality. To hell with goals, dreams, and passions. Just kidding. I want to be a Hollywood badass, truth be told.

Scripts, screenplays, and schizophrenia are defining factors of my *Glad You Don't Live My Reality*, but surface labels are often incomplete. Screw it, I'm diagnosed with several mental illnesses from schizoaffective disorder to Tourette's syndrome as I tell everyone, even the brace face lush puppet clerk at the local Circle K, just for the shock element. I dub myself the "King of Mental Illness." Despite daily symptomatic struggles and thoughts, other motherfuckers have written about me that I "radiate an authentic, effervescent, and loving spirit." And OK, I suppose that's true, or maybe I just write that myself. Who knows? Only Me. But honestly, my resilience emanates from the greatest lesson I've learned: laughter. My diagnoses and life experiences encourage me to laugh at reality as others see it. Wildly eccentric, open-minded, passionate and driven, I've got one hell of a feral imagination and my inherent traits transpose to my art, making my works some of the most original and thought-provoking of modern day.

Despite my impressive formal education and awarded honors, to hell if I'm your normal, down-to-earth guy. Meditation, Duran Duran, vivid colors, Patrick Nagel prints, and rearranging furniture are some of my favorite things. Vices include cigarettes, chewing tobacco, caffeine, obscene and inappropriate Tourettic swearing epithets, even racial ones, and sausage and green chili pizza. I sure enjoy irony, planned spontaneity, redefining myself, and change. Where do I live? In my fucking head, trapped in this cage of a body?

Fuck, what ever happened to my mind. It probably sits at some garage sale these days or on sale at the local pawn shop. Maybe at a museum. At the MOMA—The motherfucking Museum of Modern Art—maybe . . . maybe . . . just maybe . . . in my mind. It's all stuffed up there. I'm the only one with the key, says Dr C.

Time

Time for me is ill defined. We can waste time, use time, abuse time, make time, lose time. Otherwise it's open for discussion. I'm not up for another mind-fucking discussion, even if it's just some pointless convo with my own self.

Yeah, maybe I really am 38 years old—in real life, time goes fast—is it 2014? Maybe I really was born in 1976, but for any hour of the day, any day of the week, I could just as easily be 12 or 13, 24 or 30. I just as easily could be in the year 2014 or 1914. Time traveler, that's me.

August 6, 2006

Myriam:

Sorry about rushing off that e-mail last night about Thursday, I panicked. I had been in a spell from Wednesday evening until we spoke and had been missing my little kitten, Sprinkles. She had been trying to venture out on the patio here all day. I kept trying to keep her inside. Having not seen her for two days, I kept making up imaginary reasons of why she wasn't here and shortly after I got off the phone with you last night I learned that Sprinkles had fallen off the balcony down 20 stories from the oceanfront loft I just scored to get away, from persecution, and things, and that neighbor sex partner demon chick, onto the cement and died. I'm going through a rollercoaster of emotions and just need a little more time to think. Thank you for understanding.

My Santa. . . August 10, 2006

Jonathan,
I'm really sorry about your kitten. I hope you feel better soon.
Myriam

August 18, 2006

Hey Gurbz,

Hope you're doing well. I'm through the toughest part of dealing with my little kitty's death and have been thinking about you and your book deal. Hope you guys can settle on a nice cover that'll do the job—being funny and sexy at the same time. Let me know. But she must be a chick who's fucking playing with her hair—if she's not nibbling at the roots in a trichhie way. I'm a little wired on espresso this morning and waiting for my own book to come back from an editor I recently found (it's a Canadian service I looked up on the web). They did a short story for me and I think they'll work out for Broken-Hearted Jubilee: Perverted Tales . . . I like that they're anonymous, I don't have to be afraid to show my most private writing to them.

Call me soon if you can, when you're off work, we'll catch up. You know, I don't like to call anyone when I'm going through a depression or a "Jonathan spell," but I'm "cool dude" now, never a dull moment with me!!

Peace, light and subtle Tourette's syndrome.

By the way, please make me smile by adding a gentle "willow" at the end of our notoriously "us" "coffee . . . meadow . . . willow!" official ensemble tic and repeat thick thick thick. What sound vibrations! I never thought such sick perfection was possible though such utterings of stutter and nutter butter. Makes me wetter. Wear a sweater.

(Parenthetical Pet Peeve) People, usually a parent, who asks, "Where is your sweater?" (Or some other item), when they really mean "Why aren't you wearing your sweater?"

Cold. Not hot. Shite.

694

SMS

Day 1, 2006 A quick tic circa when I used to hang out with Myriam and Giggly, the Tourettic Trio

To My Future Wife:
"penis nipple asshole vagina"
Sent from my cell

Reply
   "U turn me on mightily
   Love,
   Your Future Wife"
   Sent from my cell

Doctor Whom?

I'm not necessarily Doctor Who (yet I have had many doctors, in the past, the present, and in the past yet to be; I'm one sick puppy, a mentally ill maze.) I'm not a Time Lord now, more an extraterrestrial though I might only think I am because I have a comorbid form of schizophrenia.

Band Intermission

Duran Duran, by the way, is my favorite band, other than that, rubber, after that, Post it Notes.

[Smoke Break]

I don't travel through time or space (unless I'm meditating which I am awesome at, also going out of my own body) but I am like Doctor Who as I explore the universe at random, using my extensive knowledge of science, technology, and history—the latter, like author Myriam Gurba, to avert whatever crisis I encounter. Besides, I have never even seen this show *Doctor Who.* I just looked up the summary on Wikipedia. I take the easy way out. It's not always easy, though and, like Kermit the Frog, being green is not easy. Though if you ask me, he's got more peeps than Pocahontas.

I am Myriam Gurba's Santa, so be me, not her. I've lost all my riches and glory, just not my character, and while I may not "do transsexuals" with any regularity these days, on occasion, they're still on my fave list on that slimy little porno pay-per-view site I frequent, though I don't even get off, and I mean I don't get off to anything, sexually, I just watch with fervent interest and fascination, like I do with *2 Girls, 1 Cup.* I research, I collect. I rock the mic. I do. I've got three albums out on iTunes; I'm on the charts too, man. #24 on the Albuquerque Metropolitan Area Indie Music Hit List. Shite List. Of course, the best one. Only the best for me.

The "fictional" (sure) Santa in Myriam Gurba's chapbook *Wish You Were Me.* Hell, I'm busting this one out, ah, the thoughts, the blood in my heart through the conduits of my mind, blood turning into this ink, right here and right now, and onto the printed page. Gurba's the chick who got me started on my own 500-page transgressive epic, just as she did, and as it was for her, Grove Press, all of them, they all reply the same way, "It is too long, you're not Stephen King writing *It* and you sure as hell aren't Tolstoy with *War and Peace,*" except the pubbies usually write, if they do at all . . . still, nothing. Literally, I've gotten blank pages back from two of them in the past, but hey, in Hollywood, they don't give shite about writers. There, in Hollywood, you get nothing. Just theft.

698

Queer Theory/Why I Write:

I've got this killer idea, this concept that I'm this fictional character coming out of the woodwork as a real person. Real? Here's what I write to Myriam, once I finally get the damn book that changed me, her book *Wish You Were Me*. She defined me, who I always was and still am. Santa. Nothing really changes. Not that much.

My little Facebook message to the very big fat and tall, basically as she puts it herself (I just paraphrase for her). Leave the bickering for later. Then we'll dance attendance at the opera with Chuck Palahniuk and Henry Miller (resurrected from the dead), oh and my fantasy date with the late Kathy Acker, sexy sexy sexy, I do love imperfections, ask Myriam; but I am married, now my wife is a woman, and born a woman, at least I think, and she's 25 years older than me. OK I exaggerated by a year, but hey I got the MILF (or GILF) fantasy fulfilled. Hell, yeah. Gimme gimme gimme credit. Five years married. Ten years clean and sober, but always a schizo for life. And a Touretter, big deal. The meds made me so huge. I was 285. Lost 80 pounds. Now, any old bully wants to taunt me these days, it can't be about my weight. I'll eat a hard-boiled egg and rub my big pimply 36-year-old resilient ass on them as I lay one wafting. Or I can just go off my meds for a week and go all schizo on 'em. How's that for busting stigma?

How's that for being a mentally ill artist?

I used to get these rage attacks, shite. I'll tell you, you're more than welcome to be the me I used to be. That's just not the me I am now. And don't worry I'm not here to go all hangdog evangelical on your ass. I'm just going to seduce you. Try to. Fail with glorious misery.

Zen

I don't know [fill in the blank because I can't.]

700

I am a Responsive Santa on Steroids

I am "Santa," himself, if you've even read Gurba's little book, it's fucking pioneering with all its weird and unexplored thought patterns, and pure Gurba essence, and her, her shite. I love the shite of good people.

I'm just fuckin' it, writing my own *Wish You Were ME*—A Response to Myriam Gurba's *Wish You Were Me* [*well, her*], just as bizarre, weird and as sarcastically sacrilegious, as she writes, making my "ME" just as good if not better than hers, but a total declaration of thanks and praise to all famous people, even Myriam and Corey Haim, and just as she writes about knowing famous people, so do I. Even Kevin Bacon was an acquaintance. She writes that he shite in public in front of her on Melrose? Hell on earth is funny.

Assess Up on the Cover

I'm even gonna put a photo of "Buddy the Donkey" on my cover as Myriam did with her bunny, and insert pics of M & Me with my "coffee . . . meadow" Myriam "Mona Lisa," being Santa, to me, also the piece she referenced which we wrote together, a snapshot of the "Haim original" painting, too.

Bad Days

Bad days will come but I've Got Tics. Do you?

In response to *Wish You Were Me*, and in the same vein, adding ME, Wish You Were ME, not *her* by an otherwise so-to-speak straight, out of the closet fictional character. Give me my piece, or at least some pussy, I do wish you were me, but fuck it, I love being me; you don't got a shot at being me, I'm fucking Santa Claus. Just not raping him, he's too old.

Rocking out in this schizoaffective frenzy of manic depression, voila, voila! Entirely, carrying on the story she wrote about me and she talks (even shite) about celebs and I'll have Buddy, my donkey as my cover photo, if I have any say anyway; oh, let me bicker with my own publishers so that it bothers me enough so that I can have the glory to even brag that I'd be bickering with my publishers. Agents. Entourage. Bring to the ballroom, and let's have a tea party and socialize like the gay old Truman Capote. OK, so I've only seen the movie, never read him. I do wish you were me, because I get by without reading but watching, sometimes with my eyes closed, so it's kind of like watching an audio book. Oh man, have I learned how to learn by learning in the first place, not cheating by cheating at first, to really get how to not cheat, or steal, creatively I mean, though I did steal a lollipop once when I was five. A boy, and boy did I learn my lesson fast. Mother not only beat the living pulp out of me, but humiliated me in front of the clerk at the drug store (a drug store, for my Tourette's meds).

My darling friend, an old friend, a friend who is young, but the friendship is ancient, actually. Heck, she and I go back into past life relationships and thus currently existing right now, well, you know with the parallel universe stuff and all that funky jazz. Benny Goodman comes to mind. Frank Sinatra, Judy Garland. Other singers. Something about the A Train.

Thoughts. Thoughts bombard my head, my brain. My psyche.

I am so happy today, finally, I mean as I always say—well I don't say it, per se, but I might insert it into my favorite quotes—and I think I am the author of it, but you know, when writing, the idea that everything. Yes, everything has already been written, thanks to Shakespeare, mostly, and for having to hear that in some film class back at NYU. Later, I learned it's how these things are written in new ways, so I guess all us writers are technically borrowing and borrowing. Some even steal. That's rotten. Charlie Kaufman, I mean, he and possibly Linklater (Richard, or "Rick"), though I only met him once. No, wait, twice: the first time I showed up at a private screening of the *Newton Boys* in Queens, wearing a full-on tuxedo, with bow tie and cummerbund, and a lot of speed in my system. At the time, ephedrine was actually legal. Thank God it's not anymore. People die from it, and now they've got these awful bath salts, but I've got, and thanks to God again, 10 years coming up of sobriety, and the real-person thanks goes to Mel Gibson, who is back in touch with me again. My father figure. You know Mel? Everyone knows him. Ask him. It's true. He and I have built memories together, just memories, and the resurrection of reconnecting. We haven't been in touch since 2005 or 2006. Mel saved my life back in the early 2000s. I owe him. I owe this man Mel. Calling to him, as I am.

I think he knows how special he has been in my life since January 15, 2001. The feelings are mutual, and no, I don't read any of that tabloid bull. Back when I worked in Hollywood, before my illness took over in mid-2006, I wrote with Robert Downey Jr. and Jonathan Elias, got the inside scoop from PR king, Alan Nierob. I loved that old life. Now it's gone: Joel Silver, Ed Limato. Limato is now dead, but he ran Hollywood back then. It was fun while it lasted and now some of it, some of *them*, are reemerging in my life and that's cool—you know, the fact that I did a TV pilot with Corey Haim, my roommate at the time; I was filling in for the Corey Feldman buddy role. They had parted ways then got back to being brothers. The Haimster passed, too; so did my NYU thesis instructor Gary Winick. Tic. Yikes he wasn't even 50. He took me to one of his earlier debuts once (the premiere) of *The Tic Code*, one of two films; the other was called *Maze*, with Rob Morrow. I helped train the actors with how to pretend to have Tourette's. It was fun and funny, too. I love scattered minds, this self, this Santa, freaks, and these fragments.

On to Myriam, Myriam Gurba, the award-winning author of *Dahlia Season*, as a finalist for a Lammy, a whammy, selected as a teen read by the New York Public Library, made various top-10 book lists, and won the Edmund White Award for debut fiction. See, it's this newer (2011) book, well, what they call a chapbook, a pop culture kind of pamphlet book. The story behind how these bitches came to be back centuries ago in England . . . tic, be nice. Anyway, Myriam wrote me in. Yes, she didn't say a thing to me about it, and a year later, I finally hear about her new book, *Wish You Were Me*. And so, I'm reading this cool as hell pamphlet of a book, basically, by the wildly crazy rocking small press called Future Tense Books. So I'm reading this, it's got that Gurba gay/lesbian edge, twist, twitch, shout. Shout, "Wow! I can't believe she said THAT!" I wouldn't otherwise flaunt what crack cocaine has caused me to do, sexually, (oh hell, yes, I already do) and yet, it's all coolzies. Me cry baby at the part about me. I was her Santa, and Myriam Gurba was happy to hear that I was happy to have read what she happily had written about me, a chap-ter (pun intended) on its own in the "Boyfriends" section. My wife even cried, hard, like a woman, like me. My teeth sparkled enough that I could either do my own special effects for an Aquafresh commercial or write a testimonial to all these, well, some of the how-cool-it-is to know famous people, but just as people. They turn the world; hell, my cousin was/is Pete Harnisch, my father has a better performance record than George Soros, and the list goes on, and so do I.

(Parenthetical Pet Peeve) Commercials for unappetizing products shown at meal times . . . feminine hygiene products, jock itch, yeast infections, etc.

And that's what makes all the difference. Schizoaffective alone is tough, the Tourette's that's like second nature now, who cares? So, I twitch. I pucker my lips and click.

Mood: Total Random (House)

Have you been experiencing weird dreams lately? I have. Good movie idea, *The Dream Telepathic.* Ah! Whether or not there's Pisces energy in the air, I have an extremely open mind, but can only take in so much of the "out there shite," as fascinating as it is. Must I creep in a giggle here and mention that (random, again) I could probably get a PhD in quantum entanglement [and the thoughts trail off, into Divine Oblivion.]

My imagination is exacerbated by mania, indeed made brilliant! Kind of like a mix between the great authors of our time, Julian Darius and Myriam Gurba. Myriam, if anyone as out there as me, ME, she might "get" this weird and bizarre written tic because I sure don't. But I do LOL! And might even LMAO, with my OCD, and TS, SA, Sz, but I won't fly because of TSA, but I'll support the TSA (Tourette Syndrome Association).

706

Back to Reality

Got Blessed?

In the context of "what I 'dreamed' my life story could have been" if I had crashed this party, in this live colorful life as Georgie, etc., and thus either my name would have been John, and I lived in a whole other time period, and it all would have begun with my meeting up with a prostitute with a heart of gold in 1830, say. . ." (Then the rise to glory. . .) was slanted and I ended up somewhere, in Long Beach, in New Mexico. In the US Fucking A, of all places, in a whole other life story.

Voila . . . so this is how it did happen, and maybe that was in fact my past life. After all, I am Ben, who is Georgie, and Jonathan is really, let's just say he's some guy using a pen name—maybe he, or I, will come on out of the creative closet and put a load on this obsession I haven't yet told Kelly about. Ah, Kelly and I—a happy marriage concerning two forgivers, so forgive me, I lie, I steal, and I cheat. I'm one selfish hell of a guy. I'm dammit—damn—I'm a hot damn schizophrenic self-discriminating unconventional outcast. I hide. Hell, I play hide and seek still, just so someone can say they found, well . . . me. Who am I? Benevolent Georgie. I'm David Foster Wallace. I'm dead. You're dead. We're all crazy. We are all metaphors and we are all good. Ah. We're confused, and delusional with illusions set in our minds through creative conditioning—so prior to age 7—ah, who the hell knows. Even Henry Miller, Kathy Acker and her double mastectomy and death. We all have hearts. They just seem to go astray for a while.

And I'm dying to write. Write. Write. Write. Just as Dr C (A-B-C . . . . D-E-F and even Pops, even Heidi, with the Winterbourne, they all told me, demanding I write, which brings me to Claudia (or Vivienne Babylon)—who knows. I caught her, and on hidden tape, yes, I'm a paranoid type, a safe type. I type. I am itself a safety mechanism. Jonathan. Blah! Blasphemy. Bliss. I drop a small hit of Huxley's mescaline as I read over *The Doors of Perception*—it guided me, then Hemingway, and Kerouac. Nope never read them. Audiobooks, to no avail. I'm a Wikipedia freak. I sneak a peek—those bathroom books come to mind: I poop while reading a one-page summary of *War and Peace*, and even *Beowulf*. And I confess I tell everyone I'm well-read, while I'm well-said. I'm a conniving compulsive liar, The easy way out isn't always. Easy. The speed's kicking in now, the ink bleeds into red font (errors and system overload) on to the crooked screen. I'm On the Road. I'm quick and speedy. Sped up. I'm crazy. I'm . . . somewhere, if anywhere, and can't get away from my self. Everywhere I go, I'm there, too. Fuck. Well, screw it. The metaphor of my life. An existential mind fuck. Let's call this one: *Of Crime and Passion* . . . .

Prologue

It was nothing political, although it might seem so to some. The scheme was that of any hothead who grows weary and slowly sees the light and ends by devoting himself to the cult of luxury. One very important detail: Everything can be acquired in solitude.

Everything, that is, except character.

My actions were but an act of revenge, of defense, that I may be appreciated.

It begins on the day of my 18th birthday, although there's no one else on earth who could tell you that. I am young, tall, awkward, unsure. I have taken my father's bicycle. Now that he has bought a car, the bike is pretty much mine to use. I don't mind biking much—but I prefer horse riding. I enjoy watching the tall, grassy turf slide past me, spreading over vast meadows, hills, and through lily fields. Together, we splash through small streams and rattle over the washboard of the dirt roads. I am a man on a mission. Together, we come to a stop on the grounds of the old farmhouse, the rotten old building at the edge of the property that the company has never bothered to tear down nor seems to know exists. This suits me fine, of course. As a child, I had played there in the dark cool shadows of aged wood—it was my hideaway, my castle. I slip from the saddle, tossing the reins over a well-worn post, and then walk towards the black, rectangular opening of the farmhouse door.

I blink as I step into the cool interior, adjusting my gaze to the shadows. I see a glimpse of smooth white, of naked skin.

"Close your eyes," she commands. For a moment I comply, but cannot keep my gaze from her for long.

"Close your eyes," she repeats when I look again. She stands and her beauty is before me.

My eyes grow large; I fall to my knees. "Chantal?" I whisper.

She holds her hand out. I kiss it, trembling slightly.

"Ah-ha! You have found me," she blushes and then giggles. "You must be John Marshal. Or . . . Juan Marcinel?" I shudder with shock that she knows my true name. A knowing smirk appears on her lips. "Fine, I will call you John." She shrugs. "Your friend Seth told me about you."

I stare at her mouth, unable to make eye contact. My hands are clammy at my sides, my heart pounds. "I have changed little since I last saw him," I choke.

Chantal relaxes her face and smiles. "Where are you from?"

"Nowhere of any im-importance," I stutter. "Nor is my family of any importance. I grew up in the factory."

"You are sweating," she notes.

"I'm nervous."

"Nervous? Why?" She opens her eyes widely, and I know I should relax. But I cannot.

"Because I am suddenly blind and deaf," I whisper, wiping my forehead.

Chantal giggles. "I do not believe you!" she teases.

I smile, a glimmer of wit returning to my mind. "It's not your fault, Chantal. Nature has been so kind to you."

"Thank you." She grins and then gestures for me to join her on the low bench that is built into the wall. She kneels before me, and then slowly removes my boots and begins to rub my feet.

"Now, close your eyes," she purrs, unbuttoning her shirt and revealing her small, natural breasts. The glimpse of white blinds me and I can't help but shut my lids. I slump against the wall like a dead man—motionless, my eyes to heaven.

Later, she dresses me carefully, lovingly. I am distracted, staring into space, glancing at my horse, whose eyes were fixed on me knowingly.

"Do you regret it? Is there something wrong?" she asks quietly.

"This is new for me," I acknowledge stiffly. "I am sorry." I reach into my pocket and pull out the handful of cash I had shoved there.

"Is that so?" She waves it away. "Well, now you are an expert. No more worries."

I exhale slowly, and then put the money back in my pocket. "Are you married?" I ask finally.

"No," she answers lightly.

I stretch out my arms to her. "Are you engaged to marry?"

She leans against me, her touch light, her presence warming. "You are sweet and gentle," she notes, "seductive. And, Master John, seduction is the key to all that you want in life."

"Is that so?" I ask nonchalantly. But a part of me takes heed.

"What is it that you want?" she asks cryptically.

I shake my head. "I'm not sure."

"You seem so bright, Master John," she says, looking up at me with earnest eyes. Her fingers lightly play with the hair at my neck.

"Tell me. I'll not say a word."

I look inside my own mind and sigh. "Earthly immortality," I reply.

"But that is impossible!" she teases.

"Glory," I continue.

"To achieve great praise? Heavenly bliss . . . splendor? Hmmm . . . ." She purses her lips.

"Yes." I nod triumphantly.

"The greatest man to achieve glory was Che Guevara," she says, after a moment's thought. "You know, he used a very scientific method to achieve his glory."

"Seduction?" I guess.

Chantal walks to the doorway, and then looks over her shoulder. "Che Guevara is a hero to everyone who knows about him. He started with nothing and he became everything."

"How did he do it?" I insist.

Chantal smiles as I answer my own question.

"Seduction," I say quietly.

"I know of no better way," she sings. "Could you conceive of a better way than that used by the very man who gave us our freedom?"

I wait, and then join her at the doorway.

"Perhaps I'll be joining the priesthood," I mention.

She shakes her head as I approach. "Perhaps the military. No?"

"Perhaps." I nod.

She holds out her hand, and I bring it to my lips. "I do wish you much luck, Master John," she says firmly, her eyes shining. "I would have liked, very much, to see you again. But I am off to the City in three days to be wed to a very wealthy man, and I must retire."

I start in shock, and then concede. "You have found what you want?"

"I had the right mentor." She bats her lashes.

"I apologize. I am still a little confused, Chantal."

Chantal removes a small portrait from her cleavage. It's folded and tattered. She hands it to me. "Have this," she insists.

I look at the portrait of the familiar man, the man whose face is known to so many. It is hand-signed. "Che Guevara," I breathe. "And it's signed. Is it real?"

Chantal nods. "You'll understand. I have no fear that you'll find everything you desire."

At that, she turns from me and whisks out the doorway. "Farewell, John Marshal!" she calls over her shoulder, and then she is around the corner of the house and gone.

And so my fate was set, although even without the portrait I might have eventually found my way. But from that moment on, I had no other direction.

And of course, I never saw Chantal again.

Chapter 1

In the old, beat-down back room of my father's factory—the factory he manages, but does not own—the ancient Father Padric sits in priest robes. The man's face is lined and sagging in places—his hands covered in purple spots. Sometimes I think he couldn't bear to live another year, but then he speaks—his voice is deep and full—and I think that perhaps he'll live forever.

"Hurry, John," he says with quiet authority. "Mr Roman will be here any minute."

I pull the priest robes over my head and then fumble with the Roman collar, my hands shaking. Finally, the clasp comes together and I jolt as the ground begins to shake beneath me—it growls like metal sliding against . . . the bright sheen of a guillotine blade flashes before my inner eye. I gasp and look to Father Padric, who leans unsteadily against his desk. Dust seems to rise up from every surface and dance in the air.

The mounted silver cross behind Father Padric trembles and quakes and then seems to leap from the wall.

"Father!" I cry, and in two swift strides I pull him to my side of the desk.

With a loud, resonating clang the cross plunges into the wood floor, recoils against the wall, and then falls back down, shuddering. We also shake as the earthquake's final tantrum rocks the entire factory.

When the ground is still, Padric sags into my arms. I am amazed by how light he is.

"Are you all right, Father?" I say, my voice trembling still.

"Fine," he wheezes slightly, and then coughs. "You?"

I nod. "*Ita Pater*," I say quietly, taking comfort in the familiar words.

Padric smiles.

"The earth moves to shut us up, you little cricket. You're always mumbling to yourself like you have a mouth full of cherries." He looks up. "Bookworm," he accuses.

I laugh with him, glad to shake off the last of my fear. His brows suddenly lower.

"But John, do not forget that the Mayor is a strict conservative.

Your morals have already been questioned." He turns and looks directly at me.

"Then what turned their decision in my favor?" I wonder.

Padric looks at me meaningfully. "The time you studied Theology with me," he says. He steps to me and reaches up to my collar, straightening it. "And because of your background," he says more quietly, looking me in the eye. "They want someone who will speak Spanish to the children, to open their minds to learning new language."

I scowl. The past I want to put behind me is now the only way I can step up in this world. What a joke.

"Be careful, now, with that portrait of yours," he says bluntly.

"Thank you, Father," I incline my head. "It is always kept safe."

"I still do not understand why you move always against convention," he complains. "To allow hypocrisy to grab hold of you will destroy you."

I study myself in the mirror.

Padric stands straight next to me, his back like a post. "Stand straight," he commands. "Chin up. The way you carry yourself will show your background. Think to yourself: I am confident. I am strong. I am worthy."

I mimic Padric's posture, thinking of the life that stands before me. "And Mrs Roman? What is she like?"

"Oh." He laughs. "She is a beautiful creature, of the highest moral character and virtue."

My eyes widen. "Is that so?"

Father Padric looks at me from the corner of his eye. "It is I who suggested your services to her, so do take heed of my good name," he says gently.

Have six months of your life ever been made miserable by love?

Chapter 2

In the afternoon, my father, a disheveled, poorly-dressed, pathetic shell of a man, storms into his house with a flask in his hand. He hasn't shaved or bathed for days, and the smell compels me to drop the book I was reading and exhale fiercely. Perhaps he guesses the cause, for he marches over to me, grabs the book from the table, and throws it to the ground. He grabs me by the collar, pulls me from my chair, and throws me against the door. I stumble upright and prepare myself for his rage.

"Do not lie! How did you get to know Mrs Roman?" Father screams.

"I have never spoken to her," I say quickly. "I have never even seen her, except in church."

"You have looked at her, have you not? Tell me!" he demands.

"When I am in church, I see no one but God." I lower my head, looking up at him from the top of my eyeballs.

"Mr Roman told me that his wife wanted you over there as a nanny!" he yells, confounded. "Why would anyone want you? You are as stupid as your mother was."

I stare warily, terrified. "Did he mention what I shall receive for my services?" I ask meekly.

My father moans, leans his head against the wall. "400 a week."

My shoulders slump. "I do not wish to be a servant," I whisper.

"Do you think I wanted my son to be a servant?" he roars once more. "Why can't you just work at the factory, like everyone else? You've got to learn to stand in line! Now look at you . . . you think you're better than me, don't you?"

"Why shouldn't I be better than you?" I sneer. "You're disgusting!"

My father's response is to strike me across the face with the back of his fist. I feel an explosion of pain in my cheek and for a moment I am blind.

"That's it, I am through with you! Do not bother this family ever again. Do you hear me?" he shouts.

"Fuck you!" I scream and then run to the room I share with my brothers, stuffing everything I can call mine into a duffel bag. Fortunately, there is not much.

"You are ungrateful!" my father yells. "I can't wait until Mr Roman sees how ungrateful you are."

Chapter 3

Mr Roman meets me outside the door to his house, where I stand with my duffel bag in hand, staring up at all the windows of the enormous country home. He shakes my hand like a professional, scrutinizing me with dark eyes. "Clyde Roman," he states matter-of-factly. His swift nod brings to his side the man who had answered the door, who comes to stand next to me expectantly.

"John Marshal," I return.

"Come on in, then. Alan can get your bags." Mr Roman looks around expectantly and coughs. "Erm . . . your bag, that is."

Alan sniffs and then follows me as I enter behind Mr Roman.

"I have matters to attend to in my study, John," Mr Roman says with finality. "You may wait for Mrs Roman in the drawing room."

I wonder what a drawing room is, but I don't have to wonder long.

Alan gestures for me to follow him down the main hall and then opens the third door and ushers me in with a wave of his pale hand.

The room is huge. I feel myself dissolving within this glorious room, melting into the soft, suede chairs, disappearing among the statues and candleholders of the mantel. I wonder if I should sit.

Beyond the French window that leads into a vast garden, I glimpse a colorful shadow between the folds of the long, white drapery.

She stands by the window like an angel in a dream, wearing a stunning Mother of Pearl necklace, which reflects light with the intensity of the sun. The light seems to circle her, to surround her with all colors.

The drapery blows her hair gently.

She stares at me in silence, her eyes liquid, her lips slightly parted. A slight blush rushes over her cheeks.

I stare without thinking, unable to speak.

Is she the enemy? Who is the enemy?

Mrs Roman steps closer to me and takes my hand. "Relax, my dear. Have you come to see my husband, Mayor Roman?"

"Pardon me?"

She begins again. "Are you here—"

I interrupt her. "I have come here as a . . . a childcare worker, ma'am, through Father Padric."

We two are just inches from each other. We examine each other carefully.

"You are John Marshal?" she says calmly, although her eyes betray an inner excitement.

I nod.

"I am Maribelle Roman." She holds out her hand and I shake it gently.

"It is a pleasure to meet you," I reply.

There is a long silence while we look at one another, unsure.

"So you know Latin?" she inquires.

"Yes, ma'am."

She nods thoughtfully, and then frowns. "You will not scold these poor children, will you?"

"Scold them? Why?"

"You will be kind to them, won't you? Promise me."

I smile. "Of course."

"Let us walk through the garden and discuss the children's lessons," she proposes.

I follow Mrs Roman through the French doors. The smell of fresh growing things, of air unpolluted by my father's stink, fills my head and makes me dizzy.

"But is it really true?" she says suddenly, stopping beside a fountain. "Do you really know Latin?"

I laugh quietly. "Yes, ma'am. I know Latin as well as his Reverence, Father Padric, does." I pause, looking at her shyly. "He has even been good enough to say that I know it better."

Her eyes widen. "Is that so?" She smiles a small smile and then continues walking through the blooms. "You will not strike my children, even if they do not know their lessons."

I nod. "Of course."

She glances at my hands as I clasp them together in front of me. "How old are you, sir?" she demands.

(Parenthetical Pet Peeve) Parents who teach their toddlers to use sign language to answer the question, "How old are you?"— Instead of teaching them to say the number. In other words, you get a three-year-old who shoves three fingers in your face instead of saying "three."

"Almost 19."

I come to a halt and turn to Mrs Roman. "Ma'am, I am shaking. Please forgive me." I smile pleadingly, feeling like a child.

"Whatever for?" she exclaims.

"I have never been to college. I haven't many friends. Father Padric will give you a good account of me."

She nods. "He already has."

"But if my family speaks ill of me, please do not believe them," I beg.

Enlightenment brightens her brow. "Of course," she says, resting her hand gently on my arm.

Without thinking, I pick up her hand and bring it to my lips. We both halt. I stand slowly, my gaze locked in hers once more. "I will never beat your children, ma'am. Before God, I swear it."

"Call me Maribelle," she insists.

We stare into each other's souls, oblivious to the outside world.

Just then, the sound of footsteps on the gravel path forces us to look back to the house. Mr Roman approaches, his arms swinging only slightly. Mrs Roman withdraws her hand.

"There you are, John," Mr Roman says when he is within hearing distance. "I must have a word with you before you meet the children."

With a nod and a smile, I join Mr Roman on his way back to the house. The whole way, I can feel Mrs Roman's eyes boring into me from behind.

We enter the house and Mr Roman leads me to the fifth door of the main hall. It is his study, filled with a fat leather couch and an enormous dark-wooded desk. Mr Roman walks to his desk and pulls out a cigar from a portable humidor. He lights it and looks up at me, where I stand twitching before him.

"Father Padric tells me you are grounded and well-behaved. Everyone here will treat you with respect."

"Thank you." I manage a faint smile.

"If your work is good enough, I might help settle you later on in a little business of your own."

The wild hope of someday being my own man shines through my eyes. "Thank you, Mr Roman," I repeat.

Mr Roman reaches into his desk and pulls out one of six checkbooks. He quickly writes out a check.

"Here is your first week's salary," he says. "If you do well, I'll give you the rest of the month at the beginning of next week."

"Thank you, sir." I close my hand tightly over the check, wondering what I would do with the money.

"I insist you do not hand over a single bit of this money to your father. Do you understand?"

I nod fiercely. "Of course," I growl.

"Of course." Mr Roman grins. "Now, sir, I've ordered the rest of the household to address you formally, as Sir."

He looks me up and down, his distaste showing at the side of his nose. "That jacket is dreadful," Mr Roman mutters. He walks over to a nearby closet and pulls out a suit coat. He hands the coat to me— it is the most well-made piece of clothing I've ever seen.

My hands tremble with fear of dropping it, or having it taken back. Soon enough, however, I do drop the coat. I drop it onto the couch, to make way for the shirt and pants that Mr Roman heaps on me.

"Why don't you change here, to see if it fits?" he insists. "I'll be right outside."

In short order, I am a new man—made of a soft, black suit and a simple blue shirt. I feel awkward in the clothes—the pants too high on my waist, the tucked-in shirt fluttering against my skin. I scratch at my hip as I walk into the hall.

"A perfect fit," Mr Roman announces, as Maribelle walks up behind him, two small children following behind her.

"Very handsome, Mr Marshal," she agrees.

I smile, straightening up.

"Behave yourself like a gentleman, sir," Mr Roman reminds me.

I notice Maribelle's slight smirk; she rolls her eyes behind her husband's back. I struggle not to join her mirth.

"Yes, sir," I agree. I look to the children. Despite their snub noses and carefully combed blonde hair, they remind me somewhat of my brothers. "And who might you be?" I ask.

Maribelle smiles. "The oldest is Christian," she says, touching a hand to the head of the larger child, who looks to be about four years old.

"And I'm Remy!" the only slightly smaller child pipes up.

Maribelle hushes him. "You might have your hands full, with these two." She smiles. "Now, off with you both!" she insists.

The children tear down the hallway, pushing each other playfully.

"Your duties won't begin until tomorrow," Mr Roman explains, turning back to me. "But, starting tomorrow, you are their caretaker and their teacher—you will be with them from the time they rise until the time they fall asleep, and it is your job to fill their days responsibly and usefully."

I nod carefully, feeling all of a sudden very unprepared. Then I look behind me to my old clothes, which lie in a pile on the floor. "Might I have some time to myself in my room?" I suggest.

Mr Roman nods. "Very well. I have some business to attend to in any case. Your room is just up the stairs there," he points to a dim doorway at the end of the hall, "to the right. The day starts early tomorrow—we need you up with the children at seven."

I turn to Mrs Roman, excusing myself. "Ma'am."

As I walk up the stairs, Mr Roman's voice echoes behind me. "Well, what do you think?" he asks.

I pause midway up the stairs, wanting—no, needing—to hear her answer.

"I am not as thrilled as you," she says quietly.

My heart sinks.

"What's the point?" she adds. "You will be replacing him before you know it."

I turn my face to the wall, wanting to cool my burning cheek.

"Only if I must," Mr Roman says. "In any case, I can't have my household staff looking like vagabonds."

My pride forces me to run for my room, although my shame follows swiftly behind. I resolve never to wear those old clothes—the clothes of my past life—again.

Chapter 4

I am up before the sun in the morning, splashing water on my face and shaking out my new suit. At seven exactly, I wake Remy and Christian, who tumble from bed without complaint. In short order, they are tidied up and ready for breakfast. I usher them into the breakfast room, feeling like a new man. The suit, which itched at me only yesterday, seems to mold to my movement. The house, so clean and bright and vastly different from my home, seems to breathe life into me. I feel clean and bright, too.

Mr Roman winks as I enter.

"Coffee, John?" Maribelle asks, as the boys take their seats.

I hesitate slightly, and then join them at the table, at the empty setting near Mr Roman's left hand.

Remy's face lights up before I can answer. "Can I have some coffee, mother?" he begs.

"'May I,' not 'Can I,' dear," Maribelle corrects him. She glances swiftly at me. "And no, my dear, you are too young yet."

I wink at Remy. "I'll not have coffee either," I announce. "We will both just have to wait. Coffee might make us forget our lessons."

Remy nods pleasantly, absorbed already in his eggs. "Okay," he mumbles.

Soon, the two boys have emptied their plates and begin longingly to look out the window, through which bright morning sunshine is beginning to pour.

"Speaking of your lessons, we'll begin with Latin, today," I announce.

The children moan.

"Latin is the root of all languages, both beautiful and brute," I lecture, Maribelle's gaze inspiring me to impress the children. "But I promise that we will concentrate on the beautiful and not the brute—nothing common and nothing dirty."

Remy and Christian giggle, and Maribelle leans back slightly, relaxed and seeming pleased.

I pull out a beautifully leather-bound copy of *The New Testament* and present it to the children. They examine the book with enthusiasm and excitement.

"This is the Holy Bible," I explain.

"I know the Bible!" Remy bounces in his chair.

"Very well, then, I suppose we are finished for today," I joke. The boys both cheer and I wave them to quiet. "I must warn you," I continue, "I will often ask you to recite your lessons from this book. Remy, you will be first."

Christian silently takes the book from my hand.

"Christian should go first!" Remy insists, making a face. "He likes to read."

"Excellent, Christian," I concede. "Go ahead, open it where you'd like and say aloud the first word of any paragraph."

Christian thumbs through the text.

"The New Testament is a guide for every man's conduct, word for word. If you know it by memory, then you will always know what to do when you are troubled," I explain to him.

His eyes light up with a fierce understanding.

Maribelle smiles. "Christian, why don't you choose something to challenge Mr Marshal?" she asks.

Christian opens the book to a random page. "*Pe-petite et dabi-dabitur,*" he reads with difficulty.

"*Petite et dabitur vobis quaerite et invenietis pulsate et aperietur vobis,*" I recite from memory, glancing up at Maribelle's eyes, which shine with excitement. "*Omnis enim qui petit accipit et qui quaerit invenit et pulsanti aperietur.*" I grin. "Shall I continue?"

Mr Roman looks at his wife, wide-eyed.

Maribelle's eyes are shut, her face in ecstasy.

"What does it mean?" Remy demands.

"That's the important part, isn't it?" I say solemnly to him. "It says: Ask, and it shall be given you; seek, and ye shall find; knock, and it shall be opened unto you."

Remy's eyes open wide. "Really?" he whispers.

"For every one that asketh, receiveth; and he that seeketh, findeth." I look up at Maribelle, to find her eyes locked on me. "And to him that knocketh, it shall be opened," I conclude in a hush, holding her gaze in my own.

"Do you know Horace?" Maribelle breathes.

"I am forbidden to read him. He is crude," I say shortly. "Although, I must admit I have let some of his words slip into my head on accident, yes." We share a secret smile.

Remy takes the book from Christian. "I want to try," he cries. He opens the book and strikes his finger to the page. He squints at the letters. "What does it say?" he whispers to Christian.

Christian looks and whispers back.

"*Ayit illey domna!*" Remy says proudly.

I smile. "*Ait illi dominus eius euge serve bone et fidelis quia super pauca fuisti fidelis supra multa te constituam intra in gaudium domini tui,*" I begin. "Is that the one?"

Remy nods vigorously.

"Matthew 25:23," I conclude. "You must be very ambitious, my friend."

Chapter 5

In the day that follows, Mr and Mrs Roman host a dinner party, to which I am invited. After only a short time, it becomes obvious that I am to be the main attraction; I navigate deftly through landmines—questions about my background, my family. Before long, Maribelle saves me by requesting that I recite the bible for the group, as I had at breakfast the previous day. Soon, I am less an object of curiosity and potential threat and more a performer, a simple spectacle. I am comfortable standing before them, hearing the Latin escape from my lips. If I close my eyes, it is almost just the same as being in Father Padric's study.

After everyone agrees that I am quite remarkable and an exceptional nanny, they leave. I sit uncomfortably beside Mr Roman and Maribelle, watching as the other servants clean up after the party.

Finally, Mr Roman turns to me. "Mr Marshal, sir! I would like to contract you for the next two years as a live-in caretaker and language teacher for our children."

Maribelle smiles behind her husband. And yet they both frown when I shake my head.

"No, sir," I say firmly. "If you should ever wish to get rid of me, I would have to go; an agreement that binds me without committing you is not on equal terms. I refuse to make such a contract."

Mr Roman smiles when I have finished. "You are certainly a quick one, aren't you? I must respect your reasoning." He pauses, appraising me once more. "I see a lot of opportunity ahead for you, young man," he concludes.

I nod, stifling a yawn. I am tired of his judgment. "If you will excuse me," I gesture meaningfully, "I am tired and need to sleep." As I walk past Maribelle on the way to the door, her eyes look up into mine in a sudden flash. I lock her gaze in mine, my lips curling in secret knowledge.

"Charming, isn't he?" I hear Mr Roman say, as I exit the room. I pause just outside the door.

Maribelle's response is only silence.

Chapter 6

I walk down the dirt path that winds from the Romans' home into the wooded park nearby, reading a book, when I hear movement in the bushes. Two large shadows emerge from the woods, stepping toward me forcefully but slow. As they come closer, I recognize their faces as those of boys I went to school with—Shane and Chris, the boys who had made school a living hell for me. Their eyes are filled with the casual look of vengeance.

Chris stops nose-to-nose with me, punching a finger into my chest while Shane stands guard, clenching his teeth.

"Little John Marshal, the pretty priest," Chris hisses.

"What a beautiful suit," Shane sneers. "What are you doing in such a fine suit?"

I try to move away from them, but they block my way.

"Oh, are you too good for the factory now, little priest?"

Chris grabs me and holds me in place as Shane plunges his closed fist into my nose. I collapse to the gravel path, as I am suddenly blind and deaf, praying as they kick me and grind my face into the small stones.

Finally, they leave me, beaten to a pulp, lying bloody and bruised, my clothes torn. I lie in the cold afternoon, waiting for my head to stop swimming, waiting for a reason to stand again. I drift in and out of a miserable fog until . . .

"Oh!" a woman exclaims. Cool hands lift my throbbing head and brush along my sides. I cannot open my eyes, but I know it is she.

"Do not worry," she says in a voice as cool as her hands. "Everything will be fine."

I try to nod but groan instead.

"Harold, get help," Maribelle commands. I hear an angry muttering, and then nothing more.

When I awaken again, I am warm between soft sheets. Something cold and wet is on my face. My eyes flutter open to see Maribelle, a washcloth in hand.

She sighs with relief when my eyes open. "Oh thank God," she says, quickly pressing the washcloth back to my face.

I wince at the pressure, although the cool water eases the heat of my wounds.

A young woman, wearing a maid's uniform, enters the room. "Do not worry, ma'am. I'll take care of him."

Maribelle blushes, avoiding eye contact with the woman. "That will be fine, Lauren," she says, standing and leaving the room in a rush.

Lauren picks up the wet washcloth and continues to wash my wounds. I open my eyes and stare confusedly at her.

"What happened . . .?" My voice is hoarse, strange to my ears.

Lauren puts her finger on my lips, turning my words to quiet mumbles. "Shhh. Save your strength," she whispers, her voice soothing. Then she leans over and presses her lips softly to mine. Her mouth is cool and gentle, like her hands on the washcloth.

My eyes flash open and then, like she's cast a spell over me, I sink into the pillow, exhausted, and fall fast asleep.

Chapter 7

A week later and I am back on my feet, my bruises healed and my cuts healing. My face must be presentable enough, because I am invited again to one of the Romans' dinner parties. We sit at the grand dining table, passing huge silver platters heaped with food from hand to hand. I sit uncomfortably in my still-new clothes, and pull at the lapel of my suit jacket from time to time.

"What a feast, Clyde!" one of the guests, Harold Lawrence, exclaims. "Who else would have us celebrate the birthday of the Cuban revolution?" Mr Lawrence sends a meaningful glance to me. "Those revolutionaries are right where they belong."

What does he know? I wonder rapidly. I'd thought that I was so careful . . . .

"The Lord has His place for every man. Some are born to be great men, and they prosper. Others . . ." He leaves the rest of this statement up to me to fill.

The men at the table laugh and I struggle against my rage.

"The Lord deserts them all, in the end," Mr Roman finishes quietly.

Mr Lawrence nods pompously. "Men must learn to accept their lot. If they do not accept their place, then we must teach them. Thank God that communist nonsense hasn't spread. Don't you agree, Maribelle?" He turns to his hostess and then glances at me, who sits at her left hand.

"Yes, of course," she says quietly, nervously.

My fury is too intense to bear and I stand, my eyes boring into Harold Lawrence. "You must excuse me," I say very carefully. "I have to look after the children."

I walk out of the room as gracefully as I can, still clutching my napkin with a firm grip, hearing the animal sounds of their mastication fade behind me.

Once the fury wears off and my legs are tired from pacing back and forth in my small room, I walk to my bureau and pull out the small framed portrait of Che Guevara. I stare at the picture, slowly tracing the scrawled signature with my thumb.

I shove the portrait back into my bureau when I hear the bedroom door creak open behind me. I turn to see Lauren walking into the room, as she had begun to do every night since my injury.

"You again?" I say, trying to make my irritation sound like tease.

"It's that time," she says easily. "Don't you want something to wear tomorrow?"

I stand there, wondering for the seventh time if there was some better way to do this.

"Do not be shy," she commands.

I shrug and begin to strip, handing my clothes to her one at a time. As I am removing my pants, a knock sounds on my door.

"John? I hope you were not upset by the dinner conversation," Maribelle calls sweetly through the wood. She opens the door at my silence to find me in my underwear and Lauren holding my clothes. She blushes fiercely.

(Parenthetical Pet Peeve) Underwear with worn-out elastic that keeps slipping down my hips as I walk.

"Forgive me," she croaks.

"It is quite all right, Maribelle," I say softly, glancing toward Lauren with a smile of friendship and nothing more. "Lauren is kind enough to wash my clothes every night, since I only have one suit. You have caught us at the somewhat awkward moment of exchange."

Lauren half-heartedly attempts to hide her triumphant smile.

Maribelle looks at me, satisfied with the explanation, although a small frown wrinkles her brow.

I want to reach out to her, to tell her that of course it's not what she thinks, that I could not dream to touch another woman . . . . But I can't.

"If you will excuse me now, I must be off to bed," I say carefully, trying to exude charm and reassurance, "which requires a somewhat less respectable posture."

"Of course, excuse me," Maribelle breathes, grinning slightly as she glides out the door.

Lauren follows close behind, but pauses a moment to look back at me. "Sweet dreams," she bids, with a smile that marks me hers.

I shudder slightly, and then slide beneath the sheets.

Chapter 8

My wounds healed and my heart light, I walk through the streets of town with Maribelle Roman, feeling the strength of her fingers against my steady arm, calling out to the boys from time to time when they seem to be headed for trouble.

"Are you content, John?" she asks presently.

I sigh quietly. "Not fully," I admit.

She doesn't seem too surprised. "Why is that?" she asks.

I frown as I consider an honest response. "I am not sure if happiness is my ultimate goal. I appreciate the opportunity your husband has given me, but I am always striving for . . . for more purpose."

Maribelle slows down her pace and I slow with her.

When I look over at her expression, I can see that she is blushing. "Is everything okay?" I ask, hoping that I haven't upset her.

She stops and looks into my eyes, her expression affectionate.

My heart leaps.

"No. I . . . it'll be no secret soon . . . I am the sole heiress of my very wealthy aunt, who's just died."

I nod, waiting for her to continue.

"You are so wonderful with my children . . . I would like for you to accept a small present as a token of my gratitude. It is only enough to buy some linen, a larger wardrobe perhaps. But . . ." She opens my hand with her fingers.

"Yes?" I prompt her.

"There is no need to mention this to my husband." She blushes once more. I feel myself burning with anger at her presumption.

"I may not have come from the best of families, but I am no liar, Maribelle," I say sternly. "I have never been, nor will I ever be, a man who is predisposed to secrecy." And with that, I turn and stride back the way we had come, disregarding the car that waits for us to complete our outing, determined to walk the whole way back to the manor. Perhaps by then I will no longer feel quite so angry.

"You could have shown more graciousness," she says quietly, to my retreating back.

"What?!" Mr Roman gasps loudly as I pass silently by his study later that evening. My footsteps halt of their own accord as I wait to hear Mrs Roman's response.

"I am guilty," she mutters.

"How could you tolerate such rudeness? And from a servant!" he demands.

"John has proved himself to be more than a servant," she argues quietly.

"All people of his condition are considered servants," Mr Roman interrupts.

I hear the sound of the sleek rollers of his desk drawers and the rustling of paper.

"He can't treat you this way," Mr Roman insists. "He will take the money from me; that's for certain. I will have a word or two with Master John."

Maribelle sputters. "What? Wait, Clyde, that's not what I meant."

"If this is what Master John costs me." His voice is contemptuous.

I bristle at the tone he takes with her, and then remember my own harsh words. Silent, shamefaced, I creep away from the scene.

When he offers me the money, I take it.

At our next outing, Maribelle turns to me nervously, toying with her fingertips as the children scurry behind us. "Well, are you pleased with my husband?" she says finally.

I try not to let the confusion of my emotions show in my face. "Why shouldn't I be?" I say, making my voice easy. "He has given me a substantial bonus."

Maribelle smiles in relief.

We continue on, marking a couple that passes by with their arms overflowing with books.

Maribelle finds the bookstore with her gaze. "Give me your arm," she commands.

I thread my arm through hers companionably, marveling at the lightness and coolness of her touch.

She marches me into the bookstore, and the children follow.

I look around at all the books with awe, as always. Somehow, seeing so much knowledge assembled into one space takes my breath away. Finding a new title from a favorite author of mine, I take the book from the shelf and flip to page one.

Maribelle escorts her children to the back, where there's a small play area, and hands them large, colorful picture books. On her way back, she takes her time, browsing books and picking one or two off the shelves at every pause.

As she returns to the front of the store, I glance at the price of the book and then set it on the shelf with a sigh. She unloads a stack of books into my arms.

"Now you have more books to advance their lessons," she says to my wondering gaze. She knows as well as I that I will devour these books much more hungrily than will Remy and Christian.

I smile at her gratefully.

With a pamphlet in his hand, Christian runs up to me as I sit in the drawing room, reading alone one evening after supper.

"Master John, what is this book about?" he asks.

I glance at the small book in his hands and then look at Mr Roman, who reads a paper just outside the French doors of the drawing room, on a sofa in the garden. I stand and walk to him.

Mr Roman sets down his paper and acknowledges me when I come to stand in front of him.

"Yes, John?" he says amiably.

"To provide me with material for answering Master Christian's questions about the greater world, perhaps you would allow me to take out a subscription at the bookseller's?"

Mr Roman rubs his chin. "Not a bad idea," he concedes.

"I wouldn't dare fill their heads with fiction, of course. I know you wouldn't want any of that nonsense in your home."

"So no political pamphlets, then?" Mr Roman jokes. He laughs, and I enjoy the moment of familiarity. He slaps his hand down on the armrest of the sofa. "Very well, you will have your wish," he proclaims.

Chapter 9

When the doorbell rings the following afternoon, I hear Father Padric's voice at the front door.

"I am here for Master John," he says.

Before long, Alan leads Father Padric to the drawing room, opening wide the French doors to let him into the garden, where I am giving a lesson to Christian and Remy.

Maribelle sits at the table, watching with a slight smile, while Lauren is seated nearby, polishing silverware.

"Father, what a delightful surprise," Maribelle exclaims, rising to her feet. "Would you care to join me for coffee and a pastry?"

"Thank you, but I have actually come to see John," Father Padric says, inclining his head ever so slightly.

I look up at him with surprise.

"I have an important matter of good fortune to discuss with him, and I wondered if you could spare him for the remainder of the afternoon," Father Padric continues cryptically.

"If it is important, you may certainly have him." Maribelle looks at me, her brows knit together as if with worry.

I stand and follow Father Padric to the drawing room.

"Not here," he says. "To the church."

"Certainly, Father," I answer.

"What do you mean you refuse?" he demands, looking down on me as I light the candles at the altar.

I sigh silently. "I appreciate everything you have done for me, Father. If it wasn't for you, I would not have my job and I would not be receiving the recognition for it from the whole town."

"Don't give me credit for your gifts," he says kindly. "All I did was recognize them—you have made yourself a success."

"Well, Father, I want to continue with my success. I have no wish to marry or to tie myself down." I glance up at his weathered face. "I don't want to marry for money," I say finally, my voice hushed. I feel my eyes glaze over with the thought of Maribelle. "I want to marry for love."

Father Padric walks over to me and stops my hand. He stares me in the eye, forcing me to focus, and then looks down at the unlit candle in my left hand. "Examine well what is going on in your heart, my son," he says, taking the candle from me. He turns away and begins lighting the other candles. "Don't make up your mind just yet, my dear boy," he says finally. "Think it over, and come back in a few days to give me your definite answer. She's a good girl, and pretty. And she loves you, although I don't know what you've done to deserve it."

I stare at him blankly. "Is that all, Father?" I say finally.

He waves me away. "Three days, John," he says. "Think it over."

"I don't need three days," I say with a note of finality. "I know my own mind."

When I return to the manor, I find Lauren waiting for me at the foot of the stairs. She bends swiftly once I step into the hall, dusting the banister rather than acknowledge that she's been waiting for me. I stare at her, my face a blank as I try to think of something to say. *It's nothing personal . . .?* Even I hate myself at the thought of saying those words. Instead, I walk past her expectant eyes without a word and walk swiftly to my room. She asked Father Padric for my hand; she can get my answer from him.

I hear the sound of her sobs and run the final few steps to my room.

Hours later, a soft tap sounds on my door. I look up from my book.

"Come in," I call.

Maribelle steps hesitantly into my room, and my heart skips a beat. "John, I know it is none of my concern, but . . ." She looks down at her feet, and then sighs and seats herself beside me on the bed. "Lauren told me about her proposal, and your answer. Because she is my maid, I feel a slight obligation to make a final plea in her favor."

"Do you?" I say without thinking. I continue before she can answer. "I appreciate your position, Madame, but please do not bother to make an argument. I assure you that my mind is made up."

"But, John, do you realize the extent of her inheritance? You could be making a huge mistake."

"I am well aware of these matters, Madame, and my answer remains the same." I look her straight in her lovely, luminous eyes, praying that she would understand me. "You see, Maribelle, as lovely as she is, and as wonderful as the offer seems, I do not love

Lauren."

Maribelle's lips seem to tug upward at the corners without her permission. "What part must love play in such a union? Love can develop from the prosperity that you two will share," she insists, although her eyes tell me she is lying.

I bristle. "Anyone who believes that has not had the good fortune of being in love," I say hotly.

Maribelle's eyes widen; she covers her heart with her hands as a blush covers her cheeks. "Is that so?" she asks quietly. With great difficulty, she tears her gaze from my own and leaves.

Chapter 10

Mr Roman stands at the front door, surrounded by servants who hoist his suitcases one by one. Maribelle joins him at the door followed by Lauren, who tugs at her mistress's suitcases.

"The carriage is ready." Mr Roman's voice echoes up the stairs to me as I begin to descend. "Where are Master John and the children?"

Gripping a small bag in my hand, I enter the front hall. Remy and Christian are fast behind me.

Maribelle looks up as my foot leaves the stair, as though sensing my presence. She blushes and begins to fuss with her purse.

Mr Roman looks over at her. "Dear, your face is flushed. Are you all right?"

Maribelle coughs sweetly. "This trip is so consuming. It gives me a headache every year," she responds.

Mr Roman belts out a laugh. "That's like a woman. You're always in need of repair." He turns to me. "John, be sure you have brought all you will need," he commands. "We will stay at the Hamptons estate until the summer season—there will be no back and forth."

I nod to him, and then follow as he and Maribelle leave through the front door. The servants follow behind me, carrying their and the boys' bags. Mr Roman and Maribelle sink gracefully into the front of a long limousine, while the boys and I climb into the back portion, which is partitioned from the front with an electrically operated glass window. The staff strains and groans beneath the bags, unloading and cramming them all into the trunk. The driver tugs at his gloves.

And then we are off.

When I catch sight of the Hamptons estate, my eyes widen in astonishment.

The partition is down, and Mr Roman sees my reaction. "I see you enjoy the view," he says. "The house has been in the family for generations, but we take care to keep it updated."

I nod wordlessly, staring at the enormous grounds. It looks like a park. Footpaths are lined with huge walnut trees, whose vast leafy branches rise up to staggering heights. The manicured lawn in front of the house is landscaped with fountains and gardens. Gardeners and house staff flit about the lawn, performing routine maintenance on a mass scale. At the foot of the garden lies the large estate, a humongous stone mansion with several levels and a forest of brick chimneys.

The limo pulls right up to the front door, where a crowd of staff wait to greet the family. The butler opens the car doors and gestures to the maids and houseboys behind him, who rush to grab the suitcases. Maribelle and Mr Roman exit through their doors as the boys and I climb from ours.

As Mr Roman greets his staff and receives a short report from the butler, Remy and Christian run through the front door and up the stairs. I hear their feet on the floor above as I peek into the massive entryway.

"Your room is upstairs as well," Maribelle's voice lilts close behind me.

I turn to face her.

"Come, I'll show you," she says.

After we've all settled into our rooms, Maribelle accompanies me on one of the estate's many gravel paths as the children race back and forth between the walnut trees, capturing butterflies with nets.

Christian runs up to us, proudly displaying his latest catch. "Look, Master John. Look what I caught!" he exclaims breathlessly.

I look at the brilliant little thing that bats wildly against the soft netting. "Well done, Christian." I smile. "You've caught yourself a White Admiral."

"Such a militant name for such a delicate creature," Maribelle says lightly.

We share a smile.

"Master John, come chase the butterflies with us!" Remy shouts from not far off.

"Oh yes, please?" Christian begs.

I look at the two boys, and then at Maribelle. "Only if your mother agrees to join us."

She blushes. "Oh, I don't think so."

"Do come, mother. We have enough nets!" Remy insists.

I catch her eye and turn up my hands in a gesture of innocence.

Maribelle looks at Remy and then at me. She shrugs as well, then grins hugely. "Oh, well, all right!"

Christian sprints to the field to get the extra nets. I take

Maribelle's hand in my own and tug her on to the field. We run like mad; my heart seems like it will burst from the wild joy that fills me. Maribelle smiles and her teeth seem brighter than the sun.

We collapse, laughing, into the grass, when it seems that all the butterflies have fled.

"Oh John, I haven't had such fun since—""

It begins to rain. To pour, actually.

"Oh, no!" Maribelle exclaims, holding her arms over her hair as she scrambles to her feet.

"This way," I shout gleefully, tugging at her arm. We race to the trunk of a nearby walnut. And watch for a moment as the boys stare up at the rain and then begin to look at the muddied ground with renewed interest.

"You boys get inside right now!" Maribelle calls to them, and they race each other to the front door.

Maribelle and I watch as the boys sprint to the door, laughing. Her arm rests lightly on mine. She shivers lightly with the cold, and I move my arm to her shoulders.

"Should we make a run for it?" I suggest.

She shakes her head, looking up at the rain. "Not just yet," she croaks.

I turn to her just as she looks up at me. We stand, face to face, staring into each other's eyes. I find myself leaning towards her, just wanting to be closer. Her lips part slightly as she breathes in my scent. We are less than an inch apart; the memory of the house's long bank of windows flashes before my inner eye.

I pull away, blinking. "We'd better wash up," I say finally, refusing to look at her. "Supper will be soon."

We walk back toward the house in the heavy rain.

At supper that evening, Maribelle meets my eye as I bring the boys into the dining room, and then quickly looks back at her plate.

Mr Roman seems not to notice. "Business in the city was tiresome," he says. "That is why competent men such as myself should be in power. These socialists, now, who stir up the average American with their lofty ideals, have no concept of how things must be."

Mr Roman places a piece of bread in his mouth. "They are born to do the work, and they do it well," he continues, talking with his mouth full. "But men such as myself are born to run this country, to

738

organize the workers and keep them safe from themselves."

He turns to me, and I school my features. "How did you manage with my family while I was away?" he asks.

"Rather well, although it is a relief to see your return," I say, nodding slightly.

"Yes, it's quite a relief," Maribelle echoes me quietly.

"Well, I am glad to hear it," Mr Roman booms. "I know how difficult it can be for you when I'm gone." He turns to me. "Women, you know—they don't know what to do with themselves without a man around."

I grit my teeth and smile.

Instead of responding to her husband, Maribelle looks over at me, her expression concerned.

That night, I kneel before my bed with a Bible in my hands. Staring up at me from between the leaves is my secret portrait of Che Guevara.

"Dearest hero Che, tonight I pray. You would be proud of me, Che Guevara. I have won my first battle in my own private war. Using your own tactics as I pertain them to the sin of seduction, so that I can move up and ahead. So I can reach the glory, power, and fame that you have succeeded in doing, through all that's you've done, and from where you had begun, with nothing, like myself. Dear Che, I shall continue to fight until I can claim total victory over Maribelle's heart and cuckold that self-important bourgeois fool she is married to. Then they will see."

I lift the picture from the Bible, place it into a wooden box on my night stand, and then slide the wooden box beneath my bed frame. With one final deep breath, I switch off my bedside light.

Chapter 11

The next morning's breakfast sees me sitting across the table from Maribelle, alone. Christian and Remy have already been excused and are racing across the lawn with their butterfly nets. The gardener waters the plants that grow just below the window sill beside us.

"Where has Mr Roman gone so early in the morning?" I lift a half-full coffee mug to my lips.

Maribelle catches my gaze and holds it. "My husband will not be joining us." Her voice is thick with unsaid words.

I smile mischievously.

"He is busy all day, examining the property—making sure that the caretakers have been doing their job."

I glance over at the window to see that the gardener has moved on, and then lean across the table to grasp Maribelle's arm with my hand. "Help to save my life," I whisper insistently, speaking to her heart with my eyes. "Mr Roman forbids anything to do with Che. He'd kill me if he knew I had a secret obsession with such a man, a radical Marxist revolutionary. It's like we live in another time period or something and he's not a banned book but a banned person— damn politicians. Well, most of them. See Che, he was a good man. He was no Saddam Hussein, but I must confess about this secret portrait I must keep hidden, to prevent Mr Roman from knowing about. He would, he would kill me; I'd at least lose my job. And I'm in a much deeper revolution myself, a personal one. Che inspires me." I add, "I must confess to you, Maribelle, that I have a... a portrait. I have hidden it under my mattress."

Maribelle looks down at my hand wonderingly.

"Go into my bedroom and see," I encourage her. "Slide your hand beneath the bed frame. You will find a shiny black box on the floor near the wall."

"It contains a portrait?" she breathes.

"I've a second favor to ask you, Maribelle. I must beg you not to look at the portrait. It is my secret."

"Is that so?!" She frowns at me, pulling her arm from beneath my hand.

I smirk at her reaction and nod my head. "Yes, Madame."

Maribelle glides out of her chair and leaves the room.

I watch the doorway through which she exited, biting my lip.

That evening after sunset, Maribelle and I sit out in the garden with Mr Roman and his dinner guest, Mrs Driscoll, who are engrossed in a political discussion. Mr Roman leans in to listen to Mrs Driscoll's latest point and nods his vigorous assent.

Noticing that Mr Roman is too focused on his discussion to mark his wife, I lean and whisper in Maribelle's ear. "Were you able to retrieve the box?"

She stares blankly at her husband and his guest, nodding ever so slightly.

Chapter 12

Days pass, and I walk inside from a long walk outside.

Maribelle's there. She tells me, "Mr Calvert and Mrs Driscoll are just visiting; you may feel free to join us when you like."

I incline my head. "Thank you, Maribelle. That sounds very nice."

When I enter the drawing room, Maribelle is seated on the couch with her hands in her lap, clasped around a cold sun tea. I take my seat next to her. Mr Calvert and Mrs Driscoll exchange a glance.

"It is funny seeing you here, Mr Calvert," I begin. "I was just speaking of you recently."

"Oh?" he smirks.

"Yes. You know my friend Seth?"

"The lumberman who lives in the mountains?"

I nod. "Yes. He has recently offered me a position as his partner."

Maribelle looks up in shock.

"He suggested that my friendship with you could be beneficial in terms of our future business," I continue.

"I assure you I would be most willing to help, should you ever ask."

Maribelle bursts. "Would you do that? Would you leave your pupils?"

I smile at her, without answering. The room is silent for a moment. I deliberately stretch my leg so that my foot brushes up against hers.

She gasps and starts at the shock of my touch; she drops her tea and the glass lands wrong, shattering against the floor.

Mr Calvert and Mrs Driscoll stare at Maribelle.

She turns to me. "Why did you kick me?" she demands.

I know that she's just lying to hide from them.

Mrs Driscoll smirks and turns to Mr Calvert. "Mr Calvert, may I show you the most interesting thing I noticed in the garden?" she says.

"Why, yes, I'd be delighted to follow you." His face is equally smug.

The two rise and swiftly exit. On her way out, Mrs Driscoll gives me a knowing smile.

"John, I must order you to be careful," Maribelle begins, as soon as they are out of earshot.

"Concerning my employment, you may order me all you want," I return stiffly. "Otherwise, it is my right to give you the orders." I pause a moment to let her think on this. "Madame, tonight at two I will come to your room. There is something I must say to you."

I place my finger over my lips to indicate her silence. When she nods, I stand and stride quickly from her presence.

When the clock on the side of the house strikes two, I am still awake, staring at my bedside alarm as the numbers slide into place. I get out of bed and stand up, feeling a little clumsy. When I reach the door next to mine, I put my ear to the cool wood. No noise but the sound of Mr Roman snoring. I creep to the next door— Maribelle's door—and pause for a moment before opening it.

Maribelle lies in bed with her eyes closed. The candle next to her bed is still burning, illuminating her face. After a few seconds, she opens her eyes and sees me standing before her. She sits up, pulling the sheets up to her chin. "How dare you? You have no right."

I walk over to her bed and rest my head on her knees.

"What are you doing?" she whispers. "This has gone too far!"

I raise my head and look into her eyes. They are filled both with fear and longing. I raise myself up, placing one hand at her side, the other alongside her face.

"What are you doing?!" She presses against my chest with both hands.

I duck my head and kiss her softly.

She moans pitiably, and then her lips begin to move against mine.

When we break for air, she gasps. "How were you so sure?"

I smile and wordlessly turn off her bedside lamp.

The next morning, sunlight pours through my eyelids and I am being shook.

"John! Wake up," Maribelle's voice sounds in my ear. "You have to go. Good heavens! If my husband finds out, I am dead!"

I roll out of her bed and begin to dress myself, moving slowly and carefully. "Would you regret your life, if you died?"

"Ah, very much at this moment," she answers, smiling. "But I wouldn't regret having known you."

I return her smile and then walk swiftly to the door.

"John?" she calls.

I turn. "Yes, Maribelle?"

Her face becomes a frown. "Who is my rival?"

"I beg your pardon?"

"The portrait you had me rescue. Whose is it, John? I must know."

I laugh, but then school my features. "There is no woman I love more than you, Maribelle."

I open the door wide and march into the hallway.

Chapter 13

That afternoon, as Remy and Christian engage in silent reading, I watch from the schoolroom as Mrs Driscoll and her poodle climb into the limo. She does not wave goodbye.

A few moments later, Mr Roman bursts into the room. Remy and Christian raise their heads in alarm.

"That woman is unfathomable to me," he says, turning back to the hall. "She was supposed to stay through the week!"

He turns to me. "John—just the person I was looking for."

"Yes?" I incline my head.

"As you know, it's almost July 4th. This year, Senator Brightly will be participating in the parade—she's from this area, you know, and she wishes to make a special stop at the church. It is one of my duties as Mayor to prepare the town for her arrival. It is important that we have all the clergy at this ceremony."

I nod my agreement. "Of course."

"Of course Father Padric must attend; he is the deacon, after all. But Padric insisted that he would not be willing to attend unless you agree to accompany him on the altar." He looks straight into my eyes.

"Certainly," I agree, glad that the request is all.

"I myself have another request to make of you," he continues. "Maribelle suggested that you would make a wonderful Guard of Honor for the parade. If you agree, I would like to see you carry out both duties for this celebration."

"Of course!" I exclaim.

Me, the son of a factory man, heading up the July 4th parade. How exquisite.

[Smoke Break]

Bells begin to chime as the townspeople mill in the streets. The air is filled with excitement. Still more people hang out of windows; they shout down at those in the streets, joining in the excitement. Horns blow as we near the scene; the people in the streets step back onto the sidewalks, clearing a path before us as we march down the street.

I find Maribelle watching with her children, sitting sedately on the small deck of her friend's townhouse. Her face lights up when she finds me; she smiles brightly.

The two women who stand next to her frown—one points her finger at me and the other shakes her head. Maribelle gives the two women a nasty glare, and they walk away with their noses in the air.

I lift my chin and push out my chest, which is covered with gaudy cloth and a long white sash. I return my focus to Mr Roman, who rides before me in a low car.

Behind me ride Senator Brightly and her husband in a flashy black Rolls Royce. The townspeople cheer even more loudly at my back than they had to see me come.

Soon, we arrive at the church and the procession halts. I run through the church doors, hating my gaudy parade clothes for weighing me down. Father Padric stands ready, waiting with a small bundle in his hand. It is my cassock and surplice.

"You are late. Change quickly," he commands cheerfully.

He helps me dress; his lips tighten as he catches sight of my spurs. "We must go at once. You will accompany me as I show the senator to the altar."

The enormous church door swings open. Senator Brightly and her husband enter, followed by Brightly's security officer and personal assistant.

She looks up at the high-vaulted church ceiling. "You've made some improvements," she compliments Father Padric.

He inclines his head in acknowledgment and offers her his arm. Together they walk to the altar; I follow behind with her husband, who seems a little bored.

When Padric and Senator Brightly reach the altar, the senator stares in wonder at the new installation—a brilliant work in stained glass, overlaid with a crystal cross which gleams in the morning sunshine that filters through. The face of Christ is a masterpiece, both pitiable yet ever-loving.

Senator Brightly bursts into tears at the sight. We watch with a horrible awkwardness as Father Padric pats her back. The bells of the village burst into ecstatic peals once more.

"I'm glad you like it," he says quietly.

As we leave the church, I fall into step behind the Lawrences.

"The nerve those people have," says Mr Lawrence, who is the head of the community board. "In the very Guard of Honor."

"If you ever become Mayor, dear, maybe you should appoint the valet Bishop," his wife giggles.

"This is no laughing matter," he whispers sternly. "The separation of church and state is the very foundation of this country. And now the tutor gets to play politician and priest, all in one day."

Mrs Lawrence nods. "Quite right, dear. It's shameful."

The Lawrences enter their townhouse without realizing that I'm behind them.

I exchange a glance with Father Padric, who wears a worried frown. I begin to wear my own frown when I see Lauren ducking up to the Lawrences' door and ringing the bell.

"What does she want with them?" I spit out.

Father Padric shakes his head. "She's been a very unhappy woman of late," he replies.

[Smoke Break]

That night, Maribelle turns to me as I lie beside her in bed. She wraps her arms around me and kisses me with passion. "John, do you love me with all your heart?" she whispers. "I need you to love me so . . . I've sacrificed my family and everything I've worked for, everything I thought I wanted. For you. I could lose it all."

I shush her. "My dear, it's wonderful. We're wonderful together. When I feel you next to me . . . you mean more to me than the whole world. I don't care at all about that world, anymore, except as a thing I long to escape from in order to be with you. When I'm with you, I don't worry about heaven or hell—this is better than heaven could be, infinitely better."

She smiles and snuggles into my shoulder. "I love it when you speak so. But it worries me, strangely."

"Why? Because I'm not rich, like your husband?" I begin to pull my fingers through her hair, unsnarling the tangles we have made. "I don't have the words to express the power of my feelings; I think there are none."

Maribelle rubs her hand across my chest. "John, you surprise me. I have never known anyone like you."

I move away from her. "What is that supposed to mean—'people like me'?"

She shushes me. "Take down your guard. I relate to you, John. You surprise me. You are human."

I am silent for a moment, and then speak. "During moments when you show signs of regret, the fear of being separated from you consumes my every thought."

I place my hand upon hers. "Maribelle, I love you so infinitely that my soul could never function without yours. You have intoxicated me. I could never manage to be apart from you."

Maribelle looks deeply into my eyes and then bursts into tears.

I wrap my arms around her and whisper in her ear. "Do not cry, my dear. I am not going anywhere."

Mrs Roman looks at me with glowing eyes and kisses me with her whole heart. "I love you," she sobs.

Chapter 14

When I rap on Mr Roman's door the next morning, his face is a brilliant shade of purple. A piece of paper trembles between his shaking hands.

"I was wondering if I may borrow the paper," I ask quickly. "The children want me to read to them about yesterday's festivities."

With a roar, Mr Roman picks up the newspaper and hurls it at me.

I bend down to pick it up.

As I stand, Mr Roman stares again at the leaf of paper in his hand. Then he lunges at me, swinging at me with both fists.

I duck, dancing with his punches. "Mr Roman!"

"God damn it! You son of a bitch!" he screams. He dives at my middle and knocks me to the ground, but I twist from under him before he can pin me down. "How could you do this to me?" he wails. His eyes are filled with madness.

I race out of the room, panting, unsure of what to do.

The door to his study slams shut behind me. I decide to return to the children, and their lesson.

[Smoke Break]

That evening, I take my supper with Mr Roman and Maribelle, like always. Their neighbors also eat with us, adding to the sense of normalcy. But soon the couple must leave. As Mr Roman walks them to the door, he looks back at me with an angry glare.

I grab Maribelle's arm as she turns to follow her husband.

"We must not meet tonight," I whisper as he leaves the room. "He suspects something. He's gotten a letter, I think."

I turn and walk away from her, observing a strict decorum we haven't bothered with for weeks.

That night, as the house clock strikes two, I hear a light tap on my door. I recognize the sound—I know it is her. Rather than answer her call, I turn out my bedside lamp and wait for her to leave. Is she really so ready to risk everything?

[Smoke Break]

As I approach the dining room for breakfast the next morning, I hear a loud noise from within. I peek around the corner and see Maribelle standing over her husband, who is sitting. Her hand is flat on the table, atop a piece of paper.

"Just look at this revolting thing!" she exclaims.

I pull my head back and lean against the wall beside the door.

"An ugly-looking fellow, who claims to know you and be under some debt of gratitude, handed it to me as I was passing by the solicitor's garden," I hear as Maribelle begins to pace the floor. "Can you believe it? I must ask that you send Master John back to his family without delay."

There is a moment of silence as Mr Roman presumably scans the letter. I remember the night before; how she had sought comfort and I had rejected her. She was so willing to throw it all away last night, for a moment of comfort . . . and now was even more willing to give up our affair just to hurt me.

"He's a clever lad and will easily find work elsewhere. Perhaps he can find a place with Mr Lawrence or Rob Calvert."

I hear the chair scooting backwards over the wood floor as Mr Roman stands. "Spoken just like the silly woman you are. What good is it to send him off?"

Maribelle gasps. "My honor has been outraged, Clyde! Do you know how this makes me look, how it makes us look?" Her footsteps travel toward him. "John is innocent, but we cannot allow people to think of our household as one that would condone . . ." she whispers the last word, " . . . infidelity."

Mr Roman grunts.

"Either he or I must leave this house," Maribelle declares.

There is the brief sound of a struggle. I close my eyes and grit my teeth against the urge to attack the man who would lay a hand on her.

"Do you want to create a scandal? Sending him away would only prove the rumors!" he hisses.

"Very well, then," Maribelle sniffs. "Perhaps John can take a few months' leave. He can go and stay with that timber merchant in the mountains."

"No." Mr Roman's voice is like a boulder plopped into a pond. "Everything must remain as it is. Don't you care at all about his future? What if he can't find work, because of your scandal?"

"My scandal! That young gentleman is nothing but a teacher— what do you care about his welfare? I haven't had an opinion of him since he refused to marry Lauren, merely on the pretext that she sometimes visited Mr Lawrence on the sly. Listen here: Lauren has visited Lawrence all but once and long after John rejected her. There's certainly no relationship between them, nor was there ever."

In my humble opinion, Maribelle is simply creating a diversionary scandal. I've seen no evidence to the contrary. I have not seen any letter; I have no idea what this diversionary letter might even have said, nor who is it from, to whom is it addressed. Maribelle is still but a child. Oh my. . .

Mr Roman snorts abruptly. "Ah. So there's something between Lauren and Harold Lawrence?"

"It's ancient history, my dear." Maribelle dismisses the idea.

"And you said nothing to me?" Mr Roman demands. "Was it necessary to stir up trouble between two friends just because our dear superintendent's vanity was a little puffed up?" The sound of his slap echoes out to me.

"What woman is there in our circle of friends to whom he hasn't addressed a few witty letters, with even perhaps a little gallantry in them?" she continues viciously.

Again, the heavy sound of his hand striking her flesh; the thud of her body striking the ground. "He wrote you?" Mr Roman roars.

"He writes a great deal," Maribelle sniffs.

"I want those letters at once," he demands. "Where are they?"

"In the drawer of my writing table. But I'll certainly not give you the key."

"I'll break it open."

I hear his heavy footsteps storming towards me and I duck around the corner. He rushes by, enraged.

Maribelle weeps her sorrow from the floor.

"And what about love?" she sobs. "What about love?"

I think briefly of going to her, of comforting her against her fear. But I remember that she has just been trying to force me out, and how close we have come to being discovered.

It is time for me to go.

[Smoke Break]

As I strap my only bag to the back of my bicycle, Maribelle runs out to me.

"Am I a fool for love? Is that what you think? Is that what you think?!" she demands. Tears pour down her face.

I place my hand beside her face. "Of course not." Then I turn and begin to pedal down the long driveway.

There is silence behind me, but just for a moment. Then, "John!" she shrieks. Her voice follows me onto the street.

Chapter 15

Father Peter is the deacon of a nearby county. A pale-faced man leads me into the Father's office. Father Peter sits at his desk in the back, next to a window. The sunlight falling through the window makes the valleys of his wrinkles into black streaks.

He shifts uncomfortably and pinches his lips together. "You are very late," he complains. He squints at me. "You speak English?"

"Yes sir."

Father Peter nods. "Ah! Good." He pulls a letter from his desk and nods at it.

"Padric's letter is short but sincere," he continues. "He asks that I grant you a scholarship. Do you speak Latin?"

"*Ita, pater optime*," I respond in the affirmative.

"Empty your pockets," he demands suddenly.

I dig through my pockets and pull out some spare change and a playing card. I place the objects on Father Peter's desk.

He picks up the card, looks at it, and hands it to me. "What is written here?" he demands.

I read from the card, blushing slightly. "Amanda Binet, Cafe de la Giraffe, 8 o'clock."

Father Peter looks at me crossly. "I have 320 candidates for this position, the most holy of callings. Now I am asked to overlook these young men for one who is obviously not cut out for the job." He sighs. "But Father Padric has asked a favor of me on your behalf, and he will have deserved very little after 56 years of apologetic labors if I cannot grant him a single request."

"Thank you, Father."

"Quiet! You do not even know what I'm getting at and, anyway, you are thanking the wrong man. Now, wash up and get some sleep. As of tomorrow, I will have fulfilled my obligation. And you will be leaving with me for New York City."

My face lights up in a grateful smile.

"Remember: if I recognize any failure on your part to remain competent, you will meet a very unholy fate."

I nod, unconcerned. "Yes, Father."

[Smoke Break]

The next morning, I sit beside Father Peter in a black cab. The streets of the city pass by outside.

"He has two children: a daughter and a son of 19," Father Peter explains. "The son is a superlatively elegant young man and an utter madcap; he doesn't know from one hour to the next what he's going to do. Remember, you are not in the country anymore. This is New York City."

The cab pulls up beside an enormously tall building. A sign on the gate reads: "Hotel Sinclair"

"He owns the building?" My eyes are wide with astonishment.

"Yes. He and his family live in the top three floors." Father Peter seems to smirk smugly.

We ride up a swift elevator and soon enter into an extravagant foyer. I stare in open-mouthed awe at the palatial town home.

"Do try to look sensible," Father Peter reprimands. "The servants are watching. Do you want them to think you are a country idiot? For my sake, at least, keep your lips together."

"I dare them to say anything against me or you," I respond with fervor.

A servant approaches us. "Mr Sinclair will see you now." He bows and turns, expecting us to follow.

We do.

We enter a wide, light-filled study and the man behind the desk rises. He is dark-haired, his eyes bright and searching. He sniffs. The man circles me, looking me over. I am suddenly aware that the special suit provided me by the Romans seems particularly shabby in the clean and luxurious study.

"I am giving you liberty for a couple of days. You cannot be presented to my wife before then."

"Sir, what do you mean?" I ask.

Mr Sinclair looks up and down my body. "If you must get ruined, then ruin yourself now, and I will be quiet of the weakness I show in taking you under my wing."

He looks at me with disdain. "The morning of the day after tomorrow, my tailor will bring you two suits. Be sure to tip the young fitter who tries them on." He turns and stares out the window.

The city flows away beneath us, beautiful and silent.

"By the way, do not let these New Yorkers hear your voice. If you say a word, they will find a way of making you look ridiculous. It is a special knack of theirs." He turns, looking me straight in the eyes. "Be back at noon on the day after tomorrow. Off with you now, and ruin yourself."

He holds up a hand as I turn. "Go and order yourself some boots, shirts, and a hat at these addresses." He hands me a card with three addresses written on it.

"Thank you, sir," I say stiffly.

Father Peter silently shakes his hand, and we turn to leave.

"Mr Sinclair is an active man," Father Peter explains as we leave. "He foresees everything and prefers doing things to giving orders."

I stare at the card he's given me and then pocket it. We walk back into the elevator and begin to descend.

"He's engaging you to spare him the bother of giving orders. That means you will have to know his mind before he does. Be on your guard."

The elevator door opens and Father Peter strides out quickly, leaving me puzzled in his wake.

It is of no interest what I do in the city for two days, yet on the appointed day I stand in the middle of the Sinclairs' foyer, decked out in new clothes. Father Peter accompanies me once more.

Mr Sinclair enters and appraises me with a slight smile.

"Good. You are dressed well." He gestures to a waiting servant. "Take Mr Marshal's bags to his room," he says.

Then he turns to Father Peter. "Father, would you have any objections if Mr Marshal took dancing lessons?"

"Of course not," Father Peter answers. "John is not a clergyman."

Mr Sinclair motions for me to follow him. With a nod, Father Peter excuses himself.

Mr Sinclair and I walk down a long hall. "How many shirts did you get at the linen drapers?" he asks.

"Two."

He nods. "Very good."

Mr Sinclair opens a door at the end of the hall, revealing an enormous library. At the far end, an elderly man is shelving books from a newly shipped box.

We step within.

"Very good," Mr Sinclair says again. He pulls an envelope from his inside jacket pocket and hands it to me. "Get 22 more. Here is your first quarter's salary."

He turns to face the elderly man at the back. "Samuel!"

Samuel straightens and walks over to Mr Sinclair.

"Samuel, will you look after Mr Marshal?"

Samuel nods his head and gestures me over to a desk in the corner of the library.

"This is yours, sir," Samuel says. And then he returns to shelving books.

After finding my room and unpacking my meager belongings, I bring my papers to the library and pick out a book. I read at the desk that Samuel appointed as mine. A few hours pass; Mr Sinclair raps on the desk and I jump, startled. He picks up one of the letters I have left on the table and begins to read.

"You are not quite sure of your spelling? Millennium is written with two n's. But no matter; will you come with me?"

"Certainly, sir." I am sure that my confusion shows on my face, but I stand ready to follow him.

He looks at my clothes. "I have one thing with which to reproach myself." He shakes his head. "I did not tell you that at half past five every day you are expected to dress."

"Excuse me?" I check to make sure that I am still wearing clothes.

"I mean you must change into evening wear. For dinner. But no matter—tomorrow is another day." He motions for me to follow him out.

He leads me back to the main living area, where a gathering of about 10 guests socializes in the living room. Mr Sinclair walks in, and I follow him to his wife.

Mrs Levida Sinclair is overweight and unattractive. Yet, I sense, from her poise and expression, that she's a powerful woman, used to getting her own way. I bow slightly to her.

"Mr John Marshal, I am pleased to introduce you to my wife, Mrs Levida Sinclair."

"It is a great honor." I take her hand with a gentle firmness.

"I'm sure," she says lightly. And then returns to converse with the woman who sits beside her.

I smile slightly and excuse myself as the group begins to gather around the table, waiting for dinner to be served.

A tall, good-looking young man enters the room with a bang and a loud exclamation. He is dressed in riding clothes. He walks up to

Mrs Sinclair, who stands at the end of the table. He kisses her hand.

"You always keep us waiting, Norbert," she complains mildly.

"Please accept my apology, mother. I entirely lost track of time while I was riding. But when I realized, I raced as fast as I could so that I might eat my supper while it is hot."

Norbert takes his seat next to a young woman only a year or so younger than he. "Hello, Claudia, dear sister," he says quietly.

As I watch Norbert at his seat, I notice the girl for the first time. Our eyes lock for a moment.

Mr Sinclair turns to his son. "Norbert, I must ask you to look after Mr John Marshal, whom I've just taken on as my personal secretary and whom I hope to make a man of, if that is possible."

Everyone at the table laughs at Mr Sinclair's derision.

I ignore them with a gracious smile, and then turn my head back to the young woman.

She's staring at me, rather unselfconsciously.

Chapter 16

The early morning sun pours through a window next to my desk as I file the remainder of my paperwork and type an e-mail on the laptop that Mr Sinclair has provided me. The movement of a door prompts me to lift my head. I watch with amusement as Claudia sneaks into the library through a small, innocuous door behind the shelves. She approaches a bookshelf, her hand poised to remove Voltaire's *La Princesse de Babylone*.

"Hm," I exclaim at her choice.

She turns around to see me watching her, then glares and scurries out.

The hours pass, and eventually I switch on the desk lamp. Shortly thereafter, Norbert slides down the banister of the staircase that runs from the second story landing. He runs over to me, wielding a fencing sword, and points the sword at my throat.

"There is a time in every man's life when he must put down the pen and mount the horse. This is that time, John," he commands with gravity, and then lowers his sword with a flourish. "My father gives us leave until supper." He grins.

I can see why Father Peter warned me of Norbert, but I can't help but be charmed by his youthful enthusiasm.

"What are we waiting for?" I answer.

[Smoke Break]

Later that evening, I sit at the dinner table with the Sinclair family.

"So, John, I understand that Norbert took you out riding this afternoon," Mr Sinclair begins.

"Oh yes, it was quite the adventure." I grin. "He had me on the stable's gentlest horse. But since he could not tie me to it, I tumbled off the poor mare and fell right onto the middle of the bridge."

I hear a small, choked sound, and see Claudia holding back laughter.

"The horse was afraid of me, I think. I have no problem riding." I wink at her and she bursts into happy peals, her eyes shining with merriment.

Mr Sinclair flashes his rare smile. "How charming of you to relate your misadventures to those who might otherwise admire you," he says.

[Smoke Break]

The next day, I take my lunch with Mrs Sinclair and Claudia. We eat quietly, creating an atmosphere that seems to suck up amusement like a black hole.

"The hamburger is wonderful," I say finally. "Much better than anything we have in the country."

Levida Sinclair sniffs. "John, it's veal," she explains.

I snap my lips together and chew quickly.

Later that afternoon, I receive a visit from Father Peter. He walks up to my desk as though he is used to having the run of the Sinclair household. "I see you are busy on that interminable lawsuit with Mr Friar? I just came by to see how everything was going. But you are busy, so I'll leave you be."

He starts to walk away, but I interrupt him. "Sir? Is dining everyday with her ladyship, Levida Sinclair, one of my duties, or is it a kindness on their part?"

Father Peter stops short. "It is an honor!" he declares.

I sigh. "For me, sir, it is my least favorite time of day. Even Mrs Sinclair yawns at how dull we find each other."

Father Peter's face is set as stone.

"I am afraid I will fall asleep and ruin the veal," I joke. "Perhaps you could convince Mr Sinclair that it would be better to give me a small allowance for lunch?"

I hear the sound of someone laughing behind the bookshelves. Father Peter and I turn our attention toward the noise. We see Claudia, standing with a book in her hand and smiling at me.

With a blush, she scurries out.

[Smoke Break]

"Are you almost ready, dear?" Mr Sinclair's voice echoes out to me as I walk past their suite on my way to dinner.

"Will John be dining with us this evening?" she answers.

I pause to listen.

"John always eats with us," Mr Sinclair answers.

"Yes, I know, dear. That's what I am rather concerned with. John is a lovely boy, and I see that everyone has taken to him. I myself dine with him every day."

She pauses.

"But when we have certain people over, I think that it would be best if he dined alone."

There is the clink of makeup on her vanity table and the rustling of garments.

Mr Sinclair clears his throat. "I am anxious to carry on with my experiment to the very end," he insists. "This fellow is only out of place because his appearance is unfamiliar. As for the rest, he is as good as deaf and dumb. No one will think twice about him."

With that astounding recommendation echoing in my mind, I continue down to dinner.

This evening the crowd is smaller, but wealthier. They are a pleasant group, laughing and joking with one another as they feast. Despite the general mirth, I feel out of place in the company. I look at the difference in our clothes, in their speech, and wish just to disappear.

Unfortunately, this is impossible. Claudia stares at me through the entire meal from her place across the table at me. She smirks meaningfully.

I glance swiftly at her mother, to find the lady's attention otherwise occupied, and then deliberately wink back at Claudia. She finds me amusing, at least.

Chapter 17

That weekend, Mr Sinclair treats me to his opera seats, which brings me to a lavish and close-in box that he keeps on permanent reservation. The following Monday, he calls me into his office.

When I walk in, Mr Sinclair is sitting at his desk. He stands and smiles at me. "So I hear that you are the son of a rich Texas oil merchant?" he jokes. "My box neighbors assure me that this is so."

My face twitches at my embarrassment in being caught at deception. "Forgive me, sir," I begin. "I didn't start this rumor, I swear to you. I wanted to fit in better. You see, sir . . . . To be fair and honest, I have been indignant that I do not lie. I didn't start the rumor, but I am happy to see it perpetuated. My apologies."

Mr Sinclair interrupts me. "I know, I know," he says kindly. He seems almost pleased. "It's up to me now to give some consistency to the story. But I've one favor to ask of you; it will not cost a bare half hour of your time, and of course I'll pay you."

Surprised at his understanding, I nod my head eagerly and pay close attention.

"Every evening, when there is an opera, go and stand in the vestibule when people of the best society are exiting."

I look at him with question marks in my eyes.

"I still notice at times some provincial mannerisms in you." He points his finger at me. "You must get rid of them. Besides, it is not such a bad thing to know, at least by sight, certain people of importance. Go to the box office and make yourself known. They have a pass ready for you."

[Smoke Break]

The months pass and I manage to do as Father Peter bade me—to tread lightly and anticipate Mr Sinclair's whims. In the winter, Levida, Norbert, and Claudia take a short trip to Vermont to stay at the family's ski lodge. Mr Sinclair stays behind to mind his business, and I of course stay with him.

On the day that the trio returns from the mountains, snow falls on the streets of the City. I watch from the window as people, looking like ants, scurry to provision themselves for the storm Then the limo pulls up to the door, and Levida, Claudia, and Norbert emerge. I run down to the front door to meet them.

"He is in the drawing room," I announce when they burst into the foyer, damp with snow.

After shedding their outer layers, they hurry to see him.

"I trust you had a good holiday?" Mr Sinclair asks when his family bustles into his study.

"Never the same without you, father," Claudia says shyly. She walks over to her father and claims a kiss.

"You needn't have worried about me. I had John here to keep me more than enough company."

"Is that so?"

"When he wasn't making a name for himself at the opera, he indulged me with all the latest gossip."

Claudia giggles while her mother steps forward to give Mr Sinclair a tender embrace.

"Well then!" Norbert says, giving a short wave and hurrying to the door—off on some mischief already, I assume.

Claudia turns to me. "Mr Marshal, are you coming to the Devins' party tonight?"

I shake my head. "I've not had the honor of being introduced to Mr Devin, as yet."

She laughed prettily. "Well, you have managed to make quite a reputation for yourself, just the same. Just yesterday, we saw Mr Devin on his way back from holiday, and he asked Norbert to bring you to the party."

"In that case, I suppose that I haven't a choice in the matter?" I tease.

She laughs. "Oh no, none at all."

[Smoke Break]

Snow falls as we approach the apartment building in which the Devins' penthouse resides. We enter at our finest, Norbert and I on either side of Claudia. A servant takes our hats and coats while the butler leads us to the main room.

The penthouse is stunning—with high-vaulted ceilings and a wide space for dancing in the center. Crystal and glass glint from every corner of the vast room. In the corner a seven-piece jazz band tunes up softly.

Claudia is quickly swept up in conversation with her

acquaintances, and Norbert, with a wink, begins pursuit of the most gorgeous woman in the room. I saunter into an adjoining room, finding within it a small bar and three men who lean against it, looking out at the main room with something akin to fear.

"You must agree; she is the belle of the party," one of the men says, as I walk up to the bar and quietly order a drink.

Another man laughs. "Even Louisa Charles is well aware that she's been taken down a notch."

"She seems to have full command of the pleasure she feels of her triumph," says the third, looking very hard at the doorway. "You could say that she's afraid of seeming attractive to anyone who speaks to her."

Receiving my drink, I peek past the men to see who they are talking about—although I'm already beginning to suspect.

"Why, of course!" the second man exclaims. "That's the whole art of seduction."

The third man nodded. "Her air of reserve implies how charming she could show herself to be, given a worthy suitor."

"And who could be worthy of the sublime Claudia?" the first man chimed.

"Claudia?" I whisper to myself. And then I see her.

She is beautiful. She dances gracefully with a pedigreed young man. But her eyes roam the room.

I walk toward her, mesmerized.

The music stops, and so does she. Her mouth moves in a charming apology and the young man smiles as though, by excusing herself, she has given him some great compliment.

"Come sit with me," a young woman suggests. She pats the open cushion next to her on a soft, suede divan. I sit, never taking my eyes from Claudia as she walks toward us.

"Louisa!" Claudia exclaims. "That dear boy nearly danced my legs into the ground. Look—my heels are already beginning to wear." Claudia lifts her dainty foot, and I glimpse the glowing white flesh above her knee. Then she sits beside me with a measured exhalation.

"You poor dear," Louisa drawls.

Claudia turns toward me. "Isn't this party the best of the season?"

It seems that everyone nearby turns to look at me—the man who is lucky enough to be acknowledged by Claudia.

I make my voice cold, ignoring the jealous and incredulous stares of the men that seem to gravitate toward her.

"I'd scarcely be a good judge of that, Claudia. My life is taken up with writing. This is the first party I've ever seen of such magnitude."

She nods her head, chastened. "You are a wise man, Mr Marshal. You look on all these balls with the eye of a philosopher, like Jean Rousseau. Human follies astonish but do not tempt you."

I sniff. "Jean Rousseau was nothing but a fool and a hypocrite. He failed to truly understand the nature of society; rather, he viewed it with the heart of a lackey risen above his station."

Claudia looks at me from the corner of her eye. "He wrote the *Contrat Social*."

"And while he preached the overthrow of royal rights and privileges, he went off his head with joy if a Duke altered the course of his after-dinner constitutional to see one of his friends' homes."

And with that, I excuse myself. The last thing I need is to sit around listening to the young girls' idealistic gibberish. But I walk slowly, as usual, and so I hear Louisa's next words.

"It is truly unfortunate that such a handsome young man cannot cultivate the manners and position suitable for eligibility."

Claudia exhales through her nose. "Have you not thought that maybe it is the manners and position of all these 'eligible' gentlemen that is truly unfortunate?"

I cannot hide the small smile that rises to my lips.

As I exit the room I am assailed by a man in a dark suit.

"Well John, there you are! I hardly expected to see you here," he says in an ironic voice that I immediately recognize.

"Seth!" I embrace my only real friend. "What brings you all the way to the City?"

A look of embarrassment comes over his features. "It is no matter," he responds. "Have a smoke?"

As we walk back through the great room to the balcony, I see that Louisa and Claudia have found partners once more, and are dancing side by side. Yet Claudia's eyes soon find me, and she and her young friend follow us out to the balcony before long.

"Wasn't Che Guevara some sort of a butcher, the revolutionary that he was?" she asks.

I look at Claudia with contempt. "In certain people's eyes. And yet, not so great a butcher as the then existing regime. He, at least, had a sense of justice."

Claudia sighs. "You are so young and yet so brilliant." She looks around the ballroom in contemplation.

With a wink, Seth lays a hand on Louisa's elbow and steers her off.

"There's no true passion left in this country. That's why people get so bored. The greatest cruelties are committed, yet not from cruel motives," Claudia sighs.

"That is much worse than otherwise, I should think," I contend. "When people commit crimes, they should at least find some pleasure in committing them. One cannot find the slightest justification for crime, except on such grounds."

Claudia, recognizing my zealous idealism, looks at me with longing. "I see nothing that can confer honor on a man except sentence of death. It is the only thing that cannot be bought," she says suddenly, flushing with a passion of her own.

"Anything can be bought," I answer. "Even death."

She sighs. "We have either too much or too little," she states. "Everything is either an utter disaster or truly sublime and in perfect harmony. Even the way we feel. Perhaps, in the future, things will be different."

"I doubt it very much," I say coldly. "We are as we are. We are trapped, in a way."

"Yes. We are. Aren't we?" Claudia looks dreamily at the night sky.

Chapter 18

The morning sun slowly creeps up over the window grate as I sit, typing a long message. A sound tells me that someone is standing before my desk. From the edge of my gaze, I can tell it is Claudia. I take no notice of her.

"If you could be so kind and pull a volume from the top shelf for me?" she says finally. *"The History of Man?"*

Without looking at her, I move the ladder and climb up to find her book.

"You are clearly thinking about something very interesting, Mr Marshal. Tell me, please, what is it? I'll be discreet, I swear I will."

I pull the book silently and begin to climb back down.

"What could possibly have turned you, you who are ordinarily so cold, into a creature inspired? You have a fire in you this morning," she concludes.

I hand Claudia her book. "Did Danton do well to steal? The revolutionaries of Piedmont, of Spain, should they have compromised the people by committing crimes?"

I pace before her, anguished by her ignorance. "Must a man who wants to drive ignorance and crime from this earth pass through his life like a whirlwind and do nothing but evil?"

Claudia has nothing but smiles for my passion. She loves a revolutionary, but still hasn't a clue of the torment it takes to create one. I despise her, but I want her, too.

"Is that all?" I ask coldly, and then sit back at my desk.

[Smoke Break]

In the warmth of the rare sunny winter afternoon, I head up to the Sinclairs' rooftop garden and sit myself at a table. Soon, I am gazing off into the skyscrapers, deep in thought.

"I beg you to tell me what is so interesting that it occupies so much of your mind," Claudia demands.

Where has she come from?

I sigh. "I am afraid it's not my place to even think about such things, let alone make my thoughts public."

"Oh no, you must tell me. I'm hardly public," she says with the greatest innocence.

I smile a little at her joke. "Well, as you wish. Through my position as Mr Sinclair's secretary, I have more than once written to the two lawyers arranging the terms of a marriage contract concerning Mr Bernard and yourself."

She blushes, wondering what I must think of her.

I look directly into her eyes. "Although I find your intellectual conversation most stimulating, I cannot imagine a man such as Mr Bernard receiving it with the same appreciation," I conclude.

Claudia takes a step forward and then her leg seems to crumple beneath her. "Oh, ow!" she gasps.

I rush to her side. "Are you badly hurt?"

She grimaces. "It is nothing. Probably just a sprain." She lifts her arms and I help to pull her up. "If you could kindly escort me inside?"

She leans into me and I am compelled to wrap an arm around her waist. Her arm slings around my shoulder; her chest swells as she breathes deep. And so we walk together.

[Smoke Break]

That evening, when I finish up my work on the marriage contracts, I hand Mr Sinclair the papers.

He briefly looks them over. "This is excellent work, John. You are excused until morning."

I leave, eager to have a drink before bed.

In the kitchen, I hear Norbert's voice raised. "We have learned from history that we must beware of such energy from such people. If a revolution breaks out, he will not hesitate to destroy us."

"You are such a hypocrite, Norbert!" Claudia attests. "You always treat him as though you're best friends, when secretly you're afraid."

I enter the room, and cross to the wine cupboard. I pour myself a glass of Cabernet from an opened bottle. To silence. Then I exit, feeling Claudia's eyes upon my back.

Dear Diary:

Almost Done.

[Smoke Break]

As I walk slowly to my room, I hear her light footsteps behind me. I turn when she is directly behind me.

"Oh, Mr Marshal." She looks at me with young eyes, her mind clearly blank. I raise my eyebrows and take a sip of my glass.

"We were talking about you—we were. My brother is a fool," she gasps.

"I'm all too used to fools by now," I say coolly.

She seems to struggle with herself, her mouth opening and closing. Finally, she jabs her hand into her pocket and pulls out a slip of paper that has been folded several times. "Here!" her breath explodes as she hands it to me. "Here. I didn't know if I'd have the nerve to give it to you, but I've been carrying it around with me ever since the party, and . . . well, just read it. Just read it."

Then, looking at my distant face, my amused smirk, she turns and runs back to the kitchen.

[Smoke Break]

Later the same week, Claudia storms into the library and stomps to my desk. "It has been days now, Mr Marshal, and I've still not heard anything from you in response to my letter. I demand a definite answer concerning your intentions."

She slaps a new letter onto my desk and scurries out. I read the letter, smiling. It states:

[Smoke Break]

Dearest John,
I want to speak to you. I must speak to you tonight. At 1 am exactly; see that you are in the rooftop garden.

[Smoke Break]

At quarter to one, the moon finds me pacing back and forth in the garden. I look behind me at the door. All the lights in the house are now out. I look up at the full moon which illuminates the sky.

Slowly, the door creaks open. A dark figure slips into the garden. It is Claudia—by now I know her movements. She joins me in the dark shadow of a thick bush. "You made it," she whispers gratefully.

I try to wrap my arms around her, but she pushes me away.

"No, no," she hisses. Then she starts away.

"What have you got in the side of your coat?" she demands, pointing.

"A pistol," I admit.

"Oh."

The silence passes in awkwardness.

"What have you done with my letter?" she asks finally.

"I've mailed it, hidden in a Protestant Bible, to a close friend whom I can trust."

"Good gracious! Why all the precaution?"

I can tell that she'd wished that I'd saved it, as a keepsake.

"How am I to know if you can be trusted?" I answer. "This could be a plot to destroy my spirit, or my good name."

Claudia laughs, although she does not explain why. Her laughter is low, and dangerous.

Without thinking, I pull her close to me. In an instant, we are kissing passionately in the darkness.

Chapter 19

That Sunday, I stand at the altar next to Father Peter. I look up when Claudia walks in with her mother, almost as if I can smell her presence. The two sit toward the front of the congregation. Claudia glances up at me and immediately looks away.

I stare straight at her throughout the service, unafraid, as she coldly avoids my gaze.

Finally, Father Peter makes his final remarks of the service. "Even the prophet Moses had to live by the word of the Lord in order to reach the Promised Land. And from this we learn that it is our actions that guide us to salvation."

The organ indicates that the service is over. The congregation gets up to leave.

I try to catch Claudia before she leaves the church, but she manages to escape, leaving me standing alone in front of the exiting crowd.

I glance back at Father Peter, who is frowning at me disapprovingly.

At brunch that morning, Bernard, Louisa, myself, and all the Sinclairs but Claudia are there.

"What has happened to Claudia?" Mr Sinclair asks his wife.

Levida sniffs. "She claims to have been taken ill."

"Beauty is so delicate," Mr Sinclair says jovially. "Do you not agree, Bernard?"

Bernard politely laughs. "Most definitely, sir."

"Like a fine aria, her delicacy is what makes her ever more precious," I add.

"Quite right, Mr Marshal," Sinclair congratulates me. "One can always rely on you to cleverly illustrate the phenomenon that dumbfounds one most. It is a true gift."

"Yes, you are a blessed creature, Marshal," Norbert adds with a sarcastic sneer. I glance at Norbert with annoyance; he arrogantly returns the look.

That evening, Claudia joins the company for cocktails. When she sees that I am still there, however, she immediately leaves the room. I follow her silently as she runs up the staircase.

She races into her father's game room, and then grabs a pool stick and holds it in front of her.

I slow down, holding my hands in the air as I walk toward her.

She moves away.

"I'll keep your secret. I swear," I say sincerely. "I'd never speak a word to you again, if it would ensure your reputation wouldn't suffer."

Claudia sets down the pool stick in a moment of weakness. "I cannot believe I have given myself to the first comer!" she wails dramatically.

"The first comer?!" I shout. I pull a decorative sword off the wall and point it at her neck.

She looks into my eyes and begins to tear with delight at my jealousy. She puts her hands on the sword and slowly points it away as she moves closer to me.

I look down at her in confusion.

Claudia stands face to face with me. "So I have just been on the point of being killed by my lover. John, you are truly the noblest man of our age."

She grabs my face and kisses me passionately.

Suddenly, Levida's voice calls from the hall. "Claudia, where are you, dear?"

Claudia jumps out of my embrace, startled, and runs out of the room.

I can hear Levida's voice as her daughter rushes to her. "Claudia, what is going on? Why are you so flushed?"

"I am feeling a tad warm, is all." Claudia's voice is muffled by the door, which she's closed behind her.

"There's is no time for that now. We'll be late for the curtain."

I am tired of these games; I step into the hallway.

Claudia's face drops.

"Hello, Mr Marshal," Levida says casually. "Enjoying your evening, I hope?"

"Quite."

Levida nods and then turns to her daughter. "We really must be off. Come, Claudia."

Claudia follows her mother, looking over her shoulder at me.

Later that night, I tap lightly on Claudia's door.

She opens it wide to me. "My darling," she gasps.

I embrace her in a passionate heat, leading her to the bed.

[Smoke Break]

When we are done, she looks over at me dreamily. Then, with a face grown suddenly grave, she takes a pair of scissors from her night stand and cuts off a large lock of her hair.

"You are my master. I am your slave," she intones. Her voice makes me shiver. "I beg you: forgive me for having tried to rebel. I want to remind myself that I am your handmaid. If ever again my pride should lead me astray, show me this hair." She pauses, closing my fingers over the lock. "Say to me: It's no longer a question of love; it does not matter what emotion your heart is feeling at the moment—you have sworn to obey me, you are bound to obey."

We lie together for much of that night, but when I notice the beginning of an early dawn, I rise. I pull on my clothes quietly and carefully, so as not to disturb the sleeping Claudia. Then I slowly pull the door open and leave. I leave the hair sitting in a lonely clump on her dresser.

As I'm only partway down the ladder, I hear a hissing behind me.

Claudia is framed in the doorway, clasping her bed sheets around her with one arm. With her other arm she brandishes the lock of hair. "Look what your servant sends you," she says quietly. "It's the token of my eternal obedience."

I smile at her uneasily and take the hair. Then I turn and walk silently away.

[Smoke Break]

For the next few days, I avoid Claudia with every trick I have. But one afternoon, as I'm absorbed with work at my desk, our next meeting becomes inevitable.

She walks into the library and storms over to me. "You wish to speak to me?" she demands.

I blink. "Excuse me?"

"If you have no sense of honor, you can ruin me, or at least attempt to. It won't prevent me from being sincere. I no longer love you, sir. My crazy fancy deceived me. Clearly." She storms out again.

I watch her leave, relief and disappointment warring within me.

That afternoon, after I finish with my work, Levida calls to me from the drawing room as I walk down the hall. "John!"

I stop at the entrance to the room.

Claudia is in there with her.

"Yes, Madam?" I avoid my lover's gaze.

"Will you bring me that pamphlet on the table there by the door?"

I turn to the table and accidentally knock over the vase. The vase shatters on the floor.

Levida shrieks and runs over to the destroyed vase.

Claudia follows with a small smile on her face.

"It was old Japanese porcelain," Levida wails. "It came from my great aunt, the Abbess of Chelles. It was a present from the Dutch to the Duke of Orleans when he was Regent."

I shrug. "It's destroyed forever, and so has the feeling which once was master of my heart. Please accept my apologies for all the follies such feelings made me commit."

I walk away without remorse.

Levida turns to Claudia as I go. "One would really think that this Mr Marshal is proud and pleased with what he's done."

Chapter 20

I am getting dressed the next morning when there's a knock at the door. I open it to reveal the servant Samuel standing there with a large package in his hands.

"This arrived for you, sir," he says.

I take the package from Samuel, and he leaves. I carry the parcel to my bed and tear it open. Inside is a huge stack of letters. I pull one out and begin to read.

[Smoke Break]

That evening, we have dinner with Louisa Charles, among other guests. I am seated next to Louisa and enjoy her flirtation throughout the evening. Although I can't be sure that she knows of what passed between me and Claudia, it is certain that the fading flower enjoys my attention.

Claudia watches me from the corner of her eye, full of jealousy. Her hands tremble slightly.

I pay her no mind, wrapped up in my conversation with Louisa.

"Claudia, are you cold?" Levida inquires.

Claudia's hands shake even more with her distress. "I might have caught a slight chill." Even her voice wavers. "Nothing serious."

When we retire to the drawing room, Claudia walks to the window, turning around to see if I have followed. I chuckle quietly to myself, and turn to join Louisa on the sofa.

"That is quite a story you tell," I say to her, continuing our previous conversation.

"Oh, but that is not all," she says, with a gleam in her eye, laying her hand lightly on my leg.

"No?"

"The shoes had been taken to another man to be altered for size," she continues. "Can you imagine that? I had to send a man all the way down there in the snow to pick them up for the evening!"

"What a nightmare!" I exclaim falsely.

[Smoke Break]

That night, I spend the darkness alone in my room, writing letters.

[Smoke Break]

The next day, I ride my bicycle to Louisa's home and ring the bell. The porter opens the door and I hand him the letter. Before the porter has the opportunity to close the door, I have leaped back onto my bike and am racing away.

That evening, Louisa Charles and I share a private box at the opera.

"I recently saw *Augustine Benoit*. It was not to be believed," I say, before the show began.

"I saw it, too," Louisa says. "It was wholly inferior to the novel."

"I'm surprised to hear that you've read it."

"*Augustine Benoit* is one of the best stories of its kind, which did not prevent Napoleon from pronouncing it to be a novel written for lackeys." She smirks at me.

I look at her in shock, amazed by her knowledge. Then the lights go out, and the overture begins.

The Sinclair box is several boxes down from Louisa's. Levida Sinclair is seated there, next to Claudia. Claudia twists to face Louisa's box, trying to catch a glimpse.

When the opera is done, Louisa and I stand among a crowd of theatergoers, waiting for our carriage to pull up.

"Remember, sir, that people who love me must not love a revolutionary. They may, at most, accept such men as a social necessity."

Our carriage pulls up. I follow Louisa into the carriage, feeling somewhat annoyed.

Later that week, Louisa and I take a walk in her father's garden.

"We have both avoided mention of your correspondence to me," she says. "Although I respect the sanctity of what has been left unspoken, I am slightly puzzled. How is it that you mentioned London and Richmond to me in a letter you wrote just last night?"

My face drops at my folly. I quickly rack my brains for an explanation. I look into Louisa's eyes. "It is quite simple, really," I answer finally. "Excited by the discussion of the most sublime, the most lofty interest of the human mind, my own mind, in writing to you, may perhaps have become distracted."

She smiles, satisfied. "Of course. That makes perfect sense."

Louisa takes my hand and we continue our walk through the garden.

Chapter 21

Later that day, I sit at my desk, writing. Samuel walks into the library with a letter. I see Claudia at the doorway when Samuel hands me the letter. As Samuel exits, he bows slightly to his mistress.

She sails by him, ignoring the gesture. She rips the letter from my hand. "This is what I cannot endure," she hisses. "You have forgotten me completely. Me! Your fiancée! Your behavior, sir, is shocking!"

I stand up.

She steps back, but I grab her arms and pull her to me.

Claudia surrenders to my embrace and begins to sob against my chest.

I hold her tightly, feeling a sting in my eye. "I am so sorry," I whisper.

As we make love in her bedroom that evening, I stop and look down at her. "Claudia?"

"Good heavens, what?" she pants.

"What guarantee will you give me?"

She growls at me. "Can this not wait for a more convenient moment?"

"I have to know. Before we go any further."

"I have been miserable for a month," she complains. "I never want to endure such torture ever again." Claudia pulls me down to her, and the rest of the night is silence.

[Smoke Break]

When we are at the opera the next night, Claudia leans over and whispers in my ear. "You wish for a guarantee?" She takes my hand and puts it on her lap.

I feel myself light up with joyful surprise.

She continues to whisper in my ear. "Elope with me. Let's go off to Vegas. I shall be ruined forever, disgraced. Disgrace me," she pleads.

I stare at her, stone-faced, silent.

[Smoke Break]

That night, back at the Sinclairs', Claudia sits at my desk.

I pace before her and then turn to face her. "Once we are on the way to Vegas, once you are disgraced, how do I know that you will still love me?"

I begin to pace once more. "I am not a heartless brute," I continue. "To ruin your reputation will only be a further cause for grief."

"That's not important," she insists.

I sigh. "It is not your position in society that is the obstacle; it is your own character."

Her face falls with desperate disbelief. "Then I am so unworthy of you?"

"Nonsense. You speak only nonsense! Forget these foolish thoughts; cut the cord that attaches your heart to me."

She sobs. "That would be murder." Tears stream down her face.

I come closer and lift her face up to mine. "What you are saying?" I ask gently.

"It is true," she insists, near hysterics. "We are bound by another life. Do you doubt me now? Is this not a guarantee?" Claudia smiles slightly through her tears. "I will write my father about this. We cannot go on deceiving him."

"But he'll throw me out of the house!" I exclaim, horrified.

"He is within his rights. But I'll give you my arm, and we will leave by the front door, together, in the full light of day."

I grab her arm and shake her. "You must not do this. At least put it off a few days."

Claudia turns to me. "Honor calls. I know my duty. I must carry it out at once."

"Your honor is safe," I insist. "Don't rush anything."

Claudia shushes me. "That is no longer important, my dear." She falls into my stiff embrace.

The next morning, I am asleep in my bed when a loud knock on the door suddenly awakens me. I jump out of bed and open the door.

Samuel is standing in the hall. "Mr Sinclair needs to see you. Now," he says.

When I enter Mr Sinclair's office, he is standing at the far end of the room. At my entrance, he lunges toward me. "You miserable wretch!" he cries.

But I stand tall before him. "I am no angel, that is certain. But I am a young man, and no one understands my mind except that lovable creature. We care for each other."

"Lovable? The day you found her lovable you should have run for the hills!"

"I tried. But . . ."

"But what!? My daughter is going to marry a PA? My grandchildren are going to be the sons of a nanny, a tutor?"

I stare, stone-faced, as Mr Sinclair paces quietly.

He walks up to me and we stand nose to nose. "You ought to have gone away, sir, at the first sign. It was your duty to go. You are the lowest of the low."

"You are within your right to be angry with me, but I will no longer stand for your abuse," I conclude. "I quit." I turn my back and march out.

Back in my room, I pace back and forth, not ready yet to pack. My door opens and someone walks toward where I stand. I turn violently, drawing my pistol.

It's Claudia.

I set the holster back on my nightstand. "Claudia, it would be wise for you to leave," I say brusquely.

"That's not necessary," she says softly. "I have just spoken with my father. I told him that if you left, I would leave with you." Claudia reaches out to me.

I stare at her, dumbfounded, trapped.

Before I know it, I have torn her arms from me and am running out the door. I grab my bicycle and do not stop riding until I reach the church where Father Peter resides.

Soon, I am sitting in his kitchen, drinking a warm cup of coffee and trying to calm myself.

"A troubled mind sleeps little," he notes, and then sighs. "I thought perhaps to blame myself. I thought I had guessed this love affair."

I exhale loudly into my coffee cup. "It has been over a week now. I want this to end."

Father Peter shrugs. "You are welcome here for as long as you'd like." He looks at me for a moment and pulls an opened letter from his shirt pocket. "Perhaps this will ease your temper."

I look it over quickly, breathing in the words like they are life.

"It came for you via courier last night while you were sleeping. I took the liberty of opening it in case it was important enough to wake you."

I frown. "And did you not think it important?"

"That's subjective."

My face lights up with joy as the meaning of the letter sinks in.

"I've been made a partner at Mr Sinclair's hotel! He does not wish to drive me out, but instead wishes to bring me into his family! What is subjective about that?"

Father Peter frowns as I stare joyfully at the letter.

Chapter 22

As soon as I am able, I ride my bicycle to meet with Claudia in Central Park. She waits for me in the shadow of a tall tree.

"I can hardly believe it is my John, in the flesh," she exclaims, kissing me in broad daylight.

"But how will I live apart from you when you are leaving me again so soon? Must you go this weekend?"

"I must." I brush the tip of her nose with my finger. "Do not pine for me—I will be back soon."

Claudia pouts. "I know, but it's not fair."

I smile, trying to coax a happy feeling in her brain. "You must be happy for me and our future."

"Can I come with you?"

"No, you mustn't. This is private business, and I must see to some personal matters. Don't worry—I won't be gone long."

"I will live for the day of your return."

I smile. "Good. That will be sure to keep me from staying away too long."

[Smoke Break]

Seth greets me at the front door of his cabin when I knock.

"My friend has finally become a man of class!" he jokes. "I am embarrassed at having offered you such a small position when you have achieved such riches on your own."

I smile at his humor. "Even though fate has granted me fortune, I will never forget your kindness, my friend."

Seth smirks at me. "And love? Has fate granted you that?"

"Yes, that, too," I say hurriedly.

"Love of what, though?" Seth smirks once more.

"My dear friend, your cynicism is not lost on me. If passion does not exist, then can love? I have passion with this woman. So I must be in love."

Seth chuckles. "There is no doubt of your passion, but passion can make men vain."

"What is so wrong with vanity?" I ask, conspicuously preening myself.

"Vanity, John, is the seed of loneliness."

I laugh. "Well then I am in luck. With you as my friend, I shall never be lonely."

"With vanity as your vice, you are sure to be," he quips.

I concede the point to him. "Wise Seth, my one and only friend, oh how I miss the freshness of your company. When are you moving down to the City?"

Seth shrugs and changes the subject.

I interject, "I had a dream about you, just the night before last, a dream of glory and riches. You were in the dream, but you were a woman. Can you believe that? A woman called Margaret."

"Perhaps in some other life, I suppose, but you never cease to fascinate me. I wish I could give you all the wealth, glory and fame . . . one of these days. Nonetheless, I do try. You are my only friend as well. I have always wished we could see one another more often. But circumstances are circumstances."

"Same, here, Seth. Same here. . ." I say.

[Smoke Break]

When I raise my hand to knock on the Sinclairs' door, the door opens beneath my knuckles before they can strike. Claudia, dressed all in brown and black, rushes into my arms.

I soothe her worriedly. "What is it?" I ask.

She pulls me into the elevator and breaks into heavy sobs. "It's father!" she cries. "He . . . he got a letter while you were gone and now he refuses to let us be together—he is going to remove you from your position . . . he is going to sue you for fraud!"

"What? Where is the letter? Who is it from?" I demand. "My father, eh?"

She pulls a paper from her pocket. "Who is she?" she demands. "Who is she to you?"

"Be quiet," I command. "I have no idea; certainly not your mother."

The letter is written in Maribelle's hand. My heart feels like it has turned to ice in me.

Dear Mr Sinclair,

What I owe to all that is sacred and right obliges me to approach you with the most uncomfortable of news. The sorrow I feel must be overborne by my sense of duty. The conduct about which you desire to know has been, in fact, reprehensible, and more so than

I can say.

Poor creature, it was with the help of the most consummate hypocrisy, and by seducing a weak and unhappy woman, that he sought to make a position for himself to become somebody better.

I am bound in conscience to believe that one of his methods of success in a household is to seek and then to seduce the woman who has most influence there. Under cover of a show of disinterestedness and by making use of phrases from novels, his great and only object is to arrive at securing control over the master of the house and his fortune.

He leaves behind him unhappiness and everlasting regret.

Sincerely,

Maribelle Roman

I throw down the letter and slide down the side of the elevator until I am crouching. I hear the sound of unsolvable wailing, and realize that it is me. "In her own hand!" I shriek.

"I can't believe it's true—I know you would never!" Claudia gasps. She drops to my side and wraps her arms around me.

I shake her off and stand. "Leave me!" I command. "Clearly I am the most wretched of creatures." The elevator door opens and I rush out into the lobby.

"Where on earth are you going?!" she cries.

I have no answer.

I dream that night that I am awake, and the true love of my life shoots me in the head.

Chapter 23

It is Sunday. Blind, deaf, and dumb, I stand before the old, familiar church. Inside, Father Padric's voice gives the sermon. I barge inside.

His eyebrows rise when he sees me enter, but he continues speaking. He is of no concern to me.

I walk swiftly through the congregation, my gaze fixed on my object. Soon I stand directly behind her.

Father Padric's voice ceases as he becomes distracted. I pull my pistol from my coat, thinking the most disturbing intrusive thoughts.

The letter, that letter from Maribelle, whom I have abandoned for the true love of my life, seducing my way up to glory and fame. Ah, the letter said just as much, that I do in fact use my charm and seduction, just as the young prostitute had taught me, oh so much, from the start. It is the only way to getting what we want.

"No, John!" he cries.

By some instinct, Maribelle turns to see me just as my finger clenches tight on the trigger. The gun recoils in my hand as the shot rocks the church. Maribelle gasps, clawing at the blood that flows from her chest, and sinks to the floor like a deflating balloon.

[Smoke Break]

My cell is clean, brightly lit, and impossible. A noise by the door causes me to open my eyes.

Claudia walks in.

"You again." I sigh.

"Do not be angry with me, my darling."

"I am frustrated. Please, grant me my final days in peace," I plead.

"They needn't be your final days," Claudia begs in turn.

I look at her without speaking, shaking my head.

"No harm was really done," she insists.

I stand. "You are insane!" I accuse her. "What do you know of it?"

"I am insane only in my love for you," she exclaims. Her voice quiets to a whisper. "I have consulted with one of the guards on the possibility of procuring your escape," she admits.

I sigh once more. "Stop talking nonsense and leave me be."

She smiles sadly. "I will return when you are in a better mood. Until then . . . ." She kisses me lightly on the cheek.

[Smoke Break]

I don't know what day or time it is. I am sleeping when the sound of movement comes again from the door.

"Go away!" I moan.

She slowly steps toward me. It is not Claudia. I sit up, squinting my eyes to make her out.

"How can this be?" I whisper. "I am not dead yet . . . ."

A smile graces Maribelle's angelic face. "No one told you?"

I shake my head. "This is a dream."

She shakes her head. "Many times I wished you were a better shot. Death would be a welcome guest over the pain you've given my shoulder."

I stand as the reality of the moment finally sinks in.

"You are alive, my love. I beg you, please forgive me." I sob, and bury myself in her arms.

"Who would ever have said that I would write that shameful letter?"

"I have always loved you. I have never loved anyone but you."

"Is that possible? What of your young fiancée? I read about the two of you in the society page."

I shake my head. "It is true only in appearance. She is not the mistress of my heart."

Her face glows with joy and we kiss; it is more real than anything I've ever felt.

"In a few days' time will be my trial. I am sure they will sentence me to death." I admit my fear.

"No."

I ignore her faith in the possibility of my future. What sort of future would there be for me, anyway?

"Now that I have touched you again, I am ready to face death," I admit. "And yet, I leave behind a child in Claudia's womb. Will you look after the child for me, and tell it of its father? I know that you are dead, so how might I ask you for this sort of promise? Because I do not believe you are dead. That's why. See, Mr Sinclair's hatred of me gets fixed in my son's brain."

Maribelle shakes her head. "If we were to die here and now?" she insists.

"Who knows what we will find in another life? But you must go on, and do this for me."

She sighs. "I will do whatever will make you happy."

I smile and kiss her shoulder. "I shall never have been so happy as I am now. A condemned man, together with his true love."

"You've *never* been so happy?" she smiles, looking at me tenderly.

I hold tight to her shoulder and then let her go. "Instead of clasping to my heart this lovely arm that holds me to my life, I let the future bear me away from you."

A tear falls from Maribelle's eyes.

"I should have died without knowing what happiness would mean. But instead you came to see me here, and now I remember everything I'm leaving behind."

A guard opens the door. He indicates to Maribelle that she must leave.

"I am so sorry, angel. I am so sorry," I cry. I hold her to me and kiss her one last time.

The guard escorts Maribelle out. She turns back to me, reluctant to leave.

"Swear on the love you bear for me not to attempt your life," I command. "Remember that you have to live—for the sake of my child."

She nods, her eyes glowing with tears. Then she exits, and the prison door slams shut.

If we still have sensations after our death, I should rather like to rest.

I'd overcome all of life's fears and no longer be content with the gloomy happiness that pride affords. That may be reason enough to explain why I ran headlong throughout my life without holding on to what was important to me.

Who am I to do such a thing? Look at me now. I cannot fathom the thought.

The fading tracks of your footsteps cause my wet bones to quiver in this cloudless heaven.

No End

Bonus Notes: Deleted Scenes & The Unsaid

Time passes.

I open my eyes. The room is on fire again. I remain remarkably calm. The phone rings and rings on a continuous loop until I pick it up.

"This is Ben. I'm busy, so leave a message after the click."

And Kelly, Kelly. Kelly Nolan. She still doesn't know about my obsession with Claudia Nesbitt, or, rather . . .

Time passes again.

"Georgie, I still haven't told her much about the spells that haunt me either."

"Who?"

"Kelly. My wife. I haven't mentioned a lot of things to her."

Georgie continues, "Your schizophrenic spells, and so forth, so what? Mental episodes. Mental states. Daytime nightmares. What else?

"Morbid melancholy," I say.

"Nice." Georgie slanders, "Morbid Mystical Terror. Jeez, what else haven't you told her?"

"Everything."

Poor Kelly.

An Afterword: The Day I Decided to Take Charge of My Life

I remember very clearly the day I decided to take charge of my own life. A huge dose of self-acceptance is where it began.

My editor and I have discussed further writings of fiction, yet I'll just begin here—as I call it "off the cuff"—I cannot afford to start my day with the broken pieces of yesterday. Every morning I wake up is the first day of my life. I never give up because the best way to succeed is to always just give it one more try. Healing is the journey. The destination is myself. The full recognition of all the different aspects of myself: my joy, my sorrow, my pain, my pleasure, all lead me to the source of which I am. Only by having intimate contact with this source can I experience the fullness of this, my life; only by fearlessly looking within can I embrace the landscape of my life and open myself completely to all the love and compassion that lives inside me. I let my joy, my sorrow, my pain, and my pleasure say and do what they want, while I just keep being myself.

I do, I remember very clearly the day I decided to take charge of my own life. Again, a huge dose of self-acceptance is where it began. To stop hating myself, and others, for all that they and I are not, and thus to start to love myself for all that I am and can see in others, too. Never ceasing to amaze. I've got to give myself some self-love and acknowledgement. Without my alter egos I couldn't be who I am, though they're fictional characters in my *Alibiography*.

It's been dubbed "brilliant" and it's been disliked, but once again I am by far—on a very personal note with rampant voices, hallucinations, and possibly delusions—I am my own hero, again and again. I alone, all alone, give myself 100% credit for getting through this day—more resilient, though as selfishly as possible—only to come back and, upon returning, I'll deliver more inspirational discourse.

I didn't take my own life—I gained it. I am proud of that more than I might even otherwise believe myself. As for the others who continue mocking me publicly, I can take it, hard as it is. It makes my decision to pen name a great deal of my work and art much more a wise decision. Again, I let them say and do what they want and I just keep being me, I remind myself. And just now in my inbox: "Thank you for your enormous and massively influential contributions in crusading against stigma, disability abuse, and all for better mental health services worldwide!"

While in a bad mood with yet another suicide in the family last night, missing mail, money, Internet and microphone cables, a broken iPhone (to call my doctor), and a broken swimming pool, waterslide and spa, I've been feeling ignored, blamed and helpless. My goal is to stay as positive as possible. It's been a while since any such livid frustration has surfaced. I'll be seeing my CBT doctor this afternoon, and a massage follows later in the evening. I enjoy my days the best I can—they aren't all that bad, come to think of it, it's just "life stuff." Sometimes venting is healthy (I believe so, right now, though it's just a temporary attachment to my own drama catching up with me. All others can ignore it by choice—for me, myself, just writing it out publicly can help me, at least, feel better.)

We all seem to want one another's life at times. PTSD flashbacks have been extremely rampant this past week, voices, hallucinations, as well—a lot of interpersonal family matters. I am not alone—not really at least. And I am still the "King of Mental Health," so God bless all these maladies and my mere $20 US (€60 Euro) check for international airtime for two made-for-TV movies, *On the Bus* and *Wax*.

I must say, just sitting here to let it all go mentally—none of it really matters—the losses, etc. Feelings come and go. And my two-year, fiction serial-novel series is in the works, so heck yeah! Under pen name and all royalties to charity, to avoid any expectations or disappointments (money and credit, mainly a pattern I'm fixing the best way I know how). We win or lose the biggest battles in life within our own minds. The best days of my life are the ones on which I decide my life is my own without apologies or excuses. Biscuit back it, rabbit, and flap it. It's time to start talking about mental illness, to raise awareness and erase stigma.

How simple it is to see that we can only be happy now, and that there will never be a time when it is not now. Would I trade my comorbid schizoaffective spectrum condition? No way. Never. Too many gifts come along with it. When "normies" banter and talk, I laugh to myself on a whole other wavelength. Sometimes schizophrenia sucks but other times it is the most fascinating "reality." It keeps me on my mental toes full time. Right now in this moment, I love it! With schizophrenia alone, my severe Tourette's syndrome (only now that I'm a strong and healthy adult, I must add) is entirely secondary. Thank God!

The best part of my schizoaffective spectrum syndrome is the autism other than that hypomania. Combined, the two might someday result with my "John Nash moment"—a Nobel Prize. My own take on "when we, as human beings altogether, as in a group— we question whether or not we might be going 'crazy,'" made the wrong choice on a large or small scale, made decisions that didn't pan out, feeling lost, confused or that our lives are falling apart right in front of us. We question our realities; we get shaken up as humans—not sick people, not crazy people. We learn life lessons, by taking the easy way or the hard way, and yet we will usually learn through rewards more effectively than through pain and suffering, no matter what. It's just the way it is. We either create crises that bring us to a bottom of sorts and, once we realize we've made ourselves complicit in our own unhappiness, our lives then change for the better.

I can only grow from the inside out. Nobody can teach me or make me grow, only my own self is capable. I simply decide that it's more realistic and invaluable to move on, by starting anew or just changing myself for the better. I reward myself, and, once again, I choose to make today the best day of my life! Looking at life through a child's eyes, through innocence, so that I can see and find a whole new way of what is really going on.

Are we crazy? Are we all crazy? Or are we just people doing the best we can, our "making mistakes" being proof of this? I think that human nature is, in fact inherently good. We are all good souls, all of us, even if only deep down inside. Again that's just my take on that.

And so, yes, I am schizophrenic, which is to say that I suffer from schizophrenia, also known as "split-mind disease." Even though this label has caused a lot of confusion with multiple personality disorder, which is not the same thing, the symptoms are common.

What's more, you won't find two schizophrenics who are alike. This illness affects us all differently. As far as I can tell, I'm a schizophrenic with paranoid tendencies and extreme social anxiety. Author Sylvia Plath described the mental chaos as existing within the eye of the tornado—I'm referring to her quote: "I felt very still and empty, the way the eye of a tornado must feel, moving dully along in the middle of the surrounding hullabaloo." This is my interpretation of Plath's ultimate meaning as for any such mental chaos, perhaps with some typical stream of consciousness, for example, "I try something I normally wouldn't do—I end surprising myself and find something that I might even enjoy and never regret. If it's good, it's wonderful. If it's bad, it's experience." Now that's my style as The Wizard King of Non-Sequiturs.

In times of great stress or adversity, it's always best to keep busy, to plow my own inner volcanic anger pouring all of my energy into something positive. And for me to be kind is more important than to be right. Many times, what I need is not another brilliant mind that speaks, but a special heart that listens. I release any feelings of self-rejection. I let this all wash over me again and again. I am openhearted, kind and compassionate. My self-esteem is strong. I love and respect myself. I release any feelings of self-rejection. I feel emotionally centered and balanced.

Normal people simply and completely baffle me. What's with all the body language, social cues, pettiness, and the looking in the eyes when we speak from our mouths? I'm pretty sure "normal" people are equally baffled, but better at faking it. Primeval latent core emotions volcano to the surface with centeredness; tears and elation made visible via the one-hour therapy session: priceless.

My therapist encouraged me to talk about my thoughts and feelings and what's troubling me. I was not worried. It was not hard to open up about my feelings. I have trusted my cognitive behavioral therapist for years now. We talk about daily life, challenging traumatic issues, and music, all boiling down to mindfulness and problem-solving, often working simultaneously. My CBT therapist often helps me gain more confidence and comfort in general. And some days we reach a point where we really dig deep through expression of fears and inherent emotional conditioning—for example, when asked, "How would I have preferred, realistically for [such-and-such] to have happened instead?"

And while my private life is my private life, I just had such a breakthrough the other day. I visualize the root of any breakthrough squirming and growing through the dirt, which was what had been brought to the surface. My therapist and I can only Q&A more and use today's breakthrough to enhance my quality of life in so many more areas. It was like I was an infant being parented by this infant's adult self (parent) letting the little boy in me know that this is what this means, that is what that means, and you are loved. "You have yourself; you have and are loved by me."

My therapist was only bearing witness, and prompting, encouraging, and allowing me to feel safe as the little child in me learned, for example, that the raising of a hand does not mean "I love you." In fact, the raising of the hand with a whack is wrong and I'd be better at raising my hand with a whack as I scoff at the idea. "You always have me—your own inner parent-self."

My greatest weakness lies in giving up. The most certain way to succeed is always to try just one more time. So onward, I scribble in haste from this heart, perhaps partly astray today. So be it. Albeit. When I might say I want to do something, I'm likely intending to imply that I might like to do something that is easy and convenient—that doesn't require effort or time. When I want to do something, I might rarely say it aloud, in fear of others potentially attempting to stop me, ridicule me, or simply criticize. I try to consider why I might project that other people might want to, or literally attempt to, make such an effort in stopping me. What effect might this be having upon my own need to succeed?

It's when I achieve things, large or small, it often and ironically appears to result as a reminder to others that they have not done as I have done. After all, setting and achieving goals for results would require effort on their ends as well. I'm not crazy. I'm just creatively insane! I take chances. I often tell the truth. I don't say no. I do allow myself to get to know random strangers. I tell people I love him or her. I sing and chant and rap—clap-bing-snap—at the top of my lungs and beating into yours perhaps. I cry often. I apologize when I can. I try to tell others what I really think about him or her. I often miss the mark completely. I admit it, all—all that I can.

I have befriended and dated the "wrong" people, but for the most part, I've learned from them how to better myself. I almost got divorced once. I've messed up big time and many times. I've made huge mistakes. I've learned from them. I've been grateful overall. I've won, lost and I regret none of it.

I also believe my best of friends are those who have a conversation with me that nobody else in the world could ever understand. While we're going to lose some people in order to find ourselves, unfortunately and with immense fortune—this does not include my best friends, and my audience—we're all included. . . And not that I'm leaving anybody at this time, only gaining more people, friends, and the like—the most painful goodbyes are the ones that are left unsaid and never explained. And sometimes, when you've got to go, you've just got to go.

When someone calls me a crazy freak, I just thank him or her. Nothing throws people off like a proud, polite, crazy freak. Randomly enough, as for change—moods, mania, and madness— the real spot-on secret of my real-deal change is to focus all my energy, not on fighting the old, but on building the new. As referenced in "Shoes without Heals" by Elvis Costello, I add, the opposite of love is not hate. It's indifference. The opposite of art is not ugliness. It's indifference. The opposite of faith is not heresy. It's indifference. And the opposite of life is not death. It's indifference.

I value myself for separating ability from inability with the often unspeakable daily hallucinations, voices, paranoia, and trauma that schizophrenia presents. My heart belongs to everybody and every part of me. Sometimes, I want to play hide and seek, just to hear somebody say, "I found you." There is something about being loved and protected by a parent (or guardian), knowing that I can be loved for who I am, not what I can do, or might one day become.

Unfortunately, it's not usually like this in every single situation. From time to time, my parents made mistakes during my childhood. Possibly, I was the mistake, or unwanted. But I don't know. I had every material thing that I could have ever wanted, but there was still something missing, as if I felt distanced from my parents, or misunderstood, in the ways that they treated me. At times, I had felt completely loved and accepted by my parents, but for one reason or another, they were unable to care for me, provide for me in some ways that would have been very important.

Sometimes I feel like I am trying to make up for the experiences in life that were absent when I was a child. I am . . . blessed nonetheless that it might be hatred that I'm feeling towards me, not necessarily indifference, for indifference is not even a feeling; indifference is nothing. Life can get hard. My conditions [Schizophrenia, PTSD, Personality Disorder—NOS (not otherwise specified), and, of course, my Tourette's syndrome] certainly enhance feelings, even if the feeling might be numbness.

But, I am . . . confident that I am real. I believe that I love, and I have real human feelings. I'm simply expressing my feelings. I know that I am often a very bad person a lot of times, perhaps most times. There is so much about me that I have done wrong—hurtful attacks, etc.—pure evil. I wouldn't even know where to begin—and I also don't care. Even still, I have skeletons in my closet. Time will uncloset them, I hope. I do believe I am a good person underneath it all, and a beautiful creature who happens to be a very troubled and deeply disturbed adult with an especially wounded inner child and a past full of war-like trauma, which to this day causes me to still be that sad, angry, brutal, and malicious person—I have heard it from so many people, too.

Anyone who knows me knows about the unending series of relationships that, because of me—having schizophrenia with bipolar, or not—have ended, on particularly bad notes. I only have so many issues I am literally able to take on at once, and I believe that I do exceptionally well as I work on myself, through therapy, and personal mediations, education, even speaking with the voices I hear due to the schizophrenia—both the voices of paranoia and the angelic spirit guides who I see and interact with on a daily basis.

Yes, I am literally "crazy." Schizophrenia and post-traumatic— even "presently-traumatic"—stress disorder have shaped a lot of my life, and yet, I still make my own choices. All this while I still, every day. . . [Thought trails off. . .]

If I would like Him to "know" anything about me, I so often ask God to bring me back to Baby Jesus—I want Baby Jesus to relieve the chaos, the feeling of being completely trapped in my home, in my mind, in therapy, in public, in private—I want it to end so much. I can't tell you how much. But suicide is not an option. Recovery and hope are the only options.

There's good and evil in everyone, so to speak—what I call the Angel Demon Human Dichotomy (ADHD!) I believe that I have "signed up" for all of this—all of it—for me to have, to deal with. And hopefully overcome, on my own, on my own accord—in this lifetime, and to make my next incarnation better. On that topic, I believe that I am actually the future life (reincarnation) of my father's father, my grandfather who did have schizophrenia— diagnosed in a hospital in New York—and who ended up taking his own life. I think he chose to live, but it was just a second too late. I have, in deep meditation, experienced his life, his feeling trapped, his unspeakable strange occurrences in his mind, and his self-doubt.

I do choose to post on the Net the positive things I do, the quotes, the motivational and inspirational material, along with my transgressions, even when Satan is looking over my shoulder. It's completely real for me, likely due to the symptoms of schizophrenia—yet maybe not, say some of the latest medical studies and reports. I do not write the positivity I do because my life is necessarily at peace, but often, I will post a positive quote because I believe in it, but more because I want that to manifest positivity in my life when it is lacking it.

The full spectrum of "me" is an extremely complicated one. I am just about 100% sure that I have forgiven my father, but more myself. I need to, and I need to feel, believe and think it, to live it. There is no cure for my condition—not yet—only treatment. The difference between the two is tremendous. I also have a baker's dozen other diagnoses as well. I have to pick and choose which to work on, which to heal, and which to let go. Paranoid, Paranoid, Paranoid. Delusional.

My experiences aren't real, but I can't tell. I just want to be loved for who I am, to restore the honor and protection—safety—I perhaps should have had as a little boy, but was unable to have because of natural circumstances, which on a soul level, all these absences I have chosen. All of us are different in many ways; from the clothes we wear, to our beliefs, values, needs, and wants.

I have recently taken on some healing-my-inner-child work. Who knows what's next? My father and I have always had a dysfunctional relationship, and for the most part, no relationship at all. Yet, my father is in full control of every single aspect of my life, legally— everything. The document is what I'm referring to. It basically forced me to take a vow of poverty and submission. I had no choice but to redefine my values and what things were and are really important to me. I hope to publicly disclose the living will or "trust" document at some point. It's something that nobody in his or her right mind would have signed, and yet I did not sign it. I was not in New York anytime around the time and place of my "signature" stamp. I have proof of this—phone records, e-mails, IP addresses, security camera footage, and doctor's notes as to where I was—in California at my doctor's office. A Notary Public also signed the document, yet [thoughts trail off . . .]

I believe with money comes power. And this includes such power as power over the courts, and even politics. Not millions of dollars, but billions. I'm referring to Bill Gates' kind of money and thus power and control.

There is so much I would like to say to my father and, at the same time, nothing at all. A numb feeling takes over when it comes to the thought of my father, which one might think would be very sad, unfortunate, and tragic but, again, it's no longer anger, but the numb, apathetic, uninterested, immobilized, and, if anything, callous feelings that come up. Having to accept my fate, our fates, and all the further loss, hurt, and consequences that are bound to come, by law, which will affect a large part of the world, as my father and my family are exceptionally well-known and influential public figures. They have made many seriously profound impressions and contributions through global philanthropy, for example. I have read Martha Stout's *The Sociopath Next Door*, among countless other books in order to learn some answers to "Why?" Why do my father and my family behave so mysteriously manipulating and crafty? Bordering on diabolical.

At first, it was very difficult for me to accept that my father might have, as Martha Stout calls, "no conscience." Yet, I was more relieved to see that this was actually a common character type. I was able to get a glimpse, just a glimpse, into the sociopath's mind, perhaps. If you were the father of a little boy, I would believe there's a good chance that right now, you are enjoying a very close connection with your son. He probably idolizes everything you do—dressing up in your clothes, imitating the way you read the paper or the way you stand when you talk. He tries to do everything you do and works hard to make sure he has your attention and your approval. You can see in your little boy's eyes that he is utterly convinced that you are without a doubt the ultimate man in the world . . . .

Ah. So often, I truly hate my life and who I am. I hardly trust a soul these days. Living in a perpetual state of fear and distrust—a living [fill in the blank] because I can no longer write any more at least for now. In tears for the last hour or so because of the hurt this writing causes me. Take me. Love. And, oh hell, I can write more before my doctor's appointment in 30 minutes . . . if I do at all.

There's a ton inside—transgressions, even jokes, and regarding any further transgressions, I always revert back to well, screw 'em if they can't take a joke. You are not me. I am. And I am that—purposely being vague, rather I am . . the transgressor. Blam! I know that I already have not just one, but many individuals who are 100% on my side. I have that. I know it, yet I still want it. It's as if I feel like I don't have what I know I have. This is the feeling I get. It's almost metaphorical in that I either can't see what I have or just, as they say, "Can't be happy with what I already have." But I am happy with everything that I have. Yet, I seem to still long for what I already have. This kind of idea is baffling. It's baffling me, and might seem baffling, almost paradoxical, to others.

I wonder if others feel this way. The same goes for having people on my side—I have that. I'm thinking the effects of this schizophrenia are causing this distorted view—basically the view that the good that I have might not really be good. It is good. And everything is certainly "good enough," too.

So what could this sort of schizophrenic mind trick be all about? My wife, for example, she loves me unconditionally and is 100% on my side. I seem and feel like I know this, but I still want it. Not more of it. I just want it, crave it—it's like I still want what I already have. I'm not trying to belittle, attack, or accuse anybody. I simply wonder how to cope with this kind of mind play when it occurs. Others, my wife and support team, do take how I perceive things—through my "lens"—both the good and the bad into foremost view and do respond to my needs what I want and not simply what I might want out of petty desire. Yet, I still want that. And the feeling causes me both angst and confusion—perhaps powerlessness, too. So I ask, "What is it that I'm missing or not getting here?" The "Schizophrenic Lens" can be so distorting and literally not make sense—at all.

I deserve to be heard, for one thing. Not just seen. And I have that. Other people do see and hear me, and so many fully consider all my limitations as well as my strengths and give me the benefit of the doubt when they can. Some do not, but that's just life. I don't give up. I am not giving up. I'm invested in this—though lately, I've been in that mind-set where I believe that even though the schizophrenia and the more negative impact it has had on my life and perceptions with reality—and there are many examples, most of my perceptions are common, from grief, to loss, and the list goes on.

But especially when things—especially in my own head, whether I realize it or not—are more symptomatic and not real, I think to myself, "I just want to move to the English countryside and start my life over again, altogether." You know? But I push through. If I would follow that impulse of moving away, literally, and restart everything, that would turn out to be the most devastating thing I could do. I have all that I need and want right now.

The distortion that the "lens" of schizophrenia causes, I can further illustrate, especially when under more than usual stress levels, and all of my senses become heightened, to frightening levels. The other day, my room temperature was not heating higher than 70. The thermostat read 70—not 75, as I had set it—for 24 hours. What I saw was the digital number "70" on the thermostat, where my wife—and again, I'm not arguing, blaming, or complaining—said (as I hear from others as well) that I "imagined" that. I saw 70 while my wife saw 75 on the same exact thermostat at the same exact time. I'm not "joking around" by mentioning this obvious delusion—which I fully acknowledge as such—it messes incredibly so with my already schizophrenic mind, or "lens." I know that I have Sz (schizophrenia) and I trusted my wife's perspective more than my own. But just with that little day-to-day example, am I even able to grasp the kind of impact that such a thing has on me?

Then the spiraling down from there would consist of my questioning—in complete isolation—if all individual things in my life and experiences—my friends, even my own name—to question if such things are real or not, and knowing that I could never know the answers, except by hearing it—again, perhaps through the veil of delusion—from people I trust, then trusting if the answer or they are real or if they might have said, "Yes," yet through my lens, I might hear, "No."

It's coming to get me; the voices of paranoia: the word is there, no doubt, in the dictionary. But not the feeling. Derived from ancient Greek, "paranoia" originally referred to a distracted mind. But distracted from what? The definition claims the distraction is caused by false beliefs that someone is persecuting me, or me. But if I am afflicted with paranoia, we know, wholeheartedly, that these are not delusions. People are harassing and persecuting us. Who the hell are they? Why the hell are they following us? What the hell do they want? We have become the target of a vast conspiracy stretching on invisible webs across the surface of the planet. It lives in the telephone wires, the cell towers, in the papers and even online, perhaps even inside the dictionary itself. It spills out of radios and these days, on my iPod . . . the damn TV, too. It nests in the hearts and minds of my family, friends, and loved ones. And it's coming to get me

There might be many reasons why they chose me, and why they chose you. But we were or are in fact chosen, you know? People are jealous of us. After all, we're smarter than they are. They're after our brilliant knowledge, my money, my ideas, my things, my mind, all our stuff, and so on. According to the dictionary, many of us paranoiacs have "feelings of grandiosity and omnipotence." But no book really understands, yet there are some excellent ones out there, including *Understanding Paranoia: A Guide for Professionals, Families, and Sufferers* by Martin Something-or-Other, *Delusional Disorder: Paranoia and Related Illnesses* by Alistair Monroe and *Whispers: The Voices of Paranoia* by Ronald Siegel [the latter from which I've paraphrased slightly the first page, adding my own take, given my own voices and current experiences with this diabolical perplexity. For 6 bucks, new, it's a steal.].

You and I really do possess remarkable talents as mathematicians like "The Great John Nash!" Inventors [that would be me], prophets [you?] . . . . That's why we are all so attractive and so inspired, so envied. There is nothing in life that we cannot accomplish. I haven't slept in two days and I currently fear a complete psychotic break from reality due to my own thriller-movie-style conspiracy of which I am, of course, the victim. This is no freaking joke. At this point, I am aware that my beliefs are "only the schizophrenia" but for damn sure the truth is frightening as all hell. Stuck. Trapped. No way out. But got to keep running and playing along. In code. Like an FBI agent. Like John Nash's character as portrayed in A Beautiful Mind by Akiva Goldsman.

My goal: to attain an ounce, a moment of seemingly impossible peace of mind, through complete honesty, self-love, acceptance, and self-forgiveness, and by any means necessary. I think we often stumble through life trying to force miracles, when there are miracles happening around us all the time. I began to "think that I'm thinking"—while in the midst of schizophrenic upheaval—that my only option might be, for now—and to remember upon the next day, and those that follow—to do my best, even better than my best. Perhaps acting at first so that I shall become afterwards.

While I see no way out at the moment, I trust I will get "out" and return, even if to only have another day like today again, but just not tomorrow. Positivity, an overload of it, almost forcing it just as much as I force these words out—I mean I'm really going through it now, and part of what I do—rather try to do—is to really get in there when the times are tough thus to portray these states of mind—schizoaffective, mentally ill, anxious, disturbed mindscapes—and so to bring it all to the surface . . . . Stemming from my need to write, to write as much as I can, to force it out—the letters—choosing to get out of this current state of mind to then impart what I can from the non-disturbed mind once I'm there and ultimately back to usual—the usual experiences with which I'm better acquainted. As I sit here in complete solitude, 100%, I still know that I am literally not alone. Therefore, neither are you. We are never alone. Never. Always . . . never.

Details and specific introspection might not be accessible for me to write out, as I am currently way deep, since this morning, in a spell. A sensitive schizoaffective spell—an episode; one that I will one day, very soon poke fun at in order to cope, though it sure feels like no joke right now. Yet, as I write this out, an inner laughter dawns on me—sensitivity-based—OMG kind of laughter. "Wow, this is one hand of cards I'm holding today and the worst poker face possible . . . ." But I've got to win this one.

Am I seen but not heard? Heard but not seen? I'm in complete privacy, here and now, at home. Dealing with this hand of cards. My Joker is Schizophrenia. Might have to bluff here. Well, I'm ready to throw it all in. All my chips. Taking the chance. To "Dance with Crazy . . . ." I'm going to win. I know it. This evening, I am going to take my chips and gracefully walk out of this well-fixed casino rigged in favor of the casino, not the player. I'm playing. But this is like live TV, and I'm "on the air." Live and the real deal. Playing the "Reality" version. It's the only way I can see it happening.

And that, my friends, is my 'bluff' face. However it comes out. I can't bluff the truth. I just can't. Not these days. No way at all. "Can I see the complete absurdity yet pure 'possession' that this illness has on me?" . . . Silence. "Come to think of it, my mind is the problem. The disease." . . . Remain Silent . . . Indeed, those are just thought patterns. Thoughts—that's it. Not the Word of God we're talking about.

But, wait; my mind plays tricks on me. I might not be able to trick Schizophrenia, but I can play with my mind. I'm creative and I have a wild imagination, to say the least. Let me give it a shot . . . . Let me try to laugh . . . . Okay, I cannot. Literally, on the fly, I'm smiling now. That's a sure start. One player out of the game. Wow, I did it! But it didn't feel genuine (I am writing this, as I come out of this episode, as I would on my podcast. I'm live. I'm in real time.)

Huh, time—it's coming upon 9:00 pm. I can see. A clock. Senses.

I have senses. Random thoughts coming and going like bubbles in the air. I laugh (inside), "Bubbles!" Now, as weird as this is, and as real as it is, I'm now smiling . . . Believing it's real, and that the smile is on my face because I am happy. That's it. Okay, I'm getting there. Alone, it seems, but nonetheless . . . . Another player at the table folds.

I need to return. To come out of this episode. The smile, it's still on my face. Now I really believe in it. I believe. That's a good thing! Going to try for a "lonely giggle" now, to see if I can turn this smile and giggle into an honest-to-God laugh here in my office—the Hot Club, with nobody in sight, just doing this because I want it. I want to come back. Weird? Creepy? Heck, it's been a minute now, and this smile is still on my face. Holy cow, I'm remembering—from some guided meditation I did a few weeks ago—the narrator suggested turning a smile into a full-on laugh and just keep it going until the laughter becomes me.

This would be such a bizarre series of events for me to write publicly, but to hell with it. I am self-helping and sharing it, to perhaps thousands of people whom I cannot and will likely never even see, for real, face to face. In this comfort zone, I have everything to gain. A moment of peace, if that alone will do. I feel like I'm watching a hilarious stand-up comedy show just right now. I am laughing out loud just because I want to. I need to. No matter how long I laugh. I am laughter.

Next: the "stay in the moment" idea swirls, asking me to stay, and I reply, "Yes!" Out loud, I'm saying. "I say, 'yes,' to this present moment." Nothing to lose. Nothing. I'm going for it. Going to say, to shout, I shout and laugh, "Yes!" to this present moment and then just say whatever comes next. If I can, I'll shout out anything, as long as it's positive and for my own good.

A minute has now passed and I've been sitting here on my green couch, and I feel it, believing in all of it. I ranted, smiling and laughing. I said, I yelled such things, as "I am a person!" I love who I am right now! I don't care if I have schizophrenia! I am a good person! I care about myself! I feel great! Right now, I am terrific! Right now, I don't care how weird this sounds. I'm doing my part in this, my way, and I want a mirror now! I feel happy! Now! Now! I am now! I am in the moment! I love this moment! I am sitting here talking to myself, and now I want a mirror to actually follow some of the suggestions I read about in self-improvement books, being myself and being exceptionally weird, and I want to talk to myself visually!

I often narrate aloud my moment-by-moment experiences to myself. But not like another personality. The same personality, in fact, perhaps just slightly dissociating, which is actually quite common with affective disorders such as schizoaffective disorder and bipolar disorder. No matter. Now another 5 minutes have passed and I, honest to God, just talked to myself in the mirror in the blue bathroom. I've got to say, it was hard and beyond weird, but I did it. I did it because I felt it was simply what to do and guess what? I'll have another episode—I can play around with that likelihood. I mean, I have schizophrenia for crying out loud, but I just did what I did. And I admit I feel a bit better.

I call out, now back on the couch, "I am who I am and I feel terrific! I love my life. I love. I am!" Et cetera. About 20 minutes earlier, before my most bizarre of all behaviors, looking into my eyes, in the mirror, 100% sure I was going to be sharing all of this on the Net for all to see. To see whatever my audience might, or might not see. No worries, no judgments. This is how I'm coping. And I am succeeding. Again. I'm proud. Certainly not a committable offense, is it?

Text message from my wife just came in: "Hey, I wanted to know how you were feeling. Any better? I love you." I typed back, "Getting there. Can you wait for the next post on the blog?" I hope to show it in words. Words. Weird. Words. I am being myself. I'm kicking butt. This all started after I woke up from a disastrously disturbed nap—spells, and whispers of paranoia, disjointedness. Then I got to where I am now, as I've written so far, bringing me to the "title" of my moment. This brings me to my 'this is why I do it' moment.

I remember very clearly the day I decided to take charge of my own life. A huge dose of self-acceptance is where it began. It's a very long story to put it mildly, the mere moment, which lit the spark, became my life story, the story of my new life.

I'm learning from this day-long episode of paranoia, depression (after a manic morning), voices, hallucinations, side effects, and onslaughts of disturbances.

And thus, even if I can't be better tomorrow than I am today; even If "God" was not the right metaphor, I trust what I wrote, and this is why, for example, I ran my blog, the radio show, and so on. I did it and do it for myself, for my state of mind, my own meditations on the human condition, while mine—my condition—is exacerbated with schizophrenia. I, then, with nothing to lose, do my best and that's all I can do, to put it out there.

My assumption is that many other people might have too much shame, or fear, or a job on the line, or . . . something holding them back. I understand completely if that's the case. This kind of thing is my calling—all that I do is. It's my purpose. Yes, my "calling."

On a personal note, this schizophrenia, with personality disorder not otherwise specified, autistic features, Tourette's, compulsivity, and trauma issues have plagued me for the better part of my life. This can become so difficult. So . . . so . . . so extremely difficult. Not only for me, but for those who care about me, and all others who suffer and their loved ones, too. This time, I'm learning that I am more shame-based at heart—for whatever reason—and that it takes an extremely gentle person to deal with me. I can behave in ways that might hurt others' feelings, or cause them distress. This is all derived from my being, I believe, an extremely sensitive individual—I mean to the nth degree. Extremely sensitive . . . to everything. Every little thing.

I learn through these horrible episodes and I let everyone I can in on them when I'm able, because just knowing for myself that if even one person on the other side of the earth might read this and—I don't know, but it's worth a shot—if only one person—time and space making no difference—is comforted, if anybody might not feel as alone as they might have before, and might not feel completely foreign to their own selves, and experiences—whether he or she is the CEO of a Fortune 500 company, the president of a country, or a homeless person in a shelter in a Third World country—then I will be happy. Initially I'd written, "if even one person" so there should be a then. So in a hasty fine-tuning of this stream of thought piece, I figure since the idea of helping just one person makes me happy, boom! That's what I write. But I probably have an even more eloquent way of expressing myself. Blam! Blah! Blue! Ball! Bowl!

This LSD-effect-like episode I am literally enduring right now—I'm not venting, that's not my attempt. I just want to—need to—share my experiences when others, who might, just might, have the same kinds of experiences, and might not be able to or want to share them. This is still who I am, with schizophrenia or not, and no matter what. I come through, and I will, always. I will, and I trust that everyone will, too, at some point. If not? We are altogether, at least not and never will be alone even if we never know each other. I just feel it. I just know.

I continue delivering the discourse as the unconventional mental health advocate that I believe I am, with literary galore, schizoaffective, Tourette's syndrome with Autistic spectrum disorders and PTSD. All the rest not otherwise specified, I'm still the same badass author and Hollywood sage with more to come . . .

First Draft?

As for Claudia, at last I can see her so I can be her. I can never replace her; I flipped her around with a toss and turn, letting her inside my imagination then took it for a spin. It's now been a very long time. The clarity will have finally and fully embraced me as far as I can see. Jonathan Harnisch, too, is me.

And Claudia continues to interweave with her pet peeves . . . Just for the record.

Made in the USA
San Bernardino, CA
10 February 2019